Readings in Building Library Collections

PEANUTS •

By Charles M. Schulz

Background Readings in Building Library Collections

Edited by

Mary Virginia Gaver

Volume I

The Scarecrow Press, Inc.

Metuchen, N.J.   1969

For

The Students in 610:515

Rutgers University

Table of Contents

Introduction

This anthology is intended to be used as a basis for a structured series of discussions on the principles, theory, and background of information needed by librarians in the building of collections today; in other words, it is intended to provide supplementary readings for class use. Perhaps it may also be useful to practitioners in the field for their in-service education. The primary target, however, is at the graduate level and is concerned with the broad spectrum of librarianship at all levels and in all types of library service.

The organization of the material is the result of some ten years of curriculum experimentation at the Graduate School of Library Service at Rutgers, the State University of New Jersey, during which a variety of approaches were tried out. The outline followed here has proved to be successful in work with our students in recent semesters.

Not included here are readings from Carter and Bonk's textbook Building Library Collections or Granniss' What Happens in Book Publishing, both now in revised editions and, together, treating in considerable fullness two aspects essential to the background of this subject. The justification for the present book of readings arises from the nature of the supporting literature essential for graduate study--its great diversity and the inaccessibility to the average student of much report literature--and from the desire to make available to students the equivalent of "starred readings" without the constant access to reserved book collections otherwise required. Since this book is intended for use in a multi-purpose library school, an effort has been made to balance selections by type of libraries; it must be acknowledged, however, that it has not been possible to do this in each area of the subject. It is, nevertheless, expected that graduate study requires the ability to see parallels and analogies in principles, and in other respects, across type-of-library lines. The literature of school libraries, for example, and on non-print materials is singularly lacking in specific material on building collections and yet readings on other types of libraries and other forms of materials are applicable to school libraries and to non-print materials. In other aspects of this subject, such as information on the producers of non-print materials, there simply has been little recorded. Finally, the literature of this subject is as current as the latest copy of the New York Times or Wall Street Journal. Thus, in this area of librarianship more than in some others, the student needs to be aware that "When the young professional moves into the field, prime responsibility for his learning passes from the professional school to him and to the association to which he belongs."[1]

It is hoped that the variety of readings included in this collection will provide different points of view, in many cases opposing opinions, as well as a selection of significant field studies or investigations, sufficient to give a picture of the state of the art and to provide a springboard for further study in depth and for successful practice by the beginning professional. It should also be noted that an attempt has been made to arrange the readings in each section in a logical, in several cases chronological, order.

The informed reader will recognize that some obvious "starred item equivalents" have not been included here. Such omissions are due to lack of space, refusal of reprint rights from one major publisher, and to our cut-off date of July 30, 1968.

Rutgers University   Mary V. Gaver

Note

1. Cyril O. Houle at ALA Midwinter Conference, 1967 quoted in Library Journal 92:739, February 15, 1967.

Section 1

Theory of Building Library Collections

In this aspect of his profession, I imagine the librarian of the future as a filter interposed between man and the torrent of books. In summation, to my mind, the mission of the librarian ought to be, not as it is today, the simple administration of the things called books, but the adjustment, the setting to rights, of that vital function which is the book.

> Jose Ortega y Gasset, "The mission of the librarian," The Antioch Review 21:154 Summer 1961

In the future we may expect that the routine and high-volume demands now made upon a library would gradually be divested from it, while unique services to adult education and scholarship would be expanded.

> Richard L. Meier, "The library: An instrument for metropolitan communications," In Ralph W. Conant, ed. The public library and the city. Cambridge, Mass., The M. I. T. Press, 1965. p. 87

The selections in this section provide a chronological picture of the development of a theory, or rather the long-range effort on the part of the library profession to develop a theory, of building collections. Those libraries which serve an institution (school, college and university, or special libraries) are greatly influenced in their objectives by the institutional objectives. Public librarians, however, do not serve as clearly the objectives of a particular institution and as a consequence face many dilemmas in developing a viable theory, as the selections by Wellard, Leigh, and Ul-

9

veling demonstrate. University librarians are faced, more and more, today with the realization that they can not collect everything, as reflected in Danton's final chapter. Even the definition of the nature of the collection is rapidly changing, as indicated in the statements of professional opinion from the standards for all types of libraries, but most clearly perhaps for school libraries.

This selection of background readings does not intend to recount the long history of intellectual freedom on which our concept of "free libraries" has been based. The Library Bill of Rights might, however, be viewed as the culminating statement of this concept which is accepted officially by the profession as basic to its concepts of selecting library materials. The current statements of standards reflect the best thinking of the profession on excellent collections for various types of libraries; yet, some of them are being severely criticized by some members of the profession. The research studies by Goldhor and Mueller explore some aspects of these dilemmas.

What is the role of standards in this field? What principles are stated in the literature? In what ways do these principles conflict? Overlap? To which do you give priority? What is the relation of library objectives to a theory of building collections? Are there developing principles or theories not yet fully reflected in the selections?

What in the long run determines the nature and level of the collection? Factors such as community characteristics, the quality of community and professional leadership, even the amount of money with which you have to work are all important. But behind and determining all these are the objectives of the library and your success in communicating these objectives to the citizens, the administrators, and board members who control policy.

The History of the Public Library Movement as the Basis for a Social Theory of Book Selection

by James Howard Wellard

Dr. Wellard (b. 1909) makes his home in London and his avocation is fox hunting. In addition to The Public Library Comes of Age (Grafton, 1940) he has written books in a variety of other fields including Roman Cities, The Ancient Way, and Understanding the English.

From his Book Selection: Its Principles and Practice. London, Grafton & Co., 1937. p. 71-82; Reprinted by permission of Andre Deutsch Limited, London.

When we review the foregoing historical synopsis, it is evident that there were four main trends in the public library movement, although the question of their priority cannot be categorically stated or generalized for both countries. In the case of the reformative and educational trends both were evident in varying degrees at the same time, the former predominating in England perhaps and the latter in America at the beginning of the movement. Taking them singly, however, the first trend, or perhaps impetus would be a more exact term, was the reformative one, in which the library was evidently intended to be a medium of social amelioration. Next followed a period of educational interest, during which the library was regarded by some as "an annex to the public schools" and "the working man's university."[1] This theory in its turn was gradually supplanted in some quarters by the conviction that the people must first be permitted to read the books they manifestly liked before they could be persuaded to embark upon literature "tending to moral and intellectual improvement"[2]; and so the emphasis shifted to the recreational value of reading, until the extreme democratic position was finally reached: that since the public library was a tax-sup-

11

ported institution, the people were entitled to have what they
wanted to read, whether recreational or otherwise, instead
of what any authority asserted they ought to read.   This
opinion was more or less current before the end of the nineteenth century, judging by statements such as this:

> In the first place, we try to provide the books
> people want--not those we think they ought to
> read. [3]

Now inasmuch as these theories were not independent of each other, but all four interacted in varying degrees
on public library policy, confusion sometimes arose as to
which of them represented the primary social objective of
the public library.   The confusion is also apparent in the
general attitude towards book selection wherever it is considered necessary to pay respects to all four theories, even
though the librarian must eventually prefer one or the other
of the four as the principal determinant of his policy.   In
support of this assertion, we would cite the President's addresses at the annual conferences of both the American and
British Library Associations, or the literature of public library book selection itself.

The issue before the book selector becomes less complicated only according as he defines the essential aim of a
library.   We see in the case of learned, special, and even
subscription libraries how book selection becomes clarified
by the use of a single standard.

Book selection for an engineering library is relatively
straightforward and simple, since it integrates exactly with
the purpose of such a library, which is to supply the clientele with the most authoritative works in their field.   There
is no problem here of differentiating between educational and
recreational values of trying to clarify the social issue, or
of justifying the choice by majority approval.

> While it is not easy to formulate a definition,
> there is no vagueness when it comes to the pur-
> pose of all special libraries, and it is in this pur-
> pose that they are united in their organization. [4]

The author goes on to define that purpose as the solution of
particular problems; the presenting (but not necessarily the
preservation) of relevant material; the utilization of the individual expert's knowledge and the results of special field

work; the collection and sifting of all available material for the specialist, etc.

The singleness of purpose and function which is so characteristic of the special library, is not so evident in either the history or the present organization of the public library. The aim, function, and achievement of the special library are based on a definite knowledge of the clientele to be served and the principle of utility. By a simple combination of such knowledge and such a principle, a special library's value and efficiency are limited only by material considerations of book budgets, extent of shelving, and the like.

In contrast to the simple structure of the special library (and one may include all libraries with a specialized function, whether learned or popular), stands the public library which has, partly as a result of its history, a bewilderingly complicated social purpose, with much less unanimity, it would seem, than the public school movement. [5] Public librarians, too, more markedly than public educators, have been at variance as to the fundamental nature of their institutions. This is evident from the historical analysis, and it is also likely that the divergence of views increased with the growth of the public library movement. In the earliest days in England, for instance, the reformative objective of the public library was unified and strong enough to overcome the opposition, the conservatism, and the apathy with which the movement was variously confronted. [6] Once, however, the urgency of reform diminished in England (though not necessarily because of the influence of the public library), and once the emphasis was shifted from education to recreation in America, the institution lost much of its social force.

It might seem at first glance that the purpose of these remarks was to argue for the simplification of the public library's function in terms of a particular social objective instead of accepting the confusion inevitably caused in public library policy by the interaction of several conflicting objectives. This, indeed, is an easy solution if we declare unconditionally for a wholly educational or a recreational objective. But the issue cannot be simplified to that extent, inasmuch as the public library is itself no longer a simplex organization designed to fulfil a single social need. It has now to recognize its obligations to all of the aims it has, at various stages of its history, attempted to recognize singly. It has, that is, obligations to social progress, to education, to recreation, and to its democratic structure; or, more concretely, it must be simultaneously reformative, educational, recreational, and democratic in its activities.

Of these four objectives, two, the educational and recreational, seem to be fundamental, and two, the reformative and democratic, incidental.   This may be illustrated in the case of reform by pointing out that libraries in England and America are no longer direct rivals to the public-house or saloon, as they were often intended to be throughout the nineteenth century. [7] They can, however, and must incidentally enlist their forces on the side of truth and social justice, even while avoiding the assumption underlying the reformative objective of the first libraries, that it was better for people to read anything not positively harmful than for them not to read at all.

So with the democratic principle, which as primary objective was liable to result in such policies as the Americanization and the popularization of the public library.   The former, the enlistment of the public library in the cause of nationalism, cannot superficially be reconciled with ideals of social equity, nor with the needs of groups not subscribing to such a political philosophy.   Yet the library is bound by its constitution to recognize the legitimate claims of even the smallest of minority groups if it is to be a public institution and not a political machine.

The second logical outcome of an unconditionally democratic principle may be a dictatorship of the majority and the acceptance of inferior standards as criteria of book selection. No public library, of course, has attempted to carry this principle to its logical conclusion by stocking its shelves with mass or tabloid publications and excluding any book which did not appeal to the majority.   In keeping with the tenets of democracy, a compromise was reached, the demand of the majority being recognized to the extent that they were conformable with an inarticulated conception of the social good.   This, however, is not altogether a satisfactory arrangement.

The educational objective was the first in point of time in the development of the American public library, and there have always been proponents in both the American and British movements of the subordination of the public library to the public school.   This trend reappeared in the English system in the governmental approval of the local Education Committee as the library authority in the case of county libraries. [8]

In America, the theory has become identified with a somewhat indeterminate adult education movement, but the results
on the public library book selection policy of either country
have not yet been clearly defined.

We may pause here to note the confusion of thought
which has resulted from the uncertainty and indefiniteness of
the educational function of the library.   This confusion may
have arisen from mistaking the function of the mid-nineteenth
century school libraries and mechanics' institutes in England
with that of the public library at the time of its emergence.
The school and mechanics' libraries were formal educational
or cultural agencies, the former being subordinated to the
school itself and the latter to the adult education movement
promoted by Shaftesbury and Brougham among the English
artisans. [9]   The books in these libraries, then, were formal
text books, manuals, classics, and the general reading material on which the curriculum was based.   But the popular
libraries instituted around 1850 were not intended for formal
students and could not, therefore, be regarded as a complement of the schools, although there was a prolonged attempt
to regard them as such.   Unfortunately, the popular conception of education was limited to a period of formal training
in specific institutions, but stopping short at the precincts
of the institutions themselves.

And so, when it was found that the library could not
be subordinate to one or the other of the centres of learning,
its educational function becoming more undertain and vague,
the emphasis gradually shifted to the recreational function.
The library's obligations to the initial educational objective,
however, have always been admitted in the inclusion of a
considerable proportion of informative books.   Hence even
the smallest public libraries try to include the ancient and
modern classics of literature and the rudiments of scientific
book-learning, or as one writer on book selection sums it
up, "standard works which have stood the test of time." [10]

When it was discovered, as it very quickly was, that
the public library clientele was not a group of primary or
secondary school students and that the "standard works" were
not particularly sought after, the protests of readers, the
deficiencies in circulation, and the alarm of library authorities were met by a compromise with popular taste and the
inclusion of more entertaining books.   At first, the surrender
was only partial, as the nineteenth-century fiction controversy
implies, all fiction being ruled out but other forms of imagi-

native literature admitted. [11]   Soon, however, the text-book
novelists were included, then the popular (but none the less
reputable) contemporary writers such as Anthony Trollope,
Mrs. Henry Wood, and even the prolific Miss Braddon.   Today, the selection of contemporary fiction is less rigorous,
some libraries having surrendered almost completely to the
demand for sensational fiction.

As long as education is conventionally regarded as a
formal preparation in some field or fields of knowledge, the
public library cannot be regarded as an educational institution.   It is not fitted by function to make such formal preparation, because it was not, and is not, intended for formal
students alone.   The confusion seems to have arisen from the
coincidence that a great part of institutional education is dispensed by means of books, and it was consequently assumed
that the library could dispense education with its books,
whereas all it could provide was the information on which the
formal educative process is based.   Once the full significance
of this fact is recognized--that the library is a centre of
reference and information for all groups in the community--
its aims and resources in this respect will be definitely regarded as utilitarian, and the formal educational issue will
be left to take care of itself.

But even if a redefinition of one of the library's objectives as utilitarian clarifies one particular issue, the apparent incompatibility with the recreational function remains,
and, indeed, may seem even greater.   First of all, reading
for recreation would doubtlessly include the whole range of
literature, both imaginative and scientific.   One man may
read Kant for amusement, another Edgar Rice Burroughs,
and the same man both writers, so that if the library is to
select books simply on the principle that one ratepayer had
as much right to have his reading preferences satisfied as
another, there will be no standard by which to judge the relative merits of two books so widely diverse as the Critique of
Pure Reason and Tarzan of the Apes.   If recourse is made
to the democratic principle of majority preference, the latter
will have to be selected; yet there will linger in the mind of
the librarian who has followed such a principle to its logical
conclusion certain doubts as to the advisability of his choice.

It is not difficult to identify the source of these
doubts: they will certainly arise from a realization of the
library's loftier obligations to society.   These obligations
can by no stretch of the democratic principle be confounded

with the function of those popular institutions dependent upon
the exploitation of vulgar taste.   Conversely, the public library must observe, to a greater or lesser extent, standards
of taste dictated not by the majority but based on certain
aesthetic canons.   What those canons are, it is not yet time
to discuss, but that need not prevent us from asserting the
public library's obligation to recognize them.

What this amounts to, then, is the redefinition of recreation in terms of social, ethical, and literary qualities.
In other words, the right to recreation through books provided by a rate-supported public library is fully recognized,
but it is not an individualistic right nor a vulgar form of
recreation.   The right is a collective one, and must therefore be measured in terms of social not private advantage;
and the recreation, if it is to be beneficial, must be referred
to some accepted standards of aesthetic taste.   All of these
conclusions point to the humanist principle, which recognizes
only that recreation as good which entails the healthy and intelligent exercise of the faculties.   And so it is with reading. [12]

It will be seen that this cultural limitation of recreation does not preclude the selection of even the most banal
fiction if it can be shown that such reading excites the desirable qualities in any particular reader or reading group.   It
is not impossible to conceive of a situation in which the
cheapest "thriller" would meet the requisites of healthfulness
and intelligence.   But from generalized observations it is evident that the indiscriminate supply of such books in public
libraries represents a failure either to recognize or to observe better standards of taste, and in the light of the humanist principle such a policy must be condemned as unsocial,
even if it can be defended as democratic.   As far as the
argument based on circulation figures is concerned, the only
observation necessary is that humanism does not admit the
superiority of quantity to quality; but, to the contrary, prefers the latter to the former; or, in terms of public library
policy, prizes a single good book read by a few readers to
many inferior ones read by many readers. [13]

It will be apparent at this point that a further discussion of the principles of utility and humanism as social objectives for the public library must be linked up with the
more practical bases of book selection.   For certain fundamental considerations which bridge the gap between the theory
and the practice of book selection have been touched upon,

and it is now fitting to develop them further.   We have
spoken, for instance, of social, ethical, and aesthetic standards,
or implied them in the use of such terms as "good."   We
have also referred frequently to the actual readers, either
as individuals or as groups, and they must be considered
from still another angle.   But since the ramifications of our
subject are so diverse, extending in the last analysis to the
limits of life and science, we must for the sake of precision
define the limits within which it is practical to work.   Those
limits, then, are the logical ones imposed by a tripartite
conception of the field of book selection as bounded on one
side by the book, on the second by the reader, and on the
third by the public library as the place of distribution.

Editor's note: A recent study with a similar point of view is
        Otto Kirchner-Dean, "Book selection and the democratic
        dialogue," Library Journal 91: 2755-7, Jan. 1, 1966.

Notes

1. Tyler, M. C.   "The Free Public Library in America."
        Library Journal, March 1884, p. 45.

2. Life, Letters, and Journals of George Ticknor.   Boston,
        J. R. Osgood & Co., 1876, II, 318.

3. Crunden, F. M.   "Selection of Books."   Library Journal,
        Dec. 1894, p. 41.

4. Johnston, R. H.   "Special Libraries--A Report of Fifty
        Representative Libraries."   Library Journal, April
        1914, p. 280-4.

5. Graves, F. P.   "Rise of the Common School in America."
        A History of Education in Modern Times.   New York,
        Macmillan, 1915, IV, 78-119.

See also Cubberley, E. P.   "The Battle for Free State
        Schools," Public Education in the United States.
        Boston, Houghton Mifflin, 1919, V, 118-52.

6. Cf. Part I, Chapter III.

7. See Part I, Chapters II and IV.

8. Wellard, J. H. "Introduction to a Comparative Study of American and English Library Law." Library Association Record, Dec. 1934, p. 453.

9. Brougham and Vaux, Henry Peter Brougham, 1st baron, Practical Observations upon the Education of the People. Manchester, printed by A. Prentice, 1825; and Shaftesbury, Anthony Ashley Cooper, 7th earl of, Speeches... upon Subjects Having Relation Chiefly to the Claims and Interests of The Labouring Class. London, Chapman & Hall, 1868.

10. Johnson, R. "General Policy of Book Selection." Library World, July 1915, p. 13.

11. See "Novel-Reading." Conference of Librarians at Philadelphia. Proceedings reported in the Library Journal, November 1876, p. 96-100.

12. The concepts of the two principles of utility and humanism are taken from E. A. Baker, "Book Selection: Fundamental Principles and Some Applications," Library Association Record, Jan. 1911, p. 17-29.

13. For a study of humanism in its relation to literature, See N. Foerster, Towards Standards, New York, Farrar and Rinehart, 1930, and in its relation to philosophy, Haldane, Richard Burdon Haldane, 1st Viscount, The Philosophy of Humanism, New Haven, Yale University Press.

Library Bill of Rights. Adopted June 18, 1948; Amended February 2, 1961 and June 27, 1967, by the ALA Council.

Library Bill of Rights

The Council of the American Library Association reaffirms its belief in the following basic policies which should govern the services of all libraries.

1. As a responsibility of library service, books and other library materials selected should be chosen for values of interest, information and enlightenment of all the people of the community. In no case should library materials be excluded because of the race or nationality or the social, political, or religious views of the authors.

2. Libraries should provide books and other materials presenting all points of view concerning the problems and issues of our times; no library materials should be proscribed or removed from libraries because of partisan or doctrinal disapproval.

3. Censorship should be challenged by libraries in the maintenance of their responsibility to provide public information and enlightenment.

4. Libraries should cooperate with all persons and groups concerned with resisting abridgment of free expression and free access to ideas.

5. The rights of an individual to the use of a library should not be denied or abridged because of his age, race, religion, national origins or social or political views.

6. As an institution of education for democratic living, the library should welcome the use of its meeting rooms for socially useful and cultural activities and discussion of current public questions. Such meeting places should be available on equal terms to all groups in the community regardless of the beliefs and affiliations of their members, provided that the meetings be open to the public.

The Public Library in the United States

by Robert D. Leigh

Dr. Leigh was a distinguished sociologist who, as Director of the Public Library Inquiry (1947-50), made a major contribution to the thinking of the profession which is only now being reconsidered and, possibly, redirected. In addition to this undertaking, he was President of Bennington College (1928-1941), Director of the Commission on Freedom of the Press (1944-1947), and Dean of the School of Library Service, Columbia University from 1954 until the time of his death in 1961.

From The Public Library in the United States. New York, Columbia University Press, 1950. p. 12-14; 231-235. Reprinted by permission of the Columbia University Press.

The Library Faith and Library Objectives

The Library Faith

Throughout the years librarians have transformed their concept of function into a dynamic faith. This faith has sustained the men and women who have built and operated American public, as well as university and research, libraries and the men of wealth and political position who have provided for their financial and legal support. It consists of a belief in the virtue of the printed word, especially of the book, the reading of which is held to be good in itself or from its reading flows that which is good.

Our review of American library development[1] indicates that at different periods the specific virtues to be promoted by the reading of books and, therefore, by libraries, have varied in rough correspondence with the general outlook

21

or Zeitgeist. In colonial times the Protestant revolt which
elevated private conscience to a decisive role made individual reading of the Book, if not of books, a necessary religious act.   Later, when self-governing commonwealths and a
central government were being created out of the colonies,
there was emphasis on reading as a means of providing the
citizenry with the learning necessary for a sound collective
judgment on public affairs.   As the nation expanded west-
ward and economic opportunities were broadened in exploitation of the resources of a continent, the free storehouse of
books was seen as providing opportunity for persons of ability, "otherwise doomed to obscurity by poverty," to gain
knowledge useful for their personal advancement.   As urban
life and leisure developed and the "dissipations of the tavern
and brothel" seemed to multiply, the reading of books and
building of libraries were often promoted by the town fathers
as a means of providing "more rational and profitable" forms
of amusement.   When radicalism reared its head in labor
and agrarian circles, there were those who argued for libraries as agencies to enhance stability and conservatism by
reading about the economic facts of life.   When people from
Southern and Eastern Europe, having strange customs and
dialects, seemed to be inundating our cities, the public library, with its store of books, was hopefully turned to as a
means of assimilating the recent immigrants into our cultural pattern.

The object here is not to assess the practicality or
effectiveness of these successive, overlapping beliefs in the
ameliorative function of books and libraries, but to establish
the fact that virtue in books has been the traditional faith of
the American librarian.   Interpreted modestly, in terms of
the obvious value of providing ready materials for seekers
after knowledge to serve a variety of individual purposes,
the public librarian has seen his faith justified daily in good
works.   In its more ambitious form as a belief in the power
of books to transform common attitudes, to combat evils, or
to raise the cultural level, the public librarian's faith has in
it an element of magic in words as substitutes for realities.
Recently, because of the heterogeneous output of current
print and pictures within board or paper covers, the virtue
claimed for books has had to be qualified.   At least it becomes a magic of Great Books.   But in one way or another
the tradition that books possess a precious ameliorative
quality continues to provide the public librarian with a sense
of significance in his daily work.

The Direction of Development... p. 231

Materials and Services
    The development of public libraries in accordance
with the official objectives calls for an increase of materials and expansion of services. The Inquiry's sampling of
holdings and current purchases revealed that small public
libraries--which means two thirds of them--tend to buy and
hold collections of popular current fiction more than anything
else and that these small libraries make no serious attempt,
by building stocks of popular but authoritative reference
works to "serve the community as a general center of reliable information." The sampling showed that with few exceptions adequate periodical collections including bound volumes existed in only the 6 per cent of the nation's public libraries which have budgets of $25,000 or more. It indi-
cated, further, that stocks of nontheatrical films and of music materials, including recordings, are limited largely to
the even smaller percentage of public libraries with budgets
of $100,000 or more. Government publications suitable for
popular use, which are not expensive, but are harder to select and order than best sellers, appear in quantity only in
these larger public libraries. Thus the traditional system
of small, independent public library units has resulted in severe limitations on the quantity, quality, and variety of materials available for circulation and reference in most localities.

    As long as the libraries remain small and isolated
from each other these limitations are inevitable. The development of more adequate materials and services, thus,
depends on the prior development of larger units of service
aided by substantial increases of financial support. With
larger systems and increased funds, pooled collections of
books, periodicals, and government documents of large size
can replace separate small stocks; by a system of scheduled
circulation large collections of films and records can be
made available to all the localities in a region; a headquarters reference unit and professional expert advisers on
children's reading programs and materials suitable for other
groups can serve all localities, large and small, within the
area. The library patrons in tiny villages and on farms can
have direct access to the wealth of modern library materials
and professional services now available only in the larger
and better city library systems.

    Fundamental public library service will continue to

be based on large and varied collections of materials available generally for individual borrowers and reference
workers.   But in their positive role of "stimulating" and
"furnishing expert guidance" in the use of materials public
libraries are increasingly providing special collections, programs, and other services under professional direction for
serious groups in the community with special problems and
interests.   Musicians, writers, women's clubs, business and
labor organizations, government administrative and legislative officials are among those frequently given special attention and help.   The librarians in these tasks bring to full
focus their unique skills for the benefit of important segments of the community.   Group services constitute a direction for public library activity which may wisely be expanded
as funds and personnel make it possible.

As yet the public library has not been widely used as
the official materials and program center for more formally-
organized adult education groups under the auspices of public
schools, universities, and agricultural extension agencies.
In many places, especially as larger library systems are organized, the public library would appear to be well suited to
provide the materials and sometimes the meeting centers
which these formal educational enterprises require.   Direct
functioning in connection with such adult education enterprises
would be an expansion of public library activity in line with
the accepted library objectives.

One of the oldest and most successful library services
to identified groups is work with children and young people.
It is today the major public library activity in terms of patronage and widely recognized library skill for all but the
very large city libraries.   With the emergence of school libraries in recent years, the public library is necessarily involved in restudying its service for these groups.   For the
next decade, at least, neither the public library nor the
school library is equipped or operated so as to perform the
whole function itself.   The situation calls for a positive program of co-operation on all levels between the two agencies.
The form of co-operation will vary in different localities.
But on the public librarian's part it requires full and sympathetic understanding of the increasing function and importance
of the school library in modern public education.   A desirable step toward common understanding and planning would be
to make the professional training of school, children's, and
young people's librarians identical and the posts in school
and public libraries interchangeable.   The latter change would

also require action by public library administrators to equate
the salaries, hours of work, and vacations of children's and
young people's librarians with similar positions in the school
libraries.   The disadvantage in these matters under which
public libraries labor in recruiting and keeping children's
librarians presents an acute, immediate problem in maintaining children's work in the public libraries.

The development of materials and services in public
libraries does not depend entirely on adequate sizes of units
and sufficient funds.   There are alternative directions in
which any public library, large or small, rich or poor, can
move, depending on the concept of function held by its librarian, library staff, and library board.   To what extent
shall the librarian select materials for their quality and reliability?   How much shall he concentrate on seeking out and
serving groups limited in size, but serious in their interests?
How far shall he resist the pressures of groups in the community, or of one or more of his own trustees, to exclude
from his collection serious, significant, but unpopular or unorthodox, materials?   How much in new purchases shall he
yield to the best-seller selections created by high-powered
commercial advertising?

As far as the statements of official objectives are
concerned, especially when interpreted against the background
of the whole business of communication, the direction of public library policy seems clear.   Its distinctive function is to
emphasize quality and reliability in current purchases rather
than popularity as such; to make available the less accessible
materials for serious groups in the community, however
small; to keep open a broad highway of free access to the
more daring, more provocative, often unpopular current
ideas, proposals, and criticisms, as well as the more generally approved materials.

But actual progress in this direction is not easy.   It
is one of the assumptions of the Inquiry that here lie points
of inevitable tension in public library administration, as in
the administration of other social agencies.   There are individual and social values of primary importance in making
new ideas, insights, and free critical expression as widely
available as possible through the agencies of public communication.   But in the freest societies there are some prohibi-
tions on pictures and print on behalf of safety, decency, and
morality.   The librarian, therefore, is bound to make difficult judgments of public concern in his selection and rejec-

tion of materials.   In his selection of material for reliability and quality, also, he is involved in the almost inevitable
tension arising from the differences between his professional judgments as a librarian and the opinions and preferences
of the lay members of the community.

In both areas of tension actual practice is likely to
be a compromise.   A library may decide to provide an extended service of current best sellers on a self-supporting
rental basis along with current materials selected for quality and reliability available on the free loan.   It may enter
upon a policy of gradual reduction of trashy current material on a long-term basis.   It may provide only limited access
to unorthodox publications.   The important matter to be kept
in mind is that the director and staff know what they are doing and in what direction they are going.   The rate of progress toward the attainment of the official objectives will, by
necessity, vary from place to place.

Note

Garceau, Oliver   The Public Library in the Political Proc-
     ess; a Report of the Public Library Inquiry,   New
     York, Columbia University Press, 1949.   See espe-
     cially, Chapter I, "The Foundations of Library Gov-
     ernment."   Throughout the present volume, material
     and phraseology will be reproduced or summarized
     from the Inquiry staff reports, and hereafter specific
     footnote references to them will not be made.   In the
     Appendix of the present volume there is a description
     of the sources of the material, chapter by chapter.

The Public Library - An Educational Institution?

by Ralph A. Ulveling

Director, Detroit Public Library, 1941-1968; Professor, Department of Library Science, Wayne State University, Detroit, 1968-   ; Past President of American Library Association.

From Library Resources & Technical Services 3:15-19 March 1959; Reprinted by permission of the Resources & Technical Services Division, American Library Association.

... In other words, a determination to make the library an educational instrument will readily be apparent by the quality and proportion of books provided for general readers in fields of serious adult interest. The converse is also true; a disproportionate number of books of light fiction and popular non-fiction will mark a library as a recreational agency. The former type, it seems to me, most nearly fulfills the best purpose for which public libraries were developed.

Since the basic tenets of public library objectives as put forth in our professional literature are broad, and since no library, small or large, can purchase without limit, each library must have a policy statement to guide its week-by-week selections. Once this has been carefully thought out, giving full recognition to all facets of the community's interest, the library will be well prepared to answer unreasonable criticism, and should courageously do so. Criticism may come either because certain books have been purchased or because certain books have not been purchased. In either case the complaint may be unjustified by any good standard of library service. There are cheap, worthless novels that have no place in a library even if they achieve "best seller" standing. Likewise there are books of ideas that belong in a comprehensive book collection even though most people consider the ideas impractical or unsound. Such items may be kept available but do not require promotion on the open shelf of

every branch library, or even on the open shelf of the Main
Library.

     In the past few years Detroit has repeatedly been in
the news because of a police effort to rid the newsstands of
certain paperback books.   Throughout this period the Public
Library has operated its affairs with complete independence
and without regard for decisions made by the Police Department or the Prosecutor's Office.   Time after time writers
from other cities concerned with threats to intellectual freedom have examined the Library's card catalog to see to what
extent public access to library books has been adversely influenced by the police.   In several cases these writers have
spoken to me before leaving the city and have universally
commended the Library.   It is a matter of regret to me that
these same persons have not seen fit to include such com-
mendations in their published reports on what they have referred to as Detroit's censorship.

     Because of the situation there I thought you might like
to hear the statement of book selection policy followed by the
Detroit Public Library.   Before reading it, a word of explanation may be helpful.   In Detroit the Public Library until recently was the only large library in the city.   Consequently it developed its reference-research resources to an
extent seldom found in other public libraries.   The aggregate
of books in the ten departments which comprise the Reference services is approximately one million volumes, as opposed to nearly 900,000 in the Home Reading services.   I
wish to point out, however, that books in the Reference Departments are available on call or through intra-loan to
readers who wish to take them out for study at home.

Library Objectives and Book Selection Policies--
Detroit Public Library

September, 1954

     The people of Detroit are a heterogeneous group
of nearly two million people with widely-differing
interests, educational backgrounds and native ability.   Behind or beside all of these is a mass of industrial and similar organizations, having book
needs that are quite as definite as the book needs
for individuals.   For all this vast assemblage, the
Detroit Public Library is the common book center
to which they turn, with the full expectation that

books and other material suitable to their individual needs will be available when required.

To function adequately in such a situation, the Detroit Public Library must operate as two distinct but coordinated libraries: The Home Reading Services and the Reference-Research Services.

a) The Home Reading Services provide the books for general non-specialized readers, then, through stimulation and guidance, promote their use, to the end that children, young people, men and women, may have opportunity and encouragement for their fullest development as individuals, as members of a family, as citizens. Since this service is concerned with the best personal development of people through existing knowledge, rather than with the refinement and extension of knowledge itself, its purpose in selecting books is to choose the best and the most usable that are available at varying levels.

b) The Reference-Research Services have the responsibility for preserving knowledge in its most comprehensive sense, and for maintaining open avenues for the exercise of intellectual freedom of inquiry. To carry this out, they must provide the usual as well as the obscure, the scholarly, and even the socially, economically, religiously, or politically unorthodox materials necessary for research.

The Library in choosing books applies certain standards as to quality of writing, accuracy, completeness, and integrity of the writer. In approving each title under consideration, these standards must vary, depending on the availability of materials and the availability of funds. With all the exigencies that can and do develop in the course of years, the excellence of a book selection policy will depend less on carefully defined criteria for judging books than on:

1) The careful practices established to sift and resift books under consideration for purchase, and later to reconsider any title which either the staff or the reading public feels may have been misappraised, and

2) A carefully selected staff of librarians having integrity and professional judgment of such degree that, within their field of service, they merit the same confidence accorded the doctor,

the lawyer, and the art curator in their respective fields of service.   But not every member of public will agree with every decision
made.   The best evidence of the policies being
pursued and to be pursued is in the record of
the past.

The division of responsibility between the two services
makes it possible through the Home Reading Services to select and promote vigorously the books which are deemed by
the Library to have the greatest potential for helpfulness to
people generally.   Through the co-ordinate service, access
is maintained for wide exploration by the inquiring mind without the Library necessarily putting its stamp of approval on
all the books within that service.   This does not mean that
the one million books in the Reference-Research departments
are all questionable.   Many, if not most all of them, are
such highly specialized items that the general reader would
not likely be interested in them.

Can such a division of responsibility operate outside
a great metropolitan library? I believe it can and should,
and that service to millions of readers will be bettered when
it does.   Under present professional admonitions, the very
small or the medium sized library feels a compulsion to do
everything expected of the largest library: that is, to provide and promote the best books for readers of all ages; to
provide the informational books needed by all elements in
the community; and finally to maintain open avenues for intellectual inquiry by not restricting purchases to books presenting the generally accepted ideas or social mores.   Practically, this extremely broad responsibility is economically
impossible for many libraries to fulfill, so a little of each
is done, lest the librarian be charged with dereliction of
duty.   Far more practical and beneficial, it seems to me,
would be for these smaller libraries to concentrate their book
funds on providing for materials which will meet the informational needs and books that will substantially aid the educational development of the community and let the State Library be the agency to assume full responsibility for providing the smaller local agencies, through interloan, with the
books of experimental writing and off-beat thinking, etc.,
which will at best have a very limited use.   All of this is
within the framework of existing machinery; only the interpretation of the administrators of the state libraries and the
administrators of local libraries, as Dr. Leigh pointed out
in another context, are needed to implement this plan effec-

tively. I am aware that the development of the regional organization, as promulgated in the new Standards will have
an important bearing on the problem here pointed to, but the
widespread creation of regional libraries may be years in
becoming a reality.

Up to this point, I have spoken only of the books required by public libraries for the so-called general reader
service. Let me now speak briefly on the books for study
and research by specialists.

One of the major changes that has come in the past
decade and a half to many large public libraries is an increasing need for highly specialized books, maps, reports,
and printed records generally, from around the world. Industries which are the economic life blood of cities now
compete in the markets of the world, both for raw products
and for customers. This fact has brought to the Detroit
Public Library requests for the most detailed information on
the Indians who work in the Bolivian tin mines, even on the
number and duration of their religious observances, all with
a view to determining in advance reasonable production
schedules. In another instance the call was for material on
quite another part of the world--Egypt. In that case the
need was for seasonal rainfall figures for the Nile Valley,
the extent and character of roads, the intensity of the heat,
and other factors that might have a bearing on the spraying
of cotton crops. These are cited merely as examples to
show the breadth of resources that must be available in a
large public library today to meet the completely unpredictable needs of its community.

But the breadth of information required is now
matched by the need for depth. Prior to World War II the
United States depended heavily on Europe for exploratory research. With the virtual collapse of Germany and the breakdown of established patterns of activity elsewhere on the
continent, America was forced to look to its own genius for
new developments. The story of what happened can best be
told with figures. In 1935 the total amount spent on research in this country was $200,000,000 (one-fifth of a bil-
lion). By 1941, two years after the start of the war in Europe, this had increased four and a half times, to
$900,000,000. The last year of the war, 1945, even that
high figure was nearly doubled, and by 1955 it had doubled
again. By the end of 1956 the total was six and a half bil-
lion dollars, 3300% more than twenty years earlier. This

rapid expansion was due in part to the Federal government's
spending, but only in part.   Industry has expanded its programs of research quite as rapidly as the government.   And
research wherever conducted is highly dependent on libraries.

Since university libraries are too seldom sufficently close
at hand for practical use by industrial research organizations,
many of the large public libraries are perforce having to develop their book resources in sufficient depth to support such research activities in the community.   The need for these resources has shown not only in the daily requests but in another curious way as well.   In the competition between corporations for
the highly trained talent necessary to carry on their programs,
industry has found it necessary to give the specialists being
sought, detailed information on the kind of library resources that
will be available to work with.   On several occasions the Detroit Public Library has been called on by the personnel officers
of industry for statements on the Library's holdings which they
could in turn place before their prospective candidates.

Simultaneous with the big research expansion in industry has come another change--some years ago it was usual for industrial firms to contract with universities for the
basic research they wished, and their industrial staffs were
limited largely to applied research.   Today the trend in
many places is just the opposite.   The contracts with universities are for limited testing jobs, and the industrial men
are largely concerned with basic research.   This change has
tremendous implications for public libraries in terms of resources required.

Though a reference-research collection of a million
books inevitably has tremendous strength in most fields of
learning, we know that no library can be all things to all
men.   Therefore in Detroit we have established four levels
of development to guide us in the future upbuilding of the
reference-research library, and have determined which subjects will fall within each group.   The levels set up are:

1. Subjects which will be represented to provide
    some information but will not be built up. (e. g.
    Underground literature of World War II)
2. Subjects on which a good representative collection
    for wide reading and study are maintained--in
    other words, a good working collection. (Educa-
    tion)

3. Subjects on which the broadest possible representation of contemporary materials will be maintained without attempting to assemble the earlier history of these subjects. (Chemistry, Sociology)
4. Subjects which will be developed to such a point of completeness that they may, even in the most discriminating sense of the word, be termed research collections. (Old Northwest and Great Lakes History, Automotive History, Labor)

This type of bench mark we feel is essential to an orderly planned development.

At the beginning I stated that the public library as an educational institution has a positive obligation that can be fulfilled only by positive efforts. These obligations will not be fulfilled through the negative approach of a book selection based on meeting reading pressures created by costly advertising programs which promote ephemeral and sometimes quite unworthy items. Nor are circulation statistics a gauge for measuring a library's positive influence. Therefore I say again, the public library can hope to serve an educational purpose only if its book resources represent materials that can educate and if it has a staff that can make the books meaningful. For the other facet of public library service--the specialized services--enormous expansion in breadth and depth of the book resources are necessary.

Editor's note: An interesting controversy of which this statement might be called the culmination may be traced in the following: Ralph A. Ulveling, "Book selection policies," Library Journal 76: 1170-1, Aug. 1951; ALA Committee on Intellectual Freedom, "Book slection principles," ALA Bulletin 45: 346-50, November 1951; Ralph A. Ulveling, "A reply to the CIF Committee," ALA Bulletin 46: 73-6, March 1952.

The Library's Collection in a Time of Crisis

by Margaret E. Monroe   Formerly Director of the American Heritage Project, ALA and Associate Professor, Rutgers University; currently Director, Library School, University of Wisconsin, Madison

From Wilson Library Bulletin 36: 372-4 January 1962; Reprinted by permission of H. W. Wilson Company

Library Journal in its ALA Conference issue (August), described this talk as "brilliant." For its sustained clarity of thought on a central concern of librarianship, we believe it will take its place as a contribution to professional literature of permanent value.

Professor Monroe, then president of the Adult Services Division, spoke on July 11 at ALA's Cleveland conference. Her talk opened an all-day program designed to explore "the development of the library collection and its use in carrying out its obligation in a public crisis." The problem of mental health was used as an example of such a crisis throughout the program, which was planned jointly by the Adult Services Division, the Association of Hospital and Institution Libraries, and the Public Library Association.

It is almost too pat to speak of our era as a time of crisis. What does this mean? A time of excitement? A series of emergencies; problems that must be dealt with in short order, demanding rapid analysis of difficulties and swiftly chosen solutions? Or is it a time of quandary, when the fundamental questions find no simple answers because conflicting values are involved within each problem? Is it, as Webster says, "a point at which hostile elements are most

tensely opposed"?   Or is crisis a turning point--a point after
which things are never again the same, and thus an opportunity, perhaps, as well as a danger?

What is the role of the library at these turning
points, at these moments of decision?   Is it a matter of too
little and too late?   Must the library have made its contribution long before or not at all?   "Crisis" has the tone of
heightened emotion; surely the library's contribution is one
of fact and reason.

There is a litany of purposes which public librarians
have come to repeat: research, information, education, recreation, and aesthetic experience.   Army and hospital librarians join their voices in the familiar sequence.   College and
university librarians adapt these, each to his own liking.

The role of the collection
In the first place, the library's collection contributes
information.   It must meet the informational demands which
individuals and society make on it because of the crisis.
The demands of the unemployed for books to retrain in vocational skills must be met, as well as the demands of the em-
ployer for materials to assist in the changeover within the
industrial plant.   The problems created for individuals by a
public crisis must be assisted toward solution by the provision of information.

Second, the public crisis itself must be understood,
and the library must contribute to a program of public education by supplying background information, the various analyses of the problem and their companion solutions.   These
must be available at the diverse levels of understanding required by the community to be served.   Young, middle-aged
and older citizens have different approaches to the problem
of a rapidly aging population, and materials from varied
points of view must be available.

Third, resources for research to alleviate the public
crisis must be made available.   Until the crisis is past
there is hope for a useful solution, and information is the
basic matter of the researcher.   The solutions to the problems of school integration are still to be spelled out from
the record in the literature of psychology, sociology, and
education.

Beyond the passive supplying of information, the library's collection must direct attention to the public crisis
in ways conducive to its happy solution.   The availability of
important titles, their promotion by display, the interpretation of their significance through reading lists, book talks,
lectures and discussion are among the ways of ensuring use
of the library's collection for the solution of the problem.
For example, no public issue of the moment relies more
heavily on the wide range of library techniques to stimulate
attention than the present crisis in United States foreign policy.

Finally, the library's collection must be used with individual readers to sustain attention to important aspects of
the problem.   This is essential to informed public opinion
and to readiness for decision and action.   This is the educational function of the library's collection, which is marshalled
to meet the needs of the inquisitive mind.   This is Mr. Ulveling's "prescription service." The public crisis in the
field of science--the growing gulf between the scientist and
the layman, between the scientist and policy-maker--can be
bridged only by such sustained learning on a broad scale in
our society.

Principles of Selection
Librarianship has developed two principles on the relationship of its collection to a public crisis.   These two
principles guide librarians in selecting materials of opinion
and of fact.

The first principle makes clear that in areas of opin-
ion--such as most public issues present--the best statements
of the hostile elements and conflicting values must be available among the library's materials.   A corollary has been
tentatively suggested: that the librarian should encourage the
reader to use materials representing more than one point of
view.   A related assumption has been enunciated, but not
without contest: that--in the United States--we trust readers
to identify propaganda for what it is and to make sound judgments on the relative merits of varied positions on critical
problems.   Some librarians see a fallacy in accepting the
public's discrimination as fact, rather than as an ideal essential to sound democratic function.   These librarians propose rather that readers be given an opportunity to acquire
this kind of discrimination.

A second corollary is one not often acknowledged but frequently the basis for judgment in building the library's collection. It is that in library collections serving educational and informational needs, materials are to be judged not only by their conformity with scientific fact and their sincerity of purpose. They are to be judged also by their compatibility with a few fundamental values upon which human society is based, and which have been determined by a consensus of responsible opinion distilled from all fields of knowledge over the total period of man's culture. These values have not been formulated exactly by librarians or by society; they are discerned by the sense of outrage in the educated and civilized mind when they are ignored.

The second principle which fortifies the library collection in meeting a public crisis is this: that in the areas of science and documented knowledge, the collection for information and educational uses be drawn from authoritative sources. Problems in application of this principle include, of course, the identification of "authority," and a decision in each separate field on what are truly validated facts and what really remains in the realm of opinion. Constant vigilance is needed in scanning new knowledge to redefine the legitimate areas of controversy, and in scrutinizing the library's collection for outdated materials which may deserve perpetuation as historical record but not acceptance as currently valid.

These two principles give appropriate weight to scientific fact and schemes of values in building the library's collection on any issue. In building and interpreting the collection, they obviously demand, if not a subject expert, at least a librarian conversant with the specialist's knowledge. They leave one question unanswered, however: since these two principles were developed in relation to collections to be used for information and educational purposes, how do they apply to materials for a research collection, or for recreational or aesthetic purposes?

Problems of application

The research collection is one from which materials are not eliminated for reasons of doubtful or disproven validity, or because they embody values rejected by the consensus of civilized judgment. The relevance of the research collection to public issues and to meeting a public crisis lies in its long-term contribution of fact and opinion, of the record

and its analysis and proposal, to the thinking of the specialist and of the research man.   The dilemma of the research
collection lies not in its materials but in their use by the
layman and student for purposes of information and education.

A most important question has arisen over how far
recreational materials and creative literature need conform
to scientific validity and the consensus of civilized judgment
in order to qualify as legitimate library materials.   The only aspect of this broad question that concerns us here is the
relationship of these materials to meeting a public crisis and
illuminating a public issue.   Librarians have often exempted
such materials from conformity to the details of scientific
fact (flying saucers are acceptable fictional adventure while
unacceptable as fact) and have permitted great latitude in values to materials designed to create the aesthetic experience.
The assumptions behind this practice are that the reader has
the ability to distinguish between fact and fiction and that his
personal scheme of values will enter into the reading of creative literature and become an important ingredient in the aesthetic experience.   These are highly defensible positions for
librarianship and are probably essential to the discharge of
its responsibility.   The dilemma arises as the library attempts to fulfill its information and education functions with
readers who, while literate, are in no sense judges of scientific validity or participants in the consensus of civilized
judgment.   This large body of illiterate literates challenges
the library's collection as it attempts to meet such a public
crisis as that of human relations.

So much for principles and corollaries.

Awareness of the relationship between the library's
collection and fulfillment of the library's basic purposes has
shown increasing sophistication.   There was readiness three
generations ago to exclude literature "apologetic of vice or
confusing distinctions between plain right and wrong," as the
Boston Public Library report of 1875 put it.   Librarians recognized in time that too little is known about the effects of
reading to make such exclusions automatic.   A later tendency
was to take no responsibility for the effects of reading on the
public.   This has been modified to view reader services
(such as stimulation of worthy reading interests, individual
guidance to suitable reading, development of critical judgment in literature and ideas, etc.) as the intermediary between the library's collection and the reader and what he

makes of what he reads.

The development of reader services as the intermediary between the library's collection and the reader in the past generation has developed one guiding principle for meeting a public crisis: the library should make it impossible for adults to miss the socially significant materials of their time, and--as a corollary--the library takes no responsibility for telling people what to think but does take responsibility for proposing what they shall think about. This serves well in considering the library's responsibility to public education about a public crisis.

Editor's note: See also Dr. Monroe's statement pertinent to theory of building collections "Meeting demands: A library imperative," Library Journal 88: 516-18 Feb. 1, 1963.

Library Book Selection

by S(hiyali) R(amaminta) Ranganathan
Indian librarian, author, and educator; "one of the few philosophers of librarianship" (Cur Biog 1965: 328)

From Library Book Selection. Ed. 2. Bombay, India, Asia Publishing House, 1966. p. 46-55. Reprinted by permission of Asia Publishing House, Bombay, India.

The Five Laws of Library Science

1 Books are for use
2 Every Reader his book
3 Every book its reader
4 Save the time of the reader
5 A library is a growing organism

Chapter AC

Shift in Responsibility

1 New Trend in Book Selection

Happily during the last decade or two, such things have begun to disappear in the developed countries. The Library Committee takes responsibility only to the

1 Laying down of the policy of book selection;
2 Allocation of the book fund among books and periodicals;
3 Allocation of the same among different subject areas;
4 Allocation of the same again among different standards;
5 Allocation of the same among different languages; and
6 Appointment of a Panel of Experts in different subjects
to be consulted by the librarian in making book selection.

Book Selection Committee reserves to itself also the right to
1 Review the books selected and acquired by the librarian

on the advice of the experts;

    2 Check up if its policy has been deviated from; and if necessary;

    3 Introduce changes in its policy.

The librarian

    1 Keeps informing himself, from week to week, of the books actually published and even merely announced during the week;

    2 Makes a preliminary selection from his sources;

    3 Sorts them out by subject fields, standards, and languages; and

    4 Places them before the appropriate Panel Members and takes their opinion on each book in the form of "selected," or "rejected," or "deferred."

In making the preliminary selection, the librarian gives full weight to the

    1 Actual needs of the readers; and

    2 Policy laid down by the Book Selection Committee.

He further makes a list, in which for each ultimate category of reading materials there are more items than what the library could afford to buy.   This is done in order to allow the busy members of the Panel of Experts to choose between alternatives.

2 Newer Trend

In the advanced communities, the trend has gone even further.   The librarian of a big library realises that it is futile for himself to do even the preliminary selection.   He leaves this task to the reference librarians.   For, these are the persons that are in touch with the readers.   These are the persons that can read the pulse of the readers. These are the persons that find themselves in an awkward situation when the library does not have the books needed by the readers.   The librarian comes in only after the reference librarians have done their work.   He sits with the Experts in the Panel along with a reference librarian to finalise the book selection list.

3 Purification

When this stage is reached, book selection will be purified.   It will be made free, as far as humanly possible, from the personal inclinations and prejudices of a few individuals.   It will become more realistic in the sense that what is selected will be what is wanted by the consumers.

Chapter BB

Messages of Law 2

Note.   At the end of each message the sub-section
in the text, where it is formulated, is mentioned.   Its
parent section in the text expounds the message.

Reader's Interest

EXPERT'S HELP
    2. 1 In a specialist library and a university library, pre-
pare book selection cards for currently published books of
the appropriate standard, group them under subject headings
determined by the subject-field of specialisation of the experts, and circulate periodically each group of cards to the
appropriate group of experts requesting each expert to express his selection or rejection in a specific place in the
book selection card. (Sec EB11).

PEDLAR METHOD
    2. 2 Play the pedlar by taking lists of currently published
books to potential readers.   This is essential in a specialist
library.   In a generalist library, approximate to this as
much as possible.   (Sec EB21).

SHOP-KEEPER METHOD
    2. 3 Play the shop-keeper by discussing the book needs
of each reader coming to the library, and by scanning with
him the list of currently published books. (Sec EB31).

REFERENCE LIBRARIAN'S HELP
    2. 4 Get the help of the reference librarian.   Ask him to
note the books needed by readers but not in the collection of
the library.   Make use of his notes. (Sec EB41)

SUGGESTION BOOK
    2. 5 Maintain a Suggestion Book.   Help readers to under-
stand the broad book selection policy of the library.   Scan
the Suggestion Book periodically and make the best possible
use of it. (Sec EB51).

Subject Scatter

PUBLIC LIBRARY
2. 6 In a public library, a vocational survey of the locality and the study of the subject scatter of the books used
will jointly give much help in book selection. (Sec ED61).

SCHOOL OR COLLEGE LIBRARY
2. 7 In a school or college library, the subjects prescribed for study and the subject-scatter of the books used
will jointly give much help in book selection.   (Sec ED62).

UNIVERSITY LIBRARY
2. 8 In a university library, the subjects of research and
the subject-scatter of the books used will jointly give much
help in book selection.   (Sec ED63).

SPECIALIST LIBRARY
2. 9 In a specialist library, work out the subject-scatter
in the Apupa region of the subject of specialisation, with
several sub-divisions for the umbral subject, as the basis
for book selection. (Sec ED91).

Standard Scatter

SCHOOL OR COLLEGE LIBRARY
2. 10 In a school or a college library, book selection
should care for each of the standards at which pupils or students are found in the school or in the college respectively.
Further, the proportion of the books of the different standards should be determined by the number of pupils or students found in the respective standards.   Many copies of
different text-books should be selected.   (Sec EE11).

PUBLIC LIBRARY
2. 11 In a public library, find out the few standards in
which readers are found and select books in each of the
standards.   The proportion of the books of the different
standards should be determined by the number of readers
found in the respective standards. (Sec EE21).

UNIVERSITY LIBRARY
2. 12 In a university or a research library, select only
books of a high standard leaving books of a low standard to
the college library or the public library as the case may be.
(Sec EE31).

2. 13   In a residential unitary university library, make book selection as for both a college library and a research library.   (Sec EE32).

BUSINESS LIBRARY
2. 14   In an industrial, or commercial, or other business library--a specialist library other than research library-- select more books of application including trade lists, commercial catalogues, and statistical and descriptive publications than of books of high theoretical standard, of which only a few representative books need to be selected.   (Sec EE41).

Language Scatter

PUBLIC LIBRARY IN A UNILINGUAL LOCALITY
2. 15   In the public library of unilingual locality, give the greatest representation to books in the language of the area. Select also some books in the classical language of the area and in one or two modern foreign languages, including in countries such as India, the languages of the other States in the measure of the language scatter of the people of the locality.   (Sec EF11).

PUBLIC LIBRARY IN A POLYGLOT LOCALITY
2. 16   In the public library of a polyglot locality, the representation in book selection of the different languages in use should be related to the language scatter of the people of the locality.   This applies not only to the public library system of a city as a whole but also severally to the branch library in each of its divisions or zones.   (Sec EF21).

UNIVERSITY OR RESEARCH LIBRARY
2. 17   In a university or other research library, book selection should also include important periodicals, reference books, classical works, and compendious treatises in the different foreign languages, in the measure of the importance of the communication in those languages and as indicated by the language scatter of the users.   (Sec EF 31).

VARIANT SCATTER
2. 18   Pay attention to the variant scatter of the language of the library as determined by the impression of reference librarian and by field survey.   (Sec EF41).

POTENTIAL WANT
2. 19   Do not stop with the expressed want as inferred

from the subject-scatter of accession, the subject-scatter of
circulation, and other indications of the wants of the past;
but use your knowledge of the changing social needs, the intellectual possibility, and the changing emotional wants of the
community, and select books accordingly so as to serve and
exploit such needs and possibilities.   (Sec EG11).

2. 20   Keep yourself ever alert to re-assess the potential
unexpressed wants of readers from time to time.

Anticipated Want

SCHOOL OR COLLEGE LIBRARY
    2. 21   In a school or a college library, book selection
should be done in consultation with the members of the teaching faculty at the end of each academic year so as to put on
the shelves, from the beginning onwards, of the next academic year, books necessary to meet the needs of the curricu-
lum--not merely the prescribed books but also the books
needed for preparatory, parallel, and follow-up study. (Sec
EH11).

UNIVERSITY AND RESEARCH LIBRARY
    2. 22   In a university or a research library, book selec-
tion should be done from time to time in consultation with
the members of the faculty or the research body, so as to
put on the shelves the books needed in the anticipated change
in the research activities, in good time before the changes
take place.   (Sec EH21).

GOVERNMENT DEPARTMENTAL LIBRARY
    2. 23   In a government departmental library including that
of the legislature, contemplated development schemes, legislative measures, and policy-making should be watched with
vigilance.   The department concerned should take the librarian into confidence and alert him in good time.   Book selection should be done immediately in collaboration with the
persons concerned in the department.   (Sec EH 31).

BUSINESS LIBRARY
    2. 24   In a business library, the librarian should keep him-
self informed of all anticipated developments in each of the
departments and select the books necessary to make the decision in the action of the department concerned conform to
the latest theory and practice in the matter. (Sec EH41).

PUBLIC LIBRARY
    2. 25 In a public library, book selection should be made
in anticipation in the light of the forthcoming international,
national, and local events and occurrences.   (Sec EH51).

Reference Book

PUBLIC LIBRARY
    2. 26 In a public library, select a good assortment of
reference books such as biographical dictionaries and serials,
directories of the locality and of other important cities,
travel aids such as railway, shipping, and air guides, and
tourist books, anthologies, linguistic dictionaries, and encyclopaedias of a general nature and in such of the subjects as
are of local interest.   (Sec EJ11).

UNIVERSITY OR RESEARCH LIBRARY
    2. 27 In a university or a research library, select as
many as possible of authoritative reference books in each
subject of study.   These should include bibliographies, directories of learned world, encyclopaedias, linguistic diction-
aries--particularly technical ones--trend reports, patents,
standards, and specifications.   (Sec EJ12).

LANGUAGE
    2. 28 Select reference books in English to supplement
those in Indian languages.   Further, create public opinion for
the production of reference books of all kinds in each Indian
language.   (Sec EJ21).

Survey Method in Book Selection
    2. 29 In a country, such as India, recovering from cul-
tural exhaustion and just developing thereafter, book selection will have to be based for some years not merely on statistics of issue but essentially on field survey of and personal contact with potential readers.   (Sec EK21).

Integrity of Librarian
    2. 30 High character and integrity on the part of the li-
brary profession should be brought to bear on the discharge
of its duties in regard to book selection along with an all-
round attempt to assess the potential wants of the readers--
free from any sneaking tendency to please the whims and
fancies of the individual members of the Library Authorities.
(Sec EK21).

Periodicals

PUBLIC LIBRARY
2.31 In a public library, selection of periodicals should cover a few generalia periodicals of the popular variety and some specialised periodicals bearing on the chief vocations of the people of the locality as determined by field survey. (Sec EL11).

SCHOOL LIBRARY
2.32 In a school library, selection of periodicals should cover children's periodicals capable of entertaining and informing them, on the one hand, and developing in them, on the other hand, the habit of perusing periodicals. (Sec EL12).

BUSINESS LIBRARY
2.33 In the library of a business organization, selection of periodical publications should cover the periodicals and the serials falling within the umbral region of interest of the parent body and also of a few appropriate ones falling within the penumbral region of interest. (Sec EL13).

UNIVERSITY OR RESEARCH LIBRARY
2.34 In a university or a research library, selection should cover periodical publications falling within the purview of the subject of their specialisation and also on the subjects auxiliary to them. (Sec EL14)

Continuity of Periodical
2.35 In a university or a research library, cutting down the subscription to a periodical in one year, restoring it in the next year, and cutting it down later will cause an inconvenient break in the set. Once the trial period is over and a decision is made to take the periodical, it should be continued until the standard of the periodical goes down abnormally. (Sec EL21).

BUSINESS LIBRARY
2.36 In an industrial or other business library, the continuity or otherwise of a periodical publication is best determined from year to year by the needs of the work in progress in the parent body. (Sec EL22).

CONTINUITY IN PERIODICAL SELECTION
2.37 In a generalist library, be it a public or a college or a school library, freedom may be taken in the policy of continuity or otherwise in the case of a periodical not to be

bound and preserved, according to the policy of the library.
(Sec EL23).

CONTINUITY OF SERIALS
2. 38   In the case of a serial, other than a statistical one,
it may be possible to subscribe for it at intervals, say,
every other year or once in three years.   (Sec EL24).

2. 39 In a library such as a research or a university library preserving a continuous set of volumes of a periodical,
its successive cumulative indexes should be bought as and
when published.   (Sec EL31).

NEWSPAPER
2. 40   In a public library, make a balanced selection of
newspapers--balanced in respect of their political, economic,
and social leanings.   (Sec EL41).

2. 41   Avoid selecting common newspapers for a library
other than a public library or a reading room.   (Sec EL42).

Sub-normal Reader

BLIND READER
2. 42   Bear in mind the humane responsibility to provide
books in Braille or in sound records for the blind. (Sec
EM11).

CRIPPLE READER
2. 43   Bear in mind the humane responsibility to provide
ceiling books for the cripple confined to bed. (Sec EM21).

NEO-LITERATE
2. 44   Select sound books for the neo-literates.   If they
are not already available, work for their production.   (Sec
EM31).

Chapter BC

Messages of Law 3

Note.   At the end of each message, the sub-section
in the text, where it is formulated, is mentioned.   Its
parent section in the text expounds the message.

New book
3.1   Remember to include in the book selection list new and attractive books likely to lure their readers towards some of the books of the library, failing in their appeal to readers, and thereby to increase the probability for such old books to be put back into circulation.   (Sec FC11).

3.2 To enhance the lure-effect of a new book on the old books, select such a new book as has a good bibliography. (Sec FC12).

Associated book
3.3   Select books so as to exploit the mutual dependence of books in cases, such as, a

1 Classic and the hierarchy of its commentaries;
2 Original and its translations;
3 Book on a theory and its applications;
4 Expository book and the related laboratory handbooks;
5 Law book and case studies on the law concerned;
6 Source books and treatises;
7 Original and its evaluations; and
8 Books belonging to a publisher's series. (Sec FD21).

3.4   In a school library, select books so as to exploit the mutual dependence of pupil's books and the related teacher's handbook.   (Sec FD22).

Exposition

LANGUAGE
3.5   Do not select books in a language not understood by the readers of the library.   (Sec FE11).

STANDARD
3.6   Do not select any book of a standard, which has few readers among the clientele of the library.   (Sec FE21).

SUBJECT
3.7   In a specialist library, do not select books in subjects not falling within the field of study of the library, including its fringe area.   (Sec FE31).

3.8   In a generalist library, do not select books in a subject not likely to be of interest to any reader, either for intensive study or even for general acquaintance.   (Sec FE32).

Misleading Title
3.9   Avoid selecting a book by the title alone without examining either the book itself or a review or an annotation
on it, lest its subject should be outside the purview of the library or without any interest to any reader. (Sec FE41).

Responsibility

PUBLIC LIBRARY
3.10   In a public library, the responsibility for book selection should be vested in the library staff who alone can
have the experience necessary to assess the probability for a
book to find its readers.   (Sec FF11).

ACADEMIC LIBRARY
3.11   In an academic library--be it a university, a college,
or a school library--book selection should be the joint responsibility of the library staff and the teaching staff; they
should be guided by the probability of getting readers for the
use of the book selected.   (Sec FF21).

BUSINESS LIBRARY
3.12   In a business library--such as industrial, commercial, government departmental library--book selection should
be the joint responsibility of the library and the representatives of the different divisions of the parent body.   (Sec
FF22).

Patronage Motive
3.13   Book selection in any library should be based on the
probability for readers, and should never be vitiated by consideration of patronage.   (Sec FF31).

Foreign Books
3.14   In the utilisation of the fund of a library, set apart
for books to be purchased from foreign countries, do not
make a fetish of the absolute 31 March fixed by audit or
budget.   Work on the basis of the relative time limit of
seventeen months after the sanction of the book fund. (Sec
FG51).

Sacred Trust
3.15   A librarian should regard the responsibility for book
selection vested in him as a sacred trust to be discharged in
the best interest of the legitimate clientele of his library.
(Sec FH41).

Toward an "Ideal" Book Selection Policy

by J. Perriam Danton   Professor, School of Librarianship, University of Cali-
fornia, Berkeley, California

From Book Selection and Collections: A comparison of German and American University Libraries.
New York and London, Columbia University Press,
1963. p. 131-140; Reprinted by permission of
Columbia University Press.

Despite the serious lacks and insufficiencies of present book-selection and collection-building policy and practice,
there is considerable evidence to suggest that university libraries on the whole are now building better for the future
than was the case seventy-five to a hundred and fifty years
ago. Such a pessimistic view as the following seems quite
unwarranted. "Our modern university libraries may be
larger in volume, but there is no assurance that their qualitative value will be any greater in the twenty-first century
than that of the average nineteenth century collection is for
us." Among the reasons and evidence for a more optimistic
position may be cited the very real concern of virtually all
present-day university librarians with the library's grave responsibility, and the generally far greater attention being
given to the problems, policy, and practice of book selection.

Somewhat more tangible is the evidence that more
people in libraries in Germany and in and out of libraries in
America are spending time on the business of selecting books;
that the international bibliographical apparatus even by the
fourth quarter of the nineteenth century was generally not
nearly so well developed as it is today; and that no American university library before about that time, and only a
single German one before the beginning of the nineteenth century, consciously collected for research purposes and had
the means effectively to do so. Up to approximately these
two times, respectively, most German and American university libraries grew pretty largely like Topsy. For many now
distinguished libraries, as we have seen in Chapters II and
IV, a significantly different state of affairs came even later.

Now, although the directions of university research will un-
questionably change in the future, and although new fields of
inquiry will arise, it seems improbable that our fundamental
view of research, its methods, and the materials necessary
for its prosecution will alter much, if at all.   In other
words, the original account of a creative experiment, the
governmental report on international credit balances, the author's autobiography, or the first edition of a book of poetry,
are likely to be as useful, though perhaps not always for the
same purposes, to the researcher fifty years from now as
they are to the scholar today.   Further, the library spending
$100,000, or several times that sum, for books each year
is able to buy a larger proportion of the publications it believes important than could the library of a hundred years
ago having annually only a few thousand, or a few hundred
dollars.   If these propositions be granted, it seems certain
that their combined effect will be to produce for the worker
of the twenty-first century resources very much more generally useful than the collections of 1850 are today.

Be this as it may, the evidence adduced in the previous chapters seems clearly to suggest that present policy is
somewhat deficient and could be bettered.   It is the purpose
of this chapter to attempt to outline the components of what
might be defensible as an "ideal" policy of book selection for
university libraries.   Several caveats and apologiae need
mention in advance.

The ideal is seldom a wholly, under all circumstances,
feasible and practicable solution to a problem.   The more
nearly the solution approaches a true, philosophical, or logical ideal, the more likely is this to be the case.   This consideration does not constitute a justification for silence.
Those who first proposed splitting the nucleus to wrest from
it an unlimited, that is, ideal, source of energy were no
doubt "impractical."

In the realm of ideas and of human institutions, in
contradistinction, for example, to the laboratory investigation, conditions are usually not duplicatable, and 1 plus 2
plus 3 do not always and everywhere add up to 6.   Even
though it may be demonstrable that the democratic institutions and practices of America may be the best than can be
devised for that country, it does not necessarily follow that
the very same institutions and practices can be inaugurated
elsewhere or, if they can be, that they will produce comparable results.   In other words, although the proposals sug-

gested here are believed to be generally, logically, and
philosophically sound, it is not assumed that all of them
could be adopted at all times, under all circumstances, and
in all places.

The arguments and considerations which lead to this
presentation have, in the main, been reviewed in the previous chapters and, in so far as that is the case, they are
not repeated here.

Teaching and Research Policy Statement. The university administration, following consultation with, and advice
from, appropriate academic groups, should provide the library with an official statement of policy, in some detail,
as to the institution's present and probable future program
of teaching and research. The statement should indicate the
institution's level of interest in specific areas of learning,
and the extent to which they will be supported and prose-
cuted. (E. g. , Middle Eastern languages, introductory work
only; nuclear physics, comprehensive and intensive program,
doctoral program, fullest possible support for faculty research.) Such a statement would need to be reviewed and
revised at least every decade, possibly every five years.
Without such a statement, carefully thought out, and known
to all, a really effective long-range book selection and book
collection building policy and program cannot be realized.

Development of a Level-of-Collecting Program. On
the basis of this statement and with the cooperation of the
faculty, a detailed level-of-collecting program should be developed within some such framework as that described in
Chapter V. That is, conscious judgments, on a five-point
scale, should be made and noted, for subjects and divisions
of subjects indicating the level of collecting. To be genuinely useful and effective, these judgments should probably be
rendered to the detail involved, for example, in the thousand
major classifications of the Dewey system. The development
of such a policy statement will obviously involve a good deal
of work. It will involve less than might at first appear,
however, since many judgments should result more or less
automatically from the institutional policy statement described
under the first heading. Decisions agreed upon as to level-
of-collecting for various subjects should help to insure the
building up of the library's collections in a balanced, coordinated fashion, and in conformity with the actual teaching and
research program of the institution. The policy statement
proposed here should be under fairly constant review and

should certainly be reviewed as a whole not less frequently than once every five years.   At any given time, however, relatively few collecting-level decisions would need to be substantially revised.

Budget and Book Selection Responsibility.   The whole responsibility for selection and collection building, and the entire book budget, including book money for branch, departmental, divisional, institute, and seminar libraries, should reside, legally and actually, with the university library.

Library Staff Corps of Book Selectors.   The major portion of the titles acquired by the library, or any branch, divisional, departmental, or institute library, should be, and would as a result be selected by members of the library staff--and well in advance of the clientele's need for them.

If the library has on its staff enough members with the highest subject and bibliographical knowledge, and if these individuals are given the responsibility and sufficient time for book selection, the result will be a more objectively, consistently, thoroughly built-up book collection than can otherwise be the case.   Gone, or at very least far less operative, will be the influence of special or narrow interests, and of personal bias, ignorance of major parts of the collection as a whole, the often disastrous results of personnel changes or absences.   For, with respect to book selection in such a framework, the library staff may be considered as an "administrative" continuum in a way that no academic individuals can be.   The absence or change of a library staff member is immediately known to the library administration and steps can at once be taken to fill the gap.   Not so the absence of, or change in, the putative professor-book selector who is a Civil War historian, an anthropologist, or a Gestalt psychologist.   A library staff of this kind, in short, has the knowledge; the time; the fixed administrative duty and obligation; the immediate and constant access to the necessary bibliographical apparatus; the consistency of operation and viewpoint; the knowledge of a large segment of the collection; and, more than any others, the awareness "of the total problem of the relationship between the scholar and all of the resources of scholarship," which appear to be the principal requirements, aside from adequate book funds, for the building up of scholarly libraries.

A library adding a total of 60,000 volumes a year (considerably fewer than the average of the "Princeton statistics" group) might have a cataloging staff of forty-five, of whom about twenty would be professional employees.   Many university libraries will, of course, have larger cataloging staffs; many, obviously, will have smaller ones.   Columbia in 1956 had fifty-two and a half, of whom half were professional employees.

The key to the contents of the modern library is its catalogs.   But the key is only as valuable, so to speak, as the things to which it gives access.   It seems logically possible, therefore, to suggest that libraries spend as much thought, time, and money in insuring the highest possible quality of the library's contents as they do in preparing the contents for use.   Actually, an equal amount of money might not be necessary.   A corps of twenty professional staff members with half as many clerical assistants might be sufficient. If twenty seems like an excessively large number for the tasks of selection, two considerations may be advanced.   The first refers to the present German experience and practice, as described in the first half of Chapter III.   Even the largest German group, of fifteen, is too small.   The proposed corps should carry out substantially the same tasks as the German groups, plus the activity described under the next heading, and in America, at least, would be concerned with a considerably larger body of literature, as has been seen.

A variant plan to that of having a special, separate corps of book selectors would offer several advantages.   Under this scheme, many, perhaps most of the professional staff would be assigned specific book selection responsibilities in accordance with their academic subject specializations. A fairly definite proportion of the staff members' working time would be available for the several activities which go to make up book selection.   The entire program would be under the supervision of a small group of two or three coordinators, headed by a chief of book selection.   Advanced and specialized subject competence of prospective staff would need to be a special consideration, to an extent much greater than it now generally is outside the European continent, in the recruitment of personnel for the library; it might be argued here, as it is argued on the Continent, that library staff book selectors should be as well prepared, academically, as the faculty they serve.   A program of this kind, if it should embrace most professional members of present Anglo-American university library staffs, runs quite counter to the philosophy of most Continental scholarly libraries, including those of Germany, Holland, Austria, and the Scandinavian

countries. These have long held that the task of book selection can be satisfactorily performed only by those who hold
subject doctorates. The Diplombibliothekar, for example,
in the German university library, though a library school
graduate, is not deemed qualified for book selection and is
given no responsibility for it. That this view is open to question is demonstrated by the outstanding collections which have
been built up by such institutions as the New York Public Library and the British Museum where book selection is performed exclusively by large numbers of staff members few
of whom hold the doctorate. It must be granted, however,
that these individuals commonly have two to three more years
of academic education than the Diplombibliothekar and his
counterpart in libraries of other European countries.

The advantages of this variant are several. In the
first place, it would benefit staff morale by giving many
members of the professional group a share in responsibility
for building the collection, that is, for the most important
single activity in which the library engages. Second, in the
same way, the attraction of sharing in this activity should be
a strong positive factor in recruiting. Third, staff members
not deemed by the library to have sufficiently advanced subject knowledge to participate in book selection would be provided with an additional incentive for further education and
study in order to qualify for appointment to the group of selectors. Such appointment should be considered a matter of
honor and prestige and should be clearly treated as such by
the library. Fourth, in most university libraries, size of
professional staff is such that subject assignments could be
more narrowly made under this plan. With a staff of forty
to one hundred or more, none might need to cover more than
a single subject and some subjects, as for example history,
might even be divided, one member being assigned Western
European, one the United States, and so on. Staff interest,
and attention to, and coverage of each field should, as a result, be greater than where one person had responsibility for
an entire field or even two or three fields. Finally, there
would be a financial advantage, in that such a program
should cost less in staff salaries than would the setting up
of a full-blown, separate corps of selection specialists per
se.

Some, though not the major, aspects of this proposed
program have been tried in a few American university libraries. Washington, (Seattle), for example, did so in the
1940s and 1950s. The staff, however, was organized through

a committee system, bought no books less than five years old, and never had more than $3,000 at its disposal; and the subject knowledge of prospective staff members played no part in the recruitment of staff as potential book selectors.

Faculty Participation in Book Selection. Faculty participation in selection should be encouraged and fostered and, especially, should be made more nearly universal than it is now. To this end the library staff book-selectors should be expected to devote possibly a fifth to a tenth of their total time, depending upon whether the special Library Staff Corps plan or its variant is adopted, to working with individual members of the faculty. In particular, new appointees, and those who have previously shown little or no concern for the library, should be visited, their interests discovered, their special bibliographic knowledge exploited, and offers of assistance and the strongest possible encouragement to active participation in book selection given. A program of this kind, pursued over a period of years, would result in personal acquaintance of the library staff members with most members of the faculty. Contact by mail and telephone, between personal visits, should be maintained. The closest possible contact with existing branch, departmental, divisional (or institute) libraries should also be maintained, and a maximum of collection-building coordination striven for. A special duty of the library staff members would be, in the light of the Teaching and Research Policy Statement, long-range study of predictable demands on the library, the present resources, and the resources required.

In order that this corps not work in a vacuum, isolated from other library activities, and in order that it have contact with general library problems, its members should likewise have line responsibilities which might take about one quarter of their time. If the variant plan were adopted, staff members with book selection responsibility might be spending upward of three quarters of their total working time on other duties.

Collections Built to Strength. In so far as the present and prospective institutional program permits, the university library should build on existing strengths. The argument:

A. It cannot hope to be maximally strong in all fields and subfields.

B. Therefore it must choose between (1) an aim to-

ward genuine strength in a more or less limited number of
fields and subfields, or (2) the division of available funds
more or less equitably among all possible fields, with the
result that none will have real distinction.

C. The library serves its institution in particular,
and the world of scholarship in general, better if its collections permit extensive and intensive research in some, even
though a very limited number of fields, than it does if it offers merely minimal to fair collections in many fields and
excellent ones in none. No one will be attracted to, and no
important work will be done in a library of the latter kind;
some, at least, will be in a library of the former.

D. If the library pursues the program of (B 1) it will
have limited success unless it builds on existing strength because (1) many basic, essential items will be difficult, expensive, or impossible to acquire; and (2) the task of building to excellence from limited or minimal holdings will require far more time, effort, and money than will the creation of excellence from relative strength. Nothing in the
foregoing is intended to imply that a library should not build
up to adequacy, or even to great strength an area deplorably
weak vis à vis the university's instructional and research
program.

E. It is not necessary that every university library
provide materials for doctoral study and intensive faculty research in Sumerian art, Icelandic literature, the political
history of Albania, the cultural anthropology of Nigeria, or
Polynesian land shells. If it is not already moderately strong
in such fields, the university would be well advised not to
commence programs requiring the attempt to build major library collections in them. Deliberate forswearing, at the
points where academic policy is created, has been an all too
rare phenomenon of universities everywhere. "All the evident and subtle aspects of institutional identity, sovereignty,
pride and competitiveness" have, in fact, contributed to an
opposite development. Downs makes the point thus: "As
long as universities insist upon carrying on instruction and
research in virtually every subject under the sun, frequently
in competition with one another, the libraries will be expected to support these programs by providing materials and
services. Limitations of fields, however, is a direction in
which universities have been reluctant to move. The trend
is almost invariably toward expansion, not retraction."

Aim toward Comprehensiveness. On the other hand, in fields where strength already exists and where the institutional program is comprehensive and intensive, the library should aim toward the highest degree of excellence, qualitative and quantitative, that it can possibly afford, with due regard to the ready availability of the resources of nearby libraries and the possibilities for cooperative effort. In all such fields, the aim should be toward comprehensiveness. This should be interpreted as meaning that a very good case indeed would have to be made for not acquiring any item of the graphic record deemed to be of value and which the library can afford. Any other policy but ill serves scholarship, not only of the distant but also of the immediate future. It is not believed that any man is wise enough, or gifted with sufficient foresight, to say that any document (excepting only the wholly derivative) will not be of genuine importance to some scholar some time.

This does not mean abdication from the duty, responsibility, and privilege of selection. In all, perhaps, but the minutest subdivision of a field, the library must select, if for no other reason than that it cannot acquire everything. And certainly "some things are better than others."

Current Publications versus Older Titles. Other things being more or less equal as, of course, they frequently are not, the library should prefer the current rather than the older title. Obviously this does not mean that the library would forego the opportunity to acquire a long-sought, intensely wanted out-of-print item in favor of a current, in-print volume which will undoubtedly also be readily available in the near future! Obviously, also, a library which has been unable to buy essential and fundamental works at the time of their publication (e. g., because of subsequent founding of the institution, subsequent development of a field of interest, lack of access to the sources of supply) or has lost such items (e. g., as a result of war, fire, flood) will need to pay special attention to the second-hand market. But major emphasis on current works, until all the useful ones have been acquired, is, as a general principle, preferable to a program which, buying extensively in the second-hand market, leaves insufficient funds for the purchase of current titles. The former policy, consistently pursued over a period of years, will eventually reduce the time and money which the library has to spend identifying, locating, and buying out-of-print items.

Needs of the Present and Needs of the Future.   Because of its obligation to fulfill the requirements of its present clientele, the library must acquire in considerable part
"for the needs of the present"; it must also, however, acquire for the "needs of the future"; for, if it does not now
do so, unavailability of material will later prevent it from
fully doing so.

A university's library is its most important and indispensable resource.   The material quality of that resource
is determined by the excellence of the book collection.   The
quality of the book collection depends in turn upon selection
policy and practice.   Any measures undertaken to improve
that policy and practice will result in collections better
suited to the university's educational and scholarly needs.
Even the partial adoption of the proposals discussed above
would, it seems certain, lead to improved collections.

Editor's note: Another important contribution to the develop-
        ment of theory of collections, especially pertinent
        here, is Gordon Williams, "The librarian's role in
        the development of library book collections," Library
        Quarterly 34: 374-386, October 1964.

Are the Best Books the Most Read?

by Herbert Goldhor

Director, Graduate School of
Library Science, University
of Illinois and formerly, Director, Evansville (Indiana)
Public Library

From Library Quarterly 22: 251-55, October 1959;
Reprinted by permission of the University of Chicago Press, c1959 University of Chicago.

The literature of librarianship contains frequent references to the appropriate basis for book selection--shall it be
the demand for certain titles, or shall it be their value,
either as literature or as sources of authentic information?[1]
Most libraries in practice probably take both demand and
value into consideration. But in the context of these two
approaches to book selection, the question arises: Are the
best books the books most read? To answer this question,
the Evansville, Indiana, Public Library in 1958 undertook
the investigation here reported.[2]

The Evansville Public Library and Vanderburgh County Public Library serve a population of 160,000 (1950 Census), through a central library, ten branches, and a bookmobile, with a book stock (as of the end of 1958) of 291,502
volumes. Of these, 139,220 (48 per cent) are children's
books and 152,282 (52 per cent) adult. It is estimated that
at least half the total adult book stock is in the central library building and that all adult books have been reviewed
and examined for discard at least once in the last five years.

Procedure

For the purposes of this study, only adult hard-cover
books, classified in the Dewey Decimal numbers 612-613.9,
were considered. Included were such subjects as physiology,
digestion, reproduction, hygiene, food in health, rest and exercise, and genetics. A total of 741 copies of 317 titles
were so identified, and they constitute what is here called
the "gross sample." The "value" of these books was esti-

mated by checking a number of book-reviewing periodicals, to see whether or not they were reviewed and to note unfavorable reviewer's reactions when indicated.   The resulting data were compressed into three value categories: A, for a title with three or more favorable reviews; B, for a title with one or two favorable reviews; and C, for a title with no reviews or no favorable reviews.   The intent was to place in the A group books well and widely reviewed and especially appropriate for public library use; in the B group, books not widely reviewed or not particularly appropriate for public library use; and in the C group, those books which were either not reviewed, not favorably reviewed, or considered inappropriate for public library use.   Books published in 1958 and in the library's collection were excluded from the gross sample, since they had only a minimal chance of appearing in the book-reviewing tools used.

Six main tools were consulted: the Book Review Digest (1905-58), the Standard Catalog for Public Libraries (1934, 1939, 1944, 1949 eds. and supplements), the Standard Catalog for High School Libraries (1947, 1952, and 1957 eds.), the Booklist (1904-56), the American Journal of Public Health (1927-58), and Hawkins' Scientific, Medical, and Technical Books (1st and 2d eds.).   A limited run (in no case more than six years) was available of Technical Book Review Index, New Technical Books, of the New York Public Library, and the United States Quarterly Book Review. These, however, listed so few titles in the gross sample that the results were not used.

It may be of interest to record some of the data on the use in this present study of several book-evaluation tools in checking a given library's collection.   This method is different from the traditional procedure for evaluating a book collection, viz., picking a standard list of books and ascertaining how many of its titles are held.   Such a procedure ignores books on the shelves but not on the list used for checking (except by implication); some of these books may be as good as (or even better than) some on the list.

Of 317 titles analyzed, 24 per cent were not located in any of the nine tools used; 20 per cent were found in only one; 17 per cent in two; 16 per cent in three; 13 per cent in four; 7 per cent in five; and 1 per cent each in six, seven, and eight of the lists.   No title was found in all nine.   The Book Review Digest listed 173; the Booklist, 143; the Standard Catalog for Public Libraries, 129; the American Journal of Public Health, 107; the <u>Standard Catalog for High School Libraries,</u> 40; the Hawkins list (1st ed.), 38, (2d ed.), 25; and <u>Technical Book Review Index</u> (1952-58), 18.

Findings

Of the 317 titles, 120 (38 per cent) were found to be in the A-value category, 120 (38 per cent) in the B group, and 77 (24 per cent) in the C group. No information is available on how many other titles (and of what "value") had previously been in the library's book collection but had been withdrawn and discarded by 1958. Even so, the titles on hand had been published between 1901 and 1957. The distribution of these titles by date of publication and by value category is shown in Table 1. The higher total is occasioned by the fact that in this table different editions of the same title are counted separately, while the total of 317 titles includes a unit count for each of 27 titles which are represented by more than one edition. It would appear from Table 1 that this library has managed to retain a larger proportion of the more valuable books published before 1940 (and have presumably been tested in use) than it has purchased of those published since 1951.

These 317 titles were represented by 741 copies, a mean of 2.3 copies per title, a median of 3.3, a mode of 1, and a range of 1-23 copies per title. These 741 copies were distributed by value as follows: in the A category, 50 per cent; in the B group, 32 per cent; and in C, 18 per cent. It is clear, from the data in Table 2, that the library has tended to duplicate the better books more often than those in the C-value category, particularly in the case of older titles. Thus 50 per cent of all titles in the A group have been duplicated in the collection, while only 36 percent of the B titles and 30 per cent of the C titles were provided in more than one copy. The distribution of copies by year of acquisition corresponds closely to the data in Table 2.

The total known circulation of these books was recorded from available information. This consisted of the loans noted on the book cards (in this library a summary figure of loans is typed on a new book card when an earlier card is filled up and must be replaced) and the date-due slips currently in these books. Since 1953, transaction card charging has been used in increasingly more agencies of this library, but a stroke record of circulation by year is kept on the date-due slip. Undoubtedly, some error is in-

Table 1

Classification of Titles in Gross Sample by Year
of Publication and by Value Category

Years	Total No. of Titles	Value Category		
		A No. of Titles	B No. of Titles	C No. of Titles
1901-40	128 (100%)	60 (47%)	44 (34%)	24 (19%)
1941-50	117 (100%)	56 (48%)	40 (34%)	21 (18%)
1951-57	110 (100%)	35 (32%)	42 (38%)	33 (30%)
Total	355 (100%)	151 (42%)	126 (36%)	78 (22%)

Per Cent of Value Category

Years	Total	A	B	C
1901-40	36	40	35	31
1941-50	33	37	32	27
1951-57	31	23	33	42
Total	100	100	100	100

Table 2

Classification of Copies in Gross Sample by Year
of Publication and by Value Category

Years	Total No. of Titles	A No. of Titles	Value Category B No. of Titles	C No. of Titles
1901-40	220 (100%)	122 (55%)	68 (31%)	30 (14%)
1945-50	262 (100%)	151 (58%)	82 (31%)	28 (11%)
1951-57	259 (100%)	100 (38%)	82 (32%)	77 (30%)
Total	741 (100%)	373 (50%)	233 (32%)	135 (18%)

Per Cent of Value Category

	Total	A	B	C
1901-40	30	33	29	22
1941-50	35	40	36	21
1951-57	35	27	5	57
Total	100	100	100	100

corporated in the resulting data, but there is no reason to
believe that the error distributes itself in any systematic way.
Even so, not all the books could be found in the two months
in which this study was made; and in some cases when the
books were found, the circulation record was obviously incomplete or inaccurate. In all, 160 books were excluded
from the circulation count.

In the case of the 39 titles, all copies of which were
excluded from the gross sample, 28 per cent were in the A
category, 49 per cent in B, and 23 per cent in C. Of all
160 copies excluded, 53 per cent were in the A group, 30
per cent in B, and 17 per cent in C. The remaining 581
copies of 278 titles which were available for analysis both
by circulation and by value constitute the net sample.

The total known circulation of all books in the net
sample, from 1918 (when the oldest of these books was first
loaned) to the end of 1958, was 10,389. Distribution of the
circulation figure is shown in Table 3. The differences in
average circulation per title of the books in the three value
groups is greater than can be accounted for by chance alone
$(P < .01)$. [3] But the differences in the average circulation
per copy and in the yearly average circulation per copy are
not significant.

Are the better books more read (per title) because
they are newer or because there are more copies of them?
To answer this, two further analyses were made. Table 4
shows the data on the circulation of books in the first 5 years
after they were acquired; this includes no book published or
acquired after 1954. Librarians know that new books are
read more often than old books, and Table 4 bears this out;
in the first 5 years after their acquisition the books represented in Table 4 accounted for 52 per cent of all the circulation of the net sample (51 per cent in the case of A-value
books, 49 per cent in B-value books, and 64 per cent in C-
value books). The differences between the average circulation per title of the books in the three value categories in
Table 4 are not statistically significant, nor, of course, are
the differences in average circulation per copy or in yearly
average circulation. It would appear that in the first 5 years
after acquisition the best books are not necessarily the most
read.

Table 3

Circulation Analysis of Net Sample, by Value Category

Item	Total		A		Value Category B		C	
1. Total circulation	10,389	(100%)	5,846	(56%)	3,213	(31%)	1,325	(13%)
2. No. of titles	278	(100%)	109	(39%)	102	(37%)	67	(24%)
3. Average circulation per title	37	(100%)	54	(146%)	32	(86%)	20	(54%)
4. No. of copies	581	(100%)	292	(50%)	185	(32%)	104	(18%)
5. Average circulation per copy	18	(100%)	20	(111%)	17	(94%)	13	(72%)
6. Total no. of years all copies were available for circulation	6,806	(100%)	3,507	(51%)	2,292	(34%)	1,007	(15%)
7. Yearly average circulation per copy	1.5	(100%)	1.7	(113%)	1.4	(93%)	1.3	(87%)

Table 4

Circulation Analysis of Net Sample, by Value Category,
in First Five Years After Acquisition

Item	Total		A		Value Category B		C	
1. Total circulation	5,415	(100%)	2,990	(55%)	1,570	(29%)	855	(16%)
2. No. of titles	229	(100%)	97	(42%)	80	(35%)	52	(23%)
3. Average circulation per title	24	(100%)	31	(129%)	20	(84%)	16	(67%)
4. No. of copies	422	(100%)	217	(52%)	132	(31%)	73	(17%)
5. Average circulation per copy	13	(100%)	14	(108%)	12	(92%)	12	(92%)
6. Total no. of years all copies were available for circulation	2,130	(100%)	1,100	(52%)	665	(31%)	365	(17%)
7. Yearly average circulation per copy	2.5	(100%)	2.7	(108%)	2.4	(96%)	2.3	(92%)

Table 5

Circulation Analysis of Net Sample, by Value Category,
of Titles Represented by Only One Copy

Item	Total	A	Value Category B	C
1. Total circulation	3,709 (100%)	1,621 (44%)	1,387 (37%)	701 (19%)
2. No. of titles	168 (100%)	54 (32%)	69 (41%)	45 (27%)
3. Average circulation per title	22 (100%)	30 (136%)	20 (92%)	16 (73%)
4. Total no. of years all copies were available for circulation	2,736 (100%)	1,020 (37%)	1,113 (41%)	603 (22%)
5. Yearly average circulation per copy	1.4 (100%)	1.6 (114%)	1.2 (86%)	1.2 (86%)

Table 6

Circulation Analysis of Net Sample, by Value Category,
of Titles Represented by Two or More Copies

Item	Total	Value Category A	Value Category B	Value Category C
1. Total circulation	6,670 (100%)	4,220 (63%)	1,830 (28%)	620 (9%)
2. No. of titles	109 (100%)	55 (51%)	33 (30%)	21 (19%)
3. Average circulation per title	61 (100%)	77 (126%)	56 (92%)	30 (49%)
4. No. of copies	413 (100%)	238 (58%)	116 (28%)	59 (14%)
5. Average circulation per copy	16 (100%)	18 (112%)	16 (100%)	10 (62%)
6. Total no. of years all copies were available for circulation	4,070 (100%)	2,487 (61%)	1,179 (29%)	404 (10%)
7. Yearly average circulation per copy	1.6 (100%)	1.7 (106%)	1.6 (100%)	1.5 (94%)

Table 5 shows the results of analyzing the circulation data for those books in the net sample of which only one copy was available. The differences in the average circulation per title (or copy) for books in the different value categories are not statistically significant, nor are those in the yearly average circulation. On a single-copy basis and over a long period of time, the better books are not necessarily read more often than the poorer ones.

Table 6 shows the results of a similar analysis of data for books in the net sample which are represented by more than one copy. The differences in the average circulation per title of those books in the three value categories are larger than can be accounted for by sampling error ($P < .001$), but again this is not true of the differences in the average circulation per copy in the yearly average circulation per copy. The 109 titles represented in Table 6 accounted for 64 per cent of the circulation of all 278 titles in the net sample; only half the A-value titles had been duplicated, but they accounted for 72 per cent of the circulation of all A-value titles. Similarly, 32 per cent of the B-value titles were duplicated, but their use was 57 per cent of the circulation of all B-value titles; 31 per cent of the C-value titles were duplicated, and their use was 47 per cent of the circulation of all C-value titles.

Conclusion

It would appear from the data available in this study that the best books are not necessarily the most widely read. If libraries buy good books and poor books in equal quantities, they will be read in approximately equal numbers. [4] It is to the credit of this library that, in fact, it has more of the better books (and more copies of the better titles), and therefore in net balance more of the better books are borrowed in this subject area than is true of the poorer books. But the conclusion of this study is that there is in fact a real basis for the value theory of book selection and that it is not likely that public library patrons will differentiate the better from the poorer books or read the former significantly more often than the latter.

Notes

1. For example, see Leon Carnovsky, "Community Analysis and the Practice of Book Selection,"(in L. R. Wilson (ed.), <u>The Practice of Book Selection.</u> Chicago, University of Chicago Press, 1940, p. 20-39).

2. With the assistance of Mrs. Genevieve Jain.

3. Using the chi-square test with five degrees of freedom.

4. This conclusion is supported by a study made in 1947 of 182 titles in the field of parent education, in the Urbana (Ill.) Free Library.   It was found that the annual average circulation per book of those titles listed in the <u>Standard Catalog for Public Libraries</u> or in any of four special bibliographies was greater-- but not significantly so--than the circulation of titles in the library but not so listed (see Iris Caraway, "Evaluation of Public Library Non-Fiction Book Collections with Special Reference to the Books for Parents in the Urbana Free Library" [University of Illinois Library School, unpublished report, June, 1948] pp. 33-37).

Are New Books Read More than Old Ones?

by Elizabeth Mueller[*]   Head Librarian, LaGrange
                              (Illinois) Public Library

From Library Quarterly 35: 166-72 July 1965;
Reprinted by permission of the University of
Chicago Press, c1965 University of Chicago.

How to balance the demand for new books in various fields with the competing demands for depth of the book
collection in specific areas is a complex question for the librarian. To state the problem simply: Should the librarian
be better prepared to provide the "latest book on Viet Nam"
than to provide the most comprehensive (or detailed or specialized) book on the various aspects of the Southeast Asian
conflict? When books and resources are limited, as is the
case in the small public library, the librarian must look in
part for the answer to his question in the way books are
used. Can he tell by looking at his circulation records
whether new books are used more heavily than old ones?

Little evidence has been gathered about the "age" of
books circulated in libraries. Studies which have analyzed
the circulation of books, especially fiction, as a function of
their age tend to support the belief that new books circulate
faster than do old ones. Most of these studies have been in
public libraries serving more than 40,000 people. [1] That is
a limitation, because as recently as five years ago more
than 50 per cent of public libraries in the United States
served a population under 5,000 and 85 per cent of them
were located in communities of fewer than 35,000 people.
Therefore, this study, while attempting to gather evidence
on the general question of the relation of the newness of
books to their circulation rate limited the area of inquiry to
public libraries in six different suburban communities with
populations ranging from 4,000 to 35,000.

The six communities studied were in the Chicago
metropolitan region. In the course of the study, many community analyses were made in an effort to correlate socio-
economic characteristics with various aspects of library ser-

vices and use. The communities differ widely with respect
to median number of school years completed, income distribution, and percentage of employed persons in white-collar
occupations. On the fifteen-point socio-economic scale constructed from these measures by the Northeastern Illinois
Metropolitan Area Planning Commission, the six communities ranged from a high of 1 to a low of 7 (Table 1). Attempts made in the original study to discern consistent relationships between these community indexes and library use
and service were inconclusive and they will not be repeated
in this report. However, it may be pertinent to record as
a subject for further investigation the over-all similarity of
library services despite great community variations.

The focus of this report is on the comparative circulation of old and new non-fiction titles in the six libraries.
The measurement of this difference posed some problems of
methodology. First, some basis had to be found on which
six different libraries that differed so much in size and community characteristics could be compared. The device used
was circulation rate, which was obtained by dividing the circulation for a library by the number of titles in the collection. By basing the comparison on a ratio between the size
of circulation and the size of the collection, it is thus possible to treat large and small libraries in the same table.
Thus, in Table 2, the circulation rate of 5.1 in Library I
means that the 43,700 titles circulated 222,900 times or on
the average of 5.1 times per title.

A remarkable feature of the circulation rates for the
total collections of the six libraries is the low range of variation. Library III, the only library that had a bookmobile,
was also the only one that had an annual circulation rate
over 7 for its total collection. If, however, the bookmobile's
circulation is not included, Library III's circulation rate was
6.6. In other words, the variation in the annual rate of
circulation for the collections housed in the six library buildings was less than 2.

The variation in the fiction circulation rate (Table 3),
although higher than that between the rates of the total collections, is not large either. And, with the exception of
that of Library IV, the circulation rates of the non-fiction
collections (Table 4) also have a small variation--less than
1-1/2.[2] The fiction and the non-fiction circulation rates
seem to be unrelated to the size of the libraries.

Table 1

Socioeconomic Class of Six Chicago Suburbs and the Population Characteristics From the 1960 Census Used by the Northeastern Illinois Metropolitan Area Planning Commission to Determine This Class

Suburb	Population	Median School Years Completed by Persons 25 years or Over	Median Family Income	Families With Incomes over $10,000 (Per cent)	Employed Persons in White-Collar Occupations (Per cent)	Socio-economic Class
I	34,886	12.2	$ 8,610	34.2	58.5	5
II	27,471	12.1	8,588	34.2	52.2	6
III	20,729	11.5	8,232	30.2	46.4	7
IV	10,838	13.2	12,257	64.9	80.5	1
V	8,588	12.1	8,240	30.1	54.0	6
VI	4,624	14.0	20,200	79.1	83.0	1

Table 2

Rate of Circulation of the Book Collections
in Six Suburban Libraries, 1961-63

Library	No. Titles* in Collection (1,000's)	Annual Circulation Rate
I	43.7	5.1
II	19.8	6.4
III	18.5	8.4
IV	18.5	5.4
V	8.7	5.8
VI	11.3	6.8

* For non-fiction, the cards in the shelf list were counted; librarians' estimates were used for fiction.

Table 3

Circulation Rates--Six Suburban
Libraries, 1961-63: Adult Fiction

Library	No. Titles in Collection (1,000's)	Holdings (Per cent)	Annual Circulation Rate
I	7.8	18	7.3
II	7.2	36	6.1
III	5.5	30	6.0
IV	4.9	26	4.4
V	2.0	24	5.8
VI	1.9	17	6.9

Because the circulation rates in the adult collections are so stable, the variability of the juvenile collections appears quite striking (Table 5). Even if the bookmobile circulation is removed from Library III, the adjusted juvenile circulation rate is 9.42. The variation between the lowest and the highest circulation rates of six libraries is still over 4 per year. The library having the smallest percentage of juvenile holdings (Library IV) has the largest annual circulation rate. Yet Library VI, which had the largest percentage of juvenile holdings, had a fairly high juvenile circulation, too. Neither the size of the collection nor the size of the population served seems related to this variation. This is a puzzling phenomenon, one which invites further research. The concern of the present report, however, is with the adult nonfiction collection (circulating titles only).

Table 4

Circulation Rates--Six Suburban Libraries,
1961-63: Adult Non-Fiction

Library	No. Titles in Collection (1,000's)	Holdings (Per cent)	Annual Circulation Rate
I	17.7	40	3.5
II	4.7	24	4.7
III	5.0	27	3.3
IV	7.7	42	2.6
V	2.0	24	4.1
VI	2.7	24	3.5

The following statistics were gathered from each of the six libraries for a twelve-month period: (1) total circulation of both fiction and juvenile collections and each of the eleven non-fiction sections (ten Dewey classes plus biographies); (2) the total number of "old titles" (those held at the beginning of the survey period) in each of the eleven non-fiction sections, and a listing of the "new titles" (those acquired and made available for circulating during the survey period) in each of the eleven sections; and (3) the number of times each new title circulated during the survey's twelve-month period (since libraries do not normally keep circulation records separately for new books, the information for this item was collected with the special co-operation of the libraries). [3] The data collected from each of the six libraries covered twelve consecutive months. The earliest of the twelve-month periods began January 1, 1961; the latest ended May 31, 1963.

After the data were collected, there were, for each library, three circulation figures--total, old title, and new title. But before the old-title circulation rates could be compared with those of the new titles in each library, an

Table 5

Circulation Rates--Six Suburban
Libraries, 1961-63: Juvenile

Library	No. Titles in Collection (1, 000's)	Holdings (Per cent)	Annual Circulation Rate
I	18. 2	42	5. 6
II	7. 9	40	7. 7
III	8. 1	43	13. 1
IV	6. 0	32	9. 7
V	4. 5	52	6. 7
VI	6. 7	59	7. 8

adjustment had to be made to the new-title statistics, for
theoretically, according to our definition of new titles, none
of them were in circulation at the beginning of the twelve-
month survey period.   At the same time, however, all of
the old titles were available for circulation.   Since the new
titles had been added to all six libraries at a constant rate
over the twelve-month periods, the average availability time
for a new title was six months, or exactly one-half the exposure time of the old titles.   Hence, the circulation records of the new titles were doubled in order to offset the
time advantage of the older titles.   (The doubled circulation
figure is labeled "adjusted circulation" in the tables and text
that follow.)

The old-title circulation rate for the entire non-fiction collection in each library was then compared to its adjusted new-title circulation rate.   Then the same procedure
was used to examine the old- and new-title relationship for
each of the eleven Dewey classes in all six libraries.

The summary of the old-title and new-title circulation statistics for the six libraries in Table 6 clearly reveals each library's non-fiction circulation picture.   First,
for all six libraries old-title circulation rates were quite
similar.   Second, the libraries divide into two groups--
Libraries I, II, and IV, with a high new-title rate, and Libraries III, V, and VI, with no substantial difference in the
new- and the old-title circulation rates.   The question became: What accounts for the much-augmented rate of new-

Table 6
Comparative Circulation of Old and
New Non-Fiction Titles

| Library | Old Titles | | New Titles | |
	N	Circulation per title	N	Adjusted Circulation per title
I	15, 303	3. 48	2, 420	8. 00
II	3, 897	4. 82	812	8. 45
III	4, 266	3. 57	731	4. 15
IV	7, 012	2. 56	528	9. 58
V	1, 761	4. 37	320	5. 82
VI	2, 291	3. 71	384	4. 53

title circulation in three of the libraries compared to the
other three where old and new titles circulate at essentially
the same rate?

Nothing about the communities appears to be related
to the new-title circulation differences.   Neither the size of
the population and its educational and income level nor the
extent of library use was related to the difference in new-
title circulation.   Such a result is hardly surprising but important to explore.

In comparing the libraries, the question arose as to
whether the high circulation of new titles was consistently
confined to special subjects.   Also this question is important: Were the libraries circulating a high rate of new non-
fiction alike or different in the subjects of new books that
were read a great deal?   A comparison was made of the
circulation rates of old and new titles in the ten major Dewey
classes and biography in all six libraries.   The results,
shown in Table 7, fail to show a marked concentration of
high circulation of new titles in any subject fields in Libraries I, II, and IV or any outstanding differences among
these three libraries.   Libraries III, V, and VI, while showing noticeably higher new-title circulation in some classes,
vary from each other in the classes so distinguished.

Table 7

Comparison of the Annual Circulation Rate of Old Titles With Adjusted Circulation
Rate of New Titles for Main Dewey Classes in All Six Libraries

Dewey Class	Library I		Library II		Library III		Library IV		Library V		Library VI	
	Old	New	Old	New	Old	New	Old	New	Old	New	Old	New
000's	3.5	6.3	2.5	2.0	1.7	0	3.0	3.0	3.4	1.6	2.7	2.7
100's	4.7	9.1	6.2	10.4	4.6	4.9	2.7	13.0	5.1	6.3	4.8	7.4
200's	3.6	5.1	4.6	5.5	2.5	2.3	2.0	7.4	3.8	9.4	2.9	2.7
300's	2.9	7.2	4.3	8.3	2.5	4.1	3.0	10.6	3.7	5.6	4.0	5.1
400's	2.7	9.4	5.2	10.5	6.0	1.5	3.7	5.8	3.7	5.8	3.4	0
500's	3.5	6.6	5.9	6.7	4.5	5.0	3.3	9.1	5.1	5.3	3.6	4.2
600's	4.2	6.5	5.6	11.2	5.1	4.6	2.7	9.4	4.2	6.7	3.1	6.7
700's	3.4	6.8	5.0	8.6	3.7	5.0	2.3	8.0	4.5	4.0	4.5	3.3
800's	2.4	4.3	5.1	9.7	3.1	3.0	1.9	9.9	5.0	5.3	2.9	5.3
900's	7.9	9.2	4.5	8.1	4.0	3.8	2.8	9.0	4.9	6.6	6.0	4.7
Biography	2.2	7.7	4.2	7.6	3.7	4.8	2.4	10.0	3.8	6.0	2.5	4.9

The sheer volume of new titles in proportion to the
rest of the book collection was also investigated.   Did the
libraries with the highest percentage of new titles consistently show a much higher adjusted circulation rate?   The comparisons shown in Table 8 suggest no positive correlation.
With the exception of that of Library IV, the ratios of new
to old non-fiction titles vary little, and in the case of Library IV the ratio is much lower, although it was one of the
libraries with a high circulation of new titles.

In the light of Library IV's deviation (see Table 8) the
relationship between each library's holdings and its circulation was also considered as a possible determinant of the
new-title circulation rate.   In other words, perhaps the non-
fiction collection formed a larger proportion of the total collection in the three libraries with high new-title circulation
rates than in those with low new-title circulation rates.

Table 8

Comparison Between New-Title Circulation Rate and
Percentage of New Non-Fiction Titles
in Six Libraries

Library	Percentage of New Titles in Total Non-Fiction	Adjusted New-Title Circulation Rate
I	14	8.00
II	17	8.45
III	15	4.15
IV	7	9.58
V	15	5.82
VI	14	4.53

Perhaps the proportion of non-fiction in the library
as a whole and the degree to which it circulated, compared
to the fiction collection, influenced the new-title circulation
rate.   The relevant data, shown in Table 9, show no such
relation.

Library IV, did not conform very well to the trends
cited in Tables 6-9.   In fact this library's history was a
complete puzzle: (1) it had the highest percentage of holdings

Table 9

Comparison of Percentage of Total Holdings in Non-
Fiction to Percentage of Circulation
Composed of Non-Fiction

Library	Percentage Non-Fiction Holdings	Percentage Non-Fiction Circulation
I*	40	29
II*	24	17
III	27	11
IV*	42	20
V	24	17
VI	24	13

* High new-title circulation

in non-fiction; (2) it had the lowest circulation rate per non-
fiction title; (3) it had the highest circulation rate per new
non-fiction title.   In order to find the reason for this dis-
crepancy in Library IV, its entire circulation picture was
re-examined.

At the time of this survey Library IV was in the
midst of an expansion program.   Because of this, approximately three thousand adult books were housed in the basement workroom, which was closed to the public.   About
three-fourths of these titles were non-fiction.   Except for
"controversial" or seasonal collections, none of the other libraries had a large percentage of their collection inacces-
sible to their patrons.   Yet in Library IV the non-fiction
titles housed in the basement amounted to almost 30 per cent
of the entire non-fiction collection, or about one-third of the
old non-fiction titles.   Theoretically, these books were available to the library patrons via the card catalog, personal
searching, and, finally, an oral request to the librarian.
Nevertheless, visual inaccessibility reduced book use considerably.   Evidence for the assertion was the very low old-
title rate for Library IV (Table 7) even in the divisions which
are not as timebound as science or social reform, e.g., the
100's and 800's.

Since inaccessibility had such a negative effect on the
circulation rate for old books in Library IV, the converse

might account for the high circulation of new titles in Libraries I and II. <u>Enhanced accessibility</u> of new books, in other words, may have had a positive effect on their circulation rate. After reviewing the procedures for handling new non-fiction books in all six libraries I found that three of the six libraries had special places for new non-fiction books. These were special tables or shelves where new books from all Dewey classes were displayed--and allowed to circulate--for a limited period of time before they were merged into the collection. These three libraries were, of course, Libraries I, II, and IV, the ones with high new-title circulation.

Personal observation of the circulation of each individual new non-fiction title in Library IV revealed the process. The method of classifying new titles in this library necessitated the replacement of the temporary book card at the same time a book was transferred from the special new-title bin to the regular non-fiction shelves. But the number of circulations appearing on the original circulation card was recorded on the new circulation card. Not only did this operation preserve each title's complete circulation record but it also made it possible to observe the effect of being "relocated" on a title's circulation. Frequently a new title which had circulated at least four times before appearing in the card catalog (not being cataloged was one of the criteria for being placed in the new non-fiction special collection) had not circulated once since its transfer to the regular shelves. Yet, because of my frequent visits to Library IV, I could determine for many of these titles that the actual time spent on the regular non-fiction shelves was equal to or longer than the period for which it was assigned to the special table. Although in this survey no separate record was kept of each title's circulation before transfer to the regular shelves the contrast in the circulation rate was so widespread that any exception to it could not escape notice since "before" and "after" circulations had to be added for a total circulation figure covering the survey period for each new non-fiction title in Library IV.

A similar process appears to have taken place in Libraries I and II. When new books were immediately merged with older books in the collection they were "lost," so to speak. Without the heightened visibility and accessibility that special shelving provides, new books are no more likely than old ones to attract a reader. Although this result is not too surprising, it strongly reinforces the general belief in the power of accessibility.

If, as appears from this study, the use of the library can be so affected in such specific and measurable ways, then a powerful instrument is potentially at hand for the librarian. He can shape the reading patterns of his constituents, perhaps more than he had realized, via experimentation with differential accessibility of parts of the collection. Of equal importance he can provide, through methods similar to the ones developed in this research, a way of precisely evaluating the results of that experimentation. Thus the kind of research reported here may be useful in treating these two perennially difficult problems of library service-- directing reading patterns and measuring library performance.

Notes

*The author acknowledges the assistance of Mr. Phillip H. Ennis in the preparation of this paper.

1. The study by Herman Fussler and Julian Simon is an especially detailed example analyzing by age in an academic library. See Patterns in the Use of Books in Large Research Libraries. (Chicago: University of Chicago Library, 1961).

2. The factors which caused Library IV's circulation rate to be so low will be discussed later.

3. In all six libraries the number of times each new book had circulated during the twelve-month period was found by counting its charges--automatically listed by date charged on the bookcard--recorded during the year for which statistics from each of the libraries were collected. Charges recorded for multiple copies of the same title were added together to obtain a circulation record for each new title.

Selection of Materials

American Association of School Librarians

From Standards for School Library Programs. Chicago, American Library Association, 1960.

Unless otherwise noted, all selections in this following section are reprinted by arrangement with the American Library Association, or the appropriate Division of ALA.

Basic principles that guide the selection of books and other materials for the collections of the school library include the following:

1 Administrators, classroom and special teachers, and the library staff endorse and apply the principles incorporated in the School Library Bill of Rights of the American Association of School Librarians, and in any statements for the selection of library materials that school librarians have helped to formulate for the state or for the local school system. The Bill of Rights is on page 98.

2 The library collections are developed systematically so that they are well-balanced and well-rounded in coverage of subjects, types of materials, and variety of content.

3 Maintaining qualitative standards for the selection of materials is essential. All materials are therefore carefully evaluated before purchase, and only materials of good quality are obtained.

A wealth of excellent material is available for children and young people, and there is no justification for the collections to contain materials that are mediocre in presentation and content. By virtue of their professional preparation and experience, librarians

have the special competencies that enable them to
evaluate materials critically.
They are familiar with and guided by the established
criteria for the evaluation and selection of materials.
They consult standard tools and reliable guides for the
selection of materials and go beyond the limits of
these sources whenever they have the opportunity to
examine and to evaluate materials carefully before
purchase.

4 Teachers make recommendations to the head librarian
for materials to be added to the collections of the
school library.

The teacher plays an important part in the selection
of materials for the school library. His professional
preparation and experience provide him with a knowledge of materials in his field and of the types of materials appropriate for the needs and abilities of his
students. A two-way avenue of communication exists
between the teacher and librarian, in which each re-
lays to the other information about new materials in
the teacher's field. The teacher evaluates materials
on the basis of the criteria established for materials
in his teaching area, and recommends only those materials that meet these standards satisfactorily. He
is familiar with and uses standard tools and guides for
the selection of materials, and he utilizes every opportunity to examine and to evaluate materials in his
field.

5 Students are encouraged to make suggestions for materials to be acquired for the school library.

6 The collections are continuously re-evaluated in relation
to changing curriculum content, new instructional
methods, and current needs of teachers and students.
Appropriate materials are obtained for these new developments. This process of re-evaluation also leads
to the replacement of outmoded materials with those
that are up-to-date, the discarding of materials no
longer useful, and the replacement of materials in
poor repair.

7 In order that good service may be provided for teachers
and students, materials are purchased throughout the
school year as needed, and their acquisition is not

limited to annual or semi-annual orders.

8 Final authority for materials to be acquired rests with
  the principal of the school and the head school librarian.

School library resources in schools having 200 or
more students[1]

Size of the collections

The good teacher, eager and able to make learning an
exciting adventure for his students, is continually frustrated
in his endeavors when the library resources in his school
are meager and limited.   Students become discouraged when
they cannot obtain materials easily for their classroom needs
or in their independent seeking for knowledge and for aesthetic experiences.   The standards for the size of the library's collections recommend materials in sufficient quantity
so that three aspects of a functional library program may be
realized: good service to teachers and students, the easy
accessibility of materials, and the availability of materials
on a wide range of subjects and in many forms of expression.

Books

Books are the most important of all library resources.
No well-selected book collection is ever too large for children and young people.   To provide books on all topics included in the curriculum and for all purposes of the instructional program requires a book collection of no mean size.
The scope of the collection, however, is not limited to the
curricular needs of the students.   Since the interests of children and young people, in the aggregate, are almost limit-
less and since their purposes in reading are innumerable, the
book collection in their library must be rich and extensive in
imaginative writings, in non-fiction, and in reference resources to meet their many wants.   The book collection provides a constant invitation to students to read and is a contributing factor in making reading a pleasurable and satisfying occupation.

1 Recommendations for the minimum size[2] of the book
  collections in libraries in very good schools follow:

  In schools having 200-99 students.... 6,000-10,000
  books.
      (This range for the size of the book collection is

of qualitative nature and is not to be interpreted
as being proportionate in relation to size of enrollment. For example, schools having 200 pupils
can make effective use of collections containing
10,000 books.)
In schools having 1,000 or more students...10 books
per student.

2 With collections that are large enough, books can be
made easily accessible for students and teachers. At
all times there is a sufficient number of books available for use in the school library, for classroom collections, and for withdrawals for home use. (See
Chapter 10.) Libraries in excellent schools, particularly those having 200-2,000 students, will far exceed
the minimum recommendations for size of book collections.

3 The standards for the size of the school library book
collection allow for the acquisition of duplicate copies
of titles to meet the needs of students and teachers.
It is evident from reports received from school librarians that efficient service requires two or more
copies of many titles, so that books in heavy demand
are available for students at the times when they are
most needed. Duplicate purchases are essential to
meet reasonable requests for books that are used intensively by many students in connection with their
class projects or assignments. Some titles are duplicated so that they can be made available for use in
classroom collections as well as in the school library.
Obtaining duplicate copies of titles that are popular
with students in their noncurricular reading pursuits
is highly desirable. The provision of good library
service shapes the policies to be followed for the acquisition of duplicate copies of books. Duplication of
titles, however, is not done at the expense of building
a well-rounded, basic collection of books for the library.

4 Library collections in schools having specialized curriculums in agriculture, in vocational or technical
subjects, or in similar areas meet the needs of
teachers and students for materials in these special
fields. These parts of the collection are larger and
more highly developed than in libraries in schools not
having the specialized curriculums. The special ma-

terials are provided in addition to the basic, well-rounded collection.

Magazines

Magazines form an important part of the school library collections. They contain material not found elsewhere and are a primary source of information about current events. For some students, magazines constitute their major reading fare, and this fact is treated constructively in the reading guidance done by school librarians. Students read magazines for many purposes, school related and otherwise, and it is important for students to become familiar with a wide range of good magazines. The collection of magazines is therefore large enough to permit representation of many subject and special interest areas as well as popular reading fare.

The school library collection of magazines also includes professional journals in the fields of librarianship and instructional materials. These magazines contain information that is helpful in the selection of printed and audio-visual materials and that keep the library staff informed about professional developments. They are frequently useful, too, for students.

1 Recommendations follow for the minimum number of current magazine subscriptions for the collection in the school library:

In elementary schools
(Grades K-6)... 25 titles
In elementary schools
(Grades K-8)... 50 titles
In junior high schools
70 titles
In senior high schools
120 titles

plus at least 5 titles of professional magazines in the areas of librarianship and instructional materials[3]

In the case of the elementary school library, the number of titles recommended is not restricted to magazines designed solely for the child audience, but includes some titles in the adult field that have interest and usefulness for children in the upper middle grades.

2 Schools having a special program in technical, vocational, or other areas need larger periodical collections so that magazines in the special fields are included.

3 The number of titles in the magazine collection is not
   affected by the number of students in the school.
   Size of enrollment does affect duplication of titles.
   Decisions concerning the number of magazine titles to
   be duplicated in the school library are made by the
   head school librarian and the teachers on the basis of
   need and use.

4 Back issues of periodicals needed for reference work
   and for other purposes are retained in the school library for a time span covering at least five years.
   In an increasing number of school libraries these
   magazine files are kept on microfilm.

5 The school library collection includes a general periodical index.   Large schools need more than one copy.
   Libraries in vocational, technical, or other special
   schools require a periodical index covering the contents of magazines in special fields.

Newspapers
         The number of newspapers for the school library col-
lection is determined primarily by the needs of teachers and
students.   A minimum newspaper collection consists of three
to six titles, with coverage of the news reported on local,
state, national, and international levels.   In some junior and
senior high school libraries, a newspaper index is essential.

Pamphlets
         Quantitative standards for size of pamphlet collections
cannot be formulated precisely.   For many subjects, information can be found only in pamphlets.   For some readers,
needs can be met more effectively with pamphlets than with
books.   The collection should therefore be fairly extensive,
consisting of up-to-date and useful materials on a wide range
of subjects.   The school librarian builds the pamphlet collection systematically and does not leave its development to
chance.

Films and filmstrips
         Films and filmstrips are without peer for conveying
many types of information and creative expressions.   Although a school may rent or borrow many films, it will still
need to own some films.   This principle of ownership applies
to filmstrips in even greater degree, since the costs involved
are not so high.   Effective use of these materials is made in
the classroom and also in the library or audio-visual center,

where individual students have the opportunity to make independent use of films and filmstrips in the preparation of
their assignments or for other worthwhile purposes.   The
collections of films and filmstrips are therefore large enough
to meet classroom needs and to provide a wide coverage of
subject matter for use by individual students.   Good teaching
is handicapped when the instructor has to make plans to rent
or borrow films or filmstrips a long time ahead of anticipated use, and also when these materials are not quickly
available to meet those needs that occur spontaneously in the
classroom.   In like manner, the curiosity or interest of the
individual child or young person making independent use of
these materials may not be sustained over the period of time
that it takes for the material to arrive.

Many variables affect the size of the collections of
films and filmstrips owned by schools, and hence quantitative
standards cannot be formulated that cover every situation.
Schools obtain audio-visual materials from school system centers or regional depositories and borrow or rent expensive
materials infrequently used from other sources. [4]   The following general recommendations can be made, however:

1 A film used six or more times a year is purchased by
the school.   In most instances, when rental charges
for a film during the year equal from one-fifth to one-
seventh of the purchase price of the film, it becomes
feasible to purchase.

2 It is desirable that filmstrips and recordings on many
subjects and covering a wide range of interests be
easily available in the school for use by class groups,
small groups of students, and individual students.   To
meet these needs, it is advantageous for the school
to have its own collection of filmstrips and recordings that will be used more than once during the
school year.

Disc and tape recordings
For many decades, disc recordings have formed a
valuable and extensively used part of the school library collections.   Recordings are available for use in almost every
area of the curriculum, and they are an important resource
for many noncurricular purposes of students.   To meet these
varied needs, the collection in the library has great breadth,
including recordings of music, drama, poetry, historic
events, language instruction, and many other types.   The

collection is extensive enough so that disc and tape recordings are available for use in the school library, for the
classroom on long- or short-term loans, and for withdrawal
for home use.

Pictures and slides

The library has an extensive collection of pictures
and slides available for use by students and teachers in the
library, in the classroom, and in the home.   In addition to
their value as supplementary and enrichment resources, these
collections furnish the only material available on many topics
and details.   They form an important reference tool in the
library.   Pictures are also used for displays and exhibits
in the library and throughout the school.   Some libraries
have a collection of good reproductions of paintings that students may take home on long-term loans.

Realia

The term realia is used in this book to cover such
materials as three-dimensional objects, museum materials,
dioramas, models, and samples.   Realia represent a unique
and vital source of information and appreciation for students,
and they are frequently primary sources for teaching and
learning.   The school borrows realia from individuals in the
community, museums, district materials centers, and other
agencies, and teachers and students make pieces in connection with their class projects.   In addition, it is important
that some realia be purchased for the materials collections
in the school building.   Almost every classroom needs realia
in its permanent collection of materials, and some pieces
are sent to a sufficient number of classrooms on short-term
loans to warrant their purchase.   In the school library, realia are used by students for school work and also in connection with their many hobbies and special interests.   They
are frequently so important for the last-named purposes that
it is highly desirable that students be allowed to withdraw
them from the library for home use whenever possible.

Other materials (see also pages 95-96).

The school library has a good collection of maps of
various types (in addition to those in atlases); at least one
globe is always available for use in the library.   Inflatable
globes are provided that may be borrowed for home use.
Where needed, classrooms are equipped with a globe and any
maps necessary for classroom instruction.

The school library contains indexes of community resources, trip and lecturer files, materials on local history, and other special materials useful for students and teachers.

In junior and senior high school libraries, collections of college catalogs and vocational information services are provided. These materials are needed in the school library even though similar or identical collections are maintained in the guidance department of the school.

Annual expenditures[5]

General principles
1 The standards for annual appropriations recommend a-
   mounts that are necessary for the maintenance of
   functional materials collections and, therewith, an effective program of library services for teachers and
   students. They also allow for duplicate purchases of
   materials in sufficient quantity to meet the needs of
   students.

2 The amounts recommended for the annual expenditures
   for materials pertain only to those school libraries
   where the collections of materials meet the standards
   for the size and quality of the collections that have
   been noted in the preceding pages. Where this is not
   the case, the annual appropriations will need to be
   larger during the period of time required to develop
   the basic collections.

3 It is assumed that certain factors tend to operate to
   keep sufficient balance between materials acquired and
   those discarded, so that the materials collections,
   particularly in very large schools, do not become dis-
   proportionately large. (See page 86, point 6.)

4 The figures cited apply to conditions existing in the
   year of 1960. Any changes beyond this date in the
   purchasing value of the dollar must be kept in mind
   and allowances made accordingly.

5 It is recommended that arrangements be made so that
   the head librarian has a petty cash or contingent fund
   readily available for the purchase of inexpensive materials and supplies.

Printed materials
1 Recommendations for the annual budget for printed ma-

terials in the school library collections follow:

a. Funds for books in the school library (see also
   point 1b immediately following):
   In schools having 200-249 students...
                    at least $1,000.00-$1,500.00
   In schools having 250 or more students...
                    at least $4.00-$6.00 per student

   It should be noted that the expenditure of the bare
   minimum of $4.00 per student means that approxi-
   mately only one book per student can be added to
   the school library each year.   The current cost of
   books (allowing for discounts) averages $3.00 per
   book for the elementary school library, $3.50 for
   the junior high school library, and $4.00 for the
   senior high school library.   Production costs of
   books have been rising steadily during the last
   decade, and there is every indication that these
   costs will continue to mount.

b. Additional funds, [6] as required, for:

   Encyclopedias and unabridged dictionaries. (Encyclo-
   pedias to be replaced at least every five years.)
   Magazines, newspapers, and pamphlets (see pages
   89-90).
   Rebinding.
   Supplies (see page 95).
   Professional materials for the faculty (see pages
   96-97).
   Collection of supplementary materials (see pages
   95-96).

2 Libraries in vocational, technical, and other schools
  having specialized curriculums of this nature may need
  an annual budget larger than that noted in point 1
  above.   Over and beyond the acquisitions for the general collections in the school library, special technical and scientific materials must be purchased.
  Books in these areas are usually more expensive than
  fiction or general non-fiction, and tend to become out-
  moded more quickly and must be replaced more frequently.   Magazines in the special fields must also be
  obtained as well as any special periodical indexes that
  are needed.

Audio-visual materials
     The annual budget for the acquisition of audio-visual materials, exclusive of equipment, should not be less than 1 per cent of the total per pupil instructional cost. This ranges at the present time from $2.00 to $6.00 per student, varying in general with the quality of the instructional program.

Supplies
     Funds for supplies are provided in sufficient amount for the needs of the school library program. These cover items to be used in connection with the acquisition, cataloging, and other technical processing, circulation, organization, repair, maintenance, promotion, and use of printed and audio-visual materials.

Equipment
     Funds are provided as required for the acquisition and repair of equipment needed for the effective and efficient organization and utilization of materials.

The collection of supplementary materials

     The term supplementary materials collection, as defined here, refers to those books, magazines, and other printed materials that are purchased with school funds but are not shelved with the main school library collections: sets of supplementary textbooks, dictionaries and encyclopedias for classrooms, magazines and newspapers for classroom use, and similar materials. Use of these materials should not replace or reduce the use of the school library and of the classroom collections on loan from the library.

     General principles for the effective administration of these materials follow:

1 The head school librarian has administrative responsibility for the acquisition and care of these materials, and all requests for materials to be added to the collection are to be cleared through his office. Recommendations for purchase of these materials come primarily from classroom and special teachers. The librarian's role is essentially advisory in nature, and he is serving as the co-ordinator of materials in the school. With this centralization of administrative responsibility, effective selection and optimum use of these materials throughout the school can be achieved,

and unnecessary duplication in the purchase of supplementary materials is avoided.   Materials do not
become misplaced or forgotten within the school building.

2 All titles in the supplementary collection meet recognized criteria for the evaluation and selection of
books.

3 Funds for these materials do not come out of the budget for the school library collection (see pages 93-4),
but are in addition to those amounts and are allocated on the basis of need.

4 Adequate clerical assistance is made available to take
care of the routines involved in handling and accounting for these materials.

5 It is usually desirable that a storage or depository
room be provided for the sets of supplementary textbooks so that use of these sets by more than one
class group may be facilitated.   These books may be
housed with the free or rental textbook collections or
in the stack area of the school library.

6 The materials are uncataloged and unclassified.   Simplified records of author and title entries, copy numbers
and location of copies are sufficient.

Professional materials for the faculty

Even when a school system has a centrally located and
extensive collection of professional books, magazines, and
instructional materials for administrators and teachers, it is
desirable that some professional materials be acquired for
each school building.   These materials are used for reference
as well as for general professional reading.   In some schools
parents also make use of the collection.   (Materials are not
required for the sole purpose of providing textbooks for
school personnel enrolled in college and university courses.)
Recommendations for the school-owned collection of professional materials in schools having 200 or more students or
in smaller schools having libraries follow:

1 A basic book collection consists of 200-1, 000 titles, the
number depending on the needs and size of the faculty
and the availability of other collections of professional

materials for teachers in the community.

In large schools, duplication of some titles will be necessary to provide for faculty needs and discussion groups.

2 The collection includes at least 25-50 professional magazine titles.

This core collection of magazines consists of general periodicals in the education field and a selection of other titles to represent the subject areas covered in the curriculum of the school.   Many schools will want more professional magazines, and if there is no district collection of professional materials for administrators and teachers, a larger number of titles is imperative.   (For professional magazines dealing with instructional resources, see page 89, point 1.)

3 The professional collection includes pamphlets, filmstrips, curriculum guides, resource units, and other special instructional materials as needed by the faculty members.

4 Minimum annual expenditures for the professional collection range from $200.00 to $800.00, depending upon the needs and size of the faculty and the availability of other professional materials in the community. Funds for these materials are in addition to those allocated for school library materials (page 89).

5 The professional collection is administered by the head school librarian.

6 Administrators, teachers, and librarians participate in the selection of the materials.

7 All materials in the collection meet standard criteria for evaluation and selection in the special fields represented.   The collection is kept up-to-date and functional.

8 The collection is housed best in a special room for teachers in the school library suite, or in some part of the school easily accessible to teachers, if separate space is not available in the library.   The materials can be withdrawn for home use.

School Library Bill of Rights[7]

School libraries are concerned with generating understanding
of American freedoms and with the preservation of these
freedoms through the development of informed and responsible
citizens.   To this end the American Association of School
Librarians reaffirms the <u>Library Bill of Rights</u> of the American Library Association and asserts that the responsibility
of the school library is:

To provide materials that will enrich and support the cur-
     riculum, taking into consideration the varied interests,
     abilities, and maturity levels of the pupils served

To provide materials that will stimulate growth in factual
     knowledge, literary appreciation, aesthetic values,
     and ethical standards

To provide a background of information which will enable
     pupils to make intelligent judgments in their daily
     life

To provide materials on opposing sides of controversial is-
     sues so that young citizens may develop under guid-
     ance the practice of critical reading and thinking

To provide materials representative of the many religious,
     ethnic, and cultural groups and their contributions
     to our American heritage

To place principle above personal opinion and reason above
     prejudice in the selection of materials of the highest
     quality in order to assure a comprehensive collection
     appropriate for the users of the library.

Editors note: Although a new edition of these standards has
     been announced for late 1968 or early 1969, the 1960
     edition will not be entirely superceded by it and its
     principles will still be valid.   School librarians es-
     pecially will of course wish to study carefully the new
     Standards for School Media Programs as soon as they
     are available.

Notes

1. The twelve-grade or K-12 schools having 200 or more
   students present some special problems in relation to
   quantitative standards for the collections of materials.
   If the school is large enough or otherwise can afford
   to have separate libraries for elementary and second-
   dary school students, each library can be considered
   as being comparable to a library in any other school
   having a similar enrollment and grade coverage.
   However, in schools having 200-300 students in the
   elementary grades and a comparable number in the
   secondary grades, it is not realistic to state that the
   library in every case must meet quantitative standards on a dual basis; that is, that it meets standards
   for materials for its secondary school group in equal
   extent as a separate secondary school of the same
   size, and, in addition, meets standards for materials
   for its elementary school group in equal extent as a
   separate elementary school of the same size.   Precise standards for the K-12 group cannot be formulated because of the many variables that exist in relation to the grade distribution of the student population, available funds, and other factors.   It may be
   stated, however, that total resources and total expenditures should never be less than that indicated for
   other schools of the same enrollment, and that, for
   good service, the size of the book and audio-visual
   collections should be substantially larger, with the
   annual budget for materials proportionately increased.
   The objectives and program of the library in the
   twelve-grade school are the same as those in any
   other school, and each student in the school should
   have the opportunity to use the library and its resources.

2. Exclusive of the number of books in the collection of supplementary materials (p. 95-96) and the collection of
   professional materials for the faculty (p. 96-97).

3. For recommendations for other professional magazines,
   see p. 97, point 2.

4. These comments apply also to recordings, pictures,
   slides, and realia.

5. See also footnote no. 1.

6. In some small communities where public library service
   is as yet unavailable, schools may assume the responsibility for providing adult books to the adult
   members of the community.   These should be paid
   for over and above the allowance made for books for
   children and young people in the school and should
   not be counted as part of the school library collection.   They should be considered a temporary arrangement or transition step to adequate public library service for adults.

7. Endorsed by the Council of the American Library Association, July, 1955.

State-Wide Library Resources for both Government and
Citizens

American Association of State Libraries

> From American Association of State Librarians.
> Standards for Library Functions.   Chicago, Amer-
> ican Library Association, 1963. Chap. II, p. 6-12.

The adequacy of library resources in a commonwealth
is not determined solely or even primarily by the collections
in government agencies, important as these are.   The affairs of state are obviously complex and bear upon the whole
range of contemporary life.   The informational resources
needed in the conduct of public affairs range from the obscure historical document of some event in the past of the
state, to the newest research findings in scientific laboratories.   The functioning of government in the broadest sense
includes the resources available to individuals as citizens.
The total library resources of the state must first be developed as a whole, and on this foundation a strong structure of
library service both to individuals and to government agencies can be built.

1. Each state should have a plan for developing the total
subject and reference resources which affect the economic, political, intellectual, and cultural life of the state.

The full resources needed for affairs of state in this age
encompass several million volumes.   The holdings of state
library agencies form one part of this total resource.   Collections of major public libraries and of colleges and universities are important additional portions, as are private holdings in research and industrial centers.   State library agencies should participate with other librarians and library interests in developing the plan for acquiring research and reference sources, and should take the lead in such planning
unless universities or other agencies have already exercised
initiative to this end.   The plan should rest upon clear and
specific agreements among libraries for cooperative building
of collections.   Smaller states, and those with limited resources, should consider interstate compacts for joint acqui-

sition of resources which would be available to all members
of the compact.   State-wide planning should be conceived as
a continuous rather than as a one-time activity.

> 2. The general subject resources within each state should
> include not only books but research and information re-
> ports; journals of trade, industrial, and professional
> groups; files of state and major national newspapers;
> maps; and similar materials.

Much of the knowledge needed in the affairs of state is of
an immediate and applied nature.   It is contained as much
in journals and reports as in books.   Each state faces responsibility for acquiring, organizing, storing, and developing means of rapid information retrieval of these many graphic records.   Access to them is essential for the researcher
as well as for the legislator, for the citizen as for the student.

> 3. The state through its state library agency should exer-
> cise leadership in maintaining freedom to read and free-
> dom of access to materials of varying views within the
> state.

People must have access to the full range of political, social, and religious viewpoints, in agencies ranging from the
smallest public library to the state library collection.   Efforts of self-appointed censors seeking to limit freedom to
read should be resisted.   The legal machinery for dealing
with subversive and pornographic literature exists in state
law and represents the proper means for safeguarding the
public interest.   It is incumbent upon state library agencies
to see that these legal channels are used if necessary and
to help prevent censorship of materials whether in academic,
public, or school libraries.   The basic policies which should
control access to resources reflecting various views are set
forth in "The Freedom To Read" statement and the "Library
Bill of Rights."[1]

> 4. The state should maintain a comprehensive collection
> on present and potential public policies and state responsi-
> bilities as one important unit in state-wide resources, and
> a collection which supplements and reinforces resources
> of the library systems.

This collection serves government directly and supplements local library resources through interlibrary loan.   A

few of the states maintain collections of a half-million volumes or more for this purpose, and even some of the less populous states maintain and find useful collections of a quarter-million volumes or more.   The size and scope of the general collection depend on other nearby resources, both within and outside government.   In occasional instances an existing large library, such as a municipal library, can be used for supplementary service to local libraries over the state.   In this case, the state should share in the financing of the general facility on which it depends.

5. The general resources in state agencies and the wider resources in libraries associated in cooperative agreements should be widely and genuinely available through the following means: (1) central records of holdings, (2) bibliographies and indexes of state materials, (3) rapid communication systems among libraries to facilitate location of needed information and resources, (4) interlibrary loan provisions to the extent consistent with the need for material in the holding library, and (5) duplication equipment for supplying copies of material that cannot be furnished by interlibrary loan.

Obviously there is no real value in building high-level subject and reference resources jointly in the major libraries of the state and then having them unknown or unavailable, so that the government officer, for example, is unable to get what he needs when a given problem is before the state. State library collections, holdings in large municipal libraries, college and university collections, and even private research facilities should be included in this functional network.   Library resources for government and for the state in general must not only be acquired but must be mobilized for use.

6. Subject and reference resources should also be available at regional centers within the state, at a distance which enables any serious reader to drive to the facilities, use them, and return to his home within one day.

Normally these would be existing agencies, either public or academic libraries, which broaden their usual resources and service area as they take on regional responsibilities. They should have state financial assistance to meet their regional obligations.   If suitable agencies do not exist, the state should provide branches of the state library for the purpose.   These regional centers would be part of the state network of library facilities, and in some cases might maintain special collections for the whole state on subjects of particular regional importance.

> 7. Each state should maintain a complete collection of the documents of its own government and of current documents of comparable states, plus a strong central collection of both local and federal documents.

Collections of government documents are of prime importance for historical research, public affairs, and to meet particular informational needs. The full collection for each state would normally be maintained by the state library agency, and a checklist of state documents should be published periodically by the state. Regional centers for state documents should also be developed within the state in existing libraries, and the agencies administering these encouraged to collect local publications and official reports for their areas as well. The regional document centers would logically be the libraries serving as regional reference centers (see Standard 6). Regional depositories for federal documents are also important in building document resources.

> 8. Each state should maintain a law collection covering the complete body of primary and secondary legal materials, in order to provide the best possible legal resources for the operation of state government and for the administration of justice.

The size and depth of the collection depend upon the proximity of the law library to other and more comprehensive legal collections. In practice a collection of at least 50,000-75,000 volumes has been found essential.

The collection should contain the complete primary and secondary materials of the state itself. This includes constitutions, codes and statutes, session laws and other legislative documents and materials, court reports and court rules (high, intermediate, and special courts), appellate court records and briefs, opinions of the attorney general, decisions and rules and regulations of administrative agencies and tribunals, digests and encyclopedias, citators, indexes, local treatises and practice books, publications of the law schools and bar associations, and primary materials of the local government corporations. There should be duplication of the state materials, since the law library should serve as a repository therefor.

The same categories of materials should be held for all other states, with the possible exception of local treatises and practice books, digests, legislative history materials, records and briefs, and local materials below the state level. The primary and secondary legal materials of the federal government are essential, including the reports (decisions) of all federal courts and administrative agencies, statutory materials and legislative histories, treaties, administrative rules and regulations, digests, and citators. The location of the law collection in relation to the comprehensive general state library will determine the need for the nonlegal state and United States government documents and for other nonlegal but related materials.

There should be complete coverage of the regional reporter system (reports and citators), the American digest system, annotated and selected subject reports and digests, treatises and related materials, loose-leaf services, restatements of the law, uniform state laws, legal periodicals and the indexes thereto, American Bar Association publications, annual institutes, dictionaries, form books, bibliographies and bibliographic tools, as well as a strong collection of the literature related to the law. Primary and selected secondary legal materials for the principal Anglo-American jurisdictions are necessary. The extent of the collection of international and comparative law and of foreign law will depend upon the circumstances of need and use as well as upon the location of the law library with respect to a more comprehensive legal collection in the area.

The law collection should be maintained for the judicial, legislative, and executive branches of state government and for the lower courts, attorneys, students, and the general public. If the appellate court and executive departments operate outside the state capital, branch legal collections must be maintained in these locations. The law collection should serve as a resource center for the libraries of the circuit or county courts and the bar association.

9. A strong collection of history related to the state--regional, state, and local--should exist where it is accessible to government officials, research workers, and the interested public.

It should be possible in every state to go to one collection, or to two or more closely coordinated collections, where the primary, nonofficial source materials relating to the history of the state are preserved and available. These source materials would include private manuscripts, corporate records, files of locally published newspapers, periodicals, pamphlets, maps, broadsides, photographs, and publications relating to the history of the area and its people. State historical agencies have traditionally assumed the responsibility for collecting these materials. However, where existing collections are incomplete, inadequate, or unavailable, the state should provide for collecting these materials. The purposes of this collection include both support of the intensive study of the state's political, economic, and cultural history and provision of background on current problems.

10. Each state should have an archives collection and program, for the preservation and organization of the state's own records and the records of local government.

An archival depository is necessary to preserve and service permanently valuable official records needed for the legal and administrative functioning of state government, for the verification and protection of the rights of individuals, and for historical and other research. It should include the records of antecedent colonial and territorial governments. The material should not only be stored but also arranged so that needed records can be found readily. Unless the head of the archival agency is also in charge of records management in the agencies and subdivisions of the state, he should have close working arrangements with the agency or agencies that exercise this function. Also, inasmuch as he has basic responsibility for the selection and preservation of permanently valuable records, no records should be destroyed without his approval. In states where responsibility for local archives rests with local governments, it is the task of the state archival agency to stimulate interest in their preservation and to furnish guidance in the application of proper methods.

11. Resources available within or near each state should include a full range of reading materials for the blind and visually handicapped.

Resources in Braille and in talking-book form are made available from the Library of Congress through regional centers, and books in Clear-Type can be purchased for the visually handicapped. In some states such material is provided through some agency of state government, and in others by large municipal systems or other agencies. In any case, the state is responsible for services which achieve the level set forth in "Standards for Regional Libraries for the Blind,"[2] including publicizing the availability of such resources and guidance in their use for the blind and visually handicapped. Responsibility extends to financial contribution by the state if these special resources are administered by a nonstate agency.

12. The total resources in each state should include collections of audio-visual and of other newer forms of communication which should be made available to users throughout the state.

Films, filmstrips, slides, and recordings constitute a valuable form of educational material for schools, organizations, and individuals. Newer forms of communication, such as microreproductions, and programed instruction materials are also assuming greater importance. Various plans have been developed for their coordinated provision, including state centers, cooperative pools and circuits, county units, and affiliates of regional libraries. Whatever the form of organization, the state once again has responsibility for reviewing the situation, promoting suitable facilities, and sharing in their cost, and state library agencies should take the initiative in developing the audio-visual and other programs.

13. The state should participate with other libraries in providing storage of little-used materials.

Materials which are used infrequently tend to accumulate on the shelves of public and academic libraries. Individual libraries hesitate to dispose of them because they may have some value. There should be within each state one or more centers to which such materials can be sent, one copy of which will be held if some future use is likely. This may be a storage unit within the state library, or a center elsewhere for which the state shares the cost.

Notes

1. "The Freedom To Read" statement was prepared by the Westchester Conference of the American Library Association and the American Book Publishers Council, 1953; the "Library Bill of Rights" was adopted by the Council of the American Library Association in 1948 and revised in 1961.

2. "Standards for Regional Libraries for the Blind" was prepared by the A. L. A. Round Table on Library Service to the Blind with the cooperation of the Division for the Blind, Library of Congress, in May, 1963.

Standards for Patients' Library; Hospital Medical Library; School of Nursing Library

Joint Committee on Standards for Hospital Libraries

From Joint Committee on Standards for Hospital Libraries. Hospital Libraries: Objectives and Standards. [Chicago] Hospital Libraries Division, American Library Association, 1953. Selected pages

Part I. Patients' Library

Objective

It is the objective of the Patients' Library to furnish recreational and additional educational reading materials for all patients, with the purpose of contributing to their recovery and welfare. The basic needs for the fulfillment of this objective are a qualified staff which recognizes the differences in reading tastes of the long-term and short-term patient; adequate library space with a comfortable non-hospital atmosphere; an active collection of books, pamphlets, magazines and related materials; necessary equipment for preparing materials for use and for bringing them to the non-ambulant patient. In attaining its objective, the Patients' Library coordinates with all departments of the hospital concerned with the personal welfare of the patient. It shares with other departments of the hospital the responsibility of social adjustment and vocational education of the patient. The Patients' Library promotes reading as a satisfying experience both in and out of the hospital...

Library Collection

The number of volumes in a hospital library is in relation to the size and type of hospital. The basic number of volumes for a general hospital library should be approximately as follows:

Size of Hospital	Number of Volumes
Up to 300 beds serviced	Minimum of 8 books per patient
301-500 beds serviced	Minimum of 7 books per patient
501-800 beds serviced	Minimum of 6 books per patient

Size of Hospital	Number of Volumes
801-1100 beds serviced	Minimum of 5 books per patient
1101-1500 beds serviced	Minimum of 4 books per patient

Special hospitals, such as orthopedic, children's, 200-400 bed mental and the like will need at least 25% more volumes; tuberculosis sanatoriums at least 50% more; and the 1000 bed or larger mental hospital will usually need fewer volumes than noted in the above scale...

Part II. Hospital Medical Library

Objective
        It is the aim of the Hospital Medical Library to assist and further the education, reading and research program of the professional staff of the hospital by providing and maintaining, in an adequately staffed and equipped library, sufficient medical and allied scientific literature and library services to meet the requirements of the staff in studying and giving constantly improved patient care...

Library Collection and Its Use
        The collection should conform to the most recent minimum standards established by the American Medical Association and the American College of Surgeons.

        An up-to-date collection of high quality should be maintained. In a general hospital of 100 beds or over, the collection should not be below a minimum of 1,000 volumes of medical and allied scientific literature. With few exceptions, books and monographs should have been published within the last ten years. In purchasing, stress should be put upon periodicals. The Medical Library should receive regularly not less than 25 periodicals in good standing, and own the most important medical and allied scientific indexes.

        Material should be selected in accordance with the types of service represented in the hospital, and with the quantity of educational, clinical, and research work done by the staff. The location of the hospital in regard to other medical libraries and medical centers should also govern the size of the collection: a hospital in an isolated locality needs a larger and more representative collection than one with easy access to other medical libraries.

        The collection should be made as freely available as

possible, and Medical Library rules and regulations formulated with a view to providing maximum library service.

The Medical Librarian should make arrangements for inter-library loans to provide such material as is needed by the hospital and medical staff, but not in the hospital's own collection. Similarly, the hospital should make its collection available for the same service to other libraries.

The Medical Library hours should conform to the most recent minimum standards established by the American Medical Association and the American College of Surgeons...

Part III.   School of Nursing Library

Objective
        The purpose of the School of Nursing Library is to forward the educational objectives of its particular school. Its primary function, therefore, is to aid in the education of students by maintaining an attractive and adequately equipped library which will complement, correlate, and extend the curriculum, and serve the library needs of the faculty.   Its secondary purpose is to provide stimulating, informative, and enriching non-curricular, and recreational reading material...

Library Collection and Its Use
        The library collection should conform to the recommendations of the National League of Nursing.

The number of volumes in the library depends on the size, type, and location of the school.   The hospital Nursing School Library in an isolated community needs a larger collection than a university Nursing School Library with easy access to the medical school or other libraries.

The Librarian should borrow from other libraries in accordance with the needs of her patrons and offer the same service to other libraries whenever possible.

Reference and loan material should be utilized in accordance with the regulations established by the Librarian and the Library Committee.

Ward libraries for the use of the nurses in each clinical division of the hospital should be considered part of the collection and be under the supervision of the Librarian...

Objectives and Standards for Special Libraries

Special Library Association

From Special Libraries 55: 672-80, December
1964 (sel.)

Objectives
    The Special Library Is a Major Source of Information
in the Organization It Serves.

        The special library staff is responsible for providing
the library materials and services designed to meet the information requirements of the library's clientele in fields
pertinent to the purposes and work of the organization.

    The Special Library Acquires, Organizes, Maintains,
    Utilizes, and Disseminates Informational Materials Ger-
    mane to the Organization's Activities.

        The special library acquires materials and informa-
tion for the organization's current and future needs.   These
materials must be organized for the most effective use by
the library's clientele and staff.   The library staff, when
aware of the interests of its clientele, can bring pertinent
materials and information to the attention of users before
they are requested or in direct response to requests.   Resources outside the library can also be called upon to answer
users' needs.

    The Special Library Serves All Who Have Appropriate
    Need of Its Services.

        The objectives of the library regarding whom it is to
serve and the services it is to provide should be clearly delineated, preferably in writing.   To be effective, these responsibilities must be reviewed periodically and revised in
accordance with changes in the organization's activities and
advances in library and information technology...

Collection
The special library's collection consists of the information sources that are acquired, organized, and administered for use by or in behalf of the library's clientele.

Physically, the collection may include a variety of forms and types of materials, not all of which are appropriate to a particular special library; books, pamphlets, preprints, reprints, translations, dissertations and theses; periodicals, newspapers, press releases, indexing, abstracting, and other services, transactions, yearbooks, reports, directories of organizations; external and internal technical reports; research and laboratory notebooks, archival materials; patents, trademarks, specifications and standards; audiovisual materials (photographs, slides, pictures, motion pictures, filmstrips, tape and disc recordings); and special collections (maps, sheet music, manuscripts, catalogs, legislative materials, clippings, microforms).

The Subject Coverage of the Special Library's Collection Is Intensive and Extensive Enough To Meet the Current and Anticipated Information Requirements of the Library's Clientele.

The library's collection includes all basic, frequently used, and potentially useful materials. The range of subjects covered is determined by the objectives of the organization; the depth of subject coverage in each field is governed by the nature of the organization's work. The special library administrator continually evaluates the scope and adequacy of the collection in the light of changes in emphasis or new developments in the organization's activities. Centralizing pertinent materials in the library, rather than scattering them in office collections, is important in effecting the basic goal of general accessibility of all sources of information. Occasional use of outside resources is necessary and desirable, but the criterion of immediate availability of materials demands major reliance upon the library's own resources. General reference works that supplement the library's special collections broaden the scope of the library's information services.

The Size of a Special Library Collection Depends Upon the Amount of Material Available That Is Pertinent to the Organization's Special Needs.

The purpose and use of the special library's collection influence its size. Some libraries need large reference collections, multiple copies, and works that have historical value; others have highly selective collections, keep currently useful literature only, and retain only in microform older periodical sets and items of decreasing usefulness. Many libraries discard little used materials if they are available in the area. The rate and direction of growth of the library's collection should reflect the continuing requirements of the library's clientele.

Acquisition Policies of a Special Library Must Be Established Within the Framework of the Library's Stated Objectives.

The special library administrator is responsible for establishing specific acquisition policies pertaining to depth and extent of subject coverage, types of materials, gifts, and exchanges. He is constantly alert to new sources for procuring special materials and he systematically reviews all announcements and listings of published materials. An efficient acquisition program requires sound business practices and well-organized acquisition records.

Libraries in organizations that issue publications may set up a program for the exchange of publications with other organizations. Procurement of individual titles or volumes on an exchange basis may be accomplished through a central clearinghouse or through cooperative arrangements with individual libraries or institutions. Both solicited and unsolicited gifts that add strength to the collection are desirable, provided no restrictions concerning their use or disposition are imposed.

The special library administrator can anticipate information needs if he is kept informed about all activities and future plans of his organization. Participation in planning sessions and discussions with subject specialists in the organization are essential to a continuing acquisition policy.

Books and Nonbook Materials

Public Library Association

From Public Library Association. Interim Standards
for Small Public Libraries: Guidelines Toward
Achieving the Goals of Public Library Service.
Chicago, American Library Association, 1962. p. 7-8

III. Books and Nonbook Materials

A. Every library should have a written statement of policy
covering the selection and maintenance of its collection
of books and of non-book materials.

   1. This statement should be approved by the governing
body and should define specifically what each library
expects to have in its own collection and what it expects to obtain from other sources.

   2. It should state the purposes, level of quality, and
community needs to be reflected in acquiring materials. It affirms the library's position on supplying resources on controversial subjects. From it one should
be able to learn the scope, emphasis and limits of the
collection, and the policies which govern withdrawals.

   3. The policy statement should be reviewed regularly
and revised as needed.

B. Material added to the collection should meet high standards of quality in content, expression and format and
should meet the needs and interests of the individual community.

   1. Factors to be considered in judging the quality of material are: factual accuracy, effective expression,
significance of subject, sincerity, responsibility of
opinion, durability of paper and binding, attractiveness
of the book, and legibility of print. The need for each
item in relation to the rest of the collection and to the
interests of the community should also influence selec-

tion.

2.   Selection anticipates community needs. It must go
beyond the requests of persons who use the library
regularly, and reach out to groups in the population
which are not using library materials.

C. The library collection should provide opposing views on
controversial topics.

1.   The public library does not promote particular beliefs
or views. It does provide, either from its own or
borrowed resources, materials which the individual can
examine and use to make his own decisions.
2.   Care must be exercised that groups or individuals do
not unduly influence additions to or withdrawals from
the collection. Efforts of groups to deny access to
materials to others in the community must be resisted.
3.   Material, often free, which may contain subversive,
biased, or propaganda information must be examined
closely to determine its usefulness to the collection.

D. The character and emphasis of the collection in a community library should be influenced by the existence of
other library collections in the community and area.

The community library should keep itself informed about
other book resources in the area and make every effort to develop cooperative plans for the public use or
interloan of special materials.

E. Selection of materials for the library should be determined by usefulness and should not be limited by format.

1.   Nonbook materials may be acquired to supplement book
resources. Nonbook resources include slides, films,
recordings, newspapers, magazines, reports by organizations and governments, maps, music scores, micro-
reproductions, pamphlets, clippings, and pictures.
2.   Community libraries which cannot afford certain of
these materials, and their maintenance, may satisfy
their patrons by making arrangements for borrowing
from larger libraries, using other resources in their
community or elsewhere, or by developing cooperative
services such as film circuits.

F. All materials in a community library should be actively

used.

1. A library's basic collection should contain only those items which have the most frequent and lasting usage. Books needed for shorter periods of time should be supplied by changing collections from resource centers, supplementing the basic collection.

2. A certain portion of the budget should be set aside for the rentals, contractual arrangements, and transportation costs for interloans needed to provide these changing collections.

G. Regardless of the size of the community, its library should provide access to enough books to cover the interests of the whole population.

1. Libraries serving populations from 5,000 to 50,000 require a minimum of 2 books per capita.

2. Communities up to 5,000 persons need access to a minimum of 10,000 volumes, or 3 books per capita, whichever is greater.

3. A library's total book resources should be made up of its own basic collection plus the volumes available for changing collections. The proportion may be according to the following scale:

Population	Basic Collection	Changing Collections
under 2,500	40%	60%
2,500 to 4,999	50%	50%
5,000 to 9,999	60%	40%
10,000 to 24,999	80%	20%
25,000 to 49,999	90%	10%

4. New titles purchased annually for the library's basic collection should total at least 5 per cent of the library's basic collection. The percentage of the annual purchases allotted to children's and young adults' titles would depend upon the population distribution of the community but approximately 30 per cent of the book budget is the sum usually budgeted for the children's collection and 10-15 per cent for young adults.

H. The community library should have a sufficient number of standard reference books to supply information most frequently needed.

This non-circulating collection should contain as little duplication of information as possible. Infrequently needed tools from which answers can be secured readily over the telephone or by mail from a larger or special library through some definite contractual arrangement should be omitted.

I. Each community library needs a periodical collection which should be maintained as follows:

Population	Magazines and Newspapers Received	Back files to be Kept According to Use and Indexing
under 2,500	at least 25	1- 5 years
2,500 to 4,999	25-50	1- 5 years
5,000 to 9,999	50-75	1- 10 years
10,000 to 24,999	75-100	1- 10 years
25,000 to 49,999	100-150	1- 10 years

Periodicals listed in periodical indexes should be kept longer than those not indexed. Frequent reader use balanced against storage space are the other considerations. Older periodicals should be sent to an authorized resource library from which they can be borrowed as needed.

J. Long-playing discs or recordings should be made available to local communities.

Libraries may acquire recordings by gift or through loans from a resource center, if their budgets are inadequate for this purpose. The following range size for record collections is recommended:

Population	Minimum Collection	Minimum Annual Additions or Replacements
under 2,500	acquire by gift or loan	
2,500 to 4,999	100-150	35-50
5,000 to 9,999	150-200	50-70
10,000 to 24,999	200-500	70-150
25,000 to 49,999	500-1000	150-300

K. Small libraries should not attempt to build a film collection themselves, but should allot funds to borrow films or to participate in a film circuit.

L. Systematic removal from the library of materials no longer useful is essential to maintain the purpose and quality of the collection.

  1. Outdated and shabby material should obviously be removed; discredited material deserves the same action, although this requires more judgment; and items no longer of interest should be weeded out.
  2. Material not actively used in small libraries but still occasionally needed should be withdrawn from the collection and sent to an authorized library center from which it can be borrowed for future use.
  3. Annual withdrawals from the basic collection should average 5 per cent of the total collection. In community libraries where much of the material is in a changing collection, this percentage may be lower.

M. The library should make every effort to collect local history material if this is not adequately preserved elsewhere in the community.

  Small libraries without proper facilities for fireproof and scientific preservation of valuable local history items should deposit originals at a center and if the historical information is needed, retain a photo copy or other duplicate for their own use.

N. Each community library should have ready access to materials other than its own.

  When a patron's request cannot be filled by the local library or through resources within the area it should be channeled to resource centers in library systems, large public libraries, college or university libraries, special libraries, or state libraries.

Materials: Selection, Organization, and Control

Public Library Association

> From Public Library Association. Standards Com-
> mittee. <u>Minimum Standards for Public Library
> Systems,</u> 1966. Chicago, American Library As-
> sociation, 1967. Chap. V, p. 39-48

The public library as an institution exists to provide materials which communicate experience and ideas from one person to another. Its function is to assemble, organize, preserve, and make easily and freely available to all people the printed and nonprinted materials that will assist them to:

Educate themselves continually
Keep pace with progress in all fields of knowledge
Become better members of home and community
Discharge political and social obligations
Be more capable in their daily occupations
Develop their creative and spiritual capacities
Appreciate and enjoy the works of art and literature
Use leisure time to promote personal and social well-being
Contribute to the growth of knowledge.

To provide a reservoir of knowledge and aesthetic enjoyment which supplies inquiring minds, library materials include a variety of forms:

Books	Films, slides, filmstrips
Periodicals	Music scores
Pamphlets	Maps
Newspapers	Recordings
Pictures	Various forms of microreproduction.

31. All materials should be selected and retained or discarded in keeping with stated objectives of each system.

Within the broad purposes listed above, each library should define and refine the objectives it seeks to achieve. Systems and libraries within systems must

define aims toward which they will build their collections, or aims will be defined for them by default in
what they fail to acquire.   Emphasis in collections will
change from time to time to clarify emerging issues,
and as communities change and face new problems.

Objectives need not be narrow or restrictive, but the
more definite they are the more the collection can be
built with assurance.

i. Every system and every library within the system
    should have a written statement of policy, covering the
    selection and maintenance of its collection.

    This statement should be approved and supported by the
    governing body.   It sets forth the purposes, levels of
    quality, and community needs to be reflected in acquir-
    ing materials.   It describes the scope and emphasis
    and defines the limits of the collection; it affirms the
    institution's position on supplying resources on contro-
    versial subjects; and records the policies which govern
    withdrawals.

32. Materials acquired should meet high standards of quality
    in content, expression, and form.

    Library collections comprise the most appropriate ma-
    terials selected to serve purposes and needs.   Factual
    accuracy, effective expression, significance of subject,
    sincerity and responsibility of opinions, and appropri-
    ate form are some factors to consider and at times
    to balance against one another.   The physical conditions
    of the medium used and the quality of the technical
    production are additional factors to evaluate in the se-
    lection process.

33. Within standards of purpose and quality, collections should
    be built to meet the needs and interests of people.

    Systems of libraries, both the community library and
    the headquarters unit, exist to serve their constituents.
    Materials are added because they serve agreed pur-
    poses, meet quality standards, and are of interest to
    readers and to organizations.   Selection follows from
    conscious study of the needs of all groups: among
    others, industry, businessmen, gardeners, music lovers,
    labor, the handicapped, children.

Sensitivity to interests, early recognition of needs before they are clearly expressed, and catholicity of contact and viewpoint mark the librarian who keeps the collection in tune with its public.   Selection must go beyond the requests of particular groups who have come to use the library regularly, and must appeal to segments in the population which do not as readily turn to it.

i.   The needs of the various age and interest groups in the community should be reflected in the library's annual budget allocations for resources and in the continuing selection of materials to meet their needs.

ii.   Material selected for special groups should conform to the library's objectives for these groups, and should be appropriate to their needs both in format and in literary quality.   Occasionally material not traditionally acceptable for library use may be included.

34. Library collections should contain opposing views on controversial topics.

The public library does not promote particular beliefs or views.   It provides a resource where the individual can examine issues freely and make his own decisions.

i.   The collections must contain the various opinions expressed on important, complicated, or controversial questions, including unpopular or unorthodox positions.

If a public library does not provide the means to study the several sides of issues, it is failing in one of its unique reasons for existence.   This standard does not necessarily imply numerical balance.   Controversial materials in community libraries may be limited to areas of controversy about which there is local concern.   However, it must be possible to obtain readily from other sources material representing all shades of opinion on the greatest possible variety of subjects.

ii.   Materials of the required quality, serving the purposes of the library and relating to an existing need or interest, will not be removed from the collection nor will materials lacking these qualities be added because of pressure by groups or individuals.

Care must be taken that parts of the community do not unduly influence the collections, either positively or negatively. Selection must resist efforts of groups to deny access to other segments of the community. Libraries must also resist efforts to force inclusion of materials representing political, economic, moral, religious, or other vested positions when these materials do not conform to the institution's selection policies.

35. The collection of the public library should be inclusive and contain materials which contribute to the library's purpose without regard to form.

Selection of materials for the library should be determined by usefulness and should not be limited by form. People use all senses in varying degrees in learning and enjoying. Materials which appeal to combinations of senses, particularly visual and audio, are more effective as learning vehicles than those requiring only one. Some of these will appeal to those who are not attracted by the conventional book; others will be more appropriate than the conventional book. Such resources include not only films, slides, filmstrips and recordings (both disc and tape), but also pamphlets, documents, maps, music scores, and microprint. Libraries must be aware of the values and availability of these resources and integrate them into their collections to enhance the educational capabilities of the institution.

i. The form in which materials are acquired must be appropriate to the content and use.

36. Systematic removal of materials no longer useful is essential to maintaining the purposes and quality of resources.

Outdated, seldom-used, or shabby items remaining in the collection can weaken a library as surely as insufficiant acquisitions. In time such material characterizes the whole collection, overshadowing newer and more useful purchases. Outdated materials should obviously be removed. With few exceptions, community libraries are not centers for historical research, except in the field of local history. Except for materials of special quality smaller community libraries do not ordinarily need to retain seldom-used items, for to do

so may decrease day-to-day effectiveness. Larger
community libraries whose staff and building are adequate for proper maintenance of a more varied collection may be more generous in retention of seldom-
used items.

i. Annual withdrawals from community library collections
should average at least 5 per cent of the total collection.

The community library collection should consist of
currently useful materials. The bulk of material in
the smaller community library is expendable or "dead"
within ten years.

ii. Headquarters libraries, reservoirs of quality materials from which community libraries draw, should carefully consider withdrawals and not necessarily make
them conform to numerical ratios.

iii. Withdrawals made at any level should be offered to
the next higher echelon of resources before they are
destroyed.

37. The community library stands as the first and convenient resource for all readers.

i. Materials used regularly should be in the collection of
each community library in sufficient duplication to prevent unreasonable delays in serving the needs of the
community.

The community library within relatively easy reach of
all has standard reference materials. A variety of
standard and current materials should be available in
such fields as family life, public affairs, the arts,
science, and other topics for all age groups. Magazines of both substance and popular interest and local
newspapers should be provided. In addition, a basic
collection of recordings should be maintained; and
films, if not locally held, should be available on request from the system. Other nonbook materials used
regularly should be in the local collection.

ii. The community library must be able to draw upon
large collections, to meet the needs of readers with
specialized interests and to supplement and enrich its

resources for all users.

38. The character and emphasis of the community library
    collection should be influenced by the existence of avail-
    able library collections in the community and area.

    The presence of other libraries, open to the public for
    lending or use, specializing in school, college, and
    university service, or in technology, fine arts, or oth-
    er specialized fields, should free some part of public
    library funds for other areas of interest or other ap-
    plications in these fields.   Therefore, efforts should
    be made to develop, finance, and implement coopera-
    tive plans for the public use of such special collections
    although basic book purchases in the various areas of
    specialization would still be necessary at the community
    level.

    i. Community libraries should have regular means to keep
        themselves informed about other library material re-
        sources available in the community and area in order
        to avoid unnecessary duplication and to arrange for
        their use by the public.

39. A library system must have resources covering the in-
    terests in the several communities it serves, in reason-
    able duplication to meet most requests immediately.

    In the library system of which his community library
    is a part, every person should have access to a com-
    prehensive collection of general reference resources
    and specialized materials on topics of major impor-
    tance in the region, subject resources which meet not
    only general but also individual needs and interests,
    special collections on subjects of local significance, a
    liberal quantity of the representative literature of civili-
    zation, materials relating to the history and activities
    of the region, and items in foreign languages as
    needed.   As in the case of community libraries, rea-
    sonable duplication is necessary where titles and topics
    require it, so that individuals and member libraries
    will not be delayed and frustrated in their search for
    knowledge.

    More important than total volume is rate of current
    acquisitions, particularly in a new library.   Quantita-
    tive figures to achieve an inclusive collection of this

kind will vary, but should not fall below the following
levels unless special conditions in a region make some
of the usual resources unnecessary.

i. The following quantities of materials are recommended
for system collections designed to serve populations
ranging from 150,000 to 1,000,000.

These suggestions assume that the system is designed
to serve a minimum population of 150,000 people, which
appears to ensure the most economical and effective
use of staff, collections, and funds. When the population is less, there should be the expectation that the population will increase to the 150,000 minimum within the
near future; when the collection is smaller than the
suggestions here, plans should be made to acquire the
minimum quantities suggested by massive acquisitions
from standard lists.

The system headquarters, as the immediate resource
for the community libraries, and as the principal library for a large segment of the general public in the
area, is expected to contain a wide variety and an adequate collection of currently useful materials. This
collection may be contained in one institution or it may
be divided between two or more facilities when this arrangement is more appropriate.

Acquisition for all age levels and of all forms of materials should consider special interest needs of individuals and groups as reflected in their occupations,
abilities, limitations, etc.

Books

Titles
    The headquarters should contain at least 100,000 adult
nonfiction titles as a basic collection.

The headquarters should add approximately 50 per cent
of the new adult nonfiction trade titles published in
English in the United States each year in sufficient
duplication to meet needs.

The headquarters collection should have available a
comprehensive collection of older as well as current
fiction by American and foreign authors.

Volumes

The total system collection should own resources of at least 2 to 4 volumes per capita, and at least 2 volumes per capita in areas serving 1,000,000 population.

Maintenance of system collections

Collections should be maintained by annual additions and replacements of not less than 1/6 volume per capita in areas serving up to 500,000 population; 1/8 volume per capita in areas serving over 500,000 population.

Up to 1/3 of the volumes added annually should be for children. These should be chosen on the basis of the characteristics and needs of the area.

At least 5 per cent of its annual additions should be materials of specific interest to young adults.

Pamphlets

Pamphlet collections should be developed and maintained in system headquarters in order to provide materials on new or esoteric subjects which have not yet been incorporated into more conventional printed sources.

Sufficient quantities of more generally useful items should be acquired to serve system needs. Devices should be developed to provide information to participating libraries on the availability of items in this category, and community libraries should be encouraged to organize their own pamphlet collections.

Periodicals

At least one currently published periodical title should be available for each 250 people in the service area.

Emphasis should be given to periodicals indexed in special indexing services, but acquisitions should not be limited to these.

Headquarters collections should receive all current periodicals indexed in Readers' Guide to Periodical Literature and the most frequently requested items indexed in other indexing services.

Less frequently requested items should be available from a state or regional resource center.

Indexed periodicals should be retained in their original form for 10 to 15 years, preferably unbound.

Headquarters collections should replace or supplement the original form with a microtext edition.

Community libraries should not ordinarily attempt to build extensive collections of back issues of periodicals, but should depend on the headquarters collection to service their needs for these materials.

Print-out photocopy machinery should be available as needed.

Indexing Services

Headquarters collections will plan to acquire a broad range of indexing services. Access to materials in collections is simplified by consolidated indexing services, and processing units can be relieved of much duplicative effort if these devices are properly maintained. While not all indexes are extensions of the catalog, many can be considered as such.

Services which index collections
Such publications as the Short Story Index, Index to Plays in Collections, the Essay and General Literature Index, and Granger's Index to Poetry are examples of this type. These services and the materials they index will be acquired as a part of the basic collection.

Services which index by subject
Such publications as Psychological Abstracts, Education Index, Music Index, Art Index, etc., and the materials they index will be acquired as appropriate.

Services which index by form
Such publications as Schwann's Record Catalog, Vertical File Index, etc., and the material which they index will be acquired as considered appropriate.

Government Documents

System headquarters will be a selective United States

government documents depository or have reasonably convenient access to one in the immediate vicinity, and will acquire local, state, and international documents on a selective but systematic basis.

Audio-Visual Materials

Audio-visual materials are a useful and desirable means of promoting continuing education. They are basic, independent resources in many subject areas and for many activities, rather than supplementary as they are generally considered.

The most popular forms for libraries at the present time are the conventional 16mm photographic film and 33-1/3 rpm recordings. Library collections should be planned to include other speeds and other media, such as video tape, as they become available and prove appropriate.

The suggestions following are intended for system collections with access to a resource collection at the state or regional level. When a state or region maintains the basic collection of the materials, these suggestions are not applicable.

Films

The basic film collection for the system should consist of one title for each 1,000 population served, but no collection should be less than 1,000 titles.

Selected films should be duplicated to meet needs and to supply a film circuit for the system if such is desired.

Film collections will need replacements and additions at the rate of 10-15 per cent per year.

Recordings

The basic collection of recordings for the system should consist of one disc or reel of tape for each 50 people in the service area, but no collection should contain less than 5,000 discs and reels.

Selected recordings should be duplicated to meet needs

and to supply rotating collections for the system, if such are desired.

Recordings will need replacements and additions at the rate of 10-15 per cent per year minimum.

Other Forms and Devices

Other forms of materials should be acquired as needed and in keeping with Standard 38, i.

As new forms are developed, they should be acquired by the system for testing, familiarization, and evaluation. When their value appears appropriate and useful in the community library, they should be added to the collection in sufficient quantity to meet needs.

Examples of these materials which should be considered at the present time would include:

Teaching machines and associated materials
Closed circuit television
Educational television
Transparencies
Slides
Filmstrips.

40. Each state or group of states will support collections which supplement and reinforce the resources of the systems.

Neither the community library nor the supporting system is expected to answer all the needs of all its patrons. A third level of service is needed which will provide research resources for the patron who does not have access to academic or industrial library resources. This can be done by opening the reservoirs of selected large research collections in states and regions. These can be state, university, or large city libraries, or even independent institutions.

i. Publicly supported research library collections and services will be made legally available as supporting units to library systems.

41. Organization and control provide for effective use of library materials.

Organization and control are essential to the use of a library: without them it becomes merely a collection of books in which it is difficult, if not impossible, to locate the desired information.

Organization by classification, cataloging, or other finding devices assures systematic location of materials; control systems for inventory and lending assure a continuously accurate record of holdings and fair access to many users. Organization, maintenance, and control begin with the selection of material and its introduction into the collection, continue through its useful lifetime, and provide for its removal. Much of the quality of service given in a library depends upon an effective system of organization and control. The nature of the operation, in its turn, depends upon requirements for service.

42. Processes for the selection and acquisition of library materials must be orderly and coordinated.

Information about materials in the process of being selected must be coordinated among the several libraries in a library system.

i. Within each library system there should be clearly defined procedures for coordinating and swiftly communicating information about selection of materials and status of orders.

ii. Records should be as simple as possible yet should show at any time what is on order; what has been received; current stage of preparation; and budget expenditures, balances, and encumbrances.

43. Selection of materials should be done cooperatively by representatives of all member libraries in a system.

i. Each library in a system should have regular opportunity to see, discuss, and select from the new books being published.

44. The acquisition, cataloging, and preparation of materials should be centralized.

i. Acquisition and cataloging should be centralized, either within the system or through a contract with a processing center.

Technical processing for the system may be a service
provided by a member library or may be purchased
from another library system, a government agency, or
a commercial firm.   Expert performance is assured
by utilizing specialized personnel, uniform work procedures, and time- and labor-saving machinery.   Individual libraries benefit by securing a better discount in
purchasing materials and supplies, by avoiding purchase
of expensive bibliographic tools, and by preventing
duplication of effort, thus permitting more efficient de-
ployment of staff.

45. The control of materials throughout a system should be
uniform.

i.   The user of any library within a system is entitled to
expect the same regulations regarding loans, and the
same pattern of organization in all.

46. Organization and control of materials should encompass
the needs of all the libraries of a system.

Cataloging, circulation, and other control processes
may vary from system to system.   The extent of a
system's research resources will influence the degree
of complexity of organization and control of materials.
Physical form of materials will require different treatment in cataloging, housing, and lending regulations.
The form of the catalog itself (card, book, or other)
will depend upon complete consideration of factors of
cost, complexity of system, and catalog practices already in use.

i.   Published indexes and other services available to aid
in locating information should be utilized wherever possible to avoid unnecessary duplication of effort.

47. Arrangement of materials should combine orderly location and ease of access.

The nature of the material, its use, and its permanence are factors to consider.   Books may be shelved
by any logical arrangement, such as by author or subject classification.   Other types of material may be
arranged as their format dictates.

    i. Special collections, whether temporary or permanent, which deviate from logical order should be kept to a minimum.

    ii. Materials should be arranged in logical sequence to provide access for staff and public.

48. Data to be recorded should be related to requirements for legal and administrative reporting.

    The decision on data to be assembled must be an administrative one. The general rule should be to eliminate all which are not legally required or which have no foreseeable use for administrative purposes.

    i. Data should be recorded to measure the library's collection, including number of titles as well as number of volumes; to aid in making administrative decisions; to report to official agencies; and as a record of the library's history.

Library Collections

Association of College and Research Libraries

From College and Research Libraries 20: 276-8, July 1959.

A. Books and Periodicals

The library's collection of books, periodicals, pamphlets, documents, newspapers, maps, microfilm, microcards, microprint, and other materials, must be so constituted and organized as to give effective strength and support to the educational program of the institution. The collection should meet the full curricular needs of undergraduate students and should be easily accessible to them. It should provide properly for the demands of graduate students in each field in which the institution offers the Master's degree. Also it should contain a generous selection of works to keep the members of the faculty abreast of the latest advances in modern scholarship and to assist them in their professional growth. If special programs of independent study involving a wide use of books are carried on, provision must be made for them in the library's collection.

In addition to the materials related directly or indirectly to the curriculum, the collection should contain the standard works which represent the heritage of civilization. These works should be continuously supplemented by a wide variety of books which combine timeliness with enduring value, chosen to arouse the intellectual curiosity of students and to satisfy their recreational reading needs.

There should be a strong and up-to-date reference collection consisting of the most authoritative reference works and bibliographies in all major fields of knowledge. This collection must not be restricted to subjects which form part of the curriculum, nor to publications in the English language.

The periodicals subscription list should be well balanced and carefully chosen to meet the requirements of students for collateral course reading, to provide in some measure for the research needs of advanced students and faculty, to keep the faculty informed of developments in their fields, and to afford throught-provoking general and recreational reading. [1] Newspaper subscriptions should provide news coverage at the national, regional, and local levels; they should include also one or more leading papers from abroad.   Various political points of view should be represented.   It is essential that the major journals and newspapers be kept and bound systematically or preserved in microtext form.

Printed, manuscript, and archival materials pertaining to the institution of which the library is a part should be collected and preserved.

The right of the librarian to select books and other materials representing all sides of controversial issues must be safeguarded by the institution, and any attempts at censorship from whatever sources or for whatever reasons must be resisted.

The quality of the library collections should not be sacrificed to unnecessary duplication of titles.   However, works of lasting significance or of contemporary importance should be available in a sufficient number of copies to give students a fair opportunity to examine them thoroughly.

Obsolete materials, such as outmoded books, superseded editions, incomplete sets of longer works, broken files of unindexed journals, superfluous duplicates, and worn out or badly marked volumes, should be continuously weeded with the advice of faculty members concerned.   Gifts should be accepted only in case they add to the strength of the library collections and do not carry unreasonable restrictions. President, faculty, and librarian should join in developing a policy which clearly defines what kinds of gifts are desirable for the institution and why it is important educationally to integrate them with the regular collections except in rare instances.

If funds are allocated to departments, a substantial portion beyond fixed costs for periodicals and continuations should be reserved for direct assignment by the librarian. This portion should be large enough to provide for the purchase of reference works, general publications, expensive sets, books for recreational reading, and works which cross departmental lines, as well as for correcting weaknesses in the library's collection.

Library holdings should be checked frequently against standard bibliographies, both general and subject, as a reliable measure of their quality. [2]   A high percentage of listed titles which are relevant to the program of the individual institution, should be included in the library collections.

The size of the library collections is largely determined by the following major factors: (1) The extent and nature of the curriculum, (2) the number and character of graduate programs, (3) the methods of instruction, (4) the size of the undergraduate and graduate student body, both full-time and extension, and (5) the need of the faculty for more advanced materials which cannot be met conveniently by the use of research libraries in the area.

An analysis of small college library statistics[3] suggests that no library can be expected to give effective support to the instructional program if it contains fewer than 50,000 carefully chosen volumes.   A steady growth is essential to any good college library.   The rate of growth of the library collection may slow down, however, when the number of volumes reaches approximately 300,000.   Since there appears to be a correlation between the growth of the student body and the growth of the collection, there is a convenient measure based upon observation of the development of college libraries, which may serve as a guide: up to 600 students, 50,000 volumes; for every additional 200 students, 10,000 volumes.   Part-time and extension students should be equated into full-time student figures for the purpose of such computations.   It is, however, clearly understood, that these are minimal figures and that stronger institutions will demand considerably larger and richer collections.

The library's collections should be fully organized for use.   The main catalog of the library should serve as a union catalog for all collections of the library whether housed in the main building or in college departments.   The catalog should follow the Library of Congress and American Library Association cataloging codes as standards.   Materials should be classified according to an accepted scheme in general usage and be subject to continual editing to keep the

catalog abreast of modern technological developments.   The
catalog should also be constantly revised to keep it up-to-
date in terminology.

B. Audio-Visual Materials

Audio-visual materials including films, filmstrips,
recordings, and tapes are an integral part of modern instruction, and every college library must concern itself with
them.   The library should take the initiative for providing
them, if no other agency on campus has been assigned this
responsibility.

If the library is handling the program, it should be
enabled to do so by special budgetary provisions, including
those of additional staff.   The program must be, both in its
budget and its operation, an integral part of the whole of the
library's functions.   No audio-visual program can succeed
without adequate facilities for the use of equipment and materials.

The librarian is bound by the same high standards of
selection for films and recordings that he uses for books...

Notes

1. Subscriptions should be checked against such an authoritative compilation as Classified List of Periodicals
for the College Library; 4th edition, revised and enlarged by Evan Ira Farber (Boston: F. W. Faxon
Company, 1957).   College librarians should consult
with their faculties about additions, if they consider
the coverage inadequate.

2. Two comprehensive bibliographies which have proved to
be particularly helpful for the purpose of self-evalua-
tion, are the following: Catalogue of the Lamont Li-
brary, Harvard College; prepared by Philip J. Mc-
Niff and members of the library staff (Cambridge,
Mass., Harvard University Press, 1953).   Southern
Association of Colleges and Secondary Schools, Com-
mission on Colleges and Universities, The Classified
List of Reference Books and Periodicals for College
Libraries; edited by W. Stanley Hoole (Atlanta, The
Association, 1955).   Unfortunately out-of-date, but
still useful for checking the pre-war literature in

some areas of the humanities is Charles B. Shaw,
A List of Books for College Libraries, 2d edition
(Chicago, ALA, 1931), and its supplement 1931-1938
(Chicago, ALA, 1940).

Some examples of excellent subject bibliographies are:
The Concise Cambridge Bibliography of English Literature, 600-1950; edited by George Watson (Cambridge,
University Press, 1958).   Critical Bibliography of
French Literature; edited by David C. Cabeen (3
vols. published thus far, Syracuse University Press,
1948-56).   Foreign Affairs Bibliography (3 vols. :
1919-32, 1932-1942, 1942-1952; edited by William L.
Langer, Robert G. Woolbert, and Henry L. Roberts
respectively, New York, Council on Foreign Relations,
1933-1955, and kept up to date by the quarterly bibliographies in Foreign Affairs).   The Harvard List of
Books in Psychology; compiled and annotated by the
psychologists in Harvard University, 2d edition (Cambridge, Mass. , Harvard University Press, 1955).
Scientific, Medical and Technical Books Published in
the U. S. A. to December 1956; edited by R. R. Hawkins, 2d edition (Washington, D. C. , 1958).

Also Lester Asheim and others, The Humanities and
the Library (Chicago, ALA, 1957) and Louis R. Wilson, The Library in College Instruction (New York,
H. W. Wilson, 1951) should be checked, in the latter
especially the section on teaching materials for general education on the college level.

3. See the statistics published annually in the January issue
     of CRL.

The Library Collection

Association of College and Research Libraries,
Junior College Section

From College and Research Libraries 21:202-4,
May 1960.

A. Books and Periodicals

The collection of a junior college library, consisting
of books, periodicals, pamphlets, maps, micro-publications,
archival and audio-visual materials, should be selected and
organized so as to promote and strengthen the teaching program in all its aspects. It should also seek to aid faculty
members in their professional and scholarly growth.

The holdings of the junior college library should include a generous amount of carefully chosen works presenting our common heritage. They should be supplemented by
a wide variety of modern books in the major fields of knowledge, books that should be both timely and enduring. The
collection should include in particular many works of high
caliber which will arouse intellectual curiosity, counteract
parochialism, and help to develop critical thinking. Liberal
provision should also be made for stimulating recreational
reading. The library holdings should offer a challenge to all
elements represented in the student body and assist them in
their intellectual growth.

The reference collection must be strong; it should be
up to date and broad in its coverage. It should include standard reference works in all major fields of knowledge, several periodical indexes, a wide selection of outstanding subject bibliographies, and the authoritative book lists for junior
college libraries. [1]

Periodicals and newspapers constitute an invaluable

source of reference for material on many subjects.   They
should be selected by the librarian,   with the assistance of
the faculty.   The periodical subscription list should be well
balanced.   It should include titles of lasting reference value
as well as journals helpful to the faculty or appealing to the
young college readers. [2] Periodicals of permanent significance should be bound or made available in microform.

The reading of newspapers is of increasing importance
to students in an era of world-wide political and social
changes.   Subscriptions should provide ample news coverage
at the national, regional, and local level.   Various political
points of view should be presented by the papers selected.
Permanent availability of the files of a major newspaper on
microfilm is highly desirable.

The stand of the American Library Association on the
subject of censorship should be firmly adhered to by junior
college librarians.   The right of the librarian to provide
books, periodicals, and other materials which present all
sides of controversial issues cannot be disputed.   Attempts
at censorship should be resisted no matter how expedient it
would be to comply. [3]

The following considerations will determine the size
of the library collection: the breadth of the curriculum; the
method of instruction employed; the number of students (full-
time equivalent) and faculty; the demands of the faculty for
research materials; the availability of other appropriate library resources; and the kind of student body served, i. e. ,
residential vs. commuting students.

A two-year institution of up to 1, 000 students (full-
time equivalent) cannot discharge its mission without a carefully selected collection of at least 20, 000 volumes, exclusive of duplicates and textbooks. [4] Junior colleges with broad
curriculum offerings will tend to have much larger collections; an institution with a multiplicity of programs may need
a minimum collection of two or three times the basic figure
of 20, 000 volumes.   The book holdings should be increased
as the enrollment grows and the complexity and depth of
course offerings expand.   Consultation with many junior college librarians indicates that for most junior college librarians a convenient yardstick would be the following: the bookstock should be enlarged by 5, 000 volumes for every 500 students (full-time equivalent) beyond 1, 000.

Librarians, instructors, and administrators should study carefully the latest compilation of junior college library statistics.   They should measure the adequacy of their collections against the reported holdings of junior colleges of established excellence with similar curricula and enrollments. Junior college libraries with strong financial support, a vigorous faculty, and talented leadership will forge ahead of any minimum standards.

The traditional book collection will be supplemented and broadened by the judicious selection of government documents and the many useful pamphlets now available.   Under no circumstances should junior college libraries limit their collections to books in print.   Quality paperbacks, reproducing standard works long out of print, and new processes such as photo-copying, micro-texts, and microfilms, should be imaginatively utilized.   Finally, the strength and quality of the collection must not be impaired by excessive buying of duplicates and textbooks.

The following categories of library materials should be weeded and discarded: obsolete materials and editions; broken files of unindexed periodicals; unnecessary duplicates; old recreational periodicals which do not have permanent value; and worn out books, pamphlets, periodicals, and audio-visual materials.   As far as possible, the weeding process should be undertaken in consultation with the faculty.

Gifts should be accepted only in case they add to the strength of the library collection and do not carry unreasonable restrictions.   Administrators, faculty, and librarian should join in developing a policy which clearly defines what kinds of gifts are desirable for the institution and why it is important educationally to integrate them with the regular collection except in rare instances.

The library's collection should be fully organized for use.   The main catalog of the library should serve as a union catalog for all collections of the library wherever housed. The catalog should follow the Library of Congress and American Library Association cataloging codes as standards.   Materials should be classified according to an accepted scheme in general usage.   Subject headings should be edited continually to keep the catalog abreast of modern developments. The catalog should also be constantly revised to keep it up to date in terminology.

B. Audio-Visual Materials

Audio-visual materials are an important part of modern instruction. They can play a major role in the learning process by supplementing books and other printed materials. They should be ordered, housed, and administered in the library unless another department on the campus is effectively executing this program. Audio-visual materials may include films, filmstrips, slides, tapes, recordings in music, drama, speech, and foreign languages. The same high standard of selection should be used as for books and other library materials. Faculty advice should be sought when needed.

If the audio-visual program is administered by the library, an additional trained staff member and an additional budget allotment should be provided. Whether or not these materials are housed in the building and controlled by the library staff, they should be properly indexed in the library catalogs where faculty and students can readily locate these materials...

Notes

1. Barton, Mary N. Reference Books: a Brief Guide for Students and Other Users of the Library. 4th ed. Baltimore, Enoch Pratt Library, 1959, is an excellent recent short list of major reference works. It should be carefully examined; its annotations offer valuable suggestions.

   Junior college librarians will also benefit greatly from checking the following two basic lists, even though they are not up to date: Mohrhardt, Foster E. A List of Books for Junior College Libraries. Chicago, ALA, 1937, and Bertalan, Frank J. Books for Junior Colleges. Chicago, ALA, 1954. Florida State University, under the direction of Dean Louis Shores, has begun to issue book and magazine lists for junior colleges, which are intended to supplement Bertalan's list. In addition, attention is called to the well balanced list issued by the Southern Association of Colleges and Secondary Schools, Commission on Colleges and Universities, The Classified List of Reference Books and Periodicals for College Libraries; edited by W. Stanley Hoole, 3d ed.; Atlanta, Ga., The Association, 1955. Useful suggestions for specific purposes may also be found in the Catalogue of

the Lamont Library, Harvard College, prepared by
Philip J. McNiff and members of the library staff,
Cambridge, Mass. , Harvard University Press, 1953.

Librarians of junior colleges will be well advised to
check also some authoritative shorter subject bibliographies such as The Concise Cambridge Bibliography
of English Literature, 600-1950, edited by George
Watson, Cambridge, University Press, 1958, and the
Harvard List of Books in Psychology, compiled and
annotated by the psychologists in Harvard University,
2d ed. , Cambridge, Mass. , Harvard University Press,
1955.   Also Louis R. Wilson, The Library in College
Instruction, New York, H. W. Wilson, 1951) contains
many pertinent suggestions.   Librarians in institutions
stressing science and technology will find a reliable
guide in Scientific, Medical and Technical Books Published in the U. S. A. to December 1956, edited by
R. R. Hawkins, 2d ed. , Washington, D. C. 1958.

Holdings of indexes should not be limited to sets of
Readers' Guide and International Index.   Wherever the
instructional program of the junior college makes a
broader coverage desirable, if not essential, subscriptions to other indexes should be included such as Applied Science and Technology Index, Book Review Digest, Business Periodicals Index, Education Index,
Engineering Index, Essay and General Literature Index, Technical Book Review Index, etc. ; the librarian
should aim to subscribe at least to some of the journals indexed there.   Also files of abstracting journals
such as Biological Abstracts, Chemical Abstracts,
and Psychological Abstracts will be great assets for
reference purposes.   Finally, the New York Times
Index will answer many questions of readers and help
locate materials, even if the library cannot yet afford
to subscribe to the New York Times on microfilm.

2.   Junior college librarians should have on their subscription list some outstanding foreign periodicals like
The Economist, London, Manchester Guardian
Weekly, Réalités, Paris (English language edition),
and the Times Literary Supplement, London, as a
guard against provincialism.   In general, subscriptions should be checked against such an authoritative
compilation as Classified List of Periodicals for the
College Library, 4th ed. , revised and enlarged by

Evan Ira Farber, Boston, F. W. Faxon Company,
1957.

3. The fundamental position of the American Library Associ-
    ation has been stated in the Library Bill of Rights
    adopted in 1948.   Recent lucid discussions of the sub-
    ject of censorship include those by Robert B. Downs
    in American Library Annual and Book Trade Almanac
    1959, New York, R. R. Bowker, [1958] p. 91-92,
    and Donald E. Strout in American Library & Book
    Trade Annual 1960, New York, R. R. Bowker, [1959]
    p. 129-32.   Attention is also called to the collection
    of essays The First Freedom: Liberty and Justice
    in the World of Books and Reading, edited by Robert
    B. Downs, Chicago, ALA, 1960.

4. This figure is based on the agreement of many junior
    college librarians consulted and on an analysis of re-
    cent statistics provided in College and Research Li-
    braries.

Section 2

Development of Selection Policy

The New York Public Library operates on the belief
that free men will find the truth, however devious the
route by which they approach it, or at least that they
should have the fullest opportunity to try.

> William K. Zinsser, Search
> and research: The collections
> and uses of the New York
> Public Library at Fifth Avenue
> and 42nd Street. New York,
> New York Public Library,
> 1961. p. 46

The key question was whether restrictions are being
imposed on librarians, or whether they are imposing
restrictions themselves, that threaten the citizen's
rights to easy access to as adequate a collection...
as his community, his county or his state can afford.

> Marjorie Fiske, Book selection
> and censorship: A study of
> school and public libraries in
> California. Berkeley and Los
> Angeles, University of Cali-
> fornia Press, 1959. p. viii

In this section are presented three aspects of the development of selection policy: first, the rationale for and
content of selection policies, both in particular types of libraries and for certain subject areas; second, examples of
selection policy statements not available in Carter and Bonk;
and, finally, readings on the application of selection policy
and principles of building collections in selected controversial areas.

The literature in this aspect of the subject is highly
emotional and full of ex cathedra statements; some of these

146

are nevertheless included as essential to the building of a
philosophy on the part of the beginning practitioner.   Examples include the articles by Sayers and Kister.   There
are also beginning to be available, however, a variety of
studies which provide further insight into the statements of
principle; examples of these include the studies by Bendix,
and the series published in the pages of the Library Journal
in recent years. [1]   Freeman presents a challenge to our traditional ideas of selection for public libraries and Becker
analyzes his study.   The selections by the psychologist Jahoda and novelist Pamela Hansford Johnson, contrasted with
librarian Kister's statement, provide an interesting range of
opinion on the problems of selecting fiction today.   The selection from Fiske's landmark study introduces some of the
problems in selecting material in school and public libraries;
frequently not really faced by library selectors (as confirmed also by Bendix' study), they nevertheless must be
recognized by those responsible for building collections.   Danton, Pullen and Olsen describe the situation today in university and in junior college libraries.   Bloss, Shaw and Streble
present the principles here as illustrated in branch public
libraries and in special libraries.

While the adoption of a selection policy by every library is far from being realized in practice, it is slowly
gaining ground.   The responsibilities of librarians in this
connection are discussed in more detail in some of the readings in the tenth section of this book.   The recent statements
of policy included in this section should add examples to
those now available for study by both students and practitioners and illustrate the applicability of policy statements
to a wide variety of types of libraries.

Note

1. The entire series consists of:
   " 'Problem' fiction," Library Journal 87:484-96, Feb. 1,
      1962
   Broderick, Dorothy " 'Problem' nonfiction, A second LJ
      survey... Library Journal 87:3373-8, Oct. 1, 1962
   Moon, Eric "The view from the front," Library Journal
      89:570-4, February 1, 1964
   Agler, Raymond B. " 'Problem' books revisited," Li-
      brary Journal 89:2019-2030, May 15, 1964
   Berry, John N. III "Demand for Dissent?" Library
      Journal 89:3012-7, October 15, 1964

"In, out, or neglected?" Library Journal 91:57-61,
    January 1, 1966

Intellectual Freedom

by Judith F. Krug

Mrs. Krug is Executive Secretary, Committee on Intellectual Freedom, American Library Association; her contribution appeared originally in the CIF column in the Bulletin.

From ALA Bulletin 62:659-63, June 1968; Reprinted by permission of the Editor of the ALA Bulletin.

"The best defense is a strong offense." In relating this saying to intellectual freedom, "offense" does not mean the deliberate provocation of problems for the sake of principle, but refers rather to those preparations that should be made in order to permit an effective and immediate response when and if a freedom to read problem arises. One of the most valid preparations is that of a written book selection policy. The prime goal of such a policy is to promote the development of a collection that is based on institutional goals and user needs. Using it as a defense of intellectual freedom is a secondary purpose.

A firm foundation of policy is all important for both goals. In developing this foundation, four basic elements should be considered: 1) service policy; 2) environmental characteristics; 3) collection specifications; and 4) current selection needs.

Service policy refers to those user groups which the library serves, the relative priorities assigned to the various library activities in which these patrons engage, and the nature of the service to be rendered by the collection. Information regarding service policy is necessary for the development of a clear picture of what the institution is seeking to achieve and what groups are most intimately involved in these endeavors. From this information, the library will deduce meaningful operational statements for future collection development.

To determine service policy, the institutional objectives must be clearly understood.   Ideally, these objectives are available in a public document designed to inform all concerned.   If such a statement exists, it should answer questions regarding the nature of the service the institution seeks to provide, the activities or standards most valued, the areas of endeavor or portions of society toward which it claims responsibility, and the eminence that it wishes to achieve in a field or fields.   If a broad, public statement is not available, objectives can be sought from other sources, such as the charter or law establishing the institution, its published history, board of trustees or school board reports, etc.   In the absence of written objectives, actions taken by the library or its governing body can be investigated since the institution has acted in accordance with some principle or toward some goal, even though these goals or principles may not have been codified.   One document that may prove particularly relevant is the budget.

Once the institutional objectives are delineated, the groups of people with whom the library interacts in accomplishing its objectives must be determined.   The nature of the demands these groups make upon the library should be detailed, and implications should be drawn for collection development and related library activities.   What kind of information should be gathered?   First, the various user groups must be identified.   Are the patrons children, young adults, adults, students, housewives, businessmen?   Is a breakdown needed according to the industry in which the persons are engaged?   Should the students be grouped according to educational level?

Once the groups have been determined, an indication of the relative size of each is needed.   In other words, each specific group is what percent of the total number of users?

The third type of data to be collected relates to the purpose that each group has in using the library.   Some purposes could be for recreational reading, required school reading, extra course reading, vocationally-oriented reading, research projects, teaching purposes, and for maintaining proficiency.

The purposes having been designated, one should next seek the types of materials used in accomplishing them.   Materials include books, periodicals, newspapers, manuscripts, government publications, audio devices, films, microforms, rare books, and others.

Finally, how do the library's patrons go about accomplishing their purposes? Does the patron borrow material, interact with library staff beyond the simple mechanics of borrowing, use the library as a work center, request interlibrary loans, use reproduction facilities, etc. ? The answers to each of these have implications for the collection.

The categories listed above are only suggestive. The items must be changed to fit the particular library's needs. To gather the information, however, the entire library staff should participate. By working out the areas of disagreement, the whole staff benefits, and each individual member will gain a better knowledge of the library and its patrons.

It is interesting to note that the categories used to gather data regarding the actual situation in which a library finds itself can also be used to indicate the desired state of affairs. By compiling data for both the actual and desired situations, discrepancies can be perceived and, hopefully, appropriate remedial actions taken.

Environmental characteristics refer to aspects of the user population, the institution, or the external environment that could or should influence the nature of the collection. Several examples of environmental factors, with indications of potential impact, follow. If the library is in a relatively isolated geographical area, it may be necessary to provide materials in large quantities relating to the cultural or recreational needs of users. If the library is heavily used by students from low income families, a library could conceivably provide texts related to school work. The presence or absence of library resources external to the institution has an implication for the degree of self-sufficiency or completeness of coverage sought for the collection areas. If a library is located close to local industries, the library may have to provide specialized subcollections. This listing, by no means, is complete but may suggest aspects of the general environment which could have an impact upon collection planning.

Collection specifications refer to subject areas of concern, the nature of the material desired in each, and the quantity or degree of coverage--all with respect to the ultimate collection objective. The major portions of the total library collection result from the uses the patrons make of

the materials.   The data gathered to determine service
policy and environmental characteristics will show, in a
large measure, what the library requires.   In this section
of the selection policy, each discipline should be carefully
viewed, a determination made as to the types of materials
to be acquired in each, and the depth in which materials
will be sought.   What is the total number of books currently held in each particular discipline, and is it possible to
determine the relevant number of books in print for the discipline?   If so, what percentage of total books does your library hold?   Is the percent sufficient to fulfill the needs of
your patrons?   Is it, perhaps, too large?

        This section of the policy statement will undoubtedly
be the largest in terms of actual words.   It will detail, for
each discipline, the specific kinds of materials to be included in the collection in order to fulfill the objectives of
the library and the users' needs.   Here, also, can be designated the library's policy in regard to peripheral areas of
acquisition, such as the acceptance or rejection of gifts.
By delineating such, one is not only keeping his collection
free from "junk" materials, but is also preparing against the
day when an intellectual freedom problem may arise over
such acceptance or rejection.

        Current selection needs refer to the difference be-
tween collection specifications and the present collection.
In determining what is currently needed, the desired state
of affairs which may have been detailed under service policy
should also be consulted.   Once current needs are determined, other considerations come into effect, such as the
budget of the library.   Regardless of the amount of money
available, the book selection policy should indicate, in a
fairly clear manner, which materials should be bought and
which should not.

        It is assumed that the majority of librarians believe
that a written book selection policy is desirable.   In too
many instances, however, the belief does not become reality.
Many reasons for this can be cited, including a lack of time
in which to develop a policy, a lack of interest in the actual
writing, and a lack of expected utility.   A complicating factor which possibly contributes to the situation is the term
"policy."   The word, to some, connotes a lofty statement of
noble goals; to others, it implies a written set of ordering
procedures; and to most, it is a document which offers little
guidance to actual practices in day-to-day situations.

Regardless of past failures and existing difficulties, however, the overwhelming need for a firm foundation of policy cannot be negated. The policy can, and should, relate to real world actions. It should, in effect, provide guidelines for the strengthening of a library's collection. After a close examination of the objectives of the library, its patrons, and the environmental characteristics, it seems unlikely that the collection specifications would be anything other than "real world." To keep it such, the statement must be continually reviewed since the patrons and the environmental characteristics on which it is based continually change.

Furthermore, if the book selection policy is, indeed, to fulfill its secondary purpose, that of defending the concept of intellectual freedom, it must be a viable and working document. A strong collection and intellectual freedom go hand in hand. It is less likely that problems will arise if the collection reflects the logical, coherent, and explicit statement from which it grows. This means that the effectiveness of the statement will be determined by the length of time that it has been used and the tangible results that are apparent.

In the heat of the moment, when an intellectual freedom crisis does arise, one has neither the time nor the inclination to gather and write a coherent book selection policy. This is the preparation that should have been made; this is part of the "offense."

If the Trumpet be Not Sounded

by Frances Clarke Sayers

Mrs. Sayers presented this paper as the keynote address at the California Library Association's annual conference, November 1964. She is now retired from the UCLA faculty and is noted for her many contributions particularly in the field of children's library work.

From Wilson Library Bulletin 39:659-62+, April 1965; Reprinted by permission of the Wilson Library Bulletin.

We are all in favor of free access to ideas and information, at least at the lip service level. Some of us never move beyond that level. Librarianship is only now emerging from uncertainty into an awareness of its obligation to profess a strong belief in intellectual freedom and to substantiate that profession with action, when it is necessary.

Looking back across the eighty-eight years since the founding of the American Library Association, one can see the wavering line of changing concepts and definitions of librarianship. Lawrence Clark Powell, in his fine article "Up Near the Source" which appeared in The Little Package (World, 1963), quotes an early editorial of Melvil Dewey, who saw the librarian essentially as a teacher. "Time was" said Mr. Dewey in the 1870's, "when a library was very like a museum, and a librarian was a mouser among musty books, and visitors looked with curious eyes at ancient tombs and manuscripts. The time is when a library is a school, and the librarian is in the highest sense a teacher, and the visitor is a reader among the books as a workman among his tools. Will any man deny to the high calling of such a librarianship the title of profession?"

In 1908, ALA president Arthur Bostwick, saw the li-

brarian as the guardian of morals.   Everett Moore, in his
battle cry of a book, Issues of Freedom in American Libraries, quotes a passage of his which is amusing when
read with the eyes of the present.

> Books that distinctly commend what is wrong,
> that teach how to sin, and how pleasant sin is,
> sometimes without the added sauce of impropriety
> are increasingly popular, tempting the audience to
> imitate them, the publishers to produce, the book-
> sellers to exploit.   Thank heavens they do not
> tempt the librarian.

Eight years later, ALA president Mary Wright Plummer spoke on the subject of The Public Library and the
Pursuit of Truth:

> Few librarians are entirely free in their move-
> ments when it comes to the choice of books.
> There may be a distrustful or prejudiced board
> member trying to exercize a biased censorship;
> there may be a timid member afraid of a one-
> sided community and books may have to be with-
> drawn as a sop to popular prejudice by order of
> the Board.
>
> Whether or not there is really anything untrue in
> the book, it can safely be left to profit by the ad-
> vertisement it gets in the contest--it is the library
> that loses, for some people begin to mistrust an
> institution that is afraid of a book, for a book can-
> not really and permanently damage truth--those
> who wish all argument for or against to have a
> fair field, need to be everlastingly vigilant to keep
> the umpire's mind and to have courage.

The teacher, the censor and the umpire: three faces
of librarianship that come to us from the past, each a product of the pressure of the time, as well as of the personality.   Melvil Dewey spoke at the turn of the century when the
emphasis was on the importance of popular culture;   Dr.
Bostwick trembled under the onslaught of the French novel
and the sophistication of Europe breaking upon our intellectual shores; and Mary Wright Plummer was close to present-
day concerns, and if she seems to be sure as to what truth
may or may not be, it is well to remember that she spoke
from the quiet margins before World War One.

It was the First World War that dragged us kicking and screaming into the twentieth century. The passivity of the library profession was ruffled by a deepened awareness of the library's role in patriotic service and the need for direct action in the areas of information, opinion and education. With action came the frenzied persecution of the super-patriots who found in war the ideal climate for bigotry, fear, and self-righteousness. Librarians knew, for the first time, the persecutions of the unreasonable. The brilliant reference librarian, Mary Louise Hunt, was dismissed from her position in Portland, Oregon because, as a pacifist, she had refused to buy war bonds. When John Cotton Dana, then the librarian of the Newark (N. J.) Public Library, heard of this action, he sent Miss Hunt a telegram inviting her to join his staff.

Even the staffs of large public libraries were not immune from the persecutions of the frenzied. Two young children's librarians in New York City were followed for months by members of the Bomb Squad of the New York police. They had made the mistake of attending lectures on the development of the English novel at the Rand School, the haunt of Scott Nearing and other socialists. The instructors were John and Llwelyn Powys, and a third brilliant lecturer, Gilbert Cannan, a novelist in his own right, who was to be lost to us through insanity. Franklin Hopper was the head of the Circulation Department of the New York Public Library in those years. He did not bother to tell the two young women that their resignations had been requested on the grounds that they were unfit to work with children. Being one of the two, I would never have known about it had not my friend, Agnes Cuff, been a devout Catholic. One day after Mass, an enchanting young man tapped her on the shoulder, called her by name, and revealed the whole story. He said he had begun to doubt that so faithful a worshipper could be interested in subverting the minds of children or planning to blow up the New York Public Library.

In the period between the wars, the public library was politely educational. The rallying point was adult education. It was the era of those little courses Reading with a Purpose and the studies of Dr. Thorndike, proving that any adult could learn anything, if his will to do so were strong enough. Readers' advisory services spread across the land, and some memorable leaders developed in the field: the vital Jennie Flexner of the New York Public Library, and vivid Miriam Tompkins, of Milwaukee and Co-

lumbia Graduate School.   The Sacco-Vanzetti case aroused
protest and discussion and the presidential campaign of Alfred E. Smith was argued with some bitterness, clearing the
way for a more enlightened time when the question of a
Catholic in the White House was to be answered forever with
a dazzling affirmation.

During the depression, the public library became refuge and solace, and the source of practical help and information.   But no vital program of assault upon the evils of
the time was launched by the institution.   Library funds were
cut, in many cases, and the emphasis was put upon the degree of warmth the building might furnish in a day and the
availability of chairs to accommodate the flood of readers.

New Maturity in Judgment

It was the aftermath of the Second World War that
brought the library profession to a new maturity of judgment.   The period began across the land, nobly enough, with
the Great Books Programs.   This contemplative study of the
past was interrupted by McCarthyism, and the brutal assault
upon basic freedoms; freedom of speech, of assembly, and
of intellectual freedom.   McCarthy was at last defeated, but
the backlash of the Second World War, the fear of Communism, remains to plague us.   We stand, as Gerald Johnson
describes it, in terms that delight the feminist in me... "at
the nadir of civil liberties to which nervous old women--
mostly of the masculine gender--have dragged us on account
of their obsession that there is a Communist behind every
bedpost..."

The terrifying aspect of the obsession with Communism is that the term is employed as an umbrella tag to
cover varied activities and attitudes which have little or no
connection with the political and social theories of Marxism.
Every Freedom Rider in the South is a Communist; every
teacher who tells her class about the United Nations is a
Communist; every author who explores the experience of life
and gives expression to his passionate or desolate, exalted
or depraved interpretation--every such author is called a
Communist, an obscene Communist.   Even books for children are screened for political purity, and in addition they
must be psychologically, sociologically and sexually disin-
fected before being deemed proper reading for the Bonanza-,
Gunsmoke-, and Peyton Place-oriented children of our day.
The only place where the hound of Communist fear has not

smelled out a scent is in the columns of the daily paper
which are devoted to cooking. Only recently, in the pages
of the Los Angeles Times, I came upon the receipt for
Chicken Kiev, which, as far as I know, has gone unchal-
lenged.

More desperate and tragic than the obsession with
Communism is the almost unconscious, creeping infiltration
of Communist, Nazi and Fascist techniques into American
life, as the means of assuring the triumph of one's own
point of view. We know, deplore, and are shamed by the
action of goons and the Ku Klux Klan; but the repressive
technique is now accepted as an immediate method. The
authoritative pronouncement, the demand for action, the
pressure of persecuting groups, without regard to the old
procedures of argument and debate are daily occurrences.
Certain schools of educational or psychological doctrine issue the verdict. That Little Black Sambo must be removed
from library shelves was the decision of a noted educator
in the library world, who condemned the classic because it
is not a realistic picture of Africa today. As though the region of this book ever existed in the geographies: the realm
of this book is the imagination of the child.

Even organizations whose aims are altrustic and noble
stoop to the persecution technique. In 1941, I had no sooner
returned to the New York Public Library as superintendent
of Work with Children, than a demand for my resignation
appeared in the public press. This time the pressure came
from the attitude of the Anti-Defamation League which requested all books in which any derogatory remark about the
Jew be taken from the shelves. I had refused to discard
Andrew Lang's edition of Nursery Rhymes, which contained
the line, "He sold his goose to a rogue of a Jew." It was
the now-defunct liberal newspaper P. M., which hounded me,
and published the headlines "Anti-semitic books on the
shelves of the children's room in the New York Public Library." By this time Mr. Hopper was the director of the
Library. He told me to handle the matter in my own way.
I had the last word, in this instance, for by great good luck
and the grace of God, my husband was a Jew, and I was
hardly a target for the tag, anti-Semite.

The "stupid malignity," as George Orwell calls censorship, has been, in many cases, so far-fetched, so small
minded, so out of proportion to common sense as to be a
source of purest nonsense. A California city staged a cam-

paign against Ben and Me, Robert Lawson's hilarious and
original story of Amos, the mouse, who lived in the fur hat
of Benjamin Franklin, and was really responsible for all of
Mr. Franklin's inventions and ideas. It was Amos who
thought of the Franklin stove, and it was he who told Mr.
Franklin to go fly a kite. The book was considered to be
un-American!

One of my students informed me recently that Huckleberry Finn had been banned in one high school library because of immorality; it had homosexual overtones. This was
news to me! I asked a noted authority on American literature, Dr. Leon Howard of UCLA, where this idea had originated. He knew. It had come from an essay by the critic
Leslie Fiedler, who had written, for the esoteric Freudians,
a piece called "Come Back to the Raft Ag'in, Huck Honey!"

Techniques of Terror

One cannot laugh at these absurdities, because the
techniques of terror are brought to their support. The
threat of loss of employment, the midnight phone call, the
eggs thrown at cars, the anonymous letters, the threats
against one's children, the obscene epithet, the vindictive
anger: these are not the trappings of TV terror pictures
on the Late, Late Show. These are incidents which have
happened to librarians in well-to-do and middle-class communities throughout the country.

I have been moved in my time by the voices of poets
and wise men I have listened to: James Stephens, John
Haynes Holmes, Adlai Stevenson, Martin Luther King. But
I have never been so stirred nor so filled with apprehension,
as I was at the California pre-conference meeting on Intellectual Freedom on November 2 and 3, 1964. Here I listened to Mrs. Cay Mortenson, trustee of the Arcadia Public
Library, tell the story of the persecution of that institution
which stood firm against the pressures brought to bear on
The Last Temptation of Christ, in an effort to have the book
removed from library shelves. Virginia Ross, a county librarian, told of her confrontation with the State Legislature.
Ursula Meyers, librarian of Butte County, and Hilda Collins
of Tulare, each told a tale of the pressures of hatred and
reaction. These were women brought up in the genteel tradition, engaged in a profession which has seldom been
hailed as an heroic one. But the cold, strong wind of courage blew through that meeting, and I shall never forget it.

There is a shadow of promise falling across our profession. It began to form as long ago as 1948 when the
Library Bill of Rights was published.   There followed the
ALA Statement on Labelling Books, adopted by the Council
in 1951.   Then came Freedom to Read in 1953. The creation of the Intellectual Freedom Committee in 1960, the
Newsletter on Intellectual Freedom, and now, in 1964 Everett Moore's Issues of Freedom in American Libraries--
these begin to give palpable shape to the shadow.

Librarian as Trumpeter

Is there a chance that in addition to the librarian as
teacher, censor, and umpire, the contemporary stance may
be the librarian as inciter, arouser, as trumpeter and
champion? We have no such reputation from the past.   According to Gerald Johnson in his most recent book Hod-Car-
rier (Morrow, 1964), "...the public library is the acme of
neutralism, never inciting controversy, and taking note of
its existence only when it has grown too important to be ignored." There is the opinion the general public has of us,
and indeed, there is too much truth in it.   You will remember that Marjorie Fiske in her splendid study, Book Selection and Censorship in California Libraries (1958), found that
"only one library unequivocally affirms the duty of the public library to promote communication and stimulate controversy."

I pointed earlier to our need to profess a belief in
intellectual freedom, and to substantiate that profession with
action, when action is necessary.   But if action were sustained and continuous, if it were implemented through exhi-
bitions, bulletin boards, or through all the paraphernalia of
public relations, what then? If bigotry and hate are to be
pushed back, the arena of public debate and discussion must
be open before the festering process of witch-hunting con-
sumes the community.   To carry the attack to the enemy:
does this not seem necessary to the intellectual climate of
the nation, even though your own community be calm and
peaceful?

The Great Society

It is trite and condescending for me to repeat what
the character of our time seems to be.   It is a time of such
change--each of you can see it--as to benumb the imagination.   You know the catchwords of the century: the Age of

Anxiety, the Air-Conditioned Nightmare; the Failure of Communication, the Era of Nihilism. We are no longer a Protestant, middle-class society, with fixed concepts of morality, religious beliefs, a world of fixed boundaries. Everywhere and everything is questioned, uncertain, and in ferment. It is precisely the right time to move into the Great Society, for from such circumstance there has always evolved larger visions and convictions by which men live, for a time. No other profession is as well equipped for the confrontation with the future as is our profession. Look what we have: an institution that functions above and beyond the profit motive, and pressure of competition; a profession which attracts idealists to its ranks, people who believe in the perfectibility of man, and who find in service to others a gratification of the spirit; people who relish the stirring up of communities by the circulation of ideas, notions, facts, fancies, pleasures--all the hubbub and exhilaration of reading. As people who hold to the redemptive power of books, we have books behind us, and we know them well enough to have acquired an historical perspective on the vagaries of men's minds. We have the authority of our experiences as readers, and we can command the respect of our communities for our discernment of judgment. We are vital because we function at the center of the passion and action of our time. We will have more money than we have had in the past to spend for books; more time in which to read, through automation, and in which to entice others to reading. We will be the explorers, the discoverers and the Sounders of Trumpets.

I chose for the title of this paper "If the Trumpet Be Not Sounded," in the mistaken belief that it was Francis Bacon I was quoting. But when I checked my recollection, I discovered that my quotation was not Bacon, but the Bible: First Corinthians, Chapter 14, Verse 8: "For if the trumpet give an uncertain sound, who shall be prepared for the battle?"

The conclusion is clear. It is for us to sound the trumpet, with no uncertainty, for even in the Great Society there will be those who have yet to know the magnitude of freedom.

The Berelson Report: Discussion by Martin

by Dr. Lowell A. Martin   Formerly Professor, Graduate
Library School, University of
Chicago; later at School of
Library Service, Columbia
University and Dean, Graduate
School of Library Service,
Rutgers

From Lester Asheim, Ed.   A Forum on the
Public Library Inquiry.   New York, Columbia
University Press, 1950. p. 45-49; Reprinted by
permission of Columbia University Press.

Implications for the Library's Function

These are the main alternatives in terms of the library's public.   But behind these considerations, and in the
long run determining them, are alternatives with regard to
the library's function.   And the library's function, in its
turn, must be set against the role of books and education
in America today.

The general studies reviewed by Berelson in the early
part of his volume leave little ground for being starry-eyed
on this point.   While a great amount of reading occurs in
America, its quantity may be decreasing relative to other
avocational activities; only a minor portion of it is book
reading (the library's main concern), and the majority of
books read are ephemeral and of only current interest; the
proportion of book reading to other kinds of reading is declining.   This leaves book reading in a relatively minor
position and its future uncertain.   As to the library's position, it supplies about one fourth of the books and has been
holding its place as compared to other sources of such material.

Can this sequence of statements about reading be
paralleled by statements about interest in education, leading
to a similar conclusion about its low estate?   The evidence

is fragmentary and subject to different interpretations. But except for figures showing response to required and vocational education, there is not much support for a sanguine view, much need as there is for adult education.

Against this background quite different views of the proper function of the public library are possible. One might start from the proposition that Americans like to read and that they should have a public source from which to get the necessary material. The job of the librarian, then, is to find out what the people want and supply it as economically and satisfactorily as he can. Adopting this view, the librarian must appraise his market and competition, for he is then serving the same function as other suppliers. General book reading is being subjected to pressure from many new and demanding means of diversion, but it is both too soon to conclude that such reading is necessarily entering upon a long-range decline and also too late to look upon it as an expanding market. The competition from other supliers is stiff, because many another group--the bookstore, the rental library, the magazine, the newspaper--all seek to serve the American's interest in reading. In this competition the public library has some advantages and some disadvantages. For example, its service is given at lower cost to the direct user, but it has not achieved as convenient a distribution system as has the magazine, which is placed regularly in the reader's mailbox and pre-empts a few of his evenings each week or month. With ingenuity the public library may well be able to hold its relative place as a supplier in the American scheme of reading, although in a declining and competitive market.

An important modification of this role of supplier is to emphasize the distribution of materials not well handled by other sources--a rounding out of the supply. All librarians will study the various reports of the Inquiry to see what materials are not available to the American people and to assess the possibility of library emphasis upon them.

The second concept emphasizes the information potential of the public library. Its basic proposition is that people need many facts for the conduct of their affairs and that the resources of the library can be used to supply these facts. The larger libraries have been able to acquire materials that meet at least a fair portion of the requests which arise and to assign to special posts some staff members who have become expert in extracting the information needed.   Yet the contribution of the American library as an information center is not yet great enough to show up as of any importance in nation-wide polls such as those reported by Berelson.

Another approach is from the standpoint of education rather than reading and information as such--from the aims desired rather than the commodities dispensed.   This view starts with the proposition that some adults in America are interested in one or another kind of self-improvement and that they should have a public materials center which can serve this interest.   The librarian must then define the kind of education he is to provide, the portion of this interest in self-improvement which he should or can serve, after which he can select appropriate material and encourage and guide people in using it.   He may set up goals for the library as an independent center, or he may accept the goals of educational agencies in the community and serve their needs. Even as the supply function, if it is to be appraised realistically, must be set against the reading market, so the improvement function must be related to the limited educational bent of the average American.

The weight of practice in public libraries today falls on the side of supplier, and the emphasis in the literature, on the educational function of the agency.   We seem to want to be both more popular and more purposeful at one and the same time.   While these two aims are not necessarily antithetical, they can work at cross purposes.

The smaller libraries, which comprise the bulk of outlets, buy first the materials in immediate demand and are not able to go far toward information sources and publications of permanent value.   The larger libraries have been able to build up important reference services which have caught on, grown steadily, and taken their places beside the supply activity as a regular part of library service.   Some libraries, as funds left over from these other services permit, have organized what might be called educational programs, in which a civic or cultural goal is set and appropriate materials and activities are provided, or materials are specifically furnished for a local educational group. These have been appendages to the main line of activity, usually separate in the program and thought of as extra, and they have often been short-lived.   And, just to keep the record straight, it is worth adding that some such activities have actually possessed neither vitality nor popularity and

have scarcely deserved a permanent place in the total program.

The reasons why the improvement role, which was
prominent in the origins of the institution, has not moved
more rapidly in recent years towards the center of library
activities are many and various, but foremost is failure on
the part of librarians to see it in precise terms.   It is one
thing to say that the library is an educational agency, but
another to decide just what it will educate for.   Positive
aims are needed that point toward certain goals and exclude
others and that are distinctive in relation to the activities
of other agencies.

Until such definition is formulated, the library would
be wise to let its supply function predominate, for it serves
a proven need and an established clientele; it would be unwise to reduce a tested function for an ill-conceived new
role which might command little support.   More than one
institution has disappeared in the fog of its own idealism.

If the reading studies tell anything at all about the
future, it is that the response to a more definitely educational program may well be limited.   This does not mean
that the library should turn away from such a program, but
it does warn the librarian to be clear in his mind and fairly
sure about his public before making the plunge.   I want to
be quite explicit that I do not interpret the uncertain role of
book reading and the limited impact of the library reported
by Berelson as grounds for abandoning the educational aspi-
rations of the institution, but I do believe they caution us
to be entirely clear on function and on relation to other
agencies before dissipating our energies in every likely project that comes to mind.

The future of the American public library does not
lie in thinking up new ways to entice people to read, if for
no other reason than the probability that our competitors in
the communications market are likely to beat us at this
game.   The future of the library depends upon ascertaining
the needs of the people that are not met by the expanding
communications network and in concentrating our energies
upon them.   I am convinced that such opportunities exist.

The Berelson Report: Discussion by Schramm

by Wilbur Schramm

At the time, Director of Communications Research, University of Illinois; widely known leader in investigation of television and its impact on viewers

From Lester Asheim, ed. A Forum on the Public Library Inquiry. New York, Columbia University Press, 1950. p. 53-56; Reprinted by permission of Columbia University Press.

The Reading of Adolescents

Two aspects of the libraries' publics, as Dr. Berelson analyzes them in his book, are especially peritnent in this framework. One is the adolescent period when libraries are much used; the other is the swift and rather disappointing drop in library use after the teens. Let us look at those two phenomena in the light of what we know of other communication behavior in the same years.

In the adolescent years, of course, awakened physical drives of great power are being sublimated in favor of more socially acceptable outlets. Our society postpones adulthood. It does not sanction early marriage or an early beginning of a business career at the expense of schooling. Traditionally, these drives have been transferred to an intense activity of another kind. Traditionally, adolescents have been young poets, idealists, reformers; they have gone through what Goethe called Sturm und Drang; they have argued the great questions of religion and politics; they have absorbed knowledge and acquired an intellectual impetus which has often been sufficient to carry them through the rest of life. In reading and listening, adolescents have been lusty and omnivorous, and therefore the kind of reading and listening available to them has been of the greatest importance.

166

What do we know about the communication intake of adolescents? We know that motion picture attendance is at its height in the late teens, and drops off speedily after thirty. We know that radio listening is high and that the adolescent habitually selects popular music in preference to classical, comedians and variety shows in preference to discussion and information programs. At this age there is considerably less news listening than there is twenty or thirty years later. We know that there is little newspaper reading in adolescence and that comics, pictures, and news of crime, disaster, and sports are habitually selected by adolescents. The amount of reading about public affairs, news, and editorials rises rapidly in the twenties, but is not impressive at the teen age. Indeed, I have recently studied the reading habits of 746 persons in a Midwest city without discovering one single person under 16 who was in the habit of reading editorials. Our knowledge of magazine reading during adolescence is meager, but we can judge that the chief diet is fiction and light articles. Finally, we must mention the great and, perhaps, still rising tide of comic-book reading.

We have been talking about possibly three hours of an adolescent's day. These three hours for the most part are a lien on his time which would not have existed one hundred years ago. The inescapable observation is that in the case of the average young person almost all this communication intake is devoted to what Freud called the Pleasure Principle, rather that to what he called the Reality Principle; to light entertainment and escape material, rather than to material dealing with the great questions of life. It seems evident that if the adolescent is going to fill up his tank with ideas which will sharpen his mind, enrich his background for important decisions, and make him a better equipped participant in democracy he must get much of that material from experience generated in or near the institutions of the school or the library.

Therefore, this material of Dr. Berelson's presents the public librarian with a considerable responsibility for citizen making. What is the adolescent getting out of the library? Is Reality reading made attractive to him? Is he being counseled effectively and wisely in his choice of books? Is the library co-operating with the school in filling out the more serious part of the reader's experience? These are technical questions which are subjects for library administrators, rather than for visiting social scientists, but any social scientist can see their importance.

The Limited Reading by Adults

Let us turn our attention for a few minutes to the other dramatic aspect of Dr. Berelson's analysis. This is the sharp decline in reading after the teen age. Why does it occur? Even such an uninformed amateur as I can suggest some of the reasons. Some of the previous sublimated drives are satisfied. The great timeless period of life is over; now comes the age of purposeful activity. The young adult has to make good, in business or in the home. He tends to drop longer-term activities and to concentrate on more immediate obligations. He has to paint the house, or see a good sales prospect, or feed the baby at 6:00, 10:00, and 2:00. He finds it much more difficult to go to the library, much easier to use the communications that come into his home--the newspaper that is thrown onto the front steps or the radio that can be turned on from his easy chair. He likes a passive communication experience, such as radio, that lets him do something else at the same time; or an active communication experience, such as a newspaper or a magazine, that can be taken in chunks of a few minutes each and can be discontinued at almost any time. He is not often able to settle down to several hours of uninterrupted book reading. When he goes to the library, it is more often with a specific reference purpose in view; he needs a book on how to feed a dog, or how to make a dress, or how to prepare for a different job.

The economics and sociology of leisure time are worth more study than they have received. We know that over the space of a century leisure-time activities have apparently turned from predominantly active to passive activities--from group singing around the piano, for example, to listening to the radio. We know also that expenditures for active recreations (books, travel, sports, etc.) rise sharply with economic status, whereas expenditures for passive recreations (like radio) rise comparatively little, indicating that these passive entertainments are thought of as essential to modern life regardless of economic level. The prevalence of radio sets and Pleasure Principle reading supports these economic data.

Now this presents another kind of problem to the library administrator. He must regard rather sadly and cynically the fact that his largest public is made up of children and youth, who are not yet ready for the strongest meat of a reading diet; whereas, when age and experience have made them capable of receiving the greatest books, then they no

longer come to the library.   He must also be impressed,
as are all other professional educators, with the urgency of
educating the adult generations to the rather special demands
of this age.   He realizes that we can hardly wait until a better prepared generation comes out of the schools and takes
over the key jobs in society--supposing, which may be a
dangerous supposition, that the new generation will be better
prepared.

Some Problems in Book Selection Policies and Procedures
in Medium-Sized Public Libraries

by Dorothy Bendix

Dr. Bendix is currently Associate Professor, School of Library Service, Drexel Institute

From Occasional Papers No. 55. University of Illinois, Graduate School of Library Science, May 1959. p. 26-30; Reprinted by permission of Graduate School of Library Science, University of Illinois.

Book Selection and Public Library Objectives

What does all this mean in terms of the official public library objectives, as outlined on page 2? Looking at the problem of book selection standards historically, it is clear that the educational versus the recreational function of the public library, and the "value" versus "demand" theory of book selection have contended with one another at almost every period. The importance of high quality standards for the book collection was stressed in the Post-War Standards in 1943, and in the National Plan in 1948. And in 1956, the revised Standards put it this way:

> Materials acquired should meet high standards of quality in content, expression, and format.
>
> The library continually seeks the best materials to serve purposes and needs. Factual accuracy, effective expression, significance of subject, sincerity and responsibility of opinion--these and other factors must be considered and at times balanced one against the other... Quality of materials must be related to the other two basic standards of selection, purpose and need.

(While the last sentence is open to more than one interpretation, it is assumed here--in the light of the tenor of the whole document and the personnel of the Committee--that it is not meant to qualify the first part of the statement.)

170

But as the Public Library Inquiry found, and as is
confirmed by the practices reported in this study, actual
book selection in many, and probably in most public libraries,
does not come close to the officially pronounced objectives
and standards.   Leigh sums up the findings of the Inquiry as
follows:

> Inability to meet the requirements set up by the
> official library objectives is not owing entirely to
> limited size and budgets.   It is also a reflection
> of the ideas of those in charge of library policy,
> and these seem to vary with different types of ma-
> terial.   ... with regard to books the public library
> policy in many places is not clearly distinguished
> from commercial book distribution.   There is a
> duplication of, in smaller libraries an emphasis on,
> current, ephemeral fiction and nonfiction.   It is
> difficult to justify such an emphasis in terms of
> the official library objectives.

Two additional points which have not been mentioned
so far should be discussed.   One was expressed, interestingly enough, by Ralph Munn, director of the Carnegie Library
of Pittsburgh (mentioned above as a library with high quality
standards for fiction), in his Summary of the conference of
the Forum on the Public Library Inquiry, held at the University of Chicago in 1949:

> Few of us would question the circulation of sub-
> standard books for entertainment use if there were
> also funds for the full development of the more
> serious and significant functions.   We know that in
> most libraries there are not adequate funds; usual-
> ly one or the other must be neglected.

The other point is concerned with an argument which
has gone on not only in library, but also in general adult
education circles for a long time; it maintains that you have
to take people where they are and try to lead them to higher
quality material, whether it be books or adult education
courses.

If the continued demand for low quality fiction is any
indication, there does not seem to be much evidence to support this position.   This is not to deny that, occasionally,
there may be such improvement in the quality of books read
in the case of some individuals, particularly where a library

has a highly qualified staff and puts a great deal of emphasis
on readers' advisory service, whether formally set up or
not.   However, on the whole the patrons looking for best-
sellers and similar material are very likely not to have
much, if any, contact with professional librarians--particu-
larly in libraries where the charging of books is done by the
clerical staff.   Therefore, until libraries are willing and
able to test this theory by directing the work of the professional staff towards a much more concerted effort of improv
ing the reading level of the substandard fiction fans, this
argument for lowering library book selection standards must
be rejected as a rationalization.

As for Munn's point, that if all libraries just had sufficient funds to perform adequately both an educational and
an entertainment function, few librarians would question the
circulation of substandard books, this seems highly debatable
in view of the official public library objectives.   As a matter of fact, the letter sent to the librarians with the statement of objectives included the following question: "Do the
current official objectives definitely reject the idea that the
library should, within budgetary limits, supply whatever the
public demands or asks for?"   Leigh reports that "twenty-
four thought that they clearly implied such rejection; twenty-
seven agreed that they did, but that in practice compromises
are necessary."   There were only twelve librarians (the
largest number of dissenters on any point) who considered
the objectives wrong and impractical if they did not include
provision of what the public wants.   And Leigh concludes:

> In the official objectives there is no mention of
> the terms 'entertainment,' 'amusement,' and 'es-
> cape.'   Recreation is given a strict meaning--what
> is re-creative--but it obviously includes current
> fiction which falls within this meaning of the term
> as well as publications which serve the purposes
> of enlightenment.

A few of the comments quoted by Leigh from the replies of the minority who disagreed with the official statement of public library objectives are similar to the opinion
of one of the librarians interviewed, i. e. that it is "undemo-
cratic," and even an indication of "censorship" if the library
does not respond to public demand.   However, it is implicit
in the concept of the public library as an educational institution that it sets and maintains quality standards in its book
selection and other activities.   Would it ever occur to the

spokesman for this line of thought to apply it to tax supported colleges and universities by suggesting that the curriculum be based on public demand rather than on sound educational objectives? And if not, does that mean that they do not believe in the educational function of the public library?

All that has been said lends strong support to the hypothesis stated in the Introduction, i. e. that most librarians have very ambivalent feelings toward quality standards in book selection. The following quotation from a paper given by B. R. Berelson at the Forum on the Public Library Inquiry expresses this ambivalence very well:

> On the one hand, public librarians have a set of actual objectives which have developed historically, which have been accepted traditionally, and which have been expressed in practice. They may not always be articulated--indeed, it is their peculiar province not to be--but they are nonetheless there as guides for a whole range of library activities... Then, on the other hand, there is a group of professed objectives, skillfully formulated by official bodies, which express the higher aspirations for professional service. When a request for objectives is made, they are brought forward. Thus, just as many lawyers will tell you that their objective is to see justice done, whereas they are actually out to win cases, so many librarians will tell you that education is their objective, when they are busy trying to increase circulation.

If this interpretation is correct, it now becomes clear why so few libraries, and pratically no medium-sized and small ones, have adopted written book selection policy statements although the need for such statements has been stated so persuasively and authoritatively. The formulation of a written policy statement would force many librarians to face the "split between the professed and the practiced objectives" stated by Berelson, and to make a compromise between the two.

Looking at it this way, it becomes apparent that the adoption of a written book selection policy statement--while desirable--should be regarded in its proper perspective, i. e. as part of the larger problem of bringing book selection practices closer to the official statement of public library objectives. This need for bridging the gap between the "professed

and the practiced objectives" exists in many areas of library
service, e.g. in adult education and library cooperation, to
name just a few and it is much easier to diagnose than to
prescribe a cure for it.   The following suggestions are made
in the full realization that they may, at best, be just the beginning steps in moving toward a solution.

As was mentioned earlier, book selection was considered as a fruitful object of further intensive study by the
Public Library Inquiry; the effect of "centralized" selection
on the quality of the collection, on staff morale, etc. , was
singled out as a promising subject for further research.
There are, however, several other problems in this area
which could well be studied with benefit.   One is the quality
of library holdings which order all or most of their books
pre-publication, compared with libraries which select books
on the basis of staff examination and review.   The results
of such a study would be most revealing if libraries could be
compared that were similar with regard to book budget, size
of staff, etc.   Criteria for the quality of the collection
should include both high quality and low quality material.

It might also be valuable to make a comparative study
of the quality of the book collection in libraries which have
adopted a book selection policy statement and some libraries
without such a statement, but alike in other respects.

In addition, the publication of some case studies of
libraries maintaining high quality standards in all parts of
their collection including a fairly detailed description of how
they went about making the change (i. e. eliminating substandard material) might serve as a helpful example to other libraries contemplating a new policy.   Also, as far as relating book selection to community characteristics, interests
and needs is concerned, the experience of the A. L. A. Li-
brary-Community Project should yield some specific illustrations of what is involved.

Ruth Gregory's excellent paper "Principles Behind a
Book Selection Policy Statement" which appeared in the October, 1956, issue of the I. L. A. Record, deserves a wider
audience and might well serve as the basis for discussion.
It is to be hoped that one or another of the uses she suggests for a policy statement will give food for thought to other librarians and move them into action:

The statement can be used in many ways.   It is

most useful for clarification, guidance, and the stimulation of those who are actually engaged in book selection... The statement is of particular value as an educational device for orienting new personnel in the library's policy and standards of book selection.

The policy is also useful in discussions with the citizen who thinks the library's standards are too high or too low. He may have a point if he doesn't want to restrict the rights of others. The citizen is never without the right to talk about books and the effect of the books in his own library. He also has a right to sound answers to his questions. The source of these answers could be the selection policy statement.

The statement is also valuable in dealing with groups who think they know what is poison print for other people.

Finally, it might be worthwhile to follow up the 1955 Book Selection Work Conference at Philadelphia with similar conferences or workshops on the regional, state, and local level. It is to be hoped that the relevant parts of the revised, 1956 Standards will continue to be used at such conferences and workshops as well as in library education.

Materials should be selected, retained, and discarded in the light of conscious objectives of each library.

...each library should define and refine the objectives which it seeks to achieve with its resources. These aims should be as specific as possible. Most libraries must define aims toward which they will build their collection, or aims will be defined for them by default in what they fail to acquire...

Every library should have a written statement of policy, covering the selection and maintenance of its collection of books and nonbook materials.

In this way it might be possible to gradually narrow the gap between the professed and the practiced library objectives in the area of book selection, and, thereby, bring the public library closer to performing its function as a truly educational institution.

Of "Luvs" and "Lights"

by Kenneth F. Kister   Assistant Professor, School of
Library Science, Simmons
College

From Wilson Library Bulletin 41:510-13+, January
1967; Reprinted by permission of Wilson Library
Bulletin.

Today, as in the past, some English fiction readers
continue to laugh at Tristram Shandy's missing nose or the
humorous circumstances leading to his unfortunate circum-
cision; or commiserate with that saucy bold-face, Pamela,
as she ingeniously wards off Mr. B----'s dastardly attempts
to undo her Virtue; or even see Dorothea successfully through
the plots and subplots of Middlemarch into the arms of the
handsome, youthful Will.   Fiction has been widely read and
enjoyed in England for almost three centuries, and recent
library statistics attest to its continued popularity: approximately eight books per head of population are circulated annually by English public libraries (nearly twice the comparative American figure) and, of that number, close to 70 percent is accounted for by fiction. Nottinghamshire County Library, for instance, records in its current annual report
that of the three and a half million adult books loaned in the
past year more than two and a half million were fiction titles.

However, while the classics of Sterne, Richardson,
George Eliot, et al, are read by a literary-minded few, the
vast majority of adult readers in England prefer current light
fiction to the standard classics or the serious modern novel
which, with its jarring, frequently distasteful themes and
mood of ugly alienation, is almost completely ignored. Titles
such as Take Death for a Lover, More Than Friendship,
Doomsday Creek, First Love, Murder Can't Wait and thousands of similarly innocuous novels--in British parlance,
"thrillers," "loves," and "cowboys"--have come to represent
the whole genre of fiction for much of the English reading
public. This is not to say that reading of poor quality fic-

tion is a new phenomenon in England.   Published over thirty
years ago, Q. D. Leavis' study of English reading habits,
Fiction and the Reading Public, notes that, while scant criti
cal attention has been paid to pap fiction, it has, since the
eighteenth century, "exerted an enormous influence upon the
minds and lives of the English people," and "till recently it
has superseded for the majority every other form of art and
amusement; and it forms the only printed matter besides
newspapers and advertisements which that majority reads;
from the cultural point of view its importance cannot be ex-
aggerated.   A tangle of pregnant issues is involved, question
of standards and values are raised which bear on the whole
history of taste. " Mrs. Leavis' comments are as valid toda
as they were in the nineteen-thirties.

      Reasons for the English reading public's addiction to
light novels are difficult to assess, since the whole question
of why people anywhere read at all has never been satisfactorily explored and will require basic research into man's
behavioral characteristics before accurate determinations car
be made.   Nevertheless, it is possible to point to several di
verse influences which, when viewed together, have significant bearing on reading preferences in England.   Among thes
are: 1) the English educational system which is designed--
beginning at age eleven--to produce a cultivated elite at the
expense of the majority and contributes to the pervasive public attitude that considers learning in general as slightly vulgar and pretentious; 2) the appeal of escapist fiction to poorly educated readers which, in the case of the romance, delicately camouflages illicit or frustrated sexuality under the
guise of wholesome romantic interest, allowing readers to be
come vicariously involved in situations denied them in real
life, or, in the case of the thriller or western, permits iden
tification with brutality and esoteric dangers not encountered
in daily living; and 3) the English public library, which supplies current light fiction in bulk quantity to meet the insistent public demand.   These several influences interact upon
one another, creating a dog-chasing-his-tail situation where
an inadequately educated majority of readers, the attributes
of the light novel, and the fiction policies of the public library combine to perpetuate large-scale reading of unrealisti
novels of unhappy quality by indiscriminate readers.   Or, as
Mrs. Leavis observed, the "public has acquired the reading
habit while somehow failing to exercise any critical intelligence about its reading. "

      If we allow that light fiction will still be published as

long as a market for it exists, and that the tradition-bound
educational systems in England will doggedly resist efforts
to change its pattern of producing an intellectual gentry, the
English public library would seem to be in the most likely
position to begin educating the reading public's critical judgment by supplying less light fiction and, concurrently, promoting the reading of serious fiction through the establishment of advisory services, especially since English readers
(unlike Americans) rarely build personal book collections,
relying instead upon the public library to meet their reading
needs.   This supposition, however, does not take into consideration the vested statistical interest that English librarians have in light fiction's enormous contribution to total public library circulation, or the ambivalent attitude of public
librarians toward the serious modern novel.

Quite naturally, public librarians in England prefer
to say that their job is to give readers what they want--and
if they want thrillers and loves, then thrillers and loves they
will have.   With publishers obligingly cranking out hundreds
of titles each year and booksellers accommodatingly providing weekly order forms listing the latest offerings, light fiction is looked upon as a hot commodity, stocked and dispensed to keep the customers happy.   There is the "old
dear," an elderly lady who is, by turns, lovable, cantanker-
ous, and mobile--a ubiquitous character on the English library landscape--who wants her daily "luv" or mystery story;
there is the kindly chap who exults in his garden and "snug-
gy" hearth and spends the damp winter evenings insatiably
"pressing on" with a John Creasey or Ed McBain thriller;
there is the red-cheeked housewife and mother who reads innumerable "lights" as time-out from the family wash or
worrying if Alison or Derek will pass the "eleven-plus" examination.   While occasionally English librarians will comment ruefully that "fiction stocks are being diluted by poor
material acquired to satisfy the low taste of elderly women,"
as S. C. Holliday recently did in Library Journal, most librarians in England believe that meeting the demands of this
representative cast of fiction readers is the raison d'être
of the public library.   And, if satisfying the reading public
incidentally boosts library circulation figures, so much the
better--happy readers make happy librarians.

Unfortunately, as wise men have learned, there is a
thorn on every rose and a fly in every ointment.   And, in
this instance, the supply-and-demand attitude English librarians have developed toward light fiction has blurred and dis-

torted their ability to critically evaluate the purpose and
value of serious modern fiction (the classics present no prob
lem, having been pre-selected by the passage of time).
Once librarians have decided to supply large quantities of
light fiction, supermarket standards of selection and mer-
chandising are inevitable, inasmuch as the consistently low
quality and ready availability of such novels as Escape to
Love, Dead Man Calling, and Through Panther Pass negate
the need for even the most cursory appraisal; however, when
these standards (or, more precisely, lack of standards) are
applied to all fiction, serious modern novels are smothered
and often lost among the plethora of light fiction listed by
booksellers. As one English librarian put it, the question is
not "would the works of Graham Greene, C. P. Snow, Angus
Wilson, Iris Murdock be better if there were fewer bad novels published," but rather one of evaluative standards which
distinguish among not only individual novels but levels of fiction as well. "There is a great deal of bad art, bad entertainment, bad journalism, bad advertisement," says Raymond
Williams in his survey of popular culture in England, Culture and Society, 1780-1950; he goes on to suggest that:

> clearly, the strip newspaper has to be compared
> with other kinds of newspaper; the beer advertise-
> ment with other kinds of description of a product;
> the detective novel with other novels. By these
> standards--not by reference to some ideal quality,
> but by reference to the best things that men exer-
> cising this faculty have done or are doing--we are
> not likely to doubt that a great deal of what is now
> produced, and widely sold, is mediocre or bad.

When these standards are not acknowledged or employed by librarians, distinctions between good and bad fiction become all but impossible for the English reading public.

Even more important, perhaps, is that once librarian
have decided that wholesale provision of light fiction is good
for business, enthusiasm for the product is inevitable, inasmuch as Bride's Dilemma and Make My Coffin Big represent
the reading public's fiction taste; and when librarians apply
this commercial attitude to all contemporary fiction, the
serious novel is frequently ignored or rejected as lacking the
values of the reading majority. Librarians who subscribe to
this point of view explain that, while fiction was once an important and positive literary force, the serious modern novel

has deteriorated into little more than recorded episodes of
sadistic and sensational sex and morbidity; they offer the
gloomy, Victorian judgment that today's serious fiction no
longer represents the nineteenth-century values of a Jane
Usten or George Eliot and hence--regretfully--cannot be purchased and made available to the reading public. Adjectives
such as "degenerate," "pejorative," "immoral," and "per-
verted" are commonplace descriptions used to dismiss contemporary fiction which attempts to deal realistically with society. And, it is noted, when the modern novel's values are
not corrupt and its language not ugly, it is unintelligible and
pointless and its values undecipherable.

Literary critics initially began this assault on serious
modern fiction, and librarians later took up the cry reviling
the genre and celebrating its lack of popularity with readers.
While underscoring the "reaction which seems to be developing among readers against the more sordid and lurid offerings from the publishers," they moralize (as did librarian
F. C. Tighe in his 1962-63 Annual Report for Nottingham Public Library):

> It is to be hoped that this aspect of the modern
> novel is a passing phase, for undoubtedly as an art
> form the novel can perform a most useful function
> in society, in the spreading of ideas and in the set-
> ting of standards of social behaviour. It would be
> regretable if, in the search for easy profits through
> the peddling of dreary and repetitive pornography,
> the novel should founder. Your committee have
> taken much satisfaction from the fact that there
> seems to be little demand by the public for this
> kind of material, and that in the end the best sanc-
> tion against such material is the financial one of
> refusing to purchase.

In the relative privacy of their annual reports, some
English librarians just cannot help expressing remorse that
dirty words and acts, dope addiction, insanity, and human
perversity are no longer affairs of the innermost room but
matters for public revelation and discussion. Hasn't the novel, they rhetorically ask, had its Saturday night, its glorious eighteenth and nineteenth centuries? Hasn't Sunday morning arrived, finding the novel sprawled in the gutter, rolling
in muck and filth, shouting obscenities or muttering dis-
jointed humbug? Why should the novel's Sunday morning
hangover be inflicted upon readers who are content with

lighter, happier fare?

Answers to these questions lie in understanding the purpose and nature of both serious and light fiction and, most important, the effect of each upon the individual reader. David Gerard, recently appointed librarian at Nottingham, believes that "the health of a nation, whether it knows it or not, is to a great extent registered by the mirror into which it peeks. Fiction is that mirror." Gerard, writing in The Library World for August 1964, goes on to suggest that, while serious fiction cannot help but be "genuinely disturbing" to readers, bad fiction distorts and falsifies the mirror; it "reassures and soothes; it strokes the cherished assumptions of the readers; it flatters the mediocre and puts down the proud." By casting an illusory reflection of happy-ending romance, cardboard people, always-solved murder, and ever-present violence and danger, the light novel tends to cloud readers' sensibilities until fictional fantasy and prosaic reality become intertwined, indistinguishable. And, although a brief can be argued for the light novel on the grounds of its entertainment value (just as the inanity of the "telly" or the Beatles' sound can likewise be defended), exclusive reading of light fiction subverts the public's perspective of society, its concerns, and its problems.

The serious novel, on the other hand, attempts to force readers to look at themselves as they really are, no matter how unsavory the reflections may be. Alan Sillitoe's Saturday Night and Sunday Morning, for example, is a harsh, at times nasty, novel--yet its searing criticism of English institutions and moral values is honest in intention and, therefore, valuable to English readers seeking to understand their country at midcentury. The continuing relaxation of legal censorship, especially in the area of sexuality, has allowed today's serious novelist to explore more deeply than ever before into human behavior and man's relationship to others. Increasingly, in fact, the interests of the serious novelist tend to parallel those of the social or behavioral scientist. Ralph Dehredorf's study, Class and Class Conflict in Industrial Society, deals with the sociology of social and economic stratification. So does John Braine's novel, Room at the Top. Similar comparisons could easily be cited: Doris Lessing's Golden Notebook is concerned with the present sexual and metaphysical emancipation of women; William Golding's Lord of the Flies anthropologically treats the innate bestiality latent in all human beings; David Benedictus' Fourth of June inquires into Britain's "public" school tradi-

tion; John Wain's Hurry on Down details the effects of a
crassly materialistic society on individual sensitivity. Robert
McCormick, in his analysis of recent English and American
fiction, Catastrophe and Imagination, published in 1957, calls
attention to this aspect of the modern novel, isolating it from
earlier realistic fiction:

> Events have forced the novelist to deal with mat-
> ters which previously belonged to the politician,
> the physician, the revolutionist or the historian.
> This is not to say that the novelists of the past did
> not deal with history or politics; they did.   But in
> the work of Defoe or Fielding, Dickens or Thack-
> eray, even in so fine an artist as George Eliot,
> history, politics, philosophy, sociology, all were
> submerged in the secondary layers of their novels.

It is true, of course, that, while the writer of serious fiction and the social scientist are both engaged in examining society and its components, each differs in his approach.   Whereas the scientist employs such tools as social
surveys, questionnaires, interviews, and statistical reports
and sets up controlled situations in order to gain an objective analysis leading to impartial conclusions, the novelist
operates subjectively, particularizing and intuiting the truth
about man and society as he instinctively sees it.   Nevertheless, social research and serious fiction have corresponding
intentions and significance--each attempts to give an honest
picture of society which will permit individual awareness of
things as they really are.   It was the philosopher Santayana
who conceived of science as "simply the dreaming Mind becoming coherent, devising symbols and methods."   Santayana
caught the vital connection between the intuitive and the meth-
odological, the empirical and the scientific.   C. P. Snow, the
English novelist and scientist, talked about the same connection in an interview in the Partisan Review (Spring, 1963):

> I believe there are certain things you can say about
> people in their society which are--slightly begging
> the terms but not too much--which are objectively
> true.   That is, people are like that in those places
> at that time.   Their temperaments are like that,
> and their reaction on their environment, and their
> environment's reaction on them, can be with some
> kind of accuracy stated.   Now I believe a realistic
> novelist ought to do that, often does do it.   And
> that seems to me not grossly dissimilar from the

scientific process, or a part of the scientific process...

When the dreaming mind of the contemporary novelist with serious motives goes to work and creates a work of fiction--a mirror for society--the images cast are not always pleasant.   The honest artist tells us that people are a mixed bag of tricks: vindictive and petulant as well as kind and sweet, scatological and aberrant as well as lovable and honorable.   By attempting to. wish away the unhappy realities described in modern fiction, by shrouding the mirror from public view, English librarians deceive the very readers they profess to serve.   If the English reading public is ever to develop a critical intelligence about its reading preferences, public librarians must begin not only to distinguish between good and bad fiction but also to understand and appreciate the nature, uses, and effects of both the serious modern novel and light fiction.   Eugene Ionesco, the playwright, was quoted recently as saying, "Mediocrity is more dangerous in a critic than in a writer."   He just may be right.

The Branch Collection

by Meredith Bloss   City Librarian, New Haven
(Conn.) Public Library

From Library Trends 14:422-33, April 1966;
Reprinted by permission of Library Trends,
Graduate School of Library Science, University of
Illinois.

This chapter deals with the purpose of a branch collection, its size, balance, relationship to the central library,
and policies and methods of selection. The objectives of
the collection would, obviously, be identical with those of
the branch library and as the 1956 ALA Standards put it,
the community library (including the branch) is "the unit in
the library system closest to the reader." It stocks the
most frequently used materials or those "used regularly" and
should "be able to draw upon larger collections, to meet the
needs of readers with specialized interests."[1]

This clear-cut theory of the branch library is also
expressed by Wheeler and Goldhor, "The mission of a branch
library is to give as much and as good service to as many
citizens in its area as possible." Service is defined in
small branches as "mainly... lending books [with] a high proportion of fiction, with some elementary reference work and
reading guidance." The larger branch would lend a larger
proportion of adult non-fiction and other special materials.
The branch resembles the main library in scope if not in
scale of function. The job is to "relate books... to the life
interests of people." But they also note that:

> Two main theories of branch library function have
> competed with each other. One envisages a branch
> library as a smaller-scale public library, offering
> reference and other special services as does the
> central library. The other assumes that branch
> libraries should be mainly agencies for the circu-
> lation of popular books at the neighborhood level.

185

> Both theories are valid, since they apply to differ-
> ent types of agencies... we need to distinguish be-
> tween a book distributing branch and a library ser-
> vice branch. [2]

Sealock has also a considered summary of branch
collection theory, touching a number of significant points,
and concluding that the practice has been to provide a general collection of books, without material in depth, but with
a rather wide range of fiction and general non-fiction, with
more books for children than for adults.   The distinguishing
characteristic of the branch collection, compared with other
book distribution centers such as drugstores, stationery
stores, and even groceries with book shelves, is that it is
a balanced collection served by a professional staff.   Even
the smallest branch can make a contribution to popular, informal education with a carefully chosen collection.   The
branch collection will have many calls for materials related to formal education and for general information, and a
more mobile population will require branch libraries to render a more comprehensive function that can be met with excellent fiction, authentic biography, and readable books on
current affairs. [3]

A different view of branch library purpose which, if
followed exclusively, would have a considerable impact on
the collection, was that stated by Ulveling in 1938: "the major part of a public library's opportunity to conduct a general educational service rests on its system of branch libraries." He added, "Branch libraries are not service satel-
lites of a main library, but, in their own right, they have
a definite educational responsibility... which is one of providing for the educational self-improvement of individuals." [4]

Being closest to the reader, the branch collection is
also seen as the product of community needs.   "The selection of books for the branch will be governed by the nature
of the community each branch serves... Thus there will be
a variety of types of collections in the various branches." [5]

Baltimore has the same point of view in its book selection policy, specifying that "It is around these community
functions that the average branch builds its permanent collection," although a sentence or two later this is modified
by the statement that "each branch maintains a basic collection of standard works in the major fields of knowledge." [6]

The conflict in purpose that faces branch selectors takes other forms as well. Carnovsky saw the choice as between selection "according to... a set of literary... values," or "according to... public demand," and he sees value as the only defensible policy. [7]

Lacy says that there are two major kinds of library use: "pastime use and purposeful use... By pastime use I mean that use for recreational reading that responds to a generalized desire to be entertained, a desire that might be satisfied more or less indifferently by one book or another within the range of the user's taste or by another form of recreation entirely. By purposive use I mean not only use in seeking information but also use for a particular and discriminated cultural experience which... cannot be readily replaced by a different experience." [8]

Professor Herbert J. Gans told a symposium on library functions in 1963 that there is a conflict between two conceptions of the community library. [9] The "supplier-oriented" idea argues that the library is an institution which ought to achieve the educational and cultural goals of the librarian. The "user-oriented" conception argues that the library ought to cater to the needs and demands of its users. Gans charges that the usual solution of the library has been to "uphold the supplier-oriented concept in the professional literature, but to accept the user-oriented concept in actual practice, if only to get its budget approved..." He was critical of arbitrary standards of size and program.

Library surveys provide some information about what librarians consider to be the purpose of the collection, although curiously, not as much as might be expected. In most cases, surveys tend to deal much more extensively and specifically with such matters as site, location, size of building and of collection, number of branches, and circulation, than with the purpose of the collection. One notes that branch libraries have "a clear-cut function, the supplying of materials in the whole range of everyday, down-to-earth interests..." [10] and that "Branch collections are working collections of frequently-used items." [11] Essentially, the branch purpose "is to serve the wide reading interests of the modern, active American community." [12] It is also recommended that the collection should contain both educational and recreational materials, and that the standard of quality should be high. "The public library... should stand for good reading." [13] A survey by a management firm sees the branches as the primary home-reading agency of the public library, to provide both for the general and the more specialized needs of the population. Home-reading is here distinguished from reference needs and uses. In another survey, branch libraries are defined as a means only of extending certain services of the central library and not of increasing the level of the service available, of providing greater access to materials but not increasing the scope of the resources available. Surveys also refer to the branch collection as actively changing, useful, containing fewer expensive books than central, with a higher proportion of recreational reading, with emphasis upon current reading resources and materials used by students and children.

Some questions remain with respect to the purpose of a branch collection. Is it recreational or educational, or some of each? What value if any do these slippery labels have in practice? Is there a difference between demand and need? What segment of the demand, or need, will the library consider relevant? Whose value judgment will prevail? Is there a difference between need, as expressed by the individual library user, and need as expressed (or more likely unexpressed) by the corporate community?

The second point to be looked at is the optimum size of the branch collection. The answer was thought to lie, perhaps, in the literature (books, articles, surveys) and in a brief look at practice. Textbooks and surveys, at least the dozen or so examined, seem to agree on 25 to 35 thousand volumes, although Minneapolis recommends 45,000 volumes for a branch serving 25 to 35 thousand people. The Madison, Wisconsin, study is also based on population: "minimum of 1 per capita in service area or 10,000, whichever is larger [with] growth beyond the minimum where demands justify larger stocks."[14] The per capita approach was also used in the 1943 Post-War Standards which recommended 1/3 to 1/2 volume per capita but noted that this was valid only if a substantial portion was of currently useful books, and also proposed a minimum of 6,000 volumes. [15]

Cory in his New Orleans survey recommended 25,000 as a "minimum necessary number of book titles" (my italics) for a regional branch [16] and 15,000 titles for a neighborhood library, [17] with the total number based on a formula of one volume for each six annual loans. Martin in the Dallas survey recommended "close to 30,000 volumes," for the large branch, divided into 8,000 for children, 3,000 for

young adults and nearly 20,000 for adults. [18] Greenaway in
the New Haven survey recommended for the children's collection 3,500 to 5,000 titles, and 10,000 to 15,000 volumes;
for adults, 8,500 to 10,000 titles and 12,000 to 20,000 volumes, and about 900 young adult titles, and 1,500 volumes,
or a total of 22,500 to 36,500 volumes. [19] Circulation is the
basis for the size standard proposed by Wheeler and Goldhor:
"A branch circulating 100,000 or more books a year should
have...a book stock of 25,000."[20]

Another way of finding out how big a branch collection should be in the opinion of librarians, is to look at the
shelving capacity being provided in new buildings.   For example, four Dallas branches opened in 1964 provided for
45,000, 50,000, 61,000 and 64,000 volumes.   Two Milwaukee branches opened in 1964 provided for collections of
60,000 volumes each, to serve populations of 60,000.   Three
in Tulsa were much smaller, one providing space for 12,250
volumes and two at 17,000. [21]

Apart from the question of how big branch libraries
should be, how big are they in reality?   Wheeler and Goldhor quote a 1960 report based on a sample of 162 branches
in 61 library systems which found that the median size
group was 5,001-6,000 and the modal size group was 10,001
to 20,000. [22] For the present article, a sample was taken
of 371 branches in 40 cities in 17 states as reported in the
1964 revision of American Library Directory. The sample
included only cities of more than 100,000 population, and
county or regional systems were not counted.   One hundred
twenty-one branches or about 33% had fewer than 15,000 volumes; 147 or about 40% had 15,000 to 25,000 volumes; and
103 listed 26,000 or more, with 13 of these listing 50,000
or more books.

Comparative data about size are not useful in point
of fact, since they do not take into account a whole host of
variables, such as the relative adequacy of school libraries,
the number of branch libraries in the total area or the population per branch, population density of the area served,
and most important of all, the aims and purposes or mission
of the branch collection.

It is significant and has bearing upon the purpose of
a branch collection that judgments as to size appear to be
based on population served, or on circulation, on a combination of these, or on some other unspecified factors.   One

does not find in the literature or records of performance
any indication that a branch collection would have to be of
a certain size in order to achieve adequate representation
of the basic and necessary books in the various fields of
knowledge and interest.   The way in which size is determined appears to indicate that, regardless of the fact that
the branch is spoken of as an agency of informal education,
and despite the fact that it is doubtless used in that way by
a number of people in every community, the actual practice,
administratively, is to regard it as an agency for the distribution of books for casual reading.

There is no evidence, for example, that the standards
of size were arrived at by controlled experiment.   What size
branch collection would be needed if, say, one put into practice Dan Lacy's concept of purposeful use, [23] plus an aggressive and planned exploitation by staff with leadership quality,
plus convenient and attractive quarters and accessibility?
Would it be worth investing a sum in such an experiment to
determine how big a branch collection should be?   To choose
one small area of reader interest--for example, consumer
education; one might hazard a guess that the typical branch
library might have at best ten books in the catalog and perhaps one or two of current vintage on the shelves at any
given moment.   A branch collection with that level of stock
is not apt to be able to create demand in that particular
area of informal education.

"The public library, as a social instrument in a
democratic state, has the responsibility of providing the
books which will contribute to an enlightened citizenry.   The
translation of this reponsibility into action constitutes perhaps the most difficult task of librarianship--book selection."[24]   How are books chosen for branch collections?
Practically no articles were found in the literature of the
past thirty years on this question, so it was necessary to
poll the field.   Thirty librarians in various parts of the
country, in large cities and medium-sized ones, were asked
to write a paragraph or two about policy and procedure.
The sixteen who responded were very generous and thoughtful and their assistance is much appreciated.

Several practices appear to be more or less common,
judging from this very limited sampling, and are presented
here first in summary form and then in detail.   Initial
choices are usually made by main library personnel, either
in committee or as subject selectors.   Sometimes there is

branch representation on the committee, especially if it is a
rotating one. Some responses indicated that branch librarians were "encouraged" to recommend titles, though one noted
that they were more apt to have subject than title requests.
The committee's choices for addition to the Main Library
are then usually listed, weekly or bi-weekly, sometimes by
subject, sometimes with annotations. Books are made available for examination, sometimes after or in connection with
verbal reviews by those who selected them. Practically all
libraries agree that, for practical reasons, no branch library
should stock a book that is not in the main library. About
half the libraries prepare a list "for branches only," and
some break this down into books for larger, medium,
smaller and so on. The practice seems to be equally common of opening up all system selections to branches. Various degrees of review and supervision are involved, although
the consensus seems to be that the branch librarian knows
best what his branch library should have.

"Each branch librarian decides what to buy on the
basis of reviews, inspection, budget, discards and the existing book stock and demand." "The branch librarians are responsible for choosing the items the money is to be spent
for." "Each branch librarian examines the titles and review
information... and indicates those she wishes to order for her
specific community." "The branch librarian decides... She
brings her own selections to the meeting... considers the
titles that others have brought, and makes her own selections from what the committee has approved." "Branch librarian looks at books approved for branch purchase and selects within an assigned budget."

Acquisitions regardless of method rely heavily on advance publication or approval plans. As high as 50% of
titles are purchased in this manner after the book has been
examined. In substantiating the value of particular titles or
reinforcing a staff member's review, a definite core of reviewing media is widely used. These media invariably include Library Journal, Booklist, Virginia Kirkus, New York
Times Book Review, New York Herald Tribune Book Week,
the Saturday Review, and in addition local media when available.

What proportion of the library's weekly or annual accessions is selected for branch collections? As an example,
Toledo reported that 91 non-fiction and 15 fiction titles were
chosen by one or more of eleven branches from one weekly

list of 191 non-fiction and 18 fiction titles. No other data
on this question were discovered. Toledo, by the way, has
begun preparing a bi-weekly list of branch orders, so that
Main department heads "can have a more informed idea of
what the branches decide to get. "

   The general conclusions are now examined in more
detail. Initial book selection is handled in one of three
ways: by a committee, by division or department heads,
and by subject specialists. The usual method of selection
is by a committee or the division heads. An adult book selection committee varies in composition but is usually composed of administrators, such as the chief librarian and his
assistant, the librarian in charge of branches, and the librarian in charge of readers' services. In addition to administrators, there are rotating committee members, who
include at least one branch librarian. In only a few instances were all branch librarians members of the committee. The committee meets and agrees upon specific titles
on the basis of commercial reviewing media and staff reviews. The results of the meeting are then communicated
to various agencies in the form of acquisition lists or slips.
The selection committees for children's literature work the
same way, except that the authority to purchase titles is
more frequently centralized in the children's supervisor.

   In libraries where division or department heads make
the initial purchases, these heads are individually responsibl
and there is less apt to be a meeting. The acquisitions of
the various heads are then co-ordinated on a requisition list.
In the subject specialist method, each professional librarian
is responsible for a specific area of knowledge, and he presents his acquisitions at regular meetings, which generally
include the entire staff. The subject specialist would be responsible for reviewing media pertaining to his field, and
for screening approval books in his field. Regardless of the
system of selection, the initial selection results in a pool
of acquisitions for the main library. The next step is to decide which are appropriate for the branches.

   In many cases the committee or department heads
have left the branches a free choice of any title that has
been ordered for the main library. Highly specialized items,
however, are frequently noted as such, and therefore not
likely for branch acquisition. Frequently when the acquisition list is open, a supervisor is then responsible for reviewing branch decisions.

Almost as many libraries have placed controls on the acquisition list. Usually, the individual selector or the committee as a group will decide which titles are appropriate for the main library only, and which titles can be duplicated in the branches. Some systems differentiate between which titles are appropriate for only the larger branches, and those which are appropriate for all branches. Usually the designations for the titles are not iron-clad. For special community needs there is recourse to the branch supervisor. Under the subject selector system the selector decides which titles are branch material, and in which branches to place them.

The branch librarian makes his choices from an acquisitions list or from acquisition slips which are issued on a regular basis. The books appearing on the list frequently are available in a reviewing room so that the branch librarians may examine them. Adult selections by the branch librarians generally are not closely supervised. Children's selections are usually made with the co-operation of the children's supervisor. Thus, without the aid of a comprehensive guide, the branch librarian must know the needs of his community and how to meet these needs through currently available literature.

In many systems there are automatic additions to branch collections that do not require the individual approval of the branch librarian. These additions, including reference works purchased by the Reference Department, are system-wide, such as a schedule purchase of encyclopedias. Some additions are temporary in nature, such as fiction or mystery collections that travel from branch to branch. Several systems reported using rental collections of current fiction in branches.

The branch librarian is also largely responsible for maintaining the condition and appropriateness of the branch collections, except in subject selector systems where collection maintenance (i.e., replacement, duplication, and weeding) is carried out by the subject selector. Usually the branch librarian enjoys considerable latitude in collection maintenance. However in some systems, replacements must be approved by the book selection committee, or by the branch supervisor. Frequently system-wide replacements are effected in specific areas through subject replacement lists issued by committees formed to investigate adequacy of specific subject areas in all the branches.

How are budgets allocated for branch collections? What criteria or standards are used? A study made in 1954 was based on practice in 32 cities of over 300,000 population. [25] Respondents cited a total of 20 different criteria, with use or circulation cited 24 times, special needs cited 8 times and the following, one or more times: registration, state of book collection, area served, population served, hard wear, future potentialities, type of reader, nature of neighborhood, reference use, size of building or space available, what is requested by patrons, work load, number of readers, age of branch, turnover, previous expenditure, and what each branch librarian requests. Some cities listed as many as four or five criteria for allocation; where only one was cited, it was usually circulation or usage. It would seem in general that about two-thirds of the budget goes for adult books and one-third for juvenile books. In the few cases where there was a budget for young adult books, it came out of the adult share. Not all libraries specified a percentage; some cited dollar figures for the current year.

Book funds are allocated by the chief librarian or by one or more division or department heads, sometimes with committee consultation and sometimes not. Indianapolis uses a detailed and comprehensive budget worksheet, which lists staff data including salaries, estimated service (reference questions), budget request (for each branch and department), book stock, turnover, the past year's circulation and the estimate for next year. These figures are compiled separately for adult and juvenile loans. Other factors, such as wear-and-tear in a poor neighborhood, are taken into account.

As to balance in the branch collection, the 1943 Post-War Standards recommended that children's books comprise 20-25 percent and that non-fiction comprise 60 percent of the adult collection, with the "non-fiction ratio increasing with the population of the area served." [26] Put another way, if the total collection had 25% children's books, the proportion of adult non-fiction would be 45% and fiction 30%. No guidelines were discovered as to proportion of older, standard stock and of current, changing titles; and the present inquiry has not turned up anything on a theory of duplication beyond the rule of thumb that one more copy of a popular title may be added for each specified number of reserves, such as five or ten.

Relationship to the central library is implied in much

that has been brought out under purpose of the collection
and method of selection, although one could observe diversity
on this score as well as on many others.   It is clear that
the branch collection is intended to be basically a duplicate
of whatever part of the central library collection is thought
to be most frequently or regularly used by the patrons of a
particular branch service area.   One might have thought
that every branch library's collection would be simply a duplicate of the most frequently used 10 percent of the central
collection, but this appears not to be the case.

In conclusion, this inquiry seems to have more questions than answers, questions which seem deserving of attention, but which the present inquirer lacks the information or
wisdom to answer.   It may be observed, for example, that
in both purpose and selection policy, the branch collection
is seen as needing to be responsive to its community needs
and it is clearly regarded as the responsibility of the branch
librarian to "know" those needs.   One may wonder whether
this is a realistic expectation, in terms both of time available and of perceptive skills.   What techniques or practices
are there for discovering felt needs, and how does the har-
assed branch librarian protect himself against translating demand as need?   What built-in method, other than circulation,
is there for discovering how well the community needs have
been met?   Again, what is the responsibility of the branch
librarian, as the community book person, to lead, guide, direct, stimulate and instruct the reading interests of the
users?   Is this a reasonable community expectation, and is
this concept implied in the "responsiveness to local needs"
concept of branch selection?   The hypothesis that each branch
collection is or should be unique, reflecting and responsive
to the needs of its community, ought perhaps to be tested by
more research than appears in the literature.   It might also
be worth asking how the "smorgasbord" theory of branch book
selection, with a little of everything, works out.   What kind
of branch collection results?   Finally, what is the significance of the taste of the individual branch librarian?   And
are not his taste and judgment apt to have at least as much
weight as the "needs of the community"?

Notes

1. American Library Association, Co-ordinating Committee
   on Revision of Public Library Standards   Public
   Library Service.   A Guide to Evaluation, with Minimum Standards.   Chicago, American Library Associa-

tion, 1956, p. 14, 35.

2. Wheeler, Joseph L. , and Goldhor, Herbert Practical
   Administration of Public Libraries. New York,
   Harper & Row, 1962, p. 411-412, 420.

3. Sealock, Richard B. "Extending Services." (In Roberta
   Bowler, ed. , Local Public Library Administration.
   Chicago, International City Managers' Association,
   1964, p. 258, 273-274.)

4. Ulveling, Ralph "Administration of Branch Systems."
   (In Carleton B. Joeckel, ed. , Current Issues in Li-
   brary Administration. Chicago, University of Chicago
   Press, 1938, p. 136, 162.)

5. Carter, Mary Duncan, and Bonk, Wallace John Building
   Library Collections, 2d ed. New York, Scarecrow
   Press, 1964, p. 79.)

6. Book Selection Policies. 3d ed. Baltimore, Enoch Pratt
   Free Library, 1963, p. 7.

7. Carnovsky, Leon "The Evaluation of Public-Library Facilities." (In Louis R. Wilson, ed. , Library Trends.
   Chicago, University of Chicago Press, 1937, p. 301-
   302.)

8. Lacy, Dan "The Adult in a Changing Society: Implications for the Public Library." (In Lester Asheim,
   ed. , New Directions in Public Library Development.
   Chicago, University of Chicago Graduate Library
   School, 1957, p. 59-60.)

9. Gans, Herbert J. "The Public Library in Perspective."
   (In Ralph W. Conant, ed. , The Public Library and
   the City. Cambridge, M. I. T. Press, 1965, p. 67.)

10. Martin, Lowell A. Branch Library Service for Dallas.
    A Report Sponsored by the Friends of the Dallas
    Public Library, n. p. , 1958. (Processed.) p. 71.

11. Ibid. , p. 73.

12. Ibid. , p. 74.

13. Ibid. , p. 75.

14. City of Madison Planning Department Madison's Plan for Library Facilities. n. p. , 1963, p. 5.

15. American Library Association. Committee on Post-War Planning Post-war Standards for Public Libraries Chicago, American Library Association, 1943, p. 71.

16. Cory, John Mackenzie A Network of Public Libraries for New Orleans. Survey Report, n. p. , 1963. (Processed.) p. 8.

17. Ibid. , p. 15.

18. Martin, op. cit. , p. 74.

19. Greenaway, Emerson Library Service for New Haven New Haven, New Haven Community Renewal Program, 1964, p. 8-9.

20. Wheeler and Goldhor, op. cit. , p. 412.

21. Jones, Wyman "A Foursome for Dallas" Library Journal 89:4735-36, December 1, 1964; Bartolini, R. Paul "Double Header in Milwaukee" ibid. , p. 4739; Martin, Alice B "Triple for Tulsa" ibid. , p. 4742.

22. Wheeler and Goldhor, op. cit. , p. 414.

23. Lacy, op. cit. , p. 60.

24. American Library Association. Committee on Post-War Planning, op. cit. , p. 66.

25. Booth, Sarah T. "Information About Branches in 33 Library Systems" Public Libraries 8:89-90, December 1954.

26. American Library Association. Committee on Post-War Planning, op. cit. , p. 73.

Library Systems Study for Public Libraries of Santa Clara, Alameda, and Contra Costa Counties

by Jack Freeman

Freeman and Company, Management Consulting Engineers of Palo Alto, California carried out this study for the libraries of the counties named above.

From <u>Library Systems Study for Public Libraries of Santa Clara, Alameda, and Contra Costa Counties.</u> Palo Alto, California, The Author, 1965. Sel. from Chap. II. ; Reprinted by permission of the author.

IIA 1 <u>Function, Goals and Objectives of the Library</u> (as stated for the purposes of this study)

(1) Development and maintenance of as high a Level of Service, and all its elements as listed in Section IA as desired and provided for by the community.

(2) Satisfaction of those concerned on the factors listed i the several Bill of Rights in Section IC 4.

(3) Guidance and encouragement in all patrons of the appreciation of books as books and the love of reading both for its own enjoyment and the insights this provides into the ways of man.

(4) Guidance and encouragement in all patrons of the con tinued development through reading, listening and view of cultural appreciation, knowledge, and taste.

(5) Guidance and encouragement of all patrons in continu ing self-education along desired lines of self-improve ment.

(6) Assistance in following any line of formal education b providing required and desirable back-up materials a needed.

(7) Assistance and guidance in required materials and ou lines for groups and organizations in pursuing any lin of educational content with their members.

(8) Provision of materials and guidance in their use for all recreational purposes of patrons.

(9) Provision of inspirational materials for all types of patron and the various situations facing each, and guidance in their use.

(10) Provision of sufficient easy-access, informational materials to satisfy the needs and desires of the entire community and which the community will provide for.

(11) Provision of all materials, services, and contacts in such a manner and with such ample means of notification as to insure maximum satisfaction of and participation and utilization by all concerned.

IIA 2 Function, Goals and Objectives of the Librarian
(as stated for the purpose of this study)

(1) To be an informed guide to the contents of the library and sources of information to all patrons, and patron groups, in the maximum possible satisfaction of their cultural, educational, informational, recreational and inspirational needs and wants.

(2) To be an informed and sympathetic counselor and advisor in all aspects of patrons' reading and study objectives as well as an educational guide and planner for individuals embarked on any program of self-development.

(3) To competently evaluate needs and match them with available materials.

(4) To promote the love of reading and the appreciation of books for their inspirational, human, or philosophical values.

(5) To be a competent research. [sic]

(6) To be an informed and intellectually-alive individual with wide interests such as is needed to aid in the establishment of significant collections of materials which will satisfy library goals and patron desired.

(7) To possess the capabilities and desires in broad knowledge of many fields of material, sympathetic attitude towards patrons of all kinds and ages, and wish to aid which will make possible the accomplishment of the foregoing.

IIB. Patron Interest Groups and Needs

To whom are the libraries providing service? Does the service provided match the needs of the recipients or po-

tential recipients? After considering certain fundamental
factors on the utilization of libraries and the problems existing in this regard, this section analyzes the groups which
make up the patron spectrum--recognizing that each individual fits into a number of categories depending upon his interests. Overlap is therefore inevitable, but not necessarily undesirable since each individual has different needs in each
category he fits. Since it is readily apparent that the summation of needs is greater, at the moment, than the library'
ability to fill those needs, it becomes desirable to recognize
a requirement of proportionate allocation of efforts and resources if no limited groups of patrons are to be discriminated against. Of course, the entire determinant here is
"needs," so that different communities will actually have quite
a varied application of possible materials and services which
can be almost unique to them.

*   *   *   *   *

IIC 1a Present Methods of Selection

There are three basic approaches to book selection
used in the different libraries. The first involves one or
very few selectors in headquarters or in fairly high positions
who perform all selection for the library as a whole. There
are objections to this approach on the part of the many other
librarians who don't get any chance to participate in the selection and feel therefore that an imbalance tends to exist;
there is the parallel feeling that the needs of the various patron groups--particularly at branches--are not being sufficiently considered in the what-appears-to-be arbitrary selection process.

The second method in use is that of having many selectors participating in selection meetings where all final decisions on book choice are made; in this case the participants frequently specialize by the proposed place of the book
in the Dewey Decimal System in order to present each book
to the selection meeting for decision. This approach seems
to find more favor in the eyes of the various librarians since
it strikes all as being very fair, but it too has its rather
serious drawbacks. In a large library system not many of
the librarians can be allowed to participate directly in the
process because of the great cost of the selection meeting in
terms of personnel time. The individual who has prepared
the book for discussion appears to know more about it than
many of the rest and therefore there is a very strong tendency to just go along with the recommendations of the individual
thus destroying a good bit of the purpose of the entire ap-

proach. However, the selection meeting which suffers from this then becomes so boring to the participants that many welcome reasons for avoiding the meetings; one librarian so abhors the meetings as to not be able to sleep the night before each one and to become physically ill over them. This can possibly be understood when it is realized that most of the working time of the meeting tends to involve only each participant saying how many copies of the book in question should be gotten for the library as a whole or for the branch which that individual represents. The approach still does, however, produce a feeling of participation on the part of many in a wide-spread system and it permits the accomplishment of certain administrative tasks once the individuals involved have been brought together for purposes of book selection.

The third method which is used is that involving many selectors within the framework of the library staff, but in this approach each one--also specializing in specific subjects --is completely responsible for selections in those subject areas. This method is highly satisfactory to the participants, is not as costly as number 2 or in some cases as number 1, and arrives at what appear to be equally or more acceptable choices. The librarians operating under this approach are very satisfied with it; the only problem seems to be one that is universal to the three systems, which is that there are too few librarians to cover such a wide range of material.

Of the three approaches, the third seems to be preferable from a number of points of view. All those members of the staff who are able to read critically should then be able to participate in the process (as is possible in number 3)--automatically improving it. The net result is the same as the second method it is believed in terms of end product, without the terrific drag of the going around the table for a quantity count after all have listened to just a brief explanation of the book. (It could also be argued that this listening to the brief descriptions of the books is of considerable value to the library in informing its personnel on the content of its collection; this argument cannot quite be accepted because only representatives of the library staff participate and these representatives are not the younger librarians who most need the information for the good of the library.) Another positive factor about the third method is that the person with complete responsibility for the subject area gets a closer feeling towards it and appears to do a more careful job than one who is just recommending to a group. A final advantage

is in the item of cost: the cost of the second method is
rather easy to pin down because the bulk of it is due to the
selection meeting which can be isolated as a specific cost
factor--the total can run as high as $12 per title selected.
It is more difficult to label the costs of 1 and 3 because,
unless in #1 the selectors apply themselves full-time to the
job of selection, most selection effort in all methods takes
place on the librarian's own time.

Recommendation IIC1-1:
Assign each member of the library staff who is capable
of critical reading of material to an area of subject specialization, with full responsibility for selection decisions
on behalf of the library--under the general supervision
and direction of head librarian or deputy.

In one major variation of this, Hayward schedules
reading time for selection and other purposes as part of the
work day--a fully justified practice since both selection and
collection knowledge are part of the librarian's function over
and above personal reading for personal interests.   Keeping
abreast of the vast quantities of required material can only
be accomplished through application of work time to the task.

Recommendation IIC1-2:
Schedule reading time for selection purposes as well as
maintaining collection knowledge as part of the work day.

Two other points can be listed as problems here, the
more complete treatment of which is proposed in Section III.
The first is the tremendous, hidden amount of time spent on
just finding the information of interest to the individual (under any method) on books which that individual is to cover;
each selector must at least glance through all of the available
material on every book in each selection tool received in order to discover the items of particular interest.

The second problem is that there is much that is haphazard about finding books which the library should get, with
all the help of the selection tools.   Significant over-emphasis
can result from heavy advertising of the book in the trade
media, even though the librarian attempts not to be swayed
by this.   The largest question in this direction is that of
completeness, since there are many books of great value
which later might be gotten by the library which are not located originally from library selection media.

*   *   *   *   *

IIC 1c.   Selection Policies and Questions

This topic represents the key to the entire question of selection, provisioning the library, and the resulting state of the collection.   It will be analyzed here from the points of view of the earlier mentioned "Patron Centered Library Service" and the goals and objectives of the library.

(1)   The first question which presents itself is who should perform the selection and what should be selected, two sides of the same coin.   At the present time, as indicated in the previous sub-section, the librarian basically is performing the selection and is exercising judgment as to what shall be included within the library collection.   In terms of practical fact, patrons have a significant average effect on what is selected and therefore might be included in the "who" and "what."   Although the average effect is significant, it varies from very low levels in some libraries to very high levels in others; it is even at fairly high levels in some libraries in which the statements and printed selection policy definitely reserve all right of selections to the librarian, due to some very delicately tuned librarian responses to patron desires.   Today, however, the librarian definitely performs the selection.

(2)   The next question which might be looked at without the desire of presenting a challenge with it, is just what is the right of the librarian to perform this selection?   In the establishment of libraries was this really intended to be a right of the librarian or just a matter delegated to the librarian in the face of the lack of apparently feasible methods for the owners of the library, the citizens of the community, to perform this selection themselves?   Of course there would be undoubtedly a feeling that a librarian should be better equipped than the average citizen to make logical choices between alternative materials, but this gets at the question of ability rather than right.

It certainly behooves the librarian at this point to examine the question rather thoroughly, to consider whether a group of citizens--banding together to obtain certain advantages and economies in the provision of this very desirable and necessary service--would actually wish to give over the basic right of acceptance or veto over materials which the individual providing the money might wish to read.   Of

course, such a conclusion would be of high probability if the
purpose of acceptance or veto were linked to the practical
questions of alternative ways of spending limited available
funds or the arbitration of disagreements between citizens
with different ideas, where both ideas cannot be accommo-
dated on a practical basis within the total picture.

However, if this last statement were to be close to
the truth, then logically the librarian must accept selection
not as an inviolable right, but as a matter of practical necessity, then all that is within the power of the librarian
should be exercised in order to find practical solutions, whi
will fit within the limitations imposed upon the library, for
the citizenry to make its own selections in the maximum pos
sible manner!

(3) Next comes the question of the ability of the librarian tc
     make a selection that is superior to any other means
     of performing this function.   Here there is found a
     significant divergence in the viewpoints between differ
     ent librarians (there is some divergence on the ques-
     tion of right, also).   Some hold that the ability to se
     lect books is basic to librarianship while others say
     that it is ridiculous to expect librarians to be able to
     select books and other materials which people of wide
     ly varying fields and backgrounds will find to be in-
     teresting and worthwhile.   The latter viewpoint ques-
     tions the ability of the librarian, who is generally a
     history or English major, to place himself or herself
     in the shoes of a dock-worker or a nuclear physicist
     for the selection of books of interest to either one.
     The evidence supports the latter view.

(4) It is desirable here to investigate the same question
     from a very practical standpoint.   If librarians have
     a great capability to select the "good" and winnow the
     "bad," then aside from differences caused by the vary
     ing needs of the different communities, there should
     exist a fair degree of unanimity among the different
     librarians performing the selection function indepen-
     dently.   However the data does not bear this out.   Ac
     cording to figures projected from a test of the titles
     held by each library of books published since 1960,
     and assuming a total commercial publication of books
     somewhere between 20 and 25 thousand per year, it
     was found that the 16 libraries together most likely
     purchase something greater than 80% of the titles pub-
     lished each year.   This is in the face of the largest

single purchase by any library, Oakland, being approximately 50% of the total.   This estimated value
of 19,000 titles per year purchased by the 16 libraries in concert, to put the figures in slightly different terms, indicates a good deal less than full
agreement.   Part of the degree of agreement which
does occur must be accepted as possibly due to a
power of publishers' advertising or lack of ready
availability of information on the output of certain
other publishers.   More than these, it might be due
to some bias, conscious or unconscious, which the
librarians share.   Without these factors causing a
tendency towards agreement, the degree of disagreement could be far higher than even these figures indicate.

Altogether, then, the validity of superior, highly discriminating selection by professional librarians is open to
serious question!

(5)   The figures point up another factor of considerable
      importance to the libraries and taxpayers.   This re-
      lates to the questions raised as to the considerable
      cost of selection and the effectiveness or lack of ef-
      fectiveness of selection when there is such a tremen-
      dous difference in professional opinion evident.   A
      major matter of waste is surely apparent from the
      data.

(6)   What are the rights of patrons in the matter of selec-
      tion?   The background conditions against which this
      must be considered have been indicated a number of
      times earlier in this report; the fact that a library
      does not have the "bad" will not force the patron to
      take the "good;" the function of the library is to satis-
      fy the needs and desires of the patron, etc.   All of
      this points to demand-orientation-selection of library
      materials; it's the taxpayer's money and it could be
      felt that such money should be spent more directly
      for him or for his nominee--the library user.

(7)   It certainly seems reasonable that it is a patron right
      to be served by the library on an equal basis to all
      other patrons and that library discrimination in favor
      of any one group of people or reading tastes repre-
      sents an infringement on the rights of many.   Such
      discrimination and infringement is clearly evident in
      the practices of most of the libraries; some types of
      material are not purchased at all in relation to patron

desires. The net effect has been a weaning of numbers of groups of patrons away from the library
usage--and, in some cases--away from reading altogether.

(8) The fiction/non-fiction bias has been treated briefly
earlier as has been the question of emphasis on information value as compared to book interest or reading
value. This bias shows up very definitely in the comparison of circulation figures with book budgets as
each is distributed between fiction and non-fiction.
Forgotten here is the significant information value of
fiction, its value in the program of self-development
as well as all the other values which meet the goals
of the library.

The fact that the use of non-fiction is rising in relation to fiction could be due to patrons basic needs and desires, but a question here should possibly call for some self-
searching by the librarian: "How much of this shift is due
to the driving away from the libraries of patrons who have
'read them out' (or think they have read them out)?"

(9) The bias against fiction must also be investigated
from the standpoint of basic, inherent values for the
individual. It is strange that an engineering firm
should find it necessary to undertake an outline of the
value of fiction in analyzing the activities of libraries
and librarians, since so many librarians majored in
English in their undergraduate education and many of
these concentrated in English Literature. Of course
it is sometimes that which is closest and best known
which can become forgotten in viewing "brave new
worlds."

Undoubtedly none will quarrel with a concept of great
educational value arising from reading of those fictional
works which can be categorized as all-time classics; these,
regardless of the form in which they appear, are well recognized for the broadening of background and outlook required
of an educated person. However, it is not only this which
it is wished to emphasize here; the thesis to be put here is
that almost all fictional works--again regardless of their
form--have significant value to the individual, surpassing in
total by far the general educational value of all non-fiction
combined. This statement does not represent an attempt to
demean that which is positive in the scientific, the technical,
and the professional material in the large number of fields

of specialization which now exist, but to suggest that all of
these latter put together have small bearing upon a person's
general education as well as the first molding of character
and direction for the future.   On the other hand, fiction can
be discovered as the source of much of the first knowledge
of life and all its aspects and has its place in the forming
of a good many of the patterns of life for those who take
what it has to offer.

If a summary could be made of the entire non-fiction
content of typical educational experience from kindergarten
through high school, and this summary compared to that
which would benefit a person in his general and specific
knowledge as required for a full and meaningful life in today's complex world, there would appear to be small doubt
that the former would be found to be severely wanting.   It
is even most likely a fair statement that the largest part of
the basic, factual knowledge needed in many different areas
of everyday life and fundamental education would be seriously lacking in the former, and that in no way could a person
solely so educated be considered to be an educated person.
If the school-required fictional content were to be added to
that summary then the result would most likely be closer to
the mark, but it would still undoubtedly be quite true to say
that even with this addition there are not the marks of a
full education such as might be expected below the collegiate
level.

On the other hand, considerable thought might be
given to the question of whether the possible level of education might be up to the same point if the position were re-
versed--if in place of the usual non-fiction/fiction combination, the entire concentration were put on the largest quantity and variety of fiction which could be absorbed in the
time available.   The amount of information in many very
factual fields such as English grammar, history of all sorts,
mathematical and philosophical development, word power and
almost all other usual and unusual fields of information,
available from a wide acquaintanceship with fictional writing
would most likely be astounding if gathered together in one
place; such gathering of knowledge from reading is so commonplace a thing, especially to those who are very well
read, that the total value of content is not realized fully or
appreciated by most--but take away that which was gained
from fictional reading by many of the best educated individuals and a serious gap undoubtedly would be discovered.

So, aside from all other considerations, it therefore behooves the library and the librarian to completely eliminate all bias against fiction.

(10) Within the field of fiction itself, certain definite biases show up, both in discussions with the librarians and the sampling of the holdings of the libraries. The latter, performed in a limited way at 23 agencies of the 16 libraries, provided some rather interesting information from many points of view.

In terms of the percent of the sample titles owned by the different library agencies (in their shelf lists) at the time of the study (see Table II-1) the 16 libraries showed an average holding of 95% of the Classics List, 98% of the This Year's Best Sellers List, 89% of the Last Year's Best Seller List, 51% of the Mysteries List and 35% of the Science Fiction List. (An interesting point is that most librarians appear to be highly in favor of Classics and many equally opposed to best sellers, yet the percentage of best sellers held is greater than that of the Classics--an effect of, undoubtedly, pressure from a most vociferous segment of the public.)

The most important factor showing discrimination is the definite bias illustrated against the last two classifications. One could again argue against this bias at some length that each person has a right to his own choice of reading matter or relaxation, but other factors are better dipped into here. Some few librarians feel that the needs of mystery readers and others should be supplied for the recreational enjoyment of serious thinkers needing a change of pace (ignoring the right to a change of pace, or just plain recreation, desired by manual workers and clerks), although most don't seem to go this far. The point appears to be well taken; a considerable number of PhD's who were interviewed during the course of this study did indicate that they were mystery or science-fiction fans (the bias against these in the libraries was very evident to this group and not at all appreciated). Fortune Magazine reinforces the point in an article on extremely independently-thinking geniuses who are being counted upon to change radically the face of the nation and their companies in the fields of technological development (mostly as related to space) describes them, in part, as readers of science fiction.

Although many librarians do not personally appreciate science-fiction, it should be recognized as being one of the most imaginative forms of writing that exists, and therefore falling into the category of things which the librarian should like to support, completely apart from any matter of rights or demand.

(11) In addition to bias on mysteries and science-fiction shown up in the figures referred to, bias is also evident in other areas; the light love story and the children's serial story. In both cases the librarian fails to recognize objectives different than those in his own or her own experience. The housewife or working girl who reads the light love story most likely reads nothing else; by eliminating this from the library this person is forced, not to read the "better" books available in the library, but to use other sources which might have a poorer selection than that which would be available to the library or, most likely be forced to stop reading altogether. There were many of those who had arrived at the latter point included in the interviewees in the study.

The question then becomes whether it is better for an individual to read something of which the librarian does not approve or not to read at all. Experience in teaching of language and teaching of reading shows that one of the most important points in either one is the act of reading--reading anything, but reading. If the restriction to this form of fiction is due to inability to read well, an increasingly prevalent problem, then any reading at all of this material or otherwise represents an improvement step-again, quite aside from the basic right of the individual to read what he or she desires.

(12) The feelings of opposition on the part of children's librarians to serial books is of the same nature but possibly considerably more adversely significant. Some other librarians charge that this dislike on the part of children's librarians stems from not wishing to be forced to carry the whole series once any part of it is carried; too much shelf space is taken. While this was found true to a small extent in certain instances, it is felt that practically all the children's librarians who were interviewed sincerely believe that these books are bad for the youngster. In the face of the success of children's librarians--in cooperation with grade school teachers--in encouraging many children to read books (that is, books with significant

Table II-1

Percent of Sample Titles Owned at Time of Study

	Classics	Best Sellers		Mysteries	Science Fiction	Total*
		Present	Past			
Gilroy	40	88	63	13	25	44
Mountain View	100	100	88	100	63	92
Palo Alto - Main	90	100	88	63	50	81
- Mitchell Park	100	100	88	50	13	77
Santa Clara City	100	100	88	75	50	87
Santa Clara Co. - Campbell	100	100	88	63	25	81
- Los Altos	100	100	75	63	38	81
San Jose - Main	100	88	88	25	13	71
- Cambrian	100	100	88	0	0	67
6 Libraries - Avg.	92	97	83	50	31	76
Alameda City	100	100	100	63	25	83
Alameda Co. - Castro Valley	90	100	88	38	63	79
- Fremont	100	100	88	38	38	79
Albany	90	100	75	38	25	71

Table II-1 (cont.)
Percent of Sample Titles Owned at Time of Study

| | Classics | Best Sellers | | Mysteries | Science Fiction | Total* |
		Present	Past			
Berkeley – Main	100	100	100	88	38	89
– Claremont	100	100	88	25	13	69
Contra Costa – Pleas. Hill	100	100	100	63	50	87
– El Cerrito	100	100	88	50	38	81
Hayward	100	100	100	88	63	92
Livermore	95	100	100	13	63	79
Oakland – Main	100	100	88	50	38	81
– Lakeview	85	88	88	13	0	62
Richmond	100	100	100	88	50	90
San Leandro	100	100	88	63	25	81
10 Libraries – Avg.	97	99	92	51	38	80
16 Libraries – Avg.	95	98	89	51	35	78

* Total based on arbitrary list weighting of Classics = 2-1/2 x value of each of the rest.

imaginative content and message), this one area
might be left alone.

However, since most of this is supposed to be motivated by the best interests of the child, a possible educational error must be pointed up: the possible error stems from
librarian concentration on good readers who develop nicely,
rather than on those who require considerably more help.
In one library's summer reading program, a small boy--
having found a book that he liked and having completed it--
wished to read it again to fulfill the requirement for a second book of the ten involved in the reading program; the su-
pervising librarian advised permitting him to do this; stating
that when he no longer needed the security of a book which
he had successfully read and therefore could read, he would
continue by himself.   This boy repeated the same book over
and over again until it counted for six out of the ten books
which were required.   By the time the seventh rolled around
he evidently felt sufficiently sure of himself to choose another book; for his eighth, ninth and tenth books he again chose
different ones each time, showing that he had at last weaned
himself from what was to him a very necessary prop.   Undoubtedly if he had not been permitted to repeat his first
book he would have dropped out of the program and could
have joined the growing legion of problem readers.   As it
is, today he is an active reader following very varied suggestions of the librarian.

It is suggested here that the serial book serves the
same purpose--that those who read these actually require
them as a definite stage of their development; how else can
the vast numbers of these which are sold commercially be
explained?   These are easy books to read, they represent
familiar old friends who, in some cases, are doing innocuous things which represent high adventure to many young
readers.   As more of this is read it will be found that the
youngsters involved will voluntarily shift to harder serials--
at some point the simpler serial reaches the stage of
"enough."

Ultimately, experience shows that these stories are
left altogether in favor of others of greater interest which
the librarian can suggest; but it must be emphasized that unless there is that in the library to interest each child, many
children will not be in the library long enough to receive
suggestions from the librarians.   (It must also be noted that
not all young patrons receive suggestions from librarians.)

(13) Not only should all bias against fiction in every form
      be eliminated, but this development of thinking also
      illustrates the need to emphasize the great value and
      desirability of extensive reading of fiction over and
      above all other pursuits. Organized facts can still be
      gained by research into non-fictional materials, but
      the prior extensive reading as suggested can provide
      the solid foundations for all areas of information nec-
      essary to greatest possible knowledge and educability.

      This extensive reading of fiction is not something
which can stop with graduation from grade school, since education continues, and therefore the values, insights, and
background of knowledge and understanding which fiction can
add must continue as well.   Additionally, its factual content
must not be overlooked in the search for information for patrons of all ages (in the absence of specific, factual questions)--information in a particularly palatable form.

(14) Certain conclusions corollary to those above are then
      inescapable in relation to required library actions.
      Aside from a required very basic shift in emphasis
      and major changes in collection content, much more
      would be desirable in detailed specification of both
      fictional classification and subject analysis for all
      factual matters treated in a way at all significant
      from an information point of view.   Librarians, to
      fill the needs as analyzed here, then would have to
      be able to advise patrons on reading for information-
      al background in fiction and be able to locate materi-
      als with those backgrounds and desired points of view.
(15) Along the same line of discrimination in selection of
      materials for the collection, but not in the fiction
      classification, of interest to older boys is another
      category which must be mentioned.   One of the inter-
      viewers questioned a boy of high school age who was
      apparently a high school drop-out and definitely a non-
      reader.   When the interviewer attempted to determine
      what this boy had as his interests, a spark was struck.
      He became quite excited in saying that he never went
      to the library because they didn't have the kind of
      "books" that he wanted, but that if the interviewer
      were interested he would take her to see what those
      "books" were.   Upon agreement, he took her to a drug
      store where there sat a number of boys of similar
      description to the interviewee, introduced as his
      friends--all reading avidly magazines on hot-rodders.

These were the "books" referred to earlier.   The excited descriptions of interests in this direction continued for an hour before the interviewer could break
away.

It must be pointed out once more that the reading of
anything can lead to wider interests, greater reading ability
and intensified development of boys like these.   If such magazines had been carried in the library which this boy investigated, some skilled librarian might ultimately have been able
to persuade him that additional information that he might desire is contained in various motor manuals, etc.; it is quite
clear that the druggist will never do this!

(16) It should be pointed out here that although the emphasis in this particular material is on the needs of some
who might be considered below average, the need for
the libraries to provide missing materials for the very
advanced individuals exists in like, but better recognized, manner.

(17) Review of the foregoing leads necessarily to another
very serious question, without any wish--once again--
to wave a red flag; does discrimination or bias in selection not represent a form of censorship?   It is
recognized that librarians generally are strongly opposed to any form of censorship and that normally
this term is thought of in relation to the sexual content of popular books; the censorship which is normally considered in this context is that attempted to be
imposed by self-appointed guardians of the morals of
the community--and sometimes councils and boards
are persuaded to go along with this.   (Quite a different matter than the adults referred to earlier who
wish to have the availability of sex-free materials but
are not attempting to ban the rest from the library.)
However, the basic subject of this point is not the
censorship of the sex material but that which has the
same characteristics in that it effectively bans from
the library certain classes of materials.   Perhaps the
ban is not complete but the existence of the bias constitutes an active attempt to limit or prevent many
patrons from reading that material which they desire.
These might be "fighting words" to librarians, but
some thought might indicate their approach to the
truth.

Recommendation IIC1-4:
Utilize demand-orientation-selection to add books and other materials to the library collection--guided as completely as possible by reader interests, needs and desires insofar as these can be determined; represent all types of materials in the collection in direct proportion to reader interest.

Recommendation IIC1-5:
Eliminate all forms of censorship or bias in the provision of library materials; provide every item or group of items which could be desired by any patron, to the limit of available funds.

Recommendation IIC1-6:
Utilize all materials in library programs which can be of some aid to program patrons, regardless of the field of knowledge which specifies that those materials can be of aid.

Recommendation IIC1-7:
Consider the function of the librarian in relation to the materials of the collection to be that of instructor, guide, and reading counselor and not that of selector or selection determinent except within the context of the previous recommendations.

IIC 1d Some Book Value Considerations

(1)   The first of these has been briefly indicated earlier: the question of inherent value of books vs. the commodity value of those books. Now whether books are considered to have an inherent value or to be a commodity to be supplied at the given place and time in answer to a given need depends strictly upon the goals and objectives involved; book collectors and research libraries necessarily place a great value upon the specific history, quality of binding, printing, etc. as being important to the researches of the few who wish to trace backwards precise occurrences. As has been indicated in many different ways thus far in this report, it is considered that the public library has quite different objectives than these. The public library provides to its patrons reading material with different gradation of content value and information value, but it is basically providing that which numbers of people want rather than the very few. The latter must look

to the research libraries, college libraries, special
libraries, and private collections to make the special
inquiries that go with their unusual investigations.
The general public on the other hand becomes interested in the content of the materials, but only for the
purposes outlined heretofore and not those of highly
specialized research; if one edition of the book is not
available then another is substituted.   Frequently, as
a matter of fact, if one title is not available then another covering similar material can be accepted as
substitute.   Therefore, for the public library, the
concept that books have inherent value must give way
to the concept that the library must supply the contents, the ideas and not the clothing which surrounds
them--this is a fair definition of a commodity.   Acceptance of the commodity theory eliminates the value
of any one copy and implies the need to supply to the
patron the materials themselves; in other words, if a
book wears out in the process of use, this is quite
acceptable, the only question being how to supply the
next sets of requirements as they are presented, a
physically different book being equally able to satisfy
the needs of the new patron as the copy which has
satisfied past needs of other patrons.

Of course, it can be recognized, that the maintaining
of "special" editions in the collection can still fit within the
commodity theory if those special editions are gotten for
such things as illustrations or pictures since these represent
content equally to the printed words.   It does not take a collector or connoisseur to appreciate illustrations or pictures.

Recommendation IIC1-8:
Purchase and hold materials in the collection for their
content only; avoid collectors' editions or others where
the specific copy has special value aside from that of the
words and illustrations within them.

(2) In like manner it could be considered that the public
     library has no business maintaining collections of old
     books because of their special bindings, old bindings,
     historical autographs, old sets, etc., but must be
     concerned, and devote its entire attention to the col-
     lection as a working collection--that is one which pro-
     vides for the needs of the citizenry it serves on a day
     to day, week to week, or month to month basis.   It
     would appear that special collections, regardless of

their non-content historical value, would not be consistent with this viewpoint. Special collections tend to draw off funds and effort from the serving of the needs of the many to the serving of the needs of the very few--and frequently these very few are not members of the community. This is not meant to indicate that all special collections are of no value to the public library and that, for example, the Californiana Collections of the various libraries should be disbanded, but only that the value from the standpoint of the community as a whole and the public library should be considered to be the content of these materials and not those things which would make them valuable to the collector.

The argument is put forward that if a library does not show its reverence for fine bindings and old books, it will not receive the very valuable private collections as gifts when such gifts are to be made. The question which must be asked here is whether such gifts are within the proper framework of the library's operations. As difficult as it might be to see such good and valuable collections go elsewhere, the public library--like all other organizations--must first consider whether there is any way in which the prospective gift can advance the attainment of objectives of the library as a service organization within the community.

(3) Even such things as separate Californiana Collections must be reviewed critically from the standpoint of the desirability of expanding funds and effort here rather than in some other program which might better satisfy public need.

Californiana or other historical materials and collections can very well come within the scope of the library's purpose but this is not automatic. Patron Centered Library Service requires that all such satisfy demand criteria; sufficient usage can justify the materials or collections. The next question is whether such materials (assuming sufficient use to permit the library to obtain and hold them) can justify a separate room, separate personnel, and separate rules and control as is usual for such collections--a highly doubtful matter where a number of libraries are doing the same thing. No library can afford a special, high cost arrangement where volume of usage does not create low unit costs unless there exists a desire to penalize the many for the few--the actual effect of diversion of funds unless low unit costs result.

Recommendation IIC1-9:
Purchase and maintain special, historical materials only
if justified by usage; apply the same criterion to assignment of separate facilities and personnel for such materials.

(4)   Whether stacks are to be open or closed is another
      matter of library policy which bears upon the question
      of provisioning.   The concept of the need for closed
      stacks would appear to be imbedded in the idea of the
      library as a holder or guardian of materials for fu-
      ture generations; open stacks would seem to be more
      compatible with the larger utilization of materials
      hoped for from patrons of the public library.   Today,
      the main reason for the existence of closed stacks
      lies in the possibility of theft.   Of course it must be
      recognized by the proponents of closed stacks that
      even these do not prevent theft, they only make it a
      bit more difficult.

However, if the library is to serve its patrons then
a conclusion must be reached as to whether the large number of patrons are to be deprived of the opportunity to see
freely the holdings of the library or that the few thieves be
permitted to govern the entire relationship so that, even
though held, the materials become not so important to the
operation of the library.   For the latter is the general effect of the closed stack areas.   If, however, the library is
to put in the hands of its patrons those materials which they
can best use, then patrons must get the opportunity to see
those materials in order to make their choices.   It all becomes a question of whether the dog wags the tail or the
tail wags the dog.

A Review of the Freeman Study

by Joseph Becker
Consultant in data processing and library systems; Lecturer, School of Library Science, Catholic University of America; Director of EDUCOM

From his A Review of the Freeman Study of Library Systems for the Public Libraries of Santa Clara, Alameda, and Contra Costa Counties. Bethesda, Md. , The Author, December 1965. p. 12-15, 17; Reprinted by permission of the author.

Book Selection

In this area the Study starts by saying that there is no reliable way by which a library is able to measure the adequacy of its collections to serve the public. It then proceeds to attempt to do so. Conventional methods, i. e. , standard list checking, request analysis, and circulation statistical analysis, were not used by the Study's examiners. Instead, current selection philosophy and policy were reviewed exhaustively and specific recommendations made for improvement. The over-all impression left with the reader is that the library selection process is out of phase with public need and out of date. The Study challenges the librarian's right and ability to make book selection decisions. It tends to believe that the librarian selects books in the light of his own experience or on impulse and that this conflicts with the patron's right to read what he wants. A recommendation is made for "demand-orientation-selection, " but this term is left unexplained in the text.

The importance of the selection librarian's job cannot be overstated. He has an important responsibility to spend money wisely, always keeping in mind the broad purpose and specific interests of the community he serves. The results of his judgment will stand on the shelves as permanent re-

219

minders, either of painstaking selection or haphazard gathering. The selection librarian deals with the very substance
of human communication and is continually making judgments
involving many unknowns: thus, the content value of acquired material is sometimes unknown, its future use is unknown, its relevant relationship to the rest of the book collection is unknown, and so on. Confronted with a great variety of material, a wide spectrum of potential and unknown
users, a limited budget, and the dynamics of information
communication, the selection librarian makes a judgment
which, at best, can be only a compromise. With so many
uncertain factors to take into account, it is remarkable that
libraries function as well as they do. Although systems analysts studying this problem may be able to clear out the
underbrush of extraneous issues, no one yet has come forward with a practical method for balancing the inter-relation-
ships in a clearly superior manner.

Balancing the Collection

        The thrust of comments on selection leads to the fol-
lowing conclusion: "A balanced collection cannot be built by
any amount of impulse buying, but must be the result of a
plan for creating the desired balance." This implies that no
selection plan exists now and that a systematic one should
be developed.

        In particular, the Study recommends that the public
library discontinue the practice of not buying books for its
collections merely because it suspects the titles are in local
special, school, or college libraries. This, it contends, is
an outdated practice, and it recommends that no limitation
be imposed on the acquisition of materials for patron use
despite the availability of such material elsewhere. The financial effects on county budgets of this blanket buying policy
are recognized as critical for the solution of the problem.

        Because of the inability to predict user requirements
and the restriction on dollars available for library book
budgets, the Study eventually reaches the conclusion that it
is not possible to provide everything for everyone. It recognizes that some compromise is required and urges the libraries to use every device open to them to calculate user
need.

        Sections IIC-7 through IIC-7-B use statistical analy-
sis to reveal a serious imbalance between patron demands

and <u>availability of materials in current collections.</u>   Several factors affect this problem: numbers of copies available, selection criteria, diversity of user interest, budget constraints, and space restrictions, among others.   The <u>Study</u> concludes that what the libraries have is not what the public wants.   While it presents no corrective solution, it raises the problem as one deserving further analysis.

Two minor matters discussed in the <u>Study</u> which relate to balancing the collection are: (1) The <u>Study</u> advances some convincing mathematical evidence, involving the laws of probability, to prove the thesis that buying--i.e. , by the method of predicting best sellers--is more expensive than waiting to see which books become best sellers and then buying them at the retail price; (2) the <u>Study</u> recommends that the legal restrictions which now prevent some libraries from selling unwanted books be lifted and that annual book sales be held to bring in revenue for new book purchases.

* * *

Non-book Material

Non-book material, such as magazines, newspapers, pictures, vertical files, and documentation films constitute an important adjunct to the book resources of a library.   Because of their special information value, the <u>Study</u> recommends that usage studies be made by the libraries in order to develop suitable criteria for deciding what non-book materials to buy and how to maintain them.   Some reference is made to the probable growth of micro-publishing and to its potential effect on the 16 libraries.   While the <u>Study</u> does not recommend that specific programs be initiated at the present time, it does suggest that librarians become familiar with the new media by receiving basic indoctrination and training in associated methods and equipment.   Although the comments on microfilm are brief, the <u>Study</u> evidences considerable understanding of the present "state-of-the-art." The same is true with respect to the authors' knowledge of another technical area--teaching machines.   The <u>Study</u> contends that the newer educational media are certain to have an impact on the public library, as well as on the school library.   With the acquisition of these new forms in ever-increasing number, the library will be forced to decide which methods and equipment will be most useful for making these resources available to the public.

What Should be Collected?

by J. Perriam Danton

From his Book Selection and Collections; A Comparison of German and American University Libraries. New York and London, Columbia University Press, 1963. p. 122-130; Reprinted by permission of Columbia University Press.

Current Versus Older Books

In so far as choice must be made, and some choice is almost always necessary, Should a library prefer the new current titles to the older? There are good arguments for answering the question either way.

For buying the new:
1. The demand for most books, even those of long-enduring scholarly value, has been shown to be greatest immediately after publication. If current books are not generously bought, the most immediate present interests and needs of the library's clientele will be unfulfilled; the library's position and the work of its users will seriously suffer. (Counter argument: Both the long-range value of, and the present need for, an older title may be greater than for the current one.)

2. The library can get more books for its money since it won't have to pay out-of-print prices, costs of telegrams, cables, etc.

3. Many books, not purchased on, or soon after, publication, will later be imperatively needed and will then be out-of-print, expensive and difficult, or impossible, to obtain. (Counter argument: Copyflo, Xerox, etc., can make much research material readily available.)

4. If the library year by year does successfully the task of buying all important current publications, its out-of-

222

print problems and costs will eventually become relatively
fewer.

For emphasizing the older:
    1. Despite the conscientious exercise of one's best
judgment, many current books prove to have little permanent importance; therefore, monographs should not be purchased until time has proved their value. (Counter argument: If books are needed and useful today, they should be
bought now, regardless of the judgment which time may render upon them.)

    2. Some out-of-print titles, offered the library today,
have been long sought, often for years. The opportunity to
buy these and other out-of-print desiderata, if not seized today, may not come again; or, if it comes, the price is likely to be still higher.

    3. Many, perhaps most, really important current
books are likely to be available later on in reprinted or new
editions, or in microreproduction. (Counter arguments:
Every librarian can cite a list of needed works not so available; the later edition is sometimes not as good as the earlier; the various costs and difficulties involved in acquiring,
maintaining, and using large collections of microreproduced
material must be taken into account.)

    Although, as partially suggested, some of these cate-
gorical statements are open to argument, it seems apparent
that no final answer to the question is ever likely to be possible and that universally applicable generalization, ignoring
a host of determining variables, is impracticable. The experience of the German libraries as a result of the two
world wars is, however, pertinent. In 1914-1948 and 1940-
1946 Germany was completely cut off from most foreign book
markets. Despite the most strenuous efforts, and major financial support from the Notgemeinschaft der Deutschen Wis-
senschaft and its successor, the Deutsche Forschungsgemein-
schaft, serious library lacks resulting from the two wars'
isolation existed as late as the 1940s and the 1960s respectively. Programs for the purchase of foreign journal and
monographic literature were begun in 1949 and 1951 respectively.

    Thus, a man who happened to be working at the Uni-
versity of Göttingen on the question of book selection for university libraries, found that the library lacked, among other

publications of the time, Numbers 1 and 2 of Volume VI
(1945) of College and Research Libraries. The issues were
out of print and unavailable by the time the end of World
War II made possible the resumption of purchasing from
abroad. In fact, some titles which the libraries would have
purchased on publication immediately following World War I,
when the catastrophic inflation had practically the same effect on the libraries' foreign acquisitions as the war itself,
had still not been acquired forty years later.

This experience would seem to constitute a strong
argument for a general emphasis on current publications--
even if we optimistically assume that a future war will not
again halt the international flow of print.

A further point arising out of the political and social
developments of our time, may be observed. In the 1950s
and early 1960s more than thirty new, independent countries
will establish universities. Many have already done so.
Among the dozens of universities created in such countries
since World War II, may be mentioned the University of
Ghana; the University of Karachi and Rajshahi University,
Pakistan; the University of Libya; Bihar University and the
University of Peshawar, India; the University of Dakar; the
University of Ife, Nigeria; Bar Ilan University, Tel Aviv;
the University of Sumatra; the University of Huê, Vietnam;
and the University of the Ryukyus.

In addition, population and other pressures are forcing older nations to create new universities or to bring about
the upward academic development of existing institutions.
Michigan State College and Colorado Agricultural and Mechan
ical College have become state universities. The University
of Łódź, the University Austral of Chile, the University of
Chihuahua, Mexico, the Haile Selassie I University, and the
University of the Saarland--to cite a few examples only--are
post-World War II creations. West Germany is establishing
three new universities, at Bochum, Bremen, and Regensburg
to provide for the enormously increased and rapidly growing
student population. For the same reason, California is
swiftly developing three college campuses into full-fledged
general universities and has created three new ones. England's so-called "red brick" institutions of higher education,
a phenomenon of mid-twentieth century, have steadily increased in number and have become, or are developing into,
true universities.

The point of all this is to suggest that the demand and competition for books is bound to increase in the years ahead. The increase will be especially strong because many of the new and coming universities are in countries which, as yet, produce little in the way of general academic and scholarly literature. To be sure, the demand will be for almost all kinds of print, not simply current titles, of interest to universities. But the crux of the matter is that this expanded demand is certain to cause more current publications to go out of print faster, even though edition sizes will increase with demand.

Collecting for the Present Versus Collecting for the Future

Should a university library place its greater collecting emphasis upon the acquisition of books to fill "current" needs, expressed or supposed, or should its selection policy rather be more directed toward "building for the future"? From a strict point of view, "future" obviously means anything later than "now," and therefore applies to tomorrow, next week, next month, and next semester, as well as next year and five or ten years from now. Practically, "present" or "current" may equate with "expressed" or "assumed." Thus, the books a professor indicates he will need for a seminar he is to give, or a paper he expects to write next semester, may be held to constitute examples of both expressed and current need. When, however, the library buys a book without such an expression of either current or expressed (assumed) need, it must be buying for the future. In these terms the question is far from an academic one.

It may be granted at the outset that we are not likely ever to find a hard and fast answer to it. The instructional and research programs in different disciplines, the nature and status of collections supporting them, institutional policy for the present and future, available funds, the availability of desired literature (e.g., there is little published today in Amharic, but may be much a decade or two hence); and a host of other variables prohibit categorical judgment.

It is, for example, clear that the more limited a library's funds, the less choice it will be called upon or privileged to make. Carried to the extreme, if the library's budget is sufficient only to supply demands resulting from immediate teaching and research needs, it will obviously

have nothing to spend for the needs of the future.   Conversely, a library with a very large book budget may have
the best of two worlds by being able, at the same time, to
acquire "everything" for which a specific need exists today
and much which anticipates future need.   Most university libraries fall between the two extremes.

The German library's more generally narrow, re-
search-material-oriented collecting policy, discussed earlier
in this chapter, results in the belief that most of what is
acquired is being bought both for the present and the future.
Some German librarians go so far as to maintain that this
is virtually one hundred percent the case, and there is no
reason to question their conviction.   No American university
librarian could take the same position since much of the secondary material for undergraduate teaching, recreational
reading, and reserve book collections, however much used
today, will be obsolete and of little or no value some years
hence.   Nonetheless, it seems clear, as Fussler has pointed
out, "that book buying for a large research library tends to
be very strongly oriented toward future or potential use,
even in subject fields where the institution has a current
and well established interest."   On the other hand, we may
assume that a considerable porportion of the materials acquired by any university library, even that able only to fulfill today's needs, will be useful also in the future.   The
better the library, that is, the better its collection has been
built up and the higher the quality of the material which has
been acquired from day to day, the greater the proportion is
likely to be.   This does not, of course, mean, as has been
pointed out in another connection, that the scholar fifty years
from now will necessarily use a work for the same purpose
as the scholar today.   It does mean that the important piece
of writing has enduring value.

It is axiomatic, also, that a work which gives some
assurance of being able to satisfy future as well as current
need is preferable to one which does only the latter.   This
leads to the conclusion that when choice is present, either
as a possibility or necessity, the original account is better
than the retelling of the account, the native text better than
the translation, the first edition (generally) better than the
reprint, the letters (generally) preferable to the biography
based upon them, etc.

When we speak of "satisfying current demand" we
should be quite clear that what is meant is not primarily the

purchase of a book when someone needs it. On the contrary. What we mean, or should mean, is the library's supplying of the materials needed at this particular point in time. The scholar using the ideal book collection, built up by ideal day-to-day selection, (and with an ideal budget!) would theoretically never lack a single title; everything he required would already have been secured by the library in anticipation of his needs. This is a generally accepted view, both abroad and in the United States. "In principle, a properly set up library should anticipate the researcher's every wish, so that the books he needs are already available when he requests them." The measure of the great libraries is that they approach this ideal.

As Redenbacher quite properly points out, "Inexcusable lacks would result if one were to follow the principle of waiting [to acquire material] until it was actually required or proposed for acquisition by the users." No university library known to the writer buys exclusively on the basis of present expressed demand, though a few come unhappily close to doing so. On the other hand, American university library philosophy would question in part Redenbacher's juxtaposed dictum: "Immediate demand does not constitute for the scholarly library a determining criterion of acquisition; the need (Bedarf) of the day cannot, therefore, be made the foundation of selection." If this view is carried to its logical conclusion (and unless the word Bedarf is given its secondary meaning of "desire" or "want," rather than "need"), the result is that the library puts itself in the position of claiming to know better than the user what he requires to do his work. Either that, or the library says, in effect, we will not (always) try to give you what you say you need. Either position seems from a broad philosophical and educational view, and entirely aside from any national considerations, quite untenable. Redenbacher later grants that, as "the object of use is a characteristic mark of the library, the value of utilization may be ignored only in exceptional cases." But this concession would seem to most American librarians not to go far enough.

On the basis of logic as much as factual evidence then, we might say that the library should fulfill, by anticipation in so far as it can, the current teaching and research needs of its clientele; that it should do so, in so far as possible through the acquisition of materials having permanent value and maximum probable future usefulness; and that it should, additionally, to the extent of its financial ability, buy

long-range on the basis of its knowledge of the library's
strengths and weaknesses, of the institution's future program, of faculty interests, of research trends, and of the
world literary output.

The Role of Cooperative Effort

Nothing has thus far been said, and very little need
be said, about the effects on a library's selection and collecting policy of cooperative measures and the proximity of
other research collections. The discussion to this point has
tacitly assumed that a university library will be largely sufficient unto itself, except that its need for some of the genuinely seldom-used, scarce, and unusual will be satisfied by
interlibrary borrowing. This is often the fact; Cornell, Er-
langen, Göttingen, Illinois, and Würzburg being, because of
their relative geographic isolation and distance from other
research libraries, fair examples. Very often, however, it
is certainly not the fact. Munich, but a few blocks from the
great Bavarian State Library, need not acquire research materials at the most intensive level in many fields if its students and faculty are accorded easy access to the State Library's collections. The same is true of Marburg, almost
next door to the Westdeutsche Bibliothek, containing nearly
2,000,000 volumes of the former Prussian State Library in
Berlin. The cooperative arrangements between Duke and
North Carolina; the University of Chicago and Northwestern
(with, also, the Newberry and the John Crerar), and those
embraced in the Midwest Inter-Library Center are too well
known to need detailing here. Three points may be made.
First, a library certainly need not buy the most specialized
research materials if its clientele has ready access to them
at another library in the locality; every library should, where
possible, seek cooperative agreements of this kind which
will increase its purchasing power, reduce the competition
for scarce material, and further scholarship. Second, no
library should expect another to bear the burden of its needs
except for the rare, the unusual, and the relatively little
used. A few university libraries on both sides of the Atlantic, readily admit that they do not have, on the average,
40-80 percent of the titles required for a dissertation. The
justification for these universities offering work for the doctor's degree seems dubious. And third, the extent to which
a library can afford not to acquire specialized research materials in fields of concern to its scholars, varies indirectly as the distance to a library which has those materials.

No reasonable man will object to having to spend two hours
in travel, or waiting a day or two (Princeton to Philadelphia
or New York, Mainz to Frankfurt, Ann Arbor to Detroit,
Stanford to Berkeley, Bonn to Cologne) once or twice a
year.   He will object mightily if he is asked to do so once
or twice a week, and rightly so.   And the greater and oftener his expenditure of time or the delay, the greater his
objection.   And rightly so.   If his university cannot, most
of the time, provide the materials which will enable him
effectively to do his work as a scholar, it has no business
pretending to be a research institution in the field.

Types and Sources of Material

A great deal of the writing on university library book
selection is concerned with the types or forms of material--
journals, microreproductions, rare books, newspapers, so-
called ephemera, etc. --which a library should acquire; foreign versus native literature; bibliographical sources and
criteria for the selection of individual titles; means of ac-
quisition--purchase, of various kinds, including en bloc, gift,
and exchange--and similar questions.   They are all of great
importance to the acquisition program of the library.   In the
present view, however, as suggested at the beginning of the
Introduction, they have nothing whatever to do with fundamental book-selection policy.   That policy, in a single sentence, concerns the library's provision of the materials
which will be of most value, now and in the future, for the
needs of the library's users.   The questions and matters
just enumerated, therefore, are either of a peripheral, practical, or expedient nature; or, being concerned with the "getting" of material, are both practical and chronologically subsequent to the operation of selection.   The issue here is:
Does this graphic record contain material which this library
should have?   If this question is answered affirmatively, it
matters not one particle whether the record is a book, a
journal, a holograph letter, a newspaper, a map, or a microfilm.   It matters not one particle, except in the completely
expedient matter of cost, whether it is purchased--or how,
where, or from whom--or acquired through gift or exchange.
It matters not one particle whether it is a single-sheet
broadside or a ten-volume set.   And it matters not a particle whether the record is in English, German, Japanese,
or Polish--although, granted availability of the material in
the native language this will, for obvious reasons, be preferred.

In view, however, of the tremendous value to university libraries of the materials which they receive through gift and exchange, additional brief comment on the topic may be desirable.   Gifts have been an important source of acquisitions from the very beginnings of most libraries; exchanges no less so since at least the founding of the learned and scientific societies in the seventeenth century.   Increasingly, universities themselves have become major publishers much of the output being of prime scholarly value.   The university library is commonly given a number of copies, particularly of dissertations (when printed) and of official and scholarly serial publications, to exchange for similar items emanating from other institutions.   A library may carry on as many as four thousand regular exchanges, a quarter or more of them with institutions of higher education.   The vigorous prosecution of an exchange program is obviously much to the library's advantage in view of the quality of the material received and the savings to the book budget.   Very few items secured through exchange are rejected.   Yet, to repeat, the criteria for the selection of gift and exchange material should be exactly the same as for purchased material.

Selective Acquisitions at Yale

by William R. Pullen   Librarian, State College Li-
                                brary, Atlanta, Georgia

From Studies in Library Administration Problems;
Eight Reports from a Seminar in Library Admin-
istration Directed by Keyes D. Metcalf.   New
Brunswick, N. J. , Graduate School of Library
Service, Rutgers - The State University, 1960.
p. 26-7; 34-7; Reprinted by permission of the
Dean, Graduate School of Library Service, Rutgers
- The State University.

Connected closely with the change in philosophy as to
the acquisition policy noted above was a change in the attitude as to what material would be needed in the Sterling Library.   Prior to 1951 or 1952, all of the other libraries on
the campus, with the exception of Medicine, were more or
less independent of Sterling.   At that time, there was a tendency to centralize the administration of all of these libraries under the University Librarian.   Because of this
centralization, it was possible to bring about a far better
utilization of the material among the departmental and school
libraries and the main library.   This, in turn, made it possible to reduce to some extent certain duplication which
heretofore had taken place.

At the present time, there is no written general
acquisitions policy; there is, however, a written policy for
the specific fields of juveniles, history, religion and medicine.   The last two of these have been described as "divisions of responsibilities" since there are strong school libraries in these two fields.   An attempt was made to write
a policy for state documents, but this attempt proved to be
abortive.

"Selective acquisitions" at the present time is best described as a "state of mind" rather than as an actual pro-

gram. The implementation and realization of such a program may take a number of years since it is really a long
range one. Now, there is little limitation, other than funds,
on what will be acquired for a faculty member. More definite, however, is what will be permanently retained. In
other words, more and more material being acquired is being considered expendable. The acquisition program is
geared to the University curriculum, the research needs of
the students and faculty, and the strength of existing collections. The amount of material acquired within a particular
field may be described as falling within four categories.

The first of these categories, and that of the greatest
depth, is for a field in which the Library attempts to have
an extensive and comprehensive collection. This would apply to a field in which the Library is already exceptionally
strong and is committed to remain strong--a field in which
a scholar anywhere could expect to find practically everything at Yale. It would mean collecting the "bad" as well as
the "good" material. Since the emphasis is on complete coverage, the acquisition problem is not one of selection, but
one of making sure that everything is acquired.

The second category, with less depth than the first,
would be for those fields in which the Library would want
to acquire all of the better-than-average books. The goal
of the acquisitions program in such a field would be to satis
fy the research needs of this institution. Here the selection
process begins to operate.

The third category, and still decreasing in depth,
would be for a field in which only a basic working collection
would be needed and would be for those areas in which there
is little or no research work at this institution. Within this
category, the acquisition program would be highly selective.

The fourth category, and the most shallow of all,
would be for those fields in which no work is being done at
this institution and in which little or no material would be
collected. The acquisition within these fields would be very
highly selective, since only those items of a most general
nature or those items which also had to do with other fields
would be considered.

Conclusions and Recommendations

So we see that this study has not shown concrete evidence of the effect of "selective acquisitions" at Yale since the program is still described as a "state of mind" and has not been fully implemented and realized and since the available records do not give the desired or comparable information which is needed. We feel, however, that the study has pointed up certain conclusions upon which recommendations for the implementation of the program may be based.

To begin with, an "all embracing" or "get all and keep everything" policy of acquisition does not involve the selection process beyond a decision between purchasing one or another item because of a lack of funds. The acquisition problem, rather, becomes one of ferreting out all of the material in a particular field. On the other hand, an acquisition policy involving the selection process, because of the very nature of the word "selection" itself, involves more care and knowledge or wisdom than the other. In our opinion, therefore, a program of "selective acquisitions," in order to be successful, will necessitate a clear statement of the aims and goals of such an acquisition program, the adoption of certain planning devices and the better utilization of the knowledge of experts in the selection process.

We recommend that a general acquisition policy be written for the Library and that the writing of individual policies for various fields (which was begun some time ago) be continued. It is not within the scope of this paper to present fully the arguments for written acquisition policies. Others have already done this far more ably than we could ever hope to do. [1] Suffice it for us to say, however, that every library, no matter the size, which is involved in book selection, has some guiding principles, whether they are recognized as such or not and whether they are written or unwritten, consistent or inconsistent, logical or illogical. These principles make up the acquisition policy.

We do not wish to imply, however, that such principles are easy to ascertain and set down on paper. On the contrary, they can be most difficult if they are not now clearly defined in one's mind. It may mean an evaluation of certain parts of the book collections and considerable consultation with the faculty and the university administrative officials to ascertain the teaching and research objectives of the university as a whole. The writing of an acquisition policy cannot be done overnight, and cannot be done by one person, but will involve the work of various staff and faculty members over a period of time.

Nor, do we wish to imply that any written policy will dispense with judgments and decisions on the part of the librarian in the book selection process. No selection process can ever be automatic, but must depend on the personal judgment of the librarian. If this is the case, then, what use would be served by writing such a policy? In the first place, it would tend to clarify certain principles which are not now clear and consequently would tend to make the book collecting more consistent. Secondly, such a statement would serve to inform the staff of the library of the aims and objectives of the acquisition program and thereby help develop their understanding of and cooperation in the program. Thirdly, the discussion on and writing of such a policy would also do much towards developing a faculty understanding of and cooperation in the program. Lastly, such a written statement would do much to help focus the attention of the university administrative officials on the part which should be played by the Librarian in basic decisions dealing with any changes in the scope or direction of the research programs.

We further recommend that a system of internal budgeting be inaugurated within the Library which would involve the allocation of the non-restricted book funds by the University Librarian at the beginning of each year according to the fields of knowledge and the recording by the Order Department of the expenditures by such fields. Such an allocation of funds would be solely for the use of the library staff as a planning device in bringing about a balanced and consistent book collecting program, and would not necessarily have to be made known to the faculty. Such a system should be flexible in that it could be changed by the University Librarian during the year if he saw fit and in that there would be "contingency" or "reserve" allocations to take care of the unexpected items which became available and a "general" allocation for those items which do not fall into any one field.

Such a system would mean that somewhere in the selection process, an indication of the field of knowledge would have to be made on the order request and that the Order Department would have to establish a system of record-keeping according to allocations. The latter could easily be

accomplished by filing the accession slips by fields of knowledge[2] or by establishing a simple record similar to the book
plate record now used for the several funds.

And lastly, we recommend the immediate establishment of a position within the Order Department of a selection officer for the social sciences.   Such a person would
need an advanced degree, preferably a Ph. D. , in one of the
social sciences and a library degree and/or library experience.   He should be a specialist and scholar in some field
to the extent that he would have, or soon would gain, the
respect of the faculty, yet he should be young enough so that
he would not be so specialized in his views and therefore
would be able to take an overall view of the Library's collections within this area.

Such a person would work closely with the faculty
members in the social sciences and through personal contacts
made with them in their offices and in the Library he would
arouse their interest and cooperation in the evaluation and
building of collections and the writing of acquisition policies
in their fields.   He would check bibliographies and dealers'
catalogs and bridge the gaps where faculty participation and
interest are lacking.   The work of such a person would not
interfere with that of the Associate Librarian, but would be
supplementary in nature.

The Library Administration has given some consideration to the plan, when funds permit, of adding four specialists within the Order Department: one for the physical sciences, one for the biological sciences, one for the humanities and one for the social sciences.   Such a plan may have
its merits, but we consider the immediate need to be for
the addition of one for the social sciences, since the physical and biological sciences depend heavily on the journals
and current material and since many of them have their departmental libraries.   The humanities are better provided
for through the chief selection officer, the Curators and the
heavier participation of the faculty in the selection process.

Notes

1. For recent articles on this subject see Fussler, Herman
   H. "Acquisition Policy: A Symposium--The Larger
   University Library," CRL, 14 (1953), 363-366;
   Vosper, Robert "Acquisition Policy--Fact or Fancy?"
   CRL, 14 (1953), 367-370; and Bach, Harry "Acquisi-

tion Policy in the American Library" <u>CRL</u>, 18 (1957), 441-451.

2. These are now kept for one year and filed by author.

Building the Book Collection

by Humphrey A. Olsen   Currently Librarian at Cumber-
land College in Kentucky

From Library Trends 14:156-65, October 1965;
Reprinted by permission of Library Trends,
Graduate School of Library Science, University of
Illinois.

Functioning as part of a comparatively new institution operating in many areas that have not yet been pin-
pointed, junior college libraries face many of the same problems of their own. Enrollments have mushroomed in this
country from less than 500,000 after World War II[1] to
927,534 in 1963, with the increase over the previous year
alone amounting to 13 per cent.[2] In 1963 one in every four
persons starting college enrolled at a junior college, and it
is predicted that by 1970, 75 per cent of those entering college will first attend a community college.[3] With the enrollment explosion, it now takes all the running junior college
librarians can do just to hold their own, and they will have
to run twice as fast to improve conditions.

Attention will be focused in this paper on the differences between junior and senior institutions which affect the
book collection, the characteristics of students, the facets
of the collection, book selection, the reference collection,
public documents, paperbacks, periodicals, and microforms.

One main difference between junior and senior colleges is the lack of research and research collections in the
former. This simplifies matters for junior colleges, whereas other differences add complications: junior colleges can
only influence students for two years instead of four or more as
senior institutions can, and the diversity of junior college
offerings often exceeds that of four-year colleges of the
same size. The vast majority do not even remain two years,
earlier transferring to other colleges, going off to jobs, or

just dropping out.   Instead of bewailing the fact that not all
students who attend a junior college can profit from the experience, these institutions capitalize on the situation by trying to do everything they can to help any misfits during their
short stay, whether it be a few weeks, a few months, or a
year.   The library, naturally, must do all it can to influence these persons as well as those who stay two years.

        Norman E. Tanis has pointed out the "... complex
nature of the American junior college..." and the often "bewildering diversity" of these institutions whose "burgeoning
enrollments" are usually not accompanied by adequate finances. [4]   Besides general courses and the traditional liberal
arts, junior colleges offer terminal programs, technical and
apprenticeship training, preparation for business and management, and adult programs--to mention only a few.   Besides
lacking sufficient finances, their libraries are often handicapped by staff shortages, lack of space, and the constantly
rising costs of books and supplies.   For example, in public
junior colleges the ratio of professional library staff to students in 1963/64 was 1:1,054 and in private colleges
1:325, [3] whereas the standards call for one professional staff
member for each 500 students enrolled.

        The junior college library, operating in a challenging
and little-explored territory between high school, vocational
and technical school, senior college, and the adult department of the public library, has inherited some of the characteristics of each of these institutions, but the characteristics have been put together in different proportions in a new
setting.   The majority of students, just emerging from adolescence, are from eighteen to twenty-one years old.   But
allowance must be made for make-up, noncredit courses for
those who read at the eighth grade level (or lower) or have
other deficiencies, and for an older group with no upper age
limit taking night classes.   Thus in many cases the junior
college provides a final opportunity to stimulate young adults
to develop into well-rounded citizens alert to national and
world problems and at the same time capable of enjoying literature, music, art, and other cultural activities.   The book
collection must meet the needs of these diverse groups.

        Besides taking into consideration the characteristics
of the students and the curricular offerings of the school,
junior college librarians in building their collections need to
make extensive studies of the effects of reading on students,
particularly on students who come from homes with little or

no cultural background.   For instance, a teacher or librarian may recommend a book which he has enjoyed and from
which he has profited, but how much does he really know
about its appeal to and its influence on a student who is not
book-minded?   In the past we have assumed that such a
recommendation is an important influence; but libraries today can no longer afford to operate on hunches.   Long-range
effects also must be examined thoroughly; why do many students who appear to be adequately motivated while in college
lose interest in serious reading after graduation?

Albert Lake, although a public librarian, has set
down some goals that apply equally to junior college libraries.   The central collection "...would consist of books
which have one or more qualities by which they have a-
chieved a kind of immortality or give promise of doing so."[5]
He describes a peripheral sub-collection made up of the minor novel, superficial commentaries, and trivial philosophies
(which ideally should have little or no place in the junior
college), as well as reference and other such books which
are more concerned with facts than literary value.[6]   Such
a book as Rachel Carson's The Sea Around Us falls in
Lake's first category by reason of its superb imaginative approach, and serves as an admirable introduction to the subject.[7]   Librarians should be on the lookout for similar
books.

The writer is acquainted with senior college and university librarians who strive to acquire attractively illustrated editions whenever they are available, editions such as
Heritage Press publications and the Dodd, Mead Great Illustrated Classics.   Surely it is even more important to select
such books for junior college students, many of whom have
difficulty in interpreting print.

In addition to books supporting the curriculum and
the philosophy of the school, the library should build a collection of professional books to meet the needs of the faculty,
and should also offer recreational reading.   The latter area
may be less important where public library and paperback
outlets are handy.

Today's standard of 20,000 volumes for a junior college is a far cry from that of 4,000 set by the American
Association of Junior Colleges in 1930,[8] but in the next few
years this number will doubtless go even higher as enrollments swell, course offerings multiply, honors courses

spread, and more teachers forsake the concept of a single
textbook.   Nationally only 23. 4 per cent of junior college libraries meet the present standard, and the average number
of books per student in public junior colleges is only 7. 7,
and in private ones 35. 8. [3]   In fifty of the sixty-two libraries
surveyed by the writer, for which statistics were available,
the average holdings were 16, 738 volumes, the range from
4, 000 to 41, 750.   The average number of books added for
this same group of libraries during 1963/64 was 1, 759, from
a low of 300 (in two libraries) to 4, 702.[9]   It is not surprising that the library with the largest collection added the
greatest number of books, nor that one of the libraries adding 300 had the smallest collection.

The collection should be well-balanced with the intention of covering all phases of human activity, not just those
dictated by the course offerings.   Some idea of suitable percentages for different fields can be obtained from studying
standard lists, but each school has its peculiar characteristics, and percentages must be worked out with these in mind.

For the forty-eight libraries which reported the per
cent of the educational and general budget of the school spent
on the library, the average was 4. 7, the lowest, 1. 8, and
the highest, 12. 5.   Fifteen libraries had 5 per cent or above,
with thirty-three falling below that mark. [9]   On a national
basis 47. 3 per cent spend 5 per cent or more. [3]

The average proportion of the book budget reserved to
be spent at the discretion of the librarian for buying encyclopedias, general books, and others crossing departmental lines,
etc. was 37 per cent in the 28 libraries reporting this item.
The range was from a low of 11 per cent to a high of 95 per
cent.   Nine librarians reported that 100 per cent of the fund
was spent at their discretion; four reported no formal allotment, two stated the percentage was unknown, and one each
said the amount was variable or none was allotted to be spent
at the discretion of the librarian.

Libraries usually allocate amounts annually to departments on the basis of need.   Many librarians find it advantageous to earmark a certain portion of the budget each year
to be used in strengthening a weak area.   As mentioned
earlier in discussion of how to achieve a balanced collection,
some idea of the importance of each field can be obtained
from studying standard lists, although this information must
always be modified to meet local conditions.

No individual should control entirely or almost entirely the process of selection. This statement applies to
the head librarian or to any other person, no matter how
well-trained and qualified he may be. In no single case
among the sixty-two libraries surveyed did only one person
do all the choosing. In thirty-nine libraries, however, the
head librarian had the chief responsibility for selection; in
ten libraries the teaching faculty had this responsibility. In
three libraries the head librarian shared the responsibility
equally with the teaching faculty; in three other instances
he shared equally with the other members of the library
staff, and in two cases equally with library staff, teaching
faculty, administration, and students. In five instances other library staff members had the main responsibility, but
of course this would be impossible in libraries with a single
professionally trained librarian. Forty-three stated that
students participated in selection, and in twenty-six cases a
library committee participated. Since the head librarian
in many libraries is the person chiefly responsible for selection, even though in reality his role is mainly that of coordinator, it is valuable if he has had intensive bibliographic training in at least one subject field.

Branscomb's observation about the advantage a small
library holds over a large one reads easily but is difficult
to carry out in practice: "The fact that a small library intelligently selected is a better library than a larger one
chosen without much discrimination, makes it easily possible
for a college to overcome a financial handicap by careful
planning."[10] Many times the small library is located far
from large libraries where the librarian would have a chance
to examine books before buying. The small library is more
likely to be understaffed, with fewer selection aids, and
poorly financed. Often selection must be done after hours
or in time snatched from other vital duties.

Fewer book selection aids are available which meet
the specific needs of junior college libraries than is true of
elementary, high school, and public libraries. The new entry in the field of book selection periodicals is Choice,
which, although it is slanted toward the senior liberal arts
college, was rated very useful by twenty-seven librarians,
fairly useful by nine, and of limited value by six. One librarian ignored the three categories suggested by the writer
and labeled it "useful" without any qualification. Nineteen
either had not seen it, were not ready to assess its value,
or chose to ignore that part of the questionnaire. The

writer requested librarians to list the six most valuable aids
in order of their value, and Choice garnered more first
place votes--seventeen--than any other aid, and was mentioned twenty-nine times in all. Library Journal, although
it received only ten first place votes (two of them for its
book reviews on cards), was mentioned thirty-six times, or
more than any other aid. New York Times Book Review
was placed first by nobody, yet was listed by thirty. The
Booklist and Subscription Books Bulletin: A Guide to Current
Books was the first choice of five librarians and was mentioned twenty-seven times in all. Saturday Review, with no
first or second places, totaled nineteen mentions; Publishers'
Weekly was rated first by four and was mentioned a total of
seventeen times. Publishers' catalogs and advertisements also were first choice of four, with a total of seventeen mentions. Book Review Digest received eleven votes; Book
Week, ten. The London Times Literary Supplement was
mentioned by only three librarians, but two of them rated it
first--which may suggest that many junior colleges are in-
sufficiently acquainted with this aid. New York Review of
Books was cited three times, and Wilson Library Bulletin
six times for its reviews of reference books.

Of the selection aids in book form, Charles Trinkner's Basic Books for Junior College Libraries was first
choice of all the aids in five cases, and was mentioned a
total of nine times. [11] Hester Hoffman's Reader's Adviser,
which received no first place votes, was mentioned by elev-
en. [12] Frank Bertalan's Books for Junior Colleges, probably
because it is outdated (1954) and only a supplemental list,
was mentioned only three times; a new basic edition, however, is being prepared and will include out-of-print as well
as in-print titles. [13] Subject Guide to Books in Print and
Books in Print, publications of R. R. Bowker Co., were mentioned six times and five times, respectively. Interestingly,
the Florida State Department of Education Basic Materials
series was cited by two librarians, neither of them in Florida. [14]

Of the sixty-two libraries surveyed, five reported a
continuing program of checking against standard lists, while
twenty-five others had checked against such lists since 1959.
Other librarians were right in pointing out the scarcity of
good recent junior college booklists; others stated that no library should depend too much on lists.

Thirty-five of the sixty-two libraries reported weeding

constantly to eliminate out-of-date materials. In many cases,
however, the wish is doubtless stronger than reality; of forty
librarians reporting number of books withdrawn, the average
was 205 volumes excluding two libraries which must have
been undergoing a major overhaul in withdrawing 4,830 and
3,511 volumes, respectively. [9]

Most persons agree that the library should provide
material on all sides of controversial questions, but the application of this principle to specific cases is often difficult.
How many and what books should the library have in favor
of Communism? If a local Birch Society presents the library with twenty-five books on the far right, should the library accept them and then proceed to balance them with an
equal number on the far left?

Junior college librarians can often save money by co-
operating with other libraries in their neighborhood, particularly by cutting down on duplicate buying of expensive sets
which will receive comparatively little use. They can also
make use of interlibrary loans to supplement their collections. Of the thirty-nine libraries reporting interlibrary
loans, the average for 1963/64 was forty-six. Although all
interlibrary loans were lumped together under "interlibrary
loan transactions," presumably most were loans from other
libraries. The largest number of such loans reported was
305 and the smallest was 13. Of the eleven libraries not reporting interlibrary loans, five had less than 10,000 books
each, two less than 12,000, two were near the 20,000 mark,
and one had 29,000 volumes. [9] Surely libraries with under
20,000 books could profitably use interlibrary loan.

Textbooks should be purchased sparingly and only when
no other more satisfactory material is available. Multiple
copies should only be added when their purchase is clearly
justified; this is particularly true in a small library, which
already is likely to suffer from a shortage of suitable titles.

The reference collection will never include all the
books which might be referred to for information but does
include the books most likely to be consulted for specific information. The number will vary from library to library,
but twenty-six libraries which reported this item to the
writer in 1963 had an average of 1,390 reference volumes
(excluding bound periodicals). The average ratio of their
reference collections to total bookstock was 8.4 per cent.
Since even college and university libraries feel the need for

at least one set of encyclopedias at the high school level,
such as World Book Encyclopedia, junior colleges will feel
a similar need.   Constance Winchell's Guide to Reference
Books was mentioned by eight librarians as an essential selection aid, and others mentioned The Booklist and Subscrip
tion Books Bulletin and Wilson Library Bulletin.   Because o
the high cost, reference sets should be purchased only after
careful consideration.

Documents--United Nations, national, and state--
should be acquired as needed from catalogs issued by various agencies.   But if there is a government depository near
by, the junior college library may not need to duplicate docu
ments available there.   Small libraries, in particular,
should supplement their limited holdings with pamphlets obtained free or at a reasonable price through information
furnished in the Vertical File Index.

In the sixty-two libraries surveyed by the writer,
paperbacks are purchased by forty-eight when hard-bound edi
tions are not available and by twenty-four libraries for additional copies of hard-bound editions.   Thirty-eight libraries
purchase paperbacks and have them bound, while four others
sometimes do this.   Four libraries mentioned reinforcing
paperbacks instead of binding them, even though hardbounds
are available, in order to save money, particularly in cases
where the paperbacks would receive relatively little use.
Three purchase prebound paperbacks, and two libraries have
uncataloged collections of popular paperbacks, such as mysteries and westerns.   No library reported that it was currently selling paperbacks, although one had done so in the
past but had given up the practice because of a limited staff.
As vending machines become available which will make it
possible for libraries to sell selected paperbacks, libraries
may enter this business and become a powerful force in
stimulating students to build up libraries of their own.

Dorothy Mae Poteat has suggested 122 as the minimum number of magazines for the junior college. [15]   The
fifty libraries answering this question reported an average
of 167 periodicals, ranging from 73 to 518; thirteen had
fewer than 122 and eight under 100. [9]   A survey of thirty-
two junior college libraries by the writer in 1963 disclosed
an average of seven newspapers received.   Besides local,
state, and national newspapers, every library should have
at least one foreign newspaper of the caliber of The Manchester Guardian.   Periodicals should be selected not only

with their relation to curricular offerings in mind but also
to their reference value through use of back copies by way of
periodical indexes.

Charles Joseph Benson concluded, from a study of
the use of periodicals in a junior college library, that
"More than half of the use of periodicals seems to have been
more or less unrelated to course work."[16] He felt that in
many cases "the junior college librarian might well decide
that acquisition of materials for recreational purposes unrelated to courses of instruction should be made only after full
support has been given to the instructional program."[16]

Of the sixty-two librarians queried by this writer,
fifty-nine took Readers' Guide to Periodical Literature, two
the Abridged Readers' Guide to Periodical Literature and one
received no periodical index at all. The number of subscriptions to other indexes were: Education Index, 27; International Index to Periodicals, 26; Applied Science and Technology Index, 15; Business Periodicals Index, 11; New
York Times Index, 10; Biography Index, 8; Art Index, 6;
Public Affairs Information Service, 5; Cumulative Index to
Nursing Literature, 5; Book Review Digest, 4 (doubtless
taken by many more libraries which consider it primarily a
book selection aid); Library Literature and Biological and
Agricultural Index, 3; Catholic Periodical Index, Index to
Dental Literature in the English Language, Historical Ab-
stracts 1775-1945 and Biological Abstracts, 2; Engineering
Index, Architectural Index, Accountants' Index, Christian
Science Monitor Index, Chemical Abstracts, Psychological
Abstracts, and Abstracts of English Studies, one each.

Of sixty-two libraries surveyed, five mentioned having some Xerox or other photocopies of books but did not
specify the number. Twelve libraries had microfilm copies,
ranging from 2 to 2,000 with an average of 419. Four libraries have the New York Times on microfilm; two libraries each reported having eighty-six periodicals on microfilm. The only library which reported having Microcards
had two books in this form. The argument on bound magazines versus magazines on microfilm continues; but if the library has sufficient space, bound periodicals have several
advantages. Microfilm for newspapers, on the other hand,
means added permanence, a great saving in space, and
greater convenience in use.

Junior college librarians, along with others, will

watch with interest the revolutionary library on microfiche
(3" by 5" transparent sheets) envisioned by Park Forest (Ill.)
College.   Each student will be provided with an individual
projector the size of a lunch box.   By this means the college hopes to cut the cost of a million volumes from 25
million dollars to two million. 17   However this experiment
turns out, books in something like their present form are
likely to play an important role in the junior college library's future, if the library can survive the severe growing pains and the lack of focus from which it now suffers.

Editor's note: For a discussion more directly applicable to
the four-year college see the selection by Bach.

Notes

1. Brick, Michael   Forum and Focus for the Junior College
    Movement: The American Association of Junior Col-
    leges   New York, Bureau of Publications, Teachers
    College, Columbia University, 1963, p. 24.

2. 1964 Junior College Directory of the American Associa-
    tion of Junior Colleges   Washington, D. C. , Ameri-
    can Association of Junior Colleges, 1964, p. 5.

3. Gould, Samuel B.   Letter dated April 12, 1965, includ-
    ing Summary of National Junior College Library Sta-
    tistics, 1963-64, distributed with covering letter
    from the Association of College and Research Li-
    braries.   (Multilithed; unpaged.)

4. Tanis, Norman E.   "Implementing the Junior College
    Standards," College and Research Libraries, 22:130,
    March 1961.

5. Lake, Albert "Book Selection Standards: Education or
    Communication?" Wilson Library Bulletin, 37:674,
    April 1963.

6. Ibid. , p. 672-675.

7. Carson, Rachel   The Sea Around Us.   New York, Ox-
    ford University Press, 1951.

8. Stone, Ermine The Junior College Library. Chicago,
   American Library Association, 1932. p. 53.

9. U. S. Department of Health, Education, and Welfare, Office of Education Library Statistics of Colleges and
   Universities, 1963-64: Institutional Data (by Theodore
   Samore). Washington, D. C., U. S. Government Printing Office, 1965, p. 8-59.

10. Branscomb, B. Harvie Teaching with Books: A Study
    of College Libraries. Chicago, American Library
    Association of American Colleges, 1940, p. 176.

11. Trinkner, Charles Basic Books for Junior College Li-
    braries: 20,000 Vital Titles. Northport, Ala.,
    Colonial Press, 1963.

12. Hoffman, Hester The Reader's Adviser; An Annotated
    Guide to the Best in Print in Literature. 10th ed.,
    rev. and enl. New York, R. R. Bowker Co., 1964.

13. Bertalan, Frank Joseph, comp. Books for Junior Col-
    leges; A List of 4,000 Books, Periodicals, Films,
    and Filmstrips. Chicago, American Library Associa-
    tion, 1954.

14. Florida, State Department of Education Basic Materials
    Series. 1960-.

15. Poteat, Dorothy Mae, comp. Basic Materials for Flor-
    ida Junior College Libraries: Magazines. (Florida
    State Education Department, Division of Community
    Junior Colleges. Materials Bulletin No. 22 CJC-2).
    Tallahassee, Fla., Florida State Department of Edu-
    cation, 1960, p. 2.

16. Benson Charles Joseph Study of the Student Use of
    Periodicals in a Junior College Library. Unpublished
    M. A. thesis prepared for the Graduate School of Li-
    brary Science, University of Chicago, 1955, p. 67,
    70. (Microfilm.)

17. Gorlick, Arthur "View Dynamic New College," Chi-
    cago Daily News (Red Arrow Weekend Edition), Nov.
    9, 1963, p. 3.

Collections

by Ralph R. Shaw
Professor, Graduate School of Library Studies, University of Hawaii, Honolulu; formerly Dean at Hawaii and Rutgers; Past President of ALA.

From his A Medical Intelligence Program for the National Institutes of Health. 1961. p. 36-47; Reprinted by permission of the author.

Collections

There are many collections of books, periodicals, report literature, photographs, films, and other library materials in the National Institutes of Health. While the central library is the largest of these, there are many titles in individual collections and many types of collections, such as medical photographs, which could be of general usefulness and for which there is no generally available record.

At no place in the National Institutes of Health is there a reasonably complete collection of the publications and reports issued by the National Institutes of Health nor is there any single source of information about this group of publications.

There is no central record of research in progress, either intramural or extramural, that would permit a worker in any discipline to find out what others in his discipline are doing in other Institutes that might be useful in his work. There is no central record of bibliographical projects--many of which are going on both intramurally and extramurally-- there are duplicating partial records of bibliographical and substantive projects in grants offices, in information offices, in program planning offices, in the Biosciences Information Exchange, etc., many of which involve collecting and indexing of reports and other literature, but these are nowhere brought together to give an overall picture of programs, needs and operations.

248

It is not difficult to agree that all of the present activities in collecting recorded information are essential for program purposes.   There is currently no other way by which the various program and research staffs at the National Institutes of Health can get even a minimum of coverage of the information they must have to do their jobs.   Failure to do this would leave their programs completely unsupported.   If better mechanisms were provided, and they should be, then more effective programs should and would result.

Thus while it is easy to point to many duplicating collections of books, of periodicals and of report literature, it is not possible to say that any of this represents <u>unnecessary</u> duplication of collections or work under present conditions.   In fact, in the present state of development of the library collections and services, this duplication is essential and some of it will continue to be essential for program effectiveness.

The two concerns about the library most frequently elicited in our conversations with the staff at National Institutes of Health were: (1) concern that the National Institutes of Health central library might be merged into the National Library of Medicine when that library moved onto the campus and (2) concern that the collections in offices, divisions, and Institutes might be eliminated.

As noted above in the discussion of the relationship between the National Library of Medicine and the National Institutes of Health Library, there is no basis for assuming that the move of the National Library of Medicine to Bethesda will make it possible to do away with the National Institutes of Health Library.

The matter of duplication of materials and collections on campus is a little more difficult to dispose of.   The need for materials at hand is clear.   However, one of the great arguments that has been going on for many years on college and university campuses, which is still going on and does not appear to be close to general resolution, is the question of centralization versus decentralization of library collections and services.   Generally speaking operational efficiency is raised by centralizing collections.   The reasons for this are quite obvious.   The maintenance of fewer reading rooms requires fewer staff to man them, fewer duplicate copies of reference tools, less cataloging, less checking in of periodicals, etc.   On the other hand, viewed from the point of view

of program efficiency rather than operational efficiency of
the library alone, and bearing in mind that the sole purpose
for existence of staff functions such as the library is to permit the research staff to make maximum use of their available time, any system that requires a research man to drop
what he is doing and go across campus to the library for
frequently used materials may save a few dollars in duplication of publications while defeating the purpose for which libraries and other supporting agencies exist.   It is manifestly not feasible to duplicate within reach in his own office or
section everything that each research man can and should
use.   It is equally obvious that it is wasteful to require the
other extreme, i. e. that all materials be centralized in a
single collection on campus.   The only rule that would appear to make sense is a pragmatic rule that books and periodicals used frequently enough in any one location so that it
is cheaper to buy a copy for use at that location should be
treated that way, while less frequently used materials should
be serviced from a central collection, and the still less frequently used research materials should be called for from
the National Library of Medicine, the Library of Congress,
and other comprehensive storage libraries.   This would mean
that a weekly periodical used regularly by a group might well
be purchased for the exclusive use of that group.   It might
be retained by the group as long as they have a reasonable
frequency of use.   On the other hand this does not justify
the investment in binding these periodicals because, normally, their use falls off rapidly after five to ten years and the
binding of these periodicals tends to institutionalize small library collections rather than providing live working materials in each office and each section.   Given prompt lending
and photostat service from the central library it should not
be necessary to maintain files of periodicals in individual
offices much beyond the five- to ten-year period, after which
they should be discarded.   In fact, materials bought for such
groups should, by and large, be treated as expendable materials supplementing the general collection for intensive use
for relatively short periods, after which, instead of throwing
good money after bad by binding them and housing them permanently, they should be disposed of to other libraries or in
other suitable ways.

        Another approach to determination of when it pays to
duplicate periodicals is the cost of circulating or routing
periodicals to borrowers.   Since the clerical operations of
routing periodicals from the library cost staff time and the
charging and discharging of books or periodicals on individu-

al requests probably cost 50 cents or more per circulation
in staff time, it is obvious that in addition to the waste of
research staff time by failure to duplicate periodicals when
suitable there is a substantial investment in clerical time in
the library which at some level of frequency of repetitive
circulation will become more costly than buying another copy
of the periodical as an expendable item of supply.

Assuming an average staff cost for clerical staff in
the library of 25 cents per circulation or routing, averaging
the lower cost routing operation with the higher cost individual lending operation, it would appear that a monthly magazine used three or four times a month by an individual or
group might better be bought for the individual or group as
an expendable item than be loaned from the library while
this rate of use exists.   Actually, since periodicals being
used at that frequency by one group will often be in demand
by other groups it would be necessary to buy additional
copies anyway and we might simply be overlaying the cost of
the staff for routing and for lending periodicals on the cost
for the same number of copies, while giving poorer service
since the time in transit to and from users would be time
when these periodicals are not available to the users.

While this matter has not been subjected to adequate
research, it appears quite probable that many special libraries which attempt to limit the number of copies bought
by substituting staff costs in routing may well, in a substantial number of cases, be penny-wise and pound foolish in
terms of operational efficiency as well as being wasteful in
terms of program efficiency.   This is obviously not an
either or matter; it depends to some extent upon availability
of other services such as speedy and inexpensive copying
service.   It is suggested, therefore, that in any case in
which a periodical is used as much as once a week by an
individual or group in one place it would be much more economical as well as much more effective in supporting the
program if copies were purchased for exclusive use of that
group for as long as they made frequent use of it, after
which they should be disposed of.

Similarly if a book is used once or twice a month by
an individual or group in one place, it should probably be
bought for the exclusive use of that group except in the case
of very expensive books when more frequent use would be
required to justify the purchase of extra copies.

This does not rule out the automatic routing of periodicals when the frequency of use is not great enough to
justify retention of a copy in a laboratory, or section, or
building, and some routing is now being done within divisions.

Following this logic one step further, it should be
noted that there are considerable concentrations of staff in
some of the buildings and there will be even greater concentrations of staff in some of the newer buildings. It may
very well be that approached on this same pragmatic base,
small library collections to serve the staffs in each building
might be justified in addition to the constantly used handbooks and periodicals provided in each section or laboratory.
This again can be decided in terms of needs and frequency
of use rather than on any more theoretical grounds.   The
National Institutes of Health campus is a large campus.
Time spent going to and from the library to get frequently
used materials could easily cost more than collections of
from five to ten thousand volumes of frequently used materials in each of the buildings to supplement the constantly used
materials in the offices.   These should be supplemented by
the collection of approximately one hundred thousand volumes
in the main library and the main library would, in turn, call
upon the great research libraries of the Washington area and
the country for rarely used materials.

Periodicals

Examining the particular types of materials in the collections, it is interesting to note that so far as the medical
journals, and to a very large extent the biological science
journals as well, are concerned there was almost unanimous
agreement on the part of the scientists interviewed that the
National Institutes of Health Library has an excellent collection for its purposes.   In no case was the collection judged
poor in meeting the need for medical and biological science
journals.   The collections in related fields such as physics,
statistics, and the behavioral sciences need improvement
but this improvement does not involve the purchase of large
numbers of additional periodical titles.   Some of this has
been compensated by the purchase of journals in individual
divisions for their own use.   In rare cases in which one division only is concerned with the field, the purchase of these
for the divisions only might well be continued provided there
were a central record and they were made available to others as needed.   In other cases, there is general enough in-

terest in these journals so that they might well be purchased for the central library. However, an excellent job has been done in building up the collection of periodicals and except for the matters of missing issues and binding, which will be discussed elsewhere, the library is in strong condition in this important area.

The list of periodicals currently received in the National Institutes of Health Libraries as of June 15, 1960 includes some 1,926 titles. These were checked against the holdings of the National Library of Medicine and it was found that 85 percent of them were received in the National Library of Medicine. 272 titles or 15 percent were not received in the National Library of Medicine at the time of checking. Of these, 67 were in the field of chemistry, 57 in physics, 34 in agriculture, 20 in general science, 15 in electronics, 13 in statistics, 8 in sociology, 4 in mathematics, 11 in biological sciences, and 37 in miscellaneous fields. An additional 6 were on order at the National Library of Medicine.

The important thing about this finding is that it points up that no matter how complete the National Library of Medicine may be, there are fields that need to be covered in serving the research and administrative staff at the National Institutes of Health that are outside the field of Medicine as ordinarily construed. Furthermore, the fields in which most of the nonduplicating periodicals were found in National Institutes of Health were fields in which the National Institutes of Health collection is not as strong as it needs to be to meet the needs of the research staff.

It should be noted also that almost a third of the journals received in both libraries are not covered by the indexing program of the National Library of Medicine. This means that about one-half of the journals filed in the National Institutes of Health Library, which are needed for day-to-day programs in the National Institutes of Health, represent material that the National Institutes of Health must organize for itself. While some of these are covered by other abstracting journals, such as Chemical Abstracts, many of the journals that are not covered by the National Library of Medicine indexing are not covered by other indexing services either and a considerable amount of review of the current literature would still be necessary if National Institutes of Health is to have access to the knowledge contained in the journals and serials that it now receives.

In this respect, it must be noted, however, that while it has been customary to think of the National Institutes of Health Library as a medical library, the research performed in the National Institutes of Health needs support in a number of other areas in addition to the field of medicine. In fact, the impression of many of the staff at National Institutes of Health has been that in the past the library has tended to give priority to laboratory research rather than clinical research and that requests from clinicians were not received as readily or serviced as willingly as requests from bench scientists. Whether this is true or not, it is a common enough impression to make it necessary to point out clearly that the functions of the National Institutes of Health go far beyond bench research and need support from a first-class information service, not only in the clinical areas but in related fields such as, psychology, biometrics, sociology, and numerous other underlying areas, including even laboratory design, building design and construction, and other non-medical functions which are essential to the effective performance of the various missions of the National Institutes of Health. This means that while the National Institutes of Health Library will not attempt to build a research collection in any area, it must have live, quick reference collections of some depth in a number of areas. However, as new periodicals become necessary, it is probable that with the great National Library of Medicine on campus, and with the greater use of photocopy which is recommended elsewhere, it will be possible to eliminate some of the less-used journals so that the periodical collection, which constitutes by far the largest part of the total collection, will probably not need to be increased substantially in size.

Book Collection

The book collection is quite unsatisfactory. There are many obsolete and little-used materials which do not merit shelf room and there are many books needed for day-to-day use in practically all fields which the current programs have not provided in National Institutes of Health. Insofar as major effort in acquisition is required, it will need to be concentrated on book and related materials rather than on periodical sets.

Non-book Materials

There are a number of types of material that contain information of importance to the programs of the National

Institutes of Health that are not now collected systematically even though partial and incomplete collections are maintained in a number of places on different bases and for different purposes.

In the first place, there is no complete collection of publications issued by the various Institutes. Near-print publications issued by the Institutes are, in many cases, not sent to the library and there is no archival file of these. Similarly, as pointed out above, publications resulting from extramural research supported by the National Institutes of Health are not collected in any single place and the many collections that are now maintained are incomplete.

A second category of information that needs to be collected and organized is the reports of research in progress. There are now many collections of data on extramural projects but these are not brought together in any one place. Some, such as the file maintained as part of the Biosciences Information Exchange, were limited to the first statement of a project for which a grant was made. Others are updated as changes are made in the project and include reference to or copies of progress reports, but these are all partial and incomplete and there is no place that one can get an overview of all of these publications or get access to information about what is going on intramurally and extramurally in any given field.

The collection of medical photographs produced at the National Institutes of Health contains a large amount of medical information. These might well be collected in the library and indexed for general use. The same would be true of training films.

Great need has been expressed for organization of the data obtainable from the clinical records in the National Institutes of Health. The problem of collecting, organizing and indexing hospital records is a difficult one, but in the case of the National Institutes of Health, since the primary focus in the Clinical Center is research, and since many projects require organization of the clinical records, and since the bibliographical methods used by the library have a contribution to make in the organizing of the intellectual content of medical records, it would appear that responsibility for making the knowledge and clinical records generally available must be accepted and the library should take leadership in this field.

There are miscellaneous sources of information which
are not well-represented in the library and which are important to the National Institutes of Health.   These include
governmental administrative literature which are needed for
the administrative operations of the Institutes and report literature emanating from other government agencies that applies to the missions of the National Institutes of Health.

These represent the major but not all of the areas in
which pratically no service is available at the present time.
No one else can be expected to collect the National Institutes
of Health's publications or to systematize literature on research in progress.   Information in these areas is urgently
needed.   One of the major functions of the library should be
to collect and organize these materials for the benefit of the
whole of the National Institutes of Health and its programs.

Selection of Materials

The overall policy for addition of materials to the collections has never been stated clearly.   The method of selection now in use is cumbersome and does not work in close
relationship to the personnel of National Institutes of Health
for whom the collections are built.   The book selection procedure is not satisfactory so far as book collections are concerned nor has it covered the other types of materials listed
above.

The selection routine now absorbs a very large amount
of staff time, considering the relatively small number of
books that are purchased.   At the present time, the professional staff of the library, particularly in the reference department, but including the heads of all sections of the library, is heavily committed to selection of materials and for
assigning priorities for purchase to these materials.   If the
professional staff of the Institutes could be encouraged to
handle a larger portion of the selection of materials and the
library selected primarily those items needed to round out
the collection of reference tools and if the procurement procedure could be speeded up so the staff could see the results
of their efforts in selecting materials, the collection could
be strengthened greatly while professional staff in the library
would be freed for services rather than for building the collection.

It is suggested that the subject specialist in medical

and all other disciplines in the National Institutes of Health be recruited to aid in book selection and that the primary library function in this respect be that of calling new items to the attention of the subject specialists as they appear.

The scope of the collection as outlined above should be spelled out in a written policy statement on the scope and nature of the collections, and this statement should cover collections in the library, in laboratories, Sections and in Institutes, so that the process of selection and assignment of priorities to purchase could be made largely automatic within the published canons of selection.

The book funds are currently inadequate. The periodical funds are, and should continue to be, reasonably adequate.

A copy of all National Institutes of Health publications, i. e. anything produced by or through the support of National Institutes of Health that has been reproduced in multiple copies by other than a single typing, should be required to be filed in the library and organized as part of the permanent collections of the library. Similarly, a copy of all extramural or intramural research projects approved, together with all changes in these projects, should be sent to the library for organization, permanent retention and servicing. The file copy of all audio-visual materials should be submitted to the library for storage, organization and servicing. The proposed documentation section of the library should work closely with the interested research units in developing methods and techniques for making the knowledge contained in clinical records available.

In view of the fact that the book collection is quite weak, it is suggested that a minimum of $50,000 a year be made available for the purchase of books for the central library collection in addition to the use of Institute funds for the purchase of additional copies needed in laboratories and sections of the Institutes.

What is a Special Library?

by Edward G. Strable, ed.   Mr. Strable has been Execu-
tive Secretary of Reference
Services Division and of the
American Library Trustee
Association at ALA; recently
he became Director of the In-
formation Center, J. Walter
Thompson Company, Chicago.

From Special Libraries: A Guide for Management. New York, Special Library Association,
1961. p. 1-3; 6-7; Reprinted by permission of
Publications Department, Special Library Association.

On July 2, 1909, a group of 26 librarians met together at Bretton Woods, New Hampshire, to discuss a new
form of library that had appeared on the American scene.
Before their discussions ended, they had decided that the
new form of library should be called "special library." They
placed the stamp of agreement on their conclusion, in typical American fashion, by forming an organization they
named Special Libraries Association.

Since that time, thousands of libraries that call themselves special libraries have come into being in the United
States and Canada. They have adopted this designation to
signify their difference from the three other major forms of
libraries familiar to North Americans--the school libraries
used by elementary and high school students, the general
college and university libraries used by college students and
their professors, and the public libraries used by people of
all kinds at all stages of life.

Differentiating Characteristics

Although special libraries constitute the least familiar
form of library for the general public, they are easily dif-

ferentiated from other libraries.   Special librarians usually
emphasize four or five of these distinguishing characteristics.

They are differentiated by where they are found.
Many are located in private business and industrial organizations such as banks, insurance companies, advertising
agencies, publishers, drug manufacturers, petroleum producers, and engineering firms.   Some are in associations
and societies devoted to trades or professions or having social or welfare goals.   Others are part of the framework of
federal, state, county, or municipal governmental bodies.

A number of special libraries are in non-profit institutions such as hospitals and museums.   Some are subject
branches or departments of public or university library com-
plexes, such as the business branch of a public library or
the industrial relations library of a university library system.

A recent study of 8, 500 special libraries and information centers in the United States[1] found that 25. 8 percent of
the total were located in colleges and universities, 25. 3 percent in companies, 14. 3 percent in government agencies,
4. 6 percent in public libraries, and 30 percent in other non-
profit associations, organizations, societies, and institutions.

Looking at special libraries from the viewpoint of
where they are found indicates that they invariably are units
of larger organizations; these organizations usually do not
have an educational objective as their major goal, and they
are often private organizations.

Special libraries are differentiated by limitations in
subject scope.   The larger organizations of which special libraries are units usually have specific rather than general
objectives.   This is reflected in the orientation of special
libraries to single, definite subjects or, more often, to
groups of related subjects.   Thus, special libraries are often described in terms of their subject orientation--advertis-
ing and marketing, biological, pharmaceutical, engineering,
television, real estate, chemistry, transportation, art, or
dental libraries.

Some are best described in terms of a form of material; map libraries and picture libraries are good examples.
Still others are more commonly described in terms of their

parent organizations--museum, hospital, or newspaper libraries. In every case, the common characteristic is an orientation to library materials and information that are specialized rather than generalized in character.

It follows quite naturally that special libraries are also differentiated by the kinds or groups of people who use them or are served by them. Special libraries are almost never used by "everybody," as are public libraries. They are used, rather, by people who are associated with the organizations that support the libraries and within which the libraries are located. Since the organizations and the libraries have special interests, it is to be expected that the users also have special interests and skills and represent, therefore, "specialized clienteles."

Some typical groups served by special libraries are chemists, doctors, insurance men, security analysts, lawyers psychologists, advertising copywriters, economists, engineers, metallurgists, industrial relations experts, editors, and scores of other groups whose information needs are work-related.

Special libraries are differentiated by a predominant characteristic of "smallness." All kinds of libraries come in all sizes, of course, and there are some special libraries with scores of employees and hundreds of thousands of volumes in their collections. But surveys and studies of special libraries have led to the conclusion that a majority of them, particularly those in companies, associations, and societies, employ only a few persons. The "typical" special library might, therefore, be visualized as small in staff size and, usually, small in space occupied and in size of collection.

Special libraries are differentiated from other libraries by their emphasis on the information function. While the major goals of other kinds of libraries may encompass education, recreation, aesthetic appreciation, or scholarly research, the traditional major goal of special libraries has been, and continues to be, providing information for immediate and utilitarian purposes. And, because of the nature of special libraries, information can often be provided in anticipation of the need for it.

This single-endedness of special librarianship is what first drew the group of 26 librarians together in 1909. It is the reason that "Putting Knowledge to Work" was chosen and is used as the guiding slogan of special librarianship; it is the characteristic that best defines the "special" in special library.

Determining What the Special Library Will Do: Levels of Function

This concept of levels of functions, activities, or service in libraries can be illustrated by selecting some important functions and describing how they might be performed at different service levels.   Three such functions are those that are performed in all libraries and are rather unique to libraries--the functions of acquisition, organization, and dissemination of materials and information.

The following outline describes these functions in terms of three levels of service--minimum, intermediate and maximum.   The outline illustrates that the chief differences among special libraries are due to the levels at which functions are performed.   It suggests the kinds of decisions that must be considered in determining what a particular special library will do.   Specific operations and routines are not indicated.

Acquiring Materials for the Library

As a minimum function, the special library:

Collects publications scattered throughout the organization, receives those that come automatically to the library, and checks these materials for relevancy and to avoid duplication.

Keeps abreast of the organization's general interests and needs for published materials.

Reviews announcements of new publications and selects and orders directly from the publisher.

Establishes a simple order record.

At an intermediate level of function, the special library adds or substitutes the following:

Establishes contacts with local book and magazine dealers

for expediting orders.

Begins to acquire and set up special collections of materials such as patents, internal reports, maps, and pictures.

Creates and maintains a complete order file with automatic follow-up procedures and, where feasible, takes advantage of available electronic data processing facilities and equipment.

Reviews the library's collections and builds up weak areas.

Establishes a regular system of checking with staff authorities for evaluations of publications.

At a <u>maximum level of function,</u> the special library adds or substitutes the following:

Keeps informed about the developing needs of the organization and imaginatively selects materials in anticipation of actual requirements.

Establishes personal contacts with experts and dealers of unusual publications--second-hand, rare, foreign, etc.

Prepares a written selection policy.

Sets up and maintains specialized collections, such as catalogs of executive development programs, computer print-outs, and archival material of the organization.

Note

1. Kruzas, Anthony T.   Special Libraries and Information Centers: A Statistical Report on Special Library Resources in the United States.   Detroit, Gale Research Company, 1965.

Book Selection Theory and Practice

by Marjorie Fiske

Dr. Fiske is currently on the staff of the Langley Porter Neuropsychiatric Institute, San Francisco

From her Book Selection and Censorship: A Study of School and Public Libraries in California. Berkeley and Los Angeles, University of California Press, 1959. p. 16-24; Reprinted by permission of University of California Press.

The Selection Process

Since meeting public demand is seen as a major library objective, we might expect that the gauging of community needs would be a major preoccupation. But this proved not to be true. Respondents discussed the process of evaluating the supply at great length; references to gauging needs, either of patrons or of the community at large, were brief. The evaluation of supply was often described as an elaborate, systematic, and sometimes scientific process. The gauging of needs was intuitive. "You keep a kind of file in your mind. You read a review and think about your public and how the book would fit for them." This "playing by ear" book selection procedure is used in most municipal libraries having only one or two professionals on the staff. In larger institutions, there may be group discussions or group decisions, or an order or head librarian may analyze and collate the suggestions of many staff members. But even when several staff members participate, and when special aspects of community needs are evaluated, the underlying process remains essentially the same. You "think about your public" as you "read a review."

Gauging needs. --Regardless of their position on the quality-demand continuum, all public librarians believe that the "needs and interests of the community" require consideration; but on the question of how to assess these needs there is little agreement.   Librarians in the largest systems pass over the problem lightly.   As one observed, if you buy near ly half of all books published each year, you can't help but supply most of what is wanted or needed; if some desires re main unsatisfied, there is enough money left to cover them too.   Librarians in towns of 7,500 population or less, and many of those in the next size class (up to 25,000), feel tha their first-hand acquaintance with individuals and groups in their communities enables them to gauge needs almost auto- matically.   In the communities of medium size (25,000 to 100,000), librarians who are most demand-oriented believe that the review of patron requests--those made in writing or those reported by the desk staff--constitute an adequate as- sessment of community requirements.

County librarians and municipal librarians in the middle-range cities who are not wholeheartedly demand-ori- ented express the most dissatisfaction with their methods of gauging community needs.   County librarians responsible for book selection rely mainly on reports of patron requests re- layed to them by personnel in the branches; occasionally someone from the headquarters staff goes into the field to assess turnover in various categories--but few are satisfied with such appraisals.   Heads of municipal libraries stress the importance of participation in community groups, and a number of them take desk duty now and then as means of getting acquainted with patrons and "feeling out" trends.   Per- sons from these middle-range libraries were most likely to point out that one of the greatest needs of the profession to- day is for a practicable method for assessing public interest or need.   "We really have no idea what the actual or poten- tial interest is.   I wish we could do some research," com- plained the head of a county system.   Another county librar- ian remarked, "The schools do surveys to assess needs all the time, but requests are our only survey."[1]

We might expect that book-buying decisions would be made in the light of what is now at hand either in the insti- tution's own collection or in other libraries accessible to its patrons.   Actually, such considerations are pretty much ig- nored.   Very few of the librarians studied have any informa- tion which could provide them with an up-to-date picture of how their collections are distributed among various subject matter categories.   Nearly all public and school librarians know how much money was spent for books in their institu- tions in the past fiscal year and about how many volumes (but not necessarily how many titles) were purchased. Most,

but by no means all, know approximately how many books
are in their collections (though some head librarians reported that estimates sent annually to the State Library might
be off as much as 10 percent).   Head librarians and children's librarians know the proportions spent for adult and
children's collections, and some cite rough allocations among
non-fiction, fiction, and reference materials.   But aside from
the general acknowledgment of deficiencies in technical material, few public librarians spoke of their collections in
terms of narrower subdivisions such as history, biography,
or social science.

Systematic allocations play a small role in making
decisions about new purchases.   The public librarian's attitude is epitomized by the one who said, "There is little
point in establishing categories or allocations for new purchases because you have to be flexible; public interest is
not predictable."   School librarians may say: "We do not
purchase by subject category allocations because we are curriculum oriented, and we never know when the curriculum
may shift."   Or they point out that interest in the library
differs greatly from one teacher to another, and with the
current high turnover in most school faculties such planning
would be impracticable.

Inventories have not been undertaken on a regular
basis in most institutions studied, a fact which makes the
task of becoming acquainted with a collection a rather stag-
gering one for new staff members.   Lack of specific information about a collection also affects the processes of discard and replacement which to many librarians is as important a discriminatory function as that of selecting new books.
A few public librarians have, on occasion, tried to make
spot appraisals of their collections in order to determine
gaps in various subject fields as a guide to future buying.
The most systematic of these efforts have been made by order librarians in larger county systems.   The municipal librarians in medium-sized communities who have made such
attempts soon gave them up for want of time or money.

Despite complaints about the unpredictability of the
curriculum and of faculty indifference toward the library,
school librarians are more concerned with overall appraisals
of their collections.   About half of them try periodically to
fill out each subject area with "basic" material, whereas only
one-fifth of the public librarians reported taking subject
categories into account in the process of selection.   This

greater attention to the collection as a whole, to inventory-
ing and to systematic weeding out, is more urgent and at the
same time is more manageable in the schools.   Even in a
large high school the number of volumes is fewer than in a
small town public library, and there is more dependence on
material considered to have "permanent" value, for which
guidance is available in selection sources.   County library
systems, with their inevitable shifting about of books from
branch to branch, suffer the greatest insufficiencies in collection evaluation.

　　　Evaluating the supply. --Evaluation procedures described by respondents relate almost exclusively to the selection of newly published materials.   To be sure, librarians
are occasionally faced with the necessity of building up a
basic collection or overhauling an old one, but this task is
rarely viewed as overwhelming, because the handbooks of the
profession offer both guiding principles and specific recommendations for libraries of various sizes.

　　　The selection of new materials was acknowledged as
one of the primary functions of the professional, but librarians agreed almost unanimously that they do not have enough
time for it.   The only exceptions were a few subject specialists who spend all of their time in evaluation, and head librarians in the largest institutions who delegate book selection to their staffs.   For the rest, estimates of the time
spent in book selection ranged from one-tenth to one-third
(rare) of the work week. [2]   Except for children's books, few
materials acquired for the public library are read in advance
by a staff member.   In all sizes and types of libraries, it
is the book review which forms the basis for the librarian's
evaluation of current supply.

　　　The review sources which librarians consult as a basis for becoming acquainted with the new books and for evaluating them may be divided roughly into professional sources
(ALA Booklist, special compilations of the American Library
Association, Library Journal, [3] the various Wilson catalogs),
trade or commercial sources (such as the Kirkus Service
and Retail Bookseller), and general sources including local
newspapers, The New York Times Book Review, the Saturday Review, and a number of monthly journals.   Altogether
some two-dozen printed standard sources were mentioned. [4]

　　　Public and school libraries in the largest and
smallest communities use more sources than do those in the

middle range.   An average of 12. 7 general sources are used in public libraries in cities of 100, 000 or more and 7. 6 in communities of less than 25, 000.   Only 5. 6 are used in communities falling in the 50, 000 to 100, 000 category.   Differences are less striking for school libraries, yet the trend is parallel: those in communities of between 25, 000 and 100, 000 have recourse to the fewest sources.   The head of a municipal library in a medium-sized community who remarked, "We are institutionally adolescent," may have provided a clue to this seeming deviance of the institutions in the middle range (a deviance which was also apparent in respect to gauging community needs and appraising present collections).   Such libraries are expected to fulfill most of the functions of their counterparts in the larger cities, yet their staffing patterns and their budgets resemble those in small towns.   They are rarely departmentalized, have few specialists, and are often run by persons without professional training who "grew up" in the system.   Similarly school librarians from communities in the middle range report the least time for book selection and the greatest amount for clerical or non-library functions.   In contrast, the large public and school systems are highly departmentalized, have many operational and subject matter specialists, and a sufficient budget to buy the tools they require.

The high dependence on reviews in the smallest communities is due in part to the paucity of colleagues with whom information and ideas can be exchanged.   Some of the small towns in our sample are so isolated that there can be little interchange with neighboring professionals.   And, while all libraries have fiscal limitations, a ten dollar purchase requires more careful evaluation in a book budget of one thousand dollars per year than it would in one ten or twenty times that size.

Public and school librarians differ considerably in their use of reviews: professional sources account for 63 per cent of those regularly drawn upon by school librarians, as compared with 41 per cent of those used in public libraries.   Conversely, trade journals, publishers' catalogs and other commercial periodicals account for less than 1 per cent of the sources used in schools, but for 17 per cent of those used in public libraries.   Literary weeklies and monthlies such as Saturday Review, Harper's, The Atlantic and The New Yorker, and the leading newspaper book review sections are about equally popular in school and public libraries. [5]

The most important sources for public libraries are,
in descending order of frequency of use: Kirkus' Service
(25 institutions), Library Journal (23), The New York Times
Book Review (23), one or more of the Wilson Company's
publications (22), [6] Saturday Review (21), and the ALA Booklist (20). Among schools, Wilson publications and ALA
Booklist rank first (28 and 24 institutions, respectively), with
Saturday Review (19) and Library Journal (17) coming next.
Kirkus is used only by one school librarian interviewed, and
she does not subscribe to it but occasionally browses through
issues at the public library. The school librarian, generally more concerned with the content of books and with their
impact on readers, turns for assistance to those sources
which provide the most specific information. The public librarian, generally more attentive to demand and less committed to educational objectives, turns more to sources which
have broad coverage and are timely. School librarians also
pay more attention to "basic lists" in order to review subject
matter areas for purposes of filling in or maintaining balance
in their collections. Wilson materials, the American Library
Association's A Basic Book Collection for High Schools and
special topical lists were mentioned as particularly useful by
more than half the school librarians. In discussing how and
why the various tools are used, school librarians were also
more specific than their public colleagues.

Public librarians are likely to have an ambivalent attitude toward their book review sources. There were more
spontaneous comments about the service of Virginia Kirkus
than about any other tool, and they ranged from great appreciation to great annoyance. Small town librarians are the
most grateful for this service. Some of them rely upon it
almost exclusively not only for information about what is
available but for advice on whether to purchase. "The Kirkus reviews are helpful," said one such librarian, "because
they are written from a librarian's point of view...whereas
the others review the books in a vacuum." Furthermore,
the Kirkus reviewers know, or purport to know, what is
likely to be offensive to small town library patrons. In the
words of a county librarian: "Sometimes she says 'not for
public library.' That's a flag to watch." Or, more specifically, "One thing a librarian always has to keep an eye
open for is the sex problem. I don't think any of us want
our libraries to get the reputation of having improper
books... If Virginia [Kirkus] says it's obscene, that decides
it..."

Frequently the warnings are read with misgivings, particularly in larger systems: "It's nice the way Kirkus warns if there's a question of suitability... But sometimes she does annoy me... It's funny how part of me appreciates her warnings and at the same time another part of me resents them." Reservations about the Kirkus service are particularly strong among librarians who have had professional training. To accept the service's evaluation as tantamount to a purchase decision is in their opinion, a waiver of professional responsibilities. "There are reviewers who mark a review with a 'recommended for a public library.' This is ridiculous. Nobody can select for this library except the librarian... in this community." Or again, "I don't know if you can depend on Kirkus... There's something so pat about her reviews. The tone is not of discussing and offering helpful information, but of making up the librarian's mind for her. That just doesn't appeal to me." The one positive attribute willingly conceded to this service is its timeliness (many publishers provide the firm with pre-publication proofs); that, these critical librarians believe, is the only possible excuse for using it. Conversely, the criticism most frequently applied to other sources which are considered more reliable is that they appear too late to be useful to the public librarian.

Another frequent complaint about many sources, professional as well as commercial, was that the qualifications of the reviewers are not specified, and criteria of relevance and standards are not stated. Horn Book, a review digest of children's books, is evidently an exception. It provides reviewers' backgrounds and has spelled out its criteria of relevance so consistently over the years that children's librarians allot it the same confidence they would a trusted colleague.

Librarians who have time to read the reviews exhaustively believe that if enough sources are used over a long period of time, special biases are no longer a problem because they can be recognized and discounted. But most librarians do not have time to steep themselves so thoroughly in the sources. This is one reason why review sessions of groups of librarians from one large institution or from several smaller ones are increasingly popular. Books reviewed at these sessions are previously read by the reviewer and briefly summarized at meetings, in the course of which recommendations to purchase or not to purchase are made. If there is any disagreement in the group, the chairman may

bring the matter to a vote, but decisions more frequently
are informal.   In the words of one enthusiast, these sessions are

> ...invaluable... There's no substitute for reading
> a book... because guidance is so important in work-
> ing with children...   A few minutes of oral pre-
> sentation can present infinitely more than an ex-
> tensive written review can.   Even the professional
> reviews convey remarkably little which is useful
> for guidance work.   Of course, seeing the book...
> is best, but considering the impossibility of this
> the review sessions are a wonderful substitute.

Sources other than printed or oral reviews are occasionally mentioned by public, rarely by school, librarians.
Book club choices are automatically purchased in nine institutions (including some for the children's sections), and in
three there is some reliance on the advice of dealer or bookstore personnel.   Nine spoke of visits of publishers' representatives, but opinion varied as to their helpfulness; three
find them "very reliable," while the rest believe they are
considerably less so than they used to be.   The same was
said of the publishing houses themselves.   There was a time
when much selection was made on the basis of the publisher's
reputation for specialization and reliability.   These matters
were and still are discussed in book selection courses.   But
several of our respondents observed that such information
quickly becomes outdated, and the standards and selection
patterns of publishing houses are not so predictable as they
were ten or twenty years ago.   Today, librarians may avoid
a given publisher on some such grounds as "dripping senti-
mentality" or "propaganda," but rarely will they favor one on
grounds of general reputation.   Publisher reliability is considered somewhat more consistent for children's books.

Children's material is exceptional in another respect.
Only when our respondents spoke of literature for children
did they discuss at length, or with any degree of specificity,
the standards they apply as they read reviews or the books
themselves.   School and public librarians alike seemed to
agree that reading level, adequacy of print, paper and illustrations, "developmental level," and, in fiction, "imaginative
level" (or "esthetic validity") comprise criteria which can be
applied with some degree of unanimity to children's literature.   The most specific comments about the selection of
material for children (and they are uniquely specific) came

from a high school librarian.

> Well, for example, say you're considering whether
> to buy Henry Miller or Steinbeck... Now, Henry
> Miller, I don't see that there's anything to it that
> has any constructive value in a school library...
> But Steinbeck, that's got literary value, eloquent
> prose, good character development and a social
> message.   What more can you want in a novel?

Underlying this agreement about standards for children's literature is the belief that adults read book reviews
and bestseller lists.   They know what they want; children
do not.   Children, therefore, can and should be guided "a-
way from trash" and shown "alternatives and values." "There
is enough good material [for children] so that it is inexcusable to buy bad.   Whatever the demand is, there is always
something qualitatively acceptable." Reinforcing this point of
view are two other concepts.   One is that since children do
not pay taxes, the library is not obligated to meet their expressed wishes.   The other is related to the psychology of
reading.   About one-half of the public librarians and a third
of the school librarians touched upon the latter subject.
They pointed out that librarianship has "special responsibilities" to children, and that these responsibilities become most
complex and critical when applied to adolescents.   One-half
of the school librarians who discussed this topic--as compared with one-fifth of the public librarians--believe that
books can have a harmful, even traumatic effect on readers
not sufficiently mature to cope with certain aspects of life
(references were mainly to sex and to political propaganda).
"You wouldn't try to teach Einstein's relativity before they've
had algebra," in the words of one, or, "You don't race a colt
before he's saddled and shoed."

Few public librarians believe there is any real need
for "protecting" children from books.   Most are frank to say
that their "special responsibility" is designed not to protect
children or young people but to protect themselves from parents.   Quite a number went out of their way to state their
belief that books do not harm people, that the child who is
too immature for a book will not understand it and probably
will not even read it.   A few pointed out that we really know
nothing about the impact of books, and, until we do, "If
you're going to slap their hands every time you're not <u>certain</u>
they won't get hurt, you might as well close up the library."

Editor's note: Almost equal in importance to the selections
from Fiske's study quoted herein is the material in
<u>The Climate of Book Selection: Social Influences on</u>
<u>School and Public Libraries: Papers presented at a</u>
<u>Symposium held at the University of California, July</u>
<u>10-12, 1958,</u> ed. with an introduction by J. Perriam
Danton.   Berkeley, University of California School of
Librarianship, 1959.   See especially p. 27-40 on
"The public librarian's boss" by Norton E. Long and
"The school librarian's boss" by Ralph W. Tyler.

Notes

1. Both the California State Library and the American Library Association have sponsored workshops on how
to assess community needs, but neither organization
has funds at its disposal to assist local libraries in
making such surveys.

2. Fargo, <u>op. cit.</u>, cites a 1941 U. S. Office of Education
report on a sample of eleven high school libraries
whose librarians spent an average of 5. 9 per cent of
their working time on all phases of "book acquisition"
while giving more than 40 per cent to non-profession-
al tasks "at least some of which apparently might have
been turned over to others." Our findings suggest
that "working time" considered in this breakdown obviously excludes evening homework or week ends in the
office, when perhaps a major portion of book selection for school and small public libraries is done.

3. This journal is not sponsored by any professional association but it is published and written by professionals
and is widely viewed by librarians as a "professional"
source.   Wilson publications are similarly viewed.

4. No attempt was made to compile a complete list of all
sources used at each institution; rather, we encouraged respondents to discuss those which were used
most frequently and considered most useful or reliable.   Altogether, there were 356 "mentions" of such
sources, but intra-institutional repeats were deleted,
leaving 286 references for the thirty-five systems.
The average number of regularly used sources reported from the thirty-five public libraries or library
systems was 8. 2 per institution.   In the thirty-five

schools from which data were collected on this topic, an average of 4.3 sources per school was reported.

5. A summary table of the sources drawn upon by school and public librarians will be found in Appendix A, table 8.

6. Including, variously, the <u>Bulletin</u> and the <u>Children's Catalog for High School Libraries</u>, <u>Fiction Catalog</u>, and <u>Standard Catalog for Public Libraries</u>, and their supplements.

How Baltimore Chooses

Enoch Pratt Free Library, Baltimore, Md.

From How Baltimore Chooses: Selection Policies of the Enoch Pratt Free Library. Baltimore, Md., Enoch Pratt Free Library, 1968. p. 23-6; 29. Reprinted by permission of The Director, Enoch Pratt Free Library, Baltimore, Md.

II-B-5 Pamphlets

Selection of pamphlets follows the general policies outlined for the selection of books. Because of their attractive format, brevity, and simple presentation, many pamphlets are also used widely for propaganda or advertising, it is necessary that they be carefully examined before they are added to collections.

Though many pamphlets containing propaganda or advertising are included in the Library, obviously undesirable items are eliminated and a balance of viewpoints is sought in controversial subjects. Advertising pamphlets which distort facts, intrude commercial messages unduly, or contain misleading statements are not added. Propaganda pamphlets are expected to be one sided, but those whose propagandist intent is clearly indicated by the publishers' names or statements of purpose are preferred to those which appear under imprints whose sponsorship is not clearly defined. Clear, moderate statements of viewpoint are sought on controversial subjects to balance partisan points of view. An effort is also made to avoid overloading the files with free publications of aggressive propaganda organizations to such an extent as to destroy the balance of viewpoint.

II-B-6 Periodicals

Periodicals are purchased for the Central Library, or accepted as gifts, for one or more of the following reasons: (1) to keep the Library's collection up to date with current thinking in various fields, and to provide material not available in books; (2) to supplement the book collection; (3) to serve the staff as book selection aids, book reviewing media, and professional reading. Those which are needed for reference or research are duplicated in microform for long-term use as they become available in this form.

The type of periodical most obviously needed as a source of material not in books is that which deals with current reporting, either generally or in a special field. Periodicals of this type are needed both for reference work and for general reading. Individual titles are chosen for the following reasons: accuracy and objectivity, accessibility of contents through indexes, demand, need in reference work, representation of point of view or subject needed in the collection, local interest in subject matter.

In most fields of scholarship, technical research, and creative writing, important new theories, discoveries, trends, and viewpoints appear first in journals, and frequently do not find their way into published books immediately. Even when they are later incorporated into books, they are not usually dealt with in such detail as in the original periodical treatment. As a result, the periodical references are often cited in footnotes and scholarly bibliographies. In those fields in which the Library provides books of a scholarly nature, the important journals are also needed. In selection of individual titles, the following factors have considerable weight: authority and reputation of editors and contributors, organization issuing publication, accessibility through indexes and abstracts.

Examples of other types of periodicals which contain material not found in books are "little" literary magazines of which representative titles are bought, and magazines of local interest of which a fairly complete collection is maintained.

In some fields books are not numerous; in others, periodicals give fuller or more popular treatment and thus serve to supplement the book collection. Publications of religious denominations fall in this category. The Library maintains a representative though not a complete collection of these, receiving a number of subscriptions as gifts. An effort is made to supplement the book collection also by providing at least the leading journals in most vocational fields, e. g. , resort management, writing for profit.

In selecting periodicals for purchase, the various groups in the community are considered.   For example, the leading Negro periodicals, journals of trades and professions heavily represented in the community, publications of societies and clubs in which there is considerable community interest are purchased.

For the professional use of the staff and general use by the public, the leading book trade and book reviewing periodicals are heavily duplicated.   American and foreign professional library journals are also acquired.

New periodicals of importance or on needed topics are added immediately.   Sample copies of others are examined and titles are added if they promise to be useful.   It is admittedly difficult to recognize the future importance of some types of magazines, to distinguish between those destined to a long career and those which will cease publication after the first few issues.   An effort is made to subscribe early to periodicals likely to be important, in order to save the later cost of building up back files and to avoid the expense of subscribing to many short-lived publications, with the possible exception of "little" literary titles, local magazines, or new trade magazines.

Branch libraries purchase or accept as gifts only those periodicals which are represented in the Central collection.   In branch libraries, periodical selection, like book selection, is determined by the character of the community served and the availability of space and funds.   Branch librarians select those periodicals which cover principal subjects and tend to broaden points of view of the community. Back files of these periodicals are maintained.   Selected titles are purchased for reference use only, with duplicates of some purchased for circulation.   Each branch subscribes to the Readers' Guide to Periodical Literature, as many of the titles are indexed there.   Some titles not indexed are also purchased according to local interests and needs.

Just as branch libraries do not rely on their own collections for scholarly or specialized books, so they refer patrons to the Central departments for most scholarly and specialized periodical references.

II-B-7   Newspapers

The Library's selection of newspapers is inclusive for

Baltimore, representative for other Maryland papers, and limited for non-Maryland papers.

Since local papers are important sources of information on their locality, some of it available in no other printed works, the Library acquires currently, by gift or purchase, all known Baltimore newspapers, including those in foreign languages; at least one daily from each of the other Maryland cities which have such papers; and one or more weeklies from each Maryland county. Availability of files elsewhere in this area and of other papers of the same locality is taken into consideration before old files are purchased. Efforts are made to acquire microfilm files of Maryland newspapers in order to preserve the material in fragile back files, especially of important papers representing various parts of the state, to add to the Library's files of such papers when they are incomplete, and to save space.

Because of the extremely serious space problem, as well as high cost and fragility of papers, it is the Library's policy to limit stringently permanent files of papers published outside of Maryland. Another factor which influences policy is the proximity to the Library of Congress, which has extensive holdings of metropolitan dailies and weeklies published in all parts of the country.

For reference purposes, a complete file of the New York Times on microfilm is indispensable, along with its index. Because of heavy use, newsprint files of the New York Times are maintained for the current six months. The Times (London), another indexed paper, is received on microfilm and files of the printed or filmed indexes are being acquired.

Most national dailies which represent particular points of view are not added if these points of view are represented in the magazine collection through some weekly or monthly journal. A few non-Maryland newspapers devoted to particular subjects, e. g., Wall Street Journal, are so important that permanent files are kept bound or in microform.

In order to supply readers with current issues of dailies from cities not in Maryland, the Library subscribes to out-of-state and foreign newspapers selected on the basis of quality, geographical representation, and demand. These newspapers are kept for the current month and two preceding months.

Additional copies of the <u>New York Times,</u> the <u>Christian Science Monitor,</u> and a few local papers are purchased for clipping.

Because of space limitations, cost, poor wearing quality, and comparatively infrequent use, permanent bound files of newspapers are not maintained at branch libraries.

Branches subscribe to few newspapers even for current use. Many receive gift copies of their neighborhood papers.

II-B-8 Government Publications

The Library has been since 1930 a United States depository library, receiving all documents ordinarily distributed to such depositories. Nondepository documents were received on microprint from 1951-61, and the microprint editions of depository documents have been on subscription since 1961. In addition, the Library has been through the years on the direct mailing list of many federal agencies. Selection in the field of United States documents is therefore confined to the acquisition of duplicate copies and of documents not automatically received. Every effort is made to obtain such materials from issuing agencies, by purchase from the Superintendent of Documents, through our Congressmen, or through purchase and exchange with special dealers. Documents are selected according to principles applicable to books and pamphlets--importance, need, demand. The official nature of the publications, their value as original source material, the often unique nature of their content, and the comparatively low price are important considerations both in acquiring and in preserving them. Although no longer required by law to make one copy of depository documents noncirculating, the Library tends to limit the circulation of all United States government publications to duplicate copies in order to have the information in them always available for use in the Central Library.

All official publications of the state, counties, and cities of Maryland are acquired, if possible, and preserved as source material. Duplicate copies are acquired as needed for reference and circulating use.

Publications of other states are acquired selectively, according to merit and need. The <u>Public Affairs Information Service</u> and the <u>Monthly Checklist of State Publications</u>

are regularly checked by the public department to identify valuable state documents.   In general, proportionately more publications of nearby states are acquired, although outstanding documents of any state may be added.   Because of demand, an attempt is made to keep up to date certain state documents such as state constitutions and state laws on such subjects as elections, liquor control, education, welfare, and taxes.

Except for statistical and governmental handbooks, directories, or yearbooks, government publications of other countries are not acquired regularly, but are obtained as needed.   Some foreign government publications indexed in Public Affairs Information Service are bought, and the lists of the Queen's Printer (Canada) and Her Majesty's Stationery Office (Britain) are checked to identify titles for possible purchase.

The Library subscribes to the official records of the six main organs of the United Nations (General Assembly, Security Council, Economic and Social Council, Trusteeship Council, International Court of Justice, and Secretariat); in addition other papers of the United Nations and its affiliates (WHO, ILO, UNESCO, etc.) are purchased as needed. Those which are useful to the student of current affairs are duplicated.   No special effort is made to provide a complete coverage, partly because of the difficulties of learning what is available.

II-B-13   Maps

Sheet maps are acquired by the Library to supplement those found in atlases and other books.

Free and inexpensive maps of all types are acquired from all known sources.   Many excellent maps published by government agencies are received on deposit, including publications of the Army Map Service; other United States government-published maps not on the depository list are usually purchased.   Government maps of other countries are sometimes bought, e. g., Ordnance Survey of Great Britain, Canadian Department of the Interior, sheets of the International Map of the World.   In purchasing maps, the Library stresses accuracy, completeness, and clearness, and purchases chiefly from publishers whose work is known to be satisfactory in these respects.

The general aim is to make available a representative collection of fairly large-scale maps of all countries. All states of the United States, chief American cities and towns, larger foreign cities, the various oceans, the island groups, as well as world maps on various projections are included. Among the types of maps acquired are political, topographic, soil, and astronautical. Few early printed maps are purchased (except those of Maryland) but modern maps of historic events or periods are included.

For use by groups and at meetings, a few large wall maps of the world, the continents, the United States, etc. are bought.

The Maryland Department attempts to include almost all known printed maps of Maryland, especially those of historic importance.

Book Selection Policies of the Circulation Department

New York Public Library

From New York Public Library. Book Selection
Policies of the Circulation Department. Circulation
Department Memorandum #12 Revised, 1960.
p. 10-14; Reprinted by permission of Mrs. Jean
Godfrey, Chief, The Branch Library System, New
York Public Library, New York and with revisions
as specifically requested.

Young Adult Books [1]

Although young adults are encouraged to use the entire adult collection in a branch library, a collection of special interest to this group, separately shelved, is maintained
within the adult area as an aid to transition from the Children's Room, and as a convenience for those young adults
who prefer to choose books from a small collection. Book
selection for young adults, under the direction of the Office
of Young Adult Services, has two functions: to identify
books, both adult and juvenile, of interest or use to young
adults; and to recommend the purchase of these books whether
they are shelved in the young adult collection, the general
circulating collection, or the reference collection. [1]

Every young adult collection contains books of two
kinds: girl's stories, sports stories, adventure stories, and
other simple books related to specific teen-age interests;
and a sampling of adult books to serve as an introduction to
the scope and variety of the adult collection. Books which
may answer school assignments are included only if they can
be read for pleasure by the average interested young adult.
Textbooks and reference books are excluded. [2]

The Office of Young Adult Services designates those
titles which may be shelved in young adult collections. At
the discretion of the Young Adult Librarian, a few other
titles from the adult collection, which are specifically recom-

mended for young adults, may be shelved in this section
temporarily.   The "Books for the Teen-Age" list and "Books
Recommended for Use with Young Adults," a monthly mimeo-
graphed list, serve to identify those titles which have been
approved for young adults.   The specific titles shelved in
young adult collections vary according to the interests and
needs of the users; the number of titles depends upon the
space and funds available as well as the extent of use by
young adults.

The Nathan Straus Young Adult Library contains the
Library's largest and most inclusive collection of books,
pamphlets, and periodicals recommended for young adults.
In addition to circulating material, it maintains a small reference collection, a selection of New York City high school
newspapers, and an exhibit of the books on the current
"Books for the Teen-Age" list.   Its holdings are of particular interest not only to young adults but also to librarians,
authors, teachers, publishers, parents, and other adults who
want many examples of books of tested appeal for young
adults.

Reviewing.   Book reviewing is done by the Committee
on Books for Young Adults, which is made up of all Young
Adult Librarians and is under the permanent chairmanship of
the Coordinator of Young Adult Services.   Each Young Adult
Librarian is expected to read and review books both for possible use in the branches and for possible inclusion in the
annual "Books for the Teen-Age" list.   Every new book under
consideration is read by a staff member in the Office of
Young Adult Services or by a branch Committee member, often by both.   When there is a difference of opinion, a book
has at least three readings and is discussed at meetings of
the Book Committee.

Ordering.   A minimum of 15% of the annual adult
book fund of each branch is used for the purchase of books
to be shelved in the young adult collection, as well as for
some books especially addressed to young adults which are
shelved in the adult collection.   In the absence of a regularly assigned Young Adult Librarian, the ranking Adult Special
ist on the branch staff may order these books with the approval of the Office of Young Adult Services and in consultation with the Borough Young Adult Specialist, or he may ask
that the Borough Young Adult Specialist do the ordering both
of new books and books from replacement lists.

Replacements. Books in young adult collections are tested with young adults and re-evaluated on a year-round basis. Twice a year the Office of Young Adult Services and the Committee on Books for Young Adults prepare a general replacement list of popular or useful books considered worth reordering to replenish young adult collections. Other replacement lists on special subjects are prepared from time to time in response to demand.

"Books for the Teen-Age," published each January, serves as a basic guide to the recreational reading of young adults and as a checklist for branch library use. Revised annually by the Committee on Books for Young Adults, it includes both old and new titles arranged by subject matter and covering a wide variety of interests, types of literature, and reading levels. It does not list every title in young adult collections nor are all the titles listed on it necessarily to be shelved in young adult collections. Each year the books on the current list are on exhibit in the Office of Young Adult Services as well as in the Nathan Straus Young Adult Library where they are always available for examination, not only by young adults but also by adults interested in young adults' reading.

Books in foreign languages are made available for young adult collections in response to local demand. They are read, evaluated, and recommended for purchase on the same basis and following the same procedure as young adult books in English.

Children's Books[3]

In recommending books for children's collections, the Office of Children's Services gives careful consideration to each new title and treats every edition of a recommended title as a new book. Important factors in its evaluation are good design, illustration, and format, as well as literary quality.

Each Children's Room has a circulating collection and a non-circulating Reading Room collection of books in English and in foreign languages. The Reading Room collection is composed of books chosen for excellence of format and literary style. It also contains reference books consisting of dictionaries, encyclopedias, yearbooks, and other materials necessary to provide effective reference work with chil-

dren. The circulating collection includes, in addition to
duplicates of many Reading Room titles, popular fiction, and
factual material on a wide variety of subjects covering the
essential interests of children. Materials stimulated by
school demand only are not duplicated in quantity.

The Central Children's Room maintains the largest
and most complete collection of materials for children including titles which are out of print or infrequently requested, outstanding examples of book illustration, a broad
collection of children's books in foreign languages, and a
back file of periodicals. While children from all parts of
the city use this collection, it is of particular interest to
parents, teachers, authors, illustrators, and publishers.

Each borough maintains an extensive reserve collection of children's books which may be borrowed or sent on
a rotating basis to supplement branch children's collections.
These reserve collections include books in foreign languages
as well as in English.

Reviewing and Ordering. Every children's book received in the Office of Children's Services is read, and
recommended or rejected on the basis of a staff review. All
Children's Librarians serve as reviewers.

Each Children's Librarian in charge of a children's
room has an annual book fund with which to purchase materials for the branch children's collection. The Children's Literature specialist in the Office of Children's Services and
the Borough Children's Specialists advise Children's Librarians who are ordering for the first time and order for
branches in the absence of a qualified Children's Librarian.
All orders are reviewed by the Coordinator of Children's
Services.

Replacements. The entire collection of children's
books in the Library is re-evaluated over a two-year period
by committees of Children's Librarians appointed by the Coordinator and under the chairmanship of the Children's Literature Specialist. Replacement lists, prepared on the basis
of these re-evaluations, are not limited to distinguished
books but are comprehensive lists of recommended titles in
print. They are useful in the development of collections for
new branches, as a checklist of recommended books, as an
over view of the different areas in the collection, and as an
evaluation tool. It is not intended that all titles on these

lists be in every children's room, but only those titles appropriate to the needs of each room.

Special lists published under the direction of the Office of Children's Services often serve as a guide in the replacement of children's books and in the development of children's book collections, i. e. "Stories: A List of Stories to Tell and to Read Aloud;" "Books about Negro Life for Children;" "Children's Books, 1910-1960."

Books in Foreign Languages. All children's Reading Room collections contain fine examples of children's books in foreign languages. Circulating collections usually include books in the foreign language or languages used by the neighborhood children, as well as other books which are helpful to children who are learning foreign languages.

Notes

1. The Coordinators of both Young Adult Services and Children's Services emphasize that policy relating to the selection of books in either area of interest is integrated throughout the memorandum in the general policy statements concerning the book selection philosophy of The New York Public Library. A single sample of such inclusion for example is the policy on Censorship which appears only in the general policy but applies to all.

2. The Chief of the Branch Library System advises that the following revision will be proposed for this paragraph: "Young adult collections usually contain books of two kinds: a selection of adult books to serve as an introduction to the scope and variety of the adult collection; a selection of girls' stories, easy biographies, and other simple or pictorial books related to specific teenage interests. Text books, reference books, and other books which may answer school assignments are included only if they can be read for pleasure by the average interested young adult.

3. The Coordinator of Children's Services emphasizes that policy relating to the selection of children's books is integrated throughout the memorandum in the light of our conviction that the policies of the selection of books for children are a part of the overall whole. The same is true for the selection of young adult books.

Book Provision and Book Selection: Policy and Practice

Library Board of Western Australia

From Western Australia. Library Board. Book
Provision and Book Selection: Policy and Practice
Perth, The Library Board of Western Australia,
1966, p. 14-22; Reprinted by permission of
F. A. Sharr, State Librarian, Western Australia,
Perth, Australia.

The aim of book selection is to make possible the
achievement of the objects of the lending and reference libraries set out in the first section of this pamphlet, and includes the principle of co-ordinated book stock, there explained.

The book stock of the service is therefore so chosen
as to represent as far as possible all the interests, econom
ic, social and leisure, of all the people of Western Australia in so far as their needs are not met by other agencies.

Responsibilities in Book Selection

(a) The Board. The Board determines, within the
limits of the funds available, the scale of provision and
broad questions of policy and emphasis. It does not select
individual works.

(b) The State Librarian informs and advises the Board
on policy. He is responsible for implementation of the
Board's decisions and within the scope of Board policy determines matters referred to him by the Chief Assistant Librarian.

(c) The Chief Assistant Librarian is responsible for
the book stock of the whole service:--selection, balance,
condition and discarding. He is expected to refer and
recommend to the State Librarian any matter of book selec-

tion policy and the acquisition of any exceptionally expensive work or set.

(d) Librarian: Circulation Section is responsible for--

(i) advising the Chief Assistant Librarian of any general shortage, unbalance or weakness in the circulation stock which should be corrected;

(ii) forwarding stock requests for particular titles needed in either the maintenance or development stocks;

(iii) selecting, subject to the general concurrence of the Chief Assistant Librarian, books in the circulation pool which should be bound or discarded.

(e) Librarians of subject libraries within the State Reference Library are generally responsible for the state of the book stock of the State Library within their subject fields. They recommend to the Chief Assistant Librarian within the limits of the budget allocated to them, the purchase of books, periodicals, etc. both for normal maintenance and for stock revision of their libraries, and consult with the Chief Assistant Librarian on books for binding and discard.

(f) Librarians of public libraries are encouraged to take as much part as possible in the selection of books for their libraries. Those in the metropolitan area, who can visit Headquarters, are expected to undertake the whole of their book selection themselves. A number of country librarians regularly visit Headquarters to select their books, but where a personal visit is impossible the selection is made by the professional staff of Circulation Section. In addition the State Librarian and the Chief Assistant Librarian regularly visit country libraries and discuss with local librarians the needs and interests of their districts. Reports made on these visits are filed in Circulation Section and are consulted when exchanges are being selected.

Local librarians may take part in book selection in five ways--

(i) by personal attendance to select exchange collections from the stock of the Headquarters pool;

(ii) by the submission of requests for particular titles;

(iii) by informing Headquarters in general terms, without requesting specific books, of any factors such
as local interests or activities which should affect
the selection of books for their library.   This is
particularly important in the case of librarians wh
cannot select their own exchanges and is much pre
erable to the submission of stock requests for par
ticular titles;

(iv) through the discussion of local needs with the State
Librarian and Chief Assistant Librarian referred t
above;

(v) through fortnightly meetings of metropolitan librarians held to discuss book selection.

General: Title/Volume ratio

For reference library stock, normally one copy of a
title is acquired; the title/volume ratio is therefore 1:1.
For circulation stock, on the other hand, more than one cop
is usually needed.   As the service expands more books in
total are required; this raises the problem of whether to increase the number of titles added, keeping the number of
copies of each to a stable figure, or to increase the number
of copies of a fairly stable number of titles.   Clearly there
can be no general rule applicable to all titles and types of
book; each must be evaluated individually as part of the book
selection process.   Nevertheless statistics and judgment ove
the last five years suggest that the needs of circulation stoc
can be adequately met (bearing in mind the availability of
lesser used titles from the reference libraries on request)
by the annual acquisition of the following numbers of titles
new to the stock, i. e. excluding new editions, reprints and
repeat orders: non-fiction 2800, fiction 1000, junior (fiction
and non-fiction) 1500.

While, therefore, these figures must be kept under
review in the light of changing circumstances, such as, on
the one hand, the rise of new subject interests in the State
and, on the other, the decline in numbers of worthwhile new
novels published, they offer a guide line to the scale of duplication necessary.

If the exchange system is to function, the number of

copies of a title must on the average be not more than about
one quarter to one third of the number of libraries.   Bearing this limitation in mind, it is more desirable to stock
heavily the most useful and appropriate books in each type
and subject than to spread orders over a wide range of similar titles merely to secure wider coverage.

Fiction

Novels should form a considerable proportion of the
stock of all libraries, but only novels of some value.   The
novel is a recognised form of literature; indeed the novel
and the play are perhaps the most significant forms of contemporary literature.   Novels which will broaden the experience or develop the mind of a reader should be included in
the stock; but there are some which do neither and they are
excluded.   It is better to multiply copies of good novels than
to buy indiscriminately in order to make up numbers.

A problem both in provision and in selection arises
from the marked decline in the number of new novels published in recent years.   Much as this may be regretted, it
has to be faced as a fact.   Since publishers are in business
to sell books, it must be assumed that the demand for
novels, particularly among younger people, is much less
than it was.   Even within the limited number   published,
many are of a type of little interest to many readers. These
are acquired only in small numbers.

Books for Children

In selecting books for children the aim is to provide
a good, wide and balanced stock to cater for all tastes including those of the less academic children.   The Board
does not seek actively to raise the standard of taste of children but rather to offer to children windows on a wider
world.

It is particularly desirable that books for children
should be in good editions, well printed and attractively produced so that the child may learn to value books for their
own sake and not merely as sources of information.

The first essential in a book for children is that it
should be one which appeals to children, otherwise they will
not read it with enjoyment.   When this criterion has been
met, preference is given to those books which will awaken

interests, stimulate the imagination or broaden the perceptions.   Books by certain popular and prolific authors, sometimes referred to as "pot boilers," are not emphasized but
neither are they excluded.   The basic policy of "leaving to
the reader the choice and decision as to their truth and value" is applied to children's as to adult books and it is found
that if children are given an ample supply of the best they
will themselves, after a time, reject the inferior.

Given this policy, it is essential to ensure that there
is ample supply of the best: therefore, even more than with
adult books, it is better to duplicate heavily on titles of
quality rather than to limit their numbers merely for the
sake of a wider range of titles.

School and public libraries are allies, not rivals; are
complementary, not competitive; and are both dedicated to
the one basic purpose of helping children to lead fuller, more
interesting and more rewarding lives both during their school
days and when they grow up.

The major function of the school library is to contribute to the educational programme of the school.   Here,
the needs of the child as a student are provided for by reading guidance, instruction in book skills and the provision of
reading and research materials relating to the work of the
school in the educative process.

The public library, on the other hand, provides for
the needs of the child as an individual citizen, and especially for his imaginative interests, recreational and--to an increasing extent as he grows older--informational needs.   The
public library should therefore reflect in its book selection
the following three aims:--

    (a) to afford children all the general advantages of
        the use of a library and information centre: the
        delight, self-development, amusement, inspiration
        that can be had from good books;

    (b) to create and firmly fix in the minds of all chil-
        dren that the library is a natural place to find in-
        formation throughout their lives;

    (c) to create in the minds of appropriate children an
        appreciation of and desire for books, etc., for the
        rest of their lives.

Children are always asking "why." To put this in library jargon they are seeking "information service." If the public library is to develop its full potential to help them when they grow up, and need information service, it is in the children's library that they must learn by experience that the library is a place where they can get the answers to their questions. In selecting children's books the importance of seeking out and acquiring those which will answer children's questions over as many fields as possible has to be borne in mind.

Non-fiction
General Factors

The aim in non-fiction selection is to acquire for the State as a whole as comprehensive and balanced a collection as possible on all subjects actually or potentially of interest to any significant number of citizens or for any significant social purpose. It is not, however, the responsibility of the public library service to meet the needs of students for material directly connected with their class work. If such material is of wider interest, it is proper that it be stocked, but students' text books as such, particularly elementary text books, are excluded unless they are useful for wider purposes.

The primary responsibility for meeting the needs of students and staff of academic institutions rests upon those institutions. The primary responsibility of the public library service, both lending and reference, on the other hand, is to meet the needs of ex-students at whatever level their formal education terminated. These needs may include the continuation of more or less formal studies, but more commonly comprise the practical application of skills already acquired or the development of the personal interests of the individual in connection with his business, social or cultural life. The public library service therefore places in book selection more emphasis on material having practical application or serving general social needs--at whatever level-- leaving to the university and other like bodies responsibility for the needs of pure or academic research, except in certain fields mentioned in the next section.

There are in the State Reference Library, certain collections which are of research significance. Notable among these are the collection of West Australian material in the Battye Library, the large holdings of Australian and overseas official publications related to the social sciences, and the collection of nineteenth century literary periodicals.   In such special fields, the responsibility is accepted of maintaining and developing the collection as research collections, despite the general policy set out above.

Books not in stock asked for by readers through the Request & Information Service are normally bought unless there are strong reasons for not doing so.   (e. g. a request for an out-of-date book on a subject already adequately covered and which makes no significant contribution to the strength of the stock; or for a book of a type which is not normally stocked).   If a book is not bought, efforts will normally be made to borrow it from another library if the reader so wishes, unless it falls within the ambit of the next two paragraphs.

Books published at very low prices are not purchased unless they contain information of significance which is not obtainable elsewhere.

Paper back editions are not bought if a hard cover edition is available (this applies also to fiction).

Provided the price in relation to the value of the work is reasonable, the more expensive a book the greater the need to buy it, on the grounds that the ordinary citizen would not normally be able to buy it for himself.

An important function of a major library is to acquire and preserve for posterity important books of limited appeal which might otherwise be unavailable when required in the future.   Such books are few in number but they are purchased when appropriate.

When another library in the State has a good holding in a particular subject, and is prepared to lend its material to the Board for the use of the Board's readers, selection is coordinated, as far as practicable, with that library in order to avoid unnecessary duplication.

No attempt is made to influence opinion or reading taste by emphasizing or under-emphasizing particular subjects or books for that purpose.

Subject emphasis

The aim is to build a balanced collection suitable to a public library system of this type, serving ultimately a population in excess of one million. The scale of acquisition is appropriate to this aim except in the following subjects where emphasis is above or below the norm.

Law. No attempt is made to provide a law library service. The statutes of several overseas, and all Australian Governments are held but otherwise the collection consists of books for the layman, philosophical and general works on the place of law in society together with the standard works on Australian law and on aspects of common law which are applicable in Australia.

Public Administration. Apart from the very large holding of public documents from many countries which are obtained by exchange and other means, emphasis is placed on most aspects of public administration both at central and local government level. Particular emphasis is placed on all subjects of practical application by local authorities in Western Australia.

Education. Books primarily of professional interest to teachers are not normally acquired because there are three other libraries maintained by the State Government in this field. Books on psychology, educational theory, the social implications of education and educational administration are given some degree of emphasis in view of the demand for those subjects.

Languages. Some degree of emphasis is placed on dictionaries of the languages spoken by New Australians in the State and on material intended for those learning English. A limited collection of imaginative literature in these languages is being built up.

Pure Sciences. Apart from maintaining certain rich collections in the State Library, little emphasis is placed on science except on those aspects directly relevant to a technology which is well represented.

Technology. All aspects of technology relevant to the needs of the State are represented as strongly as possible.

Medicine. Books on clinical medicine are not nor-

mally bought but hygiene, public health, pharmacology, nurs
ing and the social aspects of medicine are represented.

Engineering.   All aspects of engineering are strongly
represented in the State Library but less strongly in circula
tion stock.

'How to do it' books are strongly represented in circulation stock

Boats, Boating and Marine Engineering.   Emphasis
is placed on these subjects in circulation stock.

Agriculture.   Emphasis is placed on the practical application of all aspects of agriculture relevant to the State
including farm machinery, farm buildings, marketing and
market conditions, and farm accounts.

The Arts.   Some emphasis is placed on pottery, draw
ing and painting, particularly on books containing good repro
ductions.

Drama.   The Drama Library contains a substantial
collection of one act and three act plays in sets on a scale
of one per significant acting part and one for the producer.
These are intended for play reading.

Music.   The stock of books on music and of scores
in the Central Music Library is being developed as rapidly
as possible.   At present the emphasis is placed on obtaining
wide coverage and multiple copies are accordingly not acquired.

Australian Literature.   It is the aim to be comprehensive in Australian imaginative literature generally, and
to acquire complete holdings of material published in Western Australia, written by Western Australians or about West
ern Australia, at all dates.   The State Library is a copyright library for all West Australian publications.   Copies of
works received under copyright are regarded as being for
preservation and further copies of all works likely to receiv
any significant use are acquired to ensure the preservation
of the copyright copy.   Manuscripts of local authors are col
lected.

History--South East Asia.   Emphasis is placed on the
geography, political institutions, economy, history and for-

eign relations of South East Asia, which term is used to include India, Pakistan, Ceylon, Burma, Malaysia, Singapore, Thailand, Vietnam, Laos, Cambodia, Indonesia and the Phillipines.

The British Commonwealth.   Some emphasis is placed on the history, political institutions, etc. of the major countries of the Commonwealth.

Bibliography.   Strong emphasis is placed on acquiring materials in all aspects of bibliography.

Librarianship.   Emphasis is placed on acquiring material on librarianship from all English speaking countries.

Fine Printing.   A select collection of products of private presses and famous printers, particularly Australian, is being built up.

Manuscripts.   Original mediaeval and similar manuscripts are not normally acquired but microfilm or facsimile reproductions of manuscripts, some in colour, are acquired in small quantities for student use.

Australian Publications Generally.   The aim is to be comprehensive in Australian publications in all fields of current publication except works of purely local concern in other parts of Australia.

The Elementary School Library Collection: Selection Policy

by Mary Virginia Gaver

> From Mary V. Gaver, ed.   The Elementary
> School Library Collection.   3rd ed. Newark, N. J. ,
> Bro-Dart Foundation, 1967. p. ix-xiii sel. ;
> Reprinted by permission of Arthur Brody, Trustee,
> The Bro-Dart Foundation, Newark, N. J.
>
> Though a policy for a bibliography, this selection is
> presented as an example of policy for this type of
> library.

Scope

The Elementary School Library Collection is intended
to list the basic library materials which should be provided
in any elementary school serving kindergarten through sixth
grade.   Its purpose is to present high quality materials on
all topics included in the elementary curriculum and of wide
interest to children.   It also aims to describe a collection
meeting the standard recommended by Standards for School
Library Program (American Library Association, 1960) as
the minimum essential for a single school serving 200 or
more students--that is, 6000 volumes but more than 5000
titles. [1]   The list as a whole is built on the expectation that
it represents the minimum collection that every school should
have on the shelves of an established library.

In addition to trade books, the list also includes other
instructional materials which meet standards of quality and
are appropriate to the curricular needs of children at this
grade level, for example filmstrips, recordings and other
educational media.   This practice is in line with the policy
that the children of today need an instructional materials
center as a vital and essential learning resource for modern
educational programs. . .

The selectors have aimed to select titles for this list
on the basis of the generally accepted criteria for evaluation
of materials--literary quality, appeal to children, excellence
in format, authenticity of content, and suitability for the

range of reading abilities normally represented in an elementary school...

Policies for the selection of materials in specific subject areas, types of materials, and the like are noted below:

Materials for the reading program of the school--The elementary school library must provide as broad a selection of excellent materials covering both fact and fiction as current publishing production makes possible.   Materials on all subjects of interest to children and at as many levels of difficulty and maturity as can be provided within the physical limits of this catalog will therefore be included.   We have kept in mind the fact that the group of readers for whom this list is provided will probably read more voraciously at this period, especially in the intermediate grades, than at any other time in their lives. We have therefore tried to select those titles of real literary merit which all children should have a chance to read, as well as titles of immediate appeal, interest and social value.   On specific topics of wide appeal, we have tried to select books of many levels of reading difficulty.

Books for reading by primary grades--The vastly increased production in this area enables us to include many titles of real quality.   Children in the primary grades need many simply written books which they can read themselves, as well as books with pictures they can interpret and talk about.   There should also be books for adults to read to primary grade children, especially.   Suitability of vocabulary has been only one of many factors in selection of books for this age.   Equal consideration has been given to literary and artistic merit, plot and character development, clarity of exposition, and general excellence of design.

In this third edition two practices have been continued: (1) The inclusion of titles for pre-school use (marked N in grade level); (2) The provision of appendices giving separate listings of books for pre-school use and for independent reading at first and second grade levels.   We have however dropped the list of books in the Initial Teaching Alphabet for two reasons: (1) Our inclusion of them may have implied a recommendation of ita over traditional orthography and   (2) Recent research seems to indicate that the teacher is far more important than any current attempts to modify orthography or revise teaching methods.

There continues to be a dearth of good books, child-like in character and of excellent literary quality, which can be read by the child in third to fourth grades.

Books in series--Individual titles have been evaluated apart from the series as a whole and are included where they meet standards of literary quality, appeal and interest, pertinence to the elementary school, and authenticity. A continuing re-evaluation of series books is carried out; our findings to date indicate that the large number of titles in some series which we recommend do not overlap other titles on the same subjects. It is our conclusion the "All about" or "First books" and other series recommended here serve a valid purpose by providing balance and variety.

Abridgements and simplified versions of the classics--We have avoided abridgements and simplified versions except in those instances where the edition meets our criteria as an independent work. The classic of folk or legendary literature, translated or retold for children, has been evaluated as an original contribution and included if it meets standards of literary merit.

Literature--In this section the catalog provides a broad selection of poetry--both in anthologies and in single volumes--in order to make available ample resources for exploring the range of English and American poetry as well as the work of individual poets. The selectors feel that such materials should be available both for independent reading by children and for introduction by adults. The catalog also provides selection of versions or translations, both new and old, of works of world literature.

Human relations--Specific stories or biographies which perpetuate stereotyped characteristics or dialect, out of historical context, have been excluded. Titles are included which contribute positively and consistently to sound understanding by children of the common characteristics and needs of people of many different national, religious and ethnic backgrounds. Effort has been made to include those titles in every field which actively emphasize (through both text and illustration) wholesome attitudes of mutual respect and understanding among all people.

Religion--Books on customs and traditions of all the major
religious faiths, stories from the Bible, lives of religious
heroes, and materials on religious holidays, have been
selected where they meet standards of quality and appropriateness for elementary school use.   Books of specific religious teaching have been excluded as inappropriate, but several versions of the Bible have been provided.
An attempt has been made to balance the representation
of various religious faiths in terms of value to the school
curriculum and to children's interests.

Sex education--Materials on this topic have been included
where they meet criteria of scientific and medical authority.   Our supporting study of curricula indicates that direct teaching of this subject is still limited in the elementary schools, but we do find evidence that attention
to this subject is increasing at the sixth grade level.
Practices of making these materials directly available to
children will, therefore, need to be determined by each
librarian, in consultation with faculty and principal.

Foreign languages--Because the study of French, Spanish,
even other foreign languages is finding a place in many
elementary schools, a particular effort has been made to
provide a selection of materials relating especially to
these languages where they are available.   Trade books
written in the foreign language, and factual materials explaining cultural backgrounds, have therefore been included, as well as a selection of recordings.   Other titles
considered valuable for motivation of interest in foreign
language study have also been recommended.   Books with
line-by-line translation or phonetic spelling in English
have not been included.

Local history--Material on state and local history is essential in the elementary school library.   Although it has
proved impossible to locate books about every state which
are of sufficiently broad interest to include in this national list, many local or regional titles of general value and
interest have been included.   The individual school librarian will of course need to purchase additional sources
in terms of local needs.

Reference collection--The Elementary School Library Collection presents reference materials in a separate category, with duplication in the circulating collection where
the Selection Committee considered it essential.   A gen-

erous selection of encyclopedias and dictionaries, indexes
and bibliographies, biographical dictionaries, and the
like--sources which children in the elementary grades
generally can use effectively only with assistance and/or
instruction--and other types of materials useful for reference purposes are brought together in a separate group.
The Committee feels that it is an important function of
the elementary school library to accustom children to the
use of a reference collection.

Periodicals--For reference use, a number of periodical
titles have been recommended for acquisition in the new
library in a file at least five years in depth, along with
the indexes needed to make them effective. Periodicals
can supplement the curriculum in a special way, as for
instance, Arizona Highways in units on desert life and
weather and Beaver in units on Canadian history or geography.

Paperback books and pamphlets--Materials originally published in softcover or paperback, obtainable in no other
form, large enough to be cataloged and handled on the library shelves, have been included in the Collection when
content and style meet our criteria of quality and pertinence. Such titles have been provided in reinforced editions for library use. Many other titles listed in this
Catalog are available in paperback and are being increasingly used by teachers and librarians to provide duplicates
for the library and classroom and for discussion groups.
No effort has been made to list pamphlet materials (less
than fifty pages in length) which should be a part of the
vertical file collection of a library. The establishment
of such a resource is another responsibility of the librarian in each school.

Audio-visual materials--Since it has been the intention in
compiling this Collection to facilitate the establishment
of elementary school libraries which serve as materials
centers, this list includes a selection of recordings, filmstrips and other media. Elementary schools however do
not generally purchase films but depend on centralized
collections or rental agencies for these items; therefore
titles in this form will not be recommended. Selections
designated as Phase I (ph 1) are limited to materials for
the library's own instructional program and materials related to or derived from specific books included in the
list. Materials for supplementing the curriculum in all

areas where excellent filmstrips and recordings are available are included in Phases 2 and 3. Since there is no adequate evaluative list of non-print materials, it is hoped that these materials may be particularly useful. In this edition cards for audio-visual materials have been integrated with cards for book titles. See the preface for further information. The same criteria of suitability, excellence of format, and the like, have been applied to this type of material as to the books selected.

There are special problems in the production of various forms of non-print materials which influence their selection. For example, many of the filmstrips useful for supplementing the curriculum are issued in sets. It did not usually seem feasible to list an incomplete set, or to omit a set entirely, when only one title in a set was not up to standard. However, in a few instances, where several titles in a set were either outside the scope of this list or were judged wholly unsuitable by the selectors, the entry was made for a partial set or the recommended titles were included and treated as individual entries. In the case of recordings, selection has been limited to established producers whose work is apt to continue to be available for purchase, rather than including some worthy title which may be in the market only briefly. It is also assumed that teachers will have in their classrooms the recording sets now issued to accompany most textbook series. The musical recordings in this Collection, selected with the advice of a music educator, are therefore those which will be supplementary to these textbook series and useful for the school's total program. Other forms of non-print material, such as the eight millimeter film, are restricted for our purpose by the still limited availability of equipment and materials for elementary schools and libraries at present. We will add such new types of material as soon as it appears to be feasible.

Similarly the reviewers have given careful attention to other varieties of audio-visual materials such as transparency sets, programmed learning materials, and kits. Each of these categories poses a special problem for inclusion in such a tool as the Elementary School Library Collection. Transparencies are now becoming more readily available through commercial channels. Although many transparencies have been produced for secondary school use, the selectors are able to recommend only a few transparency sets which seem satisfactorily to meet elementary school needs.   The ease with which simple transparencies can be produced with modest copying equipment in an instructional materials center suggests a continuation of the practice of preparing these items locally as the need arises.

Programmed learning materials at the grade levels covered by this Catalog almost universally appear as text materials, which are more generally selected and used as textbooks. Kits (packaged sets) and programmed learning materials have not yet been recommended in this Catalog although schools may be adding these types of materials to their collections.   Kits most frequently are marketed as adjuncts to textbook materials, and the committee recommends that present policies for selection of such items be continued on a local or system-wide basis.   In future editions, there may be policy changes that will incorporate some or all of these types of materials as the field itself develops new techniques and approaches.

Professional materials--In addition to materials for children to use themselves, the elementary school library must serve children through its provision of materials for teachers, administrators, and parents: The list of materials recommended here is limited to those titles which we think have potential value for the classroom teacher and should be easily available in her school building.   Each library should contain a minimum of 200 titles of current pertinence to the classroom teacher's work.   There should be books, timely pamphlets, professional journals and indexes and bibliographies to facilitate a start on an investigation.

Duplication of copies--The Collection indicates those titles selected for the first phase of acquisition which should, in the opinion of the selectors, be provided in more than one copy.   In fact, it is axiomatic that multiple copies of many of these titles will be needed to assure real availability of resources in many schools.   For the later phases of acquisition of the basic collection, decision as to titles needing multiple copies should be another responsibility of the school's own librarian.   Users of this list should also note that deviations from normal grade distributions will alter decisions on what and how much to duplicate.

Note

1. For schools above 600 in enrollment, the reader is reminded that the minimum number of volumes required
would be much higher, no less than ten volumes per
student enrolled, for an adequate collection.

Principles Governing the Selection of Special
Types of Materials

Tulsa City-County Library System

> From Tulsa City-County Library System. "Prin-
> ciples governing the selection of special types of
> materials." Tulsa, Oklahoma, Tulsa City-County
> Library System, n. d. 3 p. Mimeo. Reprinted by
> permission of Barbara Hagist, Tulsa City-County
> Library System.

Audio-Visual Materials

Slides are given preference which have accompanying
scripts or information, meant to be illustrative material
for groups planning programs concerned with the study of
art.

Permanent Art Collections

Framed reproductions are selected for both the adult
and children's permanent art collection to perform an esthetic, as well as educational, function. The quality of
reproduction must be accurate in color and detail. Reproductions are chosen to represent a variety of artists
and styles, with the intent of broadening the artistic experiences of the community.

Picture File

The picture file provides a reservoir of illustrative
material to be available for historical, recreational, educational, and artistic purposes for the community at
large. Pictures are selected from books, magazines,
museum bulletins, etc., which have been otherwise discarded by the library.

Rental Art Collection

The rental art collection consists of framed original art work done primarily by Southwestern artists, selected by a special committee with training and backgrounds in art. The collection is available for rental and purchase, with the idea of encouraging the public in buying original art work, and to give serious artists an opportunity to display and sell their work.

Films

Emphasis is placed on subjects of community and national significance, particularly in the fields of intercultural relations, international understanding, and significant social problems which lend themselves to group discussion. Outstanding documentaries, subjects of general adult interest, both cultural and practical, examples of experimental techniques of film making, and productions which stimulate the creative imagination of children are also included. No attempt is made to build up an archival collection, but films which represent the history and development of the motion picture and which lead to an understanding and appreciation of this medium as an art form may be purchased.

Films produced primarily for classroom use are not included since, like other teaching materials, they are the responsibility of the schools. Highly technical material is rejected as being more suitable for a university or specialized collection. Teacher training materials are purchased only if they are suitable for wider community use. Industrial training films for a specific technique are not purchased, but general supervisory training films as well as vocational guidance films on an adult level are considered. Films including sports of wide interest may be purchased.

The System attempts to locate sponsored films of high quality in areas too specialized to warrant public expenditure, but for which a small but urgent need is felt by the community. All sponsored films are previewed by library staff before final acceptance. Deposit films must meet the same standards of selection as used for films purchased by the System.

Entertainment films such as sixteen millimeter reproductions of animated cartoons, westerns, and Hollywood features are usually excluded from the collection, but outstanding commercial films which have become film classics or which are superior adaptations from books may be purchased.

Kinescopes of significant television programs are pur chased when warranted by the importance or timeliness of the subject.

All films are previewed prior to purchase. Film content, subject matter, and treatment are evaluated in relation to their validity, lasting value or timely importance, imagination, and originality. Technical qualities connected with photography, sound tract, color reproduction, or clearness of black and white prints are examined.

Sheet Music, Scores, etc.

The music collection, answering the interests of a musically active, sophisticated community, eventually aim at a full representation of the works of standard composers, a selection of works by recognized contemporaries, and a wide range of folk music. Vocal music in cludes sheet music as well as volumes. Instrumental m sic includes scores and parts for soloists and small groups, and study scores only of orchestral works.

Editor's note: The reader should also consult in this connection Hagist, Barbara "Resistance and reluctance" Library Journal 93:518-20, February 1, 1968. This criticism of current selection policies for film libraries is by the head of the Fine Arts Department of the Tulsa City-County Library System in Oklahom

Film Selection Policy of Special Services Film Library

Special Services Section, New York State Library

From The Bookmark 25:303-6, May 1966;
Reprinted by permission of R. Edwin Berry,
Editor, The Bookmark, New York State Library,
Albany, New York.

Background

Films, along with various other nonbook media, are an integral and unquestioned part of a public library's service to its community today. Even though the cost of circulating films can be equated favorably with the cost of circulating books, the rather high initial cost of a film quite often prohibits small and medium-sized libraries from acquiring films of their own. Even if their budgets could include a few titles, there would be very little choice of subject matter in any one community. With these factors in mind the New York State Library, through the Library Extension Division, Special Services Section, embarked in 1958 on the task of building a film collection. It would serve as a State-wide resource for people in small and medium-sized communities, and in larger communities and library systems with active film collections, as an in-depth resource supplementing their film collections, thereby spreading the high unit cost of films over the State through broad usage. The funds for this program were received initially from the Federal Library Services Act and continued under the Library Services and Construction Act.

By the terms of the Federal legislation, materials purchased with these funds were for nonclassroom use. In addition to this basic mandate, film collections in several other State agencies needed to be considered. It was decided, that wherever possible, the State Library collection would not duplicate their specific fields of interest or holdings. Close liaison is maintained with the New York State

Departments of Commerce, Health, Conservation, Motor
Vehicles, Mental Hygiene, and the Division for Youth to
carry out this coordination and nonduplication of film purchases at the State level.   Where duplication may occur, it
must be justified by a broader public interest or answer
needs in other areas of interest different from or beyond
those of the specific State department's field.

Purpose

   The purpose of the State Library film collection is to
supply library systems and their members with films they
do not have, might not expect to purchase, or cannot readily
obtain.   The present film collection covers a wide range of
subjects for all age groups.   As system film collections develop, the policy and subject emphasis of the State Library
collection will be more highly selective to support the more
general collections in the systems.

Criteria for Film Selection

   All films are 16mm sound, and wherever appropriate
to the subject, are purchased in color.   Visual materials
produced primarily for classroom use are excluded.   Films
are selected for all age groups, with emphasis on subjects
of educational, social and artistic value.   As the film collection increases, it is important to compare films in one
subject area with others and in relation to the State Library's existing coverage.

   The same general principles used in the selection of
books are used in evaluating the content of films.   Because
of the powerful impact of audiovisual presentation and because the motion picture is essentially a medium for group
viewing, the selector must use, within his ability to judge,
the following special criteria:

   For Adult Films:

   1. The content should be valid, true to fact or true
      to text (if based on writing).
   2. Subject matter should be timely--pertinent to com
      munity needs or problems; or should be of such
      cultural and social value as to be timeless.
   3. The manner of presentation should be suited to
      theme and content, avoiding cheapness, conde-
      scension, preachiness, and coy humor.

4. As an art form the film should be judged for its style, imagination, originality, and other aesthetic qualities in much the same manner as books are judged.
5. The film should have unity, and be a cohesive whole.
6. If color is used, it should definitely add to the film.
7. All films should have the following technical qualities:
   a. Creative photography, sense of movement and change.
   b. Clear understandable sound.
   c. Imaginative narration or dialogue.
   d. Good print quality.

For Children's Films:

The criteria for judging children's films are similar. In addition, however, several points must be emphasized:

1. A film based on a juvenile book is judged by its success in achieving a fresh interpretation consistent with the medium. A good book does not always translate successfully to film. Occasionally a poor book can be the basis for a fine film. Care should be given to the assessment of the film for the qualities of storytelling and characterization.
2. For nonfiction materials, in addition to authenticity, emphasis should be placed on films which offer a creative experience for children.
3. There are some films which may not meet all of the foregoing criteria, but should be considered for purchase because of their motivational impetus. That is, the children, after seeing a particular film, often ask for further library materials on the subject.

For Young Adult Films:

Because the main characteristic of the young adult is "in-betweenness," many adult films and some children's films are equally suitable for this group. While, again, material should be selected that is supplementary to classroom demands, special emphasis is needed in two areas:

1. Films that deal especially with teenage problems, social, physical, psychological and economic.
2. Films that could motivate or strengthen the disadvantaged, the potential dropout, or the nonlibrary user to further concern for self-education and social development.

Factors Affecting Film Selection

The film is a language and medium in itself. But a film collection can and should integrate with and augment total library service, whether at the State, regional or local level.

As system and intersystem audiovisual centers develop or expand, the quality and content of the Special Services collection will profoundly affect selection policy at the local level. While duplication is inevitable and expected at the system level, the State Library selection policy should begin to be more highly selective and specialized, and will:

1. Collect the classical, the outstanding milestones in the motion pictures. This would include the works of pioneer and creative film makers, as well as the classic comedies and comedians. Some of this material will be very expensive and difficult to locate. This should not be an arichival collection. Some titles have both classical and archival value. Films should not be acquired because they are rare but because they have intrinsic reference value and add to the depth and utility of the collection.
2. Acquire some films because of their historical importance or their innate relation to the State's development. New York State history or American history pertinent to New York's history should be emphasized.
3. Purchase in subject fields in enough depth to assist the library systems in special program needs. To do this most effectively it would seem appropriate to purchase several films in the areas of: automation, astrophysics and relativity, alcoholism, juvenile delinquency, unemployment, industrial management, investment problems, urban development, population control, labor relations, international trade, retirement and the aged, business and management, water and air pollution, and other

problems lending themselves to group discussion.

4. Acquire a selected group of films dealing with art, drama, music, dance and related cultural subjects.

5. Procure a selected group of films dealing with librarianship, literature, publishing, information storage and retrieval, and related library and research areas.

6. Purchase representative titles of cinematographic art showing experimental camera work, direction, film editing, creative animation, sound effects and dimensions, creative color control.

In summation, the film selection policy of the State Library should ultimately parallel the policy of its book collection--the classical, the historically valuable, the expensive, the difficult to obtain, plus special subject areas covered in some depth that could support local library services to the community.

Working Book Selection Statement for the
Professional Collection

Pennsylvania State Library

From Pennsylvania State Library. "Working Book
Selection Statement for the Professional Collection." Harrisburg, Pennsylvania, Bureau of Library Development, Pennsylvania State Library,
December 19, 1966. Mimeo. Reprinted by permission of Donald C. Potter, Director, Bureau of
Library Development.

General Policy and Administration

The Pennsylvania State Library, as the Regional Resource Center with responsibility in the area of library service, shall acquire and maintain a comprehensive collection
of materials in the field of library service for the use of
Pennsylvania librarians, trustees, teachers and students of
library service, and for the use of the State Library staff.

These materials shall constitute the Professional Collection and shall be selected, organized, housed and made
accessible by the Bureau of Library Development, subject to
such agreements as are reached in consultation with the head
of all other Bureaus of the State Library.

The Professional Collection shall be under the authority of the Director of the Bureau of Library Development.
The Professional Collection librarian, assisted by the Division staff, shall be responsible for maintaining the Professional Collection and for providing reference and other services, assigning such clerical duties as are necessary.

It shall be the librarian's responsibility to check current publications for new titles, to bring them to the attention of the Director of the Bureau of Library Development,
and where necessary to other Bureau heads, and to submit
order requests to the Bureau of Technical Services.

An effort shall be made to display or otherwise bring to the attention of the staff additions to the Professional Collection, whether books, periodicals, or serials, especially new titles.

I. Book Materials

A. The Bureau of Library Development shall acquire a comprehensive collection of books in the field of library service for its Professional Collection, including:

1. Most items published in English language, both domestic and foreign

2. Selected important works in foreign languages

3. All Books indexed in Library Literature

B. This collection shall be a working one, with title duplications as necessary for advisory service and interlibrary loan demand. The collection shall be retrospective, however, as well as current, and the following methods shall be employed to secure scope and depth of coverage:

1. Current literature shall be watched carefully for new titles

2. Checklists and bibliographies shall be checked against the State Library holdings and an effort shall be made to fill in gaps in the collection

C. Duplication between the Professional Collection and other sections of the State Library:

1. Books pertaining to law librarianship acquired by the Law Library may also be acquired for the Professional Collection. However, the Law Library will be the major source of material on law librarianship, and reference requests on this subject should be referred to the Law Library.

2. Federal and State documents acquired for the Documents Section of the General Library, which it is not feasible to transfer, may also be acquired for the Professional Collection.

3. Titles ordered and held by the Bureau of Library
Development Professional Collection may be duplicated in the General Library for reference use, as
needed.   However, materials in the following fields
shall generally be held by the General Library
rather than the Professional Collection:

   a. Archives (not to be confused with materials on
   archival libraries)

   b. Bibliography and works about special areas of
   literature (e. g. children's literature)

   c. Book publishing

   d. Documentation, information retrieval; except as
   specifically related to the field of librarianship

   e. Genealogy

   f. History of the book

   g. Printing

   h. Rare books

D. An effort shall be made to secure published surveys
of library conditions in the United States and Canada,
as well as foreign surveys in English, with as comprehensive coverage as possible of library surveys of
Pennsylvania libraries.   Such surveys shall be fully
cataloged and treated as books whenever possible.

E. In addition to such items in the Documents Section,
the Professional Collection shall be the main repository for such items as pertain to the history of libraries in Pennsylvania, with the exception of those
which would more properly be placed in the rare
books collection of the General Library.

F. Basic reference titles in the field of library service
that are used frequently by the staff (such as American Library Directory, American Library Annual,
Who's Who in Librarianship) shall be duplicated so
that copies of these works shall be on hand at all
times for the use of the Bureau of Library Development staff.

G. When possible, all library science doctoral dissertations and selected Masters theses and research studies shall be acquired for the Professional Collection.
When published editions are not available, Xerox or
microform editions shall be acquired.

H. All ordering, checking, listing in a public catalog or
catalogs, as well as cataloging, preparing, binding,
etc., shall be performed by the Bureau of Technical
Services for the Professional Collection.   Processed
books will be sent directly to the Bureau of Library
Development.

II. Periodicals and Serials

A. The Professional Collection shall include a wide range
of periodicals and serials in the field of library service consisting of:

1. All domestic and foreign periodicals and serials
indexed in Library Literature

2. All periodicals and serial publications of state libraries, U. S. Territorial libraries, and Canadian
Provincial libraries

3. All periodicals and serial publications of the major national libraries throughout the world

4. Public documents of the Library of Congress, the
Library Services Division of the U. S. Department
of Health, Education and Welfare, and state documents in the field of library science

5. All library association periodicals published in the
English language

6. Such additional titles as are important to the
broadest coverage of developments in all aspects
of library service

B. Duplication between the Professional Collection and
other sections of the State Library.   Refer to I., C.

C. Such periodical titles in the field of library service
as are used frequently by the Bureau of Library Development staff (such as Library Journal and Wilson

Library Bulletin) shall be duplicated so that copies
are on hand at all times

D.   Periodicals and serials indexed in Library Literature
shall be bound and back issues retained indefinitely.
Back issues of periodicals and serials which are not
bound shall be kept for a period of five years.

E.   All ordering, checking, listing in a public periodical
and serials catalog or catalogs, as well as cataloging,
preparing, binding, etc. , shall be performed by the
Bureau of Technical Services for the Professional
Collection.   Professional periodicals shall be sent directly to the Bureau of Library Development, and
routing to staff members shall be done there.

F.   The Bureau of Library Development shall endeavor to
assist the Bureau of Technical Services to secure
periodicals and serials on exchange whenever possible,
offering the Pennsylvania Library Association Bulletin,
Pennsylvania State Library publications, and other
Commonwealth publications as the basis for exchange.

III. Vertical File

A vertical file of pamphlets and other materials within
the area of librarianship shall be maintained.   Subject
headings are selected from H. W. Wilson's Library Literature.   All materials shall be identified as belonging to the
Professional Collection and dated.

IV. Audio-Visual Materials

The Professional Collection shall include all types of
audio-visual materials which relate to the field of library
service, including all library activities and buildings, according to the appropriate media below.

A. Films, educational

1. The Bureau of Library Development shall acquire
a comprehensive collection of films.   These films
shall be housed within the Division, and arrangements will be made with the Department of Public
Instruction for their maintenance.

2. These films shall be duplicated as necessary.

B. Filmstrips

    1. Filmstrips shall be housed in the Visual Aids Section of the General Library.

    2. The Professional Collection librarian shall maintain a record of the contents of this collection and shall assist in its selection.

C. Picture collection

    1. The Bureau of Library Development shall establish and maintain a file of pictures, with emphasis on Pennsylvania.

    2. Subject headings for the picture file shall be adapted from H. W. Wilson's <u>Library Literature.</u> All materials shall be identified as belonging to the Professional Collection and dated.

D. Recordings

    1. Recordings shall be housed in the Spoken Word Collection of the General Library.

    2. The Professional Collection librarian shall maintain a record of the contents of this collection and shall assist in its selection.

E. Slides

    1. Slides shall be housed in the Visual Aids Section of the General Library.

    2. The Professional Collection librarian shall maintain a record of the contents of this collection and shall assist in its selection, with emphasis on Pennsylvania libraries.

F. The Bureau of Library Development shall establish and maintain a collection of tape recordings.

Guidelines on the Treatment of Minorities in the Selection
of Instructional Materials

New Jersey Education Association

From New Jersey Education Association Review,
November 1967, p. 20-21; Reprinted by permissio
of Norman Goldman, Associate Editor.

The New Jersey Education Association recommends
that, in addition to the standard indices of quality and appropriateness, textbooks and other instructional materials ir
all school systems, in all subject areas, and at all grade
levels meet the following requirements:

1. Give comprehensive and satisfactory treatment to
the contribution and life of various minority groups in our
society.

2. Reflect the most recent results of authoritative
scholarship and research, especially in removing myths and
interpretations which have obscured the proper history and
roles of various minority groups and their prominent representatives in American life.

3. Avoid stereotyping or condescension which contributes to unfounded, unfavorable impressions of any group;
and encourage pupils to use critical thinking and problem
solving techniques to identify tendencies toward stereotyping,
intolerance, and fear.

4. Treat with historical accuracy and frankness pres
ent and past tensions of intergroup relations, as well as the
undesirable consequences of withholding rights and freedoms
from any citizen; and present effective ways in which such
problems are and have been best solved through the interaction of individuals working harmoniously.

5. Show the cultural diversity and pluralistic nature
of our society in both textual and illustrative material (both

photographs and sketches), recognizing that merely altering illustrations does not in itself constitute a balanced treatment.

6. Recognize that fair treatment is not limited to racial, ethnic or religious groups, but also applies to the differences and diversity among urban, suburban, and rural ways of living and the variations in economic status ranging from those of lowest income to the most affluent.

7. Provide psychological support for learning by making it possible for children of minority groups to identify themselves with individuals or groups in their books, as well as provide a basis for teaching respect for the inherent worth and rights of all persons to children who might not live near nor regularly associate with children different from themselves.

8. Apply these same standards to any evaluation of the range of materials included in supplementary reading and library collections, recognizing that even greater diversity can be achieved by specialized sources covering particular individuals, groups, and intergroup situations.

The Students' Right to Read

National Council of Teachers of English

From National Council of Teachers of English.
The Students' Right to Read.   Champaign, Illinois,
The Council, 1962. p. 13-19; Reprinted by per-
mission of the Council.

A Program of Action

Clearly book censorship threatens to become a widespread problem for schools.   Teachers of English, librarians
and school administrators can best serve students and the
profession today if they prepare now to face outside pressures sensibly, demonstrating on the one hand a willingness
to consider the merits of any complaint and on the other
hand the courage to defend with intelligence and vigor a
sound program in literature.   The Council therefore recommends that every school undertake the following two-step
program to protect the students' right to read:

> The establishment of a committee of teachers to
> consider book selection and to screen outside com-
> plaints.

> A vigorous campaign to establish a community climat
> in which informed local citizens may be enlisted to
> support the freedom to read.

Procedures for Book Selection[1]

Although one may defend without reservation the freedom to read as the hallmark of a free society, there is no
substitute for informed and qualified book selection.   The
English teacher is better qualified to choose books for his
classroom than a person who is not prepared in the field.
Nevertheless, the administrator has certain legal and profes
sional responsibilities.   He must, therefore, be kept well in

formed about the criteria and procedures used in selection
and the books chosen.

In every school the English department should frame
a clear statement that explains why literature is taught, by
what standards it is chosen, what reputable and unbiased selection aids are used as guides.   If the standards used in
choosing books for suggested reading lists differ from those
used in selecting basic texts for all students, such differences should be clearly explained.   This statement should
be on file with the administration before any complaints are
received.

Operating within such a policy, the English department should--

Ask each English teacher to present his list of
choices to a meeting of the English department.
Schools without departments should organize ad hoc
meetings of qualified teachers and librarians for this
purpose.

File with administrators the list approved by teachers.

Give the teacher a chance to explain his choice if
any book is questioned.

Such a procedure gives each teacher the right to expect support from fellow teachers and administrators whenever someone objects to a book.

The Legal Problem

Apart from the professional and moral issues involved
in censorship, there are legal matters about which the NCTE
cannot give advice.   The Council is not a legal authority.
Across the nation, moreover, conditions vary so much that
no one general principle applies.   In some states, for example, textbooks are purchased from public funds and supplied free to students; in others, books are rented to students; in a few, students must buy their own textbooks.

The legal status of textbook adoption lists also varies.
These lists, at times, include only those books which must
be taught and allow teachers freedom to select additional
titles; other lists are restrictive, containing the only books
which may be required for all students.   In the absence of

widely accepted guidelines, many teachers who use lists containing books not officially adopted have found it wise, as a general rule, to label such lists "recommended" or "suggested," not "required" reading.

As a part of sensible preparations for handling attacks on books, each school should ascertain what laws do apply to it.

Preparing the Community

To handle complaints about books, every school should have a committee of teachers organized to--

Inform the community on book choices.

Enlist support from citizens, possibly by explaining policies at such meetings of parent groups as those called by the Parent-Teacher Association.

Consider any complaints against books.

No community is too small to have a group of enlightened people, often college-educated but not necessarily so, who have gravitated together because of mutual interests. Doctors, lawyers, members of the League of Women Voters, of the AAUW, of the Parent-Teacher Association, and other people interested in the education of the young might be organized into a Committee on the Right to Read or Citizens for Books. If they make their position felt through letters, telephone calls, and personal visits in defense of a besieged book, they may well cancel the protests and impress the authorities who have the power to censor.

Defending the Books

Despite both the care taken to select valuable books for student reading, and the qualifications of persons who select the books, occasional objections to a selection will undoubtedly be made. Probably no book has ever been printed to which someone could not object. Most books (even the Bible) are open to objections in one or more general areas: the treatment of ideologies, of minorities, of love and sex; the use of language not approved by certain segments of society; the type of illustration; the private life or political affiliations of the author.

Some attacks are made by persons frankly hostile to free inquiry and open discussion; others are made by misinformed or misguided persons, who, acting on emotion or rumor, simply do not understand how books are used; still others are made by well-intentioned, conscientious persons who fear that harm will come to a segment of the population if a certain book is read.

Occasionally, of course, teachers lacking judgment or inadequately prepared in literature are permitted to choose and to teach books. The complaints against selection made by such teachers may indeed be reasonable. In no sense should a committee of English teachers blindly defend the use of substandard, unliterary materials or the presentation to children of books suitable only for mature readers.

Complaints generally come by letter or telephone to a teacher, librarian, principal, superintendent, or a member of the board of education. The complaint often remains anonymous, often represents no one but himself, but is nevertheless able to stir up a whirlpool of misunderstandings. No one wants trouble or bad publicity. Regardless of the cause of the complaints, the results are often the same; the objector is placated, teacher morale is undermined, and a book useful in helping the student understand his world disappears from the curriculum.

Too many schools give in to belligerent threats of community sanctions and vague references to the backing of powerful forces. As a result, without due process, without a specific charge having been made, without a complaint having been signed, without all interested persons having been heard, students are denied the right to read. The many parents who want their children to have a broad education are victims of the few who do not.

What should be done when a complaint is made?

If the complainant telephones, listen courteously, and invite him to file his complaint in writing, but make no commitments, admissions of guilt, or threats.

If he writes, acknowledge the letter promptly and politely.

In either case, offer to send the complainant a prepared questionnaire so that he may submit a formal statement to the book selection committee. (See sample.)

Citizen's Request for Reconsideration
of a Book

Author   Hardcover   Paperback

Title

Publisher (if known)

Request initiated by _____

Telephone_____   Address _____

City _____   Zone_____

Complainant represents

_____   himself

_____   (name organization) _____

_____   (identify other group) _____

1. To what in the book do you object? (Please be specific; cite pages.)_____

2. What do you feel might be the result of reading this book?

   _____

3. For what age group would you recommend this book? ____

   _____

4. Is there anything good about this book?_____

   _____

5. Did you read the entire book?_____   What parts?_____

   _____

6. Are you aware of the judgment of this book by literary critics?_____

7. What do you believe is the theme of this book?_____

   _____

8. What would you like your school to do about this book?

   _____   do not assign it to my child

   _____   withdraw it from all students as well as from my child

   _____   send it back to the English department office for reevaluation

Citizen's Request for Reconsideration of a Book (cont.)

9. In its place, what book of equal literary quality would you recommend that would convey as valuable a picture and perspective of our civilization?

Signature of Complainant

At first, except for acknowledgment and explanation of established procedures, do nothing. The success of much censorship of this sort depends upon frightening an unprepared school into an unwise course of action.

A standardized procedure will take the sting from the first outburst of criticism. When the responsible objector learns the channels and procedures for his complaint, he is satisfied that he will be properly heard. The idle troublemaker, on the other hand, may well be discouraged from taking action.

In addition to the advantages already cited for this form, it will do the following:

Formalize and make official the complaint.

Indicate specifically the book in question.

Identify the complainant.

Reveal the size of his backing.

Require him to clarify his thinking on the book in order to make an intelligent statement on the specific objection (#1 and #2).

Cause him to evaluate the book, especially for other groups beyond the one he has immediately in mind (#3 and #4).

Establish to what extent he is familiar with the book (#5).

Give him an opportunity to recognize the criticism and intent of the book or to realize his failure to understand it (#6 and #7).

Give him, finally, alternative actions to be taken on the book (#8 and #9).

The committee of teachers to review complaints should be available at short notice to consider the Citizen's Request for Reconsideration of a Book and to call in the complainant for conference. The members of the committee should have reevaluated the book in advance of the conference and the group should be prepared to explain its subsequent findings. If the committee feels the book is justifiably available to students but the complainant remains adamant in his demand for its withdrawal, the committee should not hesitate to take the case to the newspaper or to other local news channels. The complainant by this time may have indicated his plan to do so, and the committee will often gain support by getting there first. The freedom of the press, a principle dear to most newspaper publishers, is a healthy ally to freedom to read.

Teachers and administrators in the system should recognize that responsibility for selecting the book in question lies with the teacher group concerned and should cooperate fully with the reevaluation committee, refraining from discussion of the issue with the complainant or any community group or with the press. Once the machinery has been set into motion by the filing of the request, the authority for handling the situation should remain ultimately with the administration which will act on the teachers' recommendations.

A courteous and dispassionate approach is essential in considering complaints. The American public schools, in reflecting their communities, respect a formidable opinion against any book on their shelves, but they must take great care not to be intimidated by a lone dissenter whose tastes run counter to those of the best authorities and to those of the majority of the community. At the same time, they certainly want a complainant to know that they will consider his opinion and that they welcome his interest.

Freedom of inquiry is essential to education in a democracy. To establish the climate essential for freedom, teachers and administrators need to follow book selection

ractices similar to those recommended here. Where
chools resist unreasonable pressure, the cases are seldom
ublicized and students continue to read the books. Only if
nformed groups, within the profession and without, unite in
esisting unfair pressures can our school programs in litera-
ure do what they ought to do, to transmit intact our cultur-
l heritage.

Note

. The principal concern here is for books to be used in
English classes. The more general problem of selecting materials for school libraries has already been
under study by many national groups. Much useful
information on this broader question is available from
the American Library Association.

The Freedom to Read and the Political Problem

by Wesley McCune   Director, Group Research, In
                                     Washington, D. C. ; newspaper-
                                     man, and student of right wing
                                     organizations. This selection
                                     is from a speech made at an
                                     Institute held by the ALA Com
                                     mittee on Intellectual Freedom

From ALA Bulletin 59:502-6, June 1965; Reprinted by permission of the Editor, ALA Bulletin

The portent for librarians

These major observations add up to a conclusion that
librarians will be getting a flood of right-wing material, if
it has not already been received. It may mean that the im
pact of the right wing in your areas will not be so much in
cidents of harassment of librarians as an attempt to inundate you with what we will loosely call "literature. " I am
in favor of having right- and left-wing literature on library
shelves, and I believe in presenting a balance, but the point
is that a larger bill of fare is being offered by the right
wing and it will be pressed upon you with more enthusiasm,
if not with outright fanaticism, from time to time.

I am sure that this means that librarians will want
to be able to identify and distinguish the right-wing material; this will not always be easy, because the material will
not always be marked. It will become more and more important to know the organization putting out a pamphlet or a
book. It will be much more important to know who the authors of books are and what cause they are selling. For
example, I have already mentioned the Americans for Const
tutional Action and the index they publish on conservative
and liberal issues. This organization also collects and
spends money in political campaigns, usually in the form of
putting a man in the field to help write advertising copy,
radio programs, or speech scripts.

What is not so well known about ACA is that it is interlocked substantially with the John Birch Society. Admiral Moreell is not a Bircher himself, but two of his top three other officers are identified as leaders of the John Birch Society and at least one trustee of ACA has been active in the John Birch Society. In addition, we have studied the financial support of both groups and find that at least one-fifth of the contributions to ACA come from easily recognized John Birch supporters. It is therefore important for a librarian to know, if he uses the ACA index, that this is not merely the operation of a retired admiral interested in the Constitution but is Birch-like in its nature and has connections of that kind.

Perhaps my most helpful contribution to this important meeting will be to lay out a few subpoints of this proposition that may help a librarian working his way through the right-wing material. My subpoints will deal particularly with the last three observations on right-wing activity that I have mentioned--political activity, financial support, and publications.

The first observation for librarians, in the area of publications, is that established right-wing publishers have stepped up their activities and improved the appearance of their publications, as well as their services. (We all know that a publisher may have many kinds of books in his line, right-wing and left-wing, but I am generalizing for the moment.) For example, Henry Regnery of Chicago has added substantially to its line of right-wing books and is doing a better and better job of presenting new products. The Bookmailer, which is a distributor and publisher, has made it easy for right wingers, as well as other booklovers, to get the products of the intellectual right wing. It is important to know, if you don't, that The Bookmailer is the operation of Lyle Munson, whom Robert Welch has described publicly as his good friend who has published all of the 100 books on the John Birch Society recommended list.

The John Birch Society has set up a subsidiary publishing house called Western Islands which has published such distinguished authors as Holmes Alexander, syndicated for years by McNaught. Nowhere on their books is the identification of the John Birch Society even hinted at, but the corporate connection is not hard to find.

The Conservative Book Club has recently been organ-

ized by a professional book man at the address of America
Future, Inc., which runs something called "Operation Text
book," a critical review of textbooks having too many "libe
al" messages hidden among their lines.   The opening prom
tions of the Conservative Book Club featured an author
named Victor Lasky, who is best known for his thick polit
cal biography and/or hatchet job on John F. Kennedy.   Th
club is sponsored by most of the editors of National Revie
as well as James Jackson Kilpatrick, editor of the Richmo
News-Leader and one of the organizers of the anticivil rigl
lobby; retired Admiral Radford; Howard Kershner, editor (
Christian Economics; and four conservative congressmen.
The material it sends out each month to promote its books
is among the most attractive I have seen in any field.

Second, the right wing is supplying more of its own
book reviews.   In the December 26, 1964, issue of Human
Events, an excellent right-wing publication, John Chamberlain, a veteran reviewer of books, said in his syndicated
column that a recent addition to the literature of the right
wing written by Henry Hazlitt "ought to be a big seller, bu
since the reviewing world is infested with the fashionable
enemies of the Hazlitt view of things, it probably won't ge
the notice it deserves."   That has been the right-wing attitude for a long time and perhaps should be put down to de-
monology or the conspiracy theory rather than to literary
criticism, but the right-wing reviewers are working harder
these days than ever.   America's Future, mentioned above
publishes a little pamphlet regularly with its review of
books, and its commentator, R. K. Scott, is on the radio
daily over several hundred stations with a general conserv
tive line of comment.

The Educational Reviewer, run by Russell Kirk, is
another example of increasingly greater promotion of right
wing views in book review form.   This enterprise was organized by a group called CASBO (Conference of American
Small Business Organizations) as a way of showing to the
American people the story of free enterprise.   A congres-
sional investigating committee, the Buchanan Committee,
found that the Educational Reviewer was an "ingenious contribution to the encyclopedia of pressure tactics."   It concluded: "The long-run aim of this program is obvious and
this is nothing less than the establishment of CASBO's philosophy as the standard of educational orthodoxy in the
schools of the Nation.   We all agree, of course, that our
textbooks should be American, that they should not be the

vehicle for the propagation of obnoxious doctrines. Yet the
review of textbooks by self-appointed experts... smacks too
much of the book-burning orgies of Nuremberg to be accepted by thoughtful Americans without foreboding and alarm. "

The Educational Reviewer publishes a quarterly called
The University Bookman and also run by Russell Kirk, a
leading intellectual of the conservative movement.   Other
regular, right-wing publications carry hard-hitting book review sections.   The prime example of this is Professor
Revilo P. Oliver's contribution to the monthly John Birch
Society publication, American Opinion.   Book reviews consistently get good space also in National Review.

"Nonbooks" appear

Third, the "nonbooks" are coming on stronger.   I call
them nonbooks, because they are essentially overdrawn pamphlets, but also because most of them have "nonpublishers. "
By this I mean that they have no established publishers.   I
do not mean to criticize the sudden entry into the publishing
business of any new enterpriser at any time.   The point is
that these "books" just appear from someone's living room or
even some less identifiable place.

For example, during the campaign of 1964 the book
by John Stormer, None Dare Call It Treason, reached about
8 million overnight and was published by something called
the Liberty Bell Press.   When reporters went looking for
the Liberty Bell Press, they had trouble finding it.   It was
finally discovered at the address of a beauty parlor around
the corner from the author's home in Missouri.   Obviously,
these nonbooks are being stimulated and are not being published in the usual sense of a publisher engaging in a business to see if enough people will buy a new product to make
it worthwhile for him to put it on the press and to stand behind it.   These are being created as a propaganda instrument and then called books as a way of insinuating them into the main stream of our literature.

Examples in addition to Stormer include A Choice Not
An Echo, by Phyllis Schlafly, which was designed to influence the Republican convention at San Francisco to choose
Barry Goldwater over Nelson Rockefeller, and A Texan Looks
at Lyndon, by J. Evetts Haley, a long-time member of the
radical right in Texas.   We should also mention that H. L.
Hunt, the Texas oil billionaire and operator of a right-wing

program called Life Line, privately has published three thin
paperbacks and that a man named Frank Kluckhohn, who has
credentials in the writing game, has turned out a number of
campaign-time biographies of this same general sort.

Barry Goldwater's first book, Conscience of a Conservative, which helped to make him famous, was the brain
child of a right winger who works with Clarence Manion in
Indiana and formerly worked with Father Coughlin in Detroit
He suggested that a collection of the senator's positions
would be a good idea and put the imprint of the Victor Publishing Company on it.   This turns out to be a printing plant
run by the man who suggested the book.   After runaway sale
were indicated, the imprint was transferred to a more established book publisher.

There is little doubt that we are in for more of this
type of publishing, rather than for less.   For example, an
organization called The Spirit of '76 House at Holliston,
Massachusetts, has announced that it is bringing out a book
on Vice-President Hubert Humphrey.   All indications are
that it will be written by the same man who had an article
in the John Birch Society magazine during the campaign com
paring Mr. Humphrey with Benito Mussolini.

Fourth, librarians will have a more difficult time in
classifying pamphlets and flyers, just as it is more difficult
these days to tell what a book is.   There is a tremendous
stream of miscellaneous material coming from the right
wing.   For example, H. L. Hunt's Life Line turns out a four
page publication every other day in addition to its daily radi
broadcasts and transcripts.   Billy James Hargis, who runs
the Christian Crusade in Tulsa, Oklahoma, is a very prolific pamphleteer.   He attacks everybody from Drew Pearso
to Martin Luther King and includes Group Research, Inc.
addition, he turns out many long-playing records, religious
items, and even litter bags.

The total is quite a mish-mash of propaganda and mi
information.   There is Liberty Lobby, a Washington-based
group which got into the publishing business with a campaig
tabloid attacking President Johnson, but has also done a pa
phlet sharply criticizing the former Republican leaders in th
Congress and their "Ev and Charlie show."   In addition ther
are numerous regular newsletters such as Tactics, Heads
Up, American Security Council Washington Report, and dozens of casual mimeographs addressed to "Dear Friends" fro

such people as Rev. Carl McIntire, Dr. Fred Schwarz, Gerald L. K. Smith, and others who keep the contributions coming in. The point is that these may be hard to classify but they are an important and significant part of right-wing literature. In fact, the casual letters are sometimes more revealing than the publications which have second-class privileges and the general appearance of a periodical.

Fifth, radio tapes, films, and recordings are coming in larger quantity. This probably adds no new problems to the librarian because other groups use similar techniques, but do not overlook the tapes and films as a source of the history of the right wing.

Sixth, the regular publications of the right wing are almost too numerous to mention. We have said that they are quite good in appearance, leaving out contents at the moment, but we ought to mention a few to give an example of publications which a librarian might want, or be called upon to furnish. The White Citizens Councils publish an attractive magazine called The Citizen. On the other hand, an extremist group called the National States Rights Party issues a wild tabloid called The Thunderbolt. In between you have a regular weekly tabloid called Human Events which reports from Washington and picks up most of the conservative columnists, nearly a score of them. Then there is National Review, a slick-paper, high-level intellectual publication of the Buckley family; and there are other intellectual right-wing publications such as Western Destiny or The Intercollegiate Review, published by the Intercollegiate Society of Individualists. In addition, there are regular publications of conservative groups such as the Foundation for Economic Education, at Irvington-on-the-Hudson; the American Enterprise Institute, at Washington; and the American Economic Foundation, in New York.

Seventh, there is an increasing number of awards, scholarships, and subsidies from the right wing. For example, you may find that some publication said it won an award from the Freedoms Foundation at Valley Forge and you might need to know something about this organization. It is a super-patriotic group which hands out a thousand awards a year, including some to very active right wingers but also some to nondescript schoolteachers, students, and editorial writers.

The subsidies are a little harder to root out. Some-

times they are not mentioned in the introduction of a book,
but when they are, it will be important to know something
about the organization putting up the money.   For example,
we found that an Indiana group called the National Foundation
for Education in American Citizenship had been sending
$40,000 a year to Human Events, a hard-hitting exponent
of conservatism or reaction.   In fact, the Internal Revenue
Service cancelled this group's tax exemption, presumably because it was not sticking to education.   A newer group in
Indiana, headquartered at Wabash College and called Principles of Freedom, is an open subsidy for textbooks and
other books.   It states that it plans to order 5000 books
from prospective publishers as a way of getting the books
off the ground, and it has a budget of $50,000 a year.   The
key man in this planned operation is Dean Benjamin Rogge,
who is also chairman of the board of the Foundation of Economic Education and has been a lecturer for the Intercollegiate Society of Individualists.

There are many other foundations which give stipends
to authors for learned books.   Among these, the Lilly Foundation has been quite active.   The Volker Fund has stimulated many conservative authors on many campuses to write
books which they may or may not have had in mind otherwise.

Eighth, there is a rash of strange schools and institutions.   Among the strangest are the Freedom School and
Rampart College near Colorado Springs; both might be ignored except that some quite high-ranking scholars have
journeyed there to lecture, including several members of
the Goldwater braintrust in the last campaign.   Then there
is Carl McIntire's summer school at the Christian Admiral
Hotel on Cape May, New Jersey, and Billy James Hargis'
school at the Summit Hotel in Colorado Springs.   In addition, we have MacArthur Academy in Texas and Bob Jones
University in South Carolina.   The granddaddy of them all
is probably Harding College, which has been called the West
Point of the right wing and is known for a steady stream of
ultraconservative literature and speakers.   Also, Harding
College has semi-formal arrangements with Oklahoma Christian College, Pepperdine College, and King's College.

An example of the sprouting of the new type of school
has occurred at Brookfield, Wisconsin, where the loser of
the battle to put McGuffey readers back in the public schools
set up a new institution called the Academy of Basic Educa-

tion.   The head of this school, William B. Smeeth, is also active in the Freedom School at Colorado Springs and is a "graduate" of it.

Ninth, there has been an increase in the number of free books offered librarians and private citizens.   The mail frequently brings a slender volume or nonbook with the compliments of some right-wing businessman who urges us to pass it along to someone else.   H. L. Hunt has been known to send 100 copies of his basic book, Alpaca, to small schools without even letting them know it was coming.   Retired General A. C. Wedemeyer, for instance, sent out right-wing books during last fall's campaign.   A librarian, I should think, would have to decide what to do with these gifts and would certainly want to be able to identify them quite accurately, whether he accepts them or not.

In addition to these points, you will always have self-appointed critics, professional or amateurs.   These will include demagogic politicians; these will include people like E. Merrill Root, a professor and Birch faithful who writes about alleged subversion on the campus; these will include newspaper publishers like the Hoiles; and they will include self-appointed critics like J. Evetts Haley, who a few years ago favored hanging Chief Justic Earl Warren, rather than impeaching him.

I sincerely hope that you will help all of us thread our ways through propaganda, opinion, and fact to increase our level of understanding, and that you are not hurt for your efforts.   To the extent that you fail, we will have stultification, intellectual conformity, ignorance, unheard ideas, and unread books.   These are the marks of extremism, not of the democratic process.

Election Year Tests Book Selection Policies

Dayton and Montgomery County Public Library

From This Month in your Library 9:1 and 3,
November 1964; Reprinted by permission of
William Chait, Director, Dayton and Montgomery
County Public Library, Dayton, Ohio

To an unusual degree, books have been involved in
this year's election campaign and the Library has sometimes
found itself in the midst of controversies it did not seek.
The question was discussed by the Board of Trustees at its
October meeting and the members expressed themselves as
in agreement with the policies outlined in a statement they
had been given by William Chait, the Library Director.
Parts of this follow:

The three major books in question are None Dare
Call It Treason, A Choice Not an Echo, and A
Texan Looks at Lyndon.   There are other books
in this category but the three titles above are the
ones which are creating the controversies.

None of these titles meet the criteria of the Library's book selection policy calling for authenticity of material, objectivity of approach, reputation of author and publisher, and suitable format
for circulation.   All of these books are highly partisan, published outside of the normal book trade
channels, poorly bound in paper back form and
available free or at low prices.   The Library
would not carry them except that they are controversial and we pride ourselves on our stand for
the 'freedom to read.'   We also have a need to
include in the collection the documents of our
times.

The decision was made to include these three
titles but at the same time it was decided that we

had no business giving these books special mass distribution. In keeping with our previous policy on controversial books (usually because of the treatment of sex) copies are assigned to the Main Library and branch requests are filled from these copies since we find that the demand drops considerably as soon as the titles leave the public eye. Branches do not have the space to stock unused titles.

Our general practice for all books has been to try to stock one copy for every three reserves we have, except when funds do not permit or the demand seems to be artificial or temporary. We have not exceeded three reserves for each copy of the books in question and in some cases have no reserves waiting.

The Library's Book Selection Policy, which was adopted by the Board in April, 1960, is the basis of the procedure described in Mr. Chait's statement. The following excerpts are of interest in this connection:

The primary need in a community like Montgomery County is for a general collection of books and other materials, selected with due regard to the general character of the community and to individual differences in education, reading ability, interests and needs. The Library has an obligation to supply material for increasing community awareness of local, national and international developments and problems.

Consideration is given to the demands from readers but an attempt is made to weigh specific demand in relation to the total library program and policies... Special interests are considered in acquiring materials but such interests must be reasonably broad and must be common to more than one or two individuals.

Minority viewpoints and treatments of several sides of controversial subjects, whether or not they are popular sides, may be included; however, the Library is under no obligation to furnish a public platform for every extremist who has sufficient funds to publish his viewpoint...

Materials are duplicated within reason to take ca
of permanent or even temporary demands, such a
by study groups on government or foreign affairs
but the Library cannot undertake to meet the nee
for large class assignments for any age group to
the detriment of its use by the adult public as a
whole.   A sound, readable book will be duplicate
in the ratio of one for each three reserves at the
Main Library, but extensive duplication of sensational, trivial and biased books, however popular
is not desirable.

Anyone who is interested in consulting the complete
Book Selection Policy, which covers many points beside tho
pertinent to the present discussion, may ask to see it.

Operation Abolition - A Film Review

ALA Audio-Visual Committee, Film Review Subcommittee

From ALA Bulletin 55:424-5, May 1961; Reprinted by permission of the Editor, ALA Bulletin

This review of Operation Abolition was prepared by the Film Review Subcommittee of ALA's Audio-Visual Committee. The subcommittee's reviews are published quarterly in the Booklist. Since the policy of the Booklist is to publish only reviews of recommended films, this review of a much-discussed film is published here as a special service. George Holloway, head, Educational Films Department, Free Library of Philadelphia, summarized comments from five committee reviewers and editorials from many sources in compiling the review.

Operation Abolition. Distributor: Washington Video Productions, Inc., 1637 Wisconsin Ave., N.W., Washington 7, D.C. 1960. 45 min. $100.00.

This film supports the contention of the House Committee on Un-American Activities that the Communist party is working within a pre-established time schedule on a project called "Operation Abolition," designed to destroy the committee. This film was produced and submitted to the House of Representatives as part of House Report No. 2228, and depicts the student riots during the San Francisco hearings of the HCUA May 12-14, 1960. "Films of the proceedings were taken by various news services and have been prepared and composed into a movie short by Washington Video Productions, Inc." (House Report 2228).

Commentators appearing in the film are Congressmen Francis Walter, Edwin Willis, August Johansen, and Gordon Scherer, who make the point that student demonstrations were inspired by Communist agitators.

> Among those arrested in the City Hall at San Fran
> cisco were a few trained Communist agents. The
> others were the unwitting dupes of the party, who
> had in the heat of chanting and singing performed
> like puppets with Communists in control of the
> strings, even to the point of wilfully and delibera
> ly defying law and order.

The Congressmen compare these techniques of inciting others to violence (particularly students) with the patter
of Communist-led rioting in Venezuela, Cuba, and Japan.

The film's narration follows closely the report of
FBI Director Hoover entitled Communist Target--Youth, in
which he said,

> The Communists demonstrated in San Francisco
> just how powerful a weapon Communist infiltration
> is. They revealed how it is possible for only a
> few Communist agitators, using mob psychology,
> to turn peaceful demonstrations into riots.

It must be assumed that the HCUA prepared the film or at
least endorsed it; however, no production credits appear an
where in the film. The Reporter magazine (Nov. 24, 1960)
credits much of the technical work and the narrator's voice
to Fulton Lewis III.

Much controversy has raged about this film. Probably one's reactions to it depend in some measure on one's
feelings about the HCUA and its actions. Those who sincerely and out of patriotic interests oppose the HCUA and
its modus operandi tend to feel the film is an unwarranted
propaganda tool, prepared by the committee to help sustain
itself. Another complaint is that the committee distorted th
true facts to imply falsely that Communists inspired and led
the riots. Among those organizations opposed to the film
are the American Civil Liberties Union, the AFL-CIO, the
National Lawyers Guild, and the American Friends Committee on Legislation. Editorials criticizing the film appeared
in The Reporter (Nov. 24, 1960), Christian Century (Jan. 4,
1961), New York Post (Jan. 26, 1961), Washington Post, etc
The National Council of Churches has cautioned local church
not to show the film unless providing beforehand a full and
fair presentation of facts relating to the San Francisco

events, as contained in a 35-page study document prepared by the council. The council representatives expressed concern about accusations in the film reflecting adversely upon the reputations of students and about the film's effect upon freedom of expression by implying that a criticism of the House Committee is Communist-inspired.

Organizations subscribing to the film include the American Legion, the Daughters of the American Revolution, the National Association of Manufacturers, the U. S. Chamber of Commerce, and the Department of Defense. Editorial writers endorsing the film include David Lawrence, Ray Henle (broadcaster), Paul Jones (Philadelphia Bulletin). An editorial in the Washington Star supported the film.

Considering technical criteria only, this film is unsatisfactory in several respects. There are two out-of-focus segments each lasting fifteen seconds, and on three occasions the narration does not describe the visual material or is too far ahead of events taking place on the screen. A portion of unrelated narrative described students throwing shoes and jostling police officers, and the beating of one officer with his own night-stick, but no pictures of these events are shown.

The film is not without its moments of superior reporting: Congressman Willis describing in a short clear interview the reasons for these hearings and the purpose of the HCUA; Archie Brown and the other subpoenaed witnesses shouting defiance to the committee until the chairman, not able to obtain order, requests their removal; a pathetic but humorous shot of a plump female student demonstrator bumping down thirty feet of wet marble staircase. Perhaps these few excellent scenes will appear later in a more objective and impartial documentary report of student rioting and Communist activity in the United States.

This is the first film on this subject, and perhaps necessarily exhibits the bias of its creators. After all, they are exercising their right of freedom of expression. But the use to which their film will inevitably be put by some supporters of the HCUA--whose ultimate aim undeniably is to defend our country and its constitution from the Communists --may well deny this privilege of expression to some. There is a very definite implication made by the film that all opposition to the committee is either directly Communist or Communist-inspired. A more honest documentary covering these issues would probably have pointed out that many Americans feel that the committee's actions often infringe on constitutional rights involving personal freedoms.

All five film librarians sending comments to this compiler indicated they were not purchasing the film.   It seems more appropriate that agencies other than the public library circulate this film, as for example the American Legion is doing in Cincinnati and the Christian Anti-Communism Crusade in Philadelphia.

Editors note: For related material see also Holloway, George   "Controversy on film," Library Journal 88: 513-15, February 1, 1963 (a discussion of the review quoted here) and also "Lecture hall issue raised by Birchers," Newsletter on Intellectual Freedom, March 1968, p. 18 (and also in Library Journal 93: 22, January 1, 1968.)

"Preface"

of From Radical Left to Extreme Right

by Robert H. Muller   Associate Director, University
of Michigan Library, Ann
Arbor

> From his From Radical Left to Extreme Right;
> Current Periodicals of Protest, Controversy, or
> Dissent - USA. Ann Arbor, Michigan, Campus
> Publishers, 1967. p. xi-xii; xii-xv; xvi-xvii;
> Reprinted by permission of the author.

The "Library Bill of Rights" commits librarians to a
policy of providing materials presenting all points of view
concerning the problems and issues of our times. How seriously such responsibility is taken depends on a number of
factors. Some libraries limit themselves to providing books
and periodicals that historically summarize the problems and
issues of our times. Others feel that one must go further
and make available the actual current first-hand communications from the propagandists themselves. Quite a few libraries minimize the importance of controversial materials
in order to make the library invulnerable to attack or to
avoid offense. Others limit provision to materials of quality
and exclude those publications that are poorly written, unsupported by facts, offensive, crude, excessively militant, etc.
More often than not, however, the actual reason for neglecting certain types of publication is not deliberate effort at exclusion but the plain difficulty of becoming aware of fringe
publications and how to obtain them.

As educators, librarians have a responsibility to ensure that the public has an opportunity to be informed about
all manner of ideas advocated, no matter how obnoxious they
may be to some of us. How uninformed the public is was
demonstrated in November 1965 when the Communist Party
went on trial for the second time for failing to register as
an agent of the Soviet Union. The eight men and four women

picked to hear the case before Judge William B. Jones in
the U. S. District Court of Washington, D. C., swore: they
had not read, seen, nor heard anything derogatory about the
Communist Party, and; had never read books or articles by
such conservative or rightist authors as Elizabeth Bentley,
Whittaker Chambers, Louis Budenz, J. B. Mathews, Herbert
Philbrick, William F. Buckley Jr., Gerald L. K. Smith,
Westbrook Pegler, Dan Smoot, Robert Welch, Dr. Fred
Schwarz, or Dr. George Benson; nor listened to radio pro-
grams conducted by Fulton Lewis Jr., John T. Flynn, "Life
Line," "Facts Forum," "Clarence Manion Forum," or the
"20th Century Reformation Hour."

     With rare exceptions, college and public libraries
tend to shy away from the highly controversial in their subscriptions to periodicals. They often limit themselves to
what is included in collective indexes, to magazines of culture and quality, to mass-circulation periodicals, and to a
few titles of an extremist nature that are donated by pressure
groups. The following quotation is probably quite accurate
in its characterization of public library policy:

> The public librarian's duty is to encourage the
> democratic dialogue. Unfortunately... the public
> library is committed to ideological neutrality...
> All the means of communication--newspapers, pop-
> ular magazines, radio, and television--are in es-
> sential agreement with each other. It is my con-
> tention that the ideological neutrality of the public
> library merely reinforces mass thinking. If you
> want to confirm this suspicion, check the periodi-
> cals displayed at the local branch of your public
> library. The list, with few exceptions, parallels
> the magazines for sale at your favorite grocery
> store... [1]

     The comparison is primarily designed to provide in-
formation to librarians to help them in the task of selection,
so that they can proceed, as they see fit, to create an awareness by the public of the existence of propagandistic or polemic periodicals expressing dissident, opposition, or minority opinion. Although this compilation is limited to periodicals, it should be noted that much polemic material is also
published in other forms--pamphlets, paperbacks, books,
etc.

     Excluded from this listing were those periodical titles

that seemed to be fairly widely known or well established, such as the liberal Nation and the New Republic and the conservative National Review and U. S. News and World Report. The emphasis was placed on publications that were judged to be "radical" and polemic, or that had a definite bias or orientation toward expressing opposition, dissent, disagreement, or divergence from the mainstream of opinion. It was not always easy to make this determination consistently, especially since many fringe groups or individuals regard themselves to be in the mainstream. The inclusion or exclusion of some titles may well be questioned, for instance, those that are only mildly conservative or liberal.

The first step in our effort was to identify the titles currently being published. This first step was not an easy one since available published directories were incomplete, partly out of date, or not wholly applicable. For instance The First National Directory of "Rightist" Groups, Publications and Some Individuals in the United States (and Some Foreign Countries), 5th ed., 1965, published by Alert Americans Association, contained 3,406 entries, of which over 80% were not related to periodicals and in which periodical entries were not easily identifiable. The Directory: America's Most Controversial Periodicals, published by USA Guidelines Publications 1965, contained 140 titles, some of which were not really controversial in nature and others of which were no longer published. The Agcomm Directory One listed 95 titles of interest to "libertarians." Although a few new titles were gleaned from the latter list, it also contained much that fell outside the controversial or polemic. Help was also obtained from the Labadie Collection of The University of Michigan, which receives, for purposes of preservation and research, many periodicals of the radical Left and the extreme Right. The Curator of the Labadie Collection was helpful in the winnowing and selection process. For titles not subscribed to by The University of Michigan (and there were over 40 of these), it was necessary to obtain sample copies from the publishers, which was not always an easy task.

The second step was to provide certain routine information, i. e., address, frequency, circulation (when obtainable), subscription price, the birth year or origin of publication, and its format.

The third step was to prepare a meaningful description of the content of the periodical: To do so, it was de-

cided to take three issues (more when readily obtainable)
and to have an unbiased and dispassionate summary prepared
by students employed on an hourly basis; the abstractors
were paid for in part out of a grant to the compiler from the
Jackson Social Welfare Fund, of the First Unitarian Church
of Ann Arbor.   (This fund is set up to support projects related to the advancement of "the understanding and acceptance
of the great principles of the First Amendment of the Constitution of the United States.")   The quality of the summaries
prepared by the student assistants varied, of course, depending on a number of factors.   Editing and rewriting was necessary to improve the language and also to eliminate any
bias that might have inadvertently crept in.

It was assumed that a close look at three issues
would be sufficient to give an abstractor a reliable impression of the general character and editorial policy of a given
periodical.   This assumption was based on the observation
that a periodical usually does not change sufficiently in character over a span of several years to invalidate the impression of its editorial policy gained from a sample of three issues.   A periodical may deal with different specific subject
matter from year to year; but, if it expects to hold its subscribers or readers, it can not risk too wide a deviation
from the policy position that is evident in even a small
sample.   Most people tend to subscribe to periodicals that
reinforce their predispositions; hence a periodical must be
fairly consistent from issue to issue in fulfilling its readers'
expectations with regard to biases, militancy, targets of ag-
gression, aims, ideals, fears, and hopes.

The reason for preparing summaries of the actual
content was that we aimed to avoid the kind of annotation
that was too general to be meaningful and failed to get down
to specifics.   We wanted to be sure, if possible, to cite
concrete examples of any characteristic attributed to a periodical.   The summaries were not intended to cover all the
articles and features of a given periodical, but to refer only
to those that seemed to be most typical of the periodical's
editorial policy.   In a few cases it was difficult to detect
a definable editorial policy, but in most cases the policy was
fairly evident.

The fourth step was to send drafts of the prepared
content summaries to the editors of the respective publications, along with a request to have the drafts checked for
accuracy and fairness.   Nearly 90% of the editors had re-

sponded at the time of the final editing.   Suggestions made
by those who did respond were followed whenever possible,
and some of their comments were added at the end of the
final draft of the respective summaries.

Next arose the problem of arrangement.   The summaries could, of course, have been arranged in a single alphabet, but the compiler felt that librarians might find it more
useful to have the summaries arranged simply by broad categories.   There was some reluctance to do so because of the
possibility of being accused of labeling publications and the
likelihood that some editors might not like their bedfellows.
However, by creating a "Miscellaneous" category, some of
these difficulties were overcome.

The end product is a list of titles arranged as follows:

Civil Rights and Negro	14
Left of Center	42
Miscellaneous	21
Pacifist	12
Race Oriented	13
Right of Center	61
Total	163

This classification indicates the major areas of controversy in the U. S. today.   Of greatest concern to the Right
of Center is the danger of communism and "creeping social-
ism" and the preservation of order and "free enterprise."
Some of the extremists on the Right believe in a conspira-
torial theory of current affairs under which everything they
dislike is attributed to a communist plot.   Social welfare legislation is viewed as a threat.   The Left of Center is primarily concerned with alleged injustices in the current social
and economic system of the U. S. and with fundamental ways
and means of bringing about greater fairness and equality.
Those on the Left are not necessarily followers of radical so-
cialist or revolutionist theories as is often assumed, but most
believe in planning by government action, although they do
not agree at all as to how to achieve improvements or what
model to follow.   Race-oriented publications are primarily
interested in the preservation of a pure, largely Anglo-Saxon
race in the U. S. and view the Black race, and to a lesser
extent, the Jewish people, as a threat to this objective.   Civil
rights and Negro groups strive primarily toward the better-
ment of the Negro in the U. S.   Pacifists oppose warfare,
which they view as the greatest threat to civilization, and

lend their support to peace efforts.   There is another area
of controversy, that of sexual morality, that has not been
covered in the present compilation; there seem to be very
few regularly appearing publications exclusively devoted to
promotion of a new outlook or opposed to traditional sexual
modes.   One might possibly place <u>Playboy</u> and <u>Cosmopolitan</u>
in this category.   Also not specifically covered in this compilation are religious beliefs, except atheism.

A final note to fellow librarians: If one takes the
"Library Bill of Rights" seriously, it would not seem inappropriate to try to subscribe to all the periodicals listed in
this compilation and to display them regularly on open
shelves in their library, possibly together as a special group
in a separate section of the periodicals display area.   The
total annual cost of the subscription would probably not be
much over $600.00.   Readers in many communities and on
many a campus will appreciate the opportunity to browse
among these nonconformist publications.   The display will
attract attention and will serve an important educational function in alerting people to the existence of dissenting views in
a society that has increasingly been tending toward consensus
and conformity.   If a library cannot afford to subscribe to
or give shelf space to the entire list, the summaries of the
content of the titles presented in this compilation should
prove helpful as a guide to selection.

Also we ought to keep in mind that when we deal with
such publications, the usual criteria of book selection, that
is, substance and quality, do not apply.   These fringe publications exist.   We should not bar them from the public just
because we may find them distasteful personally or uninter-
esting, or of low quality.   They are important if they have
an audience of subscribers or possibly for no other reason
than that someone is willing to provide the money to subsi-
dize them.   Their audience may vary from less than a thousand to several thousands, and while many of the periodicals
may have little appeal to the cultured and educated, we cannot afford to ignore them.

It is not sufficient for a librarian to wait until an interested party donates a subscription or until a specific title
is asked for.   It is an obligation to display as much of the
spectrum of dissident opinion as space will allow, so that
the library can serve as a sort of "Hyde Park Corner" where
free communication, a clash of ideas, becomes a conspicuous new dimension of library service.   Mary V. Gaver,

President of the American Library Association, in her inaugural address in New York in July 1966, deplored the tendency of librarians not to view "their role as being one of actively seeking and participating in the world of conflict in which we live." Hopefully, this compilation may help to counteract some of this tendency.

Note

1. Otto Kirchner-Dean "Book Selection and the Democratic Process," <u>Library Journal</u> 91:1765, June 1, 1966.

The Impact of Literature - Summary

by Marie Jahoda

and the Staff of the Research
Center for Human Relations,
New York University

From her The Impact of Literature: A Psycho-
logical Discussion of Some Assumptions in the
Censorship Debate. New York, American Book
Publishers' Council, March 1, 1954. Mimeo.
p. 42-5; Reprinted by permission of Peter S.
Jennison, Executive Director, The National Book
Committee, New York City

Summary

We have set out to look at the censorship debate fro
the aspect of psychology only. Such an enterprise is justified in view of the fact that much of the argumentation abo
censorship is based on certain psychological assumptions
about the impact of books on the minds of readers. But
throughout the centuries during which the debate has been
carried on the issue has never been exclusively psychological in nature. Social, political, philosophical and religious
values have entered into the discussion and will undoubtedly
continue to do so. This fact limits the expectations that ca
legitimately be held with regard to a psychological analysis
of these matters. It can, at best, remove some bones of
contention; it cannot settle the larger issue of censorship
once and for all.

There are other limitations to this analysis, even
within this narrowed scope. They arise from the fact that
very little psychological research has so far been conducted
which was designed directly to bear on the psychological as
sumptions and assertions in the censorship debate. Most o
the evidence that we could marshall is indirect and gets its
import from the convergence of different approaches to simi
lar conclusions. Many of the points presented in the pre-

eding pages had to be reasoned by analogy rather than by
he presentation of irrefutable evidence. This need not nec-
ssarily remain so. At least some, if not all, of the psy-
hological problems raised in the censorship debate are
menable to more systematic research for which modern
sychology has provided both concepts and techniques.

When one looks at these problems as they are formu-
ated currently by those concerned with the impact of books
n the moral level of our society, one is struck by a con-
iderable variety in definitions and assumptions. Whenever
onfronted with the problem of exploring the effect of certain
timuli on human conduct, psychologists are apt to raise the
ollowing questions: What is the effective agent? How does
his agent affect human conduct? Who is being affected?
What are the conditions which limit or enhance the effect?
And who is in a position to judge the presence or absence of
ffect?

To answer these questions sicentifically would first
require a codification of the possible types of answer to each
of them. Unless a psychologist keeps in mind a comprehensive range of all possible responses to literature, for example, he is unlikely to uncover the full process of impact.
For the absence of delinquent behavior in response to a book
which lets delinquency appear attractive does, of course, not
yet establish that there exists no specific response to it at
all.

The establishment of such a codification is in itself
a task of considerable magnitude--a task which has not been
attempted in this paper. In view of this difficulty it is, indeed, not surprising that the examination of psychological
assumptions about the impact of books made by non-psychol-
ogists yields a somewhat confused picture, in which definitions are absent or tautological, and assertions about impact
range over a wide area. One aspect, however, emerges
with some clarity from the current debate: Most people who
enter into it are concerned, first, with the impact of literary
descriptions of sexual behavior on young people. Second in
the focus of attention is a concern with descriptions of violence and brutality. As a result of reading such matters
young people, and to some extent adults, are feared to be
motivated for delinquency and to acquire socially undesirable
values and ideas. This apparent consensus dissolves very
quickly, however, when an effort is made to pin down any
one of these notions which are highly charged with subjective

value judgments.

A review of the available psychological literature sug
gested two distinct approaches to some of these problems:
First, an inquiry into what is known about the causes of
juvenile delinquency; and, second, an inquiry into the natur
of the process by which literature affects the mind of the
reader.

On the first point we have concluded that there is no
evidence available in the vast literature on juvenile delinquency which would justify the assumption that reading has
a major motivating force in it.   Experts in the field empha
size that there is no single cause for juvenile delinquency.
Most of them regard personality predispositions as they are
developed in early childhood as a necessary condition for
delinquency.   These personality predispositions are modifie
by later events.   Here, direct experiences are, as a rule,
assumed to be of greater power than vicarious experiences
such as provided by reading matter.   While there is no evi
dence that within those limitations reading of certain litera
products has a trigger function, releasing the criminal act,
this possibility cannot be excluded either, and deserves fur
ther study.

On the second point we have come to the following
conclusions: There is a large overlap in content matter be
tween all media of mass communication.   The daily press,
television, movies, radio and fictional printed material all
present their share of so-called "bad" material, varying in
the degree of reality attached to these matters.   It is virtually impossible to isolate the impact of one of these medi
on a population that is exposed to all of them.   Some evidence suggests that the particular communications to which
an individual exposes himself are probably in good part a
matter of choice.   The reader does not take in everything
that is offered but mostly what he is predisposed to take.
In the realm of attitudes, this means that adult people prefer to expose themselves to material which expresses attitudes they already hold.   A conversion of attitudes by any
of the mass media is indeed a rare event, if it occurs at
all.   Apparently, information is much more readily absorbe
from the mass media than are attitudes which do not agree
with those of the reader.

Children, who have often not yet crystallized their
attitudes, are, perhaps, more open to attitudinal influences.

These may present a particular danger with regard to those who are insecure or otherwise maladjusted, and who find in the reading of comic books an escape from reality which they do not dare to face.   The psychological function which reading fulfils in their emotional economy is the gratification of needs which are not being met in the real world.   It is likely, though not yet fully demonstrated, that excessive reading of this kind will intensify in children the factors which drove them into reading to begin with: an inability to face the world, apathy with regard to events, a belief that the individual is hopelessly impotent and driven by uncontrollable forces and, hence, an acceptance of violence and brutality in the real world.

The focus of attention in this paper has inevitably been on the discussion of the possibly undesirable effects of reading and of other mass media of communications.   Perhaps it is not entirely out of place to finish it with the assertion that the actually and potentially civilizing effects of literary products and of other mass media of communications present one of the few unquestionable achievements of our time.

"A Book List"

by Pamela Hansford Johnson   Noted English novelist and wife
of C. P. Snow. This selection
is from her book reporting on
the notorious Moors murder
trial in England.

Not so long ago, I raised a little storm by suggesting
in a letter to The Guardian, that it was not desirable for
Krafft-Ebing to be available in relatively cheap paperback on
the bookstalls of English railway stations.

Was I, then, taking a stand against the totally per-
missive and promulgating that all works should not be available to all people? To this I reply, unequivocally: that is
what I was suggesting. There are some books that are not
fit for all people and some people who are not fit for all
books.

Before I am assailed by libertarian outcries, let me
elaborate my point.

The Psychopathia Sexualis is an important work which
was written for experts in the field of sexology. If it is to
be read scientifically and not destorted by being scooped up
as a work of sexual titillation, accompanied by "Oohs" and
"Aahs," then it demands that the reader shall have made
some previous study of the subject and can take the Psychopathia as both synthesis and extension of what he already
knows. An ill-educated reader in search of excitation is
likely to get from it only some new and interesting ideas
that may provoke him to introspection of a non-illuminating
nature, to fantasticating onanism, or, at worst, to the con-

cept of putting some of the ideas into practice.   The fact is
that we are offering at random those full liberties which
would only be justifiable if offered to a far more highly educated people than we are.   It might be urged that our only
recourse now would be to step up our education in an attempt to bring us all into line with the present assumption
of our scientific-mindedness--a counsel of perfection, I am
afraid, and one not tenable for anybody with the slightest
statistical sense.   No country in the history of the world has
yet educated itself to this pitch.

It is no use for us to pretend that we are an ideal
society, fully mature, with free choice and rich leisure.
This is what we hope to become, but now are not: when we
are so, there will be no need for censorship of any kind
whatsoever.   But we are seeing the most fantastic growth of
a semi-literate reading public--semi-literate, no more, yet,
than that: and at the same time we are prepared to offer,
to minds educationally and emotionally unprepared, "total
publication" in almost every form of mass media.   This is
why we need to adjust ideal legal aims with the actual possibilities of conduct, and we cannot do this until we understand far more of what those possibilities are.

We are shouting in the dark for what we want: we
need to turn up the lights before we can understand what we
may, without endangering the structure of our society, actually have.

This is true, not only of what we are doing to the
semi-educated, but to those of us who have been luckier.   If
I understand him correctly, such is a major theme of Dr.
Philip Rieff's The Triumph of the Therapeutic, which is asking some of the deepest questions of our time.   As it is, we
have put the cart before the horse, and if the cart looks
more often like a dung-cart than is comfortable, then we
need to overhaul some of our fashionable shibboleths.

Let me make a debating point and hope that it may be
answered.   Are we to believe that all works in all medical
libraries should be offered freely (and cheaply) to the public?   If we did this, we should enormously increase hypo-
chondria and the fear of death.   That this new flood of literature would bring in the money, I have no doubt: but at
what cost?   Not a lethal one, probably; but high, nevertheless, in social terms.

I am inclined to think that it is less good to make things easy for the prurient than to make him work a little harder for his gratification.   If he feels he cannot be truly happy without reading the report of the trial of Gilles de Retz (to Sade as Pitt is to Addington) he can probably find his way, with a degree of application, to the archives of the Bibliothèque Nationale.   And a resolute attempt to obtain a ticket to the Reading Room of the British Museum may uncover for him much in any of his chosen fields.   The mere difficulty of finding the salacity he craves might be the saving of a rather irresolute, or lazy, pornographer.

Neither David Smith nor Ian Brady had received the kind of education likely to fit them for objective study, though both Brady and Myra Hindley were of slightly more than average I. Q.   Their interests were sado-masochistic, titillatory and sado-Fascist, and in the bookshops they found practically all the pabulum they needed, though one or two of their books were, I suppose, smuggled.

This library, consisting of fifty-odd books, a few of which were harmless enough, is divded sharply into three groups.   Here is a selection: but I must add that some of these works were socially and scientifically responsible in intention and not designed for study outside a specialist world.

Sado-Masochistic

> The History of Corporal Punishment
> The History of Torture Through the Ages
> Orgies of Torture and Brutality
> The Pleasures of the Torture Chamber
> Sex Crimes and Sex Criminals
> De Sade
> The Life and Ideas of the Marquis De Sade

Titillatory

> Erotica
> The Anti-Sex
> Sexual Anomalies and Perversions
> Cradle of Erotica
> High Heels and Stilettos
> Kiss of the Whip

Dealing with Fascism and Nazism

> Nuremberg Diary
> Heinrich Himmler
> Mosley Right or Wrong
> The Mark of the Swastika

There was also the copy of Mein Kampf, and, not surprisingly in the context, two books on how to teach oneself the German language.

Brady, in the box, was huffy when questioned about his library. The attorney-general offered him a list of the books which, he said, he did not wish to read out. He asked: "They are all squalid pornographic books?"

Brady: "They cannot be called pornography. They can be bought at any bookstall."

"They are dirty books, are they not?"

"It depends on the dirty minds."

"This was the atmosphere of your mind?"

"No."

It is interesting that this is the stereotype response of our time. Contemporary apologists could have done no better.

I cannot help but wonder whether, by making all books available to all men, we do not pay too high a price, if that price should be the death of one small child by torture. I shall have to return to this point. No one can prove a causal connection between what these two people read and what they did. It might have happened anyway. But if there were a causal connection, how does one weigh in the balance the libertarian principle of making all books available to all men, and the death of a child in such a fashion? I have no doubt how I weigh them.

(Both Hindley and Brady, by the way, refused to take the oath, and affirmed: about this they seemed more adamant, certainly more morally indignant, than about other, and ugly, matters. They had made their own rules and they abided by them.)

I do not want to overstate my case.

At the same time as the Moors Trial was proceeding, a housewife from an industrial district of Indianapolis, aged 47, sat in the dock with her two daughters, aged 17 and 15, her son aged 13, and two neighborhood boys, both aged 15. They were charged with having over the period of a fortnight beaten, starved, branded, scalded and ultimately murdered a pretty but obviously dim-witted girl whom the housewife had taken into her care. It was a familiar pattern. The girl had been tied to a bed, refused water or the use of a lavatory. When she wet the bed, she was beaten for dirtiness. It was the old story of deciding that a fellow creature was subhuman, and then punishing her--I suspect with moral indignation--for her supposed subhumanity.

Now I do not for a moment suppose that the accused in this trial had access to a library so diverse, or so specialized, as Brady's. Indeed, from the accounts I have read, I should be surprised to find there was a book in the house.

Yet how much violence, of permitted depravity, had they picked up in the air? There are very few intellectuals indeed who will now lend themselves to serious discussion as to whether, by mass communications of all kinds, we in the west are not poisoning that air, whether it may be due to its infection that some children die. In fact, any attempt to get them to discuss the subject responsibly and without exaggeration often drives them into a strange state of hysteria, of the curious kind of unreason one sometimes meets in religious controversy, or of total silence.

The more recent Chicago murder by one man of eight young nurses seems to me, on the available evidence, something different in kind; here a killer appears to have lured the eight into acquiescence at being trussed up for slaughter by suggesting that he only wanted money and would not hurt them. Apparently he induced five of the girls, sleeping together in a dormitory, to do as he wished, his only weapon being a large butcher's knife. There was no evidence of threat by shooting--indeed, it would seem dubious whether the murderer even had a gun. What is puzzling at this stage, with due respect for the terror the girls must have felt, was the lack of opposition to the killer. Could this present quite another problem? Could the violence in our air have persuaded these young people that the cry, "Dilly-

dilly, come and be killed," is now impossible to meet by a concerted refusal to do anything of the kind? We may all be anethetised by the air we breathe, not only into becoming murderers, but victims also. We may have been led into believing that there is nothing else for it but to put our hands up from the word "go."

The point is delicate. We have a free press, almost free dissemination in every form of mass communications: these may be the staples of our liberty.

But what is such liberty worth, without self-control by each and every one of us who profits from it?

I ask again: what is the price we are prepared to pay?

Section 3

The Library Selector's Approach to Evaluation of Materials

> Librarianship is the only profession that devotes it-
> self to bringing books into the common life of the
> world.
>
> > Helen E. Haines, Living with
> > books. 2nd ed. New York,
> > Columbia University Press,
> > 1950. p. 10.

> The library value of a book is determined by its
> real popularity, the quality and the amount of its
> influence on the intellectual life of the people who
> use it.
>
> > Pierce Butler, Introduction to
> > Library Science, with an intro-
> > duction by Lester Asheim.
> > (Phoenix Books). Chicago,
> > University of Chicago Press,
> > 1961. p. 99.

The library selector today must be competent to select materials in many forms, in a vast range of subjects,
in a variety of languages, and for many different "publics."
Competencies required to carry out such responsibilities include the ability to read speedily; an understanding of the
criteria applicable to different media and the ability to apply
the criteria; the skill to assess the potential audience of a
particular book, film, or other medium of expression; and,
finally, a high degree of skill in the use of the various bibliographical tools which are available to assist the librarian
in this task.

Criteria for assessing specific types and varieties of
materials must be considered as well as the broad policies
for building these individual bits and pieces into a collection.
As a rule, the library annotation--a conventional form for

recording the result of your evaluation--is the means by which the staff of a given library system records its decisions in these matters.   In addition, decisions must be made in accordance with the library's selection policy. Haines and the Library of Congress staff present guidelines for the composition of library annotations.

The readings in this section have been selected to present background statements on the principles of library evaluation of materials, as well as examples of forms and procedures for this task.   Stiffler discusses some of the criteria for selection in college libraries; Cox, Jones, Veaner and Pearson apply these to special forms of material; while Dr. Asheim and Mrs. Grazier give a broad picture of the status of reading today as it may affect library selection.   The chart on page 362 is intended to present one way of visualizing the variety of "publics" for which libraries must provide and select materials.

Libraries: School, College, Public, Special

Select Materials for a Range of Reading Levels, Needs and Interests

Reading Ability Level		Categories of Readers	Factors Affecting Evaluations
Pre-school	Word familiarity	Adult illiterates	Variety of languages
	Arousal of interest	Children	
Primary grade	Development of skills	Adult learner	Sentence structure-length, use, complexity
	Continuation of interest	Students	Criteria of literary quality
			Comparison to similar works
Intermediate grade	Establishment of skills	Retarded reader	Vocabulary-range, frequency of usage, familiarity
	Voracious reading	Reluctant, unhabituated reader	
Adult Level		Non-reader	Maturity of concept
Junior high school	True Story-7th gr. Readers Digest-8th & 9th gr. Standard non-technical reading	"Culturally deprived" "Disadvantaged" "Average reader" Technician "Senior citizen"	Organization of content Motivation of interest Format
Senior high school	Atlantic Monthly Harpers Fairly difficult for most readers	Specialist reader Research worker	Book – Hard bound Paper back Large print
College Level	Difficult for most readers "Intelligent layman"	Professionals	Film and filmstrip Recording & tape Teaching Machines-other media

Explanation: The items in each of the three columns in
the Chart are not listed necessarily in a continuum,
except for the first column.   The reader may identify the relationships for himself; for example, for
professionals as readers, what reading ability levels
and other factors affecting evaluations are most apt
to apply?

The Status of Personal Reading: In School

by Margaret Hayes Grazier   Mrs. Grazier was formerly
Librarian, Birmingham (Michigan) High School and is now
Professor, Department of Library Science, Wayne State
University, Detroit, Michigan

From Helen M. Robinson, ed. Developing Permanent Interest in Reading: Proceedings of the Annual Conference on Reading, University of Chicago, 1956. (Supplementary Educational Monograph No. 84, December 1956) Chicago, University of Chicago Press, 1956. p. 42-7; Reprinted by permission of the author and of the University of Chicago Press, (c) 1956 by the University of Chicago.

To develop permanent interest in reading has long been a primary objective of the reading and library program of the school.   Concern about how well the schools are achieving this objective has become widespread in recent years.   Many parents charge that the schools no longer teach children how to read or transmit to them an enduring enthusiasm for reading.   Parents and teachers fret that magazines, television, and movies are making books obsolete. Are these fears well grounded on facts of the present, or are they ill-founded on myths about the good old days?   Do children and youth read less today than they did formerly? Has the quality of their reading deteriorated?

These are difficult questions to answer even though hundreds of studies have been made during the past half-century about the reading habits of children and young people.   Differences in the test conditions and in the methods used to gather and analyze the evidence make valid comparisons about the reading of youth in different periods of time exceptionally difficult.   Yet some statements of approximate fact can be made, which may provide some understanding of the status of personal reading among children of our own and earlier generations.

Amount of Reading

One method that investigators have used to answer the question, "Do children read as much as they used to?" is to compare statistics about the number of children's books published and the number of books children borrow from the library. Such indirect evidence about the current status of children's reading appears encouraging. There has been a tremendous increase both in the number of new titles of children's books published and in the total volume of juvenile publishing. In 1925, 710 new books and 318 new editions were published;[1] in 1950, the number had increased to 1,059,[2] and in 1955, to 1,485.[3] The total number of copies of juvenile books produced in 1925 was 25,214,000,[4] and in 1945 the total number of juvenile books sold was 53,752,000.[5] Gains in the circulation of children's books from public libraries are also impressive. Circulation statistics show an increase from about 138,000,000[6] in 1938-39 to over 162,000,000[7] in 1950. Similar data are not available for school libraries, but there is every reason to believe they would reveal an equally striking gain.

Although these figures show that more books are available and are being used today than during any period in our history, they do not answer two important questions about amount of reading. Are a larger porportion of children reading voluntarily today than yesterday? Are children reading more?

Analytical summaries reported by Gray and Munroe in 1929[8] and by Gray and Iverson in 1952[9] provide a chronological comparison of the reading of children and young people. Studies made between 1890 and 1928 showed that the per cent of children who read books voluntarily increased rapidly in the primary and intermediate grades and approximated 100 in the junior high school. In some high schools, voluntary reading continued among almost all students. In other high schools, there was a marked decrease in the proportion of students who read and in the average amount of reading of those students who did read. Almost all children above the third grade read the newspaper and, to a lesser extent, magazines. The proportion of children reading them increased steadily during elementary grades and reached a high level in the junior high school. Almost all high-school students continued to read newspapers but in some schools read less in magazines.

Few major changes in this general pattern were reported in the summary of those studies made since 1940. The chief differences are the greater popularity of magazines and newspapers at practically all grade levels and the more rapid increase in the proportion of children reading books voluntarily during the elementary-school grades. The decline in book-reading among high-school students was as great as before, if not greater. Not only do high-school students read less, but fewer of them read. This fact has sometimes been misinterpreted to mean that high-school students read less than elementary school students. However, a few recent studies of both required and voluntary reading show that there is actually an increase in the total amount of reading during the high-school period because students read more for assignments.

Facts about the numbers of books read voluntarily by children and youth also provide an interesting basis for comparison of the reading patterns of today and yesterday. Gray concluded from data summarized in the twenties that the number of books read by sixth-, seventh-, and eighth-grade pupils averaged from one to two a month. [10] A survey of similar studies made during the past decade convinced him that the average number of books read by children today is not radically different from that of three decades ago. [11] Henne, analyzing studies of high-school students' reading made during the period from 1900 to the early forties, also found no marked difference in the amount of voluntary reading during the four decades. [12]

Range and Quality of Reading

Obviously, sound appraisal of children's personal reading cannot be based solely on data about how many children read and how much they read. Information about the range and quality of their reading is even more significant.

Studies made during the past half-century reveal few major changes in the range and the general subject matter of children's reading. The broad subject pattern of their reading in both fiction and nonfiction is almost identical, although the specific books and magazines read vary from decade to decade as a consequence of what is published and made available.

At all ages, children read more fiction than nonfiction and like it better. They read increasingly more difficult children's stories until the junior high school period. Between the ages of twelve and fifteen, they shift from the juvenile and teen-age story to adult fiction. For a while children read from both fields, but usually the transition has been completed by the age of sixteen. The reading of non-fiction tends to increase progressively during junior and sen-ior high school grades; this trend is particularly evident at the high-school level. In recent studies a somewhat larger proportion of nonfiction is reported in the personal reading of primary- and intermediate-grade children than in former investigations. This shift probably reflects the tremendous increase in the number of informational books published dur-ing the past decade for younger children.

If we cannot find any significant difference in range of material read by children and youth from decade to dec-ade, can we find any difference in the quality of material read? Many parents and some teachers complain that chil-dren and youth are not reading the classics today as often as they formerly did and that they are failing to develop a taste for good literature.

One approach to the question of quality of reading is through reports of favorite books. The major conclusion to be drawn from studies made during the past fifty years is that the quality of children's choices is much the same from one decade to another. Children's preferences encompass several classics and "good" modern stories, a large number of acceptable but undistinguished titles, and a few pieces of trash. The high-school students' formula is a mixture of classics and standard titles of adult and juvenile literature, adult best sellers, and very light adult fiction. Such clas-sics as Tom Sawyer, Little Women, Huckleberry Finn, and Treasure Island appear as frequently on current lists as on earlier ones. A 1955 study[13] of the favorite books of some 5,500 boys and girls in Grades V through VIII of the Chi-cago public schools indicates the range in literary merit and the division between the old and the new that are typical of children's choices. The books preferred by the boys, ranked in order of their popularity, were: 20,000 Leagues under the Sea, Walt Disney's Davy Crockett, Tom Sawyer, Homer Price, Black Beauty, Black Stallion, and World Se-ries. The girls' favorite books were: Double Date, Little Women, Class Ring, Black Beauty, Boxcar Children, Going on Sixteen, Practically Seventeen, Black Stallion, Lassie Come-Home, and Andersen's Fairy Tales.

Another recent study[14] offers more insight into the place of the classics in children's reading.   One year's voluntary reading of some 750 Chicago school children in Grades IV through VIII was analyzed to determine how many of the 300 titles found in publishers' reprint series had been read.   Although adults might not agree that these 300 titles were classics, the titles of many of the series indicated that the publishers considered them as such.   Half of the 300 titles were not read at all, and the other half were read by only 43 per cent of the pupils.   At first glance this evidence seems to support the charge of neglect made by apprehensive parents.   Before such a conclusion can be reached, however, it would be necessary to know whether any other titles were read more widely by students.   A similar study of 300 contemporary books might reveal no greater incidence of reading than was shown in this report.

Probably the most valid appraisal of the quality of reading is that based upon an analysis of individuals' total reading.   In the limited evidence of this type available about children's reading in earlier and later periods, there is little agreement about the relative amount of good or poor material.   There is agreement that the quality ranges from the classics to rubbish, but the relative portion of each in children's reading diet is still open to question.   Some investigators have found children in intermediate and junior high school grades reading a number of juvenile series of the "Tom Swift" and "Nancy Drew" variety in recent times, the "Rover Boys" and "Tarzan" in earlier periods.   Other researchers, however, report only a small number of undesirable titles on the list of books read voluntarily by children. To what extent these inconsistencies are caused by real differences in the reading of children and to what extent they are caused by children's reluctance to report books they think adults will not approve allow interesting speculation.

At the high-school level the majority of surveys from 1900 on show that light fiction predominates in the reading of students.   There exist minority reports, as exemplified by the high-level reading of the secondary-school students of the Ohio State University school, [15] that suggest the potential influence of the free yet guided reading program upon the reading habits of young people.

Any appraisal of the quality of youth's voluntary reading must consider magazines as well as books.   Most of the studies are based upon reports by secondary-school students of the magazines they read regularly or the magazines they most enjoy reading. The lists of high-ranking titles among high-school youth have changed but little over a period of years. The Saturday Evening Post, American, Collier's, and Ladies' Home Journal typify the perennial favorites, joined recently by such newcomers as Life and Look. Neither the quality periodical, such as Harper's and the Atlantic, nor the pulp magazine, like Detective Story and True Romance, appears on these lists. These preferences can be misleading. They tell nothing of the proportion of good and inferior magazines in the students' reading. That a large part of their magazine-reading may be of questionable quality is suggested by a study of the magazine-reading of some 3,000 Chicago high-school students in 1941. [16] Approximately 10 per cent of the reading was in pulps or movie magazines and another third in magazines characterized as "generally mediocre."

And then there are the comics magazines. Studies are not needed to testify to their universal appeal to children. Research does tell us, however, that the height of their popularity is reached in the middle grades. After this time the proportion of children reading them and the number of magazines read decrease steadily, although some high-school students continue to read them. Obviously, this trend cannot be interpreted as improving the quality of modern children's reading. The best that can be said about the best of the comics is that they are harmless and sometimes comic.

In Conclusion

What do all these scattered findings about personal reading add up to? Children today, as their parents and grandparents before them, read a mixture of the good, the bad, the indifferent. Their interest in book-reading starts earlier in the grades and develops more rapidly, but it declines as much during senior high school, if not more. The number of books read is neither greater nor less than it formerly was. Interest in reading newspapers and magazines has increased. This evidence may mollify our critics, but does it reassure us? What are the implications in these findings?

Does the fact that children are devoted to comics magazines, to "Tom Swift," to "Nancy Drew," give evidence only of their desire for effortless reading and vicarious

thrills?   Or is it evidence of the scarcity of books in our
libraries that appeal to their craving for adventure and excitement without distorting human abilities and values?

   The spate of books on the market today which are
thinly disguised sermons on social consciousness and charac
ter development is scarecely the kind of fare to answer children's demand for a "really good" book.   Such titles, in thei
attempt to make good citizens, may only make poor readers.
Books are not medicine to be prescribed for Bill who is too
timid, for Sue who is too bossy, for Joe who is too fat.
Let us leave bibliotherapy to the therapist and concentrate o
helping children find good books in whose pages they can los
themselves--to find themselves.

   Why do senior high school students lose interest in
book-reading?   Are we destroying youths' interest in reading
by keeping them overlong in the "junior novels" with their
patterned plots and happy endings?   Critics denounce the
stock characters and the contrived and wholesome--"disgust-
ingly wholesome"--boy-girl situations which fill the pages of
many teen-age novels which in turn fill many school library
shelves.   Are we frightening youth away from continued read
ing by insisting upon Silas Marner and The Scarlet Letter?
The best of the current adult literature gives an honest, albeit an often frank, portrayal of the world that youth must
live in and strive to understand.   Are we depriving youth of
the very books that will make reading seem worth the effort
because we fret unduly about an occasional "damn" and a
frank presentation of the facts of life?

   Should we worry because the high-school youth spends
less time in casual and personal reading as long as the total
amount of his reading is increasing?   Perhaps yes, perhaps
no.   If assigned reading is introducing him to the enjoyment
and stimulation to be found in contemporary adult literature,
and if class discussions are helping him to sense the provocation and artistry of writers who have something important
to say, the reading requirement may well be a potent motivation for permanent interest in reading.   It is highly doubtful that the student will like The Caine Mutiny less because
he is reading it for English class.

   What are the implications of the increase in magazine
reading, particularly among high-school students?   We know
magazines are far more popular with adults than books.
Should the schools buy more magazines and make greater at-

tempts to interest students in the better ones? Or are these facts a challenge to renew effort in motivating students to read books? A case might be made for the fact that much of the most rewarding adult reading is to be found between the covers of a book rather than on the pages of a magazine and that the schools are failing if they do not keep alive in students the desire to read good books.

How many people will never be readers, in the sense that they turn to reading voluntarily as a source of pleasure, enrichment, and stimulation, we know not. Certainly, we cannot be satisfied that the group of adult readers is as large as possible until such time as every child is given an opportunity throughout his school life for personal reading. The formation of sound and enduring reading patterns among children and young people is important for them, not only in 1956, but also in 1976. The reading habits formed by children and youth influence society today and tomorrow; the good society will be the society of good readers.

Editors note: One of the best introductory sources on the role of readability in evaluating materials for readers is still Edgar Dale and Jeanne Chall, "Developing readable materials," (In National Society for the Study of Education, 55th Yearbook, Part. I. Chicago, University of Chicago Press, 1956, p. 222-35.) Dr. Dale is now preparing a new book incorporating much of this material.

Notes

1. Publishers' Weekly   109:233, January 23, 1926.

2. Publishers' Weekly   159:240, January 20, 1951.

3. Publishers' Weekly   169:223, January 21, 1956.

4. United States Department of Commerce, Bureau of the Census Biennial Census of Manufactures: 1925, p. 662. Washington, Government Printing Office, 1928.

5. United States Department of Commerce, Bureau of the Census, Biennial Census of Manufactures: 1947, II, p. 358. Washington, Government Printing Office, 1949.

6. "Public Library Statistics: 1938-39" United States Office of Education Bulletin 1942, No. 4, p. 5.

7. "Public Library Statistics: 1950" United States Office of Education Bulletin 1953, No. 9, p. 38.

8. Gray, William S. and Munroe, Ruth The Reading Interests and Habits of Adults. New York, Macmillan, 1929. p. 104-5.

9. Gray, William S. and Iverson, William J. "What Should be the Profession's Attitude toward Lay Criticism of the Schools?" Elementary School Journal, 53:28-29, September, 1952.

10. Gray, William S. "Summary of Investigations Relating to Reading" (In Supplementary Educational Monographs, No. 28. Chicago, University of Chicago Press, 1925, p. 159)

11. Gray, William S. and Iverson, William J. op. cit.

12. Henne, Frances "Preconditional Factors Affecting the Reading of Young People" (Unpublished Doctor's dissertation, Graduate Library School, University of Chicago, 1949, p. 76.)

13. Schneider, Mary A. and Taylor, Marion W. "Children's Reading Interests in the Chicago Public Schools" (Unpublished Master's thesis, Graduate School, Chicago Teachers College, 1955.

14. Eakin, Mary Katherine "The Reading of Books from Publishers' Reprint Series by Children in the Elementary Grades" (Unpublished Master's thesis, Graduate Library School, University of Chicago, 1954.)

15. La Brant, Lou L. and Heller, Frieda M. "An Evaluation of Free Reading in Grades Seven to Twelve, Inclusive" (In Ohio State University Studies, Contributions in Education, No. 4. Columbus, Ohio, Ohio State University Press, 1939.)

16. Mater, Wilma S. "Sources from Which Chicago High-School Students Obtain Reading Material" (Unpublished Master's paper, Graduate Library School, University of Chicago, 1943), p. 32-34.

The Status of Personal Reading: In Adult Life

by Lester E. Asheim

Dr. Asheim is at present Director of the Office for Library Education, American Library Association; at the time when this study was done he was Dean, Graduate Library School, University of Chicago

From Helen M. Robinson, Ed. Developing Permanent Interest in Reading: Proceedings of the Annual Conference on Reading, University of Chicago, 1956. (Supplementary Educational Monograph No. 84, December 1956) Chicago, University of Chicago Press, 1956. p. 47-52. Reprinted by permission of the author and of the University of Chicago Press, c 1956 by the University of Chicago.

To establish with any certainty the status which reading holds in our society is a very subtle and difficult task. It is one with which social scientists have been much concerned and which they have tackled in many different ways. But a survey of the reading studies reported to date reveals that most of the devices now available for measuring reading are still too gross and unrefined to provide us with the kinds of insight we seek.

The kinds of measurements we make are primarily indirect ones.   They tell us something about how much reading is possible in our society much more frequently than they tell us how much reading is actually done.   Certainly it is true that the United States is particularly fortunate in almost all the correlates of reading.   A greater proportion of our population is educated; we have more leisure; our ability to pay for such amenities is greater; and the number of public libraries far exceeds that of other countries.   Yet "at any time, only 17 per cent of the adults in the United States may be found reading a book...[whereas] in England,

where schooling is far from universal, 55 per cent of the
population at any given time may be found reading a book."[1]
Thus the kinds of figures we like best to quote reveal only
that most of our people can read and that some of them do.
It does not tell us what they read, for what purposes they
read, or, most especially, what role reading plays in their
lives in relation to their other life-activities.

To find answers to questions such as these, the research device has usually been to ask the people themselves.
But to ask the people themselves about something as intangible and complex as the status of reading is to ask them
for answers which they cannot properly give. People do not
know how important reading is for them; they cannot remember accurately how many books they have read in the past
month; they do not analyze with any insight the factors which
led to their choices. It is not always that people deliberate-
ly misrepresent but that they plain do not know. Of course
misrepresentation is a problem, too, since a kind of prestige attaches to reading, and respondents are often loath to
put the worst--that is, the true--light upon the kind and a-
mount of reading they do.

Some insights, however indirect, are provided for us
by these researches. From the overall figures of publication, circulation, and sale of printed materials, we know
that reading is rapidly becoming an essential part of the
daily activities of more and more people. We know that between 85 and 90 per cent of the adult population reads a
newspaper with at least some regularity and that 60-70 per
cent read at least one magazine regularly. In terms of the
mere spelling-out of the meaning of black marks on white
paper, a lot of reading is being done throughout the United
States. As a matter of fact, literacy is assumed in our society, and a great deal of information which it is essential
that our citizens know is made available to them through the
medium of print. As a tool of survival, a basic kind of
literacy is virtually mandatory.

When we direct our attention to reading at a level
above basic literacy, we find a somewhat less encouraging
picture. The number of persons likely to be reading a book
at any given time seldom exceeds 17-25 per cent of our adult
population. If we try to limit our analysis to books of some
stature, some seriousness, some profundity, the likelihood
is that the proportion is not going to be much more than 5-
10 per cent. This 10 per cent is represented in all the other

figures of communication activities: they are the readers
of magazines and newspapers as well as of books, the viewers of television, and the audience for the theater and film,
forming what has been termed by Berelson a kind of "communications elite."[2] But they are a very small segment of
the population indeed, and there is a group just as large in
which no reading, not even of newspapers, is ever done.

When we come to the questions which try to provide
more direct evidence about the status of reading in our society ("For what purpose did you read this?" "How did you
hear of it?" and the like), we begin to get answers which
make more gratifying claims than observed reality would
tend to support. Asked why they read a newspaper, a large
number of respondents will claim something like "to be better
informed about current problems," which is exactly what we
would like to hear them say. But any pollster, or any quiz
program, or any general examination reveals how badly informed about current events the average newspaper reader
is. His newspaper-reading could be a source of important
information about the world he lives in and the decisions he
will be called upon to make affecting it, but, when we probe
beyond the high-sounding responses our reader gives us, we
find that he knows very little about the events and the issues
on which he allegedly sought enlightenment. This does not
mean that he does not read; he may not be able to name the
premier of France, but he will know who plays first base
for the Giants. It means only that his answers may not have
quite the meaning they appear to have and that we should use
extreme caution in generalizing about his motivations for
reading and the effects of it.

Similarly respondents will frequently supply (or check)
answers concerning their reading of books and magazines
which make us feel a little better about the role that reading
plays in our lives. "To broaden my view and my knowledge,"
"To keep abreast of the times," "To stimulate my imagination"--these are the reasons we often find in our studies.
So far we have not often correlated these reasons with the
actual readings themselves, but it is at least possible that
in popular reading the situation is very like that in popular
communication experiences of other kinds. The average person tends to over-evaluate that which is easily understood,
instantly assimilated and readily adapted to some practical
purpose. And since terms like "educational," "informational," "intellectual" are dependent upon the subjective standards
of the respondent, I mistrust a literal acceptance of the

reader's own evaluation of the level at which he reads and
the effects he imagines he derives from his reading. Though
it be treason, on this campus, to say so, I am inclined to
believe that the investigator's informed impressions of the
role which reading plays in society may describe it more
accurately than do the data he gathers from the readers
themselves.

These data can be used, with caution, to tell us a
great deal. What they reveal most clearly to me--in the
contradiction they present between what the respondents say
and what they actually do--is the strange ambivalence toward
reading which is characteristic of the present-day attitude
toward all things intellectual. Our respondents really want
to think highly of education, of reading, and of knowledge.
But the effects of reading, particularly of serious and important reading, are difficult to recognize, to appraise, and
to pin down. When we ask for answers from respondents,
they can reply accurately only about things which can be
weighed, measured, and held in the hand. The greatest values of reading are not of this nature, and so what our respondents tend to appreciate in reading are not its greatest
values.

It is a revealing reflection of our thinking that, on the
"$64,000 Question" program, the master of ceremonies said
to the lady who had just won the prize money for her knowledge of the Bible, "Well, all that Bible-reading finally paid
off, didn't it?" Neither the contestant, nor any member of
the audience, nor any commentator that I have seen since
then has been moved to suggest that there might have been
other pay-offs in all those years of Bible-reading.

On the other hand, there is a tradition of respect for
learning in what has been called the "book and reading culture of the West." Unfortunately the benefits of education
and of reading have come to us almost through hearsay; we
cannot, in any of the tangible ways which carry weight in
our society, prove to ourselves that they really have the
value they are supposed to have. Time and again in the interviews for our reading studies, we find a somewhat apologetic tone in the responses ("I do mean to read a lot more,
but somehow...," "I know I should read more than I do,
but..."), and always the gist of the apology is that more important and more interesting things have intervened.

Here we begin to get to the heart of the matter. Society acknowledges a certain importance to reading in its scheme of things, but it finds many things much more important. Despite its alleged respect for reading, it is just a bit suspicious of someone who does what it calls "too much" reading. In our society it would be unutterably shocking to find among our friends and acquaintances someone who did not know how to read. We also consider education to be basic, at least a high-school education and, generally, some college. But when we reach the college level, we begin to think in terms of the tangible pay-off. We state quite baldly that there are many who will go into fields of endeavor where they don't "need" a college education; that is, where the financial rewards will not be increased by education. It is clear, therefore, that financial rewards and business success are considered more important than the nonvocational benefits of higher education. Erudition, or learning (which in some societies in some periods was seen as a great good in itself), is somewhat suspect today. We can accept a man who is college educated, but we don't want it to show unduly. The well-read person is acceptable, but the bookish person certainly is not.

This odd ambivalence derives in part, I think, from our heavy emphasis on social values in the narrowest sense. Today we are concerned with group activities, with participation, with (as the Madison Avenue copy writers have it) "togetherness." But reading, unfortunately, is a kind of anti-social activity. The reader reads by himself; he seeks privacy; he closes the door. Today's parents are much more likely to be concerned about the children who read too much than they are about those who read too little. It isn't that Johnny can't read; it is just that the social environment is constantly operating to discourage his reading. His fellows don't read; his parents don't read. Except in the case of a few best sellers, he cannot even have the pleasure of talking about his reading with others, as he can about last night's television program, or the current movie, or the outcome of yesterday's ball game. And today's Johnny is, of course, tomorrow's John, Sr.

It is important to remember the child as father to the man. We cannot talk about adult attitudes toward reading without facing the fact that those attitudes have their effect on the development of the young person on his way to adulthood. In high school, and in the early years of college, our young people are beginning to look in the direction they will want to go as adults. Naturally they look to the adult world

for the models they will follow.   Consequently most of our
high schools and colleges, reflecting that adult world, place
their emphasis on the non-book aspects of education.   Would
most parents prefer to have their daughter selected for Phi
Beta Kappa or chosen as the queen of the Senior prom?
Would they prefer to have their son made president of the
honor society or captain of the football team?   With whom
would they most want their children to be popular: with
their teachers or with their fellow-students?   In most cases,
I believe, the preference would be for peer-group popularity.
How often have we heard, not only from parents, but even
from educators, that--in a university, mind you--you can
carry the emphasis on education too far!

The failure of the teachers, then, is not that they
have turned out people who cannot read.   In teaching the
technique of reading, our present educational system must
be accounted a considerable success.   What little personal
reading is done, is done by the few with the most education
--and by children.   But the child who reads has to live in
the world, and that world is essentially hostile to reading.
What the teacher has failed to do is demonstrate to the student the personal value which reading can have for him,
quite probably because the teacher himself is not really that
kind of a reader.   To answer the characteristic question of
our time, "What's in it for me?" teachers, and librarians
and parents, have sought to build up the instrumental values
of reading: "It helps you get a job." "It teaches you how to
do something." "It brings some tangible nonreading reward."
If this is all that reading does--make certain facts available
--then it is logical that the book should be displaced by
films, radio, and television.

The teachers are not the solely responsible villains,
of course.   They are merely reflecting the society of which
they are a part, and, for most people in our society, reading is not a good in itself.   It is seen as a tool skill which
may lead to other goods, but it is not its own reward.   One
does not gain prestige for being a reader; reading's value is
that it may help one to reach other goals which do carry
prestige.   Thus those who do read, read what they must or
what will have an instrumental value for them.   The drop in
book use which inevitably follows at the point of leaving
school is overwhelming evidence of this fact.

Even pleasure reading is generally undertaken less
for its own sake than as a refuge from complete inactivity.

People do not stay home to read; they read because they are forced to stay home.   They read on buses and on the sub-way, in dentists' offices, and in isolated vacation spots--on rainy days.   They did a lot of reading while in the army, but this did not fix a continuing habit.   This is not to say that pleasure reading does not give pleasure, but it is to say that, if some other diversion requiring less effort presents itself, the book is usually cast aside.

And there we have another key to our puzzle: the effort.   In any human endeavor the effort one is willing to expend is dependent upon the resulting rewards.   A young man will work very hard over a difficult technical manual if it will lead him to the job he wants.   A young woman will follow with care the charm book which is guaranteed to make her more popular.   But personal reading, in its best sense, seeks for rewards which are intangible and long-term, and thus on a second level of urgency.   If reading is to assume a more important role, the goals of our society will have to be on a higher plane than those dictated by immediacy, expediency, material values, and the easy way out.

One thing that our studies strongly suggest is that the social role played by the individual is a basic determiner of his reading pattern.   To raise the status of reading, we shall have to alter our present concepts of what constitutes an admirable social role.   The task of education, therefore, is much broader than that of teaching reading or even that of developing a deeper appreciation of reading.   It is one of making society better than it now is.   But, in a sense, this is always the task of education.

Notes

1. Dupee, Gordon "Can Johnny's Parents Read?" Saturday Review 39:6, June 2, 1956.

2. Berelson, Bernard The Library's Public.   New York, York, Columbia University Press, 1949, p. 15.

The Art of Annotation

by Helen E. Haines   1872-1961; widely respected
lecturer and specialist in li-
brary book selection; author of
<u>Living with Books</u> (2d ed. 1950)
and <u>What's in a Novel</u> (1942);
lecturer at library schools of
University of California, University of Southern California,
and Columbia University.

From her <u>Living with Books</u>. 2d ed. New York,
Columbia University Press, 1950. p. 137-47 sel.;
Reprinted by permission of Columbia University
Press, New York City.

Have you begun to detect the two main vices of
Jargon? The first is that it uses circumlocution
rather than short straight speech... The second
vice is that it habitually chooses vague woolly abstract nouns rather than concrete ones... "How
excellent a thing is sleep," sighed Sancho Panza,
"it wraps a man round like a cloak"--an excellent
example, by the way, of how to say a thing concretely: A Jargoneer would have said that "among
the beneficent qualities of sleep its capacity for
withdrawing the human consciousness from the con-
templation of immediate circumstances may perhaps be accounted not the least remarkable." How
vile a thing--shall we say?--is the abstract noun!
It wraps a man's thoughts round like cotton wool.
Sir Arthur Quiller-Couch:
<u>On the Art of Writing</u>

Annotation, or characterization of a book in a compact descriptive or critical note, is a familiar bibliographical practice. It is a feature of most of the older "literary
guides" to different fields of knowledge, of reading courses
and educational manuals, and of many works in general and
specialized literature... In writing annotations the chief es-

sentials are: condensation, sound construction, and effective phrasing. Every word must count, every sentence must be compressed to give specific, definite fact; yet at the same time there must be indication or reflection of the color, the texture, the spirit, of the book.

The writing of annotations is not necessarily a part of book selection. It has, however, a double relationship to selection, for it is a means by which the choice of books is often determined and a means by which information about selected books is put at the service of readers. So various are the uses to which it may be applied and the opportunities to which it may lead that some proficiency in the art (for at its best it is an art, demanding concentrated intelligence and expert expression) is one of the most valuable assets of any worker with books. An experienced and skillful annotator has necessarily acquired perception of book values and facility in expression...

Method of annotation varies according to its purpose. Annotations fall roughly into two classes--"readers' notes" and "librarians' notes." A readers' note is intended to impart information to the reader and at the same time awaken a desire to read the book. A satisfactory readers' note should make clear the subject of the book, its authority or special value, its treatment, and its literary quality or flavor; special features, such as important appendixes or unusual illustrations, may be noted. Such a note does not, as a rule, mention weaknesses or defects, because it assumes to treat only books that are worth reading; and it seeks to put its information into attractive and interesting phrasing. Readers' notes are most common in popular reading lists, in library bulletins, and in mediums especially intended for popular use. They are often very brief, sometimes confined to ten or a dozen words, and they are frequently misleading, in their endeavor to arrest attention and arouse enthusiasm. Among good examples for study are those appearing in Branch Library Book News of the New York Public Library.

A librarians' note has for its specific purpose the aiding of the librarian in the choice of books. It should give, with more fullness, the same information that is given in the readers' note, but in addition it should point out deficiencies, such as inaccuracy, overtechnicality, or features that would be objectionable to certain readers, and it should indicate a book's merit in comparison with other books in

the same field.   Annotations for books in specialized technical fields emphasize, of course, points of technical quality
and importance.

In all annotations brevity is especially to be considered.   Many readers' notes are limited to fifteen or twenty-
five words.   For librarians' notes, sixty words is an average length; few annotations exceed one hundred words.   The
annotations in the A. L. A. Catalog and the Booklist represen
the type of librarians' note that is now predominant.   They
emphasize the critical and comparative information that is
important to librarians and indicate suitability to different
tastes; but (especially in the Booklist and generally in fiction
annotations) they are also designed to arouse interest and
awaken a desire to read the book...

...the points essential in evaluation of nonfiction for
library selection...are: subject of the book, author's qualifications, scope, treatment, point of view, literary quality,
comparative value, class of readers it will appeal to.   To
convey this information in clear and interesting phrasing
within the compass of from fifty to ninety words is the art
of the expert annotator.   Evaluation of fiction presents
greater difficulties, but here, too, Booklist annotations offer
useful material for analysis of method and purpose.

"Readers' notes," designed primarily to attract, usually represent descriptive annotation.   "Librarians' notes,"
designed primarily to inform, usually represent critical annotation.   But the best annotation work combines the two, in
a unified, clear, and interesting characterization.   Almost
all libraries prepare and issue annotated lists of various
kinds, from the record of new books added, printed in the
local newspaper, to the carefully edited, regularly issued
bulletin that is an attractive and useful library publication.
Short popular lists for the general reader may contain not
more than a dozen titles, with a few words of comment for
each, printed on a bookmark slip; extended reference lists
or study outlines in special fields may represent expert bibliographical detail and scholarly cooperation.   In the preparation of such lists, annotations in current and standard
bibliographical guides as well as terse comments from reviews or graphic summations from publishers' announcements
are drawn upon for information, for adaptation or paraphrase.   From the evaluation of the book itself and from
this accessory material is welded the individual annotation
intended to fit a book to a reader who will enjoy it or to

make clear its usefulness to the student or serious reader in a specific field of knowledge.

To write a good annotation requires careful study of models and considerable practice. Annotations of different types should be analyzed and compared. Original annotations based upon personal evaluation of a book and prepared without suggestive material should be compared with the annotations for the same book in the <u>Booklist</u> or <u>Library Journal.</u> Such study of annotations is a fascinating exercise for anyone with a responsive mind, critical perceptions, a background of good reading, and an interest in word usage. Merits and defects are soon apprehended. Plato said, "He shall be as a god to me, who can rightly divide and define," --and the student of annotation comes to understand and share this feeling. Effective compression is contrasted with inept disunity, flexible and magnetic expression with the monotonous reiteration of a few stock phrases. The most common defects in annotations designed to attract readers are vagueness, "prettiness," and failure to convey a true impression of the book. In annotations intended to guide to serious reading, verbosity and superficiality are the chief dangers. In both types the desire to "lure" the reader often results in false emphasis.

Points to be brought out in the evaluation of a book already have been sufficiently indicated. Consider now how to weld an evaluation into a workmanlike annotation. Structure, content, and expression are the fundamentals here. They are handled differently in the annotation of nonfiction and of fiction; and there are further differences in dealing with specific classes of literature. But here only the essentials in nonfiction and fiction annotation can be considered.

Structure should be logical and unified, but may differ in plan. If the annotation opens with statement of the author's theme, this may be linked with indication of the way that theme is presented. This is illustrated by an annotation for Rourke's <u>American Humor:</u>

> The comic spirit and the part it has played in forming a national character, is the subject of this serious study. The author follows the course of American humor from its early incarnation in the Yankee peddler through its various manifestations in oral tradition, drama and literature.

If the annotation opens with a characterization of the author, this may be phrased to convey also the subject of the book: as, for Thompson's study of Mayan antiquities, The People of the Serpent:

> The veteran archaeologist, whose work in Yucatan was described in Willard's City of the Sacred Well tells the story of his forty years' study of Mayan ruins.

Exposition of theme, authority or experience of author, descriptive detail, comparative estimate or appraisal of value, appreciation of literary quality--these are all components of structure. They must not be scattered in discon nected fragments through the annotation, but, each complete in itself, built into a consistent whole. The ways in which the building is done may vary. An annotation may open with statement of theme, or with characterization of the author (as in the examples given) ; it may, especially for books of travel, open with a vivid descriptive summary of the subject; it may open with a salient short quotation from the book that conveys its purpose or flavor. There are many allowable openings, for variety in structure evades rigidity and monotony and makes the annotation more interesting to the reader. But there must be logical progression from one component to another and each component must be compact, definite, and complete. Perhaps the best formula for structure of a tragic plot--that it shall be "complete and whole and of a certain magnitude:"

> A whole is that which has a beginning, middle and end. A beginning is that which does not itself follow anything by causal necessity, but after which something naturally is, or comes to be. An end, on the contrary, is that which itself naturally follows some other thing, either by necessity or in the regular course of events, but has nothing following it. A middle is that which follows something, as some other thing follows it. A well constructed plot, therefore, must neither begin nor end at haphazard but conform to the type here described.

Content of an annotation requires first of all precision of statement. It should have exactitude as well as com pression of detail. At the same time, it should be complete rather than partial; effort must be made to convey the whole of a book instead of a single aspect. An annotation for Younghill Kang's Korean autobiography, The Grass Roof, is an example of inadequate and confused content:

> In his passage from an insular Korean village to the Western world, the author, who is now a lecturer at New York University, describes a bewildering parade of interesting characters. His biography opens the intimacy of village life to the reader so that to the discriminating the psychology of the crazy, poet uncle and the father, who uncomplainingly supported so many branches of the family, is no longer alien.

A reader will gain from this no understanding of the range and quality of a book that combines historical significance with exotic backgrounds, dramatic personal experience, and unusual literary charm. An adequate annotation would indicate each of these aspects:

> Life-story of a young Korean, born just before the Japanese invasion in 1898, who tells of his happy childhood in a little village ruled by family traditions handed down through centuries. Oppression and terror fell upon his home when Japan annexed Korea in 1910, and the boy's share in student revolutionary efforts led him ultimately to a new life in the United States. A narrative of delicate clarity, picturesque and moving, possessing also humor and poetic charm.

The content of an annotation is the substance of the component parts that are united to make its whole structure. Information concerning the author, the subject, theory, or theme of the book, the manner in which the subject is dealt with, and the spirit and quality of the work, must be distilled into clear, compact statement. In books of travel, political and sociological study, science, and other fields of specialized knowledge, an author's background of experience has special importance and should be carefully and explicitly indicated. To say of George Soule's study of Anglo-American economic interdependence, America's Stake in Britain's Future, that it offers "cogent argument," is made more significant by the specific statement that the author is "a well-known American economist and former editor of the New Republic." This individualization of an author's qualifications is a means of denoting the value of the book in relation to its general subject.

As much individualization as possible should also be
applied to the subject, so that it may be evident to the
reader in what way this book is distinguished from other
books in its field.   The usefulness of Rosinger's Restless
India, for instance, will be more evident if the annotation
mentions the documentary appendix which gives the Cripps
proposals and Indian answers and Attlee's statement of policy.   An annotation for Northrop's philosophic-cultural treatise, The Meeting of East and West, should penetrate beyond descriptive summary into the book's fundamental thesis
that the culture of the East centers on analysis of aesthetic
immediate experience, that in Western culture science and
theoretical abstractions are central, and that correlation of
the aesthetic and scientific factors in experience is the only
key to world understanding.   But an author's viewpoint is of
significance only when it affects the presentation of his subject.   That Max Eastman is an irreconcilable antagonist to
the Soviet state is important in the appraisal of anything he
writes concerning Russia, but immaterial in consideration of
his work in other fields.   Hilaire Belloc's Catholic viewpoin
should often be made clear in characterizing his writings in
history and biography, but may be disregarded in an annotation for his essays.   There must be constant discrimination
between essential and nonessential information, and only
facts that have specific relationship to the subject or author
ity or quality of a book should be included in an annotation.

Presumably, annotations are always written for
readers who know nothing of the book.   Thus they should
make as clear and definite as possible just what it deals wi
and should be phrased to convey a topic of immediate inter
est not to present-day readers only, but to future readers
as well.   In biography, indication of the dates during which
the subject lived or some clear indication of the period co
ered is desirable, unless this information is given in the
book's title.   In history, specific characterization of perio
phase, or aspect is necessary; in travel, the region dealt
with and the period covered must be noted.   In all fields
literature the annotation should bring out the most salient
facts that bear upon the presentation of the subject.

Whenever possible the quality of a book should be i
dicated simply and without too great emphasis.   For supe
ficial compilations that masquerade as authentic works so
such statement as "Popular, but not to be accepted as au-

thoritative," or "Interesting, but of slight historical value,"
is desirable, as a hint to readers who might otherwise think
they were getting a book of serious importance.   In the same
way, a work of eminent authority and equally eminent dull-
ness should receive some enlightening sentence, as "Of great
value in its analysis of original authorities, but difficult reading for the inexperienced student." Annotations for editions
of classics or standard works should state character and
scope of the editorial treatment--whether new material is included or a new point of view offered--for this is the chief
means of distinguishing between various editions of the same
work.

When a title is given in full in the entry of a book,
the annotation should not repeat the words, or give the same
information in different phrasing, or offer information that
an intelligent person could readily infer from the title itself.
It is through the bibliographical entry that the book is introduced to the reader's attention; the fundamental purpose of
the annotation is to explain or supplement information insuf-
ficiently conveyed through this introductory record.   If, however, the title of a book is obscure but has direct relation
to the book's subject or purpose, the annotation should make
its meaning clear.   Many titles are more or less cryptic,
either to stimulate the reader's curiosity or to convey a
symbolic theme; others are built upon a word or an illusion
used in the book that, in itself, is likely to be misunderstood.   An obscure title, left unilluminated by any annotation
that I have seen, is 1. Americans, in which Señor de Mada-
riaga, with the epistles of the New Testament in mind, undoubtedly sought to convey a "First Epistle to the Americans"
on the gospel of world unity.

Expression must have vigor and clarity.   First of all,
an annotation must be kept rigorously within the allotted
length, whether it be thirty-five words or a hundred.   Usually this length varies somewhat, according to the importance
of the book or the purpose of the annotation.   But brevity is
the essence of annotation writing, just as skillful and graphic
expression is its most necessary element.   There must be
logical construction and smooth dovetailing of sentences.   But
it is the substance of those sentences, the annotator's mastery of words, that gives effectiveness of appeal, precision
of statement, and conveys the quality and spirit of the book.
In all annotation writing a good thesaurus (Roget or March)
is an indispensable companion.   To shun the hackneyed
phrase, the threadbare adjective, to find the word that con-

veys the nature of a book's style or distills the essence of
its theme, to integrate its substance, quality, and value
clearly, logically, with graphic brevity, is to practice the
fine art of annotation.   Always, vague phrases, long or involved sentences, must be avoided; jerkiness and disconnec-
tion that destroy continuity of effect are equally undesirable.
An annotation should not read like a fragment from an ora-
torical disquisition, nor like a night-letter telegram.   Sir
Arthur Quiller-Couch's memorable chapter on "Jargon," in
his On the Art of Writing, is golden counsel for the annotator.   Eschew the abstract noun, the passive voice; be concrete, be active --if you can't be active, be as active as
you can.

     Certain abbreviations or contractions in wording are
sanctioned by practice.   A verb may be used with omitted
subject when the subject is the book's name or the words
"this book," thus giving a concise declarative statement, such
as "Treats of family disorganization and health problems;"
"Tells the story of American relations with Cuba;" "Describes
a journey to Lapland."   Whenever possible, avoid beginning
a sentence with "A" or "The;" do not refer unnecessarily to
"the author," or use such waste words as "The author's aim
in this book."   Articles and prepositions may be omitted in
the middle of a sentence, commas may be used to indicate
words eliminated, and other devices adapted to speed the
process of condensation; but this must be done without sacri-
fice of good form or spontaneity.   As an example of compression, effectiveness, and insight, consider the following
annotation, from Sonnenschein, of Chesterton's Orthodoxy:

          Exposition of author's religious philosophy, urging
          that an innate sense of mystery, security, ro-
          mance, loyalty to ideals and to progress, is left
          wholly unsatisfied by Logic.   Full of paradox and
          antithetical reasoning.

Here we have the essence of a book distilled into thirty-two
words.

     An annotation should not take sides on questions nor
express any strong personal opinions, nor even accept and
repeat an author's strong opinions without some qualifications
that makes it clear they are the author's views.   That is,
unless an annotator is an authority on the subject treated,
with thorough knowledge of its various aspects, it is better
to qualify dogmatic utterances.   The common newspaper

practice of disclaiming responsibility by the use of such
phrases as "it is stated," "it is asserted," is useful in annotation writing. It is better to say "apparently a fair and
judicious presentation," than to say "entirely unbiased and
absolutely fair;" better to point out that "the author says"
such and such a thing, than that "the author convinces his
readers" of the same thing, although such a comment as "a
convincing presentation" is legitimate. Annotations should
not be dogmatic; they should be devoid of any condescending
hortatory tone, and they should equally eschew an ecstatic
"come-and-read-me" appeal that is irritating to most intelligent minds. The language used should be as simple as possible; but words should be carefully chosen for their vivid-
ness and fitness, and there must be constant endeavor to
avoid monotony of effect in the annotation as a whole...

Using the Anatomy of a "Book": or
Learning to Browse Intelligently

by Patricia B. Knapp   This assignment was prepared by
Dr. Knapp for college students in
the course of her extensive research
on student use of libraries at Wayne
State University where she is Professor of Library Service. It seems
to provide an admirable framework
for examination of books by student
librarians.

From her The Montieith College Library Experiment.
Metuchen, N. J. , The Scarecrow Press, 1966. p. 242-
53 sel.

Purpose and Function of this Assignment

The purpose of this assignment is to provide a systematic framework of the external characteristics of written materials; such as books and journals, which can enable you to make
a quick preliminary judgment of their probable merit as you
encounter them in using the open stacks of the library. This
assignment, consequently, is directed toward increasing your
sense of selectivity and discrimination within that democracy of
books, the library. Because they are based solely upon the
visible evidence contained within a particular book or journal
article, the principles of evaluation in this framework cannot
provide a final or definitive judgment of the intrinsic merit or
relevance of written materials for all types of purposes, but
they can assist you in eliminating from consideration a large
portion of useless materials.

The total process of evaluating literature is complex;
this assignment deals only with a preliminary, though essential part of that process. This part of the process can only
indicate the books and journals which are most generally
quoted and used by a majority of the practitioners in various subject fields. Thus it can distinguish the better items
from the more mediocre, but it cannot distinguish the best
item for any given purpose from among the materials which
meet its criteria. Also, there are always those few unique

items which seemingly, violate nearly every external criterion of value but which still possess intrinsic merit.   No
general framework, such as that indicated here, can substitute for expert guidance or for the exercise of your personal attention to the characteristics of scholarly literature as
you progress toward becoming an independent student.

Framework for the Evaluation of Literature

        The following framework is designed to focus your
attention upon those parts of the evaluation process which
can be accomplished by a brief examination of the book or
journal as an artifact.   What can we know from an inspection of the item?   The various parts of a book or journal
article constitute a series of signals which can provide you
with important clues to the significance of an item if you
know how to interpret them.   Thus you can interpret the
significance of:

        1. The Form of the Publication.   In a physical sense,
we can readily determine whether the item is a book, journal or pamphlet, whether it is large or small in overall dimensions and whether or not it is long or short in length.
In terms of its intellectual form and design, we can determine whether it is a monograph, a novel, a research report,
an epic of the proceedings or some professional meeting of
conference.   Each of these forms, and many others we could
have mentioned, exist to fulfill a recognized need and we
must distinguish among them if we are to realize the intention of their respective authors and publishers.   All books
and journal articles are not created equal and not every item
that claims to be scholarly shall enter into the kingdom of
knowledge.

        The basic communication function of the journal is to
provide the first reports of scholarly research and theoretical discussions.   A second function is that of presenting reviews of current books, abstracts of articles, comments on
material in current periodical literature and reviews of special areas.   Thus journal articles provide the latest, up-to-
date opinions and data upon developments within the various
subject disciplines.   Book in monographic form, on the other hand, are usually less current than journals, but generally are more reliable, authoritative and comprehensive.
Pamphlet literature is a special class in itself providing a
means for extended discussion of highly current topics, generally in a controversial manner which soon have only a

historical value.

The choice, then, of the particular form of literature you select while browsing depends upon the needs of your specific topic or problem. It is rare that only journal articles or only books will meet all the informational needs for a Monteith assignment. Depending upon the characteristics of your topic, then, there is a form of literature which is more likely than others to convey the type of information you need. Within that form of literature, be it a book, journal article or a pamphlet, there are authors whose recognized competence entitles them to more respect than other writers, and likewise there are differences among publishers regarding the quality and integrity of their respective publications.

The first "principle" or rule of evaluation, consequently, states that we must know what kind of material we are reading and we should know this as early in the process as possible, preferably before we begin to read it extensively. But how can we be expected to know what sort of material we are reading before we begin to read? (In this discussion we are focusing upon the characteristics of books because they are the most mature and elaborate form of literature. Journal articles and pamphlets share many of the same features possessed by books, so our remarks may be applied with qualifications to all the forms of literature which you will commonly encounter.)

We can know what kind of a book it is upon the basis of information obtained from what is conventionally called the "front matter" of a book. The front matter consists of the title page, table of contents, preface and introduction. These are signals which the author gives us to indicate what he intended his work to say and how he wanted to organize it. Thus, our second set of clues is:

2. The Title Page. The title page is to the book what the face is to the human being. It is the principal means by which we can quickly identify a given item of literature. Just as the human face is composed of parts, each of which contributes to the total impression we have of a person, so the title page of a book has parts and each one contributes to the judgment we can make of the book. The main elements of a title page are the author, title of the book and the location and name of its publisher.

a. The author.   Within Western cultures, the author has traditionally been the predominant facet around which we have identified and organized our intellectual systems and the literature which has documented these systems.   Thus most books, especially those of a scholarly nature, generally try to give evidence of the qualifications of their respective authors by indicating: 1) academic degrees he holds, 2) institutional affiliations and position, viz. Jacques Barzun, Ph. D. Dean of the Graduate School, Columbia University, 3) previous books published and any other information that can be indicated briefly which lends credence to his implicit claim of competence.

b. The title.   The title serves various functions.   In an elementary sense, it serves to distinguish one book from another.   Substantively, however, it can provide us with many clues as to the purpose and intention of the author and assists us in the judgment of whether to stimulate the reader's curiousity or to convey a symbolic theme; others are built upon a word or an allusion in the book that, in itself, is likely to be misunderstood.   In expository writing, however, authors generally take considerable effort to make their titles as accurate and descriptive of the contents of the work as possible.   A well chosen title provides clues as to its manner of treatment by the author.   In many cases, titles are complemented by sub-titles which provide further clarification of the purpose and contents of the work.

c. The publisher.   The publisher is an important clue to the quality of a book.   As agents for placing books into the public domain, publishers have a legal responsibility for them as well as an economic stake in their success.   Consequently publishers try to select manuscripts of high quality which will also find an adequate market.   Within the world of knowledge, however, there are simply too many subject areas for each publisher to cover individually.   There is, accordingly, a "division of labor" among publishers with each of them tending to specialize in certain subject areas.   Within these areas, publishers try to establish their reputations for quality and completeness of coverage.   Thus within each major subject field, there are certain publishers who issue a disproportionate number of the better works in that field. Judgment as to who these publishers are comes with experience in using the literatures within respective fields, but even there the pattern changes as new publishers try to get a foothold in expanding their sales.

The above remarks apply particularly to the commercial publishers, i. e. , those firms which use their own risk
capital to publish books on the open market for a profit.
A sub-variety of commercial publishers is the vanity press.
The vanity press is composed of firms who receive payment
from authors for the publication of their respective books.
If the sales of the books are sufficient, sometimes the author is able to get his money back, but few vanity presses
have best sellers.   Generally, the quality of books from vanity presses is inferior to that from other commercial houses
or university presses but nevertheless the vanity press performs a valuable social function in keeping open a freedom
of expression which can be limited to the economic considerations of commercial presses or by the academic conservatism of university presses.

Another type of publisher which is becoming increasingly more important for the dissemination of scholarly materials is the university press.   University presses are supported and operated by universities as an integral part of
their social responsibility to the scholarly community and to
the general public.   The function of the university press is
to place in the public domain of knowledge the work of scholars or other significant literature which cannot be distributed
profitably by commercial publishers.   University press books
and other materials, accordingly, are usually of high quality,
but they occasionally have their "dogs" also.

The last general type of publisher is the government,
especially the various agencies of the U. S. government.   As
an effect of the expanding role of government within our society, the various agencies at the local, state and federal
levels are important sources of information on virtually every
aspect of our culture.   Like information from any other
source, government documents must be carefully evaluated
for bias, completeness of information, sources of data and
by the general criteria we use for judging any other item.
Merely because an item is a government document does not
give it any special claims for adequacy unless it is supported
by these general criteria; on the other hand, merely because
it is a government document, we should not dismiss it as a
piece of political propaganda, although some of them are.

d. Date of publication.   Depending upon the form of
literature involved, the publication date of a book is of varying importance.   In standard and current inspirational and
recreational literature date of publication is of minor im-

portance, as the value of the book depends not so much on
its timeliness as on its literary quality.   In informational
literature, however, date of publication is generally quite
significant in indicating the present value of a book.   A book
written by a lady doctor on mental health in 1925 would be
of little value in an analysis of current trends in mental
health care today.

Knowledge of the date of publication of the individual
works of a given author is frequently useful and often necessary for an adequate interpretation of their significance within the intellectual growth and sometimes radical change in
the viewpoint of an author.   Freud, for example, changed
many of his viewpoints during the course of his career.   In
interpreting any of his works, it is useful to know at what
period of his career it was published; the same thing, of
course, can be said for the work of any serious scholar.

Determining the date of publication of a book, in a
legal sense, is not difficult because on all copyrighted material it must be indicated on the back side of the title page.
The copyright date, however, is always later than the actual date or time during which the book was written.   A
closer approximation of the time that a book was actually
written may often be indicated by the date on the preface or
introduction which is usually the last thing an author writes
before sending his manuscript off to the publisher.   The
copyright date and the date on the preface or introduction
may both be different from the date which publishers frequently put on the title page itself.   This "imprint date"
simply indicates the date that the publisher printed the book
and it may legally be up-dated every time a new printing is
made, even though no changes were made in the text itself.

e. Edition.   The "edition" of a book is the whole
number of copies of a book printed any time or times from
one setting of type.   A given work may be reprinted many
times, but unless there are substantial changes in the text
the edition does not change.   However, unless the changes
in a text are any but the most trivial, the publisher will
want to see that they are legally protected with a new copyright and to be able to call the work a "revised and enlarged" edition, second edition or some similar notice. Thus,
a work that has gone into two or more editions carries with
it a certain presumption of intrinsic merit since it has obviously been accepted by many people within its subject field.
For example, Alfred Marshall's Principles of Economics, a

standard classic in the field, which was originally published
in 1890, is still being used in its eighth edition which was
issued in 1920.   Even though it is obviously an "old" book,
the fact that it has gone through so many editions should be
a signal that here is a book that many people considered
worthwhile.

3. The "Dedication" in a book.   Following the title
page of a book, many books contain a dedication of the work
to some person or persons whom the author wishes to honor
by his work.   Historically, this practice is a carry-over
from the days when the authors had patrons, either the local
lord or later a wealthy member of the aristocracy, who supported their work.   Today, while most of them are fairly
innocuous homages to wives, children or mothers, a significant number of them still attempt to indicate some sense of
intellectual indebtedness to persons who have influenced the
author.   For this reason they may be a signal indicating the
possible biases or value systems of the respective authors.

4. The Preface.   The preface comes next.   It is
usually written by the author; if not, it may be shifted to
some other person.   In modern times, it is usually a succinct statement of the need which the book is intended to
serve, a statement of the author's purpose, possibly a detailed analysis of the way in which the book should be employed.   It may contain acknowledgements for help received
by the author in his work, or for professional courtesies extended to him.   Prefaces are therefore not to be ignored,
for the whole benefit you get from a book may depend upon
principles for its use there set forth.   The preface is usually more specific than the introduction, to be discussed later,
but the two often exchange some functions.   If the preface
states the method of use or the circumstances for which the
book is written, it is an essential guide to choice, suitability, and use.

5. Tables of Contents.   Tables of contents are "maps"
to the terrain of a book.   They are just as useful in the
first reading of a book as a road map is for touring in
strange territory.   There are many, many kinds of tables
of contents.   In novels, the table is useful chiefly to tell
you at what page each chapter begins and its title, but in
such works the chapter titles are likely to be imaginative
rather than descriptive.   Since novels are usually read
wholly and straight through, there is little lost except the loving
care which some novelists expend upon their chapter titles.

Other types of works, such as informational literature, furnish a table of contents by which the reader can
find with greater assurance that part of the book which concerns him.   It affords a conspectus, or mental survey, useful in orienting the reader in the larger field of which his
interest is a part.   He may thus save himself blunders of
comprehension while picking up clues about the general drift
of the book which enable him to understand more fully, remember more easily, and read more swiftly.

6. List of Illustrations.   In an illustrated book, the
list of illustrations usually follows the table of contents.
The ordinary reader will find himself confronted with no
real difficulties in using it unless the arrangement is unusu-
ally inept.   In some few books, the list of illustrations may
distinguish "illustrations" from "plates," the reason being
that special illustrations, particularly colored matter, require special processes, and appear as unnumbered inserts
rather than as numbered pages.   Be prepared to accept and
use many similar variations of techniques in the list of illustrations, but consider the list when you are choosing a
book so that you may know how well the work fits your
needs.

7. Introductions.   Introductions to books present a
major problem when one is determining the usefulness of
the book to prospective readers.   In general, they should
provide just what their name implies.   They may, however,
say little to guide the reader if such directions have already
been committed to the preface.   They may be (and usually
are) written by someone other than the author.   Sometimes
the identity and value position of the author of the introduction is a better clue to the merit of a book than is the author of the text.

Specialists who prepare for publication the works of
another man, which is to say "editors," not uncommonly produce introductions which may of themselves become somewhat monumental pieces of writing for their style or for
their content.   The field of foreign language studies often
produces works in which the text is merely a matter for
practice reading, whereas the introduction contains the essential treatise on grammar and syntax which makes the text
itself comprehensible.   The "introductory matter" of Webster's Collegiate Dictionary (only twenty pages) is as necessary to the full use of the work as any part of the volume
which follows it.

8. The Body of the Text: Typographical Layout and other Features.

a. Heads.   Within the body of the text, there will not be found as much uniformity of practice as in the "front matter" of title page, table of contents, etc. , for the infinite variety of its purposes calls for many different methods of presentation.   But there are a number of devices commonly used to aid the reader to more efficient use of the work.

In a book of thoroughly conventional kind, divided into chapters as it usually is, further subdivisions may be desirable.   One common practice is to print at the top of every verso (left hand page) the title or an abridgement of it, and at the top of every recto (right hand page) the titles of the chapters.   Many books, notably text books, employ other typographical devices to signalize topics and their divisions, and thus offer two very important advantages.   Since they afford you the easiest and readiest means of acquainting yourself with the scope and content of a chapter before you read it through; the rate at which you read and the accuracy with which you remember are both greatly improved.   Books which are not read through but consulted only in part, such as handbooks and other types of reference books, must, if they are not to absorb too much of our time, provide a ready means for "finding the place."   This need may be met by an analytical table of contents or an index; if these are not well executed, the running heads and similar devices become all-important.   Learn to recognize and use them in your evaluation of the potential merits of a book.

b. Notes, foot and otherwise.   Within the body of the text there arises a constant need in certain kinds of books for footnotes, which commonly serve any of three or four functions.   1) In the first place, the writer may wish to provide necessary information for the reader without interrupting the flow of his remarks.   A brief explanation of a point which might remain obscure or cause misunderstanding, particularly when definitions are needed, is a common function of the footnote.   2) A second is that of developing a footnote, [in which] the author can throw out a suggestion, indulge in a reminiscence, or give some part of his work a completeness which in the text would be only an annoyance.   3) Footnotes are also the readiest means of providing cross references within various parts of the text without disrupting the progressive development of the argument or series of propositions the author is attempting to establish.   4) A fourth and fundamentally important use of the footnote is to cite the source of material taken from other books; and it is necessary at this point that we anticipate a later section dealing with book lists or bibliographies. If the author has provided at the end of his work a separate, formally alphabetized bibliography, he can refer to any book in it by means of a condensed footnote.

Not all books present bibliographies as separate entries. Many professional periodicals require that the writer give the author, full title, city and year of publication, and other pertinent information in a footnote appended to the first passage requiring such documentation. All subsequent footnotes referring to that book are likely to be much condensed, and they will commonly employ abbreviations which it is necessary that you should know.

An author's "style" of footnoting, i. e. the extent to which he uses them, his purposes in so doing, the kind of sources he depends upon--does he depend upon first hand, primary sources or does he cite secondary sources and what are their quality--provides us with a quick basis for judging the probable scholarly merit of a book. Since styles in footnoting vary with the personal predilection of authors, the mere absence of footnotes does not condemn a book as being unscholarly, but the presence of an inept style certainly can.

c. Appendixes. Many times authors find that several points in the text would profit by expansion or more detailed treatment, but that a footnote does not furnish adequate space. In such cases, they may grow to any desired length and appear as appendixes, the first major division following the text. There is no imaginable limit to the kinds of appendix which the reader may expect to encounter. He will find charts, diagrams, maps, brief treatises on methodology and other pertinent subjects, reproductions of original documents for comparisons, tables of statistics. The advantages offered by this means are very often ignored because, having finished the text, the unwary reader is likely to clap shut the book and stretch himself with the satisfaction of accomplishment. These parts of a book, self-effacing as they may seem, are not to be ignored because of their location, but sought out in their suburban retreats like skilled though remote advisers.

d. Glossaries. The reader in any field is likely to

find himself faced with the need of developing familiarity
with a new set of terms.   To fit this need many books
furnish an alphabetical listing of terms which should not only be consulted as the need arises, but learned so that the
entries become a part of the reader's ordinary working
speech.   The glossary is an incomplete lexicon of words
that fit a special need created by the subject matter of the
book.

e. Bibliography.   The discussion of footnotes anticipated the treatment of the bibliography, which conventionally
follows the glossary.   It has many purposes.   It is, first of
all, an indication of the fundamental soundness of the work
you are reading if it is a list of works consulted by the author.   No writer in any field will risk his professional
standing by producing a book which presupposes the examination of source material and predecessors without detailing
his materials.   2) In the second place, since bibliographies
are also intended for the reader's convenience and to aid
him in his own studies, some writers go beyond the "works
consulted" kind of bibliography and try to present a list as
complete as humanly possible of all the material which may
be found anywhere dealing with a given subject, even though
the author makes no claim to having examined all of it.
Such bibliographies go far beyond the mere listing of books,
accessible or rare.   They list diaries, journals, letters,
portraits, manuscripts, notebooks, public documents and records whether found in the private collections of enthusiasts,
in libraries or museums, or merely among the personal effects of chance possessors.

The forms observed in most older bibliographies show
very little variation from certain standard procedures.   It is
common to list "original" or "primary" sources separately
from "secondary" sources.   A primary source is any kind of
document believed to furnish direct evidence or information
based on personal knowledge.   Secondary sources are the
books and other materials derived from original sources;
they must be taken into account, for they represent an ac-
cumulating body of data, interpretation, and correction.
Some bibliographies will make further distinctions in form,
listing manuscripts, diaries, and the like separately from
printed material.   Some, in giving the works consulted, separate conventionally bound books from periodicals, and these
in turn from general reference works like encyclopedias, but
this practice is not universal.

Increasingly today, as Sherman Kent indicates in
<u>Writing History</u>, scholars are veering away from the old
practice of uncritically listing all the books they consulted
for a given project.   More and more are they using the
"note" as the proper vehicle for bibliographical information.
The note, besides being infinitely more useful than the barren alphabetized book list, is more pleasant and informing
both to write and to read.

In essence this bibliographical note is a short critical essay about the materials which the author has used in
writing his study.   Author's name, book title, publication
dates, and so on are all incorporated into running sentences.

Arrangement of the material within a note, or any
sort of bibliography for that matter, ought to follow one general pattern.   Within this large scheme personal preferences,
and the peculiar demands of the material will make the detail of every note different from the last.   The general pattern is simple.   Every note should be made up of at least
two (and sometimes three) main sections.   The first of these
(when it is used) is apt to be the shortest, for it is the one
which deals with bibliographical aids.   That is, it starts
with a discussion of bibliographies and bibliographical articles
and essays which cover the literature of the topic.

The second section is the most important for it is
here that the author discusses his sources.   He should describe them in the order of their weight and their closeness
to what he believes the truth.   His description should consider the form of the materials--whether printed or manu-
script--where they are to be found, the state of their preservation, their completeness, how they are sorted, indexed,
catalogued, or calendared.   In the last analysis it is the
topic of the essay which determines what is and what is not
source material.

The third section comprises the so-called secondary literature; it should contain all material which cannot be positively identified as source items.   It too should be subdivided into
at least two subclasses: monographs and general works.   If
newspapers and journals of opinion, autobiographies, memoirs,
and diaries have been used and if they are not classable as original sources, they should come in this section in their own sub-
class.

While an author may misuse the scholarly functions
of both footnotes and bibliography, together they form an ex-

ternal index of some of the sources and influences which
contributed to his work.   The pattern they prescribe give us
clues for judging the quality of workmanship and probable
merit of the item.   For example, if a book or journal article was published in 1961, but no footnotes or bibliographical
references were later than, say, 1940, we have reason to
suspect the item or, at the very least, it is a signal for us
to investigate why the author did not use any later literature.
It may be such an esoteric topic that no significantly relevant literature has been published since that time, on the
other hand, the author may have actually written it in 1940
and only now published it without bothering to revise it--
stranger things have happened in scholarly publishing.

Another kind of clue is the relative dependence upon
primary as compared to secondary sources and also upon
monographic literature as compared to journal articles.
Given the demands of specific topics, the peculiarities of
literature in various subject areas and the variations in the
personal styles of authors, there is no general rule as to
what proportions should pertain in these ratios; for the purpose of a quick evaluation of a book or journal article, we
should simply be sensitive to the fact that some balance
should be maintained among them.   The more that we know
about the substantive problems in a given subject field and
about the generally recognized authorities who have published
works in the area, the more significant will be our scanning
of footnotes and bibliographies.   Of course, practitioners
may not share any consensus about a ranking of the major
subsantive problems or who the "generally recognized authorities" are within any given subject field but finding out those
details is part of the fun in mastering a discipline.

f. Indexes.   An index is the back door to a book.
Essentially, an index is the book reduced to its essential
themes, places, topics and persons mentioned therein.   The
one purpose in making an index to any book is to make all
the information in that volume fully available to any reader
without delay.   This is a comparatively simple matter as
far as it concerns references to names of places and of
people--though even these can present difficulties--but some
skill and experience are required wherever it is desired to
make references to ideas and define and indicate the different aspects of a subject.   Indexing, in fact, is no mechanical process; if it is to be of use, it requires thought and
consideration in every phase of its construction.   Since all
the uses to which a work may be put cannot be predicted,

the index must by its completeness attempt to anticipate
everyone's questions. Obviously, this is an impossibility,
but a good index provides a sufficient range of entries for
discovering whether the specific items of information we are
seeking can be located within a particular book. The usefulness of many otherwise valuable books has been seriously
impaired by the lack of an index or by a poorly designed
one.

The above listed parts are the major elements of a
book. Obviously, not every book you will encounter will
have all of them. Taken together they make up a typographical "model" of the book as an instrument of communication. Until now, we have discussed each of these parts
separately, but our judgment of the probable merit of a book
will be based upon the total impression it makes upon us.
In other words, it is the relationship between these parts
and their common consistency which provides us with the
basis for our judgment. For example, if the author's qualifications on the title page are set forth impressively and if
the title promises us something like an "Intellectual History
of Western Civilization," but the table of contents indicates
a vaguely defined scope covering only the intellectual history
of certain periods in England and the United States, the footnotes only referring to generally known secondary sources
and the bibliography limited in its coverage, our obvious
conclusion would have to be that there was a gross incon-
sistency between the promise of the author's qualifications
and the title and the actual accomplishment of the text.
Thus, even in our quick evaluation of books and journal articles while we are browsing in the library, if we are perceptive we can detect a certain proportion between the various parts of a book, a certain fulfillment of expectations
which the various parts of a book or journal article cause
us to develop. How many times all of us have spotted a
catchy title on the shelf, a new cover on a book, only after
examining the table of contents, a quick flip through the footnotes and a glance at the bibliography to decide that this
item is or is not for us. If we have a little more time,
perhaps we dip into the preface and introduction and look up
a few key terms in the index.

In any event, we do go through a decision-making
process in selecting books and journal articles, bring to
bear our prior knowledge and attitudes along with the new
impressions we have gained from our brief scanning of the
item. The more adequate our background knowledge and the

more sensitive we are to the bibliographical characteristics of written materials we have indicated in these notes, the more efficient our use of the library will be.

Bibliographical Note

The problems we have considered in these Notes are covered extensively in the literature on the art of reading and in some books on research techniques. A "how-to-do-it" book which still retains its value and "message" after many years is Mortimer J. Adler's How to Read a Book: The Art of Getting a Liberal Education (New York: Simon and Schuster, 1940; also available in a more recent paperback edition.) Another how-to-do-it book which was useful in writing these notes is E. Wayne Marjarum's How to Use a Book (New Brunswick, Rutgers University Press, 1947.) Of the books on research techniques, the best brief, but admirably adequate treatment may be found in Sherman Kent's Writing History (New York: Appleton-Century-Crofts, 1941.) A more extended treatment of essentially the same themes may be found in Jacques Barzun and Henry F. Graff, The Modern Researcher (New York: Harcourt, Brace and Co., 1957.)

A Philosophy of Book Selection in Smaller
Academic Libraries

by Stuart A. Stiffler   Associate Librarian, Hiram
                               College (Ohio)

From College and Research Libraries 24:205-8
May 1963; Reprinted by permission of Association
of College and Research Libraries, ALA, Chicago.

What theoretical guidelines should the librarian adopt,
then, if he is to assume an active role in book selection?
Every institution presents its unique problems.   The points
included in any sound book selection policy statement are
basic.   What are the educational aims of one's institution?
What is the general trend in departmental and in total enrollments?   What are the specific trends in research and
teaching interest within each department?   What is the pattern of curriculum development?   What is the proximity of
one's institution to other book collections?   The introduction
of Honors programs and the generally increased emphasis
upon independent study is, for example, a development which
can significantly alter one's total purchasing program.

As a background for selection these policy considerations should be tied in with a carefully written estimate of
the strengths and weaknesses of one's collection.   The more
detailed and specific this can be made, the better; but in any
case, it will have to be constantly amended and expanded
with changes in curriculum and faculty and with the continuing evaluation of the collection.   But, beyond this, what general applicability can theoretical considerations have for the
numerous individual book collections, each with its own requirements?

In the first place, a book is always, ideally, evaluated originally, or in review, by the librarian on its own
merits.   He utilizes his own knowledge, consults staff or
faculty members and checks standard bibliographies, check
lists and reviews.   The librarian remains ultimately responsible for the qualitative character of his book collection.

He may on occasion think it necessary to express a negative
opinion of a book or to summarize reviewers' professional
consensus to the individual who requests such a book.   And
he must retain the ultimate authority to reject a book under
consideration.

But with exceptions to be noted, a volume should not
usually be selected exclusively on the basis of its individual
merit.   The questions must be asked, what is the relevance
of the book to our requirements in terms of the educational
aims of our institution?, in terms of student and faculty interests?, of the level of demand and enrollment in the various courses?, of the relative strengths in the collection as
defined in one's written evaluation of the collection?, of the
degree of specialization and level (or type) of treatment of
the volume in relation to the clientele served?   Decision for
purchase of most volumes must be based upon careful assessment of the multiple selection criteria involved.

To select a book without reference to these extrinsic
criteria will, in the long run, materially decrease the general utility of the collection to the library's public.   As a
general underlying principle it is important to view the library collection not as composed of isolated book-units, de-
riving their organic character only from physical proximity
and the residual subject analysis provided by the classification system, the card catalog, indexes, and printed bibliographies.   In a substantive sense a book collection is not
composed of books as physical objects in space, but rather
it consists of ideas or themes, events, interpretations having some structural coherence in terms of collective treatment in the total body of material selected and analyzed.
By "structural coherence" is meant that the ideational content
of a given volume is viewed, insofar as possible, in its
manifold relations to the corresponding or related content of
all other physical units in the collection.   This criterion
should be qualified, as shall be explained below, by the ad-
mission of books relatively comprehensive and self-contained
and which further appear as significant idea-complexes
around which to build.

The well selected book collection, then, poses a complex problem in applied social epistemology.   Accordingly,
the librarian must be sensitive to the evolving organization
of knowledge, and to the interrelationship of the ideas, the
events, and the broader themes which he is evaluating.
This "sensitivity" involves not only some sense of the logi-

cal organization of knowledge (considered as idea, event, or theme) but of the associative or analogical element which, since it is involved in research and imaginative thinking, is ultimately a factor in the analysis and selection of books.

Now it follows as a corollary of the fact that the collection as a whole possesses its own distinctive structural characteristics that the individual book is not, typically, a self-contained unit of knowledge. Anyone who has worked with books knows that the book is not often a comprehensive, logically and coherently organized vehicle of expression, precisely fitted to a researcher's need, even when the subject in view is but one clearly delimited aspect of a broader topic. Further, most library users naturally select a research topic without reference to the topic's compactness or unity of treatment in the materials which constitute the library collection.

From the researcher's point of view the scattering of information on a research topic is the result of the natural divergence among patterns of definition of subject, of logical organization, of level and mode of treatment, and of canons of pertinency as conceived by himself and by the authors of that body of material of potential use to him. This divergence is complicated by the cumulative growth (and sometimes the obsolescence) of knowledge which may, in itself, alter with time the effective ideational relationship of a given volume to related volumes in the collection. This scattering effect is ultimately a result of subjective differences in modes of thinking together with the social growth of knowledge and the changing pattern of its physical organization. The librarian can only hope to reduce somewhat the dissimilarity in the mental pictures of authors and library users by judging books against some operational conception of his clientele's subjective type of mind. The difficulty in applying this approach with any great precision should not, however, be a matter of great concern. The complete elimination of "cross purpose" between author and library user is not the ultimate goal. Since a basic element of research is the imaginative reorganization of recorded thought, absolute subjective correspondence would eliminate the possibility of research itself.

If the book is to be of maximum value it must, then, be judged on the basis of its ideational content viewed within the context of the internal structure of the collection and the external requirements of the clientele. Otherwise it is conceivable that one may build a collection of excellent book with but very few topics or themes reliably treated in depth. Brooks Adams' observation of fifty years ago that "men of liberal education have collected libraries who have never been taught to generalize... When a book is supposed to have a certain degree of merit it is deemed worthy of purchase, almost regardless of subject"[1] is probably still true of the practice of many librarians today. In sum the physical units which collectively constitute the treatment of even delimited topic are typically numerous and often physically scattered in terms of the formal classification structure. Even when expertly performed, the organization of subject analysis cannot be expected to remedy the deficiencies of book selection without close attention to the structural characteristics of knowledge. For this reason I think that even in small collections with limited budgets the indispensable standard of the "well-balanced" collection should not be made a fetish. The list of authors or broad topics almost automatically selected should not be too extensive or too rigidly adhered to. Some imbalance in coverage may have to be tolerated in planning for selected coverage of a few specialized ideas, themes, or events.

Several categories may be enumerated which should help organize in the librarian's mind the evaluation and selection of books. Before considering these general categories, it should be acknowledged, that, in order to reduce the scattering effect discussed above, some books will immediately eliminate themselves by virtue of the public to which they are addressed, or, more specifically, because of their degree of specialization, or the level and type of treatment they exhibit. Although some may be selected if specifically requested or if judged to be of standard or seminal importance, most will be quickly eliminated. The degree of a book's specialization in relation to the size of one's collection or, more properly, the size of the collection in the specialized subfield which the volume treats is an initial consideration.

The categories may be enumerated as follows:

1. First, there are books whose selection is, in most academic libraries, quite properly determined by the formal structure of the selection process. The faculty selects these books subject to the informal advice and review of the librarian. These volumes may, of course, be valuable from the point of view of the criteria outlined below. But such

coincidence must be considered to be considerably fortuitous.

2. The second category consists in the works of "standard" authors which are selected almost automatically. To permit flexibility the list should be informal and not too extensive. Generally speaking, the less significance critical opinion attaches to an author, the more the author's subject and style should be immediately considered in relation to the interests and tastes of the libraries publics and, ultimately, the more attention should be focused upon the intrinsic merits of the book itself.

3. The third category includes books selected on specialized subjects, themes, ideas, or events (qualified by mode of treatment). Books on certain subjects--depending upon local interest and demand--may receive priority consideration for purchase. This category may, however, sometimes be chosen without reference to immediate demand in order to add depth to selected ideas, themes, and events on which some demand may reasonably be anticipated. Automatic buying on topics should, however, be carefully controlled by the pattern of changing needs and by the merits of the book itself. Where demand is very heavy or published material is scarce, critical standards may on occasion be lowered somewhat.

4. The fourth category is made up of miscellaneous material, added for symmetry or for "rounding out the collection" and overlaps to some degree with category two, "standard" authors. Priority consideration within this category should be given to books for which anticipated demand may be determined with some assurance. Although these judgments are difficult at best, by noting the pattern of student and faculty interests and by analyzing curricular trends one may choose well within this category. Types of material which may be subsumed under this category include standard or classic works for which there is continuing demand. Also included are books in fields which have been developed in the past but which have receded in relative importance because of changing personnel or changing interests and because of curricular changes. This latter material should be "kept up" by the librarian to the extent that the budget allows, as the area in question may well again emerge within the purview of faculty or student interest. Or these books may attract research interest from allied fields or may be used for papers in freshman English courses.

5. The fifth category is normally small in relative
financial priority but nonetheless vital in qualitative importance.   It encompasses new books which do not fall within
the first four enumerated categories.   These materials
should challenge the full range of the librarian's insight, re
inforced by a certain measure of educated guessing.   This
category may be designated as including those works which,
although apparently not of immediate interest to students an
faculty, appear destined to become standard or definitive
surveys of a subject field, of a theme, an idea, an event.
These are not selected purely intuitively, however, but in
part upon the intrinsic merits of the volume in relation to a
logical projection of needs and interests of the library's put
lic estimated from all available evidence.

These points then may be summarized as follows.
The librarian always should bear an active responsibility in
the development of the book collection.   This responsibility
should rest upon an evaluation of the differential strengths
of his collection in relation to the interests of his clientele
and to the educational aims and curricular trends of his institution.   To implement effectively this responsibility, ther
should be established as basic assumption in the librarian's
mind a clear conception of his book collection as an organi
body of knowledge with its own peculiar structural organiza
tion.

The competent selection of a new book title, especially in institutions with very limited resources, frequently
involves the consideration of multiple determining criteria.
Each new title, consequently, might be considered in terms
of the categories of valuation here outlined.   The specific
nature of the decisions which may be deduced from these de
termining guidelines must be dictated by the local situation.
A survey program of current reviewing and indexing publica
tions should be established to provide a consistent and rational implementation of these guidelines to the book selection program.   It is the frequent complexity and the consid
erable element of subjectivity involved which should make th
selection process a constantly interesting and challenging pr
fessional undertaking.

Note

1. The New Empire   New York, Macmillan, 1902, p. xxvi.

EFLA EVALUATION

Film Title: Running Time_____
Subject-Matter Field: Date Produced_____
Producer:
Purchase Sources:

So.____ Si.____ B & W____ Color____ Sale Price____

Rental____ Free____

Evaluation Institution: Date of Evaluation_____
Names and Titles of Evaluators:

Synopsis: (About 75-100 words, as detailed as possible.
          Do not use producer's summary.)

i. List the possible audiences, and the purposes for which the
   film could be used. Rate probable value for each purpose.

		Value			
Audience	Purpose	Low			High
1.		1 2 3 4 5
2.		1 2 3 4 5

ii. Recommended age level: primary_____,

    intermediate _____, jr. high_____, sr. high_____,

    college_____, adult_____.

iii. Structure: (organization, editing, continuity)
                                        1   2   3   4   5
     Picture quality: (clarity, framing, color, etc.)
                                        1   2   3   4   5
     Sound, quality: (audibility, voice fidelity,
                      music, effects)   1   2   3   4   5

iv. Comment and General Impression: (Note here any special
    points as to authenticity, creativity or attitude; also a
    brief statement of how the film affects you. Use back of
    sheet if necessary.)

v. Your estimate of the value of the film: Poor____ Fair____
   Average____ Good____ Very Good____ Excellent____

411

Annotations

Library of Congress.   Reference Department

From Library of Congress. Reference Department.   General Reference and Bibliography Division.   Bibliographical Procedure and Style.
Washington, Library of Congress, 1954. Appendix
C.   Annotations, p. 99-101 sel.

While many bibliographies rightly may be prepared
without annotations, others require these additional elements
for a variety of reasons, such as the following: (a) entries
are not self-explanatory;   (b) achievement of the complete
purpose of the work requires interest supplied by annotations;
and (c) the scope of the bibliography justifies time and effort involved in supplying annotations to aid potential users
rapidly to assess the value of individual items.

Successful annotations are not evolved from the application of dogmatic rules.   Instead, they reflect knowledge,
judgment, awareness of relative importance, and good taste
on the part of the person who writes them.   The greater the
bibliographer's mastery of the subjects concerned, the more
latitude to which he is entitled in preparing his annotations.
There are, however, degrees of excellence in the special
skill required for writing satisfactory annotations.   For that
reason a section on annotations is provided to indicate material gleaned from the literature of the subject and to be
used for purposes of orientation and review...

II.   Checklist of specifications.   When writing annotations
the bibliographer will find it wise to keep before him
a checklist of specifications from which to select those
applicable to his work at a given time.   The literature
of annotating yields the following suggestions for such a
list:

1. Avoid repetition of information already explicit in the
entry being annotated.

2. If the authority of the author has a bearing on the usefulness of the work, give his title or state his experience.

3. Confine coverage of topics to those significant for the purpose of the bibliography and avoid the inclusion of extraneous ideas.

4. State the scope of the work, employing terminology susceptible to successful indexing in relation to the subject of the bibliography.

5. Give the author's central thesis if it is possible to do so in few words.

6. Explain qualifications requisite to the successful use of the item, e. g. , knowledge of advanced mathematics, statistical analysis, theoretical economics, etc.

7. Indicate limits imposed by dates or periods covered.

8. Call attention to the individual slant of the book, if important, e. g. , "Techniques described apply to microfilm made according to British standard specifications. "

9. In exceptional cases that justify particular attention or involve conflicts of opinion quote from or cite an important review, abstract, or reply by a recognized authority.

10. Point out features of importance, such as documentary appendixes, indexes of sets, bibliographies, and extensive illustrative and graphic material.

11. Compare the work in question to another publication of similar or contrasting purpose, if such comparison is an aid in establishing scope and purpose.

12. Omit evaluation according to personal opinion of the bibliographer, but supply objective facts on which the user may base his own opinion.

13. Compress the annotation into the fewest possible words, considering 30 to 60 desirable and over 100 prohibitive unless a review, not an annotation, is called for.

14. Omit redundant annotations if the authority and importance of the work are obvious from the author and the title, e. g., in the case of historic documents, laws, treaties, etc.

15. Explain in the preface, and if necessary state in different words in a note at the beginning of the bibliography, any puzzling stylistic usages, and the omission of annotations, which might impress the user as an evidence of superficial treatment.

III. Style. Two clearly marked styles used in writing annotations represent the extremes of several choices open to the bibliographer. These are: (a) the conventional literary style; and (b) the clipped, telegraphic style. Both styles may be used in the same bibliography according to which is best suited to individual items.

A. Conventional style. Those who choose to annotate in this style must use the best possible idiomatic English in sentences that are clear, complete, and readable. An opening sentence expresses the principal point of the annotation, while transitional words and phrases lead on to other sentences embodying subsidiary ideas. A conclusion or climax of sorts then adds emphasis to a graceful and polished piece of writing. The peculiar virtue of this style, if its art has been thoroughly mastered, is that it lends itself to persuasive writing which helps to stimulate interest and fix attention. It is particularly well adapted to the annotation of books selected for complete reading. Works chosen not for thorough reading but for consultation in the course of study and research present a different problem and bring to light difficulties in the use of the conventional style. Quite justly the annotator may feel that he loses precious opportunities to present information useful to serious students, while he struggles to be urbane, elegant, and interesting in 30 to 60 words. He may decide, therefore, that the telegraphic style is the one best suited to his purpose.

B. Telegraphic style. When this style is followed, introductory words, phrases, and sentences are omitted. Articles, adjectives, and adverbs, when they are not essential to clarity of meaning, are dropped. Familiar abbreviations of technical bibliographical

terms, e. g. , bibl. , p. , v. , cf. , etc. , legitimately
may be employed.   Elliptical expressions and compact phrases are substituted for complete sentences,
while connective and transitional elements tend to be
eliminated.   Frequently no period appears until the
end of the annotation is reached, although in such a
case semicolons may be used between independent
expressions within the annotation.   While it is difficult to avoid the monotony that results from repeated
use of nouns without verbs, and vice versa, which is
an inevitable result when this style is used, at its
best it produces a workmanlike effect, with a refreshing lack of ostentation.   So brief and direct a presentation of essential facts may be welcome to specialists and scholars already thoroughly familiar with the
trends in literature of a subject field.

IV. Form.   An annotation, in the form of a paragraph, is
placed after the main body of the entry in a bibliography, following the necessary supplementary notes. When
space is at a premium in a long bibliography, it may
even be necessary to coalesce notes and annotations in
a single highly compact paragraph.   In such a case,
great care must be exercised to avoid confusion from
compression that becomes cryptic.

Filmstrips: Selection, Evaluation, Cataloging, Processing

by Carl T. Cox

Director, Teaching Materials
Center, State University College, Cortland, New York

From Wilson Library Bulletin 38:178-82, October
1963 (sel.); Reprinted by permission of Wilson
Library Bulletin, New York City.

What Is a Filmstrip?

Filmstrips, sometimes called slide films or film-slides, have been defined several ways in recent education and library literature. Perhaps the clearest definition is found in the audio-visual text by Brown, Lewis and Harcleroad.

> Filmstrips are composed of a series of still pictures and titles or captions placed in sequential order on 35mm film from 2 to 6 feet long with sprocket holes on each side. They are commonly between twenty and fifty frames (individual pictures) in length, although they may be as long as 100 frames. Filmstrips are produced in black and white or color... Most filmstrips are produced in 'single-frame' size, with each individual frame 3/4 inches high and 1 inch wide across the 35mm width of the film.

Sound filmstrips can be defined as filmstrips which are accompanied by some form of recorded narration. The narration, which may be on a disc or tape recording, discusses each frame of the filmstrip. A signal indicates to the projectionist when to move to the next frame.

Filmstrips have become an important teaching material because they have strengths not found in other devices. Cross and Cypher list the following advantages of filmstrips:

1. They make it possible to show pictures at a rate of speed of projection controlled by the projectionist and adjustable to individual group needs.

2. Provide projectable material easy to handle. ... easy to store, always ready to use.

3. Provide projectable material arranged in sequence for showing.

4. Provide a visual or pictorial medium which can be adapted to use by individuals, small groups, or very large audiences.

5. Provide a good source of projectable material at low cost.

6. Provide material which can be projected effectively in a room which is only partially darkened...

7. Provide material to suit a very wide range of instructional needs because of their low cost and the fact that many producers have made filmstrips in virtually every subject area.

The advantage of price should be emphasized. The black and white filmstrip costs from $3 to $4; a color strip from $5 to $7; a sound strip from $7 to $11. These prices make it possible for most schools to acquire a sizable collection of filmstrips.

Disadvantages must also be recognized. The pre-set sequence of the filmstrip may be its greatest disadvantage. This requires the showing of the pictures in a given order when a particular group may wish to view the pictures in a different sequence or may wish to see only selected frames. Another weakness is that when one frame becomes out of date, the entire filmstrip is outdated. A third weakness lies in the fact that filmstrips are easily damaged and difficult to repair.

Although the sound filmstrip may be more authoritative than one narrated by the teacher, it presents disadvantages not found in the silent strip. It is very difficult, if not impossible, to stop a sound filmstrip for discussion and then restart with sound and picture synchronized. When this happens, the confusion created may destroy the effectiveness of the entire projection.

Selection Aids

There are several sources which can guide teachers and librarians in selecting filmstrips. These sources are discussed below in three groups: guides, periodical listings and catalogs.

Guides to Filmstrips

There are three basic guides which should be considered in a discussion of filmstrip selection aids. Of historical importance is Vera Falconer's <u>Filmstrips: A Descriptive Index and Users Guide</u>, which is described by Rufsvold as follows:

> More than 3000 filmstrips released before January 1, 1947 are included in Vera Falconer's <u>Filmstrips: A Descriptive Index and Users Guide</u> (New York, McGraw-Hill, 1948). This is the best source of critical evaluations of educational filmstrips produced prior to 1947. It contains a detailed discussion of the nature of filmstrips, criteria for selection, and the use of filmstrips in education.

The majority of filmstrips produced since January 1, 1947, have been listed in H. W. Wilson's <u>Filmstrip Guide</u> (6). This is by far the most important listing of filmstrips and should be available in every materials center or library. Through its third edition, 1954, <u>Filmstrip Guide</u> contained an annotated list of filmstrips arranged by Dewey decimal classification. It included a title and subject index and a list of filmstrip producers. The third edition was kept up to date by annual and cumulative supplements. The supplements, starting with the <u>1955-1958 Revised Supplement</u>, are arranged by title and have a subject index. The supplements do not include strips of fiction, fairytales, folklore nor those produced by the United States government as did the third edition.

For each filmstrip listed in <u>Filmstrip Guide</u> and its supplements, the following information is given: title, producer, date, physical description, price, grade level, annotation, Library of Congress card number, if available at the time of printing.   Prior to the 1955-1958 Revised Supplement, a Dewey classification number could also be obtained through Filmstrip Guide.   The Guide is invaluable as a cataloging aid as well as a selection aid.

Unfortunately, it was discontinued with the 1962 supplement...

Educators Guide to Free Filmstrips is also a valuable selection aid.   The Guide lists filmstrips which are available to schools on a free-loan basis.   Twenty-eight of the 643 titles listed in the 1962 edition can be retained by the school without charge.   Arrangement in the Guide is by broad curriculum areas with separate title, subject and source indexes.

Periodical Listings

Virtually all audio-visual journals list new releases and have reviews of new titles.   Many professional periodicals regularly list titles of new filmstrips.   Among these are Elementary English, The English Journal, Grade Teacher, Instructor, Journal of Health, Physical Education and Recreation, The Science Teacher, Social Education, and Social Studies.   No attempt has been made to include audio-visual journals.

Catalogs

Catalogs from producers and distributors offer an inexpensive and indispensable selection aid.   Materials centers should have a file of these available for faculty use.   Filmstrips will usually be listed in catalogs before they are listed in other sources or reviewed in professional literature.   The materials center should, in addition to maintaining a collection of catalogs, have its name placed on the mailing list of the major filmstrip producers.   This will enable the center to receive immediate notification of new materials.   Lists of producers are available in Filmstrip Guide or in texts on audio-visual education.

Evaluation Techniques

The selection aids cannot evaluate filmstrips in light of local needs.   The evaluation of filmstrips is the joint responsibility of the faculty and librarian in charge of the materials center.   Ideally, grade and subject matter teachers and the librarian would preview the strip as their time permits. Then a preview could be held for the group. After watching the filmstrip, the teachers and librarian should discuss it in terms of these six criteria. Does the filmstrip...

1. Enrich the instructional program?
   Filmstrips must be closely correlated with the instructional program. They should be designed to introduce new material, to supplement facts acquired through the use of textbooks and other printed sources, to increase appreciation, to test learned skills, or to review subject matter.

2. Meet grade level needs?
   A filmstrip must suit the grade level for which it is intended through its content, its choice of illustrations, its interest level, its conceptual level, and its vocabulary level.

3. Prove authoritative?
   Editorial integrity is as important in a filmstrip as in any teaching material. Facts must be accurate, ideas must be reliable, illustrations must be representative and the information presented must be up to date.

4. Prove educationally sound?
   Filmstrips should follow accepted learning patterns through the presentation, discussion, and review of materials presented. The subject presented should be adequately covered. Students viewing the filmstrip should be encouraged to seek additional information in other sources.

5. Prove technically sound?
   The topic covered by the filmstrip should be appropriately presented in filmstrip form and the illustrations, photography and captions should be clear.

6. Fill a local need?
   The filmstrip should fill a gap in the school's collection or should enrich an area which is widely used. Unnecessary duplication should be avoided...

Film Evaluation

by Emily S. Jones

Miss Jones is Executive Director of the Educational Film
Library Association

From her Manual on Film Evaluation.   New York,
Educational Film Library Association, 1967. p. 3-
4; 7-9; 22-3; 31;   Reprinted by permission of
Educational Film Library Association, New York
City.

Definition of Terms

When discussing Evaluation it is important to be clear
about what it is.   There are a number of different ways of
describing and giving an opinion about a film, and each has
its own function.

Note.   Film notes appear commonly in various magazines and other publications, and in selected lists of films
in a particular subject area.   They are brief and descrip-
tive--usually only two or three sentences which are limited
to a synopsis of content and sometimes an indication of use
or audience.   The only critical judgment factor involved is
in including the film in the list at all.   This may be an important factor, if the list is a highly selective one, compiled
by a person or committee of experience and knowledge.
Most film notes are simply catalog listings, derived primarily from the information supplied by the producer.

Appraisal.   An appraisal is the result of a systematic
rating procedure, usually employing a detailed rating form.
Various elements involved in the film are identified, and
each one rated by the viewer according to a pre-determined
scale.   A number of different appraisal scales have been developed and used for a variety of purposes.   Part I of the
EFLA American Film Festival Rating Sheet is an appraisal
form.   ...   The advantage is that ratings of a
number of individual viewers can be brought together and

averaged to indicate a group response, without the actual
coming together or joint discussion by the viewers.   The
disadvantage is that there is little or no allowance for the
special qualities of creativity, imagination, or stimulation
which are inherent in outstanding films.   This is why the
Festival Rating Sheet has Part II, a subjective rating.   Appraisals are particularly valuable for straight-forward instructional or information films, and are therefore used
chiefly by school systems.

Review.   A review is one man's critical opinion.   It
is the exact opposite of an appraisal, since it presents the
personal reactions of an individual.   For this reason it
should always be signed.   Theatrical motion pictures, and
the so-called independent or new cinema productions, are
thoroughly reviewed in the public and specialized press, but
there are almost no real critics of the non-theatrical film.
Signed reviews do appear in Film News, but they tend to be
rather bland.   The ALA Booklist has reviews in the quarterly issues, done by a committee of public library film librarians, but oddly enough they are not signed.   The new
Film Library Quarterly published by FLIC (Film Library Information Council), plans to have many reviews in each issue.   The Landers Reviews are valuable primarily because
of the very detailed description of content, rather than because of any critical opinion expressed.   A review reflects
the tastes, experience, opinions, and prejudices of the reviewer.   Generally, reviews are far more interesting to read
than appraisals or evaluations, simply because of the human
angle.

Most people setting out to report on films write either
notes, with no critical aspects, or reviews, abounding in
personal reactions.   A review is valuable entirely to the degree to which the writer is qualified as a critic.   He is
speaking only for himself, and readers must know something
of his characteristics in order to decide the value of the review to them.   A critic has greater freedom than an evaluator to point out good and bad aspects of films, to hail a new
masterpiece or denounce a disaster.   The danger is that he
may come to believe that only he knows the answers, what
he likes is a good film, and what he dislikes or finds boring
is necessarily bad.   In other fields, this is balanced by the
profusion of critics.   Each reader is free to find the critic
whose tastes agree with his own, and be guided accordingly.
In the non-theatrical film field, critics are so few that any
reviewer who sounds authoritative can convince film users

either that he is right, or that reviewers are no good.   What
is needed is more and better critics.

Evaluation.   An evaluation is the carefully considered
opinion of a qualified group or committee, as to the scope,
usefulness, and quality of a given film.   The evaluation should
state what the film is about, who could use it, for what purpose, and should give the evaluators' opinion of the value of
the film to the suggested audiences.

Whether the individual members of the evaluation panel
personally enjoyed the film is less important than their group
estimate of its probable reception by others.   It takes training and practice to develop the skills of a good evaluator.
This book is intended as a help towards that end.

Why Evaluate?

The process of evaluation is time-consuming, and requires concentration and skill on the part of the evaluators.
Why go to all that trouble?   It's a lot easier to run off the
film whenever one or two people in the department have half
an hour or so to spare, and jot down a quick note--"great,"
"dull," "informative," "colorful," or "ugh."   That sort of instant opinion is easy, and practically useless except to the
person actually screening the film, and it won't be much use
to him unless he has a better memory than most people.

The point of evaluation is to provide useful information to potential film users.   Over ten thousand 16mm films
are released each year.   Many of them are specialized, with
limited distribution, but the number that any film user may
be interested in may range from the hundreds to the thousands, and that is only new releases.   Probably 75,000 different films are available, and the film user cannot possibly
screen even just those which are listed as being in his subject area.   A good film evaluation is a sort of verbal preview; it tells the potential user enough about the film to give
him some basis for selection.   From the evaluation he can
decide whether it is worth his time to find out more about
the film, possibly to send for it for preview, or find out if
it can be rented or borrowed locally.

Theoretically, the description of the film in the catalog of the producer or the major distribution sources should
be a good guide.   Unfortunately, the description is often too
brief, or misleading, and naturally it has no indication of

quality.   Also, even the best and most detailed producer's guide may not cover the usefulness of the film for the particular audience or purpose the user has in mind.   The evaluation helps to point out ways the film can be used, and may warn of dangers with a particular audience--a narration that talks down too much for teen-agers, or inclusion of scenes that would be offensive to certain groups.

Because film is a tool, as well as a communication medium, and an art form, it is often necessary to use a film which is not flawless.   The usefulness may outweigh the technical deficiencies, or the need for visual information may be more important than an insistence on creative qualities. But there is no excuse for settling for a second-rate film when a first-rate one is available.   For this reason, it is essential to know not only what the film can be used for, but also how well it does its job.   If there are several films on the same subject, an evaluation of each can be a great help in selecting the right one.   Effectiveness may depend on the content, the treatment, or the technical quality, and the evaluator must learn to indicate these to the user.   Quality includes not only whether the camera was in focus and the exposure correct, but other aspects which are dealt with in the section "What Makes a Good Film."

Evaluation is a way to make films more useful to more users, and to improve the quality of film use along with the quality of the films themselves.

What Is a Good Film?
(Reprinted from Using Films, edited by J. L. Limbacher)

All film programmers are engaged in a constant search for good films.   Faced with a constantly increasing number of available titles and with widely diverging opinions about them, some people yearn for a universal set of criteria or an authoritative check list of "approved films."   But the great variety of kinds of films and type of audiences make any such easy answer undesirable.   Each program planner must select his own films, and the degree to which he makes the right selection will be the measure of his success.   There are, however, some helpful pointers which may aid him in attaining skill in this difficult but fascinating art of film selection.

A Good Film for Whom.   The first prerequisite for good program planning is to know your audience.   Children,

teen-agers, young marrieds, community leaders, and senior
citizens all react differently.   Different levels of education
and sophistication are as important as age levels.   Only experience can teach the programmer just what his audience
will like, and he must always be alert to extend their taste
outwards and upwards.   A group which likes the ordinary
commercial travel film can also be interested in the documentaries of Julien Bryan or Harry Atwood; those who ask
for animated cartoons of the Mickey Mouse or Mr. Magoo
type can also be intrigued by the more experimental techniques of Norman McLaren or John and Faith Hubley.   But
it is a fatal mistake to try to impose the taste of the programmer on an audience; in fact, it is a sure way to lose
the audience permanently.

Even when there have been highly enthusiastic reviews
or evaluations of the film, the programmer should screen it
himself before he shows it to an audience.   There may be
unexpected pitfalls in the way of scenes which are offensive
to some members of the community, or the reviewers' standards may differ radically from those of the intended audience.   One man's humor is another man's corn, and a film
hailed by one critic as bold, imaginative experimentation may
seem to another simply an example of inept, amateur attempts at filmmaking.   If the film is likely to be controversial, the programmer should know it--not to avoid controversy, but to be ready to guide it into constructive channels.

A good film for its audience is one which can speak
directly to those who are to see it--not too obvious, not too
obscure; one which can bring its viewers something new--a
new insight, a new idea, new facts, new experiences.

A Good Film for What?   Films are made for all kinds
of purposes, and the user should know what the producer's
purpose was.   However, the user's purpose may be quite different.   This will not prevent the programming of a film
originally intended for another use, provided the use is valid.
For example, travel films are usually sponsored by a country or a transportation company, and their purpose is perfectly clear--to make the viewer want to go to the place
shown.   But a group of hospital shut-ins, with no possible
chance of a trip to a far-off country, might well find the
travel film a window on the world they will never see.   The
Aluminum Company of America made a film called Color and
Texture and Finish, intended to be shown to industrial de-
signers to encourage them to use more aluminum in the prod-

ucts they designed.   The film has been very popular with
many audiences because of its exciting visual approach.

If the film is to provide information, then the information should be accurate and up-to-date, presented clearly
and interestingly.   If the film is to develop attitudes and
opinions, then it should be persuasive and convincing.   If it
is to present works of art, the photography should be outstanding; if it is about music, the sound recording should be
of the best possible.   (The quality of sound reproduction in
the average 16mm film and projector is not very high; if high
fidelity is what you want, use a fine recording, not a film.)
And if the chief purpose is to show a fine film--art for art'
sake--then extra care is needed in selection.

A film showing can backfire if the wrong film is selected.   A famous example was the showing by the Russian
government of the Steinbeck film about the dust-bowl mi-
grants in jalopies on their way to California.   The authorities intended to demonstrate the down-trodden condition of
the American working man, but the Russians flocked to see
it, much impressed that in the U. S. even poor men had auto
mobiles.

How Important Is Technical Quality?   The film user
has a right to expect certain minimums of technical compe-
tency.   Photography which is in focus, properly exposed,
and well composed; a sound track which is clear and understandable even on a portable projector; the whole film put to
gether to make its point without omissions or redundancy--
the average film should be a reasonably professional job. But
there are occasions when flaws in technique are over-shad-
owed by the importance or vitality of the subject matter.
Footage of news events, or of anthropological studies in remote areas, may be vivid and exciting even though technical
ly it suffers from the difficulties faced by the cameraman.
First films by young filmmakers are often crude technically,
but have something to say and say it effectively in spite of
technical limitations and exaggerations.   As long as the defects do not impair the viewer's comprehension or enjoymen
an imperfect film can be put to good use.

On the other side of the coin, technical virtuosity
brings its own complications.   An audience of would-be film
makers will watch enthralled the brilliant innovations of an
advanced experimental film, but technique for its own sake
soon bores the general public.   Really beautiful photography

will hold more people longer than the very experimental material, but a long film made up of beautiful shots without either physical action or emotional development has a static quality which skillful editing could have enlivened. Many highly competent cameramen are unable to edit their own material--it hurts them to cut out a fine shot or a difficult scene, and they need the perspective of the editor to determine how it will look to an audience.

The best films are those in which the filmmaker had such control of his medium that he used its full resources to express what he had to say without his audience becoming aware of the details of the technique. A film should be a visual experience, and audience attention should not be distracted by either poor or show-off technique.

What About Emotional Quality? A good film should have the power to evoke a response from its viewers. The kind of response will depend upon the kind of film, and is often unpredictable, but the programmer who shies away from any film involving an emotional reaction is cutting his audience off from all the best films. The emotions aroused by a good film are of many kinds--interest, excitement, envy, dismay, alarm, anger, sympathy, enjoyment. Too many films made for schools or for public information seem to have removed all traces of human emotion, presumably because a straight catalog of facts cannot be criticized as biased. The result is a large number of films which fail to achieve their purpose because a viewer does not remember a movie which bores him. The same philosophy may produce films in which emotion is removed from a situation which demands it--for example, a film on marriage counselling intended to persuade young people to postpone early marriage in favor of a college career showed the young couple sitting down with a minister to tabulate the desirable characteristics of marriage partners and reaching a conclusion on the basis of the tabulations. The conclusion may have been sound, but it was invalidated by the acting of the engaged couple, who gave no indication that they were in love, nor of the notorious effect of love on the reasoning process.

The obvious ability of the film to arouse emotions in the propaganda film has obscured its power in other types. The enjoyment of sheer beauty is a legitimate purpose in film viewing; so is the excitement of interest in an intellectual theory. If the film leaves the audience just exactly where it found them, it hardly qualifies as a good film.

Pointers to a Good Film.   Films and audiences are
both so varied that no hard and fast rules can work uniform-
ly in selecting a good film.   However, there are a few questions that the programmer can ask himself at the preview
screening which may be of help.

1. Does the film make good use of the film medium--
    does it do only what a film can do, rather than
    trying vainly to be something else (a book, a lec-
    ture, a stage play, a series of still photographs?)

2. Does it have something to say, and know how to
    say it?

3. Does it have value and interest for more than a
    special, limited audience?

4. Does it leave the audience wanting to see more?

5. Is the film honest, both in content and in tech-
    nique?

6. Does it evoke a response from the viewer?

How Can You Spot a Great Film?   All the foregoing
remarks apply to the considerable number of good films.
More and more good films are becoming available, and even
the most discriminating audience should be able to find a continuous supply of good films.   But the number of great films
is small, and it always will be.   Masterpieces are not plenti-
ful in any field, and films are still young, compared with
books, plays, paintings, and other works of art.   The non-
theatrical field is particularly poor in really great productions, because the rewards of filmmaking go to those in the
theatrical or entertainment field, and the filmmakers have an
understandable desire for recognition and financial security
which is hard to find in 16mm films.   Fortunately, from time
to time great films appear, and take their place among the
classics.   Any knowledgeable film user can name a dozen or
so--Nanook, The River, Boundary Lines, The Quiet One--
the lists will differ slightly, but many of the same names
will turn up over and over again.

It is easy to recognize greatness in a film frequently
referred to as a classic.   But what about a new, unheralded
film?   How can you know that you have just seen a great one
The answer to that question is both simple and complex.   Of

course you know--but how you know remains mysterious.   By
instinct, by radar, "by the pricking of my thumbs?" Perhaps.
Later, it is possible to write a critical evaluation, or an exhaustive analysis; but a great film is recognized by its proper
audience instantly and wordlessly and remembered vividly and
long.

Selecting films is a time-consuming, sometimes exasperating job; finding good films makes the job worth doing;
discovering a great film is the pot of gold at the end of the
rainbow.

Writing the Synopsis

A very important part of the evaluation process is
preparing a synopsis of content.   Since the purpose of an
evaluation is to tell the reader what the film is like, it is
first necessary to tell him what is in it.   The EFLA form
says, under the Synopsis heading, "About 75-100 words, as
detailed as possible.   Do not use producer's summary."
Most films can be described well in less than 100 words, but
it takes skill and practice to give an accurate and vivid verbal picture.   The warning about the producer's summary is
because most catalog descriptions are too brief, and often
misleading.   "A fascinating picture of the struggle between
man and nature" is not a factual description.   "Report on recent explorations in Antarctica, covering the landing of equipment, establishing base camp, carrying out research in
weather studies, and a trip to map previously unknown territory" is far more useful.   Catalog descriptions or promotion
flyers also tend towards flowery adjectives "An exciting and
beautiful film," "dramatic experience" "heart-touching story."
These may (possibly) be true, but leave them out of the synopsis and save them for the Comment section.

Because the writing of a good, clear synopsis requires
considerably more time and care than the filling in of the
rest of the Evaluation, it is helpful to assign the synopsis to
one member of the committee for each film, and move the
responsibility around, so that no one person has to do all of it.
During the screening, the synopsis-writer should take notes
specifically on content, and then should write the synopsis
after the discussion which follows when the film has been
completed.   If several films are to be screened at one session, each member of the committee should have one assigned, and then a time be set aside at the end of the session which can be used for synopsis writing.   Ideally, of

course, the synopsis writer should see the film at least
twice, but this is seldom possible.

The first sentence of a synopsis is the hardest to
write. It should summarize the content of the whole film
clearly enough so that readers not concerned with the subject
can skip the rest of the Evaluation, and go on to one more
relevant to their needs. The temptation is to begin with a
phrase like "This film tells" or 'this film shows." Since
such a repetition gets monotonous and eventually irritating
both for the evaluators and for those who read the evaluations, it is better to skip the first words and get down to the
business, even at the risk of writing an incomplete sentence.
Here are a few samples:

> A social history of the United States in the depression
> era, compiled from newsreels and other contempo-
> rary footage.
>
> How prejudice against other groups, races, and na-
> tionalities has developed in man, and how it can be
> combatted through education and understanding.
>
> The theory of sets in mathematics, presented in car-
> toon form for elementary grade students.
>
> The life cycle of an insect with complete metamor-
> phosis, using time-lapse photography and animation,
> as well as regular photography.
>
> Dramatized version of the Poe story, with actors in
> stylized costumes and settings.

Notice that in most of these opening sentences not only
is the subject of the film indicated, but also the technique
used. The synopsis should always make it clear just what
kind of film is being discussed--standard photography with a
narrator ("voice over" in technical terms), dramatization with
actors and recorded dialogue ("lip synch"), compilation of
newsreel and other footage, animation, puppets, models, in-
conography (motion picture photography of still photographs
or art work, also called filmograph), documentary with sound
recorded in the field, specialized photography such as time
lapse or microphotography, etc. Often a film will combine
several of these techniques, and the synopsis should indicate
which ones.

The more absorbing a film is, the harder it is to
write an accurate synopsis after one viewing. If the producer has provided an outline of the script, or even a copy
of the narration, it is relatively easy to reconstruct the con-

tent, but this is rarely the case.   One method to make sure
nothing has been forgotten is to jot down during the screening
a key word or phrase for each sequence of the film.   Just
as books are divided into chapters, films are divided into sequences.   Usually (but not always) the sequences are marked
by fade-outs.   This means that the scene on the screen gets
darker until it disappears, and then a new scene becomes
visible as the screen brightens again.   A sequence is a group
of scenes centered around an event, an idea, or a development.   It should be easy to find a key word or phrase to
identify each sequence, but the synopsis should be written up
as soon as possible after the screening, or the jottings in the
dark may be meaningless at a later reading.   A sample list
of sequences might read:

> seashore--dawn
> men launch boats
> at sea, nets ready
> putting out nets
> hauling in
> fish on board
> return
> unloading
> men return home

The film described here is obviously very simple, but
it is easy to omit something in a simple synopsis, and it is
all the more fatally easy to do it in a complex film.   It will
not be possible to describe each sequence in a paragraph
totalling under a hundred words, but if all the information is
on hand, the synopsis can be as short or as long as is
needed.

If possible, the person writing the synopsis should
check on correct spelling of names or exact dates mentioned
in the synopsis before the report is published or distributed.
If the film is accompanied by a teacher's guide or descriptive folder, the difficult names, places, dates, or technical
terms may be found in it.   The subject area specialist on the
committee can be very helpful at this point.

When writing the synopsis, keep the user in mind.
Are your evaluations to be read by teachers?   By specialists
in a particular field of interest?   By the general public?   By
film librarians selecting films for rental or purchase?   Try
to tell the reader what he needs to know--give him the clearest possible idea of just what the film is about, and by what

means it tells its story. If space is limited, as in the
EFLA Evaluations, it is necessary to use a terse, almost
telegraphic style. If more space is available, the phrasing
can be smoother, and more detail may be included, but it
should still be concise. Rambling, wordy descriptions are
almost worse than the too-brief one-line notes so often found
in catalogs.

Try to keep all qualifying adjectives out of the synopsis. The producer's blurb will of course be full of them--
"this exciting film, with its outstanding photography, presents
a unique picture--" The synopsis is no place to comment on
the "fine photography" or "dull and repetitious treatment."
Save those remarks for the Comment section at the end.

Re-Evaluation

One evaluation by one committee does not necessarily
provide the final word on the quality and usefulness of a film.
Ideally, every film should be viewed by two or three separate committees, unaware of each other's reports, before
any result is published. Unfortunately, shortage of manpower
and screening time makes this impractical for all but a few
controversial films in the regular EFLA Evaluation Program,
but films for the American Film Festival are screened
twice--once during the pre-screening process, and, for those
which survive the first screening, again at the Festival itself
before the Blue Ribbon awards are made.

There are several reasons why re-screening is desirable. There are marked differences of approach in different kinds of committees--a school group reacts differently
from a public library or film society committee; a committee meeting by itself may reach a conclusion unlike that of
a group screening with a sizeable audience present. Geographical differences are also a factor, as are economic and
ideological groupings. Two or three complete evaluations
from different sources will give a more accurate picture of
the range of opinion, although of course the final combined
report will be much less neat and conclusive.

Special Projects. It is sometimes necessary to take
a second look at films previously evaluated because of a
special need. For example, a school which had evaluated
elementary science films in the context of the regular classroom program might wish to re-evaluate them with the needs
of the slow learner in mind. Many community agencies have

been looking for suitable materials to use with disadvantaged students of all ages; in selecting films added weight must be given to such factors as vocabulary level and the economic and racial backgrounds of the protagonists.

Time Marches On. All films which are kept in active use should be re-evaluated periodically. It is obvious that films about space exploration go out of date rapidly, but it is less obvious that social attitudes change, as well as teaching methods. Films have a surprisingly long life, and there are classics which will always be the backbone of the film collection, but too many libraries are giving shelf space and cluttering up their catalogs with films which should have been retired long ago--either because there are better new ones available, or because the information or attitude of the film is hopelessly out-moded. It is easier to re-order a title which has been used for five or ten years, and therefore is in all the lists of "Suggested Materials," or which the teacher or chairman knows will not have to preview, but it does not make for the best use of the film medium. A good method when screening a new film is to show also, to the same committee, another film in the collection on the same subject which is five or more years old. The comparison will not necessarily favor the new title, but it will mean that at least some of the older films will be looked at critically from time to time. Such re-evaluation should consider also technical quality. Standards of the selection committee, and of the field of motion picture, should both have been raised, and the evaluators may be surprised to see what they, or their predecessor, thought was good filmmaking a few years previously. A second look can be a very educational experience.

Editor's note: For additional background guidance the reader is referred to James L. Limbacher, "Film evaluation and criticism" ALA Bulletin 58:42-7, January 1964.

Selecting the Recording

by Mary D. Pearson   Mrs. Pearson is Head of the
                            Art, Philosophy and Religion
                            Department of the Long Beach
                            (California) Public Library

From her Recordings in the Public Library.
Chicago, American Library Association, 1963.
p. 6-11, 15; Reprinted by permission of the
American Library Association Publications Office.

Judicious record selection includes consideration of
physical values as well as of subject content. It involves
questions concerning sources, surfaces, and speeds. Record
selection is similar to that of book selection. It includes an
awareness of best materials available, a budget adequate to
the goals of the collection, and an endeavor to meet the
needs of patrons with the material chosen. The formula giv-
en as an American Library Association standard for public
libraries is:

> For nonbook materials... physical and technical
> excellence... must be considered. Quality... must
> be related to the other two basic standards of se-
> lection, purpose and need. [1]

Translated to actual practice, the formula implies the
need of an evaluation of each record on its own composite of
qualities. An over-all check list such as "100 Best Music
Classics" cannot be used to start a recordings library. Even
when the best recordings are indicated for each title, the
recommendations may soon become dated. The librarian also finds that some basic music is not yet represented by a
satisfactory recording.

The urge to have a well-rounded collection is one
that must be tempered with patience. The collection should
be developed gradually as recordings that meet the criteria
are released. The following specific selection aids and gen-

eral suggestions on building a record collection should be helpful.

Selection Aids

A librarian must engage in a "treasure hunt" to find the most useful material for his particular collection. A suggested first step is to ask to be put on mailing lists. Current catalogs of many dealers are listed in the periodical, Notes. Advertisements in ALA Bulletin, Library Journal, and other periodicals are also a good source of addresses and so are news items about recordings in newspapers and periodicals. Patrons sometimes receive announcements of noncommercial recordings from their colleges, churches, and societies. Recordings news from all sources should be welcomed and used for a file of sources for unusual records. Such a file can become a fund of information to which even the local dealers will refer.

All of the aids mentioned below, as well as additional ones, are listed with annotations in the bibliography of selection aids at the end of this chapter. The publications should be kept near the recordings desk for the convenience of both patrons and staff. A glossary of the technical recording terms used by manufacturers, dealers, and librarians appears on pages 143-47.

Catalogs and indexes. Catalogs of long-playing records are often distributed free of charge by record dealers. The monthly Schwann Long Playing Record Catalog is the most widely available. If librarians have difficulty in finding it, they may subscribe to it directly. The publisher accepts subscriptions from dealers and libraries but not from individuals. Schwann attempts to list all LPs that are currently available at dealers. It does not include records sold on a subscription basis, those sold direct by the artist, and noncommercial items. In addition to an alphabetical composer listing, the catalog contains a separate subject grouping. Stereo recordings are so indicated. New releases are noted in detail in a separate section printed on colored stock. The following month the former new items become brief entries in regular alphabetical order, followed by a date that refers to the date of the original full entry. These date references, initiated in December, 1957, make all subsequent issues a reference tool to the date of issue. Librarians find them helpful in determining the contents of a multiselection recording or in establishing an approximate date to

look for a review.   Other features that make the catalog an
asset to patrons and staff are the abbreviations indicating the
language of a vocal recording, the up-to-date price list, and
the symbol signifying the final appearance of an item in the
catalog.   This symbol alerts the librarian to order if a to-
be-discontinued recording is desired for the collection.

Another catalog, Schwann's annual Artist Issue, lists
currently available LPs by performer or performing group
and is also obtainable from record shops.   It is helpful in
determining available works of serious musicians and occasionally in verifying name entries for the library catalog.
Libraries are fortunate to have these free aids to record
buying.

A set of trade catalogs compiled primarily for dealers
by One-Spot Publishers is also available.   Several services
are offered as part of the catalogs.   Libraries may wish to
subscribe to the two of them, One-Spot Classic Guide and
One-Spot Numerical Index.   The One-Spot Classic Guide has
monthly revisions of releases by title, performer, and composer and a few subject categories, such as the spoken word.
It covers over 100 labels, which represent most of the current production of serious music on Extended Plays (45 rpm)
and LPs.   The title listing of selections, with cross indexing by secondary title and translations, is especially helpful.
As with many record catalogs it becomes a reference source
for much more than the obvious question about the availability of a recording.   As an aid to ordering, cataloging, and
music reference it is used by both patrons and staff.   Single
copies are available at $2.25.

The One-Spot Numerical Index lists the contents of
the catalogs of over one hundred major companies by record
number.   Libraries frequently find it desirable to review
works being produced by a particular company; this type of
information is shown here in chronological order.   The service costs $3 a month with its monthly supplements and bi-
weekly revisions.

Most record companies have their own catalogs for
the consumer and for the record trade.   The latter are numerical listings, which are covered also by the One-Spot
service.   The largest companies charge for their numerical
catalogs but have free descriptive catalogs or lists for the
consumer.   The free material is distributed by record

stores and individual producers.   The catalogs of larger
companies are often only announcements of the latest releases or certain types of recordings, but those of smaller
companies include all the records they produce.   Even
though the Schwann and One-Spot catalogs are excellent tools,
it is advisable for a library to keep a current file of individual descriptive catalogs, and any free numerical ones, of
many serious music producers and of all non-musical producers that would be of interest to patrons.

Distributors specializing in children's records have
catalogs that will help supply teaching needs.   If a request
is made on official library stationery, Children's Music Center, Children's Reading Service, or Educational Record Sales
will send a catalog without charge.

Announcements.   Direct-mail announcements are another source of information about recordings.   Some valuable
LPs, available only from the artist or producer, are advertised only by such mailed announcements.   Examples are
some of Richard Dyer-Bennett's ballads and Columbia University's productions from the Center for Mass Communication.

Reviews.   Reviewing aids for recordings are as indispensable to the library as those for books.   Most of the
library's buying is done on the basis of reviews.   Since no
one reviewing aid covers all of the important releases, it
is wise to use several sources.   By doing so the librarian
develops a broader basis of criticism.

Periodicals are the chief source of reviews.   The
Music Library Association publishes a quarterly index to reviews in almost thirty magazines in its periodical Notes.
This is a primary reference tool that will save much searching through individual periodicals to find an elusive review.
Some of these periodicals--as Atlantic Monthly, Consumer
Bulletin, Consumer Reports, Harper's, Library Journal,
Musical America, New Republic, New York Times, Reporter, and Saturday Review--are in most library collections.   Notes's system of indicating the rating given by reviewers focuses attention on the best recordings.   Periodicals recommended as next purchases for record reviews are
American Record Guide and High Fidelity.   The large number of reviews and the information noted about recordings
and equipment place them first in special recordings periodicals for the United States.

In the past timely information about children's records
has been difficult to find, but a loose-leaf reviewing service,
Children's Record Reviews, is now filling the need. It reviews material of interest from preschool through elementary
school. The approach is practical: the speed, price, manu-
facturer, and commercial number of the recording and a full
description of the contents are given. Charge for the service is $12 a year. Since educational records remain avail-
able longer than the usual commercial recording, this file
should become increasingly useful.

The Audio Cardalog service is probably of more interest to schools, but it should be known to libraries as another source of recordings information. It costs $25 for a
year's subscription, which includes 400 cards in ten issues.
The service covers educational recordings (phonorecord and
tape) from elementary school through college, and its form
is the 3 x 5 punched card that can be interfiled in a recordings catalog as the recordings are acquired. Information on
each card includes the recording label, a short synopsis, appraisal, suggested use, a rating by the editor, and suggested
subject headings for cataloging.

Books that evaluate recordings are also useful references, even though some of the records may have become
unavailable. Some of the best book references are those for
particular subject areas, such as voice, chamber music,
and orchestra.

Auditioning. More records are published yearly than
can possibly receive critical reviews or even a notice. This
means that the librarian needs to develop a critic's ear and
upon occasion select a recording without a review. Confidence in one's judgment is nurtured by noting personal reaction to a new recording and then reading what the critics say.
The professional critic will have technical reasons for his
decisions, but his conclusions may often be similar to the
layman's. Good judgment in the selection of recordings
comes from hours of listening.

Auditioning before purchase, when trying to fill a specific subject need, is done usually with records from the
local dealer. Although the local dealer may not get the bulk
of library orders, it is wise to establish rapport with him.
He will be aware of customers that have developed as library patrons, and sometimes will turn to the library for
reference aid. In turn, the librarian may be allowed to take

out his records to audition.   The dealer may have special demonstration records for this purpose, or he may allow auditioning from regular stock not in sealed covers.

The auditioning of entirely new titles after purchase may be done by the record librarian alone or with other staff members.   Defective records occur so rarely that it is not necessary to audition for defects.   More important to consider are the special uses of the record and the aid to the cataloger when printed information is not adequate for cataloging purposes.   The staff member who shares the responsibility of record auditioning will recommend recordings to patrons with spontaneous enthusiasm.

Patrons' suggestions.   Valuable suggestions for purchases frequently come from well-informed patrons.   Specialists in music, languages, children's records, and other subjects can make the recordings collection more distinctive by their recommendations.   The problem is usually the budget, for each specialist likes to see more material represented in his field.   The librarian must temper the requests with available funds and judgment.   Requests from non-specialist patrons sometimes are for performances that are not outstanding, or for titles that are not desirable.   It is well to investigate each request, however, and report the decision to the patron.   Often a countersuggestion by the librarian will satisfy the patron.

Gifts

Some recordings collections have been started by gifts resulting from an organized drive, spearheaded by a citizens' committee cooperating with the library.   Such a start assures community interest in the collection and plants the idea for future gifts.   Some collections have been sponsored by a music or a service club.   But even when the collections are not begun with gifts, libraries usually can expect to receive offers of gifts once they are started.

As with books, the decision of what to accept must be left to the librarian.   The recordings must meet the criteria for selection.   Sometimes it is necessary to audition them before acceptance, but usually the title or the appearance of the record will determine whether it should be kept.   Gifts should be graciously acknowledged or declined as the occasion demands.

Large collections of music recordings on 78s may be offered now that many people are replacing them with LPs. Some of these 78s are of commercial value, but unless there is ample room, or the library wishes to develop a historical collection, they should be accepted sparingly. Most public libraries could use another copy of popular numbers such as the <u>Nutcracker Suite</u> or <u>Scheherazade.</u> The gifts that seem useful can be accepted with processing kept at a minimum. Some libraries accept 78s in albums and shelve them by composer or title of a collection. Some salvage albums and sleeves of 78s to reuse for LPs that have broken through their packaging. The size of the gift, library space, and the needs of the collection will be determining factors in the policy of accepting 78s.

Good public relations affect the number of superior LPs offered as gifts. Patrons who are grateful for the library service have been known to buy records for the library, to give important records to the library after taping for their own pleasure, or to share their Christmas gifts or hasty purchases. Records are so much a matter of individual taste that a recording rejected by one patron may be just what is needed by another.

Acceptance of 45s will depend on the library's decision of including this speed in the collection, but an offer of particularly desirable titles may be the turning point in their favor. Many patrons will enjoy them. Gifts of acceptable content and condition should be considered at any speed...

Talking Books for the Blind

Failing eyesight brings renewed interest in recordings, and requests for talking books for the blind frequently come to the recordings desk. The record librarian should be informed as to who qualifies for the talking books and who distributes them. A catalog from the Library of Congress, Division for the Blind, will give this information.

The records are a service from twenty-six regional agencies. There are also state agencies that lend talking-book players. Application for the service is made by the individual patron, and all loans come directly to him. There are many who ask about recorded books who do not qualify for the service, because they still have some sight or are only temporarily without use of their eyes. The library collection of commercial recordings can be of inestimable value to them.

Note

1. American Library Association, Public Libraries Division.
    <u>Public Library Service: A Guide to Evaluation, with
    Minimum Standards.</u> Chicago, American Library As-
    sociation, 1956, p. 32.

The Crisis in Micropublication

by Allen B. Veaner

The author is Chief Librarian, Acquisitions Division, Stanford University Library, Stanford, California and Chairman, Subcommittee on Micropublishing Projects, Resources Committee of the Resources and Technical Services Division of ALA.

From Choice 5:448-53, June 1968; Reprinted by permission of Peter M. Doiron, Editor of Choice

Unlike conventional publications, micropublications are essentially an invisible product. Short of examining each and every individual frame in a roll or on a fiche, there is no way a purchaser or user can evaluate the bibliographic and technical characteristics of this type of nonbook material. Even a small micropublication project consisting of one reel of film or a few dozen microfiche would require a time investment beyond the capabilities of the most dedicated acquisitions librarian. In practice, the situation is much worse, because most micropublications aggregate dozens, hundreds, and perhaps thousands of reels or fiche. For example, a recently proposed micropublication project for Latin American material is estimated to eventually total 20,000 reels of film.

Since no librarian can evaluate micropublications exhaustively, he must lean heavily upon the publisher's technical competence and reputation. Established micropublishers are anxious to protect their good will, just as are established publishers of conventional materials. Unfortunately, this desire is not characteristic of every micropublisher, and there seem to be some micropublishers who make available inferior products out of carelessness or lack of knowledge of technical and bibliographical standards. A ready acceptance by the library community of an inferior product perpetuates these inferior practices.

The number of micropublishers has grown enormously within the past few years, especially with the advent of
increased Federal support for collection building in university and college libraries. A real technical and bibliographic problem exists. Since it is difficult to detect a poor
product in the first instance, and serious defects often do
not show up until months or years later (when an angry faculty member or student complains of an illegible or missing
page, or when images have faded owing to faulty processing), how shall the acquisitions librarian protect himself and
his limited book funds from possible exploitation?

The Resources Committee of the Resources and Technical Services Division of the American Library Association
recognized this problem quite early, insofar as it applied to
the university and research libraries. Accordingly, in 1958
the Resources Committee established a standing Subcommittee on Micropublishing Projects. Rapid, recent growth in
the micropublication industry has naturally extended the scope
of the Subcommittee's interests. Among the Subcommittee's
responsibilities are the following:

1. To serve as a coordinating agency for both libraries
   and publishers of microforms.
2. To advise on the desirability of proposed publishing
   projects.
3. To recommend projects needed by the academic community.
4. To take appropriate action to ensure a desirable
   quality of reproduction and adequate bibliographic control.

It is specifically with this last named responsibility in
mind that the Editorial Board of Choice has agreed to collab-
orate with the Subcommittee in establishing a reviewing
mechanism for micropublications likely to be considered for
purchase by college and university libraries. Just as is now
done with books, Choice's Editor will acquire review copies
of important micropublication projects. Choice consultants
will appraise the content value (e. g. in the case of a reprint,
is it still valuable or has it been superseded). With the Library Technology Program providing the necessary laboratory equipment, arrangements are being made for professional, qualified technical evaluations. Both reviews will be integrated and published in Choice at the same time. The
Subcommittee is grateful to the Editorial Board of Choice
for making available to it this reviewing mechanism which

will extend to acquisitions librarians the same invaluable services now furnished them for book materials.

Reviews of prospectuses and/or micropublications must take into account content, bibliographic, administrative, and technical factors. To aid in judging micropublications, the Subcommittee has developed a checklist of evaluation criteria for each of these major aspects. The principal criteria are cited below, along with references to appropriate U. S. A. Standards Institute standards.

Criteria for Evaluation

A. Bibliographic Criteria
   1. Does the publisher furnish external finding aids?
      As catalog cards, unit cards or full sets?
      LC cataloging and/or ALA entry rules?
      Is cataloging complete or shortened? If shortened, what has been omitted?
      As printed booklets prepared by the Publisher? If so, is a specimen furnished?
      As an existing published list or bibliography? Is the list still in print?
   2. Does the publisher furnish internal finding aids?
      A checklist of the contents of each reel on each reel?
      A catalog card preceding each item on the reel?
      An eye-legible bibliographic target preceding the first item on each reel?
      Numbered frames for manuscript materials?
   3. Do the editions microphotographed coincide exactly with those described in the finding aids, or are variant editions published?
      If variant editions are offered, does the publisher so state for each variant?
   4. Will the producer collate the original material in each title; does he identify gaps? What plan does the producer indicate for filling in gaps?
   5. Will the publication represent the total corpus of material cited in an external bibliography? If not, what criteria will govern the actual selection? Best edition? Availability? Convenience for producer?
   6. In what sequence will the material be issued? Random? As material is available? In chronological sequence? In the sequence of an already issued external finding aid? Whatever the sequence, is it suitable to the material in the project?

7. Is there an editor responsible for the bibliographic aspects? Is the editor a scholar competent in the field at hand?

8. Will the producer identify the owning library for each title he films?

B. Administrative Criteria

1. Does the publication duplicate existing projects? If so, is the new publication superior in any technical sense? In any bibliographic sense?

2. Is the publisher of established reputation? Has he proven his competence by previous issuance of satisfactory microforms?

3. Will the publisher furnish samples of his product for preliminary evaluation and/or technical inspection?

4. Is there a definite terminal date to the project? Is there a definite delivery schedule?

5. Is the publisher's announcement an actual offering of goods definitely to be furnished or available for immediate delivery, or is it merely a prospectus to gather subscribers, following which the publisher will decide whether to embark upon the project?

6. What is the publisher's policy regarding replacement of portions of the file which later prove technically deficient? What provision does he make for ordering replacements for damaged, worn out, or lost portions of the buyer's file? Is the buyer assured of reasonably priced replacements?

7. What provisions does the publisher make for safeguarding the master microcopy from which publication copies are made? Does he maintain an intermediate master for generating working copies? Does the publisher report his master films to the National Register of Master Microforms?

8. Will the publisher furnish portions of the publication in reasonably sized units for those libraries not wishing to buy the entire file?

9. Can the publisher furnish hard copies of any selected title in the project? Will hard copies be printed on permanent/durable book paper and be issued ready for immediate use by a library (i. e. without need for adding paper covers unless so desired)?

10. Does the publisher provide a sound time payment plan for smaller libraries?

11. For long-term projects, is there provision for cancellation or termination by the subscribers? What are the terms of these provisions?

C. Technical Criteria
    1. Does the publisher cite established bibliographic or technical standards to which he certifies adherence? Does he cite <u>Specifications for Library of Congress Microfilming</u> or <u>Microfilm Norms</u>?
    2. Does the publisher warrant that his product is free from residual sodium thiosulfate (hypo) in accordance with U. S. A. Standards Institute specifications for permanent record photocopies? (PH4. 8-1958).
    3. If no to question 2, will the publisher submit samples of his work for chemical testing?
    4. Does the producer warrant that his product is compatible with available readers and reader/printers commonly in library use? Does the producer specify the reduction ratio employed for the material?
    5. Does the publisher issue his product complete and ready for immediate use without further processing by the library? Specifically:

    Is film correctly spooled on reels meeting U. S. A. S. I. specifications? (U. S. A. S. I. Standard PH5. 6-1961).
    Does film have specified leader and trailer needed for easy threading of readers? (U. S. A. S. I. Standard PH5. 3-1958).
    Is film boxed in cartons of acid free and dust free cardboard?
    Are boxes carefully and legibly labeled to indicate contents and sequence?
    Does the publisher guarantee adequate packaging and safe arrival of microforms?
    What is his previous performance in this regard?

    6. Will the publisher undertake camera and processing work on his own? If so, is he technically qualified to do so? If not, does he name the agencies to which the work will be contracted? What is their competence?
    7. Does any film show evidence of chemical stains, scratches, or other physical image impairment?
    8. Are images evenly and regularly placed on film, so that the user need not readjust his reader as film is advanced?
    9. Is all the material photographed? Or are pages cut off at top, bottom, or sides?
    10. Is everything in sharp focus, or is there evidence of blurring?
    11. Is the film wound correctly on reels so that images are projected right side up?

Neglect of established guidelines and accepted good practices easily makes the librarian or scholar a victim of ignorant or careless technicians and camera operators, or of shady entrepreneurs anxious to cash in on quick profits from micropublication schemes. Unfortunately, with the exception of the largest professional producers, malpractice is often the rule rather than the exception.

Example One

A publisher issues manuscripts on several reels of microfilm. In his prospectus he neglects to inform the purchaser that page after page of the original documents are water stained or burned about the edges, making reading of the material extremely difficult, a problem compounded by the high contrast of microfilm. The publisher further places the reels in cardboard boxes of such poor quality, that when a reel is removed, it is already covered with so much dust and dirt that it immediately is scratched when placed in a reading machine. The publisher, in an act of either carelessness or stinginess, also neglects to supply enough blank film at the beginning of each reel, so that when the reel is loaded into the reader, the first image cannot be viewed. Finally, the publisher's staff affixes to each box a label which gives a title completely different from the title announced in the prospectus. The prospectus also states that a printed index is being prepared by another organization, but there is no evidence of any coordination between the micropublisher and the index publisher. Indeed, the frames of the microfilm are not numbered, so it is doubtful the index would be of much use even when it is prepared.

Example Two

Another publisher issues a prospectus for micropublication of complete runs of some 20 different periodicals. While he does specify the number of reels which the project will take up, he neglects to inform the user that all the periodicals are reproduced at a very high reduction on 16mm film. Only when microfilm arrives in the library is it learned that images on the reader screen will be much smaller than life-size, to the user's great discomfort. Examination of the film itself reveals cut off portions of text, poor focus, and uneven image placement.

Example Three

A third publisher employs the technical services of a highly competent microreproduction laboratory located in a distinguished institution with a reputation of worldwide excellence. Despite this honorable association, the publisher insists upon distributing his microfilms without reels, on the grounds that the user can easily spool the film himself. This may be compared to an automobile dealer requiring the buyer of a new car to go to a tire store, buy his tires separately and mount them himself; were this the case, the number of new cars sold would certainly be smaller than it is. This same micropublisher also does not supply enough leader and trailer to thread reading machines, and has only recently begun to place identifying labels on the outsides of the boxes containing the films.

Example Four

A fourth publisher announces a proposal to publish large numbers of printed books in microfilm. He provides no technical information on his project, nor does he affirm adherence to the <u>Specifications for Library of Congress Microfilming</u> or the American Library Association's <u>Microfilm Norms</u>. Correspondence with the publisher reveals that he intends to use a reduction ratio far higher than that normally employed in academic microreproduction laboratories, a reduction so high that the image will be much smaller than the screen size of most library reading machines. Further analysis shows that the cost of this project is far higher than the price of a similar project, which in fact provides similar books on film at a much lower reduction ratio.

Example Five

A fifth publisher announces micropublication of a large number of important regional historical works. While there is every reason to believe that this publisher's technical work will be of good quality, he neglects to provide the user with any apparatus for the bibliographic control of the titles in the project. As a result, each purchasing library must, at great expense, do original cataloging on all 50 titles, whereas if from the start the publisher had provided a good, detailed checklist or sets of catalog cards, most of this needless work and trouble could have been avoided. The publication of numerous monographs in microform is not a service to scholarship if the buying library cannot economically in-

form its users of the fact that it now possesses additional
resources.

These examples are considered routine; they do not
exhaust the possibilities.   One could go on and on citing
dozens of poorly conceived micropublication projects.

The first step in many micropublication projects is
the issuance of a prospectus by the publisher.   It is intended
that the evaluation criteria shall be equally applicable to the
prospectus as well as to the actual product itself.   Although
it is not always the case, a lack of specificity or lack of
indication of adherence to established standards within the
prospectus may be indicative that the project itself is defective with respect to one or more criteria.   In fact, in many
instances, it may be more important to review the prospectus than the actual product.   The prospectus is the first key
to the worth of a micropublication project.   Evaluation of
the prospectus is the acquisitions librarian's first task.   He
may decide not to buy the project; this decision could have
actual benefits far outweighing the supposed benefits of purchase as suggested by the copywriter responsible for the
prospectus...

Editor's note: This article is the first step in Choice's
            program to review selected micropublications--card,
            fiche, film.   Until now no regular reviewing of these
            materials has been initiated, and Choice hopes that
            the forthcoming microform reviews will provide a
            sense of sanity in a confusing field of acquisition.
            More colleges are using microform today, and future
            developments like portable, versatile readers will in-
            crease use and force circulation which will raise de-
            mand for both technical and content quality.   To meet
            the "Crisis in Micropublication," three American Li-
            brary Association groups (Subcommittee on Micropub-
            lishing Projects, Resources Committee of the Re-
            sources and Technical Services Division; Library
            Technology Program; Choice) have agreed to cooperate
            in promoting and improving current standards.

Section 4

Aids in Selection of Materials--
Retrospective and Current

No librarian could make a satisfactory selection in
every field of literature, without guidebooks representing the specialized study and knowledge of
those familiar with the material in each field...
He who has learned where to look for the recorded
knowledge of his subject is no longer an amateur
but a proficient in the use of books.

> Helen E. Haines, Living with
> books. 2nd ed. New York,
> Columbia University Press,
> 1950. p. 63-4

All the bibliographical knowledge and skill that one
can muster are required to identify trade information, to
evaluate, and to make decisions on the acquisition of library
materials for any type of library, from the elementary
school level to the most sophisticated network. This section focuses on searching techniques, provides an overview
of essential trade bibliographies, and presents reviews of a
limited group of library selection aids essential for professional work.

The selector must learn to use trade bibliographies
skillfully in order to make effective plans for supervision of
searching by technicians; he must also know how to make
maximum use of such aids as publishers' catalogs and announcements; and he must know how to use critically the selection aids and review media developed by, and for the use
of, the library profession. Many of these review media,
focus on "library values" not necessarily considered by general review media, and the reviews included here point out
a number of these values.

Background for Acquisition Work

by Gertrude Wulfekoetter   This is a shortened version of
a chapter in Acquisition Work:
Processes Involved in Building
Library Collections (Seattle,
University of Washington, 1961)
by the author, who was at the
time Assistant Law Librarian
in charge of Technical Processes, University of Washington Library, Seattle

From Library Journal 86:522:6, February 1,
1961; Reprinted by permission of R. R. Bowker
Company and of the author.

If an acquisition librarian wishes to do really good
work, he should have not only a good general professional
background but a specialized one, too. Of prime importance
is a knowledge of publishing and the book trade.

An acquisition librarian who has not visited a large
printing establishment, a well-organized publishing firm, a
good book bindery, and a large jobber's place of business
should do so in order to gain an understanding of the processes and terminology they use. Seeing such businesses in
operation can do much more than reading or checking glossaries in helping one to understand them.

With such a background the reading of one or two of
the good and fairly comprehensive recent publishing histories
in the English language, [1] some of the well-written histories
of individual firms, and at least one of the good books on
the business of publishing[2] will be helpful. In order to keep
up to date the knowledge gained from this reading, it must
be followed by constant checking of current issues of book
trade periodicals, such as Publishers' Weekly for the United
States, and British Books (formerly Publishers' Circular)
and Bookseller for Great Britain. This reading cannot be

allowed to lapse, for anyone out of touch with such trade
journals for any appreciable length of time is amazed at
changes which have occurred in the publishing and book
world. The vital statistics of publishing and book firms are
astounding; births, deaths, marriages, and divorces occur
without interruption and must be watched closely if one
wishes to keep abreast of them.

Publishers' Weekly is primarily a publishers' and
booksellers' tool, but librarians use it constantly for news
of the book world and listing of new books. In its columns
are occasional histories of publishing firms and bookstores,
usually timed to coincide with the celebration of some anniversary, as well as articles about the book trade in various
countries, notes of new publishing houses and amalgamations
of older ones, of new bookstores opened and older ones
moved, modernized, sold, or discontinued. Statistics of
publishing, valuable to acquisition librarians who must make
budget estimates or plan purchasing in relation to the published output in various fields, appear in the Annual Summary Number, issued usually the third week in January.
The last issue in January includes a list of firms whose publications have been reported in Publishers' Weekly during
the preceding year. Often this roster, including names of
both prominent and obscure firms, yields the hard-to-find
address of an unfamiliar publisher. Each weekly issue contains an annotated alphabetic listing of newly published books
and pamphlets. Since the fall of 1959 the listing of many of
the books not only includes the Library of Congress card
number but also full LC descriptive cataloging information.

To become familiar with the workings of the American antiquarian book trade the Antiquarian Bookman, an out-
growth of the former antiquarian book section of the Publishers' Weekly, is most useful. Although the issues are
made up largely of advertisements of books wanted and books
for sale, the weekly issues regularly contain news notes and
articles on subjects of interest to antiquarian dealers and
acquisition librarians.

The monthly British Books and weekly Bookseller give
acquisition librarians much the same type of information for
Great Britain as does Publishers' Weekly for the United
States, except that the listing of books does not contain the
cataloging information now included in PW. British Books
is the older publication and was once the main standby for
information in regard to British publishing, but the Book-

seller is now more nearly comparable with Publishers'
Weekly. Both periodicals contain short articles and news
notes about publishing and the book trade as well as advertisements and lists of new books; both have Fall and Spring
Announcement Numbers somewhat like those of Publishers'
Weekly, but the Bookseller, a Whitaker publication, has fuller
lists of recently published books than does British Books,
lists which are the basis of other Whitaker publications, the
monthly Current Literature and the quarterly and annual
Cumulative Book List.

      In addition to these histories and periodicals, direc-
tories help familiarize acquisition librarians with the book
world of today. The latest edition of the American Book
Trade Directory, published triennially by Bowker, and kept
up to date by the ABD Weekly Information Service, another
Bowker publication, and Clegg's International Directory of
the World's Book Trade, published at intervals in England,
are primarily tools of the book trade, but they are likewise
invaluable library tools, particularly for acquisition librarians wishing to broaden their knowledge of the book world.

      American Book Trade Directory is largely a list of
book outlets arranged by cities and towns, but it also includes lists of book clubs, American representatives of foreign publishers, and other groups. The later editions of the
Literary Market Place, another Bowker publication, contain
some of the same information intended primarily for authors,
not for the book trade or libraries. The Book-Buyers Handbook, published by the American Booksellers Association,
despite its promising title, is of little use to acquisition librarians, since it is a list of American publishers and the
discounts they grant to bookstores, discounts not applicable
to libraries. The British Booksellers Handbook, a trade
tool published annually since 1945, is on the other hand most
helpful to acquisition librarians, since it lists publishers,
booksellers in various fields, and publications of book trade
interest.

      The valuable specialized American book trade direc-
tory by Scott Adams, The O. P. Market,[3] is now completely
out of date. No other directory of specialized antiquarian
bookdealers has really taken its place, but the AB Bookman's
Yearbook: the Specialist Book Trade Annual, does have an
annual subject list of antiquarian and specialist bookdealers.

      North American librarians wishing information con-

cerning booksellers in Latin American countries have found
Cleggs' International Directory, even when up to date, is
not inclusive enough.   It was an awareness of this fact that
motivated the Assembly of Librarians of the Americas,
meeting in Washington, D. C. , in the spring of 1947, to recommend that its Inter-American Committee on Acquisitions
attempt to bring up to date (and keep up to date) the list of
Latin American booksellers, the last edition of which had
been published by the Pan American Union in 1945.   As a
result the Pan American Union began publication of a revised list in the numbers of the Pan American Bookshelf and
its successor, LEA, from July 1948 to November 1949.   The
difficulty of keeping this directory up to date, to make it
really useful, very probably was one of the factors which
led to the inception of the annual Seminars on the Acquisition of Latin American Materials in 1956.   The curiously
individualistic nature of publishing in these Latin American
countries, as reported by those making a survey for the
Latin American Cooperative Acquisition Project[4] perhaps accounts for the basic difficulties encountered in keeping up to
date in regard to Latin American bookdealers.

To round out acquisition librarians' knowledge of publishing and the book world they should be familiar with one
or two glossaries which explain the meaning of terms used
in these fields.   The Bookman's Glossary, published by
Bowker and frequently revised, includes definitions of the
more commonly used terms, as does Harrod's The Librarians' Glossary. [5]   To supplement them Orne's Language of
the Foreign Book Trade[6] is helpful.

National and trade bibliographies

Equally as important to acquisition librarians as
knowledge of publishing and the book world is a knowledge
of bibliographies.   The more comprehensive ones, the national and trade bibliographies, are those of greatest importance for acquisition librarians, and the ones with which
they will work most.   National bibliographies are alphabetic
or classified lists of material published within a country;
trade bibliographies are comprehensive or selective lists of
such publications with trade information added, sufficient to
enable anyone to order material from them.

Although it is impossible to cover the whole field of
such bibliographies here, mention must be made of some of
the more important current ones in English and of ways of

finding others.   Some countries have a long bibliographic
history; others have just made a good beginning.   The need
for comprehensive national bibliographies has been a subject
of vital concern throughout the world for over a century; it
has been the topic of discussion at many meetings, and the
subject of many professional articles, but, as in other fields,
it took the impetus of World War II to bring concerted action for their improvement.   The first frontal post-war attack on the subject was the Conference on International Cultural, Educational, and Scientific Exchange, held at Princeton, New Jersey, in November 1946.   The concensus of this
conference was that Unesco and other agencies throughout
the world should do all possible to stimulate the publication
of national bibliographies in those countries which had relatively none and the improvement where necessary of those
that did exist; other conferences held from then through 1950
added other recommendations. [7]

From the time of this conference in 1946 the Library
of Congress and Unesco worked closely together.   It was decided, early in 1947, that the Library of Congress would
bring up to date Lawrence Heyl's list of existing national
bibliographies.   This was done, and the new list began publication in the Library of Congress's Quarterly Journal of
Current Acquisitions in August 1949 and continued through
February 1951, with supplements in 1951, 1952, and 1953.
A later revision, made by Helen F. Conover and published
by the Library of Congress in 1955, is a most helpful, descriptive list of those bibliographies in existence at the time
of its compilation in 1954.   For the acquisition librarian
wishing to keep up to date on new national and trade bibliographies the latest edition of the Guide to Reference Books
(ALA) and its supplements, and the listing in the current issues of the Unesco Bulletin for Libraries and Stechert-Hafner Book News will be most helpful.

Another product of the Princeton conference and its
successors in the joint bibliographic survey of the world, of
which the revision of Heyl's list was a part, was the brief
survey of the development of national bibliographies from
1844 to the outbreak of World War II, made by Mrs. Murra
of the Library of Congress and included as an appendix to
the first volume of the joint bibliographic survey. [8]   This
brief study is an excellent short review of earlier national
bibliographies for acquisition librarians.   For a more comprehensive study of national and trade bibliographies up to
the time of its publication (1928), Van Hoesen and Walter's

Bibliography: Practical, Enumerative, and Historical has not
been replaced; Linder's recent Rise of Current Complete National Bibliography, [9] although not as inclusive, does contain
later publications.

Prior to the Princeton conference the United States had
fairly comprehensive bibliographic coverage in the Library of
Congress catalog, the Catalog of Copyright Entries; the various
H. W. Wilson publications, including the Cumulative Book Index;
Publishers' Weekly (Bowker); Publishers' Trade List Annual
(Bowker); Public Affairs Information Service Bulletin; the lists
of federal and state publications; and some specialized bibliographies. Relatively shortly after the conference (in 1950) the
Library of Congress expanded its monthly Author Catalog and
began publication of its supplementary Subject Catalog; in 1953
it added three other parts, appearing somewhat less frequently,
its Maps and Atlases Catalog (which was incorported in the
main catalog in 1956), Motion Pictures and Filmstrips Catalog, and Music and Phono-records Catalog. In addition to
these parts of its catalog the Library of Congress in 1951
began the publication of Serial Titles Newly Received, which,
in 1953, changed its title to New Serial Titles; this, while
not really a national bibliography due to its inclusion of
world-wide publications, gives the United States its most up-
to-date list of American serial publications.

To broaden these Library of Congress enlargements
of the American bibliographic picture the most recent addition is the monthly American Book Publishing Record (Bowker), begun in February 1960, to give a current classified
listing of material included earlier in the firm's Publishers'
Weekly.

For British publications, for which acquisition librarians had been dependent on the annual English Catalog of
Books with occasional cumulations and Whitaker's Cumulative
Book List (quarterly and annual), together with the monthly
British Books and weekly Bookseller, mentioned earlier as
book trade tools, the most important recent addition has been
the British National Bibliography. This weekly, begun in
1950 with its quarterly and annual cumulations, is a classified list of new British publications, including books, pamphlets, and periodicals, and is published at the British Museum by the Council of the British National Bibliography,
Ltd.

Book evaluation and selection aids

Book evaluation and selection aids form another group
of bibliographies of great value to acquisition librarians.
For assistance in book selection and in checking material
chosen, acquisition librarians quite naturally turn to the several current bibliographic and book selection aids, the ALA
Booklist and Subscription Books Bulletin, the Book Review
Digest (Wilson), the American Book Publishing Record or
BPR (Bowker), and the bibliographic section of the issues of
the Library Journal for evaluation of and information concerning the majority of current books. The subscription books
section of the Booklist and Subscription Books Bulletin is useful for the same type of help in regard to subscription and
reference books. In helping to select books for approval
shipments and securing books wanted by publication date, the
acquisition librarian needs to be familiar with such prepubli-
cation guides as Bowker's Books to Come, . . .
. . .   the Virginia Kirkus Service Bulletin
and the Retail Bookseller, and also, perhaps, for British
books, with Books of the Month, with which is incorporated
Books to Come and Books and Art, [10] and British Book News.
Acquisition librarians are often asked to suggest the best
edition available of certain standard works and for this they
should know about Orton's Catalog of Reprints in Series
(Scarecrow Press), a frequently revised publication, and the
quarterly Paperbound Books in Print. For juvenile books
the latest edition of the Children's Catalog is helpful, and
other publications in Wilson's Standard Catalog series are
useful. The annual Textbooks in Print, formerly the American Educational Catalog (Bowker), identifies textbooks issued
by publishers not represented in the Publishers' Trade List
Annual, thereby filling an oft-recurring need.

For selecting, checking, and ordering nonbook materials, such as maps, films, and other audio-visual material,
as well as less frequently desired and more highly specialized material, such as autographs, valuable aids exist.
Some of these guides not only list the material itself but also suggest sources through which it can be obtained. A listing of the most recent aids, sometimes separately published
books, sometimes valuable periodical articles, is to be
found in the issues of Library Literature.

If possible, some of this background for acquisition
work can and should be gained before attempting to do the
work. However, the professional information which an ac-

quisition librarian uses daily grows by accretion, through reading and consulting professional and trade periodicals and by finding and using bibliographic, book selection, and evaluation aids of all kinds. Valuable information is also constantly gained through personal contacts and correspondence with people who want library material and others who can supply it. It is this constantly growing background which makes an experienced acquisition librarian valuable to a library.

Notes

1. Hellmut Lehmann-Haupt, L. C. Wroth, and R. G. Silver The Book in America; a History of the Making and Selling of Books in the United States (2nd ed. ; New York, Bowker, 1951); Frank A. Mumby, Publishing and Bookselling; a History from the Earliest Times to the Present Day (4th ed. ; London, Jonathan Cape; New York, Bowker, 1956); and Svend Dahl, History of the Book (1st English ed. ;   New York, Scarecrow Press, 1958).

2. Chandler B. Grannis, editor What Happens in Book Publishing (New York, Columbia University Press, 1957), and Hellmut Lehmann-Haupt, The Life of the Book; How the Book is Written, Published, Printed, Sold, and Read (New York, Abelard-Schuman, 1957).

3. Scott Adams The O. P. Market; a Subject Directory to the Specialties of the Out-of-Print Trade (New York, Bowker, 1943). o. p.

4. Cf. Stechert-Hafner Book News for March, April, May 1960.

5. Leonard M. Harrod The Librarians' Glossary; Terms Used in Librarianship and the Book Crafts (2nd ed. ; London, Grafton, 1959).

6. Jerrold Orne The Language of the Foreign Book Trade: Abbreviations, Terms, and Phrases (Chicago, American Library Association, 1949).

7. Helen L. Brownson, comp. "Recommendations and Results of International Conferences on Scientific Information and Bibliographic Services." American Documentation, 3 (1952) 29-55.

8. Kathrine O. Murra <u>Notes on the Development of the Concept of Current Complete National Bibliography:</u> Appendix to UNESCO/Library of Congress Bibliographical Survey, <u>Bibliographic Services, Their Present State and Possibilities of Improvement: National Developments and International Planning of Bibliographic Services</u> (Washington and Paris, 1950), 2 v.

9. LeRoy H. Linder <u>The Rise of Current Complete National Bibliographies</u> (New York, Scarecrow Press, 1959).

10. This is an amalgamation of <u>Books of the Month,</u> published for 75 years by Simpkin, Marshall, with <u>Books to Come,</u> which began publication in 1944 and <u>Books and Art,</u> which originated in 1957.

Use of a Publishers Catalog File in a Special Library

by John Gaddis

A student paper based on work
experience in the Field Research Laboratory Library of
Socony Mobil Oil Company,
Dallas while the author was a
student at University of Texas

From Special Libraries 54:514-16, October 1963;
Reprinted by permission of Publications Dept.,
Special Libraries Association.

The term "publishers' catalog" as used here means
any kind of printed material distributed free of charge by a
book publisher or dealer describing his publications and including a price list. This paper discusses the reasons why
a special library found it necessary to set up a file of publishers' catalogs, how the file is organized and used, the
problems the library has encountered in using the file, and
the improvements that could be made to facilitate its use.
An examination of library literature indicated a lack of published material on this subject, and a survey of public and
university libraries in the Dallas area did not indicate any
extensive use of publishers' catalogs. This article is therefore limited to a discussion of one special library's use of
publishers' catalogs, but it is felt that the information may
be of value to others.

Necessity for File

The Socony Mobil Field Research Laboratory Library
serves a research staff of 155 technical people. Because of
the nature of the research done at the Laboratory, speed is
a most important factor in the acquisition of books for the
library. The median time lag between the date of order and
receipt of the book now stands at 28 days, and the library
is constantly seeking means of further reducing this lag. The
library does virtually all of its ordering directly from pub-

lishers.   In an eighteen-month period it contacted 440 different sources for 1,900 book orders.

The Field Research Laboratory Library organized its file of publishers' catalogs because the standard bibliographic tools to which the library subscribes are not designed to meet certain needs of an acquisitions librarian.   The library subscribes to: Cumulative Book Index, Monthly Catalog of U.S. Government Publications, Books in Print, Technical Book Review Index, Library Journal, and Monthly Index of Russian Accessions.   In addition, the 460 technical journals and the 30-odd abstracting journals received in the library supply much bibliographic data on current imprints.   To meet the specific needs of the acquisitions librarian these tools would have to provide:

1.   Immediacy in listing new publications.   Notices in advance of publication are of the greatest value to the library.   It is desirable that at most no more than two weeks elapse between the date of publication and receipt of a publication announcement in the library.

2.   Coverage in depth of both new and out-of-print publications within the library's field of interest.   The library purchases material from a large number of sources and to be informed of new publications of only the well known scientific publishers is not enough.   The library must also be aware of the publications of lesser known publishers, for example, The West Texas Geological Society.   Since the library must often attempt to procure out-of-print publications, broad coverage of OP dealers and agencies is also important.

3.   Descriptive annotations as an aid to book selection.   It is important for the library to know as much about a book as possible before ordering, but the title often gives little indication of its contents.   The library cannot spend the time required to order books on approval.   To achieve maximum usefulness, a bibliographic tool should provide some kind of subject analysis of the book, even if just an abstract or partial table of contents.

The standard bibliographic tools do not meet all of these requirements.   Publishers' catalogs, however, do meet them and have several unique features of their own.   For example, bibliographic information concerning a certain book can frequently be found faster in a well-organized file

of publishers' catalogs than in the more conventional bibliographic tools.   Catalogs are especially valuable for locating
prices quickly.   For libraries that do not subscribe to Publishers' Weekly or Publishers' Trade List Annual, a file of
publishers' catalogs would seem to be a virtual necessity.
No other source of bibliographic information provides information about new books as rapidly, and catalogs often provide a fuller description of books than do other sources.
Libraries that do subscribe to Publishers' Weekly and Publishers' Trade List Annual probably still find it necessary
to maintain a file of catalogs, though the file could be smaller than that of a library that does not subscribe to these
tools.   Finally, a point of importance to libraries that operate on a limited budget is the fact that publishers' catalogs
are free.   If a file can be organized so its maintenance will
not be expensive, considerable savings can be realized.

Use of the File

        The Field Research Laboratory Library's file of pub-
lishers' catalogs is at present used for four purposes:

        1. Bibliographic tool.   Publishers' catalogs are often
the only source of bibliographic information for obscure or
recent publications.   An examination of 150 recent orders
showed that in 45 cases the publishers' catalog file provided
the only available bibliographic information about the publication.   In almost all cases, the author, title, edition, series,
place, and date of publication can be obtained from a publisher's announcement.   In addition, announcements of publications in a series or set can often serve as a record of
the library's holdings of that series or set.

        2. Order information.   Publishers' catalogs are an
important source of order information, especially since the
library does a large amount of its ordering direct.   A publisher's address can always be obtained from the catalog.
This is a particularly valuable feature since Cumulative Book
Index no longer gives complete listings of publishers' addresses.   The price of the publication, and occasionally its
Library of Congress card number, are also given.

        3. Reference tool.   The file is an aid to the refer-
ence librarian in determining what publications certain publishers have issued or in determining what publications make
up a particular set or series.

4. <u>Stimulating use of the literature</u>. For several years the library has routed publishers' announcements of new books to members of the research staff working in the field covered by the books. This was done to stimulate researchers to use the scientific literature. In a study conducted over a six-month period, it was found that 192 announcements were routed to 562 people (an average of 2.9 people on each routing slip). Of those 192 routed announcements, 126 were returned with an order for the item described. Another study is in progress to determine whether a correlation exists between the number of announcements routed and the number of books ordered. Preliminary data indicate a negative correlation. In view of this evidence that scientists learn of new publications from sources other than routed publication announcements, the library has discontinued routing such announcements pending further studies of this use of publishers' announcements.

Organization of the File

The Field Research Laboratory Library's file of publishers' catalogs presently occupies eight legal-size vertical file drawers with a total of 11 linear feet of space. This file contains leaflets, folders, and flysheets. Arranged on shelves are 32 linear feet of Princeton files, containing catalogs in pamphlet form. As of August 1962, 415 separate sources of publications were represented in the file. The file is organized as follows:

Classification	Number of Sources
Commercial publishers and dealers	95
Societies and foundations	85
University presses	28
Federal and state government agencies	88
OP dealers (books and periodicals)	41
Business services	42
Maps and globes	16
Russian publications	11
Journal subscription agencies	9
	415

From five to ten items are added to the file each day and two to three man-hours per month are spent in maintaining it.

Annual requests for catalogs are sent to publishers
and dealers by means of a form letter.   Catalogs are received daily, and date-stamping and prliminary weeding of
extraneous and duplicate material takes place at this time.
Selected catalogs and announcements are then routed to members of the research staff thought to be interested in specific
titles.   Catalogs not routed are filed.   The folders and
Princeton files are arranged alphabetically by publisher within each classification.   Finally, routed catalogs that are returned to the library are filed with routing slips after items
requested have been ordered.

Problems and Possible Improvements

Several problems still exist, all of which create difficulty in retrieval.   The most troublesome problem is that
of weeding to eliminate duplicates, superseded announcements,
and rarely-used items.   The only serious weeding presently
being done is an annual removal of duplicates.   A more frequent and more rigorous weeding policy needs to be established, but before this can be done, the following questions
need to be answered:

1. How long should leaflets and flysheets be kept in
the vertical file?   At present they are kept indefinitely.
Some of the items represented in these announcements have
long since been listed in annual catalogs.   These announcements could, therefore, be discarded.

2. How long should annual catalogs be kept?   Does
an occasional request for an older work justify retaining old
annual catalogs?

3. How long should the catalogs of OP dealers and
other special lists be kept?

4. How can these three kinds of weeding be done with
the least possible time and effort?

A second major problem concerns the physical form
of the catalogs.   They appear in a multitude of shapes and
sizes that can be broken down into at least five major categories: 1) pamphlets (with stitched or stapled binding);
2) leaflets (several folded unbound pages);   3) flysheets
(single-page announcements);   4) postcard announcements;
and 5) publishers' catalogs on cards.   At present, pamphlets
are placed in the Princeton file, and everything else is put

in the vertical file. A more clearly defined policy for handling this material is necessary.

A third major problem is a lack of consistency in the classification scheme. As the file is now set up, the classification of some categories is according to the kind of publisher and in others according to the type of publication. Although this classification system worked well when the file was small, the present size of the file is such that a revision is needed. Retrieval is also made difficult by the lack of a subject approach, except through familiarity with publishers' specialties.

Consideration of the above problems suggests several improvements that could be made, both by the library and by the publishers, that would contribute to making the catalog file more useful. The library could: 1) establish a more frequent and more rigorous weeding policy; 2) establish a more definite policy on the handling of different forms of catalogs; and 3) improve its classification scheme.

Usefulness of the file could be improved if publishers could: 1) standardize the form of catalogs; and 2) provide a better subject approach to their catalogs.

The Field Research Laboratory Library's file of publishers' catalogs is a necessary and vital tool. An estimated 25 to 35 per cent of the orders processed by the acquisitions librarian can be bibliographically verified only through use of the file. Without the file, book delivery time lag would be increased, while the library's awareness of new publications would decrease. The file is used frequently enough to justify the time and space required to maintain it. Until a bibliographic tool that can meet the special needs of the library appears, maintenance of the file will be a necessity.

From A Searcher's Manual

by George Lowy   Bibliographer, International En-
                                  cyclopedia of Social Sciences,
                                  New York City

From his A Searcher's Manual. Hamden, Connec-
ticut, The Shoe String Press, 1965. p. 39-50;
Reprinted by permission of The Shoe String Press,
Hamden, Conn.

III.   Use of Bibliographies and Catalogs

If the work is not found in the main catalog of the library or the outstanding-order file, the searcher must verify
the doubtful entry, as it is not always possible to rely on entries in dealers' catalogs or on request cards.

Requests for library material reach the acquisitions
department in various stages of completeness--some with full
and accurate details, and some merely confused notes or haz
remembrances.   When incomplete information is given, in or
der to acquire the material wanted in the shortest possible
time and with the minimum of correspondence, first of all
complete and exact data must be located, checked, and noted.
The searcher can use a variety of bibliographic sources to do
this.

However, before we can consider the use of bibliographic sources in searching work, a short description and
some distinctions among them must be made.

The most important tools of verification are the bibliographies.   A bibliography is a systematic listing of books
sharing common characteristics.

The essential features of a bibliography are that it shall identify, with a certainty sufficient for its purpose, the book that it lists; that it shall describe it in accordance with generally accepted criteria; that it shall list books systematically, even though merely through an alphabetical arrangement; that the books so listed possess certain common characteristics; and that the listing be addressed to some recognizable purpose. There are many types of bibliographies, but three stand out as especially important from the searcher's viewpoint: national, general, and trade bibliographies.

The national bibliographies are the chief working tools for verifying books. In theory, the national bibliography gives a complete and up-to-date record of all the printed output of its country or language in such a way that items may be traced by either author, subject, or title. Thus it records not only books and pamphlets but also government publications, theses, maps, music, filmstrips, and other audio-visual materials. In practice, a publication of this kind seems to be feasible only in a country with a relatively small output of printed matter. In countries where more publishing is done it is customary for the special classes of material (e. g. , government documents and pamphlets) to be treated either selectively or not at all in the current national bibliography.

Some current national bibliographies are based on material received in an institution in accordance with a law making it compulsory for copies of all new publications to be deposited there. If this legal deposit is strictly enforced, the resulting national bibliography benefits accordingly.

Other national bibliographies are based on the voluntary submission of publications or relevant information by the publishers to the editors. This method can work quite efficiently (as it has in Germany) or it can result in only partial coverage.

Many different methods of arrangement have been adopted in national bibliographies. Some are classified, some are in dictionary order, others are in author order. Some cumulate into volumes which, with the passage of years, become useful tools for retrospective searching.

Regardless of their form and scope, national bibliographies are lists of works published in a country; or, in a

broader sense, of works about a country, by natives of a
country living in that country or elsewhere, or written in the
language of that country.

Another class of printed bibliographies is the general
bibliography. (A great many general bibliographies are
called catalogs. Well-known examples of this type are the
Library of Congress catalogs and the British Museum catalog.) A general bibliography is a list of books not limited
to a specific period, locality, subject, or author. As distinguished from a national bibliography, it is a list which
records, describes, and indexes the resources of a collection, a library, or a group of libraries. Although it reflects merely the acquisitions of one library or a group of
libraries, it has enormous bibliographic importance for the
purpose of identifying books.

If the general bibliography represents the collections
of several libraries it is called a union catalog. The National Union Catalog, for example, represents the holdings
of the Library of Congress and more than 750 other North
American libraries.

Similar to union catalogs are the union lists which
record (usually in book format) the periodicals, newspapers,
or other materials of special type held by a group of libraries and assist not only in identification but also in location; they also contribute to coordination of acquisition. The
best known example in this country is the Union List of Serials.

Trade bibliography is the term used to describe bibliographies compiled primarily to aid the book trade by supplying information as to what books are in print or on sale;
when, where, and by whom they were published; and their
price. Publishers' catalogs; records of prices paid at sales;
weekly, monthly, or annual lists of new publications; lists of
books in print are among the bibliographies that fall within
this class. (National bibliographies could technically be considered trade bibliographies since they are generally issued
under publishers' auspices.)

The most frequently used bibliographic tools are:

1. The National Union Catalog... (NUC)

2. The Cumulative Book Index (CBI)

3. <u>Books in Print</u> (BIP)

4. British Museum, Department of Printed Books, Catalogue of Printed Books... (BM)

5. Paris, Bibliothèque Nationale, Département des Imprimés, <u>Catalogue général des livres imprimés: Auteurs</u> (BN)

These and other bibliographic tools are discussed in Part Three.

More and more academic libraries use the Library of Congress proofsheet file for verification. At the Columbia University Libraries this file is arranged alphabetically in annual cumulations. Selected proofsheets are kept for cards issued during the current year and two preceding years.

Search starts with the year which covers the date of the book (usually the copyright date). If a proofsheet card is found that fits the book in all details it is removed from the file.

Assuming that one bibliographic source may contain more information than another and that the time for searching varies considerably with the source used, a definite sequence of usage of bibliographic tools should be sought.

The first source to consult for a very recent English-language trade item is <u>Books in Print.</u> If adequate information is not found, the desired data may be located more easily from the Library of Congress proofsheets or <u>The Cumulative Book Index.</u> If still further information is needed, the search continues in <u>The National Union Catalog.</u> Experience indicates that adoption of this searching sequence for current English-language items gives the best results.

Some exceptions to the procedure above are followed because of certain idiosyncrasies of the sources. For example, the publications of an obscure scientific society would rarely be listed in BIP. Therefore, one would waste his time searching there.

When an entry is verified in a reliable source, the searcher revises the request card or dealer's catalog in order to give a full and correct entry. If he has found new

information about the work, he goes back to the main catalog as well as the order files and rechecks to see whether
the library has the book under the revised entry. If he finds
nothing, he can then report that the library does not own the
work.

Verification also gives the searcher an opportunity to
fill in the gaps if inadequate information is given on the order request, e.g., lack of place or date of publication,
price, publisher, whether the work is part of another set.

The extent of bibliographic verification also differs
from library to library. In a great number of academic libraries every item is verified bibliographically if it is possible (for instance, in the libraries of the University of California, Syracuse University, Johns Hopkins, Oberlin College,
etc.). Johns Hopkins not only tries to verify everything regardless of cost but, if it is not possible to do so, the dealer or publisher is requested to identify the work before shipping. The Indiana University Library also verifies everything except some items such as maps and some atlases.
At the University of Minnesota Library exceptions are allowed
at the discretion of the chief acquisitions librarian or the
head of the book division if items are not found after a reasonable search. At some other universities verification generally depends upon the price of the publication. New York,
Stanford, Princeton, and other universities follow this principle. At the University of Pennsylvania Library the verification depends on price, selector, urgency, amount of bibliographic information given, and whether or not a source is
noted. At Yale as little as possible is done in verifying less
expensive material. At the University of Michigan Library
very inexpensive items are not verified. Items are frequently ordered without verification if there is little or no doubt
about the correctness of the main entry and little or no
doubt that the item is not in a series for which the library
has a standing order. At the Columbia University Libraries
not every single item is verified bibliographically; verification depends on the price, the reliability of the dealer, the
publication's date, and the nature of the entry. Entries for
books not yet published cannot, of course, be verified. The
exceptions are American trade books which can be checked
in the spring, summer, and fall prepublishing announcements
in Publishers' Weekly. The searcher must be able to use
his own judgment; however, items costing over $10.00 are
verified.

Summary

Bibliographic verification is a process of checking bibliographic details sufficiently to identify any library material which is to be requested or ordered. It should cover the author, title, publisher, place of publication, year of publication, edition, series note, number of volumes, parts, and/or supplements, and list or estimated price. The most frequently used tools of verification are national and trade bibliographies as well as big library and union catalogs.

IV.   Illustrative Searches

An understanding of the contents of reference tools and a logical analysis of the item itself will result in the best search. Without such a background, the searcher may conduct merely an unsystematic handling of volumes.

The following examples are given to emphasize the place of evaluation and logical analysis in searching.

Checking the "Weekly Record" in one of the issues of the Publishers' Weekly, the searcher encountered the following item:

> Rosenberg, Arthur. Imperial Germany; the birth of the German Republic, 1871-1918. Tr. from German by Ian F. D. Morrow. Boston, Beacon, 1964.

After carefully searching the outstanding-order file as well as the public catalog, he reported that the library did not have the book. This was a fact: This edition was not in the library. However, he did not pursue the matter and, not being experienced, did not make the logical analysis which is a necessity in bibliographic searching. Therefore his report was not accurate.

What should have been the logical procedure in this case? The searcher should, first of all, have noted that Rosenberg's work was a translation from German.

Experience indicates that publishers sometimes change the title of a translated work; different editions of the same work, even by the same translator, may appear under various titles. It is not necessary to be fluent in a foreign language in order to find the original title and possible translations of a work. The card catalog corner-mark system will provide ample guidance for this.

If the searcher had used this approach he would have found that the library had several copies of Rosenberg's work under the title <u>Birth of the German Republic</u>, translated by same person. This information naturally should have been reported.

When translations are indicated in the item, careful checking will many times uncover relevant bibliographic data.

Searching means more than the mechanical checking of the card catalog; it could be illustrated by another example. The entry in the dealer's catalog was:

> <u>Blue book. Report of H. M. commissioner... connected with the war in South Africa.</u> (Appendices to the Minutes of Evidence taken before the Royal Commission on the war in South Africa). 2 v. 1903.

This item was searched under the following: (1) Blue book, (2) Report,   (3) South Africa--History,   (4) Royal Commission,   (5) Minutes.

The searcher's decision was to start the search in the card catalog under <u>Blue book.</u>   There was no such entry. Before turning to the reference tools he focused the search on the organization which issued the report, knowing, however, that "Commission" or "Royal Commission" is not a distinctive heading.   Any country could have such a body.   It doesn't require wild imagination to decide that "H. M. [His or Her Majesty's] Commission" refers to Great Britain. Putting together the pieces and checking the item under "Gt. Br. Royal Commission on the war in South Africa," he found the work in the card catalog.

Consequently, whenever an organization, government bureau, or commission is the publisher of a work, the searcher should not overlook this possibility as a starting point in his checking.

A French antiquarian dealer's catalog included an entry which read:

> Lefebvre, Georges.   <u>Etudes orléanaises I.   Con-</u>

tribution a l'étude des structures sociales a la
fin du XVIIIe siècle. Paris, Commission d'hist-
oire économique et sociale de la Revolution en
vente à la Bibliothèque nationale, service de com-
mandes, 1962.

Due to the fact that a personal author's name was
given, the searcher started his work from that. When he
was not able to verify the item under the author's name, he
proceeded to search for the publisher as a main entry. Here
there were two possibilities: "Paris. Bibliothèque Nationale.
Commission..." and "France. Commission ... de la Revolution." The work was found under the latter.

Another order request was given in the following way:

80 masterpieces from the Gold Museum. Bogotá,
Banco de Republica, 1954.

The item first was checked in the library's main catalog under the title. After failing to find it, the searcher
used the Library of Congress catalog for verification. The
question was where to start the attempted verification. The
chain of thought was the following: The content of the book
is the description of masterpieces held by the Gold Museum
in Bogotá, so the most likely entry should be a corporate
one under "Bogotá. Gold Museum." The Library of Congress
catalog did not list an entry for "Bogotá. Gold Museum."
However, command of the Spanish language indicated to the
searcher that perhaps "Gold Museum" might be in Spanish,
i. e. , "Museo del Oro." This conclusion was correct; the entry was "Bogotá. Museo del Oro." After rechecking the
card catalog the searcher found that the library already
owned the work.

Occasionally the subject approach proves to be the
most useful. This was used for the following entry in a
dealer's catalog:

Tipos Populares do Refine Antigo. Rio, 1954.

A preliminary search of the card catalog indicated nothing,
and a subsequent search of the Anuario Brasileiro likewise
proved fruitless. Finally, the subject approach in LCC
yielded--under "Brazil. Social conditions"--a reference to
"Wanderley, Edward," as the author of a work whose contents were similar to those of the above-mentioned title.

Upon rechecking the 1954 volume of the <u>Anuario Brasileiro</u> under "Wanderley, Edward," the item was found.

Another example of the subject approach is described below. The request reached the acquisitions department in the following way:

<u>Encyclopedie Grande de la Belgique du Congo</u>

Logically the searcher started under the title. However, there was no card under this title in the main catalog. For verification the searcher used a wide range of reference tools, including subject bibliographies, without success. At this point he turned to the subject approach. First he checked under "Congo. Dictionaries and Encyclopedias," further under "Belgium. Dictionaries and Encyclopedias." Under the latter entry he found the item with a correct title: <u>Grande encyclopedie...du Congo</u>. This, of course, was in the library.

A faculty member sent the following suggestion for purchase:

<u>Memoir famiglie nobili delle provincie Meridion-ali d'Italia</u> Conte B. C. Gonzago.

No imprint data, punctuation, or further information was included.

The searcher's analysis was the following: (1) The item should be checked first under the title in the library's main catalog. If the library had the book there should at least be an added entry for the title. However, no title entry was found in the catalog. (2) As the next step he checked the name indicated in the descriptive part of the title. It could be considered as the author or the editor of the work. This approach also failed to give the necessary result. (3) At this point the searcher came to the right conclusion that he must verify the entry by means other than the card catalog. Since no date was given, the book was checked not in a national bibliography but in a general catalog. The Bibliothèque Nationale catalog was picked as an appropriate reference tool because the item probably was published in Italy, and BN is strong in Italian holdings. BN listed a name "Gonzaga, Berardo Candida," close to the spelling given by the faculty member, and gave a cross reference to "Candida-Gonzaga, Berardo." (4) Experience indicated that names in Romance languages are often entered differently in English bibliographies.   Therefore, the searcher consulted the Library of Congress catalog to check on possible differences.   And indeed in LC he found a cross reference from "Candida-Gonzaga" to "Filangiere de Candida Gonzaga"--the author of the work.   It was then only a matter of routine to establish the correct entry.

The example below illustrates the title approach to searching.   The request was:

> Ballens, J. C.   The states and the metropolitan
> problem.   1956.

Because the publisher and price data were missing, BIP was checked first without success.   The searcher then continued in CBI, but there was no entry under the name "Ballens." The searcher knew that CBI is a good source if only the title of a work is known.   Therefore, he also checked under the title and found the requested item together with the important reference to the main entry, which was "Council of state governments.   The States and the metropolitan problem. "

Summary

As we can see from the examples above, bibliographic searching is a fascinating work involving a knowledge of cataloging techniques, familiarity with a wide variety of reference tools in many languages, and an ability to interpret order requests.

The Bitter End

by Ashby Fristoe   Chief, Acquisitions Department,
                                    University of North Carolina,
                                    Chapel Hill

From Library Resources & Technical Services
10:91-5, Winter 1966; Reprinted with permission
of Executive Secretary, Resources and Technical
Services Division, ALA

As the flood of new books increases, so too does the
effort required to process the books. In a large university
library a not inconsiderable part of this processing is taken
up by searching. In searching, a skilled, well-trained clerk
takes an order card for a title, frequently not in correct
bibliographic form, and attempts to locate the exact title in
LC form in a standard bibliographic tool. Having located it,
he then corrects the title on the order card so that he can
determine whether the library already owns the book or has
it on order. Rigorous attention to detail not only prevents
duplication, it ensures that the dealer can identify and supply the specific book ordered.

The searching process, as described above, appears
fairly simple. Unfortunately, this is not always true. Regardless of the number of the tools the library might have,
it is most unlikely that all titles will be located in every
search. Furthermore, searching in all the bibliographic
tools available in a large research library would be very
costly.

Searching to the bitter end is costly or may be unnecessary, and it would appear that there must be an optimum number of tools to be searched. In addition, the sequence in which bibliographic tools are searched has considerable bearing on the results of the search. * Without be-
laboring the point, it is fruitless to search for titles that
have not yet been published, in bibliographic tools which list

only titles already published. Also, if a library receives and files Library of Congress proof slips and if they arrive before the monthly issues of the <u>National Union Catalog,</u> it is a waste of time to search the monthly issues of the <u>NUC.</u>

Also bearing on the question of searching sequence is the fact that it is best to search in the most productive place first, ending sequentially with the least productive place. If, for instance, 60 of 100 titles were found in the monthly issues of <u>NUC</u> and only 20 of the same titles in the LC proof-slip file, it would be wrong to search the full 100 titles in the LC proof-slip file first. The former sequence adds up to 140 searches, while the latter demands 180 searches for the same yield.

The question of the depth of searching also has relevance because all searches, even if unsuccessful, must end somewhere. The problem is to determine where the search should end. If there were 100 bibliographic tools to be searched and if experience had demonstrated that one could expect to find 79 titles in one tool, 19 in another, and the remaining 2 buried somewhere in the other 98 tools, then it seems reasonable to limit the search to the first two productive tools.

Another element of the searching problem that looms large in the minds of many librarians is the verification of entry. Much extended searching is done in the name of "verification of entry;" much of it is pointless, though undoubtedly strangely satisfying. It is really not likely that a dealer's desire to sell will be seriously affected by an order not in the correct LC form. It is almost certain that he will send the correct book whether it is written:

> Nabokov, Vladimir Vladimirovich, 1899-
> Lolita. New York, Putnam, 1958.
> or
> Nabokov, Vladimir V.
> Lolita. New York, Putnam, 1958.
> or
> Nabokov, V. V.
> Lolita. New York, Putnam, 1958.
> or even
> Nabokov, V. Vladimirovich
> Lolita. New York, Putnam, 1958.

Furthermore, when the card catalog shows a 1958 Putnam

edition on hand, any good searcher would mark this as a duplicate.

The many "Smith"-type entries and confusing corporate author entries are potential problems, but many of these can be screened out from the routine searching process. It is true that, without a standardized form of author entry, some scattering of orders in the order file may occur for the same title, and some duplication could occur. This is not always crucial. What is important is the determination of a proper balance between effort and product. The searching process should be designed for the large bulk of uncomplicated entries; simple entries should not be pressured into a complicated process designed to take care of the exceptional and complex.

To find answers to the problems of depth and sequence of searching, it was decided to take one group of 100 order cards, picked at random from current (1965) American imprints, search them in standard bibliographic tools, record the information as to where located, and from this information determine the optimum searching sequence and depth. American imprints were chosen because they represent one of the largest single categories of material ordered for the library in which this study was made, and because older imprints are much more frequently located in the cumulated NUC volumes, and therefore pose less of a problem.

Each title was searched in each bibliographic tool and the results kept in tabular form. Many of the titles were found in each of several tools. All 25 titles found in NUC were included in the 40 titles found in the LC proof-slip file. The bibliographic tools searched and the number of titles found in each tool are as follows:

CBI (Cumulative Book Index) (March and April 1965	37
LC proof-slip file	40
NUC (Jan. and Feb. 1965)	25
BPR (American Book Publishing Record) (Oct., Nov., Dec. 1964 and Jan., and Feb. 1965)	14
PW (Publishers' Weekly) (1, 8, 15, 22, 29 Mar. 1965)	13
PWA (Publishers' Weekly Announcements) (Mar. through July 1965 Interim Index to Forthcoming Books)	33

One difference between NUC and the LC proof-slip
file which might have some bearing on the results of searching is the fact that, whereas the cooperative copy prepared by
a large number of American libraries appears in NUC, it is
not included in the LC proof slips. This would, of course,
tip the scales in favor of searching first in NUC. Interestingly, of the 100 titles searched in this study, not one of the
25 found in NUC was cooperative copy.

When the 100 titles were searched through all six
tools in a random sequence, the results shown in Sequence
A were obtained.

Sequence A

Sequence	# Searched	# Found	# of Units per Tool	Total # of Searches Made
1st-- LC PS	100	40	1	100
2nd--NUC	60	0	2	120
3rd--BPR	60	1	5	300
4th--PW	59	0	5	295
5th--PWA	59	26	1	59
6th--CBI	33	4	2	66
		71		940

The figures in the right hand column are the result of multi-
plying the number of issues of each bibliographic tool in
which the search was conducted by the number of titles
searched. For instance, in the third step, when 60 cards
remain to be searched in BPR, there are 5 issues of BPR,
Oct. 1964 through Feb. 1965, in which the 60 cards must
be searched. This represents a total of 300 separate
searches to be made just in step 3.

This "Bitter End" search located 71 titles after 940
searches, but a detailed examination of the results revealed
that, with one exception, every title found in NUC, BPR,
and PW was also found in the LC proof-slip file. (The one
exception was found in CBI.) It was obvious that these
three tools should be eliminated. This was done, and
searching in the remaining tools by varied sequences yielded
the results shown in Sequences B-G.

Sequence B

Sequence	# Searched	# Found	# of Units per Tool	Total # of Searches Made
1st--LC PS	100	40	1	100
2nd--PWA	60	26	1	60
3rd--CBI	34	5	2	68
		71		228

Sequence C

Sequence	# Searched	# Found	# of Units per Tool	Total # of Searches Made
1st--LC PS	100	40	1	100
2nd--CBI	60	9	2	120
3rd--PWA	51	22	1	51
		71		271

Sequence D

Sequence	# Searched	# Found	# of Units per Tool	Total # of Searches Made
1st--PWA	100	33	1	100
2nd--LC PS	67	33	1	67
3rd--CBI	34	5	2	68
		71		235

Sequence E

Sequence	# Searched	# Found	# of Units per Tool	Total # of Searches Made
1st--PWA	100	33	1	100
2nd--CBI	67	27	2	134
3rd--LC PS	40	11	1	40
		71		274

Sequence F

Sequence	# Searched	# Found	# of Units per Tool	Total # of Searches Made
1st--CBI	100	37	2	200
2nd--PWA	63	24	1	63
3rd--LC PS	39	10	1	39
		71		302

Sequence G

Sequence	# Searched	# Found	# of Units per Tool	Total # of Searches Made
1st--CBI	100	37	2	200
2nd--LC PS	63	12	1	63
3rd--PWA	51	22	1	51
		71		314

An examination of Sequences B through G reveals that Sequence B produced the 71 titles for the least effort. Sequence D is almost as good as Sequence B, but the fact that only 26 of the titles found in PWA had not yet been cataloged by the Library of Congress favors B over D.

Sequence B is an improvement over Sequence A by a factor of four. Using an estimate of 30 seconds per search and a wage scale of $1.90 per hour for a searcher, it costs $3.60, or 5¢ per title, to find the 71 titles using Sequence B. In contrast, it costs $14.75, or 20¢ per title, to find them using Sequence A.

If the library ordered 10,000 current American titles per year, and if the search were made to the "bitter end," the searching would cost about $2,000 per year as opposed to $500 for Sequence B.

Some unpublished imprints may be ordered under this system without absolute verification, but these imprints might be ordered in any case even if they could not be located in the "bitter end" search. As a matter of fact, many unverified imprints are ordered without duplication occurring. As for titles found in PWA and ordered without verification, by the time they arrive from the dealer, the proof slips will, in many instances, already have arrived for use by the cataloger. Also, it is relatively easy for a trained searcher to put in correct LC form a title which cannot be found during the searching process. It is certainly far less expensive than a search to the "bitter end" justified either on the basis of ensuring the title is in correct LC form, or just because many different bibliographic tools are available in the library.

The above study suggests that for current American imprints ordered for a large university library the optimum searching depth is three bibliographic tools arranged in the sequence, LC proof-slip file, Publishers' Weekly Announcements, and Cumulative Book Index.

Editor's note: For comparative purposes, see Lazorick,
     Gerald J. and Minder, Thomas L.   "A Least Cost
     Searching Sequence." College and Research Li-
     braries, 25:126-28, March 1964.

Current Reviewing of Children's Books

by Zena Sutherland

Mrs. Sutherland is Editor of
the Bulletin of the Children's
Book Center, University of
Chicago and also Children's
Book Editor for the Saturday
Review

Selection from her "Current Reviewing of Children's Books," Library Quarterly 37:113-118,
January 1967; Reprinted by permission of the
University of Chicago Press, Copyright 1967 by
the University of Chicago

Although most of this audience is surely familiar with
the policies and procedures of Booklist, Bulletin, Horn Book,
and School Library Journal, it may be useful briefly to review.

The ALA's Booklist, which is published every two
weeks save for August, is indexed in each issue and the index cumulated twice a year. There are separate sections
for children's and for young adult books; the editors choose
only books they recommend for purchase. Advisory voting
lists are sent out each week for each list to a dozen young
people's librarians who, because of their own situation, will
have had an opportunity to see the books. Especially recommended books are singled out in the list for small library
purchase. A statement of its policy was made in a 1953 issue of Top of the News giving the criteria used as a basis
of evaluation and stating that the annotations point out short-
comings that may limit the usefulness of the book, and that
they make comparisons when possible with other books on
the same subject.

The Bulletin's reviews are based on assessments
made by the editor and reviewed by a committee of librarians and teachers meeting weekly. To assist librarians who

have no opportunity to examine books, in making their selections, non-recommended books are reviewed.   The Bulletin
uses a six-symbol code for evaluation, and the opinions of
faculty members who are subject experts are sought when
needed.   The Bulletin is published eleven times a year and
indexed annually; the back cover lists professional material
each month.   In December, a list of titles recommended in
the calendar year is included.

Horn Book is published every two months with an index in each issue and annual index.   It includes articles and
reproductions of illustrations; it reviews only books it recommends, the signed reviews being written by staff members.   In addition to regular sections for various age groups,
Horn Book includes any special heading that may seem useful, even if only one review is given under the special heading.   Mrs. Viguers, the editor, said in a meeting reported
in the May issue of the 1963 Library Journal, "While fortunately libraries do use the Horn Book as a help in buying
books, we also hope that they make the Horn Book available
to parents, since it is geared to individuals as well as to
library groups wanting recommended books."[1]

At the same meeting, Miss Davis of the School Library Journal stated that the main purpose of the publication
was "to serve as a buying guide, particularly for average
and smaller public and school libraries throughout the country.   Our appraisals are not intended to be definitive literary reviews, nor an attempt to pick out the distinguished
books of the year."[2]   School Library Journal is published
monthly from September to May.   It is indexed in alternate
issues, the book it has recommended during the year being
included in a separate annual publication, and it includes
articles and professional news; its signed reviews are written by almost a hundred librarians and library supervisors
throughout the country.   A small panel of librarians serves
as advisors for each issue, occasionally deciding on publication of a second review.   School Library Journal reviews
all books it thinks will be seriously considered for purchases
by librarians, marking books of special merit with a single
or a double asterisk.

It seemed to this investigator fairly apparent that to
follow in a third survey the same procedures that were used
by Mrs. Anderson and Miss Galloway would produce corrob-
orative evidence--perhaps to the point of monumental redun-
dancy.*   Clearly, the methods they used--the application of

lists of criteria to a comparatively small number of reviews--produced a detailed content analysis but could not give at the same time a broad picture.

In 1965, there were 2,473 juvenile titles published. In examining the reviewing of books in that year, I have chosen not to analyze 1965 titles, but 1965 reviewing. Some of the titles listed in Publishers' Weekly in 1965 were, of course, reviewed in 1966, and some of the reviews published in 1965 were reviews of 1964 titles. Since the pattern of time lag repeats each year, there seemed no reason to pursue the 1965 titles.

Media used were the Booklist, published by the American Library Association; the Bulletin of the Center for Children's Books, published by the Graduate Library School of the University of Chicago; Horn Book Magazine, published by Horn Book Incorporated, and School Library Journal, published by R. R. Bowker Company.

There were 2,299 books reviewed by one or more of the four media. Of these, 1,501 were reviewed by only one publication. The largest number in this category was found in the School Library Journal--927 books. Titles reviewed only by the Bulletin were 350; Booklist, 139; and Horn Book, 85. Books reviewed by two of the four media totaled 466; School Library Journal, 405; Booklist, 203; Horn Book, 175; the Bulletin, 149.

In the category of books covered by three out of the four media, out of a total of 238, School Library Journal covered 211; Booklist, 198; Horn Book, 176; and the Bulletin, 129. Only 94 books out of the total of the 2,299 reviewed were covered by all four of the media. Of the 2,473 titles published in 1965, School Library Journal reviewed 1,619; the Bulletin, 748; Booklist, 608; and Horn Book, 530.

One of the problems for most reviewers has been the increasing number of science books--among them, books on fairly technical subjects, or on advanced research, or on the new mathematics with which many of us are unfamiliar. Today, young people are reading books on cryogenics, biochemistry, and computers at a level that would not too long ago have been considered adult material.

Therefore, it is of interest to consider the coverage given science books. It is a low percentage. Out of the 94

books reviewed by all media, only 4 were science titles, a
shade over 4 per cent; 12 per cent of the books reviewed by
three media were on scientific subjects; 13 per cent of the
titles reviewed by two media; and in the case of books covered by only one of the journals, the figure was 12 per cent
--the last three very close percentages, all three times as
high as the percentage of science books reviewed in the all-
four group.

Of the 4 titles in that group, none was in the physical sciences, reflecting the tendency in each group toward a
preponderance of reviews of books in the area of the natural
sciences.

Another area of interest was the amount of fiction
versus non-fiction. Of the books reviewed by one medium
only, 721 titles out of 1,501 were non-fiction. Of the 466
titles in the two-media group, 244 were non-fiction. Of the
238 books reviewed in the three-media category, 105 were
non-fiction; and there were 28 non-fiction titles in the small
group of 94 books reviewed by all four media.

There was unremarkable agreement on reading level.
Five reviews each in the Bulletin and in the Booklist gave
levels that differed to any noteworthy degree from those given
by the other three media in the 94-book review. Horn Book
does not give the close definition of reading level as a matter of policy. Although it is difficult to calibrate agreement
when the four media assign for one book junior and senior
high school, grades 6-9, grades 7-10, and just "Biography,"
it is possible to say that there still exists, as there did in
Mrs. Anderson's study of ten years ago, the highest degree
of agreement between Booklist and the Bulletin.

It is interesting to see that in the list of 94 books
thirty-two publishers are represented--one with 12 books--
and eleven publishers with only a single entry. One indication of the publishers' interest in reviewing is the increasing
use, in their catalogs, of lists of media whose recommenda
tions of individual titles are noted in a system of coded sym
bols.

What emerges from this compilation of facts, comparisons, and judgments? No journal gives complete cover
age, and no one of the four so intensively scrutinized is
without some flaws. There are some constant facts, such
as the wide coverage of the Library Journal and the person

al tone of the Horn Book, to which Mrs. Anderson referred
as being "characterized by a note of enthusiasm in contrast
to the more studied and objective tone of the reviews in the
Booklist and the Bulletin of the Children's Book Center."[3]

There are some differences of opinion: Mrs. Anderson finds that appeals to the reader are usually noted; Miss
Galloway does not. I find more comparison with other books
on the subject--perhaps this is a developing trend. Mrs.
Anderson mentions the fact that, in Horn Book, "page references to authors and titles of children's books include advertisements as well as the reviews, with no distinction made
in the index as to whether a review or an advertisement is
indicated."[4] Advertisers are now indexed separately. The
Bulletin, once able to review all of the books it received,
now receives more of the larger amount published, a fact
that has resulted in a larger percentage of recommended
books out of its total reviewing.

Most reviewing media have been forced to give up
something--series books usually being the first to go. Some
media have found that they needed to increase their staffs.

The nature of the inadequacies in current reviewing
would indicate that those inadequacies are only partially su-
perable. A co-operative arrangment combined with a proliferation of media for special areas would help. So would
governmental or foundation subsidies. Eventually, the computer will come to the help of the librarian selecting books,
but that is not imminent.

Examination centers may have increased, but there
are still many librarians who have no opportunity to examine new books. Virginia Haviland says, in an article written in 1961,

> Small libraries, without approval copies at hand,
> must usually rely on printed reviews and approved
> lists and on visits to the bookstores and exhibits.
> The need for a variety of reviews with their dif-
> ferent emphases and coverage is greater for the
> small library than it is for the larger one with an
> orderly system of reviewing. There is special
> help in the "For the Small Library" recommenda-
> tion in Booklist; in the unfavorable as well as fav-
> orable verdicts expressed in both School Library
> Journal as well as the Bulletin of the Center for

Children's Books, with a helpful key also in the
latter to "marginal" and "special" values; in the inclusion of illustrations from books and a scientist's reviews in the Horn Book.

For the small library, even more important guidance than that of the current reviews (and, says a
one-man department, it is "less difficult and time
consuming") is that offered later in selective lists
and in catalogs with annual supplements, in which
entries are starred and double-starred.

ALA's annual "Notable Children's Books" appears
each spring; the Horn Book "Fanfare" summary is
printed in its August issue; during Book Week and
before Christmas many lists of the year's outstanding books are printed by large libraries and newspapers.   No single summary or review medium is
sufficient, but a number of them together become
a substitute for reading and examination of the
books themselves. [5]

Virginia Haviland also mentions the system of comparative reviewing that was used by librarians of greater
Boston.   Part of current reviewing practice is certainly a
lively exchange of opinion.   At the Children's Services Division meeting in New York, a panel of three editors and three
reviewers discussed policies and books.   The questions from
the floor made it clear that CSD members were anxious to
talk about "controversial" books.   With the advent of books
like Harriet the Spy and Dorp Dead, there has been sounded
an acid note in exchanges of opinion--a note some find moderately distressing.   These books seem to be a reflection of
our literary times, perhaps a reflection in juvenile literature
of Salinger and Kerouac.   We do not need to agree on the
merit of a book, but in making acid comments about a conflicting opinion we are indulging in internecine pyrotechnics
that are less than instructive or dignified.

It is also apparent that there is need for clarification
of the terms we use, both in evaluations of books and in descriptions of books and their audiences.

Perhaps the "controversial" or "trend" books are over-
analyzed; so, perhaps, are the beginner books.   Let's face
it: some of them are delightful, some of them are deadly
dull, and the rest--which is the largest number--vary from

innocuous mediocrity to pedestrian usefulness that verges on
textbook sterility.

There are so many books published; how does a reviewing journal decide what to include and what to omit?
Clearly, for some users, the journal that reviews non-recommended books serves a need. For some, the reviews of
only recommended books is sufficient. Certainly a librarian,
or a teacher, or a parent who is selecting books should
ideally use all of the media available and should also, ideally, know the policies and the tone of each publication he uses
and be aware of the special values or the limitations of each.

The user must also evaluate the medium in terms of
its intended audience. The tendency in newspapers and some
magazines to describe 2 or more books in a comparative review seems perfectly acceptable for its audience of individual subscribers. They do not need the decimal classification
of Booklist; librarians do. They do not want School Library
Journal's information on binding; librarians do. Young parents need to be reminded of old books; young librarians are
likely to have the old books and be stunned by the spate of
new books. They need information and critical evaluation
and some discussion.

There are readers for all books of merit. In a meeting of the New York State Library Association at which four
reviewers spoke and conducted a question period, a librarian
asked, "Why does the Newbery-Caldecott Committee pick
Newbery Award winners that sit on the shelves and just
don't circulate?" Mrs. Viguers volunteered a succinct answer to the effect that we surely want Shakespeare in every
library even though not everybody enjoys Shakespeare.

The problem of the reviewer's audience was also
touched upon by some booksellers during a recent ALA Conference. The booksellers collect reviews and take them a-
long on their trips, but often discover that the librarian or
supervisor is not interested and prefers the salesman to select the books. To these men, there were two problems in
reviewing; one, that reviews were not objective enough; two,
that they failed to consider the wide disparity in levels of
sophistication and reading ability in different geographical
areas. It seems difficult to solve the latter problem. One
can hardly grade a book 4-6 with a note that it should be
used in primary grades in backward areas.

This is one of the things the user of reviews must judge. The reader should know the consistent practices of the media he uses. And reviewers must avoid the pitfall of assumptions. Let me give two examples. These are comments from reviews in a sample of a proposed new paperback review service.

Speaking of Arthur Goldberg and his career: "Thus when he writes a history of the labor organization it can be viewed as a definitive work." And this: "The account start when the author was ten years of age, so its appeal to a young reader is assured."

Today the need for reviews seems greater than ever. There are more books, there are more libraries, and there has been loosed an abundance of money. Circulation figures have risen sharply. Between 1960 and 1965, Booklist circulation rose 45 per cent. Helen Kinsey, editor of the "Children's Books" section, says that over half the subscribers are now school libraries. Mrs. Viguers reports a tripling of Horn Book subscriptions in the past eight years, and the increase has been approximately the same for the Bulletin. Hilary Deason said that to his surprise and pleasure the new quarterly review, Science Books, had reached a circulation of 5,000 in its first year.

The Detroit Public Library has announced that its list of books, published monthly, is now available to subscribers and will include two lists, "Books Approved for Purchase," and "Considered but not Included." The Virginia Kirkus Service is a hardy perennial, and Young Readers' Review is growing nicely. The regular or special-issue reviews in educational journals and science magazines are more and more mentioned in lists of review media. And there is a flourishing proliferation of the bibliographies and selected lists mentioned by Miss Haviland--including her own list, Children's Books 1965. [6]

It seems reasonable to conclude that 1967 will bring as many new books for children and young people as did 1965 and 1966, and that most of these books will have some review coverage. Probably there will be relatively few books reviewed in many media, and those few will be books of good quality that merit, but do not need, comparative assessments. Possibly the need for such assessments will lead either to co-operative reviewing or to some practical division of responsibilities; certainly this need will eventually be

met in part by the acceleration that will be gained by using
such mechanized processes as the future will bring.

Notes

1. "Book Reviewer's Summit Conference, the Big Four
   Speak" Library Journal 88 (May 15, 1963), 2072.

2. Ibid. , p. 2069.

3. Anderson, op. cit. , p. 46.

4. Ibid. , p. 37.

5. Virginia Haviland "Search for the Real Thing" Library
   Journal 86 (December 15, 1961), 4334.

6. Virginia Haviland and Lois B. Watt Children's Books
   1965 (Washington: U.S. Government Printing Office,
   1966).

*Editor's note: Mrs. Sutherland is referring here to two
   studies discussed in the first half of her article:
   Evelyn Anderson, "A Study of Some Reviewing Media
   of Children's Books" (unpublished Master's thesis,
   Graduate Library School, University of Chicago, 1957)
   and Mabel Louise Galloway, "An Analytical Study of
   the Extent and Nature of the Reviewing of Juvenile
   Books in Eight Journals and Newspapers..." (unpublished Ph.D. dissertation, Teachers College, Columbia University, 1965).

Boston's Horn Book Magazine

by L. F. Willard

From Yankee 29:51+ January 1963; Reprinted by
permission of Yankee Magazine, Dublin, New
Hampshire

Bought any children's books lately? Traumatic experience, isn't it? What Johnny would like to read, you
think he probably shouldn't; what you think he ought to read,
he probably won't. And there are so many books--where do
you start? According to Publishers' Weekly, around 1600
titles are published each year in the children's field. Unlike
adult books, many of these continue to sell for years, so
that at any one time the number of children's books to choose
from staggers the imagination.

A small publishing firm in Boston's Copley Square
has been meeting this problem of selection head-on for more
than thirty-eight years through its Horn Book Magazine and
other publications. The Horn Book Magazine applies high
literary standards in its judgment of children's books. Its
reviews are widely used as a guide for home, church, school
and public library collections, selecting the best of the torrent of fiction, fairy tales, beginning readers, animal stories
science books, travel books, picture books, and others pour-
ing from the presses each year.

Mrs. Ruth Hill Viguers, present editor of The Horn
Book Magazine (published bi-monthly), is able to print about
500 reviews in a year's time. She receives virtually every
children's book published. "Several hundred books published
each year are really bad," she says. "They are badly written, condescending, talk down to the child. Then there are
the follow-the-leader books--some publisher brings out a book
with a really fresh idea, the book sells, and dozens of other
publishers jump to bring out their own book like it, almost
always inferior." Mrs. Viguers does not review a bad book,

preferring to use the space to bring a good book to public
attention.

In addition to book reviews, The Horn Book Magazine
publishes articles which are informative, inspirational and
sometimes controversial. In one article a Harvard education
professor may challenge librarians to show courage and creativity in selecting books to appeal to the more hard-shelled
adolescents. Another article may present a detailed analysis
and espousal of the works of a writer for children whose
books The Horn Book editors feel deserve to be rescued from
impending obscurity. Other articles vary in content from an
account of the collection of Ethiopian folklore to anecdotes
from the hunt for material on the mysterious Japanese water
elves known as "kappas."

A recent issue of The Horn Book Magazine carried an
article on an outstanding Russian poet whose goal is to encourage childhood happiness. In the article, written by Miriam Morton of Santa Monica, the poet, Kornei Chukovsky, is
quoted as saying:

> All children between the ages of two and five be-
> lieve (or yearn to believe) that life is meant only
> for joy, for limitless happiness, and that this be-
> lief is one of the most important conditions for
> their normal psychological growth. The gigantic
> task of the child in mastering the spiritual heritage
> of the adult world is realized only when he is sat-
> isfied with the world that surrounds him. From
> there comes his incentive and strength to wage the
> struggle for happiness which the individual carries
> on even during the most trying periods of his life.

Such articles are typical of the high calibre writing
which is available to The Horn Book editors, not only from
this country but internationally. This is only possible because of the wide respect held in literary fields for The
Horn Book and for its editors. Mrs. Viguers has devoted
her entire life to children's literature. She is a graduate of
Willamette University in Salem, Oregon, and of the School of
Library Science, University of Washington, Seattle. After
her graduation from Library School, she was a children's librarian in the New York Public Library, serving in that capacity in various departments between her years abroad.

She spent three years in Europe, first to organize the

library of a girls' school in Madrid, Spain, then in charge
of work with children in The American Library in Paris.
Later she went to teach in the Boone Library School in Wu-
chang, Central China. There she married Richard T. Viguers, who was teaching law and economics in Central China
College. When her husband came to Boston in 1947 as administrator of New England Center Hospital, Mrs. Viguers
became associated with Simmons College. She teaches Children's Literature in the School of Publication and Storytelling at the Library School.

During the summer of 1959 Mrs. Viguers conducted
a two-week workshop in writing for children at the New
Hampshire Writers Conference. Last year she returned to
Madrid to survey the library she organized early in her career. Despite her busy schedule, she still finds time to
write. She is co-author of Macmillan's A Critical History
of Children's Literature, and one of the compilers of Illustrators of Children's Books, 1946-1956. The others who
assisted on this book were Marcia Dalphin and Mrs. Bertha
Mahoney Miller, editor of The Horn Book until 1950, and
now president of The Horn Book, Inc.

The Horn Book's small staff of editors which provides
all of the reviews includes, in addition to Mrs. Viguers,
Virginia Haviland, Reader's Advisor for Children at the Boston Public Library (just across the square from The Horn
Book offices); Margaret Warren Brown, Coordinator of Elementary School Libraries in Wellesley, Massachusetts; and
in charge of science reviews, Isaac Asimov, a scientist and
writer of science fact and fiction books. Margaret Scoggin,
Coordinator of Young Adult Services at the New York Public
Library, writes a department of review of adult books for
young people.

Miss Haviland is well known internationally as an authority on children's books. She is the author of a series
of fairy tales published by Little, Brown and Company. She
is a member of the jury for the Hans Christian Andersen international children's book medal, and a member of the executive committee of the Children's Librarians in the Public
Libraries Section of the International Federation of Library
Associations. She also was in Europe last summer, but on
different assignments from Mrs. Viguers. Miss Haviland
spoke at Library Association meetings in Edinburgh, Scot-
land, and Keele, England.

The Horn Book got its name from the early 17th century lesson book. Its cover is decorated with Randolph Caldecott's "Three Jovial Huntsmen," to indicate that the magazine hunts down and blows the horn for fine books. It had
its beginning in 1924 at Boston's Woman's Educational and
Industrial Union, where a young woman named Bertha Mahoney (now Mrs. Bertha Mahoney Miller) had been operating
a unique "Bookshop for Girls and Boys." In 1936, The Horn
Book, Incorporated, headed by Mrs. Miller, bought the magazine. She was its editor until 1950 when she retired from
that position. Miss Jennie D. Lindquist assumed the editorship. When she resigned in 1958, Mrs. Viguers was appointed editor. The original eighteen-page magazine has
grown to 112 pages and has a world-wide circulation and
enormous prestige.

In August each year The Horn Book devotes the entire issue to the year's two top award-winning children's
books--The American Library Association's Newbery Award
for distinguished writing, and the Caldecott Award for distinction in illustration. In this issue the author or illustra-
tor tells about making the book, and other articles give facts
on the lives of the winners and other information on the creation of these outstanding books.

Some of the articles which have appeared in The
Horn Book Magazine have been compiled by Norma R. Fryatt
and published as a book entitled: The Horn Book Sampler.
Among other books published by The Horn Book are Books,
Children and Men by Paul Hazard, and Newbery Medal Books
and Caldecott Medal Books.

Max Lerner, social historian and author of the monumental America As A Civilization maintains that "a child
reared without good books and ideas goes out into the world
with a vacuum in him." To The Horn Book staff, the need
for "blowing horns for good reading for children and young
people" is as urgent today as it was when Bertha Mahoney
first sounded the call to the hunt almost forty years ago.
For today it is easier than it ever was to pass by a good
book in the ever-increasing deluge of children's books en-
gulfing bewildered parents, teachers and librarians faced
with the all-important task of filling that vacuum Max Lerner
speaks about.

Reviews of <u>BPR; The American Book Publishing Record</u>,
v. 1- Feb. 1, 1960-New York, R.R. Bowker Co.
$10 per year.

From <u>Library Resources & Technical Services</u>
4:257-60, Summer 1960; Reprinted by permission
of Executive Secretary, Resources & Technical
Services Division, ALA

University Library Viewpoint

This year witnesses the birth of a new monthly bibliography to aid librarians and scholars in keeping up with
the current book publications in the United States. The new
publication, <u>BPR; American Book Publishing Record</u>, aims
to be "a complete and accurate record of American book
publication." Volume 1, number 1 lists books issued in the
United States for the month ending February 1, 1960. Each
issue of <u>BPR</u> is compiled from the previous month's "Weekly Record" section of <u>Publishers' Weekly</u>. Thus we now
have a trade bibliography (<u>PW</u> and <u>BPR</u>) which reports the
publication of the country's books speedily and cumulates the
lists once every four or five weeks--a very useful selection
and ordering tool indeed.

By means of special arrangements with book publishers and the Library of Congress, the listings in <u>PW</u>
(which subsequently appear in <u>BPR</u>) are prepared using LC
card proofs. In addition to the entry and descriptive cataloging, LC furnishes Dewey classification numbers and LC
subject headings. The editors of <u>PW</u> use this cataloging information to prepare their listing, adding the price of the
book, other pertinent trade information, and a descriptive
annotation.

The distinction between <u>BPR</u> and other trade tools
previously available to us is that <u>BPR</u> uses Library of Congress form of entry. This represents a major and long-
wished-for change in an important segment of our bibliographical apparatus. Uniformity of entry in catalogs and

496

bibliographies has been a dominant dream and goal of American librarians for many years, and the dream certainly has practical logic behind it. Who cannot see sound reasons for having the same form of entry in the catalogs and book lists prepared and used within one library? By a simple extension of this reasoning, the uniformity of entry in the main national bibliographical apparatus is equally desirable, though admittedly more difficult to obtain and control. For achieving a major step toward this goal BPR and the R. R. Bowker Company are to be toasted and congratulated!

It is unfortunate that our congratulations must be tempered by reservations. For there is a serious flaw in this otherwise fine addition to our bibliographical apparatus for book selection, ordering, cataloging and reference operations. In his foreword to the first issue of BPR ("The Birth of a National Bibliography") Daniel Melcher describes the background of apparent needs and the negotiations which led to the creation of BPR. Mr. Melcher does not explain, however, why PW has not used the LC entry as it was furnished on the LC card proof. In the transfer to PW the LC entries have been modified and omissions have been made. The most serious alteration is the omission of the author's dates. Other alterations, such as the substitution of commas for periods, are perhaps less serious. But they also leave one with the question as to whether the alterations were intentional or the result of unfamiliarity with library cataloging practice on the part of the PW editors. These alterations will badly curtail the use and value of BPR in the normal library ordering and cataloging operations. For those libraries that integrate ordering and cataloging operations by "pre-cataloging" as books are ordered, any editorial modification of the LC entry eliminates BPR as a possible pre-cataloging tool.

Mr. Melcher states in the foreword to the first issue of BPR that "it is now entirely possible to catalog as well as select and buy from PW's current entries." (Italics are mine.) Unfortunately, as applied to the first two issues of BPR, this statement will not hold true for most college and university libraries. Rules of entry for the cataloging of books have been codified and widely accepted by American libraries, including the Library of Congress. Unless LC entries are reproduced exactly and entirely in PW, in BPR and in the card catalog of the Pawebipor University Library, we do not have uniformity of entry, but only approximate uniformity of entry, quite a different thing in the lives of scholars and librarians.

Until one knows whether the modification of LC entries is the result of PW editorial policy or merely an editorial oversight, it is impossible to predict the future value
of BPR as a cataloging aid. But it is obvious that the Bowker Company has assembled the elements to produce a unique
and potentially invaluable addition to our national bibliography. We hope that the policy and the future issues of BPR
will realize Mr. Melcher's hope and intention for "The birth
of a national bibliography."--Eugene M. Johnson, Acquisition Librarian, University of Nebraska Libraries, Lincoln.

From the Public Library

In February of this year, the BPR (known also as the
American Book Publishing Record) joined the ranks of the
other alphabet bibliographical tools for the American book
trade: PTLA, BIP, CBI, PW. This is not the only "New
Deal" connotation, as the BPR is the first American book
trade tool to recognize the inter-dependency of all technical
process functions and the togetherness of operations in this
field. With the proper care and nourishment, the BPR has
the possibilities of being the tool in this area.

The BPR is a monthly cumulation, in Dewey Decimal
numerical arrangement, of the book announcements which appeared during the previous month in Publishers' Weekly's
"Weekly Record," plus an author and title index. The February BPR covers books listed in the January, 1960 issues
of PW's "Weekly Record." The "Weekly Record" itself has
recently expanded its services by supplying Dewey Decimal
classification numbers through the cooperation of the Library
of Congress. Moreover, during 1959 the "Weekly Record"
began listing all publications in hard covers or consisting of
49 or more pages. This increased the number of titles
listed and correspondingly increased the items available to
be listed in the BPR.

There are four possible areas of application of the
BPR in a library; reference, book selection, acquisition, and
cataloging.

In a public library, the least important of these uses
seems to be reference. This is not surprising as the BPR
was not primarily designed as a reference tool. In spite of
this, there are, however, several possibilities of reference

use, i. e., a local medical book store, which has requests
for books not listed in PTLA or CBI, might be helped in its
search for a publisher. A club woman vaguely remembers
a review of a book she read in last Sunday's paper, and the
library assistant is able to locate it through the author-title
index of BPR, without thumbing through all of the Publishers'
Weekly since the last fall or spring announcement issues.

Public libraries, except for the large research institutions, will find the BPR of greater use in book selection
than in direct service to patrons. This will be true irrespective of the size or type of public library. In a large,
departmentalized public library, the head of a department,
say Art, will use the BPR to survey her field; while in the
small library, the librarian will check to see how her section of shelving containing art books measures up. This use,
though, is at best retrospective, a means of checking gaps
in collections after ordering from other sources.

BPR's publisher and its editors are most enthusiastic
about the use of the BPR as a book selection tool. In the
introduction to the first issue they say,

> ... generalists and specialists alike can do their
> checking without the irritation of occasionally mark-
> ing the same book twice (a definite possibility in
> dictionary catalogs like the Subject Guide to Books
> in Print and the CBI, which are really intended to
> aid those who know what they are looking for,
> rather than those who know not what they see, but
> want to 'keep up. ').

While the BPR does have use as a book selection tool for
public libraries, it cannot be a primary one. The fact that
the BPR appears at monthly frequencies will hinder its use
as a primary book selection tool. There are even specialists who cannot wait a month to check what is currently
available in their field. The annotations are another point
at which the BPR falls short as a selection tool. Reviews,
not annotations, are preferred by public librarians in considering books for purchase. Perhaps the BPR could best
be defined as a tool to check book selection, rather than a
book selection tool.

The forte of the BPR lies in the technical services
fields of acquisitions and cataloging; more especially in a
coordination of these two activities. Here for the first time,

in one place, can be found (for items in the American book
trade) the author, title publisher, address, price, Dewey
classification number, and Library of Congress subject headings, plus an annotation. With a few exceptions, this covers
all the information that is needed in a public library to acquire and catalog. This almost complete inclusiveness of
ordering and cataloging information could make the BPR an
ideal tool for cooperative processing centers.

It is extremely helpful to have again a monthly author-
title index to the "Weekly Record." This has been sorely
missed by librarians, acquisition and reference people alike.
Now that this index appears in conjunction with the expanded
information in the Publishers' Weekly listings, it is doubly
useful. Dewey classification numbers and Library of Congress subject headings are easily discovered. To realize
the full potential of the index, though, why not one that is
truly cumulative? By the end of a year, although it is less
than 52, twelve is a large number of issues through which
to search.

The editors mention that "the cataloging of books ordered can begin at once, either directly from the entry, or
through the use of the LC card order number given in the
entry." Here is a sensible, economical approach for all public libraries. The large public library, with equipment and
resources, needing volume, can proceed along the lines
taken by Robert Kingery at New York Public; to reproduce
photographically the entry in PW or BPR for order information, temporary catalog cards, and, possibly, for permanent
catalog cards. When the "cataloger's camera" is perfected
and priced within reach of all, these benefits will be available to all libraries. In the meantime, a smaller public library can obtain the advantages of the order-cataloging information appearing on LC proof cards, without spending the
approximately $85.00 or so for the cards.

It would be most beneficial, but probably difficult, to
include also in the entries in the BPR, subject headings
(Sears?) of a nature more suitable for a small general public library than are the Library of Congress subject headings. Just as cooperation with the Library of Congress produced LC subject headings and Dewey classification numbers,
could cooperation with another agency provide for the inclusion of such subject headings? It should not be too difficult
however, to include LC classification numbers as an aid to
those libraries not using Dewey. This is not as important

in the public library field as in college and university libraries, but nevertheless should be done to increase the potential of the BPR.

Although the official report of the "Cataloging in Source" experiment seems to have once more turned this dream into an hallucination, it is still worth considering the BPR in relation to CIS as pertains to public libraries. If Library of Congress classification numbers are included in the entries in BPR, the information available from both sources, BPR-CIS, would be essentially the same. The continued omission of LC classification numbers in the BPR would leave this information available only under CIS and certainly points to the need, especially in the research library, for CIS.

The information necessary for order-cataloging coordination in a library would be available in PW sooner than under CIS and at about the same time in the BPR and CIS. If a public library participates in the "Greenaway Plan" or by some other method obtains books pre-publication, the balance would swing the other way and CIS would be the more important source. A catalog card photographically produced from the BPR or CIS would have a much neater format by the latter, although the former would include an annotation, a feature very helpful to some public libraries. The BPR anticipates listing 15,000 titles in 1960, while LC estimates it would process 30,000 titles a year in a permanent, full scale CIS program. Thus, CIS has twice the potential of the BPR. This factor cannot be taken too lightly in weighing the relative merits of these two programs. At this stage of development it appears that the BPR and CIS would complement, not supplant, each other. The former serves as a means of quickly supplying vital order-cataloging data; the latter not only permits, with the "cataloger's camera," the quick and economical production of catalog cards, but also supplies order-cataloging information for twice as many titles.

The BPR will cover all books listed in PW. This is all books of 49 or more pages, excluding the cover, plus any hard bound books. However, it does not include many government publications, some imports, nor much of what is not distributed through normal book trade channels. While this is a definite drawback in making the BPR a "complete" bibliographical tool, it is not as much of a hindrance in the public library (except large research) as in others. This limitation is probably insurmountable under the present organization of the BPR. It is to be hoped however, that the editors will eliminate the other fore-mentioned deficiencies; lack of LC classification numbers and an index cumulative month to month; and investigate the possibilities of providing headings usable by the general public library.

The use of the BPR in public libraries, especially as pertains to technical processes, will be limited only by the imagination of the librarians themselves. --George N. Hartje, Supervisor, Technical Services, St. Louis Public Library.

From the School Library

At the outset it should be stated that the usefulness and relative cheapness of this service are incontestable. Whether it is the answer to all cataloging problems for school librarians is another matter.

The advertising for the new publication stated five reasons for subscribing to the BPR:

"Miss none of the books being published in your field" and "Save time by looking only under the subjects that interest you" are good arguments for the specialist; but if there ever were a "generalist" in the library profession, it is the school librarian whose interests are as broad as those of a small public librarian, whose subject fields include all branches of knowledge, and, to a larger extent than is generally recognized, all levels of reading difficulty. For us, using BPR for subject fields means using the whole periodical--all sixty-two pages of the third issue!

"Take care of cataloging as you select" brings up the whole messy problem of simplified classification and subject headings, simple brief cataloging as practiced in school libraries, and, most confusing of all, the growing tendency to use the-author-as-he-appears-on-the-title-page (or pseudonyms) in school and public library cataloging. Besides, in large school library systems with central cataloging, the librarian doesn't catalog and the central cataloger doesn't order; in this situation, BPR becomes a useful adjunct but no more helpful in its way than the ALA Booklist.

"Check back on books you have ordered from other selection media." Here, for a central cataloging office, is

the most valuable purpose of BPR: to verify call numbers
and subject headings, authors, illustrators, and series.

"Simplify ordering"--perhaps, but each library and
school system has its local tangle of red tape about ordering; and each librarian her own rooted habits about keeping
information on possible order cards, and she is not likely
to rely solely upon even the most useful new publication. In
school libraries a relatively small proportion of an order is
composed of current publications. Because a budget is never
large enough for all of the library needs and wear and tear
is excessive in a school library, perhaps 50-60 percent of
any school's order is for replacements, duplicates, and recent books perhaps published a year ago and only reviewed
within the current school year. The need for information
about books published within the month is less than in other
types of libraries.

The monthly form, with the very brief indexing by
author and title, means that the librarian will have to use
twelve different issues by 1961; a cumulated index seems
needed to make the tool as useful as the Booklist. Perhaps
we could dare to suggest inclusion of cross references from
pseudonyms to real names. But especially I wonder who is
ever going to classify that simple and rather popular book,
Landis Story of the U. S. Air Force Academy, in
358. 4071178856. (Sounds like a Social Security number.)
Typographical errors bring one up short; a sculptor might be
surprised to find Salt's Teaching Physical Education in the
Elementary School in 731. 7322 (sic) on page 29 of number 3.

School librarians not only use relatively simplified
classification (even the 8th edition of the Abridged Dewey is
modified in many systems), but they tend to use subject
headings out of Sears and the Reader's Guide when a new
subject arises, and to adapt them to curriculum uses. We
know that "True Books" and "First Books" are juvenile literature, but there is no quicker way to puzzle a child than to
add that subdivision to every subject in the catalog. That is
one reason why so few school libraries find LC cards useful, and why Wilson cards are relatively universal.

In spite of all this carping on details, BPR will prove
a useful aid if utilized in connection with existing tools and
with due regard for its peculiarities and complexities. It
probably cannot take the place of evaluative review periodicals for selection, and the cost will make it a luxury for the

individual school library. --Catharine Whitehorn, Cataloger, Central Cataloging Unit, Division of School Libraries, Baltimore Public Schools.

Savior and Nemesis

by John G. Veenstra   A "Letter to the editor" written when
the author was Director, Department
of Libraries, Universidad del Valle,
Cali, Colombia, S. A. He is now at the
University of Florida Library School,
Gainesville

From Library Journal 90:4650-2, November 1, 1965;
Reproduced by permission of R. R. Bowker and of
the author.

Far too little has been written in the literature of
Latin America about Libros en Venta and the importance
this book has for all of us. In a sense it has become a
savior for many libraries and librarians and a nemesis for
the bookseller. It has also become the indispensable guide
for reference and acquisitions work as well as a selection
guide for all faculty members.

In a world where books are published unpriced and
the costs are never clearly established or defined for the
public in general, the guide is necessary in purchasing any
books. Salesmen run rampant and publishers' sales forces
are overstaffed and each person works on a commission basis. Since publishing in most Latin American countries is
minimal, the majority of the books have to be purchased
from other countries, with Spain dominating the field. Since
nearly every major publisher of Spanish books has agents in
each country and these agents have exclusive contracts, the
prices can vary considerably from country to country. In
Colombia, for example, the cost for Aguilar books is generally twice the price in Spain. The same is true for books
of most publishers in Latin America and Spain.

Sometimes our joy tends to be sardonic with the visits of agents. As we discuss their prices and then lead
them to the nearest copy of Libros en Venta and show them
the list price, they insist that we have to buy our books
from them since they are exclusive agents. The solution is
to buy through booksellers in the different countries and thus
obtain the books at list price. As we explain this to the
booksellers, they become somewhat crestfallen, but so far

505

all have accepted with understanding our need to purchase at best price.   In fact this system has caused so much dissension among book agents in Colombia, there is some hope they will revise downwards their extremely high prices. Their gains must be tremendous since they receive the books at a discount from list price and sell the books at 150 percent to 200 percent over list price.

For our faculty and students Libros en Venta has also been very well received.   Various professors have used the subject guide to find out what is available in Spanish, and whenever we hear the gripe that there is nothing available in Spanish, we are pleased to be able to show them Libros en Venta.

The Universidad del Valle has recently established a faculty of education.   In selecting a basic list of books available in education, Libros en Venta was indispensable. We also are using this bibliography in all areas to better our collection.   In fact we have substantially reduced the high percentage of books purchased in English, much to the relief of our students and faculty.   Still, the average remains about 50/50 Spanish books and English books.

At the same time, I would be remiss in not mentioning the use made of the magazine Fichero Bibliografico Hispanoamericano as a supplement to Libros en Venta.   Each issue is checked by our professors and our acquisitions section and new material purchased.   To keep us current, this magazine in combination with Libros en Venta make a pair that should be in every library in Latin America.

50 Years of Service to Libraries

by Edna V. Vanek

Miss Vanek is almost "Miss Booklist;" she has been on the staff since 1942 and Editor since 1952

From ALA Bulletin 49:13-14+ January 1955; Reprinted by permission of the Editor, ALA Bulletin, Chicago

This month, January 1955, The Booklist observes its fiftieth anniversary of publication and fifty years of service to libraries. Originally published eight times a year, The Booklist has grown to twenty-three issues a year and has increased steadily in circulation until it has over 12,000 subscribers in 1955. Through its widespread use it has become one of the best-known of the many publications of the American Library Association.

Founded by the Publishing Board of the Association in January 1905, The Booklist has throughout its fifty years of publication maintained the purpose for which it was created: to be "a current buying list of recent books with brief notes designed to assist librarians in selection."

From the thousands of books published annually, The Booklist selects those which in content and style are suitable for library purchase.

The method of selection used by The Booklist is one of its distinctive features. Although the reading, final selection, and annotating of books are done by The Booklist staff at ALA Headquarters, the selection of the books listed is made to a large extent with the collaboration of a group of practicing librarians--specialists working in book selection for adults, young people, and children in public and school libraries in various parts of the United States and Canada. These cooperating librarians are sent a weekly checklist comprised of books received from publishers by The Book-list office during the current week. By their votes and comments the librarians indicate those books which, in their opinion, should be listed in The Booklist as suitable for library purchase.

From the beginning The Booklist has been intended primarily as an aid for the small or medium-sized library. To help the smallest, or those libraries most limited in funds, The Booklist staff makes for each issue a more selective listing, "Suggested for the Small Library," of those titles which, in their opinion, most libraries will benefit by having. While all books listed in The Booklist are recommended for library use, the selection is not intended to be a list of books that every library should buy nor a list giving a balanced subject selection in each issue.

Changes in the content of The Booklist reflect various aspects of library development. The Booklist endeavors to anticipate or to keep abreast of developments and to fill the resulting needs. One of the earlier developments--that of service to younger readers--was recognized from the beginning by a separate listing of books for children. Indication of grade or interest level was added soon, reflecting the libraries' awareness of the need to draw finer distinctions in children's capacity to read. In 1921, when interest in school libraries was growing and The Booklist was endorsed as a book selection aid by the Library Department of the National Education Association and the National Council of Teachers of English, The Booklist initiated a special high school list. Unannotated lists for high school use grew into annotated lists of books for young people as public libraries made separate collections for teen agers. In 1946 a separate section of books for young people was established in The Booklist, giving full recognition to the growing literature for teen agers but with the main emphasis on the careful selection of adult books for young people.

Over the years additional sections: Forthcoming Books, U. S. Government Documents, Free and Inexpensive Material, and Series and Editions have become regular features of The Booklist, each separate listing having been started to help simplify the librarian's selection.

Recent lists of foreign books are not an innovation. As early as 1907 a note called attention to a list of German books, and special lists of foreign books have been an intermittent feature for many years, interrupted by war, and perhaps occasionally by waning interest, but provided whenever the need was voiced and conditions permitted.

Special subject bibliographies have also been a periodic feature. One of the earliest, in November 1905, was a fourteen-page "Christmas Bulletin." Others in more recent years have been on public personnel, mental health, photography, and books of Canada.

Even the index to The Booklist reflects changes made to give greater service to libraries. The annual author, title, and subject index, initiated in 1923, replaced the author, title annual index dating back to the first volume. Each issue now contains an author, title, and subject index in response to requests from subscribers. When finances permit, The Booklist hopes to fill the recurring demand for more frequent cumulations of the index within each volume.

The appearance like the content of The Booklist has been altered at intervals in the interests of timeliness and functionalism. The new format of the January 1, 1955 issue is the fifth for The Booklist. Its original small size was stoutly defended for its convenience for carrying in men's pockets and ladies' handbags but in spite of protests the size increased in 1917. In 1927 and again in 1940 the entire format was redesigned. The 1955 design brings a new cover, and a more flexible makeup.

Realizing the limitations of time and staff--especially in the small library--the ALA Publishing Board helpfully included cataloging information in the first issue of The Booklist. Decimal classification, subject headings, and Library of Congress card numbers have always been given. The cataloging information given now in every entry in The Booklist is intended for use by libraries of all sizes. The Booklist uses Library of Congress cards for authority on form of entry and repeats subject headings and decimal classification as given on L. C. cards whenever the information is available. The latter are modified for some entries in the Children's Books section. The practice of including full classification and subject headings for adult entries is designed to permit libraries to modify the data to suit their individual needs. Since September 1953 The Booklist has also noted all the titles listed for which H. W. Wilson Company catalog cards are made. This service is intended especially for school libraries and the smaller public libraries.

The Booklist is a self-supporting publication operating within the Publishing Department of the American Library Association. Like numerous libraries and library projects The Booklist was started with the help of a grant from Andrew Carnegie. In 1902 Mr. Carnegie gave to the American Library Association the sum of $100,000 to be used for bibliographical and library aids. With the income from this gift the ALA Publishing Board founded The Booklist.

The Booklist is today, after fifty years of publication, only one of the many services carried on for libraries by the American Library Association. As a publication of the Association it is administered by the Executive Board and its advisory committee, the ALA Editorial Committee, through the Publishing Department. The Executive Board, like the ALA Publishing Board, which founded The Booklist, and The Booklist staff hope to keep The Booklist responsive to the needs and interests of libraries and of continued service.

From The Booklist 61:401-2, January 1, 1965;
Reprinted by permission of the Publications Office,
ALA

Sixty years ago the American Library Association
Publishing Board, "with the cooperation of many librarians,"
published the first issue of the A. L. A. Booklist, "a current
buying list of recent books with brief notes designed to assist
librarians in selection."

Ten years ago when we observed its fiftieth anniversary The Booklist had 12,000 subscribers. Now as we observe its sixtieth anniversary we are pleased to report that
the magazine has not only enlarged its title and scope as a
result of a merger with Subscription Books Bulletin, and increased its coverage of new books, but that its circulation
has increased considerably. The January 1965 issues will go
to more than 27,000 subscribers.

The steady increase in subscriptions through the years
reflects the growth in number of all types of libraries--pub-
lic, school, and college. The greatest increase is in school
libraries since service to children was the first area in
which libraries met the challenge of the population explosion,
and more school libraries have been started than any other
type. Over half of the subscribers to The Booklist and Subscription Books Bulletin today are school libraries.

To keep pace with the increase in U. S. book production and the needs of libraries for more materials at all age
levels the "Booklist" has increased its editorial and reviewing
staff to 10 professional members; the "Subscription Books
Bulletin" assistant and the advertising manager are in addition to the editorial and reviewing staff.

All the editorial and reviewing staff have had experience in school or public libraries, or both, and all are
therefore able to evaluate books in terms of subject needs

and reading interests. To keep themselves in touch with
trends in reference needs and reading interests and with curriculum developments as well as to benefit from the experience and judgment of other book selection experts the "Booklist" staff obtain the opinions of librarians actually engaged
in book selection for adults, young adults, and children in
various parts of the country. These opinions are obtained in
two ways: by sending a weekly list of the books received in
the "Booklist" office for review to the consultants, who indicate by symbol or comment their opinions of whatever books
they have seen, and by receiving from several large libraries the weekly or bi-weekly record of their buying.
Separate buying lists are received for the three age groups
just as the "voting lists" or opinion sheets sent by the "Booklist" office are directed to specialists in the respective areas.
These opinions from the field are recorded in the "Booklist"
office and are taken into consideration by the reviewing staff
when the books are being evaluated. The opinions on children's books and books for young adults are especially valuable for keeping the reviewers alert to current needs and
interests of children and young adults in school and public
libraries.

     The editorial and reviewing staff, those working with
adult books, children's books, and books for young adults,
follow a proved evaluative procedure that has evolved over
the years. About 45 percent of the current annual 26,000-
to-27,000 American book title output is received for consideration in the "Booklist" office. All books are examined by
the staff, the majority are carefully read and evaluated, and,
if a book is selected for review in the "Booklist" and thus
recommended for library buying, an annotation is written for
it. The "Booklist" editorial staff makes the decision as to
whether or not a book is reviewed in the "Booklist." About
35 percent of the books received and considered are reviewed in the "Booklist." Each book is evaluated on its own
merit, for authenticity, style, and achievement of purpose.
Factors also taken into consideration are its presentation of
a point of view, the qualifications of the author, the appeal
or lack of appeal of the subject for a general audience, comparison with standard or other recent books on the subject,
and the limitations in use it may have in a library.

     Although "Subscription Books Bulletin" is now, after
its merger with The Booklist in September, 1956, an in-
separable part of The Booklist and Subscription Books Bulletin, it has retained its distinctive processes of evaluation

and reviewing. The 35-member Subscription Books Committee represents general reference and various special subject
areas and all types of libraries and services including those
for children and young adults. The committee is responsible
for the content and writing of the reviews. The chairman
selects the titles to be reviewed and assigns them, and the
entire committee participates in the preparation of the reviews. The secretary of the committee is a member of
The Booklist and Subscription Books Bulletin staff and is responsible for channeling the reviews and materials among
the committee and for submitting the review for publication.

The Subscription Books Committee's reviews may recommend or not recommend a book for purchase. These
carefully detailed and documented evaluations have not only
influenced the standards of subscription publishing but have
also gained the respect of both librarians and publishers.

Like all other institutions today The Booklist and
Subscription Books Bulletin is affected by mechanization. Although the reviewing is not yet done by machines, the subscription records have been converted to an IBM punch-card
process for more efficient service.

Mechanical aids, new forms of teaching, and new
methods of communication and storage of knowledge are features of this age that no one would underestimate, but their
effectiveness is still dependent to a large extent on the
printed word. And books are still a convenient vehicle for
the printed word. As long as books are basic, The Booklist and Subscription Books Bulletin looks forward to helping
librarians by serving as a selective guide to the new books.

CHOICE: Books for College Libraries, Its Origin,
Development, and Future Plans

by Richard K. Gardner

A paper read before the College and University Librarians Section, Southeastern Library Association, October 30, 1964 at which time Mr. Gardner was the founding editor of Choice; he is now Lecturer, Case Western Reserve School of Library Science

From Southeastern Librarian 15:69-75, Summer 1965; Reprinted by permission of Cora Paul Bomar, President, Southeastern Library Association.

On October 1, 1958 Verner Clapp, President of the Council on Library Resources, wrote to David Clift, Executive Director of ALA, that there seemed to be a need for a book selection medium for college libraries. He remarked that the Shaw list had served this purpose but was outdated. "The extent of the need is indicated by the avidity with which the Lamont list was bought up. It has given way to the Michigan list; but the Michigan list is available only to those who wish to purchase a set of cards or a microfilm thereof." (And I might add, at prohibitive cost.) "In all these cases a large investment of work was made only to incur the immediate commencement of obsolescence."

In April of 1959 a two-day conference was convened in Chicago at which some 30 librarians and publishers met to discuss the problems involved. It seemed to be the consensus of this meeting that both a retrospective basic list and a current selection service were needed. No agreement could be reached on which was needed the most or which should be started first, although Leon Carnovsky remarked:

As I look back, I think that, if at the time the Shaw list was published there had been established a serial to do the temporary evaluating and the listing of books, we would not have any problems today. Looking into the future, we have the promise of a new list. Where do we go from here? I think attention must be paid to the listing, evaluation, and recommendation of contemporary titles to college libraries. This is a continuing problem that a new list will not solve.

Following this 1959 meeting, committees were established to explore further these needs and in November of 1961 a grant of $150,000 was made by the Council on Library Resources for the publication of a book selection service at the college library level. Unfortunately, another year and a half passed before someone foolhardy enough to take on the job of editor was found, and it was not until July of 1963 that an office for what eventually came to be known as CHOICE: Books for College Libraries was set up on the campus of Wesleyan University in Connecticut.

II

The purpose of CHOICE, as has been stated many times, is to assist college libraries with a book and periodical budget of less than $30,000 a year with their book selection. This includes 72 per cent of all academic libraries. Actually, I feel rather strongly that our main goal should be to help those with even smaller budgets, primarily the 60 percent of college libraries that have less than $20,000 a year to spend. We hope that university libraries who serve an undergraduate student body, public libraries who also serve a student clientele, and high school libraries, particularly in those schools which offer courses for advanced college placement will also find CHOICE useful. In fact, it is absolutely essential that we have other subscribers than just colleges and universities, as the 2,000 American colleges and universities do not represent a large enough market to support a magazine such as CHOICE, and we cannot always depend on subsidies from foundations.

It is an appalling fact that in the period between 1959 and 1963 there was a 73 per cent increase in the number of books published in the U.S. To cull through the more than 25,000 books a year now being published for those of primary interest to undergraduate collections is a tremendous

task. If CHOICE is going to publish reviews of as many
books as possible the reviews must be fairly brief. It is
perhaps fairer to call them annotations. We are very much
interested in having our reviewers place a book in relation
to others already available on the same subject. In order
to obtain such evaluations, we must have people who are
subject experts, who know well the bibliography of their own
fields. For this reason, we have turned to the academic
community, and more specifically, to professors teaching at
the undergraduate level, for our reviewers.

While we attempt to be as current in our reviewing
as possible, this is not our primary goal or consideration.
If we were to publish reviews prior to or on the date of
publication, we would have to do more of our reviewing from
galleys. Since there are many changes made at the galley
stage, particularly in non-fiction books, we and our reviewers are reluctant to use them. We must, therefore, wait
until review copies of the finished book become available.
Thus, we will never be as prompt in our reviewing as the
Library Journal or the ALA Booklist. On the other hand,
since the majority of our reviews appear within two or three
months of publication date, we are far in advance of the
scholarly journals, many of whom do not review books until
a year, sometimes even two years after the date of publication.

III

I thought it would be interesting if I described how
we work in the editorial offices of CHOICE and how we have
gone about setting up the magazine. At the present time,
the editorial staff consists of an editor; two assistant editors, one for subscriptions, promotion, advertising, and production and the other for reviewing; and two editorial assistants, who help edit the huge number of reviews which
we are having to cope with every month. We also have a
clerical staff of five.

Our first task on establishing the editorial offices
was to recruit our reviewers. We set about this by sending out requests to college librarians all over the country
who were known to us, asking them for the names of faculty
members in their schools who did a good job of book selection for them and who might be interested in participating in
a nation-wide book selection project. We made it clear that
we wanted undergraduate teachers, and, therefore, initially,

we did not solicit reviewers from the big universities. As
time has passed, however, we have acquired a number of
university faculty through recommendations from various librarians and also due to the fact that some of the college
professors have moved on to new jobs in universities. Furthermore, announcements about CHOICE which appeared in
AAUP Bulletin, Scholarly Books in America, and on the education page of a Sunday edition of the New York Times
brought in volunteers from all over the country. We now
find that many of our reviewers are recommending their
friends to us. A few librarians who felt that their faculty
were just too busy to participate in such an enterprise have
been surprised at the response of the faculty.

We are, in general, using younger faculty just out of
graduate school who still have the bibliography of their fields
very fresh in their minds. Many of these instructors find
that reviewing for us is a good way to build up their professional libraries, and although we can make no payment for
their services other than the book that they have reviewed,
we are able, from time to time, to give them extra copies
of books which come to us or copies of works too advanced
for undergraduate libraries. Since we only ask for a very
brief review, we have told them that they are free to go on
and do a much lengthier one for a scholarly journal if they
have such an opportunity.

We give our reviewers specific instructions about the
length and style of the reviews that we want from them. We
ask that they be very specific in their comments and that, if
it is at all possible, they compare the book with a work already published. This they seem to be doing very well. To
date, we have recruited 1, 470 reviewers. We are now in
the process of weeding out a few who have been unable to
meet our deadlines or who have not come up to our standards. A few have also withdrawn of their own free will because of pressure of other duties. Therefore, we continue
to be interested in new reviewers and I want to urge all of
you to submit names of interested faculty members to us at
any time. While certain colleges such as Birmingham-
Southern, Sewanee, Randolph-Macon, and Agnes Scott are
well represented on our reviewing staff, many of the southern schools are not and we would like to have a wider representation from this area.

Another of our first steps upon opening the editorial
offices was to establish contact with all of the major pub-

lishers in America. During the fall of 1963, I personally
called on over sixty of the large publishing houses in New
York, Boston, and Philadelphia to inform them of what we
were planning and to request review copies from them. The
cooperation of the publishers has been extremely good. The
Association of American University Presses and the American Book Publishers Council sent out notices to all their
members asking for their full cooperation in this new venture since they felt it would be as valuable to publishers as
it was to librarians. To date, only one major publisher has
failed to supply review copies--a technical book publisher
who is primarily interested in classroom adoption of textbooks rather than library sales.

        In visiting the publishers, I set forth our reviewing
policies, which are these: we are primarily interested in
books for student rather than faculty use. Thus, we are not
interested in certain advanced texts, particularly in the science and technology fields. With the humanities and social
sciences, it is much more difficult to draw the line, and we
probably tend to publish reviews of more books that are suitable only at the senior or first year graduate level than in
other areas. We are omitting certain subjects, notably
gardening, home economics, and vocational literature. We
are including business and elementary engineering because
these subjects are taught in many junior colleges and in som
liberal arts institutions. For the present we are reviewing
only American publications, plus those of the University of
Toronto and McGill University Presses, both of whom are
members of the Association of American University Presses.
We are interested in trade books, texts, and reprints. In
the latter case, whether we review the book or not depends
largely on how long the book has been out-of-print and
whether we think it needs a new evaluation. Some of the
most favorable comments coming to us have been about our
reviews of reprints. We consider paperback books for review on the same basis as hardbound books. That is, if it
is an original, it receives just as much consideration as if
it were in hard covers. If it is a reprint, it all depends o
how long it has been out-of-print.

        Once the books are received in the editorial offices,
we examine each one of them and weed out the titles which
obviously are of no interest for college libraries. If there
is any doubt in our mind, we send the book out for review.
We have classified our reviewers by subject field on punche
cards and thus are able to match the book with a qualified

reviewer quite quickly. We find that it is much easier to
assign books to reviewers who have been very specific about
what they want than to the person who says he will review
anything in American literature, for example. The fact that
we have had, to date, very fine relations with almost every
one of our reviewers, I think is largely due to the fact that
we have been very careful not to send a man a book which
is the least bit outside his area of interest. We plan on a
four-week schedule, one week for the book to reach the reviewer and three weeks for the writing of the review. Unfortunately, the U. S. mails are not all that they should be,
and we find books taking as long as four weeks to get from
Connecticut to New Jersey. We provide the reviewer with
a self-addressed, stamped envelope in which to return his
review so that he does not even have to pay for a postage
stamp.

Once the reviews arrive back in the editorial offices,
they are culled once again, and those reviews which state
that a book is of no value for a college library collection
are filed away and are not published. All the other reviews
are edited for publication. This type of work has proven to
be the most time consuming of all our operations, although
as time passes, more and more reviewers are attempting to
be as brief as possible and at the same time contribute as
much information as they can. As most of you are aware,
we publish both pro and con reviews, unlike the ALA Booklist. Perhaps there are not as many negative reviews as
we might like, due to lack of space, but if we feel that there
is going to be wide publicity about a particular book which
our reviewer feels is very bad, or if the book is an expensive one where a great deal of money could be wasted, we
will attempt to find space for a negative evaluation. We also attempt to publish the review when it suggests other titles
which may be purchased in place of the badly reviewed book.

IV

I should like to make some comments on the functions
of CHOICE and how it might be used in the book selection
process of a library. Some of these things I may have said
earlier but I think it is important to summarize them here.
We are attempting to:

1. Provide a selection service designed specifically
for use by undergraduate college libraries (but which we also
feel should be of value to all libraries serving college age

students and the increasing number of public library patrons who are college graduates and who need to continue with their education in this day and age).

2. Provide a current service that selects publications in relation to a basic collection by means of comparative reviewing.

3. Aid in increasing the proportion of quality publications in college and community libraries by insuring that no important publication is overlooked.

4. Aid in preventing inferior publications from being purchased.   (The money saved on this item alone should pay for a subscription to CHOICE.)

5. Provide a reminder of the need to purchase new editions of the basic reference serial publications.

6. Assist librarians in ordering in fields in which they are not qualified by educational background or experience.

7. Assist in the selection of books that do not fall within the province of one single teaching department (for example, city planning).

8. Aid in preventing extreme over-emphasis or neglect in any one subject field and to substitute for faculty advice in departments uninterested in library book selection.

9. Provide an authoritative yardstick by which the librarian can measure the quality of his faculty's as well as his own book selection.

We already have indications from several campuses that CHOICE is assisting in developing a new cooperative relationship between the library and the faculty. It is helping to secure increased interest and recognition of the library by the administration, faculty and students, and thus is creating a considerable improvement in the image and status of the librarians on their campuses. With this improved image it should help to develop an increasingly important role for the librarian and his staff in book selection on campuses where the faculty has heretofore almost completely controlled library book buying.

I must emphasize very strongly, however, that CHOICE should not be used as a rigid buying guide. We cover no English publications so no college librarian should neglect his reading of the Times Literary Supplement. Other well-known selection tools also have their place in selection activities. All libraries must tailor their collections to the needs of their curriculum, students and faculty. No two schools are exactly alike and this fact must never be lost sight of in building up a library's collection.

V

There have been many questions coming in to the editorial offices about our rather high subscription price, particularly in view of the fact that we have received a grant from the Council on Library Resources. I must say that the approximately 1, 900 subscriptions which we have to date are far from the 4, 000 or 5, 000 needed to make this a self-supporting venture. The grant money is fast being used up to make up the deficit. In fact, we will have used over half of it by the end of this fiscal year. This is $100, 000 a year operation and we have felt $20 to be a fair price considering all the work that is being done. Any reduction in subscription price would mean a reduction in the number of pages in the magazine and, therefore, in the number of books we could evaluate each year. (We started out with the intention of reviewing 2, 500 books a year. We will, undoubtedly, have reviewed over 3, 000 by the end of Volume One. I would estimate that next year we will review nearer to 3, 500, if we keep on at our present rate.)

At a recent meeting of the Editorial Board, it was voted to institute a multiple subscription rate so that more libraries could subscribe to multiple copies for distribution to interested faculty or staff members. Thus, beginning with Volume Two, a second or third subscription costs only $10 each. The initial subscription price will remain at $20, but two subscriptions cost only $30 instead of $40, and three subscriptions $40 instead of $60.

We have also been asked if it would not be possible to publish reviews on cards as does Library Journal. Unfortunately, this is just not economically feasible until we get more subscribers. In this regard, may I ask you to do a little promotion for the magazine among your friends in the public or school library fields. Those in these fields who have begun to subscribe are very enthusiastic about the mag-

azine. An example of this occurred just three weeks ago
when, at a meeting of the New York State Library Association, Katherine O'Brien, the Head of Adult Services in the
branches of the New York public library system, remarked
that she could not get along without CHOICE and was recommending subscriptions for all her branch libraries. Note
that this was not the 42nd Street Reference Library that she
was referring to, but the many smaller branches scattered
throughout the boroughs. Similar comments have come from
other public library subscribers, but we need to become
much better known to public librarians than we are at present. Anything you can do to help will be much appreciated.

VI

I know many of you may be interested in what plans
we have for the future. At the moment, our main attention
is turned to the development of a retrospective basic list
along the lines of the old Shaw or Lamont lists. Originally,
it was planned that once CHOICE became established, the
staff would be expanded and that work would begin on developing such a retrospective list. This would undoubtedly require additional foundation support, but ALA felt that this
could be obtained. Once this retrospective list was published, CHOICE would be used as the basis of cumulations
to the basic list much in the same manner as Winchell's
Guide to Reference Books has been kept up-to-date.

However, some months ago we learned that the University of California, which has been in the process of building up collections of some 50,000 monographs and 15,000
volumes of periodicals for three new campuses, was interested in publishing the shelf list of this collection. Since
this would, undoubtedly, be available for publication much
sooner than any list we could draw up ourselves, it seemed
to us that we ought to try to work out some method of cooperation with the University. We were very concerned that
any list published not be the work of just one faculty, as
most of the faults in the Lamont list can be attributed to the
fact that it represents the point of view of one school only.
Thus, we proposed to the University of California that each
section of their list be reviewed by teachers at other undergraduate institutions around the country. They readily
agreed to this and the work is now about 60 per cent complete. We have used professors at a wide variety of institutions, all of them known to us at CHOICE as extremely
knowledgeable in their fields. In a few cases, we have been

able to use librarians who possessed doctorates in a subject field. An example of this is Dr. Helen Sears, the librarian of Wells College, who started out her career as a professor of Spanish and who continues to teach in addition to her duties as librarian.

If all goes well, this list should be ready for publication within the next year, and at that point, CHOICE will take over responsibility for the publication of supplements. We would anticipate that these would be published at three to four year intervals and would be a culling out of the best books reviewed in the monthly issues of CHOICE.

The Editorial Board of CHOICE is also considering expansion of the magazine into other areas such as foreign publications, particularly in literature; the evaluation of new periodicals, of audio-visual materials, and of English language publications issued outside North America. However, any expansion of the magazine will have to await an increase in subscribers since the present editorial staff is already swamped in just trying to keep up with American publications. We do welcome suggestions and comments at any time from our readers and I can assure you they will be given the most serious consideration.

"The New Shaw" or "UC/NC"

by Sol M. Malkin   Editor, owner and publisher of
                                    <u>Antiquarian Bookman</u> (Newark,
                                    N. J.) and himself bookman
                                    extraordinary

From <u>Antiquarian Bookman</u> 39:2378, 2380, June 5,
1968; Reprinted by permission of the author

Voigt, Melvin V. & Treyz, Joseph H. editors and
compilers. <u>Books for College Libraries</u>: A selected list of approximately 53, 400 titles based on
the initial selection made for the University of
California's New Campuses Program and selected
with the assistance of college teachers, librarians,
and other advisers, lg 8vo [or sm 4to or 8-1/2 by
11"]. ix, 1056 p. $45. American Library Associ-
ation (50 E. Huron, Chicago 60611).

It was sometime in 1961 that rumors first began flying in the book world that a gigantic acquisition program was
in the making at California to provide basic library needs
for 3 new UC campuses (Irvine, Santa Cruz, and San Diego).
Soon thereafter, the master list, which eventually contained
over 50, 000 titles (some 60, 000 vols in all), was being referred to as "The New Shaw"... Reference was of course to
the long outdated Charles B. Shaw's List of Books for College Libraries (ALA 1931). (Just as some bookdealers delight in annotating their catalogs with [often erroneous] assertions, "Not in Sabin, Evans, Church, etc, " library specialists have almost always proudly noted "In Shaw")...

[This is a shame, because the present work can--
and deserves to--be judged on its own merits. The fault is
perhaps the editors: the title does not lend itself to any
simple acronym or initialism! Voigt-Treyz is just too much
a mouthful--try that on your piccolo! Surely, librarians engaged in so basic a work should have simpler names, or

first pick a catchier acronym and then make the title to
suit! BCL and/or V-T just doesn't click; perhaps UC/NC
is more euphonious!]

The work itself is a project developed by the ALA
Editorial Committee in close cooperation with the librarians
at the U of California (San Diego). The list itself was developed from the initial selections made for 3 new undergraduate libraries in UC's New Campuses program, under
the direction of Melvin J. Voigt (UC/SD university librarian)
and Joseph H. Treyz (formerly head of the NC program,
and now asst. librarian at U of Michigan).

There have of course been many other lists between
Shaw and this UC/NC, notably Harvard's Lamont, Michigan,
Princeton, etc. but all were essentially "parochial" for specific needs. The present work, however, does not claim to
be "a list of the best books" or a "basic list for any college
library" but rather a "list of monographs designed to support
a college teaching program that depends heavily upon the library, and to supply the necessary materials for term papers and suggested and independent outside reading. It contains some information on all fields of knowledge, including
areas not in a college curriculum. Within the limits of the
allocation, each area contains some scholarly monographs
for the use of the faculty and exceptional undergraduate students. The collection is expected to satisfy independent intellectual curiosity (and recreational interests) of students
and faculty."

This proud purpose has been most admirably fulfilled
by UC/NC--and we're getting to like that initialism better
than ever, and even if no one else uses it, we'll continue
because it will often so be referred to in AB! To be sure,
every bookman has his own favorite titles and abominations.
To be fair, UC/NC has almost all our pets and few of our
hates. But it is idle to quarrel with omissions or inclu-
sions. There are limitations even within a thousand pages.
Thus, "the list contains no periodicals, newspapers, music
scores, phonograph records, microfilms, slides or pictures.
Aside from bibliographies there are few pamphlets. General
college textbooks are omitted except those which are outstanding because of their content or bibliographies."

Bookmen will have no quarrel with method of selection of titles, which were made "without regard to their
availability from publishers, and approximately one third of

those included are out of print. [Emphasis is ours: this
means 17, 800 o. p. out of 53, 400! This corresponds to Lee
Ash's o. p. graph in the July 4, 1966 AB, p68-69]. Usually
the hard-cover edition was listed, even if it was out of print
and a paperback edition was in print. The paperbacks included are primarily those that have been published only in
this form. Out-of-print titles are not indicated, because of
rapid changes which would make such information obsolete in
a short time. "*

[*Oh, how we disagree, and we do think that most
bookmen will certainly quarrel with this assertion. Triple-
X UC/NC presumably first sent out its special lists to publishers and wholesalers, later to library dealers and specialists, etc, and then as almost a final resort to AB for
the many o. p. books it still had not been able to obtain, and
we were most thankful that we had not been deluged with full-
page lists of many thousands of titles. (This has always
been AB's policy and advice to librarians: try the regular
sources first and use AB only as last resort). When we
first heard of plans for publication of complete list, a "New
Shaw," etc. we urged that o. p. titles be indicated by asterisk, dagger, or any kind of distinguishing symbol, and we
received the same reply quoted in above statement. When
Bob Vosper visited AB's quiet madhouse, we begged him to
use whatever influence he had as UCLA librarian and as
ALA president to have such a symbol used for o. p. titles.
That was our Big Misteak [sic]. We know of the close cooperation among the UC libraries but we had underestimated
the rugged independence of each campus!... And so now many
thousands of publishers and reprinters, wholesalers, library
specialists and general dealers will have to check many
thousands of titles to find out whether the books are o. p. or
in print... Despite all the hullabaloo about antiquarian reprints, this is only a minute fraction of all the o. p. titles.
How much easier it would have been for every bookman to
have a simple symbol for o. p. titles! And how much easier
it would have been for bookmen to check a much smaller
number of titles as to their current availability...

[Another important defect in UC/NC is that work de-
liberately goes only up through 1963 pub dates, although we
believe the original lists went up to, if not also including,
1965. Reason is simple--even though fallacious, ALA also
publishes ACRL's current book-review monthly, Choice ($20
sub), which was "launched" in March of 1964 (with CLR subsidy) and has submerged since then with more than its alot-

ted 3 times. [Choice has also reprinted as a "special supplement" its "Opening Day Collection" ($5) of a piddling 1776 books "which should be on the shelves of every academic library when it opens its doors" [sic]... Librarians require professional standards... Bookmen should demand equal professional standards from librarians]

Above are not quibbles, but definite defects in a most important and useful tool in every bookman's armamentarium. We cannot think of a single library, from the largest to the smallest, that will not profit from its constant use, even in the unlikely circumstance that every book listed was available in the library. We cannot think of a single dealer, from the top library specialist to the smallest dealer, who will not profit from its constant use, for sale in shop or by catalog. Even the seemingly high price is illusory: it comes to less than a tenth of a cent a title--surely a minute cost for any bookman!

We must also note that titles have been listed by the Library of Congress classification, which is becoming increasingly popular with all bookmen. [Dewey system may not be dead, but it is certainly moribund]. A UC/NC title is entered only once; we noted no cross-references. The list is indexed only by author and subject, and not by title. (Subject index was weak, and users are advised to refer to LC Catalog Books: Subject). The "Z" section (bibliography and library science, etc) is necessarily limited and quite weak in many fields. [No Streeter Americana Beginnings!] Winchell (w/supplements) is much better, and it's time for a new ALA complete edition. Also needed is a new ALA ed of Hazeltine's Anniversaries and Holidays (1944), etc. We can personally testify that AB's Literary Anniversaries is one of the most carefully read and checked features. But this should be a job for ALA's 30,000-Odd librarians, not just for AB's "mere" 5,500 bookmen!

And now for the most pleasant part of our frank "trade" review. It's way past midnite, way past our deadline, mam has long since given up on us, and preparing for a full 24-hour day after a full 18-hour day, but we've been waiting for UC/NC for many months, and our review copy arrived only a few hours ago--in time for this issue, thanks to Jack Hagopian--and it was promptly delivered by our Newark P.O.--bless 'em, we're neighbors, just across the street, and AB is their favorite "client"--and we'll still be reading, checking, reminiscing over old favorites, and cluck-

ing over omitted pets, long after we've sent some 100 pages
of text down the chute--that's AB's secret:" our printer--
bless 'em all!--is on the ground floor and AB is the floor
above, and while we're getting our six hour sound sleep
they'll be working, and bright and early we'll have the proofs
even though only one eye will be open, t'other may make it
by noon...

       All kinds of encomia to bookmen--librarians Voigt and
Treyz! Est, est, est--to mix up our classics! (We only
regret that they felt impelled to omit symbols for o. p. titles
and to omit some titles from their original lists).   Honors
once more to Verner Clapp for the $45,000 CLR grant to
ALA to prepare and publish the list.   Unfortunately, we take
too much for granted LC's many services, including its processing dept which provided catalog cards or cataloging copy
without charge for the shingling of individual cards into page
form, ready for offset--not beautiful, but quite readable.   To
the hundreds of specialist librarians who worked on specific
lists all due honor.   If at times they allowed their preferences [and/or prejudices] to show, they were entitled...   To
the ALA Editorial Committee and ALA Publishing Dept, we
retract any unkind words we may have said in the past...
At long last, we have "The New Shaw"--or better UC/NC--
and all bookmen will be profoundly grateful.   To paraphrase
the slogan of The New York Times: "If you're not with it
[UC/NC], you're not in it"...

From Choice 4:797-8, October 1967; Reprinted by permission of Peter Doiron, Editor, Choice: Books for College Libraries, Middletown, Conn.

Voigt, Melvin J. and Joseph H. Treyz. Books for College Libraries: a Selected List of Approximately 53,400 titles Based on the Initial Selection Made for the University of California's New Campuses Program and Selected with the Assistance of College Teachers, Librarians, and Other Advisers. American Library Association, 1967. 1056 p 66-30781. 45.00

In this period of new college libraries and burgeoning older ones, bibliographic guidelines are needed. Books for College Libraries is a mandatory source. Begun in 1960 as the core collection (some 75,000 titles) for the four University of California's New Campuses and under the direction of Joseph Treyz, national publication along the lines of Michigan's undergraduate list was always in the future plans of Voigt and Treyz. In 1963-64, CHOICE was born as a periodical "New Shaw" with the hope it would contribute to a basic list. CHOICE and the New Campuses Program decided to cooperate on the venture. Treyz and the New Campuses people agreed to submit subject portions of the total 75,000 titles to subject specialists primarily recommended by CHOICE editors (some 37 CHOICE reviewers did the final consulting along with other selected authorities). Treyz and his able assistant, Miss Charlotte Oakes, again correlated matters and definitely assisted in the delicate book selection that arrived at 53,410 titles.

While the content creation of the "New Shaw" was going on, the American Library Association sought and obtained permission to print and publish this basic list from the Regents of the University of California.

(Supplements to Books for College Libraries are being investigated by CHOICE and its Editorial Board. Such periodical additions and revisions are necessary if the library profession is, indeed, to have a continuing "New Shaw. ")

This reviewing period was tedious. One rule of thumb was the list would cut off at January 1964 in order to tie in with CHOICE which began publication that year.

Published with the assistance of a $45,000 Council on Library Resources grant, the list is an adumbrated Library of Congress classification printed offset from shingled varityped cards. The entries cite author, title, edition, publishers, date, pagination, L. C. order number. Price or o. p. status is omitted. Titles include both English and foreign language publications.

Despite the magnitude and importance of this creative list to book selection, some faults do exist. First, the author and subject indices are not enough; a title index would be of great help to users accustomed to approaching catalogues by title. Also, some proofreading errors in the indices (both cite L. C. classification number, not page number) prevent rapid and easeful use. Second, the shingled columns are not consistently justified.

More important is the fact that this list, besides replacing bibliographies like Lamont, Michigan, or Julian Street, resurrects a truer base for liberal arts library collections. In the final analysis, Books for College Libraries represents no one school since its many consultants (revising some areas as much as 40 percent) refurbished it to the point of being more useful to more libraries on an interstate or inter-college level.

The subjects covered (Literature and Language-- 17,203 titles; History--10,006; Social Science--11,101; Religion, Philosophy and Psychology--4,779; Fine Arts-- 3,977; Science--5,083; General and Reference--1,261) lend undergraduate librarians an effective contemporary in developing and possibly welding their book collections. The small college library will be goaded onward and upward by the selections; the larger libraries will employ it as a value measure. Books for College Libraries also supports four-year schools expanding in special ways (e. g. Home Economics).

Invaluable is the incentive B. C. L. has instilled in the hearts of reprinters. Reprinters are scouring the entries for possible publications; trade houses are planning to reissue o. p. titles on their backlists. Carpings aside (o. p.'s not designated), Voigt and Treyz have influenced needed publishing, and libraries will prosper that much more.

Refinements of this basic list are already in order and supplements will serve as the necessary correctives so that the B. C. L. may continue to keep pace with changing fashion and scholarship. Books for College Libraries is a major publishing effort; all those associated with it merit gratitude from the library profession.

And Then There Were Three

by Mary K. Eakin

Formerly on the staff of the Children's Book Center, University of Chicago; now Librarian, Youth Collection, State College Library, Cedar Falls, Iowa

From Library Journal 91:424-8, September 15, 1966; Reprinted by permission of R. R. Bowker Company and the author.

Junior High School Library Catalog, Rachel Shor and Estelle A. Fidell, eds. 1st edition, H. W. Wilson Company, 1965. 768pp $20.

Junior High School age girls have sometimes been described as having a yo-yo in one pocket and a lipstick in the other; the same can be said for junior high boys, substituting a pocket comb for the lipstick. In like manner, the junior high school student's reading ranges from the very elementary to mature, adult writings, and it is this range which creates so much difficulty in compiling a booklist for junior high.

In the past, librarians have depended on the Children's Catalog and the Standard Catalog for High School Libraries as the basic tools for selection of books for grades seven through nine, and these were quite satisfactory in that they covered the entire range of books with any possible interest for junior high school students. The most frequent complaint was that neither list was entirely satisfactory alone, and the junior high school librarian was forced to use both volumes in order to build a well-rounded collection.

Now H. W. Wilson Company has published a third catalog, aimed at the junior high school library. As in the other two, the arrangement of this catalog is in three parts. Part I is a classified arrangement according to the Abridged

Dewey Decimal Classification, giving complete bibliographic
information about each book plus suggested subject headings.
Part II is an alphabetic index by author, title, subject and
analytical entries. Part III is a directory of publishers and
distributors. There are 3,278 entries for which full information is given. As in the other Wilson catalogs, entry is
by the author's name as it appears on the title page, with
see also references to other forms of the name or to pseudonyms used by the same author.

Of the 3,278 titles listed, approximately 26 percent
are not included in either Children's Catalog or Standard
Catalog for High School Libraries; 36 percent are in both;
14 percent are in Children's Catalog only, and 24 percent
are in Standard Catalog for High School Libraries only.

The 26 percent not found in the two earlier catalogs
represent, for the most part, works by writers of so-called
"teen-age" books, many of them of only average merit. It is
questionable how much value there is in listing multiple titles
by authors such as Joe Archibald, Rosamond DuJardin, Anne
Emery, and Walter Farley, at the expense of eliminating
titles by better but less prolific writers. The total coverage
is heavily geared to books published specifically for the junior high school level, with only a relatively few titles
stretching up into adult books or down into elementary grade
books. Even among the junior high books listed, the selection is extremely conservative. The librarian who depends
entirely on this selection aid will end up with a collection
that will offend few adults (school board members or parents)
and will satisfy or stimulate few students.

Apparently the editors had intended to produce a fairly selective list. In the preface, they say,

> Considerations of size and cost of the catalog and
> its supplements inevitably limit the total number of
> books which can be included... Furthermore, since
> the primary purpose of the catalog is to serve
> many thousands of very small schools and libraries
> which have few other book selection resources and
> often extremely limited budgets, and since it is
> essential to keep the catalog within the price reach
> of these small libraries, it is realized that larger
> libraries with greater staff and facilities may need
> to augment the titles in the catalog through their
> own efforts.

This philosophy, however, would justify a collection of far greater range, and less duplication than the present volume represents. In fact, its limited and conservative selections pose the greatest problems for small libraries. It almost seems that the Junior High School Library Catalog is intended to compensate for the decision made at last to upgrade the Standard Catalog for High School Libraries by including in the latter good, mature adult books, especially fiction. The junior high school list seems to promise the more timid librarians (high school as well as junior high): "Never mind. If the high school catalog frightens you with its 'controversial' titles, you can always resort to the junior high catalog. It includes nothing you need ever worry about." It is unfortunate that the junior high school catalog should be starting out subject to exactly the same kind of criticism that has been leveled at the senior high school catalog for so many years--not enough emphasis on the truly good, contemporary writing and too much emphasis on the innocuous.

Users of the Wilson catalogs have come to accept the fact that few, if any, titles published during the year that the current edition is published will be included (i. e. , the tenth edition of Children's Catalog, published in 1961, has few 1961 titles). This is understandable in terms of printing schedules. However, it does seem strange that since the 1965 Junior High School Library Catalog could include six 1965 fiction titles, they are ones of such mediocre quality. Only one of the six has received consistently favorable reviews; two have not even been reviewed in the standard reviewing tools; one is an abridgment of an adult novel frequently read by junior high students in its original form; and one is an adequate but by no means first choice book by an author who has numerous other, better works listed. Since some of these books received their first reviews as late as May of 1965, it seems reasonable to assume that the committee would have had access to other 1965 books which had been reviewed by May and are of much better quality.

There is little justification for complaint about the inclusion or exclusion of individual titles in a bibliography such as this one, since everyone has his own personal likes and dislikes which color such judgments. However, one does tend to question the inclusion of a very juvenile edition of Aesop's Fables when there are numerous delightful adult editions available which would add to the reader's appreciation of the work as having adult as well as juvenile implica-

tions. The same criticism can be made of the overabun-
dance of abridged and special young people's editions of good
adult writings which most junior high school students can
handle in their original form with little difficulty. And why
include the Abridged Reader's Guide, thus limiting the student's access to information about the wider range of good
adult magazines which should be available in the school or
in the local public library? These are just a few criticisms
of the volume which can be raised in terms of its tendency
to downgrade the reading of junior high school students in
terms of both the quality of the young people's books included, and of the dearth of good adult titles.

It would be easier to evaluate this volume if the reviewer also had access to the 1966 Children's Catalog and
the 1967 Standard Catalog for High School Libraries since
presumably the new catalog will serve to alter the first two.
As it now stands, however, the excessive duplication of titles
seems to make it an unnecessary tool for libraries already
owning Children's Catalog and Standard Catalog for High
School Libraries. If, as has been hinted in the preface,
there is a planned cutback in the Children's Catalog to eliminate many titles on the 7-9 level, with increased coverage
of K-6 books, and a cutback of "j" books in the Standard Catalog for High School Libraries, with an increase in mature,
adult titles, then there will be need for a volume aimed at
the junior high school level. However, the librarians who
have complained about having to consult two volumes for adequate coverage will not find their problem changed. In fact,
junior high school librarians will need to use all three catalogs to insure a well-balanced collection serving students at
both ends of the reading level continuum. Elementary school
librarians will still need both the Children's Catalog and the
Junior High School Library Catalog, and high school librarians will need both the Junior High School Library Catalog
and the Standard Catalog for High School Libraries. In the
face of the increased number of books being published each
year, such a proliferation of book selection tools is not unreasonable, and, in fact, probably desirable. The real problem will come from the quality of the list presented for the
junior high school level and from librarians who depend solely on one of these lists, thereby limiting their collections in
range as well as in quality of coverage.

Because of the high degree of duplication with Children's Catalog and Standard Catalog for High School Libraries
and the questionable quality of many of the titles not dupli-

cated, the Junior High School Library Catalog is not recommended for libraries already possessing the Children's Catalog and the Standard Catalog for High School Libraries
(whether these be in elementary, junior high, or senior high
schools). If, in the future, there is a drastic change in the
latter two lists which results in a gap at the 7-9 grade level,
then librarians now using just these two may want to consider adding the junior high school list. For junior high
school librarians this will mean using all three; for elementary and senior high school librarians it will mean adding the junior high list to the elementary or senior high
school list, as the case may be. Under no circumstances
is the Junior High School Library Catalog recommended as
a book selection tool which can stand alone.

Section 5

Popular and Scholarly Reviewing Media

At least half the reviews published in the United
States are scandalously bad. Well, if you press
me, more than half.

> Bernard DeVoto, "The easy
> chair," Harper's Magazine
> 195:26, July 1947

Criticism of the current state of reviewing in America has in the past ten years been copious to the point of
satiety, acrimonious, and apparently has had little effect on
practice. The readings in this section present a capsule
history of reviewing by a novelist-journalist of the past generation and articles which discuss a variety of special as-
pects--reviewing in special fields, attention paid to translated works, a test for bias, and the publisher's attitude
toward reviewing. In addition, actual reviews in chronological order (including some pertinent correspondence) are presented, for comparative study, of two books: a best-seller
arousing considerable controversy and a professional publication related to the subject of this book, on which a range
of professional opinion was generated. At what point in the
reviewing would you make a decision? What criteria are
met (or not) by the series of reviews?

What is the importance of reviewing to the library
selector? Of what significance are reviews which appear
with a time lag of one or more years? Is there a difference in the value of reviews for different types of libraries?
What kinds of materials of importance to library selectors
are not reviewed at all, or very little? Is there any evidence for the charge of relationship between advertising and
reviewing of specific titles? If it is still true that most reviewing is generally favorable in tone, in what ways and for
what purposes should library selectors use reviews?

Selections from

The Reviewing and Criticism of Books

by Frank Swinnerton   Prolific early twentieth century
British novelist; most recently
London correspondent for
Publishers' Weekly

From his The Reviewing and Criticism of Books.
(9th Dent Memorial Lecture) London, J. M. Dent
& Sons, Ltd. , 1939. Sel. pages.

Definitions

You will notice that in choosing a title for this lecture I made a distinction between criticism and reviewing.
This was because I believe that while a reviewer may be a
critic and his criticism a review there are differences between what a man will write as his first word and what he
will write as his last word upon any given book or author.
Whereas reviewing is, on the whole, an immediate and pro-
visional estimate of performance, criticism, in the words
of Arthur Symons, 'is a valuation of forces. '

I do not see how the distinction can be avoided. The
critic, whatever the work of human knowledge or imagination before him may be, is sure with the greatest of English critics, Coleridge, that 'the ultimate end of criticism
is much more to establish the principles of writing, than to
furnish rules how to pass judgment on what has been written
by others. ' He might add 'or than to pass judgment on that
work as it is first apprehended. ' That is, criticism, properly regarded, is an exploration of the mind of man. In
Coleridge's case a never-ending exploration, and in ours also, unless we are seduced by one of the infallible systems
introduced by modern sciolists. The reviewer, confronted
with the same work, which the critic regards as a manifestation of the soul, is called upon to tell the world whether
it has instant and calculable merit as a book. The critic
is a philosopher; the reviewer a man with a pair of scales
in his hand. . .

Old-time Reviewers

I have reminded you of the sins of reviewers a hundred years ago. The sins were arrogance and impudence,
you remember.   But while these sins flourish to-day, and
while they do so under the cloak of superior culture and superior standards, they are not the sins most remarked in
the modern reviewer.   Circumstances then were different
from what they are now.   There were fewer books.   There
were fewer critics and periodicals.   And there was more
time in every department of life for consideration.   The review of Lord Byron's early poems, for example, which pro-
voked the author to write English Bards and Scotch Reviewers appeared one year after the book's publication.
The powerful English reviewers of that age, Macaulay and
Croker and Jeffrey, wrote at leisure, and if they could not
claim to be without political bias they could at least pretend
that they had given omniscient consideration to whatever they
discussed.   They were not critics (compare Macaulay on
Boswell with Carlyle on the same subject, and stand amazed
at the difference in penetration); they were readable encyclopaedias.   They probably consulted a few obvious authorities,
cast the light of their own judgment upon the subject, read
the book they were to review, and wrote an essay.

They often used a book merely as a peg for learned
or pseudo-learned discourse; but they always suggested that
they knew more of the subject than any man who had given
ten years to the study of it, or as if, when they testified
to the genius of a poet, a dramatist, or a writer of novels
(do not forget that Walter Scott extolled the novels of Jane
Austen, without, however, showing by any sign that he had
read Mansfield Park), they had been able to consider his
work as a whole or in relation to the body of kindred or
contemporary literature.   It may often have been bluff; but
these men established a tradition of reviewing in England.
The reviews they wrote were collected in book form, and
those of Macaulay are among the most famous, brassy,
and stimulating of all narrative essays in the language.
Furthermore, they had power.   They were not the makers
of permanent reputations; but they attacked ferociously, and
they gave standing to whatever .they praised...

Reconciliation of Criticism and Reviewing

It was Sainte-Beuve who first reconciled criticism
and reviewing.   And Sainte-Beuve was the first man to ap-

proximate to our modern star reviewers.   It was his habit
to devote twelve hours on each of five days a week to the
preparation and writing of his one article, to give a further
day to the correction of his proofs, and then to take a day's
holiday.   His article appeared every Monday, and it dealt
as a rule with a single book, very much as Mr. Desmond
MacCarthy's article in the <u>Sunday Times</u> appears every Sunday and deals with a single book.   When writers bewail the
fact that we have no contemporary Sainte-Beuve, they either
forget Mr. MacCarthy or intend that some invidious comparison should be drawn; but as far as I knew there is at present nobody except Mr. MacCarthy who continues a tradition
so valuable in its unhasting commentary on a single new
book at a time and its effort to reconcile criticism with
hebdomadal journalism.   It was Sainte-Beauve's aim to be a
disinterested 'naturalist of minds.'   He never referred to
canons or principles, axioms or the first class; he represented, in spite of much learning and great experience, a
point of view which I may describe as the humane, in opposition to the academic or doctrinaire.   This is the reason
why he was a better critic than the aesthete and the dilet-
tante.   Strangely enough, he was more interested in the work
before him than in any exhibition of his own superior knowledge or in any abstract conceptions of Art or Literature.
A pragmatist, you say?   At any rate, the first ideal reviewer.

        If Sainte-Beuve lived nowadays I think his task would
be more difficult than it was in the eighteen-forties.   I cannot tell you how many books were published annually in his
lifetime; but I feel sure that he had not to deal with any
sort of proportion of fourteen or fifteen thousand, every one
of which carries somewhere upon its person the statement
that it is big, stupendous, superb, a revelation, and a wow.
I am confident that he did not receive the acres of puff paper upon which present-day publishers commit propaganda
for their forthcoming masterpieces.   I doubt if he ever saw
a publisher's advertisement, or dined with a member of the
Publishers' Advertising Circle.   He had an easier life.   He
reviewed the books he wanted to review.   He took his own
time over them.   His lines were not ransacked for quotes.
In those days the book trade was not organized.

Changed Conditions

        How have the conditions of critical reviewing altered?
Well, the kinds of book to be published have changed, as

well as their numbers. Whereas novels were then comparatively few, they are now many. Books of memoirs appeal,
perhaps, to as many readers as they did in the eighteen-
forties; but they do not appeal to as many people as a new
novel by Mr. Brett Young. Poetry, in one of its fluctua-
tions, has ceased for the moment--for the moment only--to
be considered important. Above all, library subscribers
would take little heed of an article by Sainte-Beuve. They
would think it far inferior to one by Mr. Clifton Fadiman.
Living at a speed so much higher than their fellows of the
past, they strongly resemble eaters and drinkers who have
lost their palate. For them, everything must be more highly spiced than it was. Reviews have to snap. They must
be short, slick, outspoken, up to the minute. What's new?
What's its kicking power?

        This demand for spice began a long time ago. It was
a part of that arrogant impudence of which Coleridge complained (but if I mention to you that I believe the arrogant
impudence was aimed at the epics of Southey and the more
rural pieces of Wordsworth you may, if you are thoroughly
modern, feel that arrogant impudence must have been the
voice of posterity speaking out of time). It was at the back
of what used, in the last century, to be associated with the
Saturday Review, when outrageously dishonest and destruc-
tive reviews were written and printed of all sorts of books,
some of which have now become classics. I don't know if
any of you have chanced to read, for example, the Life of
Froude, by Herbert Paul. There you will find the evidence
against Freeman, whose attacks upon Froude--printed as
reviews in the Saturday Review--spread a belief, still widely
held, that Froude unscrupulously cooked quotations and mis-
represented facts; whereas the truth is that Freeman knew
nothing of the Tudor period, relied entirely on what he could
pick from other men's researches, and libelled a man whose
standard of scrupulousness and scrutiny of unknown and in-
credibly crabbed manuscripts, was far in advance of anything previously known to English historians. We have our
Freemans to-day. They function in journals especially pretentious of culture.

The Hack Review

        What is the alternative to the destructive review? I
shall be told that it is the hack review. And it is true that
as the nineteenth century advanced the hack review tri-
umphed. It was unsigned; it was dull, vapid, commonplace,

and timidly cordial. At one time--those were days when
publishers were just beginning to advertise more freely, and
so to support literary journals which printed little beside re-
views--it crept over a new book very much as an inky spider
creeps over a piece of paper. It was very correct; it took
a strict moral line, so that the heroine of a novel who
stepped just over the line of the drawingroom carpet caused
a shiver of horror to travel through every tedious word of
disapproval; it gave with one phrase what it took away with
the next. It had no ability to distinguish between the original and the derivative. And when one had read it one did
not care whether one read whatever book it spoke of or not.
The hack review is still with us. It will always be with us.
I will tell you in a moment why that is so.

Reviewing by Literary Stars

But first of all I want to speak of another branch of
reviewing by literary stars. I do not pretend to have studied this question closely; but (omitting consideration of Theodore Watts-Dunton, who was a tiresome and long-winded
first-reviewer in the old Athenaeum) there were two or three
men who used to give books a certain topical value by writing under their own names in prominent positions in their
own papers. One man who did this was T. P. O'Connor.
He would gut the book and add some comments of his own,
some of them reminiscent, some of them paraphrases of
what he had just read in the book he reviewed, some of them
laudatory. Many readers were delighted. They felt they
had been brought into contact with the books and their authors; and a few of them would take the further step of getting those books for themselves, to continue the acquaintance. This was decidedly, from the point of view of authors
and publishers (neither of whom care much for criticism,
since what they both need is the freer circulation of books),
a step in the right direction. T. P. had his vogue.

Still more influential were the reviews of Dr. Robert-
son Nicoll, who figures as Tomlinson Keyhole in H. G.
Wells's satire, Boon, and who used in the British Weekly
the pseudonym of 'Claudius Clear.' Nicoll was a very
shrewd and able book-taster, one of the first men of his day
to recognize young talent as soon as he saw it, and one of
those who were bold enough to speak of this talent without
waiting for a lead from somebody else. He used a method
similar to O'Connor's, but his comment was always more
pointed, and an adverse review by him used to cause--let

us say in the nineteen-hundreds and nineteen-tens--considerable talk in our trade. Less talk was caused by anything said by Nicoll's friend and contemporary, Clement Shorter, and more laughter; but Shorter, too, was an influence, a book-lover, a man who sighted talent early and cultivated the acquaintance of greater men than himself. These three commenters on new books were powers in their day. They preceded the star reviewers of a later generation. They made books 'news.' For that reason they were straws showing the way the wind was blowing. Please do not forget this. The publishers were beginning, if not to organize, at least to feel the breeze of competition. They were beginning to do a little more than print some books and ask the booksellers to magnificent banquets before they handed round the order sheets.

Reviews as News

I have suggested that these three men were the pioneers, not so much of star reviewing (because obviously famous lights had sometimes reviewed books before O'Connor and Nicoll and Shorter), as of star news reviewing. The old discreetness, which we may regard as glorified hacking, had filled many an anonymous column; these men both signed their reviews and brought them into prominent places in their journals. So did Sir Edmund Gosse, a social figure, a historian and pseudo-scholar, and a patron of artists. So, in a lesser way, did W. L. Courtney, who was a more substantial man than Gosse, but lacked his air. Gosse wrote about all sorts of books. If anybody feels disposed to grumble at the enthusiasm of modern reviewers for new novels, and to sneer at them for discovering a masterpiece a week (it is an unwarranted sneer, based upon glimpses of publishers' advertisements, and in reality a back-handed testimony to the exploratory skill of publishers' advertisement managers), let him look up the catalogue at the back of an old Heinemann book, and read what Edmund Gosse said of Hall Caine. It will be a salutary experience. I need hardly add that Heinemann quoted only the best; but as one who writes both new novels and reviews of new novels by other men I must admit that my mouth waters in envy. To have such words written of oneself! To be bold enough to apply such words to another! Those were days of the publishing world's springtime.

Gosse gradually ceased to extol Hall Caine. He became, in the intervals of acting as Librarian to the House of

Lords, a reformed character, and grew reminiscent about
the Brownings and other no longer existing poets of his
youth and maturity. Eventually he wrote a chaste and polished article every week for the Sunday Times, and it was
at one time the habit of literary-minded men to read what
he said in that paper before turning to see what J. C. Squire
was saying in the Observer. The Sunday newspaper as an
organ of literary opinion, and as a field for publishers' advertising, rose high above the horizon.

For a period these were the only visible stars,
though Robert Lynd had succeeded R. A. Scott-James as
Literary Editor of the Daily News. But one day--I do not
know how it happened; but I think that following their first
acquaintance he must have read Books and Persons, a collection of certain notes printed almost weekly in A. R.
Orage's wonderful review, the New Age--Lord Beaverbrook
invited Arnold Bennett to contribute a regular article on new
books to the Evening Standard. I think I must be right, but
I do not doubt that I shall hear of my wrongness, in believing that apart from the introduction of big business into publishing by Victor Gollancz, the advent of Arnold Bennett as
a star reviewer did more to change the aspect of the book
world than any other post-War event. The whole system of
book-reviewing underwent an overhaul.

Reviews and Advertising

It did so for this reason. I can remember that when
I was in my teens the two daily newspapers which gave most
space to reviews of new books were the Daily Chronicle and
the Daily News. These papers carried some publishers'
advertising, and they also contained reviews of new books
written by competent and sometimes celebrated persons. In
the Daily News, for example, Gilbert Chesterton often
frisked through the pages of a book and improvised an article upon a phrase which had struck him there; while many
a writer now known to us all turned his hand to the task of
estimating contemporaries. Whether the News and Chronicle were the first papers to depart from anonymity I cannot say; but if they did so they must have been following the
inclination of the hour, and even the Manchester Guardian,
while for the most part keeping to initials, would sometimes
use the reviewer's full name in relation to an important
book. Other newspapers took a less cordial view of literature. The Daily Telegraph printed many reviews; only
Courtney's, I believe, were signed. The Times has always

preserved anonymity.   The <u>Athenaeum</u> buried all its contributors.   Reviewing in the first twenty years of this century was ill paid; the work of men whose names were largely unknown to the public.

Now under the stress of competition all newspapers
were compelled to raise more revenue from advertisements.
Publishers had always been allowed space at lower rates
than those paid by brewers; and these were increased.   Publishers felt that they were no longer able to keep pace with
the new rates.   And as the papers could get plenty of advertising elsewhere, and as they also had to extend the variety
of their contents, to catch women and illiterates and the new
products of national education, the space available for the
reviewing of books was restricted.   Reviews grew shorter,
more insignificant.   One sometimes lost sight of them altogether among the pictures and the advertisements of clothes
and bottled foods and tobacco.   Anonymity reigned again.
Very few troubled to see what Mr. Nobody thought of this or
that.   Only the big-selling novelist was sure of early attention.

<u>Arnold Bennett</u>

Arnold Bennett changed this.   I am well aware that
those who in his lifetime received much kindness from Arnold Bennett have joined the snobs in reviling him since his
death.   I know that because he remained unimpressed by the
antics of our cultured quacks he has been accused of fighting the battles of Philistinism against the First Class.   But
I will not here express my opinion of Bennett's detractors.
I will only say that he made new books news.   He caused
them to be read by people who had never previously bought
books in their lives and had never bothered to take out a library subscription.   He sometimes praised what was inferi-
or: it is done all the time by his condemners, who are
criticasters to a man.   The fact remains that he created a
new excitement about books; that he gave revived authority
to reviewers of every sort; that as long as he was alive the
<u>Evening Standard</u> was seen every Thursday by all who were
interested in living literature...

No such consideration deters those same juniors and
peers from attacking the successful writer at every turn.
He is fair game.   But the cause of the attacks is envy; it
is not (as it is supposed to be) a noble refusal to compromise with the highest standards.

Worst Kind of Reviewing

The highest standards are never the foundation for what seems to me the worst kind of reviewing, that of ardent propaganda for a particular set or that of systematic belittlement of authors outside the set, and especially authors whose greater attractiveness has brought them wide popularity. This sort of reviewing, with its suppressions, its misrepresentations, its constant sycophantic references to favoured names, its yawns at whatever sells more than seven hundred copies, its pretence that certain genteel writers belong to the class of Donne and Marvell, and that others are no more than hucksters, is a low form of politics. It assumes that one may justifiably be a cad for one's school. To it, rather than the oft-repeated charge of venality in the popular reviewer, is due the loss of authority in the modern review.

Alleged Venality

On the subject of this alleged venality, much could be said. And a great deal has already been said. Reviewers are commonly believed to use the word 'masterpiece' by rubber stamp. I shall not deny that they often use adjectives with great recklessness. In writing previously on this subject I said that they are affected by what may be called the perishing of adjectives, which includes the loss of effectiveness suffered by the word 'good' and the fact that a whispered word of praise is unheard amid the bawling of 'stark,' 'glorious,' 'stupendous' and the like. But there is also the competition in capital letters and the furious wish to be first to acclaim something new or slightly out of the ordinary. For this I think editors must take some of the blame. I have been told by two reviewers that their responsible employers estimate quality in the reviewer by the quotes they see from his reviews. There is the bad trait in a reviewer that he likes to see himself quoted--and he will never be quoted unless his words have a blaze and lustre beyond those of other reviewers. There is the degree to which the reviewer may be influenced by what the publisher tells him. There is the fact that although no pressure may be brought to bear upon him by his advertising manager he knows that a total loss of advertising by his paper would mean the total loss of his job. These are some of the reasons for mild venality, or for highly coloured adjectives, excessive attention, falsification of the value of the book extolled.

Pressure of Publishing Organization

They represent the increasing pressure of publishing organization upon the literary contents of a periodical. Long ago, when I was in the trade, I noticed one day that a reviewer who had been in the habit of exhibiting himself at the expense of certain new books was no longer contributing to his paper. I asked why. I was told that publishers, being sick of his continued crabbing of their books, had signified an intention of withdrawing support from the paper. The reviewer went. Now I think that was deplorable; because if English publishers were to carry this action farther English reviews would be as worthless as the reviews in the French press, which are bought. But as long as the reviewing of books is governed, as to space, by the quantity of publishers' advertising bought in each issue of the periodical, it must be clear that persistent slating of new books will be the exception.

I do not say that persistent slating would be a good thing. It is the easiest form of reviewing. The most difficult form is the tolerant which avoids mush. I draw attention to the fact that for one man who can praise with apparent conviction, there are fifty who can slate with fury. Practically any undergraduate can slate. It is because inexperience knows no control. The undergraduate has energy, a vocabulary, impatience, and a recently learned infallible test for his reading. He is not a critic; he does not know why an author writes his book in one way rather than another; he does not care. His attitude is like that of the lover in the song:

> If she be not fair to me,
> What care I how fair she be?

He proceeds to be unfair.

Attitude of Older Reviewer

But what of the older reviewer? What should be his attitude to the mass of new books? Is he to say that only certain kinds of book are worthy of praise? Or is he to say that many kinds of books are entitled to praise, but that particular examples of those kinds are faulty? If the latter, and I think the latter is the true course for the reviewer, by what measure is he to work? Is he to say: This is a long biography, and long biographies are out of date; therefore this long biography is tedious? Is he to say: This history is written with the object of exculpating some person hitherto reputed a tyrant, or of telling how the poor people lived, whereas it has always been the habit of historians to take a different line, and therefore this history, being tendentious, is no good? Is he to say: This poetry is not like Milton's and is not as good as Shakespeare's; therefore it is vile and eccentric? Or is he to say: This is modern, and so excellent; biased, and so a social criticism; long, and so a relief from the recent snip-snap biographical sketch?

I think he should do none of these things. Sainte-Beuve thought he should do none of these things. Sainte-Beuve said: 'The critic should have no partiality, and should take no side.' This means that the critic--and you understand that I have slipped for the moment, following Sainte-Bueve, into the use of the word 'critic' when the word 'reviewer' is intended--should present himself to any book with an open mind, and that he should judge each book on its own merits.

That is to say, he should <u>submissively</u> ask: What is the author's plan?

Does this book fulfil the author's plan?

Is it a good plan; an original plan (using the word 'original' in Hazlitt's sense, and not as indicating exhibitionism)?

Has the book style; that peculiar suggestiveness of knowledge and understanding, and reserves of temperament which we can call 'quality' or 'texture'?

Is it a <u>book,</u> in the sense that only this author-- never mind whether I like it, or relish its attitude or its argument or its type--could have written it?

If the answers to these questions, which it must be understood are to be put so tentatively that they are hardly there at all, insinuate themselves satisfactorily into the attention, the book may be assessed; but what I wish to make clear is that the reviewer should first of all be receptive to the book as it is. He should read it with what Coleridge calls 'a willing suspension of disbelief,' giving it every chance to make, as a whole, its effect upon his imagination. His imagination, remember.

For it is with his imagination, the depths of himself, and not with his culture or the superficies of his mind, that he should judge. He is not debating; he is assaying. And unless he allows the book full use of his profoundest attention for as long as he is reading it he is yielding nothing of any value to the author, who may well be his superior. He has this first duty to the author: it is very important...

Receptivity, of course, does not imply the abdication of judgment; merely its reservation. It means that whereas the dab critic opens a book with his mind made up, sees a misprint or a tedium or a tolerance, and writes insultingly of the talent of any writer who allows misprints, tediums, and tolerances to disfigure his pages, the true critic sees all, but permits himself no mental comment until he is at the end of the book and can set misprints and tediums in their proper proportion. Proportion is the critic's need; withdrawal from dogma; a recognition that from a culture different from his own may come work--sometimes unwelcome--of extraordinary quality. The reviewer can approximate to the critic if he can get behind the book to the author, and behind the author to the essential force which has produced the work in question. He will not slate in a hurry. He may learn; he may admire; he may demur; he may shake his head; he may say 'here, but for the grace of God, go I'; he may exclaim at wasted labour; he will rarely, even in a bad book, find the author wholly worthless. It is his business to find the vital speck in that author, in that book; it is not his business to dwell meaninglessly upon the difficulty of the search.

For the reviewer, besides having responsibility to the author, stands here as representative of the public. He is prospecting, not on behalf of posterity, but on behalf of the readers of his paper. They want to know, first of all, what the book is about, and whether it is a book they would like to read. In a very minor degree do they want to know what one reviewer thinks of himself as a reader of it. So the reviewer, doing justice to the author, then does justice to the reader. If he is imaginative enough, he will give all readers an impression of the book, and will indicate the quantity and quality of its success in pleasing himself. He is an interpreter.

This involves no compromise. The reviewer is at full liberty, when he has done justice to the book, to kill it with his intelligence. But intelligence, in reviewing, is not

enough.   It must be supported by imagination--a quality
greatly lacking, as a rule, in the intelligentsia--by taste, by
humour, detachment, experience of men and books, and tolerance.   The spiteful reviewing of the highbrows is an abom-
ination. The slobber of the ecstatics is repellent.   The la-
boured piecework of the hacks is never equal to work of any
originality whatever.   But the irresponsible reviewer is as
bad as the back-scratcher.   He only inverts the sin he
loathes; he does not restore the balance.

Conclusion

        Well, I have done.   I have told you that there is no
such thing as an absolute standard of literary excellence.   I
have told you what Coleridge and others have said about criticism and about reviewers.   I have shown how reviewing has
developed from some date about a hundred years ago until
to-day.   And I have discussed a few of the problems of reviewing.   Chief among these problems is the number of new
books which must be reviewed.   Next comes the difficulty of
assessing the value of these books, which I say can only be
done by the reviewer's intuitions of immortality, beauty, and
virtue.   Third, is the severe difficulty of relation between
publishers' advertising and the space devoted to books in the
periodical press.   I do not think I can usefully add anything
more; and therefore I shall leave you to consider for your-
selves what changes, if any, in the art and practice of reviewing are either possible or desirable, and what hope there
is of reviewing (it has never yet been seen on land or water)
which avoids the rival evils of academicism and subservience
by means of sympathy, judgment, and rigorous but acceptable
candour.

Book Reviewing for Middle-Brows

From Times Literary Supplement, September 17, 1954, p. lviii and lx; Reprinted by permission of Times Newspapers Ltd., London, England

The middle-brow book review in the United States appears in some 250 newspapers, which devote regular attention to books, as well as in half a dozen magazines for the general reader. In all the newspapers, and in such magazines as Time and Newsweek, new books are considered as news and treated as such. Genuine criticism--the examination of the corpus of a writer's work, the relation of a new book to other books or to ideas, or a re-examination of some past work--is so rare in the middle-brow reviews as to be virtually non-existent. What the middle-brow review offers its readers in place of criticism is a brief summary of the plot, accompanied occasionally by the reviewer's opinion of the work in hand. As in British newspapers, brevity is generally the keynote in reviews, and a review of more than two or three paragraphs is exceptional, although the British practice of grouping together several unrelated books in a single review is not followed. Most reviews are favourable, since the average book editor prefers to use his limited space to give news of good books rather than to warn readers against bad ones. An exception, of course, is the occasional fall from grace of a Hemingway or some writer of similar stature. Most book reviewers and book editors are newspapermen (many of them older men retired from the news sections, editorial pages and even the sports columns to the less arduous duties of the book page); others are librarians or university professors. Unknown in the United States is the professional writer who does regular book reviewing.

Standing above all other publications in its treatment of books is the New York Times. In the excellence of its editing, the thoroughness of its coverage and the quality of its reviews it has no rival. Although published in New York City and distributed as part of the regular Sunday edition of

the newspaper, the New York Times Book Review has an
enormous influence among the reading public of the East
Coast from New England south to North Carolina, and an impressive circulation throughout the rest of the country. In
addition to its Sunday section, the newspaper has, under
separate editorial control, a daily book review column conducted by Mr. Orville Prescott and Mr. Charles Poore. Mr.
Prescott is probably the country's most influential book reviewer. In spite of his dislike for naturalistic books and
his reluctance to review controversial ones, he brings his
readers a cultivated taste (including a special fondness for
good English historical novels) enhanced by a quality which
he alone among his colleagues seems to possess: the capacity for enthusiasm.   There was a time in American reviewing when a single reviewer--an Alexander Woollcott or an
Edmund Wilson--could make a book a best-seller.   That sort
of influence is lacking to-day, but Mr. Prescott sends more
readers into bookshops and libraries than any other reviewer.

* * *

        Second in influence to the New York Times is the
New York Herald Tribune, one of the three newspapers with
a separate book section.   Like the Times, the Tribune is
read throughout the country.   With a smaller corps of reviewers and less space than the Times, the Tribune covers
fewer books and makes less effort to publish its reviews in
good time.   The daily reviewing for the Tribune is done by
Mr. Lewis Gannett, the "Dean of American book reviewers,"
whose interest in American history and in nature books has
won him a loyal following over the years.   His co-reviewer
is Mr. John K. Hutchens, a comparative newcomer to the
task of daily reviewing, but an experienced book editor and
commentator on books whose deft and lighthearted reviews
are increasing in popularity.   And it is safe to say that no
one in the United States seriously interested in books--
writers, librarians and other book editors--fails to read either the New York Times or the New York Herald Tribune.

        The third separate book section is the Chicago Trib-
une's "Magazine of Books," the mid-Continent's most influential book medium.   The Chicago Tribune publishes a great
many brief reviews and devotes much of its space to its
staff of literary columnists.   The Tribune is an articulate
champion of Middle Western culture and a sturdy opponent of
what it considers an East Coast plot to foist avant-garde literature and over-realistic writing on an unsuspecting public.

Ranking fourth in national importance is the San Francisco Chronicle, whose book editor, Mr. Joseph Henry Jackson, has guided literary taste on the Pacific Coast for almost twenty-five years. In addition to editing a book section of approximately eight pages, for which he writes a column of literary news every Sunday, Mr. Jackson also conducts "The Bookman's Notebook," a review column which appears five times a week in the San Francisco Chronicle and the Los Angeles Times, two of the Coast's most important newspapers. Mr. Jackson has an inevitable predilection for books dealing with California and other parts of the West; but his judgment is respected and his influence is great. Apart from these four papers, there are no others carrying daily book reviews of their own or with weekly book sections of more than one or two pages in size. Two papers may be instanced as typical of the reviewing that appears elsewhere in the nation. First of these is the Dallas News. The book editor of this Texas paper is Mr. Lon Tinkle, a professor of romance languages at Southern Methodist University. Like Mr. Jackson on the Coast, Mr. Tinkle is the literary arbiter of Texas, and his activities are by no means confined to the book page. Books by Texas authors have first claim to attention on his page, but he is a man of wit and urbanity and it is his continual championing of good writing that has helped to make reading more fashionable in Texas than it is in most of the forty-eight states. The second important book page is that of the Providence (Rhode Island) Journal. Under the editorship of the poet Winfield T. Scott and his successor, Mr. Maurice Dolbier, this page has become the first in New England and is considered by many to be the best in the country. Mr. Dolbier has brought together a staff of good reviewers, and his page offers demonstrable proof that, under a good editor, a group of excellent local reviewers can be assembled and, as it were, rubbing against each other, produce consistently fine reviews. It is in the pages of the Providence Journal that middle-brow reviewing makes its closest approach to criticism.

No discussion of book reviewing in the United States would be complete without mention of Carl Victor Little, the enfant terrible of the Houston (Texas) Press. Now in poor health and no longer reviewing regularly, Mr. Little boasts that he is the only book reviewer in the world willing to back up his reviews. A reader who buys a book on Mr. Little's recommendation and finds it less than it was represented to be may return the book to the reviewer and receive in its place another volume of equal cost. Mr. Little

also combats space restrictions by offering to give telephone
reviews of any books not treated at length in his weekly
column.   In addition to those already mentioned the best
newspaper book pages are to be found in the following newspapers: Birmingham News, Cleveland Press, Columbus
Dispatch, Dayton News, Louisville Courier-Journal, Miami
Herald, Milwaukee Journal, Minneapolis Tribune, Norfolk
Virginian-Pilot (the only paper to run a regular column of
poetry on its book page), Omaha World-Herald, Richmond
News-Leader, St. Louis Post-Dispatch and Winston-Salem
Journal and Sentinel.

        Many local book editors, as well as some newspapers
without book editors of their own, make use of one or more
nationally syndicated book review services.   The most widely used of these is "The Literary Guidepost," a column conducted for the Associated Press by Mr. William G. Rogers.
Mr. Rogers reviews five books a week, and also covers
every important New York event in the fields of art, music
and ballet.   In spite of this seemingly impossible undertaking, Mr. Rogers manages to produce some of the country's
best reviewing, and he is known for the sympathetic attention he gives to younger writers.   His column is available
to more than 1, 700 papers, but is ordinarily used by fewer
than fifty of them--a figure which indicates the apathy of the
average newspaper editor to book news when there is not a
local book editor to prod him into providing space for it.
Of the other syndicates most important is the Saturday Review Syndicate, run by The Saturday Review magazine, but
with its own reviews, done usually by Mr. John Barkham.
About thirty-five papers in the United States and Canada
make use of this service.   Smaller in the number of papers
using them are The Sterling North Weekly Book Review Service; "The Literary Journal," distributed by Classic Features;
and the column of Van Allen Bradley, a reviewer for the
Chicago Daily News, whose reviews appear in various other
newspapers in the Middle West and upper South.   The United
Press, the leading competitor of the Associated Press, sends
four or five short reviews weekly to many newspapers, while
the King Features Syndicate supplies a weekly review column
written by Mr. Clark Kinnaird and used in the Hearst newspapers.

        Hundreds of magazines, ranging from America (a
Jesuit weekly) to The Rotarian, from Glamour (a magazine
for young women) to The Combat Forces Journal, give regular attention to books of interest to their readers, but six

magazines which appeal to the general reader of books rank above the rest in influence, if not always in the quality of their reviews. The two news-magazines, Time and Newsweek, cover, in the country's only unsigned reviews, from three to six new books each week. In spite of a fondness for the detailed description of a book, which represents the ultimate in non-criticism, Time's reviews are widely respected and can be markedly influential. Time, seeking to elevate its readers' tastes rather than to cater to them, is generally impatient with the popular best-seller, while it is hospitable to poetry, criticism and other works of narrower, but deeper, interest. Newsweek, whose book department is at present undergoing a change of editors, has in the past staked out as its particular area of interest Americana, especially books dealing with regional history.

There are two monthly magazines, Harper's and the Atlantic Monthly, with small but literate circulations. Appealing to the upper middle-brows, both magazines avoid in their book sections any taint of the highbrow. In the Atlantic its editor, Mr. Edward Weeks, writes a personal essay which occasionally deals with specific books while his colleague, Mr. Charles Rolo, writes short reviews of the month's important titles. In Harper's the reviewing has been done by Mr. Gilbert Highet, a professor of classical languages at Columbia University.

Another important home of middle-brow reviewing is the New Yorker, which has declined considerably in prestige and influence since the days when its reviews were being done by Mr. Edmund Wilson and Mr. Clifton Fadiman. Occasional New Yorker reviews are done by Mr. Brendan Gill, who, in spite of his infrequent appearances as a reviewer, is considered by many to be the most able critic in the field. Synonymous with middle-brow book-reviewing in the United States is The Saturday Review, a transatlantic counterpart of John o' London's Weekly. The magazine only recently, and significantly, dropped the word "literature" from its title. Concerned with international affairs, records and drama, as well as with books, The Saturday Review retains a large and loyal audience, composed in no small part of librarians and teachers, who depend upon it as their chief source of news of books.

An important aspect of middle-brow book discussion is the "book news" column, a variation of which appears on almost every book page and the most popular of which are

those written by Mr. Harvey Breit of the <u>New York Times</u>
<u>Book Review,</u> Mr. John K. Hutchens of the <u>New York Her-</u>
<u>ald Tribune,</u> and Mr. Bennett Cerf in <u>The Saturday Review.</u>
These columns, composed in part of interviews, in part of
literary gossip, reflect a national curiosity about the personalities behind the news in any field.   Another indispensable adjunct of the average book page is the best-seller list.
The most influential of these are the two in the <u>New York</u>
<u>Times Book Review</u> and the <u>New York Herald Tribune,</u> and
the one prepared by the trade publication, <u>Publishers'</u> Week-
<u>ly,</u> and widely reprinted throughout the country.

       In general, middle-brow book reviewing in the United
States is a labour of love.   Except for the larger sections,
most newspapers do not pay their reviewers and some do not
even permit them to keep the books they have reviewed.   Unlike his high-brow counterpart, the middle-brow reviewer
gains from his work no academic preferment or chance for
advance publication of work in progress.   His reward is usually the satisfaction of seeing his review in print.   But the
integrity of these reviewers <u>as</u> reviewers cannot be im-
pugned, and their reviews, while perhaps lacking in critical
quality, rank high as journalism, which is all that most of
them ever attempt to be.

The Serious Literary Review

From Times Literary Supplement, September 17, 1954, p. lxiii; Reprinted by permission of Times Newspapers Ltd., London, England

Literary reviews abound in the United States. When, however, as here, the adjective "serious" is added to the title of an article dealing with them, their numbers are notably reduced. Many, though, remain--too many for mention in a brief comment--which are close to that uncertain dividing-line separating "serious" from "popular."

Of those that, issue after issue, justify both the terms "serious" and "literary," each has, at least in the eyes of its sponsors, its individual character and reason for existence. Nearly all, however, share certain conditions, have certain characteristics in common. One of these is that the serious review in the United States is almost invariably a quarterly; another, that--also almost invariably-- the title of the quarterly proclaims attachement to a given region or institution. And where the title does not make the announcement, copyright line does, as, for example, with The American Scholar, which is the organ of the Phi Beta Kappa Society. Except, however, for those published south of the Mason and Dixon line, that always self-conscious region, this localization is carried little farther than the cover. Most, whatever their beginnings, aim at national, not sectional, influence. The Yale Review, for one, adds to its main title a supplementary line, "A National Quarterly;" The Virginia Quarterly Review, "A National Journal of Literature and Discussion," and so with others.

* * *

In spite of these qualifications, the use of the local name continues, new journals following the example of the older ones. It must do so; it is a condition of survival. In the United States no serious review is wholly self-supporting. Even when for a year or two income rises, it can

be counted on with dismal certainty to fall again. Subscribers, taken altogether as a class, form a group numer-
ically insignificant when contrasted with those of any of the
larger weeklies. And advertising, that main prop of publication, conforms to the subscription list. Subsidization from
somewhere, then, is a necessity. The "somewhere" re-
solves itself almost without exception into one of two sources
--the large foundations, the universities. The foundations
(the Rockefeller Foundation in particular) have been consistently generous in providing for the expenses attendant on the
beginning of publication, and have helped out along the way;
the required yearly support comes usually from universities
and colleges. The Virginia Quarterly Review depends not
on the State of Virginia but on the University of Virginia,
an organ of that state; The Sewanee Review on the University of the South. The Pacific Spectator here stands a little
apart from the rest in that it draws, not on one institution
but on twenty, scattered the length of the three Pacific
Coast states.

Another likeness, this time not financial, among the
serious literary quarterlies is the large space given by most
of them to the formal book review--a space so large as to
raise question in a reader's mind as to why these sections
are relegated to the back pages and why they are set ordinarily in type smaller, less easy of reading, than are the
articles preceding them. Is there tradition only here? Or
economy? If it is economy, it is furthered by another cus-
tom common to all--one forced on them, indeed, by the ra-
pidity with which new books tumble from the presses. Half
a dozen biographies, half a dozen novels or books of verse
are made the subject of a single consideration, a paragraph
or two for each. The book that is permitted to stand alone
must be one that the editors of the quarterly concerned regard as of outstanding importance. Which books are so
chosen, what treatment is accorded to them and to the others
under review marks a chief cleavage between one group of
American serious reviews and another. It is the cleavage
between those editors who define "literary" as applying solely to the arts and almost wholly to the printed word--The
Sewanee Review, The Hudson Review, The Kenyon Review--
and those who give the term a broader meaning and include
in their columns discussions of national and international
politics or economics--The Yale Review, The Virginia Quarterly Review, The Pacific Spectator, The American Scholar.
This last named has lately passed so far over from the arts
to public affairs that in the Spring issue of 1954 only one

article, and that doubtfully, could be named "literary" though "philosophical" might be applied, also doubtfully, to several.

* * *

Whatever their differences, there is one article of faith remaining which all members of both groups hold in common. All give importance to poetry. All publish freely from the work of living poets, offer abundant comment on that work and evaluations of it. Beyond this, difference in definition, reinforced by a no less great difference in tone, affects the entire content of each quarterly in either group. Nowhere is this effect more readily assessed than in the voluminous book sections already mentioned. The Yale Review--not the oldest of American literary reviews but one which, under Helen MacAfee's editorship, became a kind of doyen among them--may stand as an example on the one side; The Hudson Review, which in a brief life has spread its influence widely, on the other.

Reviews in The Yale Review tend to be moderate in tone, to give evidence of the reviewer's erudition, to be written oftener than not by persons already eminent in the field covered by the works with which they deal--Mr. Alvin Johnson, a notable present-day liberal, reviews a biography of Robert LaFollette, a notable liberal of a day just past. A pair of books on the English Parliament are reviewed by Miss Mildred Campbell, author of The English Yeoman and chairman of the History Department at Vassar College. These are typical. The position of the reviewer, the fact that he will be held accountable by his professional fellows for the fairness and penetration of his comment--these make for sober estimate, tend towards qualified judgment and away from black-or-white pronouncements.

* * *

Reviewers for The Hudson Review, on the other hand, write usually in provocative fashion, deal in unstinted denunciation, in unstinted praise, and as a result take to themselves--or seem to take--an authority which can be exemplified only by quotation. One example must serve--the review of a novel, The Disguises of Love, by Robie Macaulay. The book was given the distinction of an entire review to itself, was favourably presented by the reviewer, who explained it to readers as a narrative "... in which... accounts of homosexual relations are disguised as accounts of heterosexual relations," since, owing to American prudishness, "... our authors have no choice but to metamorphose

gender. " Therefore the heroine's name, Frances, the reviewer points out, is to be altered to Francis by any dis-
cerning reader. In the following issue of the quarterly the
author of The Disguises of Love denounces at length this
misinterpretation of his story, rejecting it in toto. Frances
is Frances, none else. No homosexuality is involved or suggested, the reviewer's "disclosures are fake. " This indignant disclaimer might perhaps be expected to disconcert the
reviewer? Not at all. The protesting author, he answers,
"is not the first novelist to have builded better than he knew
or will admit. " He, the reviewer, is "not to be scared out
of a critical reading of a novel by the author's waspish insistence that it is not his reading. " All this makes lively
reading. What nourishment it provides for readers is open
to question, but there is no doubt about what it reveals of
the reviewer's self-confidence, of his sense of final authority. Many of the reviewers, as also many contributors of
the articles appearing in this group of quarterlies, exhibit
something of the same authoritative attitude, one ballasted
often by a weight of Freudian doctrine and guided by a pro-
found absorption in the symbol. The example just given is
an extreme one, but it by no means stands alone in its ele-
vation of the reviewer's opinion over the writer's.

The differences dividing review from review inside
a group are subtler than those which separate the one group
from the other--subtler and more subject to swift alteration.
They are largely the result of individual editorial attitudes,
the tone, and even the substance of the publication tending
to change with a change of editors. There are, though, a
few distinguishing marks to be found. The American Scholar
has instituted an "American Scholars' Forum" which brings
together several people, more or less prominent, for informal discussion of a previously suggested topic, the discussion being recorded--perhaps a little to the damage of its
informality--for later appearance in the magazine. This
quarterly differentiates itself, too, by having reduced many
of its references to new publications to brief notices; in one
issue there were twenty-eight of these as against five reviews. The Pacific Spectator, published almost within sound
of the western ocean, carries a department, "Asian Literature, " containing articles and stories translated from the
work of contemporary Japanese, Iranian, Indian and Filipino
writers. It has no formal review section but instead publishes in the body of the magazine articles dealing with aspects of contemporary writing. The Virginia Quarterly Review makes a skilful admixture of the sectional with the in-

ternational.

* * *

A visiting Englishman, Mr. Ian Wilson, writing lately of his impressions of the United States, complains that he
finds earnestness everywhere, a tendency everywhere among
Americans to what he calls a "hand-on-heart" attitude. It is
an odd characteristic to be attributed to a people traditionally humorous, but a survey of the reviews in either group
goes some way to confirm him. If it does not reveal quite
what was discovered by Mr. Wilson's transatlantic glimpse,
it does show a certain sense of mission and of the emotional intensity which accompanies such a sense. What is accomplished by that sense of mission and the resultant emotional pressure--what is the worth of the serious review--is
open to varying judgments. Whatever the basis of judgment,
however, it must, like all those concerned with publication,
fall into two parts--a judgment which estimates immediate
accomplishment and one which concerns itself with ultimate
influence.

Immediate accomplishment--or the lack of it--can be
measured with some accuracy. Judged commercially, the
reviews are negligible; no one of them can live without subsidy. Judged by numbers of subscribers, they are negligible,
too, though here with two qualifications to be stated presently. In the field of their main interest, however, they are
important in some ways which are not easily disregarded.
One of these is the present aid they give to imaginative writing; to the building up of the writer not yet established, or
the one who, because of the nature of his talent, will never
have more than a small public. All the reviews publish
some stories as well as much verse. Lacking the outlets
they provide, the exceptional, the unconventional poet or
story-writer, who, as it is, meets difficulty and delay
enough in getting a hearing, would find the attainment of
that hearing harder still. The "little magazines" help, but
it is largely through the reviews that the generally unacceptable work of one decade becomes the acceptable of the next,
and a new unacceptable talent appears to be supported.

* * *

Those reviews which include discussion of public
questions perform for these the same service. And, doing
so, they have an advantage over their more prosperous contemporaries. Where there is no expectation of profit there
need be no timidity. And, fortunately for the nation as well

as for the individual publication, neither patron university
nor patron foundation has shown an inclination towards censorship. It was noted in an earlier paragraph that, with
the serious reviews, judgments based on size of subscription
list were more than usually subject to error. For this there
are two reasons. Free libraries, whether public or collegiate, usually have one or two or more of the reviews in
question on their shelves. And since quarterlies call for a
larger expenditure per copy than do magazines of more frequent appearance, their library use is increased proportionately. And, secondly, such subscribers as quarterlies have
are likely to be strategically placed for the influencing of
opinion. Ministers, college professors, zealots in behalf of
one or another literary cause--remove these, and what remains in negligible indeed.

It was an American scholar of the earlier years of
this century who said, "When I look at history in the terms
of fifty years, I despair; when I look at it in terms of five
hundred, I do not." In a lesser time measurement, but in
the same terms, the serious literary quarterly looks forward
to making its final impress on the civilization within which
it has developed.

R. S. V. P.

by Zena Sutherland
This comes from a little leaflet distributed by the Corporate Library Service of Holt Rinehart & Winston

From Owlet Among the Colophons 2:1-2, September 1967; Reprinted by permission of Office of Corporate Library Services, Holt Rinehart & Winston, New York City

"What," I was invited to answer, "is the responsibility of the reviewer?" What is most important? Blank as the paper in the typewriter, I sat. And sat, and sat. Finally decided that of all the responsibilities the reviewer has, the major one is not taking oneself too seriously while taking the job very seriously indeed.

Reviewing books offers a splendid chance to pontificate, and the more one is excited (pro or con) the more one is liable to sound opinionated rather than informed or convinced. There's a fine line between them; mea many times culpa, I fear. One of the most educational--and humbling-- experiences for a reviewer is to give editorial advice, which I do occasionally. Having seen what a good editor has done to the raw manuscript one's read makes very, very clear the patience, intelligence, and experience that have gone into the finished book.

This may sound ridiculous, but I think it is imperative to read the book. It doesn't happen often, and it is not liable to happen in responsible review media, but there ARE times when a review is all too clearly the result of a hasty scanning of the book--or a dependence on jacket copy--or both. Let's face it, most jacket copy is intended to make the book sound enticing, not to give a measured analysis of literary worth.

One ought, also, to judge each book on its own merits.

If a prolific author turns out a good book a year about little
Nancy's family and friends, and book number ten is as good
as book number one, it is a good book. It shouldn't be
dismissed because it seems to the reviewer (who has read
the preceding nine) that it is like the others. It is. It is
also an entity; to the child who reads it, it is a good new
book.

One must consider the needs and the probable experience of the audience; in this case, I mean not the readers
but those who select books for the readers. If one is writing reviews for parents, there is no point in comparing older
books on the same subject and suggesting that this one will
bring a collection up to date. If one is writing for teachers
or librarians, of course they want to know this. For one
thing, they have (sob) budgets. It IS important that the reviewer know the literature that exists, however, as a standard for comparison.

Three minor, but not unimportant, things come to
mind. The reader may be entertained by quips and sallies,
but if they are caustic and uninformative, or if they are too
personal, I feel they are out of place. And if THAT isn't
opinionated, what is?

Then there is the price of the book. It is most definitely not the reviewer's responsibility, in my opinion, to
say, "This is too expensive for what it offers." Let the purchaser decide if the book is worth it to him; he may have
a passion for expensive full-color illustrations or feel that
life is barren without everything in print on the subject of
cryogenics.

Third, the suggestion of an age or reading range--
most review media give some such indication, and I hope
that this is understood by purchasers to be a suggestion
rather than a mandate. Young people read books intended
for them, they dip into long-past favorites, they absorb difficult material in pursuing special interests, and they browse
through books only part of which they can--or want to--ab-
sorb.

Now, to get down to the core of the reviewer's responsibility, what does his reader want to know? Well, he
wants to know what the book is about, and he usually wants
to know if you think it is good, and why. Or not good, and
why. Sometimes it is easy to give a synopsis of the plot,

sometimes not. Often a complicated plot, if divulged in full, may tell the reader more than he wants to know. In compressing the story line, one must be careful to give an accurate and balanced impression.

The reader want to know something about format and illustration, perhaps about the type or the binding, certainly about the style of writing. If the book is nonfiction, how reliable is the information? How up-to-date? Are the illustrations near the text to which they refer; do they have adequate captions; do they agree with the text? (Sometimes they don't.) Has the index been carefully compiled?

If the book is fiction, are the characters believable, and is there a consistency in characterizations, relationships, and motivations? Does the story line hang on contrivance or coincidence? Is the dialogue natural or stilted? It's easy enough to spot melodramatic action, stereotyped characters, purple prose or hackneyed poetry, and (grr) conversation that is used as a vehicle for informative homilies. And it is easy, at the other end of the spectrum, to describe the book that is perceptive, honest, and beautifully written. It's the books in between that demand the most attention from the reviewer.

Certainly a serious responsibility is the weighing of strengths and weaknesses in such a book; one has an obligation to make a balanced statement. One has, also, the obligation to recognize one's own bias about genre, or about subject, or style, or any aspect of the book. The reviewer should be able to keep in mind those qualities that appeal to children and young people while being aware that their subject interests need nourishment and their literary discrimination needs guidance.

Elizabeth Nesbitt, in the summer of 1966, read a paper on "The Critic and Children's Literature" at the annual conference of the Graduate Library School at the University of Chicago. Her comments are a precise and eloquent summation for those who read reviews and those who write them.

> Creative literature has, in the past, and should in the present call forth creative criticism, and this should be as true of children's literature as of adult. Criticism may manifest itself in various forms. In the form of the book review, it should

serve a utilitarian as well as a stimulating purpose. In this form, it must deal not only with the
truly great but also with the near great and with
that which misses greatness altogether. And always, with whatever it may be concerned, it must
establish, with clarity, preciseness, and enlightenment, the quality or lack of quality of the writing
in question. If criticism is to have the effect upon children's literature that it should have, that is,
the effect of convinced acceptance of children's literature as an integral and significant part of the
total body of literature of any country, then it
must not only, in Arnold's words, 'learn to know
and progagate the best,' it must also learn to know
and discourage the worst.

Zena B. Sutherland is editor
of The Bulletin for the Center
of Children's Books and author
of History in Children's Books.

Observations on Specialized Book Reviewing

by Mary L. Allison

After a career in a variety of publishing positions--with Publishers' Weekly, encyclopedia projects, Educational Film Library Association--the author is now Publications and Public Relations Director of Special Libraries Association

From Stechert-Hafner Book News 19:93-95, April 1965; Reprinted by permission of Dominick Coppola, President, Stechert-Hafner, Inc.

During the past few years there has been a spate of harsh criticism directed against some of the most respected library and literary reference tools. The New York Times Book Review, the third edition of Webster's International Dictionary, and the Encyclopaedia Britannica, for instance, have been roundly trounced for their banality, limited coverage, lack of scholarship, commercialism, inaccuracies, and mediocre writing. On the other hand, the New York Review of Books, which started during the 1963 New York City newspaper strike, has become an established biweekly, The Association of College and Research Libraries began publishing Choice: Books for College Libraries in March, 1964, the New York Herald Tribune's Sunday Book Review is syndicated to the San Francisco Examiner and the Washington Post, and it has even been suggested that librarians initiate still another book review magazine for their profession. All these criticisms and innovations testify to the interest and concern of readers, writers, librarians, booksellers, and publishers about the current quality and quantity of book reviewing in the United States.

Thus it is surprising that there has been so little comment about the book reviews appearing in the trade, professional, and technical press. Surely this is an area as

567

deserving of objective examination as the popular book reviewing media, for it is only in these journals that books
produced for limited, specialized audiences are ever reviewed or even mentioned. Many of the same criticisms of
poor selection and uneven writing can justifiably be applied
to reviews in specialized periodicals; some others are
unique, the most common probably being the long time lag
between the publication of the book and the appearance of a
review. Another important consideration is the relationships
that exist between the specialized publisher, editor, reviewer, and reader (buyer). Their responsibilities and roles in
the specialized reviewing process differ, it seems to me,
from those involved in trade reviewing for the general public.

A physicist learns about new works in his field in
Physics Today, a metallurgist consults the "new books" section of Metals Review, and a business executive finds titles
concerning practical solutions to administration problems in
Business Management, while librarians, especially those who
select books for users with strong subject interests, scan--
or certainly should--reviews in a variety of trade and professional journals. Although there are a number of fine
specialized selection aids, such as Technical Book Review
Index, the "New Books Appraised" section of Library Journal,
Insurance Literature, Stechert-Hafner Book News, and New
Technical Books, librarians responsible for building subject
collections for industrial, commercial, government, university, or research libraries must also cover the current periodicals in their subject areas. I have sometimes wondered
how many editors of technical and business periodicals are
fully aware of the importance of their book reviews to their
librarian readership.

I rather suspect that many of them do not realize
that frequently it is the librarian, not the scientiest or scholar or sales manager to whom a journal is directed, who
makes the decision whether or not to buy a certain book.
Those responsible for acquiring and strengthening the subject collections of public, university, research, and special
libraries are as guided by reviews in making their selections as are librarians purchasing general-interest books for
children, young people, or adults. A review in a subject
journal is usually far more persuasive and indicative of the
coverage, treatment, and value of a new book than direct-
mail advertising circulated by the publishers, and librarians
with limited book budgets are apt to wait until a likely title

is reviewed before making a final decision about purchasing
it.   A wider recognition of this fact by editors--and publishers and their advertising agencies--might serve as an
impetus to expand the book review sections of technical and
trade journals.

Some publishers seem to regard specialized journals
as second-class members of the book world, for they rarely
provide galleys or review copies of new books in advance of
publication as they do to the popular reviewing media.   This
is probably the principal reason reviews are so late appearing in technical and professional journals.   In all fairness,
however, it must be pointed out that many specialized book
publishers are small or of a nonprofit nature and cannot afford the luxury of dozens of extra sets of page galleys or
of distributing a large quantity of free finished books prior
to publication.   Another inhibiting factor is that many technical volumes contain photographs, formulae, graphs, tables,
or other illustrative matter that is added after the type has
been set, and a publisher is understandably reluctant to have
galleys reviewed without this graphic material.   Furthermore
many specialized titles are printed by the offset process in
which the production of galleys is more complicated than in
letterpress printing.

Another serious charge against publishers is that they
are often guilty of not taking the trouble to search out the
specialized periodicals that should review their specialized
titles.   This is particularly true of the larger firms that
only now and then publish in certain subject areas or infrequently produce basic reference tools.   Speaking from my
own experience as the editor of Special Libraries, I have
frequently been annoyed at having to write a publisher requesting a review copy of a new book dealing with some aspect of library science.   One would think that an alert publicity department would automatically send new books on librarianship to all the major library journals, just as it
would circulate new novels of major writers to the popular
reviewing press.   I must admit, however, that during the
past eighteen months five large commercial publishers have
begun sending appropriate books to Special Libraries without
being asked--sometimes they have even been advance copies!
--so perhaps this situation is improving.   For small or society publishers that often do not have full-time or professional promotion staffs, the challenge of improving their distribution of review copies is admittedly more difficult than
for commercial publishers with large advertising budgets and

staff.   However, any publisher issuing specialized volumes
should be able to compile a list of suitable reviewing media
by investing in the current edition of Ulrich's Periodicals
Directory or the recently issued Standard Periodical Directory, both of which list journals by subject categories.

The debate about whether book reviews should be primarily descriptive or critical is as applicable to specialized
reviews as it is to popular reviews.   In my opinion a review
of any type should be both descriptive and critical--one without the other is dissatisfying and frustrating to the reader.
In this connection a distinction should be made between a review and an annotation or news item.   The former should be
descriptive and critical and be signed; the latter is usually
very short, purely descriptive, and is unsigned.   Despite
their brevity, however, carefully prepared book notes serve
an extremely useful function when they give complete bibliographical data, including price and availability, and succinct-
ly summarize the content and objectives of a book.   Technical and trade journals, particularly those of a news nature,
are inclined to treat new books in this brief manner.

In contrast to the editorial staff member who prepares descriptive book notes based on publishers' dust
jackets or promotional material and a quick thumb-through
of the volume, a book reviewer should conscientiously read
the entire work, for only then can he be objectively critical
as well as descriptive.   With specialized books this is a
longer and more laborious task than reviewing a novel or
popular nonfiction.   In addition, the specialized book reviewer must pay particular attention to the accuracy of the
information presented and the validity of the ideas or methods discussed.   He must keep the basic purposes--stated or
not--of a work firmly in mind as well as the technical competence of the intended audience.   He must be able to distinguish clearly between theory and application and to compare the factual statements and personal point of view of the
author with the facts or opinions set forth by other authorities.   The specialized book reviewer should know what the
author has done to qualify him to write as an expert, and
he must be knowledgeable about the subject matter under discussion.   Like the reviewer of general books, he must evaluate the organization of the material and discriminate between
original and derivative ideas.   He should be aware of the
niceties of book production and be prepared to comment on
format, illustrations, binding, layout, and quality of the
printing as well as the adequacies of any indexes, bibliogra-

phies, appendices, or other supplementary data. And finally
he must have the skill to express himself intelligently on all
these points in lucid, cogent prose.

Unfortunately most reviewers--technical or general--
do not possess all the qualities of the paragon sketched
above. Dr. Alvin Weinberg has frequently deplored the "dull
way in which they (scientists) express themselves," and the
now famous report bearing his name states:

> This Panel is gravely concerned... that so many
> American scientists and technologists can neither
> speak nor write effective English, that the new
> language of science and technology is turgid, heavy
> and unclear.

Thus it is not surprising that so many book reviews prepared
by subject specialists are written in a pedestrian, unimagina-
tive way and are abstract-type reports on content alone, with
little critical evaluation of the author or his material. This
is particularly true of reviews written and published in the
United States. British journals tend to carry livelier reviews that are fuller of comment and written with more verve
and enthusiasm, witness, for example, the outstanding reviews in Nature.

Although somewhat behind the scenes, another important contributor to the specialized book reviewing process is
the journal editor. He is the one who decides which books
will be reviewed in full, which will be noted as news items,
which will be ignored. A sound knowledge of the interests
and needs of his readership helps him make these decisions
for, like the publisher, he has an obligation to inform the
technical and professional people in his subject area of pertinent new published information. Then there is the task of
selecting a competent reviewer. This act is faught with intangible considerations, in addition to the obvious ones of
subject knowledge and writing ability. For instance, the editor should know if the potential reviewer is a colleague or
competitor of the author, or if he has other commitments
that will make it difficult for him to read and review the
book within a reasonable time. And finally, the editor must
decide how much and in what way he will edit the reviews he
receives. My own position is that editorial treatment of full-
length reviews in a professional journal should be restricted
to changes necessitated by space limitations or style rules.
The reviewer himself should assume full responsibility for

his statements and presentation and stand ready to justify
them to the reader, the author, and the publisher.   This is
the reason any review of a critical character should be
signed and the reviewer fully identified.   A perspicacious
reader and potential buyer evaluates the reviewer as well as
the review, the author, and the publisher.

At this point several general observations by Anthony
A. Martin, Assistant Director, Carnegie Library of Pittsburgh, should be of interest.   He has edited Technical Book
Review Index for the past eight and one-half years and regularly scans the twenty-five hundred scientific, technical,
trade, and professional journals received in the Science and
Technology Department of the Carnegie Library.   Mr. Martin, who is most knowledgeable about the current status of
specialized book reviewing, commented in a recent letter:

> On the basis of competence of the reviewer, his
> literary ability, knowledge of the literature of the
> field, and honesty, the best reviews of scientific
> and technical books appear in the journals of the
> learned societies of both Britain and America.
> There is little difference to note between these two
> sources.   The greatest improvement in the last ten
> years is the increased promptness in the appear-
> ance of the reviews.
>
> However, reviews in trade journals in both these
> countries are quite dissimilar.   In both instances
> poor to excellent reviews are to be found, yet re-
> views in British trade journals are as a rule
> consistently better.   Far too many American "re-
> views" are merely a rehash of the publisher's
> blurb, a statement from the preface, or a sum-
> mary of the table of contents, written or copied by
> a lowly member of the editorial staff.
>
> The British trade journals have their faults also.
> Two items of information in which the prospective
> reader or purchaser is more interested--date of
> publication and pagination--are frequently omitted.
>
> Yet perhaps the greatest dishonesty is perpetrated
> by some of the American and British publishers of
> trade journals who also publish books.   It is the
> very rare occasion when their books are critically
> reviewed in their own journals.   It must be pointed

out also that a disproportionate number of their own books appear on the book review page.

While Mr. Martin speaks from broad experience with journals specializing in science and technology, some of his remarks are equally applicable to the library publications I peruse regularly. Like him, I have been impressed with the high quality of the reviews in the British periodicals, which are longer, more thoughtful, better written, and more critical than those in the library journals of other countries. This statement requires qualification, however, for I refer principally to reviews of professional library literature. In general, reviews of books prepared and published for librarians as practitioners of special skills tend to lack comparative judgment, broad perspective, and critical insight and to accept new volumes at their face value.

A curious dichotomy seems to exist in some library journals, especially those that devote considerable space to reviews of fiction, biography, travel, science, children's, and other specialized books, as well as to the literature of librarianship. The reviews in the former categories may be informative, well written, and evaluative, for example, the splendid brief reviews in Library Journal's "New Books Appraised" section and Antiquarian Bookman, which are often marvels of succinct, pithy, perceptive, and knowledgeable writing. Reviews of library literature, on the other hand, are all too frequently merely a mediocre summation of the volume's contents. British librarians seem to have the gift --or is it perhaps the interest, tradition, or courage?--of appraising their professional literature as critically and analytically as they do that of other subject areas. Librarians in other countries might well endeavor to emulate the English introspective approach to reviewing library-oriented books.

Specialized journals are increasing in number at an astonishing rate in response to the "information explosion," and as part of this same "explosion" more specialized books are being published that deserve more and better reviews. All concerned--authors, publishers, journal editors, reviewers, readers, librarians, booksellers, and book buyers-- have a vested interest in improving the quality, coverage, and speed for the specialized book reviewing process.

Note: The opinions expressed are those of the author and should not be construed as reflecting the policies of Special Libraries Association.

Bias in Book Reviewing and Book Selection

by Henry Regnery
It is often charged, without any
evidence being offered, that libraries tend to purchase liberal
books and pass over conservative ones and that the leading
book review media show the
same bias. To initiate a meaningful discussion of this thorny
subject, Henry Regnery, the
well-known conservative publisher, was invited to substantiate these charges.

From ALA Bulletin 60:57-62, January 1966;
Reprinted by permission of Editor, ALA Bulletin

Mr. Regnery comments on the following article:

The question of bias in the selection of books by
librarians has been discussed by many people on
both sides of the fence. It is, of course, of concern not only to those of us professionally involved
with books but to everyone, for such bias is a
form of censorship and, therefore, interferes with
the free communication of ideas. In the ALA
Bulletin (June 1965), Wesley McCune of Group Research, Inc. , if I understood him correctly,
seemed to be saying that free speech and the existence of the Republic itself were being threatened
by the increase in the quantity and quality of pamphlets, journals, and books reflecting a 'right-
wing' point of view; I am now asked to write an article for the Bulletin 'touching on the reasons why
the American Library Association appears to be
biased, what librarians are doing that stimulates
the belief that they suppress certain points of view,
and what books [I] think are not being given a fair

play in library circles.' Ervin J. Gaines, of the Minneapolis Public Library, who suggested that I write the article, said he came to me because of my 'own predilection for a conservative point of view.'

I have no objection whatever to being called a conservative, provided it is clearly understood what is meant. But my first reaction to the suggestion that I write on why ALA appears to be biased was to say no. I have no reason to believe that ALA either is or appears to be biased, and I have no competence whatever to discuss the subject. After some reflection, however, it occurred to me that it would be interesting to see if I could confirm an impression I have had for a long time: that the leading book review publications, particularly those on which librarians chiefly rely, are biased, specifically toward the liberal point of view, and that books reflecting a conservative position are often either unfairly or inadequately reviewed.

I decided that the best way to approach the problem was to select pairs of comparable books and then to see how the reviewers had treated them. The publications I chose were the New York Times Sunday book review section, Library Journal, and the Booklist and Subscription Books Bulletin. I also checked such publications as Atlantic, Saturday Review, and Christian Century. To bring in too many publications would be confusing, and it seemed legitimate to generalize from these three, since the Library Journal reported in 1962, based on a careful survey, that these publications, with the Kirkus Service and Saturday Review, were the five most used by librarians for selecting books. Library Journal also reported that 32 per cent of the librarians polled relied solely on published reviews in purchasing controversial books, and 19 per cent on a combination of published and staff reviews. In addition the opinions and general position of the New York Times are very close to those of a whole group of other newspapers and magazines, including Harper's, Atlantic, and the Washington Post. In view of this, it seemed to me that a study of the manner in which a representative list of books was reviewed in these publications would shed some light not only on the direct question I have raised--bias in reviewing--but also on the related question--bias in library purchasing.

The selection of books was more difficult. To make
the comparison of reviews meaningful, the books would have
to be comparable on the basis of subject, quality, competence, standing of the authors, and time of publication. I
sought the advice of a number of people--critics, a professor of philosophy, a professor of political science, etc. The
list we finally agreed on met the criteria I have mentioned
reasonably well, but it wasn't possible, as I had originally
hoped, to confine the list to books published within the last
five years; however, the oldest book was published in 1954,
and only six were published before 1960. Finally, of course,
the pairs of books to be compared had to be written from a
conservative and a liberal point of view.

Before going any further, I should make clear what I
mean by "liberal" and "conservative." The most useful definitions of these two positions with which I am familiar are
the "syndromes," as he calls them, worked out by James
Burnham in Congress and the American Tradition (see below).

Conservative	Liberal
1. Belief that government in- volves nonrational factors; distrust of ideologies.	1. Confidence in the ability of rational science and democrat- tic ideology to solve all prob- lems of government.
2. Belief that human nature is limited and corrupt.	2. Belief in the unlimited po- tentiality of human nature.
3. Respect for tradition.	3. No presumption in favor of traditional usage.
4. Belief in the diffusion of sovereignty and power.	4. Willingness to waive the principle of diffusion of power if thereby progressive forces or goals are furthered.
5. For representative, medi- ated government.	5. Tendency toward plebisca- tary democracy.
6. For States' Rights.	6. Minor concern with or even disapproval of States' Rights.
7. For the autonomy of the various branches of the central government.	7. Belief that the autonomy of the branches of the central government hinders solution of major social problems.
8. Greater solicitude for the limits than the powers of government.	8. More solicitude for the power of government to ac- complish progressive goals than for limits of government.

Conservative	Liberal
9. Belief that American constitutional tradition embodies principles that are intelligible and of permanent value.	9. Interpretation of the American Constitution as instrumental, its meaning wholly dependent on time and circumstances.
10. For decentralization and localization.	10. Belief that decentralization and localization often interfere with the solution of modern problems.
11. Presumption in favor of private enterprise.	11. Critical attitude toward private economic enterprise, and positive belief in government economic control plus some measure of government ownership.
12. Primary philosophic concern with individuals in their private capacity, rather than with the nation or the collectivity.	12. Belief that the expansion of governmental activity aids the attainment of the good life.
13. Presumption in favor of Congress as against the executive.	13. Presumption in favor of the executive as against Congress.

The Affluent Society, by John Kenneth Galbraith
(Houghton, Mifflin, 1958).
The Humane Economy, by Wilhelm T. Roepke
(Regnery, 1960).

These two books fill the requirements I listed for meaningful comparison almost perfectly. Galbraith is a professor at Harvard, a former ambassador and adviser to President Kennedy; Roepke is a professor at the University of Geneva and an adviser to Chancellor Erhart; Galbraith is a Keynesian, Roepke a staunch defender of the free market and balanced budgets; both are skillful writers. Library Journal recommended the Galbraith book for all public and college libraries; the Booklist was equally warm in its recommendation, calling it "stringently honest... well grounded in economic history." The Times pulled out all the stops-- a front page review by a warm admirer of the author.

The Booklist didn't review the Roepke book, and while Library Journal was respectful, it was hardly effusive: "... more dazzling than illuminating... interesting but hardly

convincing... Recommended for large educational and public
libraries." The Times review, which began on page six, was
also respectful, declaring that "if anyone in our contemporary
society is entitled to a hearing it is Wilhelm Roepke." Then
it went on to consign him to the liberal Dark Ages: "If conservative thought cannot cope with the great fact of social
mobility all over the world, it can offer little for our guidance despite its devotion to liberty." Saturday Review, however, gave the book an excellent review, "...an able, hard-
hitting, and well-written account of the century old conflict
between mass society and humanist culture."

> Reflections of an Angry Middle-Aged Editor, by James
>   Wechsler (Random House, 1960).
> Rumbles Left and Right, by William F. Buckley, Jr.
>   (Putnam, 1963).

William F. Buckley, Jr., and James Wechsler provide another sharp contrast in their positions and in their
books. Wechsler is editor of the liberal New York Post, the
angry young radical of the 1930's; Buckley is the editor and
founder of the conservative National Review and author of
God and Man at Yale, which, appearing a year after his
graduation, shook the liberal establishment to its foundations,
and particularly the equanimity of Yale University. Library
Journal called the Wechsler book "a thought provoking book
for all libraries." The Booklist used the phrase, "a stimulating appraisal." The Times review by Emmet Hughes became quite eloquent, "...a passionate pamphlet in the best
sense of the word... Yet the more striking fact is that so
impassioned a statement is so largely rich in fresh insights,
so largely free of the snares of caricatures and cliche common to many an editorialist's polemic."

I was unable to find a review of the Buckley book in
Library Journal; the Booklist described it as "political and
social criticism designed to tease and annoy liberals, may
amuse or instruct readers of either liberal or conservative
persuasion..." In the Times it was reviewed by the Washington correspondent of the Christian Science Monitor, who
characterized Buckley as "this latter-day Don Quixote of the
right" and concluded, "Mr. Buckley is an American exotic of
the far right, who wins some sympathy for his frankness and
boldness since, in this sorry world, the heterodox are always laughed at, whether right or left."

A Piece of My Mind: Reflections at Sixty, by Ed-
    mund Wilson (Farrar, Strauss, 1956).
Occasions and Protests, by John Dos Passos
    (Regnery, 1964).

Both of these books are collections of essays. The
Booklist and Library Journal recommended both books, and
I think no one, whatever his position, could question either
the fairness or adequacy of their reviews. The Times reviews of the books, on the other hand, were distinctly partisan. "Mr. Wilson has given us a piece of his mind for nearly forty years now--and very lucky we have been to be in his
audience... we find ourselves hoping that he will continue to
give us a piece of his mind for many a year to come." The
Dos Passos collection of essays was reviewed on the front
page of the Times by the young English novelist, John Braine.
Like many liberals, Mr. Braine much prefers the Dos Passos
of The Big Money and Manhattan Transfer, who wrote for
The New Masses, to the man who writes for National Review
and is concerned about different bosses than those who bothered him in the twenties--now it is labor union bosses. According to Braine, Dos Passos "has become an unauthor, he
doesn't exist any longer." Occasions and Protests, he decided, "... is a sad drab book." For all the length of the
review, it said very little about the book itself--it consisted
largely of the reviewer's expressions of disapproval of Dos
Passos' alleged changed attitudes.

Senator Joe McCarthy, by Richard Rovere
    (Harcourt, Brace, 1959).
McCarthy and His Enemies, by William F. Buckley,
    Jr. , and Brent L. Bozell (Regnery, 1954).

This next subject, the late Senator Joseph M. Mc-
Carthy, usually brings forth an emotional response. Library
Journal recommended the book by Richard Rovere "to all libraries as a helpful journalistic portrait," and the Booklist
called it "readable, informed, important." It was reviewed
in the New York Times by Anthony Lewis, who called it "an
appraisal without apology," and although Mr. Rovere used
such words as liar, barbarian, seditionist to describe Senator McCarthy, the Times reviewer also said that the judgments of the author "are given without rancor." The reviewer pointed out that the book "lacked factual support," but
this didn't stop him from coming to the conclusion that it was
"uncommonly sensitive and accurate." The Buckley-Bozell
book fared reasonably well in Library Journal and the Book-

list; both reviewers found the book well written and recommended it, but with some reservations.   In the Times it was
reviewed by William S. White, who dismissed the book without attempting to meet its carefully reasoned, documented
argument "as a bald, dedicated apologia for 'McCarthyism.'"

> Deadlock of Democracy, by James MacGregor Burns
>   (Prentice-Hall, 1963).
> Congress and the American Tradition, by James
>   Burnham (Regnery, 1959).

The two books by James Burnham and James Mac-
Gregor Burns are both on American government, the first
pro-Congress, the second inclined to a strong executive at
the expense of Congress.   The Booklist reviewed them both,
fairly and accurately; Library Journal recommended the
Burns book but did not, insofar as I could discover, review
the Burnham book.   The Times gave the Burns book the full
treatment: a 1700-word review by a most sympathetic critic
beginning on page two and ending with "a striking analysis
...; bold recommendation...; and a readable journey through
American history." Burnham, who fears the growing concentration of power in the executive and defends Congress as
the bulwark of our liberties, fared much less well in the
Times.   The 1000-word review by Professor Lindsay Rogers
of Columbia, on page fourteen, remarked, quite irrelevantly
to the argument of the book, that it contained "echoes of the
Liberty League of 1934 and the America Firsters of 1940"
and concluded with the cheap and unworthy remark, that if
Mr. Burnham was 'not an amateur in the matters he considers, he is plowing fields that have only recently become
familiar to him."

> Danger on the Right, by Arnold Forster and Benjamin
>   Epstein (Random House, 1964).
> Suicide of the West, by James Burnham
>   (John Day, 1964).

The book by Forster and Epstein would have been
greeted by howls of "McCarthyism" and "guilt by association"
had it been titled Danger on the Left and been written by two
members of the John Birch Society.   As it was, it was received with uncritical enthusiasm.   "A copy of this book belongs on the shelf of every person active in the civic life of
the nation, just as a manual of poisons belongs in the medicine chest," intoned the Times.   Both the Booklist and Library Journal recommended it, the Booklist calling it "in-

formative, readable..."

The Booklist, on the other hand, called Burnham's
Suicide of the West an "inconclusive, emotional attack," but
in its Young Adults Section recommended it to "high school
students who have a philosophic bent." Library Journal described it as "an honest attempt to understand some... contemporary political phenomena," recommended it for college
and university libraries, and described its author as a "dynamic conservative." The Times didn't find room to review
it, but the New York Review of Books called it "puerile as a
birchite pamphlet" and the Atlantic, while acknowledging
Burnham as "a thinker and writer of great gifts" said that he
"manages nevertheless to be persistently wrong-headed when
he comes to deal with politics..." meaning, of course, that
he doesn't agree with the Atlantic.

>The Great Crash 1929, by John Kenneth Galbraith
>   (Houghton, Mifflin, 1955).
>The Great Boom and Panic, by Robert T. Patterson
>   (Regnery, 1965).

The two books on the 1929 crash don't provide as
sharp a contrast as some, but I thought it would be interesting to compare the reviewer's reaction to a book by an economist who uses the 1929 crash to bludgeon the Republican
Party and the capitalist system, with his reaction to one by
an economist less interested in proving a theory than telling
what happened, and whose views are in the classical tradition. The Galbraith book was reviewed on page three of the
Times, very favorably, by a member of the Times editorial
staff. The Patterson book was not reviewed. Library Journal reviewed both books adequately and fairly; I could find
no review of either book in the Booklist.

>The Democratic Prospect, by Charles Frankel
>   (Harper, 1962).
>The Conservative Affirmation, by Wilmoore Kendall
>   (Regnery, 1963).

The books by Charles Frankel of Columbia University
and Wilmoore Kendall of the University of Dallas, formerly
at Yale, are worth comparing because both are concerned
with political theory, and both authors are recognized as
prominent spokesmen of the liberal and conservative positions. The Frankel book was reviewed in the Times by
Brand Blanshard, as sympathetic to Frankel's position as

any writer could wish, who thought it "... a little too full of
the abstractions of the philosopher. Yet it is full, too, of
the generous concern and wise asides of a good doctor, sitting with his thermometer and stethoscope at the bedside of
a distinguished patient." A very pretty picture, and one calculated to fill the reader with the feeling that in spite of the
"abstractions of the philosopher" there wasn't much wrong
with Mr. Frankel's book.

     Mr. Kendall didn't fare quite so well at the hands of
the Times, where his book was reviewed by William S.
White. Mr. White found The Conservative Affirmation
"... an exasperating but far from trifling book, streaked with
brilliant perception but strained by harsh oversimplification."
Mr. Kendall, obviously, doesn't have the bedside manner of
Mr. Frankel, and what were "abstractions of the philosopher"
in one case became, presumably, "harsh oversimplifications"
in the other. The Booklist and Library Journal reviewed and
recommended both books; Library Journal said that the
Frankel book "should be in every library" and suggested that
the Kendall book gave a synthesis "which should make it useful in at least medium-sized and large libraries."

> The Professional: Lyndon B. Johnson, by William S.
>   White (Houghton, Mifflin, 1964).
> Barry Goldwater: Portrait of an Arizonan, by Edwin
>   McDowell (Regnery, 1964).

    My next pair of books involves political candidates and
are therefore a severe test of the objectivity of the reviewers.
Library Journal "highly recommended" the White book on
Johnson and used the phrase "recommended for wide purchase" for the McDowell book on Goldwater. The Booklist
did not review the White book; it recommended the McDowell
book as a "slightly more up-to-date presentation of Goldwater's qualifications" than an earlier book. The Times did
not review the McDowell book, but gave its cover to the
White book. The following is characteristic of the review:
"the best written and most compelling portrait of Mr. Johnson that has so far appeared... the outstanding performance
has the ring of truth."

> The Liberal Papers, edited by James Roosevelt
>   (Quadrangle Books, 1962).
> The Conservative Papers, edited by Melvin R. Laird
>   (Quadrangle Books, 1964).

I concluded my investigation with The Liberal Papers and The Conservative Papers and was pleasantly surprised at the result. Library Journal gave each book about 150 words; The Liberal Papers was "highly recommended" and The Conservative Papers "recommended for any library." The treatment by the Booklist of both books was equally fair. In the Times, both reviews appeared on page three; both were fair, objective appraisals, The Liberal Papers reviewed by August Heckscher and The Conservative Papers by Joseph M. Lalley, book review editor of the conservative quarterly, Modern Age.

Does all this prove my impression that the leading review publications are biased, and does it reveal bias on the part of library purchasing? Based on the ten pairs of books I have chosen, I don't think there is evidence of decided bias on the part of the two professional library publications, but I think that rather consistent bias is indicated on the part of the New York Times. I am sorry to concentrate on this one publication, but if a similar examination were made of Harper's, Atlantic, the Washington Post, Book Week, or the New York Review of Books, the results would be about the same. It should be said, of course, that the New York Times has as much right to review books in the way it wants to as I have to publish the books I like, but that isn't the subject I was asked to discuss. One source of bias in the case of the Times is the choice of reviewers: a liberal reviews the liberal books, and in every case but one a liberal reviewed the conservative books.

It does not necessarily follow, of course, that a liberal cannot review a conservative book objectively and fairly, but in the case of books involving strongly held, controversial opinions, it would be rather unlikely that a man who disagrees with the author would give his book an entirely objective review. In this connection it is instructive to mention that when it became known that Book Week had asked William F. Buckley, Jr., to review Theodore White's book on the last presidential campaign, the editor received a flood of protests from people who felt that Buckley couldn't possibly review the book objectively. I have never heard that these people objected when, for example, Arthur Schlesinger, Jr., was asked to review one of Buckley's books.

The fact that William F. Buckley, Jr., was asked by Book Week to review the White book and Joseph M. Lalley by the Times to review The Conservative Papers is an indication, we may hope, that the situation is improving, and in actual fact, it isn't quite as bad as some of those on the conservative side would have us believe. The Dos Passos book was reviewed on the front page of the Times unfavorably and, in my opinion at least, unfairly, but it was reviewed, as many other books have been, which reflect the conservative position. Some of us may not always like the Times's choice of reviewers, but many do, and we can all be grateful that a book-reviewing publication of its completeness and professional competence exists. It is unfortunate that there is no comparable publication reflecting the conservative point of view.

As for bias in library purchasing, that could be demonstrated only by making an actual survey of books in libraries. To mean anything, a large sample of both books and libraries would have to be used, which would be more than I could undertake. A questionnaire was sent to 22 libraries in Illinois inquiring whether copies of 22 selected books were in their collections. These included most, but not all, of the books I have discussed. The results were inconclusive. The Chicago Public Library, not surprisingly, had all the books. The replies from the other libraries gave no indication of bias that I could see.

Since I am human, I am sure that my investigation of bias in reviewing has not been completely objective, but I did try to make it as objective as possible. The results were reassuring, at least to me, and rather different from my expectations. Quite frankly, I had thought that I would be able to demonstrate far more bias than proved to be the case. I think that bias is indicated reflecting a liberal point of view in reviewing, but the conservative position, all things considered, is given a fair chance. The liberals enjoy a strong and commanding position in the communication of ideas, but a conservative who has something to say can still get a hearing.

Editor's note: A much earlier study on the library selection aspect of this topic is C. L. Haselden, "Social attitudes of librarians and the selection of books on social issues," Library Quarterly 20:127-35, April 1950.

The Author and His Audience (Sel.)

An anniversary volume produced by the publisher in celebration of 175 years of publishing.

From The Author and His Audience; With a
Chronology of Major Events in the Publishing His-
tory of J. B. Lippincott Company. Philadelphia,
J. B. Lippincott Company, 1967. p. 42-8 (sel.);
Reprinted from The Author and His Audience,
copyright (c) 1967 by J. B. Lippincott Company.
Reprinted by permission.

Another conspicuous feature that distinguishes book
publishing from other enterprises is book reviewing. In
cities from Boston and points even farther east to Los Angeles and Honolulu, newspapers review books regularly--once
a week, or in New York and a few other large cities, at
least a book a day, plus a weekly book section that covers
dozens or scores of new titles. Many magazines, weekly
and monthly, review many books. Other industries have
trade journals that comment on new products, and in fact
newspapers will describe new merchandise of all sorts if
they think their readers are interested. Much space is given
regularly to new models of automobiles. But here the space
is devoted to description, not to criticism--unless there is
independent criticism to be reported, as when in 1966 the
subject of automobile safety was ventilated in Congress and
in Mr. Ralph Nader's book, Unsafe at Any Speed. But Mr.
Nader was not writing as a newspaper critic. Reviewers
employed by newspapers and magazines, either as staff members or free lances, are expected to express their opinions
of the books they review. When an opinion is unfavorable,
it may cause distress to the publisher and anguish to the author, but unless it is demonstrably unfair, prejudiced, or inaccurate, publishers and experienced authors swallow their
disappointment and realize that to complain in public would
have the effect merely of calling attention to the original re-

view on the part of readers who might have missed it. What other business welcomes, even invites, criticism of its products, knowing that the rough must be taken with the smooth?

What is a review for? Specifically, <u>whom</u> is it for? And what is it supposed to do for those who <u>read</u> it? There is a venerable definition which has acquired the characteristics of a cliché through repetition; it runs as follows. A review should answer three questions. What did the author try to do? How well did he succeed? Was it worth doing? Another axiom is that reviews are written for readers, to give them the information they require to decide what books they are interested in reading.

The trouble is that a review may admirably fulfill the foregoing functions and be dull reading itself. To be interesting, a review needs style; it should reflect a personality and still be unprejudiced. There are always some reviewers in general practice who can regularly write reviews that genuinely interest their readers and tell them how to choose what to read out of the avalanche of publications. To avoid being misinterpreted, perhaps this essay should choose its examples from reviewers who have retired from regular reviewing; Orville Prescott and John K. Hutchens; the late Joseph Henry Jackson and Lewis Gannett; Clifton Fadiman and Charles Rolo.

All these men have written regular columns or departments of newspapers or magazines. Their readers came to know their tastes and their personalities. Unlike the Phelpses and Woollcotts, whose enthusiasm was indiscriminate, they wielded all the more influence with their favorable reviews for the contrast of their frequent expressions of coolness, of distaste, sometimes of opinions altogether devastating. Quite different is the situation of the free-lance reviewer. He is called upon by the editors of magazines or of the book-review sections of newspapers to take assignments for reviewing, one book at a time; and while some free lances gain the confidence of editors sufficiently to become regular reviewers--for The New York Times Book Review, Saturday Review, Book Week, New York Review of Books, or whatever--even then their choice of books to review is restricted to those the editor offers them. And while there are frequent and striking exceptions, generally the influence of their reviews depends on the influence of the paper or magazine.

The converse is that the influence of the paper or magazine in book reviewing is in the long run the resultant of the abilities and standing of the individual reviewers. The book-review editor's job is not easy. When he finds a reviewer who can write professionally and interestingly, he grapples him to his stable with hoops of steel. But the editor who is trying to produce a publication that reviews books for its readers must often have occasion to feel frustration and chagrin. Even his best regular reviewers cannot always be counted upon. They go on trips; they become engrossed in their own work and have no time to spare. They get bored with an oversupply of mediocre books about which there is nothing interesting or new to say. Sooner or later, being inveterate if not compulsive readers, they discover an exciting new author, an important new book, and back they come. But meanwhile and otherwise, the editor must be looking out for new talent.

Quite obviously competitive is the review by an author of a book similar to the one under review--perhaps another treatment of the very same subject. An editor who assigns a travel book to a reviewer who has written a travel book on the same territory may delude himself that he is giving his readers an expert opinion--he is more likely to be committing an indefensible atrocity.

One obvious hunting ground is inhabited by professional writers. At least they can write. But they cannot necessarily review books by other writers. Sometimes it is difficult for a novelist to be altogether objective and impersonal about the work of a contemporary novelist. Frequently a novelist reviewing another novelist's work will overcompensate and praise lavishly. Logrolling, apparent and real, will go on as long as logs are floated to paper mills. On the other hand, a novelist reviewing another novelist's work may have too professional a point of view, and may criticize the author for not writing another kind of novel than the one he intended to write, and indeed did write. The inherent unfairness of this kind of reviewing is difficult for the reader to see through, because it is perfectly honest.

Another obvious game preserve is that of the colleges and universities. Members of college faculties are indispensable as reviewers of new books in their special fields of interest--history and biography, economics and politics, art, science, literary history and criticism. All reviewers love to review books of literary criticism and all review editors

think these books are congenitally important.   A vast amount
of laundry exchange goes on in this area, especially among
teachers of literature.   Perhaps the readers outside of academic life come to feel that they ought to be interested.   As
to other subjects, most college teachers can judge a new
book in their field on its merits, objectively.   Not infrequently, however, professionalism has the same danger as was
noted about novelists in the preceding paragraph: the author
is judged by what the reviewer thinks his intentions ought to
have been.   And rare indeed is the book of history or biography written by an author who is not a college teacher--
worse, not even a doctor of philosophy--that can get a fair
hearing from members of the union.   It would be unfair not
to mention that there are notable exceptions.   Allan Nevins,
for instance, came to the academic world from journalism
and for many years, in addition to teaching and writing his
own distinguished and voluminous works, did a vast amount
of reviewing, and never unfairly--indeed, he could always be
interesting and fair simultaneously; a rare achievement...

        To return to reviewing.   Many college teachers, es-
pecially those with their reputations still to make, are eager
to review books.   Reviewing gets their names into print; it
may be the first step in publishing as an alternative to perishing.   Now it goes without saying that the way to attract
attention quickly is to demonstrate superiority.   In book reviewing, there are only a few ways to demonstrate superiority.   One is in style, another is in judgment; nothing is better than a combination of the two.

        Now fastidiousness is admirable if genuine.   But noth-
ing is more easily faked.   The reviewer who is too sophisticated to be taken in by what other readers admire; the reviewer who is careful not to set his own sails before he
knows which way the academic wind is blowing; the reviewer
who knows how to express patronizing tolerance--he is the
one who can call attention to himself, to his discernment,
his resistance to bluff, his fastidious superiority.

        And every one will say,
        As you walk your mystic way,
        "If that's not good enough for him which is
            good enough for me,
        Why, what a very cultivated kind of youth this
            kind of youth must be!"

Our reviewer has forgotten his Gilbert and Sullivan; so has
the editor who prints his stuff.

Out of this one-upmanship there quickly develops a peck order in criticism. The critic who sees more wrong with a book than the next critic gets a higher place in the peck order. Not just _any_ book--it must be a book which has been praised, is popular--and not merely popular with the undiscriminating. The thing to be superior to is the respectable and popular book-club selection, the book read with pleasure and even absorption by hundreds of thousands of readers literate but not "literary;" bookish but not critical; intelligent but not "intellectual;" cultivated* but not "cultured." These unfortunate readers have been cleverly designated as "middlebrows" in a term coined by an editor of a middlebrow magazine.

It is important to distinguish reviewing from criticism. A review is an ad hoc, journalistic exercise. Its function is to relate the book to its immediate audience. Criticism goes deeper and attempts to achieve an importance beyond the immediate. Reviews are written for people who have not read the book; criticism for those who have. Reviews are ephemeral; criticism may last as long as Aristotle's Poetics. Therefore it is natural that academic reviewers should try to elevate their endeavors into the realm of criticism. But this is dangerous. If criticism is to have enduring value, it must be significant (in the cant word of contemporary criticism, meaningful) to more than an immediate audience. It should be significant to more than one generation. Criticism is at its best in the work of such distinguished men as Edmund Wilson and the late Van Wyck Brooks, in which new books seldom if ever provide the subject matter.

* The connotation here being different from Gilbert's, in the quotation above, perhaps the distinction suggested between "cultivated" and "cultured" should be illustrated: a cultivated field, a cultured pearl. Anyhow, Gilbert meant "cultured" but needed the extra syllables.

Common Ground - An Editorial

From Times Literary Supplement, June 15, 1962, p. 445; Reprinted by permission of the Times Newspapers Ltd., London, England.

It seems strange that literary critics, who are popularly supposed to be quite sharp-witted, should be so loth to examine their own situation and consider just what they are doing. Criticism in the large academic sense is an inexhaustible subject (if only for its practitioners), but the structure and limits of the critical press, the merits and dangers of book reviewing as done week by week, the forces that encourage or threaten the conscientious reviewer: all this has been left virtually undiscussed. Weekly criticism as done in this country is something that we have taken for granted, at least since 1945.

Much the same is true elsewhere; so far as the standards and conditions of his activity go the weekly critic has had to guess for himself. It was thus a real innovation when the French Syndicat des Critiques Litéraires summoned the international colloque of critics which met in Paris last week. Here, under M. Yves Gandon's stimulating chairmanship, French reviewers and men of letters came together with representatives of fourteen other countries to examine the critic's situation in the modern world. How far can he and his editor cope with the books put before them? Do they get enough space? Are they paid properly? Can they compete with criticism on radio and television? What do they do for international understanding? And what, if anything, can they be said to achieve?

The answers given were various, as might be expected of a group of critics and editors drawn from many of the chief European papers on both sides of the iron curtain yet a number of common features emerged. Nobody except the west German rapporteur (Herr Krämer-Badoni) felt that the critical resources in his country were adequate to cope

590

with the increasing flow of new books. Only in eastern Europe and in the most prosperous British papers is the reviewer paid well enough not to need a second employment; it is indeed where he cannot live by criticism alone that the best criticism is done. A major French critic on a regular contract can earn perhaps 1,500 N. F. a month (or about Ł 1,350 a year); a reviewer writing for one of the main west German dailies will be paid between 80 and 150 DM. per hundred lines of typing, or Ł 6 to Ł 13 for a thousand-word article.

In France and Germany it is common for notices of a book to appear over a period of some months following its publication; English editors usually try to keep more up to date. French publishers send their review copies direct to likely critics; their English colleagues leave this to the editors concerned. In Spain reviewing, and in fact the whole literary scene, is bedevilled by censorship. In France books have won a place on radio and television where elsewhere they are still slightly uncertain intruders. In Poland and Czechoslovakia, and still more so in the U. S. S. R. , an effort is being made to improve contacts between writers, critics and the general public by drawing the non-specialist reader into the discussion of literary problems or of individual books.

The question of reviewing works in foreign languages was repeatedly discussed. In France this is rare, despite the efforts of individual critics such as M. Jean Cathelin; in the Dutch and Scandinavian papers it is on the contrary the rule, the Nieuwe Rotterdamsche Courant for instance being liable to issue special supplements of twelve to fourteen pages on foreign books, often very expertly reviewed. The same problem is evidently present in the minds of Soviet editors, who find themselves faced with a growing number of books in the minority languages of the U. S. S. R. and are taxed to find Russian (as opposed to local) critics who are competent to review them. What is, however, slightly discouraging, for those who see Switzerland and Belgium as possible models for the multinational Europe of the future, is to find that the critics in these countries, instead of trying to look at their literature as a polyglot whole, turn outwards to that larger literary world, notably German or French, of which their own particular language group feels itself a part. There is no Swiss paper or literary periodical that treats the country's three main languages on a common footing--even typography will depend on outside affiliaations--while of all literatures to be discussed in the French-language Brussels press Flemish evidently comes last. Familiarity with other cultures, it seems, can breed deliberate ignorance as well as contempt.

Such concerns emerged all the more clearly from these discussions thanks to the use of a common language--French--by all but one of the participants, and many of them were expressed in a series of resolutions which were hurriedly but unanimously adopted at the end. Like the various papers read and the debates on them, these will in due course be published by the very capable officials of the French Syndicat. In effect they say, in terms that are addressed to editors, proprietors and publishers as well as to fellow critics:

> (1) That a country's or a publisher's literary standing must be judged by the quality, not the quantity of books produced.

> (2) That it is time for a careful study of the trend towards publication of more and more titles each year.

> (3) That more space needs to be given to reconsiderations and critical second thoughts.

> (4) That reviewers in provincial papers often do excellent work without getting much credit.

> (5) That conscientious reviewing, being unlikely necessarily to attract new readers or stimulate advertising, is to be pursued for its own sake and for its long-term influence on a paper's reputation.

> (6) That all imposition of censorship is bad.

Such tenets are simple and perhaps a little utopian, but they form the nucleus of what might develop into an international critical charter. If, as was proposed and unanimously accepted, further meetings are held in Brussels and/or in Prague it should be possible to extend these basic principles and so to fight the tendencies which are at present in many different countries pushing criticism in the direction of reporting, gossip, religious and political moralizing or plain advertisement. There are only two provisos: there ought to be some American reviewers or editors pres-

ent, and surely more than one English representative should
be induced to attend.

Reviews of: Why Are We in Vietnam?

by Norman Mailer   New York, G. P. Putnam's
Sons, 1967. $4.95

Mailer's Texas-to-Alaska Talkathon

From The Christian Science Monitor, September
14, 1967; Reprinted by permission from the
Christian Science Monitor (c) 1967, The Christian
Science Publishing Society. All rights reserved.

It is almost impossible to consider a Norman Mailer
novel without considering Norman Mailer. Take "Why Are
We in Vietnam?"--his latest talkathon in the shape of a
novel. It really has no independent existence of its own. It
really has no independent existence of its own. It lives only
as the latest installment in a kind of running autobiography.

Readers are practically forced to develop a personal
response--a sort of Aunt Polly-Huck Finn relationship--to-
ward Mailer ("Tarnation, that's a good boy if we can just
civilize him"). But by now old Norm knows all the moves.
No one's going to get him in shoes. He plays the 44-year
old barefoot boy to unwashed perfection.

Mailer's current escapade is a book-length scatalogi-
cal monologue by an 18-year-old Texan calling himself D. J.
A disc jockey who is all obscene chatter and no records,
D. J. floats down a heavily polluted stream-of-consciousness
while narrating the often scabrous details of a bear hunt in
Alaska with his Texas-rich father and friends.

The general point of D. J.'s diatribe seems to be that
Americans, in Alaska or Vietnam, are a violent, guilt-ridden, and thoroughly insecure people. There is little doubt,
at any rate, that D. J. is violent, guilt-ridden, and thoroughly insecure, and being a bit of a bully besides, he is deter-

mined to impose therapy on all listeners by forcing them to confess that yes, his hangups are their hangups too.   Such are the ways of the tough guy as artist, not excluding Norman Mailer.

Mailer has a marvelous nose for the phony and a roaring, ham-fisted style of disposing of it--usually along the throw-out-the-baby-with-the-bath lines.   Organization men, cagey old white hunters, Southern womanhood all get savaged.

There is humor in Mailer's total assault on American character but no other visible sense of perspective.   A passing random insight can become for the next few perfervid pages the basis of a whole new cosmology.   To adopt his own metaphor of the chase, rabbits become grizzlies just because Mailer is chasing them.

At a time of general alarums and calls to crisis, he is, of course, an in-tune voice; hysteria passes for plausibility these days.   The pity is that Mailer has the ability to do much more than just reflect with numbing fidelity the excesses of his age.

What once looked like a great talent. . . .
. . . . Eric Moon, Editor, Library Journal

From Library Journal 92:3056, September 15,
1967; Reprinted by permission of R. R. Bowker
Company and the author.

What once looked like a great talent now seems to be
in an advanced state of decay. This is Mailer's worst novel,
and a strong candidate for the worst novel of the year. Os-
tensibly about a hunting expedition in Alaska, the story is
narrated (spewed might be a more accurate word) by a foul-
mouthed Texan teen-ager, Ranald Jethroe, alias D. J. , disk
jockey to the world. The book pretends, however, as in its
title, to deeper or wider significances, and in the more than
200 pages of invective and ridicule aimed at Texas and Tex-
ans it appears that Mailer is using Texas as a microcosm of
all of America's current ills. The language--a field day for
the four-letter word--conveys only evidence of Mailer's own
sickness as a novelist. It is to be hoped that he will recover
but the malady, in this "novel," is at an advanced stage.

From Potpourri by Phoebe Adams

From the Atlantic Monthly 220:143-4 October 1967;
Reprinted by permission of Donald B. Snyder,
The Atlantic Monthly, Boston, Mass.

Norman Mailer's novel Why Are We in Vietnam?
(Putnam, $4.95) is fierce, funny, and tightly organized. Per-
haps as a result of turning The Deer Park into a play, Mr.
Mailer has learned to build his sermon into the plot instead
of goofing off periodically into the pulpit. The book also contains, I believe, a percentage of dirty words unequaled except on certain washroom walls. Mr. Mailer has reason for
these words. His first-person narrator, a youth who calls
himself DJ (for Disc Jockey to the Universe) is "a humdinger
of a latent homosexual highly over-heterosexual with onanistic
narcissistic and sodomistic overtones, a choir task force of
libidinal cross-hybrided vectors." This is DJ's malicious
and imaginary version of diagnosis by his mother's psychia-
trist. His real trouble is rather more simple. With a dis-
creetly lecherous mother from Norleens and a status-grab-
bing father from Tex-ass, DJ sees the world organized by
his elders as a mixture of (let us stick to civil euphemism)
sex and sewage. His vocabulary is limited by this view, but
within its limits, precise and consistent. It is also repetitious, and what Mr. Mailer accomplishes by the repetition is
unusual. First comes the inevitable disappearance of any
meaning at all from these overworked words. Then they acquire a new meaning, or at least a new authority, as Mr.
Mailer's persistent hammering at them compels the reader
to accept DJ's vocabulary as the articulation of normal, accepted reality. The book's style in other respects is a
wickedly clever parody of Salinger, Burroughs, and Barth,
full of puns, ironic scholarship, bits of old jokes, learned
paraphrase, burlesque scientific jargon, juvenile slang, and
slapstick Texas dialect. The whole compilation is a mockery of the current tendency among critics to count intricacy
of style as intrinsically meritorious. (Actually intricacy is
meritorious, from the critic's point of view; it proves that

the author has really been working hard, which gives the
critic one solid point to take a bearing on.)

      The literary spoof is merely titivation, however. Mr.
Mailer's real target is American society, which DJ sees as
a constant struggle for what his father would call success,
meaning face, meaning the right to kick an inferior and get
away with it: a right to be won by any means available and
subsequently described by the winner as the result of disinterested and heroic action. Specifically, DJ and father go
hunting in Alaska, accompanied by DJ's friend Tex and two
of father's flunkies, one of whom lugs along a cannon fit to
stop a charging rhino at ten feet. He can hardly hit a
mountain with the thing, but technically he has outgunned the
boss, a social error that casts general murrain. Father,
soured by the firepower question, nags the guide unreason-
ably about grizzly. The guide, a distinguished old D. Boone
type, judges correctly that what this crowd wants is not
sport but loot. He contemptuously helicopters them all a-
round the Brooks Range, rings them with bodyguards, and
silently packs up and flies out the slaughtered beasts. The
dead animals are real, but the rest of the affair is a fraud--
cheap thrill, safe danger, make-believe courage, results
guaranteed or your money back. By the end of it, the two
boys have resigned from the system. Vietnam is not mentioned until the last page of the book, and Mr. Mailer could
have made his point without ever mentioning it at all.

Montgomery County Bars New Mailer Book...
Footnote by Librarian Hirsch...
Libraries say Mailer was judged on merit...

From Newsletter on Intellectual Freedom, January 1968, p. 1; Reprinted by permission of the Washington Post, Washington, D. C. and Leroy C. Merritt, University of Oregon, Eugene

Montgomery County's public libraries have refused to stock Norman Mailer's new novel, but the County Council was assured yesterday the decision was not related to Mailer's political activities or personal life.

William L. Sollee, a Rockville resident, wrote to the Council asking for an inquiry about the decision not to purchase the controversial book Why Are We In Vietnam? He enclosed favorable reviews of the book from The Washington Post and the New York Times.

Robert A. Passmore, assistant to the county manager, said library officials told him the decision was based solely on the book's literary merit.

Mailer's novel consists almost entirely of an account of a bear hunt in Alaska. Although Vietnam is mentioned only on its last page, some critics view the work as an allegory of the United States involvement in the Asian war.

The decision not to purchase Mailer's book was prompted by two reviews by library staff members. Jane Hirsch, an assistant librarian at the Bethesda branch, wrote: "Sorry this one is beyond me. This is either a classic or nothing at all."

Mary Dulany, coordinator of adult services, added a recommendation against purchase of the book to her finding that "this is such a poor book that I am not willing to inflict it on our borrowers." She added, however, that "it is important as a demonstration of the uses of language."

George Moreland, director of County libraries, said the system has six of Mailer's books, but rejected The Deer Park because "it isn't a good book," and said the same rule was applied to the new volume.

Moreland backed up the library's decision by saying that public libraries in New York, Baltimore and Washington have rejected the book although it is available in Prince George's County Libraries.

Footnote by Librarian Hirsch

In the Oct. 25 story regarding the decision of the Montgomery County Public Library not to buy Norman Mailer's Why Are We In Vietnam?, phrases from book reviews made by librarians were quoted out of context. As one of the librarians quoted (or partially-quoted), I would like to make my position on book reviewing and on the Mailer book clear, not only in self-defense but also so that citizens of Montgomery County will be assured that this librarian considers book selection a serious and important responsibility, and decisions on books which I know will be controversial are not taken lightly.

My "review" was in reality more of an inter-office memo, intended to convey disappointment in the book and my desire that it be read by many staff members before a decision was made. The entire memo expressed my viewpoint that Why Are We In Vietnam? is a very poor book, it is badly written, boring, repetitious, and of no discernible literary or social value. If anyone except Mailer had written this book, I would have had no doubts, but because Mailer is, in my opinion, one of the greatest living American writers, I was loathe to take an absolute stand. However, I do feel each book a writer produces should be judged as a separate work, and if my word had been the final one, the greatness of The Naked And The Dead and Cannibals and Christians would not have redeemed Why Are We In Vietnam?

As to the charges that Mailer's use of "obscene" language and his political views were the deciding factors, the first statement shows a complete ignorance of modern literature and what is available in public libraries; the second gave me the only laugh in the whole situation. Here I'd thought

I was the noisiest dove in Bethesda.

Libraries Say Mailer Was Judged on Merit

Why is Norman Mailer's new novel, Why Are We In Vietnam?, being rejected by many public libraries in the Washington area?

It's not that the book is so politically far-out or shockingly racy, say the librarians. It's just that Mailer's latest effort strikes them as worthless.

Library officials in Montgomery, Fairfax and Arlington counties and Alexandria said they have decided not to buy the book.

In Washington, the book has been "tentatively" rejected and no change in that decision is in the offing.

Mailer in Wilmington...

From Newsletter on Intellectual Freedom, March
1968, p. 19; Reprinted by permission of Editorial
Director, Wilmington Journal, Wilmington, Del.,
and Leroy C. Merritt, University of Oregon,
Eugene

The technique of selecting books for purchase by the
Wilmington Institute Free Library as described on Nov. 24
requires some discussion and some protest.

The committee which rejected Norman Mailer's newest book admits its decision was made without reading the
book on the basis of condemnatory reviews. Whose reviews?

Mr. Christopher B. Devan, director of libraries, is
quoted, "It wasn't just the words. The whole book has no
valid purpose. It is a bad novel." This judgment, if he has
not read the book, is someone else's which Mr. Devan has
chosen to impose on the entire community using the library.

That a book review is critical should in no way be
equated with a recommendation by the critic that it not be
made available to readers who wish to make their own evaluation or wish to read it despite the critic's opinion. Especially with respect to an author of Mailer's previous achievements, all of his new works should be available in the public
library.

Admitting that available funds must limit purchases,
decisions by a small committee which effectively restrict
what adults will be permitted to read are a serious matter.
The library selection committee must, of course, select,
yet its selection is actually an arbitrary censorship imposed
on the community.

The article stated that public libraries in New York,
Baltimore, and Washington have also refused to purchase

602

Mailer's newest book.   Do the libraries tell this to each
other?   Do they band together to ban books?   I have phoned
the main New York City Library on Fifth Avenue; it has the
book in question in circulation.

Let our library continue, if it must, its policy of
marking some books V (for venal, or verboten, or vulgar)
and producing them only on demand rather than placing them
on the open shelves, but let the library not ban these books
totally.

Perhaps the list of books considered and rejected for
purchase by the committee should be published along with the
list of their acquisitions.

Bernadine Z. Paulshock
(Letter to the Editor)
Wilmington Journal, 7 December

Editor's note: In connection with the problem of reviewing
current fiction, see also John C. Pine, "Minor masterpieces and ghastly mistakes," Library Journal 87:497-
500, February 1, 1962 and also Mr. Pine's letter
quoted on p. 604.

Caveats and Contradictions

by John C. Pine

Readers Advisor, The Smithtown Library, Smithtown, New York

and "A Reviewer Replies"

From Library Journal 90:3828, 3830, October 1, 1965; Reprinted from Library Journal, copyright (c) 1965 by the R. R. Bowker Company, with the permission of the author and R. R. Bowker Company

In a review of Christopher Isherwood's novel about a sexual deviate, A Single Man, in the September 1, 1964 issue of Lj, Ervin J. Gaines, although admiring Isherwood's "clarity, wit and lean style," recommends the novel with "the caveat that the theme may give offense." Looking up the word in my battered Webster's Collegiate, I found that caveat meant exactly what I feared it meant: "a caution; warning; admonition."

For some time now a question has nagged my conscience. Why are there so many caveats, so many warnings and admonitions, sprinkled throughout the fiction reviews which appear in Lj?

A classic example would be the July 1963 issue. Reviewing John Rechy's City of Night, Lloyd W. Griffin writes that the novel is "a cool, level, extremely graphic picture of a piece of subcultural Americana as true, unfortunately, as the facets of America revealed by Tom Wolfe or Robert Frost." Sounds good, doesn't it? And indeed we recall having seen other favorable reviews of the book. But wait! Mr. Griffin is not yet done. He must also warn us that it is "a kind of Cook's tour of sexual perversion and homosexuality which would probably cause no end of trouble for certain libraries" (italics mine). This sentence is clearly designed to put librarians on their guard and can have no other effect than to reinforce whatever apprehensions they may al-

604

ready have concerning the book.   Is not Mr. Griffin just as guilty of voluntary censorship or pre-censorship as any of the timid librarians flushed out by Marjorie Fiske in her famous report of a few years back?

In the same issue of Lj, we find a review of John Cleland's Memoirs of a Woman of Pleasure, better known as "Fanny Hill," written by none other than the distinguished editor of the Library Journal himself, Eric Moon.   Mr. Moon adopts the same cautious approach as Lloyd Griffin. He gives qualified and grudging praise to the book and decides that "college and university libraries should certainly include this book as a hardy survivor of the literature of the period, and public libraries with substantial collections should probably have it too.   But others had better be careful," Mr. Moon warns ominously (italics mine), "a great many 20th Century puritans will find grossly offensive this elegant product of an elegant but licentious age."

Now the editor of Lj writes fearless editorials in that unstuffy, indignant style of his that has won our admiration, severely chastizing the censors and would-be censors both inside and outside the profession.   And not so long ago he devoted an entire issue to this whole area of what he likes to call "problem fiction" (Is he making it a problem?), an issue to which this writer is proud to have contributed.   But shades of Mrs. Grundy, how can he vehemently denounce every manifestation of censorship--and especially the voluntary censorship illuminated by the Fiske Report ("the kind of anticipatory internal censorship through nervousness," as he so strikingly puts it)--in an editorial and yet when it comes to the very immediate and specific task of reviewing one of these "problem novels," turn right around and plead caution to the librarians in the field who may well be looking to him for (and have every right to expect) real guidance and support?

I would certainly appreciate it if the writer of the editorial "Coalinga to Philadelphia" (see Lj, July, pp. 2980-81) would explain this apparent contradiction between theory and practice in the pages of Lj.   Perhaps it might even make an interesting subject for an editorial.

A Reviewer Replies

The purpose of reviews in Library Journal, as I understand it, is to aid librarians in the selection process.

The selection process, again as I understand it, involves a consideration of both the book and of people. At least, I have always thought that librarians were supposed to select books with people (their public, defined any way you want to define that) in mind. Thus, it seems reasonable to me for a reviewer, not only to comment on the content, quality, and style of the book but, where this is obvious, to say something about any elements in the book which are calculated to elicit certain reactions from certain segments of the public. To warn librarians that selection of a book is likely to cause repercussions is not the same, in my language, as to say "don't buy it." If I mean "don't buy it," I say "don't buy it." I happen to believe--and have said often--that the librarian who is doing a good job of book selection is bound to open himself up to controversy and repercussions. But I also believe that part of the service the book selector expects--and deserves--from us is at least a hint that he should be prepared for such problems if he buys certain books which receive any kind of recommendation from us. I admit, sadly, that in some cases, a warning has the unhappy effect of frightening off the already chicken-hearted, but I do not know that deceiving this latter group by omission is much of a solution for their particular ailment. --Ed.

Reviews of Library Surveys

Ed. by Maurice F. Tauber
and Irlene Stephens. New York, Columbia University Press,
1967. $13.50

From Klimberger, Joseph. "Library surveys examined," Library Journal 92:2903, September 1,
1967. Reprinted by permission of R. R. Bowker
and the authors.

The late Dr. Ernest Jones once remarked that 50 per
cent of the people undergoing psychoanalysis do not need the
treatment, but should be able to help themselves. Worse,
however, he observed, is the fact that the far greater percentage of the practitioners of psychoanalysis are not
equipped for the task. Such skepticism in relation to library surveys apparently did not particularly trouble the
participants in a Conference on Library Surveys, held at
Columbia University, June 14-27, 1965, co-sponsored by the
Committee on Library Surveys of ALA's College and Research Libraries Division and Columbia's School of Library
Service.

The editors of this volume have done a fine job organizing the papers read by the various expert participants
covering a great many aspects of survey methods and special approaches to problems of library surveys. The book
contains a most instructive review of the history, origin,
and evolution of the survey in various types of public and
academic libraries as well as discussions of procedures and
descriptions of measuring instruments used in evaluating resources, technical services, building programs, personnel,
and other important aspects of library service today.

Very few critical remarks, however, cropped up in
these fine academic discussions, and one is almost relieved
to find an occasional hint of doubt about present practices.
A refreshing tone of uncertainty comes with Lowell Martin's

607

remark,

> I am constantly astonished at the number of library
> surveys commissioned in recent years. This no
> doubt reflects a healthy self-criticism on the part
> of librarians, and a faith in formal planning.   At
> the same time, I confess to a somewhat jaundiced
> view of the trend, and find myself asking--is this
> survey necessary?"

Andrew Geddes also voices some skepticism in his
paper:

> The surveyor unquestionably is hired as the author-
> ity; it is expected that he will cure all of the ills
> of the library.   Yet, in fact, many of the problems
> he will face are new to him.

Although the reviewer understands that some of these
points were explored in discussion groups following the delivery of the formal papers, the conference as reported did
not delve into practices prevalent in current library surveys.
For example, the question was not raised as to why a self-
survey by the experienced staff of the library would not be
preferable to the new approach of employing an often ill-informed "outsider" whose survey might overlook many important issues and developments.   The conference skirted the
fashionable exchange game: "If you recommend me for a library survey, I'll recommend you, and we'll both earn a
nice fee. " Neither did the conference examine the dangerous
implications of the fact that a few so-called professional library consultant firms are taking a decisive role in the shap-
ing of the future of our libraries, a point briefly mentioned
in Mr. Geddes' paper.

Has the library profession become so insecure that we
have to accept directions and the last words of wisdom from
a few self-appointed judges?   A list of consultants is available from ALA.   What are the criteria used to have one's
name placed on this list?   Is the taxpayer's money spent
wisely through handing out large amounts to surveyors to
produce superficial and ill-documented pieces of work?   A
second conference following this high-minded academic exercise is needed to deal with all the practical problems of use
and abuse of surveys.   The "what" of surveys has been examined; the "why" and "who" still remain unanswered questions.
--Joseph Klimberger, Nassau Lib. System, Garden City, N. Y.

Surveys and Reviewers

by Larry Earl Bone

Assistant Director, Graduate
School of Library Science,
University of Illinois, Urbana

From Library Journal 93:15 January 1, 1968;
Reprinted by permission of R. R. Bowker and
the authors.

The negative review of Tauber's and Stephen's Library
Surveys in the September 1 issue of Library Journal (p. 2903)
made me anxious to receive my copy of the book. As a participant in the conference at which these papers were given,
I remembered them as being highly informative. Consequently, I was disappointed with Joseph Klimberger's one-sided
and superficial review.

In basic courses in book selection, we teach students
that a review, if it is to serve as a selection aid, should indicate and evaluate clearly a book's contents and not merely
air the reviewer's own special prejudices. Only in the first
two paragraphs of his review does Mr. Klimberger deal with
a specific evaluation of the papers themselves; in the remainder of the review, he seems concerned only with his
personal objections to surveys.

Mr. Klimberger has every right to question. In fact,
even though he is not a recognized authority on library surveys, he could have performed a valuable service for his
readers with a balanced critical evaluation of the book's contents. This, however, he did not choose to do--and he has
weakened whatever case he has against surveys.

Furthermore, Mr. Klimberger's review leaves a definite question in my mind as to whether he read the book
carefully. For example, he says, "The question was not
raised as to why a self-survey by the experienced staff of

the library would not be preferable to the new approach of
employing an often ill-informed 'outsider'..." As I read
this, I wondered if my memory had failed me.   The question
of the self-survey, I thought, had arisen on several occasions
during the conference.   So when my copy arrived, I checked.
Surely enough, the subject of the self-survey appears in five
different papers.   In fact, Janet Bogardus, in her paper on
"Special Libraries," suggests quite clearly why the self-survey is not as valuable in that type of library.   "The self-
survey," she says, "whether by librarian or by the planning
or other management division within the firm, is not, I think,
likely to be very productive in the small special library.   If
the librarian had new or better ideas, presumably he would
have tried them.   Attention from the management is likely to
revolve around cost-cutting or space-saving objectives."

  Mr. Klimberger dismisses the conference as a "high-
minded academic exercise." If I correctly sensed the atmosphere of the conference, however, those present (of whom
Mr. Klimberger was not one) considered it more than that.
The discussions following each of the papers proved that the
participants regarded it as a forum in which they could deal
with "practical problems of use and abuse of surveys," which
Mr. Klimberger so desires.   As such, the book deserves
consideration for addition to any professional collection because of the wealth of material it brings together on this important topic.

Review

by Robert B. Downs

From College and Research Libraries 29:160-2
March 1968; Reprinted by permission of Executive
Secretary, Association of College and Research Li-
braries, American Library Association, Chicago,
Illinois.

The present collection of papers by leading lights in
the somewhat esoteric world of library surveys is based upon a Conference on Library Surveys, held at Columbia University in June 1965. The expanding interest in the general
theme is shown by the recent publication in England of a
work with the same title, Maurice B. Line's Library Surveys,
subtitled An Introduction to Their Use, Planning, Procedure,
and Presentation.

No fewer than seventeen speakers contributed to the
Tauber-Stephens compilation, among whom one recognizes
such veteran surveyors as Guy Lyle, Edwin Williams, Leon
Carnovsky, Donald Bean, Lowell Martin, Stephen McCarthy,
Morris Gelfand, Frances Henne, and Walter Brahm, as well
as a surveyer of surveys, E. W. Erickson. From such a
group, we would expect a diversity of views, and we get it.

Background for the series is provided by Guy Lyle in
his article exploring "the origins and evolution of the library
survey." Lyle selects for extended comment a half dozen
"landmark surveys" of the past ninety years, placing them in
their proper historical setting and reviewing their methodology and accomplishments. Beginning with the special government report issued in 1876, Public Libraries in the United
States, the story continues through the ALA Survey of Libraries in the United States (1926), Wilson's The Geography
of Reading (1938), Joeckel and Carnovsky's A Metropolitan
Library in Action (1940), the Public Library Inquiry (1949-
52), and institutional library surveys, exemplified by the
pioneer Report of a Survey of the University of Georgia Li-

611

brary (1939), by Louis R. Wilson and others.   Lyle also
considers the place of the self-survey (as do a number of the
other contributors) and evaluates the influence of the Carnegie
graduate library school on the development of surveys.

The rather bewildering variety of library surveys
merely demonstrates that they are designed to serve different functions.   Thus we have comprehensive investigations,
such as those listed by Lyle; studies of library collections;
of technical services in libraries (sometimes subdivided by
analyses of acquisition procedures, cataloging, classification,
applications of automation, etc.); library use; building and
facilities; general administration; budgets and finance; personnel; and of types of libraries--academic, public, school,
special, and state--all considered by experts in the Tauber-
Stephens work.

The complex matter of surveying library collections
is treated in depth by Edwin Williams, whose Resources of
Canadian University Libraries for Research in the Humani-
ties and Social Sciences has had an enormous impact on
Canadian library development since its publication in 1962.
The prolific output of reports on collections is examined by
Williams from the points of view of purposes, methods, and
results.   The methodology is still far from standardized, but
Williams provides some useful guidelines.

The editors are the authors of a chapter on another
popular area, "Surveys of Technical Services in Libraries."
Tauber's seasoned approach, conditioned by innumerable investigations in the field, comes out in a detailed discussion
of the choice of the library consultant, the literature of such
surveys, reasons for, how to conduct processing surveys,
and a review of three typical processing surveys: those of
McGill University library, Dallas public library, and Nassau
library system.

An old hand with another kind of survey, Leon Carnovsky, looks at studies on the use of library resources and
facilities from the points of view of circulation trends by
type of agency, by classes of material, and by reader. While
circulation statistics are relatively easy to come by, Carnovsky emphasizes the difficulties in their interpretation.   Particularly complex is any meaningful study of library reference work.

Library buildings and facilities are of basic importance, because of the large sums of money involved and their bearing on the general effectiveness and efficiency of the whole library operation.   This type of survey is examined by Donald Bean, who writes from a background of many years of commercial consulting.

In other chapters, John A. Humphry deals with surveys of budgets and finance, Lowell Martin with personnel, and Stephen A. McCarthy with administrative organization and management.   Five contributors concern themselves with surveys of types of libraries, and E. W. Erickson concludes with a convincing review of the value, effectiveness, and use of the library survey as an instrument of administration.

The Tauber-Stephens work is the first full-scale investigation of an increasingly important branch of library science.   No significant aspect of the multifarious field is omitted.   Experienced surveyors and those planning any type of survey will find in the compilation a variety of helpful discussions on the methodology, purposes, limitations and uses of the library survey in its many manifestations. --
R. B. Downs, University of
Illinois.

Review

by Margaret E. Cockshutt

From Ontario Library Review 52:53 March 1968.
Reprinted by permission of Editor, Ontario Library
Review, Toronto, Canada

In 1965 the Columbia University School of Library
Service and the Committee on Library Surveys of the Association of College and Research Libraries sponsored a four-
day Conference on Library Surveys, held at Columbia University. Seven Canadian librarians were among the Conference
participants. The Conference papers have now been published for the benefit of all librarians, and form a welcome
addition to our professional literature.

The book is divided into two principal sections. Part
One, "Use of the Survey Method," contains papers on methodology and applications in such problem areas as library collections, technical services, library use, buildings, budget
and finance, personnel, administrative organization and management. While such areas are common to all types of libraries, the illustrations are chiefly from the academic and
public library fields. Part Two, "Special Approaches and
Problems of Library Surveys," presents papers on applications in different types of libraries. The section ends with
a perceptive discussion of the value, effectiveness and use
of the survey as an administrative and educational device in
the academic library and the library school. There is also
a curiously isolated appendix, chiefly containing questionnaires which are interesting and useful in themselves but only one of which is cited in the papers as being included in
the volume, and there is an index which is aggravating and
misleading because of its incompleteness.

Inevitably the papers are uneven in their interest and
value for the reader; inevitably and often desirably there is
duplication as ideas are examined from different viewpoints.

Some of the contributors have given a greatly simplified outline of procedures, some have attempted to identify principles and relationships, and some have given extensive illustrations from their own survey practice. In the best papers there is an emphasis on the objective measurement and evaluation of a library's performance in terms of its own purposes and objectives. Standards which have been set and accepted by the profession are therefore seen as yardsticks against which an individual library or a library system may be evaluated, rather than as goals in themselves. As Guy Lyle has noted in his background paper, "in no small part, the development of survey technique has been a problem in applying the research methodology of science and the social sciences to the study of library problems."

This book will not satisfy the novice surveyor as a "how-to-do-it" textbook. Several of the individual papers are excellent, but the chief value of this collection lies in the frequent insights which it gives the librarian on the interrelationship of the objectives and evaluation of library service, the tenuous balance between scientific measurement and subjective expert judgment in the survey of performance, and the complex administrative network which must be perceived and untangled in even the simplest survey. For those whose libraries are to be surveyed this book will be required reading.

Section 6

Evaluation of Collections

Evaluation ... signifies describing something, in terms of selected attributes, and judging the degree of acceptability and suitability of that which has been described.

Elizabeth P. Hagen and Robert L. Thorndike, "Evaluation," IN Encyclopedia of Educational Research. 3rd ed. New York, The Macmillan Company, 1960. p. 482

The evaluation of collections lies at the heart of the professional responsibility of the librarian, but is a relatively recent concept in the literature. Waples' pioneering text outlines a method which is ideal but also exceedingly difficult to apply in practice. A variety of other methods for carrying out this responsibility are described in the readings in this section, including use of checklists of approved titles, checking holdings against citations in important sources, checking availability of materials on the shelves, and checking for saturation or reader satisfaction.[1] The identification of levels of collecting and the marking out of boundaries which a specific collection ought to meet (illustrated by Mrs. Welch's student paper) have proved to be especially appropriate for use with university collections, but are also applicable to other types of libraries. Studying the distribution of collections by date of copyright as in the Blasingame study appears also to provide a method which gives a different insight into the quality of collections, especially for libraries within an area system or at differing levels in a state network.

The second group of readings is intended to supply examples of some of these methods as applied in a variety of types of libraries, and to differing types of materials or subjects.

What are the limitations or advantages of each method of evaluation? Are there others which have proved useful? What is the responsibility of the professional staff member in this task? Of the outside specialist or consultant (as in the case of the Toronto survey)? What specific competencies are required in order to carry out such a task? What are the implications of the current idea of the "instant library" for the librarian's role in evaluating and developing collections?

Although there is no dearth of standards and guidelines for the evaluation of school library/media collections, as well as many examples of quantitative evaluations of collections for such agencies as accrediting associations (unpublished), there is a real dearth of published examples of collection evaluations. What is seriously needed is examples of evaluation of <u>media</u> collections, using methods illustrated in this section and others pertinent to collections in schools.

Note

1. See also p. 1181 for the reading by McColvin on this particular method.

Quantitative Criteria for Adequacy of
Academic Library Collections

by Verner W. Clapp and Robert T. Jordan

Mr. Clapp was President (now
Consultant) of the Council on
Library Resources. Mr. Jor-
dan, formerly on the staff of
CLR, is now librarian at the
Federal City College, Washing-
ton, D. C.

From College and Research Libraries 26:341-80,
September 1965; Reprinted by permission of
Executive Secretary of Association of College and
Research Libraries, ALA. Note that corrections
called for in C&RL, Vol. 26, No. 5 have been
made in the text.

The authors challenge accepted doctrine which asserts that the adequacy of an academic library
cannot be measured by the number of books which
it contains. Out of their feeling that the Standards
for College Libraries and the Standards for Junior
College Libraries are inadequate for estimating the
size (in volumes) required for minimum adequacy
by libraries of institutions of higher education of
widely differing characteristics, they developed new
formulas for this purpose. These formulas attempt to identify the principal factors affecting
academic needs for books and to ascribe suitable
weights to each factor. The authors then illustrate
the application of the formulas to specific institutions, and conclude that while the results are useful, further research is needed. They end by suggesting specific topics for such research.

Can the adequacy of the collection of an academic library be measured by the number of books which it contains?

Respectable authorities say "No!"

"The adequacy of the college library's collections cannot be measured in quantitative terms," asserts a well-known
textbook in the field of college library administration. "To
judge a collection superior or inferior on the basis of the
volume holdings," it maintains, "is as absurd as rating a college on the basis of its enrollment."[1]

Regional accrediting agencies agree. "The actual
number of books which a library contains is not a stable
measure of the adequacy of the library."[2] "More important
than the total number of books in the stacks is the extent to
which the selection of volumes accurately reflects the needs
of the institution as defined by its educational task."[3] "It
will be noted that no mention is made here of required mini-
ma for... library holdings ... The adequacy of each institution's resources must be judged in terms of its program."[4]
"Every [academic] library must ... be evaluated in its own
setting rather than by comparison with general patterns or
norms, because each library must support a particular educational program."[5] And similarly the Northwest Association,
1957, and the Western Association, 1963, while concerned
for the "adequacy" of the academic library, provide no yardstick for the measurement of that quality.[6,7] The only regional association which makes an obeisance in the direction
of a quantitative measure (but in a manner which approxi-
mates mockery) is the Southern Association:

> The book and periodical collection should, by qual-
> ity, size, and nature, support and stimulate the
> entire educational program... the following should
> be used as a reference: Library Statistics of Col-
> leges and Universities. Annual Analytic Report...
> In using this reference, institutional authorities
> should consider it a serious danger signal if the
> library regularly falls in the lowest quarter of any
> of the categories analyzed.[8]

When, as in these cases, standardizing authorities
omit or refuse to set standards in quantitative terms, the
budgeting and appropriating authorities who cannot avoid
quantitative bases for their decisions, are compelled to adopt
measures which, though perhaps having the virtue of sim-
plicity, may be essentially irrelevant.[9]

It is not surprising, in consequence, that the Standards

for College Libraries adopted in 1959 by the Association of
College and Research Libraries of the American Library Association, while properly placing primary emphasis upon quality and the means for achieving it, should also include suf-
ficant numerical criteria to meet to a degree the need for
quantitative standards.

Specifically, these Standards provide that fifty thousand
"carefully chosen" volumes may serve as the minimum for
the library of a college of up to six hundred students (full-
time equivalent); that "steady growth" is essential but may
slacken when the collection reaches approximately three hundred thousand volumes; and that for each two hundred students above the initial six hundred there should be an additional ten thousand volumes.   It is emphasized that these are
minimal figures. [10]

The Standards for Junior College Libraries, likewise
promulgated by the Association of College and Research Libraries, are similarly insistent upon quality, but similarly
offer some quantitative assistance.   They require that an institution of up to one thousand students (full-time equivalent)
should have a minimum of twenty thousand volumes exclusive
of duplicates and textbooks and suggest that this figure should
be increased by five thousand for each additional five hundred
students beyond one thousand.   Again, it is emphasized that
these are minimal figures. [11]

In neither case, however, are the suggested quantitative criteria convincing in the sense that they rest on demonstrations of actual numbers of books required for specific
educational purposes.   Instead, the suggested figures admittedly reflect the accidentals of college library statistics (without indication of how this reflection is effected) or agreement
among librarians consulted.   The requirements for additional
books are based in one case upon an apparent "correlation
between the growth of the student body and the growth of the
collection," and in the other simply upon "consultation with
many junior college librarians." Finally, the Standards for
College Libraries are by definition inapplicable to institutions
stressing advanced research or granting degrees beyond the
Master's, while the Standards for Junior College Libraries,
although recognizing that institutions with a multiplicity of
programs may need minimal collections of two or three times
the basic figure of twenty thousand volumes, do not state at
what point this requirement takes effect.

The present authors recently needed formulas for producing estimates of the size required for minimum adequacy by the library collections of a number of academic institutions of widely differing characteristics. It was important that these estimates should carry conviction to the planning, budgeting, and appropriating bodies concerned. Available standards were found unsuitable for producing the desired result. Accordingly, an attempt was made to develop formulas in which separate account would be taken of the principal factors that affect the requirements for books in connection with academic programs, and in which each factor would be weighted in a manner capable of being related to and justified by practice.

The results of this attempt, though admittedly but a beginning and needing much improvement, were found useful for the purpose for which they were designed, [12] and are consequently presented here as of possible wider interest. They invite exploration of the conditions which affect academic needs for books, of the relative weights which should be attached to the various controlling factors, and of the basic hypothesis itself--namely, that it is possible to provide a meaningful quantitative measure of adequacy in library collections.

Formulas for Estimating Size of
Academic Library Collections
Required for Minimum Adequacy

The minimum size required for the adequacy of an academic library differs from institution to institution depending upon the combined effect of the variables constituting the controlling factors in each case. Among the most important of these are:

The student body--size, composition (graduate or undergraduate, full-time or part-time, resident or nonresident, etc.), scholastic aptitude, socio-economic and intellectual background.

The faculty--size, involvement in research, "library-mindedness," etc.

The curriculum--number of departments of instruction, number of courses, proportion of laboratory to literature courses, number of undergraduate "majors," number of fields of masters' and doctors' degrees, number of professional schools, etc.

Methods of instruction--extent and use of textbooks, assigned reading, independent study, honors work, etc.

Availability of suitable places for study on the campus.

Geography of the campus--proximity to metropolitan areas, to other large libraries, etc.

The intellectual climate--inducements and distractions to study, etc.

It is obvious that these factors differ widely in their susceptibility to measurement. Only those that can be most easily and meaningfully measured were given places in the following tables which constitute the formulas.

Notes on Table 1

The formula presumes that even liminal or minimum adequacy can be achieved with its assistance only if all material is carefully chosen with a view to the purpose to be served, and the weeding program is as active and realistic in relation to needs as is the program of acquisition.

Averages. Because of wide disparities in the extent of the literatures of various subjects, the figures suggested by the table must be considered as averages of the literatures of subjects of academic interest. It is not too difficult to estimate the size of a collection for work at a given level in a single subject; it is when the library is required to serve the interest of many users at many levels in many subjects, as in an institution of higher education, that estimates of size become difficult.

Interdependence of factors. No factor represented in the formula will be operative in isolation; each is dependent on others. For example, it is not suggested that 240 monograph volumes are sufficient for an undergraduate field of concentration (line 5). Obviously, there will be contributions to each field of concentration resulting from each of the other variables (lines 1 through 4).

Microcopy. The table presumes that most of the materials estimated in lines 1-4 will be in full-scale format.

Table 1
Formula for Estimating the Size for Liminal Adequacy
of the Collections of Senior College and University Libraries

(1)	Books		Periodicals		Documents	Total
	Titles (2)	Volumes (3)	Titles (4)	Volumes (5)	Volumes (6)	Volumes (7)
To a basic collection, viz.:						
1. Undergraduate library	35,000	42,000	250	3,750	5,000	50,750
Add for each of the following as indicated:						
2. Faculty member (full-time equiv.)	50	60	1	15	25	100
3. Student (graduate or undergraduate in full time equivalents)	...	10	...	1	1	12
4. Undergraduate in honors or independent study programs	10	12	...	...	...	12
5. Field of undergraduate concentration--"major" subject field	200	240	3	45	50	335
6. Field of graduate concentration-- Master's work or equivalent	2,000	2,400	10	150	500	3,050
7. Field of graduate concentration-- Doctoral work or equivalent	15,000	18,000	100	1,500	5,000	24,500

Even here, however, some of the less-frequently-used material (such as back files of newspapers) may be in microcopy. With respect to much of the little-used research material to be added in accordance with the estimates contained in lines 5-7, "adequacy" can be achieved with almost as much efficiency through the use of microcopy as with full-scale material. The table assumes that fully cataloged material in microform will be measured in volumes as though it were in original form.

Title-volume ratios. The title-volume ratio employed for books (columns 2 and 3) is 1:1. 2 which falls between that (1:1. 37) found to obtain in the National Union Catalog[13] and that (1:1. 15) which is found in the Lamont library catalog. [14] The ratio used for periodicals (columns 4 and 5) has been set at 1:15 (cf. the note on line 1, column 4). For documents (column 6) a title-volume ratio does not seem to be meaningful. In consequence, the total sizes of collections obtained by using the table are expressed only in volumes.

Line 1, Column 2. The figure of 50, 750 volumes suggested as capable of providing threshold adequacy for an undergraduate collection derives authority from experience in the actual construction of lists for this purpose. The most important of these lists have been:

List	Date	Titles Listed
Shaw[15]	1931	14, 000
Lamont[14]	1953	39, 000
Michigan[16]	1964	56, 550
California[17]	1965	55, 000

The Shaw list was a pioneering effort which set the pattern and the standard of excellence. The Lamont list was the first to be related to an actual undergraduate library, but it had many faults. The Michigan list learned from these. The California list (under construction at the library of the University of California at San Diego) has not only benefited from previous experience but has been executed under auspicious circumstances. The Library Council of the University of California recommended that the three new campuses currently being planned each have seventy-five thousand-volume libraries at opening day, since the experience of the growing campuses, Irvine in particular, suggests that it is difficult to give adequate service with a smaller collection. The California list, in consequence, provides for about sixty thousand volumes of monographs and fifteen thousand volumes of serials.

Line 1, Column 4.   The figure of 250 periodical titles is supported by the Michigan list which includes 245 such titles and the California list which provides for fifteen thousand serial volumes representing nine hundred titles, of which the three hundred most useful are in runs of twenty or more years.   Furthermore, the figure of two hundred and fifty is 50 per cent of the number of titles covered by the following standard periodical indexes published by the H. W. Wilson Company, without which no (general) American library can expect to render adequate service:

Titles Indexed

Readers' Guide to Periodical Literature	
(selected general and nontechnical periodicals)	130
International Index	
(social sciences and humanities)	170
Applied Science and Technology Index	200
Total	500

Line 1, Column 6.   The figure of five thousand documents would admit the most important publications of the U. S. Congress, the Bureau of the Census and other federal executive agencies, the United Nations and its specialized agencies, states of the United States, etc.

Line 2.   If the library which provides merely threshold adequacy for undergraduates is to permit the members of the teaching staff to keep up in their subjects even liminally, the collection must be enriched for their benefit.   An enrichment amounting to fifty titles (e. g. , three per year for sixteen years), one periodical subscription and twenty-five documents per faculty member would seem to be a minimum. [18]

Line 3.   The undergraduate library represented by line 1 takes no account whatsoever of the size of the student body.   As this increases, the number of copies (not titles) will have to be increased.   At the suggested rate of twelve volumes per student, every book in the undergraduate library could be duplicated by the time that studei.' body had risen to 4, 230.   In other words, there could then be, if desired, two identical undergraduate collections, each serving 2, 115 students.   It is more likely, of course, that all 4, 230 would

use the same library but that the books more in demand
would be supplied in multiple copies.

    Line 4.   The typical student in an honors or inde-
pendent study program may read or use hundreds of books
each year.   However, since the criterion sought here is
merely threshold adequacy, a very low figure is used.

    Line 5.   The undergraduate collection (line 1) will
rarely have as many as several hundred titles in each field
in which an undergraduate "major" is offered.   By contrast,
"basic lists" for such subjects typically include two thousand
and more titles (see note on line 6, below).   Accordingly,
the reinforcement suggested here, amounting to only 17 per
cent of this quantity, is very modest.

    Line 6.   At the point at which graduate work is of-
fered leading to the master's degree or its equivalent, the
collection must assume some of the characteristics of a research collection, albeit at the lowest level.   The quantity
of material for addition here is suggested by the numerous
"basic lists" which typically include two thousand and more
titles, e. g. :

Anthropology[19]	2, 000
Area studies (Asia, Africa, Eastern Europe, Latin America)[20]	7, 000
Art reference books[21]	2, 850
China, modern--economic and social development[22]	2, 000
Communism--books in English only[23]	2, 500
Electronics[24]	2, 000
Physics[25]	1, 883
United States of America--life and thought[26]	6, 500

    Line 7.   These 24, 500 volumes represent but a frac-
tion of the literature of any but the most recently-developed
subject, and can ordinarily be expected to present a subject
only in its most recent aspects, neglecting historical development.   Yet as recently as 1955 one of the most literature-
based of the learned professions adopted twenty thousand
volumes as a passing grade for its training centers in the
United States, [27] and even in 1964 sixteen of these centers
still had fewer than thirty thousand volumes.   It is also true
that the literatures of several disciplines support each other,
as chemistry, biochemistry, physiology, anatomy, neurol-
ogy, psychology, and other related sciences contribute to

make a medical library.

Notes on Table 2

As with Table 1 it is presumed that all material will be carefully selected--and weeded--with reference to the purpose to be served.

As with Table 1, also, the formula provides only for a minimum. When it is seen, e. g. in the notes on lines 2 and 4, out of what this minimum is constructed, few institutions should be willing to stay there.

Averages. Similarly as for Table 1, the figures suggested here must be construed as averages. Obviously, courses in court stenography or in conversational Spanish do not require the same library support as courses in theatre or decorative arts.

Government publications. No special provision has been made for these; to the extent included, they would be considered as books or periodicals.

Title-volume ratios. Same as for Table 1.

Line 1, Column 2. Similarly as for the senior colleges, there have been attempts to prepare basic selections of books for junior college libraries, of which the more important are as follows:

List	Date	Titles Listed
Mohrhardt[28]	1937	5, 300
Bertalan[29]	1954	4, 000
Trinkner[30]	1963	20, 000

The earlier of these are out of date, and none is now authoritative. It is consequently not possible to give to the initial step in the formula of Table 2 even the degree of empirical support which is available for Table 1. The development of such support would be an important step toward the improvement of the standards for junior college libraries.

Line 1, Column 4. The number of periodicals is arbitrarily set at one half the number for the four-year colleges.

Line 2. This provision amounts to fewer than two

Table 2

Formula for Estimating the Size for Liminal Adequacy
of Junior or Community College Libraries

(1)	Books		Periodicals		Total
	Titles (2)	Volumes (3)	Titles (4)	Volumes (5)	Volumes (6)
To a basic collection, viz.:					
1. A collection to support a two-year general education or liberal arts (transfer or university parallel) program	12,500	15,000	125	1,875	16,875
Add for each of the following as indicated:					
2. Faculty member (full time equivalent)	30	36	1	15	51
3. Student (full time equivalent)	...	4	...	1	5
4. Subject field of study, either transfer or terminal, in which courses are offered beyond the standard general education or liberal arts transfer program	100	120	3	45	165

books per faculty member per year (if spread over sixteen years) plus one periodical. [18]

Line 3. This item provides for additional copies (not titles) required by the size of the student body. At the rate suggested the basic collection could be duplicated by the time there were 3,375 students. This figure obviously needs testing in practice.

Line 4. This item provides for each additional subject at the rate of six titles per annum with replacement over a sixteen-year period. [18] In this connection, it may be noted that for the diversified program of the community college as contrasted with the narrower one of the junior college, the recent Rutgers Guide has the following to say:

> The community college library should probably be larger than that of a comparable-sized four-year liberal arts college... because a greater amount of materials is needed to maintain the diversified programs offered by a comprehensive community college. [31]

Examples of Application of the Formulas

In Tables 3-5 the formulas of Tables 1-2 have been applied, by way of illustration, to the data for a number of academic libraries. Because of the untested status of the formulas, the names of the institutions have been withheld unless there seemed to have been no risk of an unjustified pejorative judgment.

In Table 3 it is possible to compare, for four senior college libraries, the calculations resulting from the formula of Table 1 with those for additional volumes suggested by the Standards for College Libraries (viz., increments of ten thousand volumes, additional to the basic collection of fifty thousand, for each two hundred students beyond an original six hundred). It may be noted that the Standards are easier on the stronger institutions and harder on the weaker than is the formula of Table 1.

In Table 4 are found certain libraries with enormous collections which are nevertheless found short of minimum adequacy by the formula of Table 1. Can this be possible?

Table 3

Application of Formula of Table 1 to Selected Senior Colleges

(1)	(2)	(3)	(4)	(5)	(6)	(8)	(9)	(10)	(11)	(12)
1. Oberlin	215	2,370	600	25	10	147,000	900,000	+512	138,500	+550
2. Swarthmore	110	975	250	20	10	114,000	245,000	+115	68,750	+256
3. Antioch	100	1,725	430	20	1	96,300	129,000	+34	106,250	+21
4. ...	90	2,200	220	25	2	103,000	65,000	-37	130,000	-50

The source of adverse judgment is found principally in column 7 (number of doctoral fields).   Thus, library no. 9, with 1.67 million volumes, offers the doctor's degree in sixty-two fields as contrasted with Illinois' sixty fields supported by 3.6 million volumes.   The interpretation to be put on the table, therefore, is not that the collections rated minus are in an absolute sense "inadequate," but that they are inadequate in relation to the programs which they are attempting to support--in other words that the institutions have overextended themselves in relation to the available library resources.

The libraries represented in Table 5 without exception possess collections exceeding the basic minimum size required by the Standards for Junior College Libraries, and in some cases their collections are several times this basic minimum.   In spite of this all but two fail to meet the threshold of adequacy prescribed by the formula of Table 2.

In Table 5 it is possible to compare the findings of the formula of Table 2 with those of the Standards for Junior College Libraries (viz., increments of five thousand volumes, added to the basic twenty thousand, for each five hundred students beyond the original one thousand).   Two more institutions in the list are found adequate by the second than by the first criterion.

Notes on Table 3

32-36   Source of data, Tables 3-5:   Various, see footnotes. All data are for 1962/3 or 1963/4, extrapolated for some items for some institutions from prior years.   Student and faculty figures have been reduced, in some cases arbitrarily, to full-time equivalents.

Column 1:   Senior colleges; no. 4: A state-supported senior college.

Column 2:   Faculty (full-time equivalent).

Column 3:   Students (full-time equivalent).

Column 4:   Honors students (postulated at 25 per cent of student body for nos. 1-3 and 10 per cent for no. 4).

Column 5: Fields of undergraduate concentration-- "major" subject fields.

Table 4

Application of Formula of Table 1 to Selected
State-Supported or State-Assisted Universities

(1)	(2)	(3)	(4)	(5)	(6)	(7)	(8)	(9)	(10)
1. Illinois	3,150	30,275	3,025	200	125	60	2,683,000	3,635,000	+35
2. Michigan	1,800	22,000	2,200	130	90	66	2,456,000	3,250,000	+32
3. UCLA	1,500	18,000	1,800	80	70	39	1,634,000	2,000,000	+22
4.	900	10,000	1,000	70	50	33	1,257,000	1,350,000	+7
5.	375	9,600	960	90	60	2	477,000	412,000	-14
6.	240	4,700	470	34	16	2	246,000	195,000	-21
7.	900	14,400	1,440	70	45	29	1,202,000	865,000	-28
8.	300	9,300	930	60	30	1	340,000	236,000	-31
9.	2,200	30,660	3,066	165	100	62	2,555,000	1,670,000	-35
10.	470	11,400	1,140	85	55	5	567,000	360,000	-37
11.	300	5,360	540	50	30	3	333,000	266,000	-30
12.	500	13,300	1,330	100	55	5	600,000	268,000	-55

Column 6:   Fields of graduate concentration--master's work or equivalent.

Column 8:   Size (volumes) of collection calculated by the formula of Table 1.

Column 9: Size (volumes) of actual collection.

Column 10:   Difference between columns 8 and 9 expressed as a percentage of column 8.   Plus indicates that the actual collection is larger than required by the formula; minus that it is smaller.

Column 11: Size (volumes) of collection calculated by the formula suggested by Standards for College Libraries.

Column 12:   Difference between columns 9 and 11 expressed as a percentage of column 11.   Plus indicates that the actual collection is larger than required by the formula; minus that it is smaller.

Notes on Table 4

Source of data: See Table 3.

Column 1:   State-supported or state-assisted universities.

Columns 2-6:   Same as for Table 3.

Column 7:   Fields of graduate concentration--doctoral work or equivalent.

Columns 8-10:   Same as for Table 3.

Notes on Table 5

Source of data: See Table 3.

Column 1:   Junior or community colleges; nos. 3-7, junior or community colleges in California, Michigan and New York.

Column 2:   Faculty (full time equivalent).

Column 3:   Students (full time equivalent).

Table 5
Application of Formula of Table 2 to Selected
Junior or Community Colleges

(1)	(2)	(3)	(4)	(5)	(6)	(7)	(8)	(9)
1. Wright Branch, Chicago City Junior College	215	5,700	30	55,580	68,600	+23	67,000	+2
2. Los Angeles, Calif., City College	600	11,100	45	99,300	104,600	+5	121,000	-14
3. ...	80	1,380	14	28,785	26,500	-8	23,800	+11
4. ...	370	12,375	50	92,300	76,100	-18	133,750	-43
5. ...	100	1,125	14	28,785	22,000	-24	21,250	+4
6. ...	227	4,750	50	55,702	42,000	-25	57,500	-27
7. ...	245	3,810	30	49,500	34,800	-30	48,100	-28

Colum 4:   Subject fields of study beyond standard general education or liberal arts transfer pattern.

Column 5: Size (volumes) of minimum collection calculated by formula of Table 2.

Column 6:   Size (volumes) of actual collection.

Column 7:   Difference between columns 5 and 6 as a percentage of column 5.   Plus indicates that the actual collection is larger than required by the formula; minus that it is smaller.

Column 8: Size (volumes) of collection calculated by formula of Standards for Junior College Libraries.

Column 9:   Difference between columns 6 and 8 as a percentage of column 8.   Plus indicates that collection is larger than required by the Standards; minus that it is smaller.

Conclusion

The adequacy of an academic library collection may be difficult to determine, but there is no mystery about it. The difficulty arises simply from the quantity of detail and number of variables involved, far beyond the capability of any visiting committee to assess merely on the basis of easy observation or sampling.

Yet every scholar has a notion of what in his own field constitutes adequacy for various purposes--undergraduate instruction, graduate teaching, advanced research, etc. This notion can in every case be expressed in concrete terms, i. e., in terms of a list of specific books.   The contents of the list can in turn be made the subject of agreement or consensus of a number of scholars in a field.   And the adequacy of an entire library is made up of the adequacies of its parts.

The best yardsticks of adequacy are therefore those to which we have become accustomed--the book-selection list and the specialized subject bibliography, frequently reviewed and brought up to date by experts and in the light of use. But to apply these yardsticks is, at the present time, something else again: manual checking and searching procedures are involved--slow, tiresome and costly.

Yet it may be foreseen that, with the advent of electronic catalogs the checking of a book-selection list or bibliography will become the mere routine of a mechanical
process.   Not only will evaluation of collections be simplified thereby, but collection-building procedures will be assisted.   The end result will be gains in the quality of collections.

The formulas described in this article have been developed in an attempt to find a method for estimating the
size for minimal adequacy of academic library collections
more convincingly than can be done with existing criteria.
It may be validly objected that little more has been accomplished than to transfer the locus of conviction from an unknown whole to the unknown parts of which the whole is composed.   This may be readily admitted while calling attention
to the fact that to break an estimate down into components
is standard practice for convincing budgeting and appropriating bodies.

In any case, the attempt to identify and weigh the
factors which affect the need for books in academic situations reveals gaps in our knowledge, to the filling of which
research might profitably be directed.   Among the questions
requiring answers are:

What are the tests of adequacy of an academic library
collection?

What is learned from experience regarding the contents of an undergraduate collection of minimum adequacy?

How are these contents affected by variable factors
such as geography, curriculum, teaching methods, intellectual climate, etc. ?

What constitutes adequacy for particular kinds of material at various levels of use--e. g. , periodicals,
government documents?

What constitutes adequacy for the needs of faculty,
honors students, etc. ?

What correlation, if any, exists between size of student body and size of collection?

Is there a renewal or replacement cycle?   What are
its characteristics?   Does it affect acquisition, weeding, or the estimates of cost of collection-building?

What constitute adequate resources for graduate work
and research in various subjects and at various
levels? [37]

Questions similar to the foregoing may be asked with
respect to the collections of junior and community
colleges.

Notes

1. Lyle, G. R.   The Administration of the College Library.
Ed. 3. New York, H. W. Wilson Co., 1961. p. 399.

2. Association of College and Research Libraries.   Committee on Standards: College and University Accreditation Standards--1957.   Chicago, ACRL, 1958. p. 11.

3. North Central Association of Colleges and Secondary
Schools.   Commission on Colleges and Universities,
Guide for the Evaluation of Institutions of Higher Edu-
cation, 1961. p. 16.

4. Middle States Association of Colleges and Secondary
Schools.   Commission on Institutions of Higher Education, Characteristics of Excellence in Higher Education and Standards for Middle States Accreditation,
1957, p. 3.   Also op. cit., footnote 2.

5. Gelfand, Morris A.   "Techniques of Library Evaluators
in the Middle States Association." College and Research Libraries, 19, July 1958, p. 305-30.

6. Northwest Association of Secondary and Higher Schools,
Guide for Self-Evaluation and Accreditation of Higher
Schools, 1957, p. 9.

7. Western Association of Schools and Colleges.   Accrediting
Commission for Senior Colleges and Universities,
Statement of Standards, 1963, p. 2.

8. Southern Association of Colleges and Schools. College
Delegate Assembly, Standards, 1962, p. 31.

9. For example, in California a formula for the annual book
    fund of the state colleges provided four books per
    student for the first one thousand students, two for
    the next four thousand, etc. A recommendation to
    change this formula proposed the provision of forty
    books per student by a certain date. But neither
    formula is directly related to the quality of the li-
    brary. Program for the Development of California
    State College Libraries (n. p. , August 1962). p. 2-3.

10. [American Library Association. Association of College
    and Research Libraries] "Standards for College Li-
    braries." College and Research Libraries, 20, July
    1959, 274-80.

11. [American Library Association. Association of College
    and Research Libraries] "Standards for Junior Col-
    lege Libraries." College and Research Libraries,
    21, May 1960, 200-206.

12. Clapp, V. W. and Jordan, R. T. The Libraries of the
    State-Assisted Institutions of Higher Education in
    Ohio--Their Maintenance and Development--Guidelines
    for Policy. Prepared for Academy for Educational
    Development, Inc. Washington, D. C. , 1964.

13. Williams, E. E. "Magnitude of the Paper-Deterioration
    Problem as Measured by a National Union Catalog
    Sample," College and Research Libraries, 23,
    November, 1962, 499, 543.

14. Catalogue of the Lamont Library, Harvard College
    Harvard University Press, 1953.

15. Shaw, C. B. A List of Books for College Libraries
    American Library Association, 1931.

16. University of Michigan. Undergraduate Library Shelf
    List. Rev. ed. Ann Arbor, Michigan, University
    Microfilms, Inc. , 1964.

17. [University of California at San Diego. Library, List
    of books selected for the libraries of three new cam-
    puses of the University of California.] In prepara-
    tion for the press.

18. The observed tendency for stable and continuing aca-

demic libraries to double in size every sixteen years
that is associated with the name of Fremont Rider
suggests that sixteen years represents a period at
which the collections of such libraries require a substantial degree of renewal. Accordingly, this period
is here adopted for the cycle of renewal for the additional materials purchased for faculty, etc.

19. Mandelbaum, D. G. and others, eds. Resources for the
Teaching of Anthropology; Including a Basic List of
Books and Periodicals for College Libraries Compiled
by Rexford S. Beckham with the Assistance of Marie
P. Beckham. University of California, 1963. 2,000
titles.

20. American Universities Field Staff A Select Bibliography:
Asia, Africa, Eastern Europe, Latin America. (AUFS,
1960); Supplements, 1961, 1963, 6,000 titles in basic
list, 500 in each of the supplements.

21. Chamberlain, M. W. Guide to Art Reference Books
Chicago, American Library Association, 1959. 2,500
titles, 250 journals, 100 series.

22. Yuan, T.-L. Economic and Social Development of Modern China: a bibliographical guide New Haven,
Human Relations Area Files, 1956. Over 2,000 titles.

23. Kolarz, W. Books on Communism; a Bibliography
2d ed. London, Allen & Unwin, 1964. Approximately
2,500 titles, restricted to English.

24. Moore, C. K. Electronics: a Bibliographic Guide
Macmillan, 1961. Over 2,000 titles in 68 subject
areas.

25. American Institute of Physics Check List of Books for
an Undergraduate Physics Library New York, AIP,
1962. 1,883 titles.

26. U. S. Library of Congress, General Reference and Bibli-
ography Division A Guide to the Study of the United
States of America Washington, U. S. Government
Printing Office, 1960. 6,500 titles.

27. Association of American Law Schools Proceedings
1955, p. 325.

28. Mohrhardt, F. E. A List of Books for Junior College Libraries Chicago, American Library Association, 1937.

29. Bertalan, F. J. Books for Junior Colleges Chicago, American Library Association, 1954.

30. Trinkner, C. L. Basic Books for Junior Colleges Northport, Alabama, Colonial Press, 1963.

31. Merlo, F. P. and Walling, W. D. Guide for Planning Community College Facilities New Brunswick, N. J., Division of Field Studies and Research, Graduate School of Education, Rutgers--The State University, 1964. p. 34.

32. U. S. Office of Education Library Statistics of Colleges and Universities, 1962-63. Institutional Data Washington, U. S. Government Printing Office, 1964. Supplement Chicago, American Library Association [1964].

33. American Colleges and Universities 9th ed. Washington, American Council on Education [1964]

34. American Junior Colleges 6th ed. Washington, American Council on Education, 1963.

35. Junior College Directory Washington, American Association of Junior Colleges, 1964.

36. The World of Learning, 1963-64 London, Europa Publications, 1964.

37. Downs, R. B. "Development of Research Collections in University Libraries" University of Tennessee Library Lectures No. 4. Knoxville, University of Tennessee, 1954. p. 1-15. Distinguishes four stages in the progress of a collection--the general information collection, the well-rounded reference collection, the fundamental research collection, and the comprehensive and specialized research collection.

Editor's note: See the application of this formula in the article by Blanchard, p. 680 ff.

Building a Strong Reference Collection

by Thomas J. Galvin   Director of Students, School of
                           Library Science, Simmons
                           College, Boston.

From Choice 3:279-82, June 1966; Reprinted by
permission of Executive Secretary, Association of
College and Research Libraries, American Library
Association

If American colleges and universities currently have
any one thing in common, it is change.   Visit any campus,
urban or rural, vocational or academic, large or small, and
the person who greets you, whether president or professor,
librarian or student guide, is almost certain to open the conversation with "right now we're in a period of transition."
There follows a description of what the institution will be like
five, ten, or twenty years from now.   What is planned for
the future usually involves two elements--growth and diversification.   It is difficult to imagine that anyone associated
with higher education today could conceivably be unaware of
the first of these.   The second, diversification, while perhaps a bit less obvious, is equally, if not more, important
to those who must provide adequate library service to the
academic community.

The phenomena of growth and diversification appear to
be interrelated.   Today's academic planner usually wishes to
provide not merely space and instructional facilities for
larger numbers of students, but a wider variety of educational options for them to pursue.   At the post-high school level,
the single purpose academic institution is passé.   Trade
schools are renamed technical institutes, and offer preparation for any one of several vocational specializations.   Colleges that formerly concentrated on a single professional or
occupational objective such as teaching, accounting or agriculture, now must offer, in addition, curricular alternatives
in the liberal arts and sciences.   Towards the opposite end

641

of the educational status spectrum, we find the small university (sometimes defined as a college that has grown top-heavy with graduate and professional schools) assuming research commitments that equal or exceed its teaching mission.

The implications of all this for the collections of the academic library are painfully obvious.   New and changing curricula and the growth of faculty and staff research activity necessitate systematic review, expansion and strengthening of book, journal, and document resources.   The task is an especially complex and expensive one with respect to the reference collection, and accordingly demands particularly careful planning if an orderly development of reference resources is to occur.   Reference titles tend to run to multivolume sets which, while relatively inexpensive in consideration of the amount of useful data they contain and their long-term informational value, are comparatively costly on a title-by-title basis when measured against the general run of library purchases.   Both the library and the college administrations have the right to expect that the reference staff will not only recommend purchase of new or standard reference works that need to be added to the collections, but also that they will develop buying schedules for groups of titles that allow for realistic budgeting over a three-, five-, or ten-year period. The library director must insist that the reference staff assume this kind of responsibility, and should logically question the acquisition of any expensive reference book if the staff cannot show that its purchase is clearly consistent with a systematic plan for strengthening the reference collection as a whole.

To the library director falls the difficult job of deciding what portion of the book budget is to be allocated for purchase of older or standard works to support new or expanded areas of the curriculum and, in turn, how much of the appropriation for such retrospective purchase should go towards reference materials.   An encyclopedia or two, a modest run of a national or trade bibliography, a large atlas, or a few back volumes of a periodicals index can cut a painfully large slice out of the fiscal pie.   If the college is newly established, or many new programs have recently come into existence, if the faculty has labored for years under the handicap of a meager book collection, growth of which has been retarded by lack of space or funds, a decision to earmark a substantial part of the book budget for reference materials may generate a major public relations problem for the library administrator.

Logic demands, however, that under such circumstances, the reference collection be given initial priority in a retrospective buying program. The ACRL Standards for College Libraries stress the fundamental importance of a strong reference collection, especially in terms of the need to make general and subject bibliographies available as an aid to overall collection development. If regional or professional accreditation is a matter of institutional concern, and if an accrediting visit is in the offing, one should anticipate that the visiting team may be making use either of the ACRL Standards or of guidelines derived from them, and that the reference collection will be subject to careful scrutiny. Anyone looking at an academic library in this kind of evaluative way can appreciate the fact that a strong general book collection, reflecting depth in all curricular areas, cannot be brought into existence overnight. The evaluator has every right to expect, however, that a reasonable plan for strengthening book and journal resources will exist, and that the reference collection will contain the bibliographies and indices needed to facilitate identification of standard titles to be acquired for general and special subject collections. Moreover, book and informational needs must somehow be met over the period of years that is usually required to bring a substandard book collection up to the level where it can provide the bulk of the materials asked for by students and faculty on a day-by-day basis. During such a transitional stage, a strong collection of bibliographical reference sources can serve as a key to unlock the resources of other libraries, both within and outside the local area.

The development of a detailed plan for building up the college library's reference collection ought, basically, to be the job of the reference staff, subject, of course, to review by the library administrator. It is always a complicated process irrespective of the size or complexity of the institution that the library serves. Increasingly, academic libraries are turning to consultants to survey reference holdings and create buying lists. Such a consultant study can result in a valuable set of purchase recommendations that will carry real weight with the college administration.

Sound planning for the systematic expansion and rejuvenation of the reference collection will normally embody several distinct phases. Among these are: (1) a review of existing holdings; (2) consultation of standard guides to reference materials to identify lacunae in the collection and to create a list of titles for possible purchase; (3) analysis of the curriculum, both existing and proposed, and identification of informational and reference needs of students, faculty, and staff; and (4) development of a buying list and systematic purchasing plan.

In reviewing the existing collection, it is important to make sure that all titles of obvious reference value have indeed found their way to the reference shelves. The Mental Measurements Yearbook is a good example of a reference source that, for some mysterious reason, is often found buried in the psychology section of the general book collection. It is at this stage that holdings should be checked to make certain that the latest editions of standard reference works have not been missed in the acquisitions process in past years. Serial holdings should also be surveyed and compared with the collection of indices to make certain that optimum correlation has been achieved.

Most of the standard guides to reference sources are well-known and need merely be mentioned rather than described in detail here. Among the retrospective guides, Winchell and Walford, with their supplements, Hoffman's Reader's Adviser, Jenkins' Science Reference Sources, the Enoch Pratt Library and Southern Association of Colleges and Secondary Schools lists are widely used to identify likely titles for purchase. Wallace Bonk's recent study, Use of Basic Reference Sources in Libraries (Department of Library Science, University of Michigan, 1963) suggests many titles that reference librarians in a variety of libraries have found valuable. These retrospective guides must be supplemented by current review media such as CHOICE, The Booklist and Subscription Books Bulletin, Library Journal, and the Wilson Library Bulletin. Each of these is oriented towards a slightly different audience, so that their lists and reviews of new reference books bear a complementary relationship to one another. Publisher's Weekly helps to round out the picture of available reference titles from which selections may be made, and consultation of its "announcement" issues is essential if one is to avoid the embarrassment of buying an expensive older edition, only to discover, a month after the bill has been paid, that it has been superseded by a new one.

The use of standard lists as buying guides involves certain hazards that have been widely discussed in professional literature. It is important to be aware of the scope, in-

tended audience, purposes, and limitations of any bibliographic guide if one is to make intelligent use of it. The proper
way to use such lists is as a reservoir of titles from which
specific items are <u>selected</u> for purchase in the light of the
instructional interests and informational needs of the college.
Failure to observe this stipulation often results in purchase
of large and expensive reference sets, not because they fulfill any particular existing or anticipated need of the institution, but merely because they appear in one or another of
the standard lists. Such misuse of book selection aids would
be merely ridiculous if it did not frequently result in tragic
waste of precious book funds. It is for this reason that curriculum analysis and faculty conferences are essential to the
development of an effective buying program.

It is obvious that a formal review of the teaching and
research programs of the college, both as they presently exist, and as they are planned for the future, can have values
for the library staff far beyond the immediate context of reference book selection. One must, however, not depend entirely on advice from faculty or staff either to establish priorities in purchasing, or to make selection decisions about
individual reference titles. Many faculty members lack
familiarity with newer reference sources in their own fields,
and only a handful are knowledgeable about the general reference sources that are the workhorses of the reference department. Ralph Shaw, in his 1961 survey <u>A Medical Intelligence Program for the National Institutes of Health,</u> reminds
us "that simply asking the research staff what they would like
to have does not necessarily provide a full guide to what they
would use if it were available." Finally, the ACRL <u>Standards</u>
call for, I think correctly, a reference collection that "must
not be restricted to subjects which form part of the curriculum."

The last, and most difficult phase in planning a reference buying program involves preparation of buying lists
reflecting purchase priorities. It is not possible to establish universally applicable guidelines for this purpose, since
decisions about individual titles must ultimately be made by
the reference staff in the light of their best evaluation of
local conditions and needs. Sources known to provide kinds
of information that have been sought unsuccessfully in the
past by students or faculty will clearly rate high priority.
If the library contains no general, multivolume, English language encyclopedia that is less than four years old, the reference book purchasing plan should provide for a current

printing of the oldest encyclopedia, and systematic replacement of the others at regular intervals in the future. A realistic replacement schedule for annuals, titles that appear regularly in new editions, and other continuously revised works ought to be included. For reasons already noted, general and subject bibliographies, indices to periodicals, and subject field literature guides are of particular value in compensating for a limited general book collection.

Dividing reference book funds equally among subject areas towards the end of achieving a "balanced collection" is not <u>always</u> the soundest approach. "Building to strength," even at the expense of subject areas that are under represented in the reference collection, may, under certain circumstances, make greater sense in the initial stages of a purchasing program.

Limitations of space make it impossible here to do much more than sketch in the general outlines of a procedure for surveying reference holdings. Any plan or purchase list that emerges from this process must reflect an awareness of available reference resources in the local area, so that needless duplication with the holdings of public, other academic, and accessible libraries is avoided. Finally, it must be flexible, to provide for those future informational needs that even the most careful study of curricular and research interests will fail to anticipate, and modifiable in the light of future trends and patterns in reference book publishing.

The Faculty and the Development of Library Collections

by Maurice F. Tauber   Dr. Tauber is Melvil Dewey
Professor of Library Service
at Columbia University. Among
his many surveys and studies
is the evaluation of Columbia
Libraries, from which a section is quoted on p. 702 ff.

From The Journal of Higher Education 32:454-8,
November 1961; Reprinted by permission of the
Managing Editor, The Journal of Higher Education,
Ohio State University Press, Columbus, Ohio.

One of the assumptions upon which librarians of academic institutions work is that book collections should be developed with the active participation of faculty members. In
some institutions, there have been notable cases in which
individual faculty members have taken the responsibility of
building collections in their special fields. On a smaller
scale, a few faculty members in other institutions have considered it their duty to recommend the purchase of books
that were of importance to the departmental collections as a
whole. Unfortunately, many faculty members are willing to
leave these activities to their colleagues.

During the academic year 1957-58, the writer had the
opportunity of participating in a self-study made by the Columbia University Libraries. [1] One of the important tasks
of the subcommittee working on this project--a subcommittee of the President's Committee on the Educational Future
of the University--was to evaluate the present weaknesses of
the collections in specific fields in which the University was
interested from the standpoints of instruction and research.

Such an evaluation for a group of libraries having over
two million volumes was not an easy task. The subcommittee, however, was determined to give all full-time faculty

members, and a selection of the part-time teaching staff,
an opportunity to express themselves on the problems they
faced in connection with library resources.   Since it was
recognized that in a large university the selection of books
is an activity that must be carried on by the library staff as
well as by the faculty members, the assistance of the departmental librarians was essential.   Moreover, it was considered necessary to get some estimate of the difficulties of
students in their efforts to obtain materials needed for course
work and research, particularly in gathering data for their
dissertations.   In the full report of the subcommittee, an
analysis of the information derived from these sources is included.   In this brief paper, special attention is given to the
role of faculty members in developing book, periodical, and
other kinds of collections.

In the questionnaire sent to the faculty members, the
subcommittee suggested five levels of completeness that could
be used as the basis of faculty and library-staff appraisal of
existing library collections and as a guide in establishing ac-
quisitional policies.   These levels were as follows:

1. Basic-information collection, for a subject that
falls outside the scope of present instruction, yet
within which readers may need minimal resources to
aid their understanding of, or their work with, materials properly within the scope of their studies.

2. Working collection, which conveys existing knowledge of the subject in broad outline, including its
main historical aspects; adequate for the needs of undergraduate courses

3. General-research collection, adequate for the
needs of graduate students in the subject, since it includes the major portions of the materials required
for dissertations and other independent research

4. Comprehensive collection, which embraces all
the materials in the general-research collection in
addition to a wider selection of books, periodicals,
and other materials having value for current research,
and also the works needed for historical research in
the subject, in all pertinent languages, though not
necessarily in all editions, or in translation, with inclusion of considerable documentary and original source
material

5. Exhaustive collection, which seeks, so far as is
reasonably possible, to include everything written on
the subject, in all languages, in all editions and translations[2]

Obviously, to apply this scale effectively, knowledge of
subject fields by specialists is essential to supplement the librarian's information.   It was hoped that the faculty members
would participate fully in this evaluation.   However, because
of regrettable pressure for the completion of the survey, the
percentage of returns was not so high as had been anticipated.   Of 2,250 questionnaires sent to faculty members, including part-time and clinical professors, 709 were returned
in time for use in the study.   Of this number, 644 were
fairly complete.   If the part-time and clinical groups are excluded, the percentage of return was approximately 15 per
cent higher.   In certain fields, however, the returns were
not sufficient to assist the subcommittee in making satisfactory analyses. [3]

Yet it should be observed that the faculty members
who answered the questionnaire provided a body of useful
data.   There is no point in examining the returns in this
brief statement.   But time after time the subcommittee members were pleasantly surprised to find that those faculty members who might have been considered too busy to concern
themselves with an elaborate questionnaire that required considerable time to complete turned in full forms, sometimes
supplementing their replies with additional typed pages.

In the table provided for the evaluation of resources,
faculty members were asked to pinpoint the field as narrowly as possible in terms of their specialties.   They were asked
to name the languages which should be included.   The countries issuing the publications were to be listed.   For example,
should Japanese and Mexican publications dealing with a period of German literature be included?   Finally, types of materials were to be listed in cases in which form in relation
to content applied.   In addition to books and periodicals, attention was called to other serials, government publications,
manuscripts, newspapers, dissertations, films, and so on.
What was being sought was elements in collecting which might
together serve to formulate an acquisitions policy in the
fields of concern to the University.   There were exceptions
that might well be made in the application of the policy.
Moreover, there was clearly no intention of reducing flexibility in collecting or of setting up rigid programs.   The

librarians, however, have had a long period of struggle with their consciences as to how far they should go in collecting in their areas of library responsibility.   Even within teaching departments, there was not always agreement as to how limited funds should be spent.   The analysis of the resources by the departments provided an opportunity for soul-searching that they had not had before as a group, even though there had been some guidance through strong departmental librarians.   In some instances, deans and directors of units of the University indicated that they had no real worries about the development of the collections, since they had full confidence in their librarians.   Not only were they willing to allow the librarians to buy or otherwise acquire for present needs, but they took seriously any recommendations of the librarians for building resource materials in areas that might be considered peripheral at the time.   In a number of instances, the librarians have been able to prepare the way for the installation of new courses, the expansion of limited curriculums, and the furtherance of research on advanced levels.

Undoubtedly, the extent to which a library staff includes individuals who are so conversant with the fields of their responsibility that they can anticipate future needs on the scale necessary for collecting is an important factor in the strength of personnel.   The need for such librarians has been recognized; how to attract them to librarianship is another matter.

It is doubtful, however, whether university-library collections can be built up as effectively without the complete co-operation of faculties as with it.   It is especially doubtful where such matters as the acquisition of micro-reproductions instead of originals and co-operative specialization in collecting among a group of libraries are concerned.   Both of these represent policy actions in the formulation of an acquisitions program.   In both approaches, there appears to be increasing interest on the part of faculty members, even though there is still a strong desire to have materials close at hand.

In the light of the interest of trustees and administrative officers in the rising costs of library service, it may be worth while to promote a positive program of faculty participation.   The obligations of the university and library administrations and the faculties for the future systematic development of the collections at Columbia, as suggested in the survey, are not new to library literature.   Nevertheless, they merit the constant attention of the groups involved, if building of collections is to be more than guesswork.   The obligations are as follows:

1. Faculty members, at the time they are recruited by the University, should be selected with some regard for their ability to strengthen the library collections.

2. Teaching departments and schools should establish library committees or appoint departmental representatives who can serve as liaison officers with the libraries.   The younger members of the departments are likely to take an active interest in this work, but the responsibility should not be restricted to them.

3. Sufficient funds should be allotted to interest faculty members in making recommendations for the collections; each department should be aware of the fund available to it for the year.

4. The libraries should have a positive program for encouraging faculty members to participate more fully in the acquisition program, but faculty members should be willing to reconsider recommendations that appear questionable on a long-range basis.

5. The faculties of departments and schools should work closely with librarians in justifying to the administration their need for adequate funds to purchase library materials for instruction and research.   Analyses of holdings for specific subject fields are essential.

6. The library needs for support of new courses should be examined carefully by faculty members and librarians, and the extent to which older materials should be acquired must be determined on the basis of available funds or special moneys required.

7. Whenever possible, faculty members should take an active role in obtaining gift collections for the libraries that bear an appropriate relation to the current or potential programs of the University.

In a large university, it is likely that some faculty members will not perform satisfactorily.   The administration then has the responsibility of providing library personnel with the language and subject competence necessary to do the work required. With the increasing enrollments facing academic institutions of the future, the importance of libraries, never really questioned by faculty members as a body, will be greater than ever. The faculties will require their students to use libraries to the utmost. In order to do effective work, faculty members must ensure that the libraries of their institutions are equipped properly to give the support that will be indispensable.

Notes

1. The report of the subcommittee, The Columbia University Libraries, was published by the Columbia University Press in 1958. The questionnaire to the faculty members consisted of two parts, one relating to library problems in general and the other to the resources of libraries. The subcommittee was composed of C. Donald Cook, Richard H. Logsdon, and the writer of this paper, who served as chairman.

2. Suggestions for developing these levels were obtained from various sources, but primarily from the John Crerar Library's Acquisitions Policy (Chicago: The Library, 1953), and from Policy on Scope and Coverage [of the] Army Medical Library (Washington, D. C. : Government Printing Office, 1951).

3. A follow-up of this study is being made by C. Donald Cook in a doctoral dissertation in the School of Library Service, Columbia University.

Selection from Checklist for Review and Evaluation
of Technical Libraries

by Christopher Glenn Stevenson

Manager of Technical Information, Batelle Memorial Institute,
Pacific Northwest Laboratory,
Richland, Washington. The
checklist is based on work performed under United States
Atomic Energy Commission Contract AT (45-1)-1830

From Special Libraries 58:108-9, February 1967;
Reprinted by permission of Publications Dept.,
Special Libraries Association, New York City

5. Reference Resources

a. What is the total number of volumes in the library collection including those in branch libraries and in self-main-
tained indefinite loan collections? Books_____ Bound jour-
nals_____

b. Total subscriptions including office copies, if any_____
  Number of titles   _____
  Library subscriptions, including branches
   if any   _____
  Number of titles   _____

c. What is the estimated size of the technical report
collection? _____ Reports (titles)   _____
Reports (copies)_____

d. Estimate how many of the reports (titles) in the
collection are: Locally originated_____ Offsite
originated_____

e. Does the library handle classified reports? ____ Yes

____ No. If yes, give approximate percentage of the report collection that is classified____%.

f. In addition to books, periodicals, and technical reports, does the library maintain files of:
Standards and Specifications   _____
Trade Catalogs   _____
Reprints   _____
Photographs   _____
Other   _____

g. Does the library have the major bibliographic tools in the technical fields pertinent to the organization's main interests?

h. Does the library have a general reference collection?

i. Has the availability of other materials in the geographic area been taken into account in building the library collection?

j. Does the library receive at least one copy of each of the following types of material representing significant research and/or development done by the organization? Formal research and development reports? Informal or internal technical reports? Technical articles submitted for publication? Patents? Technical speeches? Technical reports prepared by subconstractors of the organization? Others?

   Strengths:

   Weaknesses:

6. Selection and Acquisition Practices

a. Is the library responsible for the procurement of all reference materials (books, journals, reports, pamphlets, government documents, etc.) required by the installation?
____Yes____No. If no, give details:

b. Does the library have a strong collection of bibliographic tools to support the selection and acquisition of materials?

c. Is the library staff consulted in the selection of vendors and evaluation of vendor bids for the library's business? Give details:

d. Is the final decision regarding items to be acquired the responsibility of the library and its staff?   Give details:

e. What provision is made to permit the technical and scientific staff to recommend library purchases?

f. What procedures have been established to permit the library to order publications directly?   Give details:

g. Do the purchase procedures allow for prompt ordering of materials when speed is necessary?

h. What is the average time lapse between order and receipt of domestic trade books?   Comments:

i. Does the library participate in a publication exchange program?

j. Does the library make use of coupon services for procurement of patents, society papers, etc. ? ____Yes____No.   If no, give details:

k. Does the library take advantage of deposit accounts for procurement of government publications, photocopies from New York Public Library, etc. ?____Yes____No.   If no, give details:

l. Does the library participate in duplicate exchange programs?

m. Are site employees permitted to purchase books through the library at discount prices for their personal use?

Strengths:

Weaknesses:

7. Organization and Maintenance of the Collection

a. Are the library's materials cataloged and organized in logical, easily understood ways which will permit rapid retrieval of information?

b. Does the library attempt to develop by creation or adaptation special systems for organizing and cataloging materials of special types or interest?

c. Are library materials cataloged, indexed, and/or abstracted promptly?

d. What is the backlog of uncataloged or unindexed materials?

e. Are there clearly developed criteria for the selection of technical reports to be cataloged?

f. Do circulation records permit prompt location of all items on loan?

g. Does the library require terminating employees to return all "permanent loans" or "desk copies" for the reassignment to other site personnel? Comments:

h. Is there a program for retiring or microfilming little used materials?

i. Does the library have a policy to determine which journals will be bound and which will be kept unbound?____Yes ____No. If no, give details:

j. Are periodicals, and other long-life material to be retained on the shelves, promptly and securely bound?

k. Is the collection culled periodically to eliminate less valuable or duplicate copies of materials?

Evaluation

by Douglas Waples

Dr. Waples, one of the pioneers in library research, is
now Professor Emeritus,
Graduate Library School, University of Chicago

From his Investigating Library Problems. Chi-
cago, University of Chicago Press, 1959. p. 94-6;
Reprinted from Investigating Library Problems by
Douglas Waples by permission of the University of
Chicago Press (c) 1939, by the University of Chi-
cago and of the author.

Book selection. --The public library selects publications of any kind and on any subject which the readers demand and which meet a certain minimum of literary excellence.

This is an assumption by means of which the library's book collection is often judged. It will be noted
that the foregoing remarks on circulation apply to the one
critical clause in the sentence, namely, ''which the readers
demand.'' This clause is a joker, which can easily rob the
criterion of any meaning save that which the librarian
chooses to read into it. If he estimates the strength of the
readers' demand by the relative number of readers demanding each type of publication, the standards of selection may
sink to the level of the newsstand or rental library and still
meet the letter of the criterion. Should the librarian, however, seek to justify the highest standards, he may select
only the best of the publications which any reader demands.

It is plain that every library must make its own best
compromise between these two extremes. The former would
fill the shelves with racy fiction and the latter would fill
them with technical monographs and belles-lettres, many in
foreign language. It is also plain that each library should

657

base its compromise on the highest threshold of literary excellence the community will tolerate, and the same goes for the clientele of the school library, college library, or specialized library.

A sound evaluation of the library's collection must accordingly comprise three steps, in addition to those suggested for evaluating the library's financial support and its circulation. First, it is necessary to construct from appropriate bibliographies some sort of check list for use in comparing the accessions of a typical year with the titles published. This will involve some method of group-rating whereby at least three levels of excellence are represented by from ten to thirty titles in each of the major types of fiction, branches of nonfiction, periodicals, and other areas of publication.

The second step will compare the titles of the check list with the titles accessioned during the year or years selected for study. Results of the comparison will indicate the level of excellence which the accessions in each class represent. The reliability of the results will naturally depend upon the reliability of the check list as a sample of the year's publications.

The third step will compare the circulation of the titles accessioned at each level of excellence. The more recently the titles have been accessioned, the more satisfactory will be the identification of relative circulation as found on the first book card. The results of this comparison will show the level of excellence which the circulation attains in each class of literature examined. A highly desirable refinement would be to determine the degree of excellence for each class of publication and each distinguishable group of readers. The breakdown by readers is not possible, however, from existing library records. Readers must be sampled directly to obtain it, much as the readers of the New York Public Library were sampled by W. C. Haygood. [1]

Such in bare outline is a procedure for the evaluation of any book collection in terms of the library's present clientele. Any satisfactory analysis of circulation would extend the evaluation by further comparisons with the local bookreading population as a whole, which will doubtless include readers of the better, as also of the worse, publications, who do not use the library.

Assistance to readers. --Our last example of assumptions concerning library values which deserve investigation may be taken from the somewhat vague but much advertised aspect of library work called assistance to readers. Such assistance takes many forms and is not easy to evaluate except as certain assumed effects are singled out for examination. Of such effects perhaps the most tangible may be found in the assumption that the staff teaches readers to make efficient and independent use of the catalog and other apparatus for finding a desired book and the desired information in the book.

It is perhaps debatable whether readers in a public library are more "assisted" when they are taught how to help themselves than when they are presented with the books they want. In a school or college library, however, it is reasonable to suppose that the reader's increasing skill in the use of reference tools is an important indication of a value he obtains from the library. If then the student undertakes to determine how well the reader has benefited by instruction in how to use the library, it is clear that he must use other methods of evaluation than those thus far mentioned in this chapter, namely, individual judgment, group rating, and comparison. The additional methods he will require are the more technical and elaborate methods of testing and experiment.

Note

1. Who Uses the Public Library? See p. 8, n. 2.

Surveying Library Collections - Methods

by Edwin E. Williams   Energetic analyst of library collections and resources; Assist-
ant Librarian, Harvard University.

From Maurice F. Tauber and Irlene Stephens, eds.
Library Surveys. New York, Columbia University
Press, 1967. p. 28-34, 41-5; Reprinted by per-
mission of Columbia University Press.

Methods

    Statistics, it seems safe to say, are used in surveys
of collections more consistently than anything else; if a general library survey says anything at all about library collections, it is almost sure to mention their size. In some
cases there are good reasons for doubting that further information would contribute very much. There are widely accepted standards for minimum sizes of school, college, and
public libraries, below which, in the judgment of professional organizations or accrediting bodies, it is impossible to
provide the variety of materials required for adequate service. If the surveyor is examining a library or group of libraries falling substantially below the minimum, and is recommending that a state or regional system be established in
order to make satisfactory collections available to communities too small to support libraries of the minimum size, he
may well rest his case on statistics and standards. [28]

    Above the minimal sizes, standards normally specify
a given number of additional volumes per capita. The surveyor can also compare the library or libraries he is examining with those of other communities or institutions that
seem to have similar needs. He can use, both for checking
against standards and for comparison with other libraries,
such additional quantitative statistical data as the number of
volumes acquired per year, the annual expenditures for books,
and the number of periodicals currently received. Per capita

calculations and comparisons are normally made for these items as well as for the size of the collection.

While surveys of collections cite quantitative statistics more frequently than any other facts, they normally and quite properly warn that these figures may be misleading and that quality is more important than quantity. They may well admit also that uniformity has not been achieved in methods of counting library holdings, [29] and that many a library has discovered errors in the figures it has been reporting.

Obviously, then, it may be rash to base conclusions on quantitative statistics alone, uncorroborated and unmodified by findings based on any of the survey methods yet to be considered. A cynic might assert that statistics are almost universally used because they are easy to obtain, appear to be clear and unambiguous, and may impress the innocent reader. Nevertheless they are usually significant; "size," as Tauber has said, "does tell something."[30] There is normally a high correlation between the size of a library, its usefulness, and (if it is an academic library) the quality of the institution it serves. [31]

Statistics can also be used in checking the balance of a collection; for school libraries, in particular, there are recommended percentages for each major subject. [32] No one would advocate blind acceptance, but such standards are useful to the surveyor, who ought to examine any substantial departures from the norm and judge whether they seem to be justified by particular local needs. In addition, it may be useful to analyze the collection or portions of it by date of publication. [33]

Though surveys of use are to be considered at a later session, it may be noted here that an ambitious effort was once made at Hamilton College to use circulation statistics as a basis for evaluation of the book collection. There, twenty-five years ago, it was found that three fourths of the titles borrowed during one academic year were borrowed only once, and this was regarded as strong evidence that the collection was reasonably adequate. [34] This might be more convincing if comparisons with other college libraries were possible. As computer-based operations become more common, the alert surveyor may find it relatively easy to obtain statistics of this kind.

List-checking has been widely used by surveyors as a check on statistical data and as a means of assessing the quality of collections. More than 400 lists and bibliographies were used in the University of Chicago survey alone,[35] so enumeration is out of the question here, but something should be said of the types of lists most commonly employed.

Accrediting bodies have prepared or designated lists in some cases, and specific lists are suggested by some library standards. [36] State authorities have issued approved lists for school libraries. Then, of course, there are numerous lists originally prepared to assist libraries in book selection--many of them for children and for schools, the ALA Catalog, [37] the Standard Catalog, [38] the Booklist, [39] and Booklist Books,[40] the Mohrhardt[41] and Shaw[42] lists, and now Choice. [43] Both Mohrhardt and Shaw, it might be added, have often been used in public as well as in college library surveys. A wide variety of lists of best books, prizewinning titles, and annual selections of all kinds have been used. [44] In at least one public-library survey the catalogue of the Columbia University Press was checked. [45] Specialized bibliographies of all kinds have been used by surveyors of research libraries. Special attention has been given to reference works, and the standard bibliographies--particularly Winchell[46] or selected titles from Winchell--have often been checked. Sometimes, because it was believed that a high correlation can be assumed between general holdings and holdings of reference works, [47] only the latter have been checked; in other surveys, for similar reasons, only lists of periodicals have been used. Periodicals are especially important in research collections, and surveys have used various periodical lists prepared for special types of libraries, lists of titles covered by some of the indexing and abstracting services, Ulrich, [48] and, particularly popular with surveyors, Charles Harvey Brown's lists of most frequently cited journals in certain scientific subjects. [49]

Surveyors of individual libraries have normally depended on ready-made lists of the kinds suggested above, but lists have been specially prepared for use in a number of the multilibrary studies. The Public Library Inquiry attempted, in both fiction and nonfiction, to distinguish between best sellers, and notable and important books; comparing acquisitions of these with acquisitions of periodicals, documents, films, and music, it found evidence that popularity had influenced public library collections of books much more than their collections of other materials, for which quality had been the major criterion.[50]   A special list of "expensive books" was checked in Chicago and Westchester surveys.[51] Other ad hoc lists include Eaton's[52] for current political science, Martin's[53] for social problems, and Waples'[54] for social science.   Strunk, surveying musicological resources, used a list of only forty-five periodicals, historical works, and critical reprints,[55] while Ruggles and Mostecky, for their survey of Russian and East European publications in American libraries, prepared a list of 2,400 titles based on bibliographies compiled outside the United States--a procedure designed to make sure that the adequacy of American resources would not be measured against a standard reflecting the deficiencies of these resources.[56]   For the Canadian survey, a handpicked list of only 240 periodicals was used in comparing the strength of libraries relative to one another,[57] but the University of Chicago, assessing its holdings against the total that might be desirable, produced a list of 32,000 serial titles.[58]

Desiderata have not been listed on this scale by any other survey.   Yet, unless the examination is as thorough as this, it is evident that any lists used by the surveyor must be regarded as samples.   There are many books that would be desirable in a college library in addition to those on a Shaw list; if one checks the list, one assumes that there is a correlation between the percentage of listed books held by the library and the percentage of other desirable works that are in its collection.[59]   Such an assumption is obviously unsound if the list in question has been used as a buying guide; hence Shaw lists can be expected to lose their value for surveying purposes even before they go out of date in other respects, and one cannot use the same accreditation list year after year any more than one can use the same examination questions.   Moreover, unless a library is very small or weak, a desiderata list based on any ready-made selection will not go far toward filling in the gaps.

While list-checking is commonly a means of qualitative evaluation, it has sometimes been used in multilibrary surveys to obtain quantitative data, for example, to determine the total number of different titles represented in a group of libraries or to discover the extent of duplication between their collections.[60]

Some surveys, it has been noted, have dealt with library collections merely by calling attention to the fact that their size falls far short of minimum standards.   This, it was suggested, may be enough to make a case for regional organization; perhaps it can also be justified in the general survey of a public library on the ground that, if a sound acquisition program can be instituted, the library will soon contain the recent books that ought to be in it, and these, after all, are of first importance.   Research collections are a different matter, but fortunately there are faculty members whom the surveyor of college and university libraries can consult by means of questionnaires or interviews or both. Ideally, he can hope to base his findings on the expert opinion of men who know their subject, have a broad knowledge of its literature, have intensively used both the library he is surveying and many others, and have also kept themselves well informed of the degree to which the library is meeting the needs of their students, undergraduate and graduate.   In practice, of course, the surveyor does not find such men in every subject, and the individuals he consults do not always agree.   Even in the largest university there will be some important segments of the collection in which, temporarily, no one is particularly interested.   If one man in a department has been depended upon to build up the relevant collections, he will probably know more about the library's holdings in his area than anyone else, but may well be unconscious of deficiencies or indifferent to them; indeed, they will be deficiencies that have developed because of his lack of interest in certain subdivisions of the subject.[61]

If time were available it might be desirable to have each professor fill out a questionnaire and then to interview him in order to provide an opportunity for amplification of his written comments and clarification of questions they might have suggested to the surveyor.   In practice, something less than this is normally the best that can be managed.   An interview may seem particularly desirable when the professor's reply to a questionnaire seems to be contradicted by his colleagues or by other evidence.

Perhaps little need be said of questionnaires except that brevity and clarity are virtues.   Members of the faculty have sometimes been asked to estimate the cost of filling gaps in collections of books, current subscriptions, back files, documents, and other materials.[62]   While this may produce specific figures for which the surveyor need not assume personal responsibility, it is not clear that professors are particularly well qualified to estimate such costs.   On one recent occasion at least, when a professor thought he was proposing expenditure of "a few thousand dollars" for newspaper microfilms, he turned out to be asking for at least two hundred thousand dollars.

Though the professor may be no more infallible as a prophet than as an estimator of costs, there seems to be no better oracle whom the surveyor can consult regarding trends in research and potential future needs. A survey in progress at Harvard is emphasizing these questions in the hope that, just as it built up strong Russian resources long before Slavic studies became fashionable, the Harvard Library can succeed in anticipating some major demands of research in the twenty-first century.

Students also have been questioned in large numbers by some surveyors. [63] When questions deal with their failures to obtain what is wanted, it may be doubtful whether one is measuring legitimate demands or those resulting from poor choices of thesis topics. It must also be recognized that a faculty and student body of the highest quality may ask for much more than even a very strong library can supply, while a mediocre community may be relatively well satisfied with poor collections. [64]

There is one other thing that many surveyors do, though it is so manifestly unscientific that little has been written of it. This is to go into the stacks and look over the shelves. While there, the surveyor may judge the physical condition of the collection, estimate roughly the size of its various parts, and perhaps form some opinion of how well recent publications are represented in it. [65] Anything more depends entirely upon the experience of the surveyor and the acuity of his perceptions.

Notes

28. An excellent recent example is John A. Humphry, Library Co-operation, The Brown University Study of University-School-Community Library Coordination in the State of Rhode Island. Providence, Brown University Press, 1963.

29. Downs, Robert B. "Uniform Statistics for Library Holdings," Library Quarterly, 16:63-69 (1946); A. F. Kuhlman, "Two ARL Approaches to Counting Holdings of Research Libraries," College and Research Libraries, 21:207-11 (1960); Eli M. Oboler, "The Accuracy of

Federal Academic Library Statistics," College and Research Libraries, 25:494-96 (1964).

30. Tauber, M. F. "The Importance of Developing Australian Library Resources." Australian Library Journal, 10:115-21 (1961).

31. Jordan, Robert T. "Library Characteristics of Colleges Ranking High in Academic Excellence," College and Research Libraries, 24:369-76 (1963). George Piternick. "Library Growth and Academic Quality." College and Research Libraries, 24:223-29 (1963).

32. Fargo. The Library in the School. Henne, Ersted, and Lohrer. A Planning Guide for the High School Library Program.

33. Fargo. The Library in the School; George Walter Rosenlof. Library Facilities of Teacher-Training Institutions, New York, Teachers College, 1929--Contributions to Education, 347; Elizabeth Opal Stone. "Measuring the College Book Collection." Library Journal, 66:941-43 (1941).

34. Stieg, Lewis. "A Technique for Evaluating the College Library Boon Collection." Library Quarterly, 13: 34-44 (1943).

35. Raney. The University Libraries.

36. Association of College and Research Libraries. Committee on Standards. "Standards for College Libraries," College and Research Libraries, 20:274-80 (1959); also the same Committee's "Standards for Junior College Libraries." College and Research Libraries, 21:200-6 (1960). The Southern Association's list was used by Mark M. Gormley and Ralph H. Hopp. The Sioux Falls College Library: A Survey. Chicago, American Library Association, 1961.

37. ALA Catalog, 1926. Chicago, American Library Association, 1926, and Supplements.

38. Standard Catalog for Public Libraries. 1934 and later editions. New York, H. W. Wilson Company.

39. The Booklist. Chicago, American Library Association

1905-.

40. American Library Association. Booklist Books. 1919-
    1940.

41. Carnegie Corporation of New York. Advisory Group on
    College Libraries. A List of Books for Junior Col-
    lege Libraries. Comp. by Foster E. Mohrhardt.
    Chicago, American Library Association, 1937.

42. Carnegie Corporation of New York. Advisory Group on
    College Libraries. A List of Books for College Li-
    braries. Prepared by Charles B. Shaw, Chicago,
    American Library Association, 1931; and also Charles
    B. Shaw, A List of Books for College Libraries,
    1931-38, Chicago, American Library Association,
    1940.

43. Choice. Middletown, 1964-. An issue was checked by
    Leon Carnovsky; also his The Racine Public Library,
    An Evaluation and a Consideration of Selected Prob-
    lems (1965).

44. For an interesting group of lists, see Frederick Weze-
    man and Robert H. Rohlf. Hopkins Public Library,
    Hopkins, Minnesota, A Survey and Recommendations
    for Future Development and Planning (1962).

45. Baltimore, Enoch Pratt Free Library. The Reorganiza-
    tion of a Large Public Library.

46. Winchell, Constance M. Guide to Reference Books.
    Seventh ed. Chicago, American Library Association,
    1951, and Supplements.

47. McEwen, Robert W. "The North Central Association's
    1943 Survey of College and University Libraries."
    College and Research Libraries, 4:253-56 (1942/43).

48. Graves, Eileen C. Ulrich's Periodicals Directory.
    Tenth ed., New York, R. R. Bowker Company, 1963.

49. Brown, Charles Harvey. Scientific Serials. Chicago,
    Association of College and Research Libraries, 1956
    --ACRL Monographs, 16.

50. Carnovsky, Leon. "Measurement of Public Library

Book Collections." Library Trends 1:462-70; (1952/53); Robert D. Leigh. "The Public Library Inquiry's Sampling of Library Holdings of Books and Periodicals," Library Quarterly, 21:157-72 (1951); Robert D. Leigh. The Public Library in the United States. New York, Columbia University Press, 1950, p. 76-91.

51. Carnovsky, Leon. "The Evaluation of Public-Library Facilities." In Louis R. Wilson (ed.). Library Trends, Chicago, University of Chicago Press, 1937, p. 286-309; Carleton B. Joeckel and Leon Carnovsky. A Metropolitan Library in Action, A Survey of the Chicago Public Library. Chicago, University of Chicago Press, 1940, p. 311-13, 425-26.

52. Eaton, Andrew J. "Current Political Science Publications in Five Chicago Libraries: A Study of Coverage, Duplication, and Omission." Library Quarterly, 15:187-212 (1945).

53. Martin, Lowell. "Public Library Provision of Books About Social Problems." Library Quarterly, 9:249-72 (1939).

54. Waples, Douglas, and Lasswell, Harold D. National Libraries and Foreign Scholarship, Notes on Recent Selections in Social Science. Chicago, University of Chicago Press, 1936.

55. Strunk, W. Oliver. State and Resources of Musicology in the United States. Washington, American Council of Learned Societies, 1932--A. C. L. S. Bulletin, 19.

56. Ruggles, Melville J., and Mostecky, Vaclav. Russian and East European Publications in the Libraries of the United States. New York, Columbia University Press, 1960--Columbia University Studies in Library Service, 11:228-49.

57. Williams. Resources of Canadian University Libraries. p. 10, 74-80.

58. Raney. The University Libraries. p. 4; Robert B. Downs. Guide for the Description and Evaluation of Research Materials. Chicago, American Library Association, 1939. This book contains extensive lists;

it was originally prepared for use in the survey of
resources of southern libraries, and has been checked
in several later surveys, including Richard Harwell,
Research Resources in the Georgia-Florida Libraries
of SIRF.   Atlanta, Southern Regional Education Board,
1955; and Louis R. Wilson and Marion A. Milczew-
ski.   Libraries of the Southeast.   Chapel Hill, University of North Carolina Press, 1949; Eugene Hilton.
Junior College Book List.   Berkeley, University of
California Press, 1930--University of California Publications in Education, VI:1.   This book was also useful in several surveys, cf., Douglas Waples, "The
North Central Association's Study of College Libraries," College and Reference Library Yearbook,
2:85-89 (1930), and Douglas Waples and E. W. Mc-
Diarmid, Jr., "Comparison of Book Selections in Li-
braries of Teachers Colleges with Those of Liberal
Arts Colleges," in United States Office of Education,
National Survey of the Education of Teachers, Washington, Superintendent of Documents, 1935--Office of
Education Bulletin, 1933:10, 5:233-40.   Many public-
library surveys have used lists of material particularly relevant to the community in question, cf.,
William Chait and Ruth Warncke, A Survey of the
Public Libraries of Asheville and Buncombe County,
North Carolina, Chicago, American Library Associa-
tion, 1965; and Ralph R. Shaw, Libraries of Metropolitan Toronto (1960).

59. Stieg.   "A Technique for Evaluating."

60. Carnovsky, Leon.   The St. Paul Public Library and
     the James Jerome Hill Reference Library, A Study
     of Co-operative Possibilities (1960). A. F. Kuhlman.
     The North Texas Regional Libraries.   Nashville,
     Peabody Press, 1943; Merritt.

61. This may be a weakness of the Bibliographical Planning
     Committee of Philadelphia.   A Faculty Survey of the
     University of Pennsylvania Libraries.   Philadelphia,
     University of Pennsylvania Press, 1940--Philadelphia
     Library Resources, I.

62. Among surveys for which this was done are A. F. Kuhl-
     man and Icko Iben, Report of a Survey of the Univer-
     sity of Mississippi Library, University, Miss., 1940;
     Maurice F. Tauber and William H. Jesse, Report of

a Survey of the Libraries of the Virginia Polytechnic
Institute, Blacksburg, Virginia Polytechnic Institute, 1949
Maurice F. Tauber and Eugene H. Wilson, Report of
a Survey of the Library of Montana State University,
Chicago, American Library Association, 1951; Louis
R. Wilson, Robert B. Downs, and Maurice F. Tauber,
Report of a Survey of the Libraries of Cornell Uni-
versity, Ithaca, Cornell University, 1948; Louis R.
Wilson and Raynard C. Swank, Report of a Survey of
the Library of Stanford University, Chicago, Ameri-
can Library Association, 1947; and Louis R. Wilson
and Maurice F. Tauber, Report of a Survey of the
University of South Carolina Library, Columbia, University of South Carolina, 1946.

63. Examples are Donald Coney, Herman H. Henkle, and
G. Flint Purdy, Report of a Survey of the Indiana
University Library, Chicago, American Library As-
sociation, 1940; and the Tauber-Cook-Logsdon survey
--Columbia University, President's Committee on the
Educational Future of the University: Subcommittee
on the University Libraries. The Columbia Univer-
sity Libraries, A Report on Present and Future
Needs. New York, Columbia University Press, 1958
--Columbia University Studies in Library Service, IX.
There is an account of this survey, Maurice F. Taub-
er. "The Columbia University Libraries Self-Study."
College and Research Libraries, 19:277-82 (1958).

64. Cf. G. Flint Purdy. "The Evaluation of University Library Service." Library Quarterly, 12:638-44 (1942),
in which an attempt at evaluation on the basis of use
is made. Interlibrary loan requests have also been
studied--Donald E. Thompson. "A Self-Survey of the
University of Alabama Libraries." College and Research Libraries, 8:147-50 (1947).

65. Sample shelves have been checked in detail--cf., Fred-
erick Wezeman. Public Library Service, Ramsey
County, Minnesota, A Survey and a Plan. St. Paul,
Ramsey County Public Library, 1958, p. 17-25.

The Scope of Toronto's Central Library (Selections)

by Lee Ash

Library Consultant and specialist in evaluation of collections, with a wide range of abilities and interests (including membership in the Society of American Hypnotists!)

From The Scope of Toronto's Central Library. Toronto, Canada, Toronto Public Library, 1967. Mimeo. p. 5-7, 44-7; Reprinted by permission of H. C. Campbell, Director, Toronto Public Library

The Criteria

Any research problem is best begun by the construction of a series of hypotheses which at the outset anticipate the purposes of the proposals. Hypotheses should, of course, be couched in such terms that the components can be tested by the accumulation of pertinent data that will prove or disprove the validity of the stated concepts.

In Toronto, changes in the growth of the community served now and to be satisfied in the future by the Public Library are easily apparent. An ever-growing population of diverse cultural elements, a rapidly changing economy--locally, and in relation to neighbors in Metro, to the Province and, indeed, to the Nation--are facts of life in Toronto. Any alert library board and library administration would feel that it was necessary, in the light of such changes, to face-up to the challenges of the legal charges that are implied by such an evolution of community growth. This has been the response of the Toronto Public Library.

As a result of consideration of data now at hand and of the implication of related surveys (such as the Woods and Gordon study of the reference use of the Library in 1958, the Shaw report on Libraries of Metropolitan Toronto, 1960, and the St. John report on the Provincial library situation published in 1966) the Library administration, with the endorsement of its Board has proposed the following hypotheses:

1) That the Toronto Public Library must take responsibility to provide publicly accessible reference and information materials, including nonbook research materials, such as would be used to support study through the first level of graduate education, the Master's Degree in some fields and even beyond this in other fields.

2) That the Library's bookstock, special collections, periodical holdings, and all other resources for reference and information, are inadequate to meet reference and information demands at this time and those which can be anticipated for the next two decades of community growth and change.

Definition of Terms

That part of the first hypothesis concerning availability of resources is stated in the Public Library Act.

The second hypothesis, based on an a priori administrative decision that the Central Library Division of the TPL is to serve as a reference and information center, posited the need for specific analyses of the collections and recommendations for future growth and support of such a program.

In order to approach these problems it was necessary to survey several factors. We had to know, first of all, the character of the collections, their depth of coverage, completeness, and information value. A study of this kind also required answers to such questions as numerical sufficiency, quality and selectivity, physical condition, and the need to weed the collections for preservation, discard, or storage of seldom used materials.

Another postulate for this survey has been recognition of the changing community requirements and their relationships to the proposed increase in the Library's stock of reference and information materials. This meant a study of the public accessibility policies of other libraries and special collections in the orbit of the TPL's geographical area

which will, in part, help to determine TPL's future responsibilities to the community. Indeed, this study is likely
to become an exceedingly important influence on the pattern
of TPL's collecting and service program, especially when
the cost of the development of collections is acknowledged.

Some modification of necessary recommendations for
the expansion of collections or services can be expected in
the future though as the Library begins to take full advantage of an effective system of Canadian bibliographical controls such as the Metropolitan Bibliographical Centre, printed
book catalogues, and other keys to resources.

The Character of the Collections

Two approaches have been made. First, there has
been an overall subjective view of the collections by the surveyor whose findings are recorded in the following pages.
Second, more refined analyses of the collection produced
special sampling techniques to reveal the character of the
Library's holdings with reference to dates of publications
and language representation (although no thorough review of
this last was planned since there is such obviously poor representation). These samples have been measured numeri-
cally and graphically to indicate some special strengths and
weaknesses. *

Other checks on the collection were made, particularly a comparison of holdings against titles noted in available selective bibliographies of each subject field which TPL
elects to strengthen. The Chief Librarian proposed that
this chore would be undertaken by the members of the Central Library Book Selection Committee and this was the major part of the self-survey undertaken by the staff of the Library. An analysis of this kind, though not definitive nor
necessarily the most perfect (since it cannot take into special account factors like national--that is, Canadian--or other
special points of view) was the easiest to complete in the
time allowed and, begun by the first of December 1965, was
finished by the end of June 1966. This project gave staff a
refreshing insight into the quality of their collections and an
opportunity to build Desiderata Lists which may be prepared
for computerized analyses and ordering for primary and secondary acquisition. We have given an outline of first steps
here and subsequently the Library will determine what techniques will be used to investigate the other matters we have

noted.

Good collections are expensive but poor ones are ex-
travagant and wasteful.   Nevertheless, it is foolhardy for a
consultant to propose a complete plan for development of resources; the local staff must undertake this task and at TPL
has demonstrated a willingness and some ability to do the
job which will be a continuing one.   All the surveyor can do
is give some guidance or assistance and try to keep the
cars on the track.   My proposals stem from the staff and
from my own careful examination of the shelves, but they
must be interpreted by the administration.

———————

Following is my personal evaluation of the quality of
the Toronto Public Library's Central Library book collections, including collections in the City Hall Branch, the Music Library, and the Language and Literature Centre.   It is
a consideration of the total representation of holdings, by
"Dewey Tens" of materials found in all subject sections or
special collections of the Central Library and the three
branches just listed.

*   *   *

770-779--Photography

The General Reference Section remarks "Very few
books.   Send patrons to Fine Art Section," but the latter's
staff notes that its circulation collection is only fair while
the reference collection is poor, and "Except on the amateur
level, the collection is inadequate."   It becomes obvious that
with an ever-increasing demand for this kind of material the
TPL is not serving its public's needs in one of the most
popular fields of interest.   Especially important is the need
for the Library to subscribe to more than two photography
periodicals.

At this point I should remark that the photography
material in the Science & Technology Section (both 500s and
600s) has the dubious distinction of its antiquity and although
in the past year a few useful modern titles have been added,
not nearly enough has come into the collection to keep apace
of this fast-changing subject.

The Music Library

780-789--Music

The General Reference Section is the only place in the Central Building with any reference materials. These can be used to answer only superficial reference questions, but are of sufficient variety to meet the needs of most high school students.

The most complete and informed evaluation of the Music Library collection (housed in its own building at 559 Avenue Road) has come largely from observation of the staff of the branch and enlarges on the surveyor's limited observations and inability to comment on the subject except in the most general terms--as a music lover.

There is an excellent collection of Music biography (classed as 780), notable for its English language titles, but advanced reference work requires more primary source documentation.   Most of the foreign language material is in this part of the collection only because no English translation is available.   Music history is well covered, including a good collection of older standard works as well as books representing contemporary scholarship.   All the principal music encyclopaedias and dictionaries are in the reference stock of the branch, including major titles in French, German, and Italian.   Bibliographical reference works and guides to music collections in other institutions are helpful in locating source materials, and the Library is developing a good collection relative to Canadian music and musicians.

The sections of the classification dealing with opera and church music are good, but only fair with regard to instrumental music.   There is no doubt that these need to be supported by a wider spread of representative periodical titles.   Sacred music is in only small supply but sufficient to meet current demands and even heavier reference use if the resource were generally known among local church musicians.

There is some representation of musical comedy materials in the Theatre Collection (782) but not enough for historical reference.   The field is not covered extensively in the Music Collection either, outside of general encyclopaedic reference books and the most standard items, such as Gilbert and Sullivan, Rodgers, Friml, Kern, etc.

In all classes, Jazz is not strong except in some of the older and more traditional schools of writing. Young musicians in Yorkville have complained to the surveyor that the Library's collection of printed materials "just isn't with it," and that the record collection seems to have complacently avoided most of the far-out experimental music. This is the only expression of severe criticism that has been raised with regard to the Music Collection (except for the paucity of current periodicals of a more specialized nature), and it may also be a serious one since much new Canadian music will stem from the thoughtful Yorkville-type youngsters who need the breadth of scope that a modern jazz collection can give them if they are to have a good grounding in this vital contemporary art.

As in most public libraries, "current demand for opera is seasonal and most requests for vocal scores can be met." Advanced reference workers do need more orchestral scores than the Library is able to provide, but the demand is not an intensive one.

Along with jazz, for which the Library's resources have been remarked on as inadequate, there is a great demand for folk songs and here at least insofar as North American music is concerned the resource is adequate except, I am told, with regard to French Canadian songs. Be that as it may, the collection could be strengthened by the addition of other foreign language materials, and by greater interest in contemporary protest songs.

Piano music, it is reported, meets demands well, with emphasis having always been put on the acquisition of original material rather than transcriptions (which, of course, have their proper place in a collection such as ours). Organ music, on the other hand, has been neglected, "most of it was obtained through a donation and needs filling in with collected editions and modern works;" still, there are a few interesting items among the older scores. The performer is fairly well served by the String Music section which "consists of numerous parts for string instrument and piano or collections for strings alone," but the advanced reference worker would find little of source material here that would be unusual.

Orchestral music, in full score or parts, "meets the demand from students for study scores and from the amateur performer for chamber music," and some persons doing more advanced work "would find the miniature scores convenient for study." Not much can be said for the Library's representative collection of music for Wind or Percussion instruments, "the quantity is not great but is acquired as it becomes available."

On the whole the Music Collection is useful and its devoted users frequently comment on its excellent service and interested assistance to patrons. The presence of a particularly good circulating and reference collection of recordings (with the exception of the need for contemporary jazz) enhances the Music Library's work, as do the special files of reference materials of an ephemeral nature--clippings, photographs, programs, etc. It should be noted that the Music Collection is 90 percent a circulating collection, although according to the Chief Librarian, it has a very low annual circulation (20,000 a year) for its 25,000 volumes. This means that as a reference source it is more useful than if it could only be used for consultation. "I think this is the point that patrons appreciate when they comment on it," says Mr. Campbell.

Only the Music Library replied substantively to the Library's invitation for staff to comment on the survey, and even though I do not agree completely with the following self-appraisal as it touches matters of adequacy, the comments are helpful and indicative of the kind of staff reaction that is attentive and can be useful:

> I would agree that a wider spread of representative periodical titles is needed to back up any claim we might hope to make of adequacy in our field, even though the need is not supported by public demand. However, as in other fields, appetite probably comes with eating.

> Sacred music, contrary to the report, is in very large supply, rather embarrassingly so, since the demand falls so far short. Our shortcomings there, if shortcoming it is, is that we do not supply sets of anthems, cantatas or oratorios suitable for choir use. It is an area we do not wish to invade and for which the demand has been extremely small.

> Jazz in both the scores and records has been ex-

cluded chiefly for two reasons: lack of money and
lack of space, particularly for material of a somewhat ephemeral nature which, under traditional library methods, would be largely outdated before it
was processed and available. Now that money and
space are being added to us, jazz is to be added
to the collection, with better results, we hope,
than have been experienced by some libraries we
have consulted.   There are upwards of two-dozen
albums in the collection, from Carawan's 'We shall
overcome' to the 'Sing out' reprints which take
care of most of the current folk-song and protest
material as it is published.   Since the singers are
all busily writing 'original folk songs' neither the
publishers nor we could hope to keep up with the
output.

There are 26 books of French-Canadian folk songs
as against 37 others in the Canadian section (these
include some Indian & Eskimo albums) which proportionately seems fair enough.   For many years,
only French-Canadian material was available, so
that we are well pleased that the English-Canadian
is coming into his own at last.   Our total folk song
collection is in excess of 500 volumes, exclusive
of sheet songs & choral arrangements, and includes Egyptian, Basque, Japanese, Chinese,
Ukrainian, Hungarian, Flemish, etc., as well as
the more common languages.   Where possible, we
buy a volume with both the original text and an
English translation.

The organ section is very large but has been allowed to coast along for several years because of
its size.   However, many new items have recently
been added, both in the historical and modern
fields.

This is true of all sections of the music classification.   As I mentioned in my comments on the
general chapter of the Ash report, the increased
budget and new addition to the Music Library co-
incided more or less with the beginning of the Ash
Survey.   Many collected editions are on standing
order and arriving rapidly in the Technical Services Division--the Reference Section is increasing
by leaps and bounds--even the woodwinds and

brasses have grown considerably in numbers.

Modern classical music, even of the far-out variety is well represented--Berio, Boulez, Bussotti,
Foss, Ligetti, Stockhausen, etc., in scores, and
records are being bought as they are available.

Much of this is not visible at the present time as
space in our present quarters is at a premium,
but all members of the staff plus a full time music cataloguer are working hard to provide the
shelves of the music library extension with a collection that in scope as well as depth will be more
than adequate for most musical needs...
                    Ogreta McNeill, Head.

---

* Source tables and graphics not published in this volume
    are deposited at the Toronto Public Library and are
    available for further study by interested persons.

Planning the Conversion of a College to a
University Library

by J. R. Blanchard

University Librarian at the
University of California, Davis;
prepared for presentation to
the officers of the Rockefeller
Foundation

From College and Research Libraries 29:297-301,
July 1968; Reprinted with permission of the Editor,
College and Research Libraries, ALA, Chicago

Many new university libraries are being rapidly
developed out of older, small college collections.
Methods and standards available for the planning
of such libraries include the Clapp-Jordan formula
for book collections and standards for buildings
and book collections used by the State of California. Professor Robert Hayes of the school of
library service, UCLA, is preparing a formula
for the development of collections in University of
California libraries. Methods used in planning for
the development of the University of California library, Davis, are described.

The painfully sudden and explosive development of
many small, usually bucolic, undergraduate and specialized
colleges into full-scale universities in this country and a-
broad has been a remarkable phenomenon since World War
II. Some institutions have literally doubled their enrollment
annually over a period of years with student bodies increasing from a few hundred to ten or twenty thousand persons
in a relatively short period. In addition, numerous and
completely new colleges and universities with great aspira-
tions and mostly hope for assets have been started in tropi-
cal forests, asphalt jungles, raw prairies, and in the mazes
of suburbia. In several notable cases new satellite campuses have been seeded by existing older campuses.

range library plans should be prepared which include estimates of needs for book collections, space, staff, and funds.

As a case study, it should be useful to examine the
methods by which planning for educational institutions and libraries has been undertaken by the State of California. The
urgent need for greatly expanded educational facilities in California became obvious shortly after World War II and resulted in three very important and seminal planning documents. [4] These studies showed clearly that great quantities
of new students would soon inundate the state's institutions of
higher education and that it was mandatory to enlarge existing
colleges and universities and to start new ones. The last and
most important of the studies, A Master Plan for Higher
Education in California, 1960-1975, resulted in legislation
which officially recognized California's higher education system which is based on junior municipal colleges, state colleges, the university, and independent colleges. Each type
of state-supported institution has a specific task although there
is much overlapping of function. Entrance requirements vary
from the junior colleges, which accept graduates of all ac-
credited high schools, to the university, which accepts about
the upper 12 per cent of high school students. Junior colleges
prepare students for vocations as well as for transfer to the
state colleges and universities. The state colleges provide
general academic work through the master's degree in most
basic disciplines and also train many of the teachers for the
state. Besides a general curriculum, the university gives
particular attention to graduate work, research, and professional training in such fields as law and medicine. Total enrollments in 1958 were 225,615 with 661,350 expected by
1975. There are now nine general campuses of the university as compared to two, Berkeley and UCLA, in 1951. State
colleges have grown to about seventeen.

The studies gave little specific attention to libraries.
However, in the Restudy of the Needs of California in Higher
Education the following guidelines were recommended.

1. Library reading stations for one-fourth the students
should be provided. Thirty net square feet per station should
be allowed which would also provide for library work space.

2. .10 net square feet of space per volume for the
first 150,000 volumes decreasing to .05 net square feet for
the second one million volumes.

It is clear that all over the world, including the United States, there is a great need for thorough planning, based on reasonable standards and guidelines, in connectio with the library systems of such new and rapidly growing i stitutions. Standards for library buildings have been avail able. Planning for book collections and library services h been difficult as there has not been available in the past we devised, clearly defined, and widely accepted standards and guidelines. Fortunately, the Clapp-Jordan[1] formula for bool collections, which has now been widely promulgated, will be useful as will other recent efforts to create meaningful stan ards.

Before library standards can be used, however, an institution must first make basic decisions about its purpose, academic program, and size. The various factors that have a bearing on library needs listed in order of priority include the following:

1. The academic program. Undergraduate programs require relatively small library collections. Graduate programs, particularly at the doctoral level, require heavy investments in large book collections. According to a recent survey[2] at the Joint University Libraries, graduate students and faculty there require library services costing 4.8 times more than undergraduates.

2. Quality. This is a factor that is hard to determine. The fact that a good library is important in relation to the quality of an institution is widely accepted and was clearly noted in an important study recently published by the American Council on Education.[3]

3. Size of enrollment. This factor must be considered, but it should rank below the academic program and quality as a factor, particularly as far as book collections are concerned. Institutions should not plan library facilities based largely on the size of the enrollment.

4. Other library facilities available in the area. Too much weight is often given to this factor. An institution must eventually develop a library to meet its basic needs and other libraries if available should only be depended upon for seldom-used special materials and for the partial support of certain research projects.

Once the above factors have been determined, long

3. State colleges: Thirty volumes for each full-time student for the first 5,000 students plus twenty volumes for each full-time student beyond 5,000 students. University: one hundred volumes per student for the first 10,000, seventy-five volumes for the second 10,000, fifty volumes per student beyond 20,000.

These guidelines were admittedly rule of thumb and were devised quickly by an advisor who based them on library facilities and collections as they existed at certain institutions. Although they were partially inadequate, they were used as standards for several years and still have much authority. As far as the university is concerned, they were replaced in part by A Plan for Library Development[5] issued in 1961, prepared at the request of President Kerr, and the Unit Area Allowance for Libraries[6] prepared by a special committee of librarians and architects in 1966.

Within the University of California system the Davis campus represents very well the growth of a specialized campus into a general university. An examination of its library development might be fruitful in coming to conclusions about how library planning in such a situation should be handled and what mistakes should be avoided.

From 1909 to 1951 Davis was a college of agriculture started originally as an offshoot of the Berkeley campus. In 1951 a College of Letters and Science was initiated at a very modest level. At that time, Davis had about eighteen hundred students, all in agriculture except for a handful in the College of Letters and Science. The academic program in agriculture was a strong one with a doctorate provided. Major emphasis was placed on research. The library had eighty thousand well selected volumes, about 80 per cent of which were concerned with the biological sciences and agriculture. No firm, long-range plan had as yet been prepared for the library or the campus in general. It was assumed, however, that the College of Letters and Science would remain small and would emphasize the basic sciences. With these limitations in mind, efforts of the library staff for the next few years were largely focused on building up the scientific collection, although some attention was given to basic material needed for the social sciences and humanities. Much dependence in these years was placed on the large university library at Berkeley.

Library growth was accelerated in 1959 when Davis

was designated a general campus.   At about that time an acquisitions code was devised for the library which emphasized
that the development of the book collection should be based
on the academic program.   A library long-range building
program was prepared.   Unfortunately, both of these documents were based on inadequate information about the future
academic development of the campus, which was still somewhat uncertain.   By 1961 it became clear that Davis would
become a general university in fact as well as name, that
graduate work in practically all basic disciplines was to be
provided, and that professional schools of law, medicine,
engineering, and possibly two or three others would be created.   It was also at this time that the previously noted A
Plan for Library Development was issued which stated that
Davis and the other emerging general campuses of the University should have at least five hundred thousand volumes
on hand by the year 1970-71.   This figure for Davis was
later increased by President Kerr to nine hundred thousand
volumes.   Using this document, plus a published academic
plan for the Davis campus, it was now possible for the library staff to do its planning work with some assurance.
The planning had four principal aspects:

Collection Development.   It was agreed at the beginning that selection of material should be a joint faculty and
library staff endeavor.   Subject specialists on the library
staff worked with faculty members in preparing want lists
based on standard bibliographies and the needs of the academic program.   Goals for the numbers of volumes to be
processed each year up to 1970-71 were estimated.   Priority in the expenditure of book funds was given to the needs
of new graduate and professional programs particularly in
the fields not formerly emphasized on the campus.

No acceptable quantitative factors for estimating the
size of book collections were available in 1961.   However,
Professor Robert Hayes of the University of California's Institute of Library Research is now developing a set of factors based in part on the Clapp-Jordan formula and experience at the University of California.   Librarians at the Davis
campus in preparing material for Professor Hayes reached
the following conclusions about quantitative factors.

1. A basic core collection should be developed of at
least fifty thousand volumes, but preferably consisting of
seventy-five thousand or even one hundred and twenty-five
thousand volumes.   The Clapp-Jordan formula suggests an

"undergraduate library" as a starting point with a minimum of fifty thousand seven hundred and fifty volumes. The core collection would include general reference works, bibliographies, volumes supporting basic general reading requirements and a general periodicals collection (assuming that bound periodical backfiles would be counted as monographic volumes). Selections for this basic library could be based in part on Michigan's undergraduate library[7] and for the new campus program of the University of California. [8] The latter program involved the simultaneous development of basic undergraduate libraries of seventy-five thousand volumes each for the new San Diego, Irvine and Santa Cruz campuses.

2. Additional volumes should be added for each academic program as follows.

a. Seventy-five thousand volumes for each new college and professional school.

b. Approximately one thousand to fifteen hundred volumes for each undergraduate major. The Clapp-Jordan study recommends three hundred and thirty-five volumes for each baccalaureate program. However, the Davis librarians believe these requirements should be higher particularly for programs that include fields with high literature requirements such as history, English literature, and political science.

c. About five thousand volumes for each master's program and twenty-five thousand volumes for each doctoral program. The Clapp-Jordan formula calls for three thousand and twenty-four thousand five hundred volumes respectively for master's and doctoral programs.

3. Volumes needed based on student enrollment. It is recommended that approximately ten volumes be added for each undergraduate student and twenty volumes for each graduate student. As stated earlier, book collection requirements must largely be based on the academic program; however, additional copies of basic works are required as the student enrollment grows.

4. Volumes needed based on the number of faculty members and research in the institution. It is recommended that about 200 volumes for each faculty member and 100 volumes for each professional research staff member be added by the library.

Notes

1. Clapp, Verner and Jordan, Robert T. "Quantitative Criteria for Adequacy of Academic Library Collections" CRL, 26, September 1965, 371-80.

2. Unpublished report by the Joint University Libraries (Nashville, Tennessee).

3. Cartter, Allan M. An Assessment of Quality in Graduate Education Washington, D. C. , American Council on Education, 1966.

4. California. Committee on the Conduct of the Study of Higher Education in California. A Report of a Survey of the Needs of California in Higher Education Submitted to the Liaison Committee of the Regents and the State Department of Education (The Strayer report, Sacramento, 1948); Liaison Committee of the Regents of the University of California and the California State Board of Education. A Restudy of the Needs of California in Higher Education (Sacramento, 1955); A Master Plan for Higher Education in California, 1960-1975: (Sacramento, 1960).

5. California. University. Office of the President, A Plan for Library Development. 1961.

6. California. University. Committee on Library Space Standards. Unit Area Allowances for Libraries, 1966.

7. Michigan. University. Library. Undergraduate shelf list to December 30, 1963. Ann Arbor, University Microfilms [on microfilm, cards, and xerox].

8. Voigt, Melvin J. and Treyz, Joseph H. Books for College Libraries. Chicago, ALA, 1967.

Book Collections in the Public Libraries of the
Pottsville Library District

by Ralph Blasingame   Formerly State Librarian of
Pennsylvania; Professor,
Graduate School of Library
Service, Rutgers - The State
University of New Jersey

From his Book Collections in the Public Libraries
of the Pottsville Library District. Pottsville, Pa.,
Pottsville Free Public Library, 1967. p. 50-53;
55-7; 61-4. Reprinted by permission of Jane L.
Hess, Director, Pottsville (Pa.) Free Public Library.

The below-median showing of the Pottsville fiction collection is probably a reflection of total size (59,009 adult
non-fiction volumes as of Summer, 1965) rather than conscious development of the Library's role in the community.
Inspection of the collection reveals a large number of titles,
many light love and mystery stories, many very old titles,
and many book-club edition duplicates, apparently donated.

Table 2 is self-explanatory. However, the information presented in it must be read with knowledge of a particular collection and the objectives of the library.

Science Collections

Table 3 presents the date distribution for the science
holdings of the libraries in the Pottsville District, together
with the date distribution of starred science titles listed in
the Standard Catalog for Public Libraries. Summarizing the
data in this Table, we find that:

Two libraries have collections with at least 50% of the
items copyrighted within the most recent five-year interval.
(The collections in these two libraries, plus two others,
show a higher percentage of titles in the 1961-1966 time

Table 2

Percentage Distribution of Adult Book Collection by Dewey Classification
for the Public Libraries in the Pottsville Library District,
with median based on 10 other Pennsylvania libraries, tabulated for another study

	Median	Pottsville	A	B	C	D	E	F	G	H	K
Fiction	37.2	22.2	51.9	59.1	56.2	53.1	31.3	72.7	63.3	40.6	46.4
Non-Fic.											
000	.75	.7	.3	.2	.2	.2	.5	.2	.3	.3	.3
100	1.6	1.4	1.4	1.2	.6	.8	.8	1.3	1.0	1.5	2.2
200	2.65	3.1	1.6	2.0	1.3	1.6	2.9	1.3	1.4	5.0	4.4
300	6.8	6.2	4.0	4.7	3.2	4.0	12.1	2.6	4.7	6.8	6.9
400	.55	.9	.8	.6	.1	.7	3.0	.6	1.0	.9	1.0
500	3.05	3.4	1.7	3.0	2.8	2.1	6.1	2.6	2.5	3.9	3.4
600	5.5	5.4	4.4	2.6	4.4	3.5	6.1	1.8	4.9	5.3	4.7
700	4.4	6.9	2.9	2.0	2.0	3.0	1.2	1.0	2.4	3.1	1.7
800	8.8	11.3	8.5	6.7	4.5	5.7	13.2	3.7	5.4	5.7	11.0
900	21.2	24.9	17.8	14.0	15.9	16.0	21.2	9.3	11.0	15.9	16.3
Reference	5.15	10.9	4.7	3.9	8.8	9.3	1.6	2.9	2.1	11.0	1.7
No. of vol.	19,372	59,009	6,208	8,261	4,431	3,538	8,314	2,166	12,087	11,347	7,496

Table 3

Percentage of Science books held by age distribution

Library	In last 5 years 1961-66	In last 10 years 1956-66	1955 or earlier	1950 or earlier	1940 or earlier	1925 or earlier	Number of volumes
Pottsville	12.1	21.7	78.3	71.0	50.2	24.0	1,768
A	9.4	15.6	69.7	68.6	35.4	19.7	98
B	36.0	50.8	46.0	38.8	24.8	10.8	249
C	56.4	89.7	10.3	7.7	2.6	0	125
D	50.0	64.8	35.1	32.4	16.2	2.7	74
E		8.0	92.0	88.0	78.0	56.0	500
F			92.8	89.2	77.0	49.0	57
G	19.0	27.2	70.7	63.2	48.3	27.2	302
H	35.9	45.2	54.6	40.6	34.3	21.8	448
K	6.0	6.0	90.0	86.0	74.0	46.0	250
Standard Catalog*	24.2	50.0	49.6	19.6	5.4	.3	329

* Starred titles listed in the Standard Catalog for Public Libraries

period than does the Standard Catalog for Public Libraries.
It must be noted again that the basic volume of that Catalog
was issued in 1958, and also that the number of starred science titles in the Catalog is larger than the number of science volumes held by three of these four libraries.   Thus,
Library D which shows 50% of its science collection in the
latest five-year time period actually has only 37 volumes as
compared with 79 in the Standard Catalog for this period.
On the other hand, Library H with a 35. 9% showing has 159
volumes for this time period.)

     Two libraries have no science books published within
the most recent five-year interval; one lacks books published
within the last ten-year interval.

     In six libraries, more than two-thirds of the science
books are copyrighted 1955 or earlier (more than 10 years
ago).

     These six libraries hold more science materials copy-
righted before 1925 (more than 40 years ago) than materials
copyrighted since 1960.

     In short, in a field where the rate of progress and
change has been almost incredible, the majority of books
available in the Pottsville Library District are old enough
that they probably contain misinformation, or at least out-
moded concepts.   In some localities, the reader turning to
his public library for information will find an iron curtain on
all scientific discoveries since the development of Sputnik.

Religious Collections

     Religion is another field in which older materials re-
tain value, and the date distribution of the collection should
reflect this fact.   At the same time, many new discoveries,
such as the Dead Sea Scrolls, have brought about new interpretations and the impact of social change and upheaval has
exerted revolutionary changes in this field, as much as any
other.

     Table 5 presents the date distribution of the religious
collections.   In view of the small size offered by the starred
titles in the Standard Catalog for Public Libraries in this
subject field and the even smaller size of many of these collections, the percentage of current titles held must be related to the number of volumes held.   Library C and Library

Table 5

Percentage of Religious books held by age distribution

Library	In last 5 years 1961-66	In last 10 years 1955-66	1955 or earlier	1950 or earlier	1940 or earlier	1925 or earlier	Number of volumes
Pottsville	4.2	8.0	92.0	86.7	70.8	51.5	1,541
A	4.3	19.4	69.1	52.9	31.3	21.6	94
B	19.8	34.0	58.9	50.8	34.7	27.9	163
C	26.3	36.8	63.2	47.4	10.6	5.3	61
D	26.7	42.7	55.2	35.6	14.2	1.8	56
E		9.1	90.9	84.8	66.7	54.5	231
F	3.6	17.8	78.6	75.0	67.8	53.6	28
G	5.4	12.0	78.6	69.6	52.8	27.6	172
H	29.8	42.0	56.0	33.2	15.8	8.8	570
K	3.0	6.1	88.2	86.6	74.5	51.7	330
Standard Catalog*	19.8	52.2	47.4	28.8	7.2		166

* Starred titles listed in the Standard Catalog for Public Libraries

D, for example, exceed the "norm" in percentage of titles held for the 1961-1966 time period, but the percentage represents only about 15 volumes. Relating percentage to number of volumes, it is apparent from Table 5 that the majority of libraries in the Pottsville District are failing to provide current materials in the field of religion. One library has no recent titles and four others offer less than a dozen items copyrighted within the latest five-year interval. The adult reader seeking information on the ecumenical movement, the changes taking place at the Vatican, the "Honest to God" debate, or the young person who might be stimulated by some of the new attitudes and fresh approaches beginning to appear in the literature, will not be served by these libraries.

The low percentage holding of titles copyrighted in the 1956-1960 time period, compared with the Standard Catalog, suggests that the collections ought to be checked for gaps in holdings. At the same time, the very high percentage holding of older materials (1940 or earlier, and 1925 or earlier) suggests that the older items in these collections should be reviewed to be sure they still have validity and usefulness.

Application

A few simple calculations may be applied to any collection to estimate the expenditure necessary to bring the collection to the desirable levels set forth in this report. These calculations have been worked out for one local library in the Pottsville District to provide an illustration not only of method but also the magnitude of the problem suggested by this application. Library B has been selected for this example because it is one of the larger and older established libraries in the district, follows a careful selection policy, and at the same time is neither decidedly good nor decidedly bad in terms of age and subject distribution of the collection.

1. Determine the total size of book stock necessary to meet State Standards.

   Applying the present (1958) standard of 1 volume per capita, Library B should have 14,181 volumes. The standards specify a collection of 6,000 volumes for smaller communities.

2. Determine appropriate distribution of book stock by broad categories, adult non-fiction, adult fiction and juvenile, as these relate to the role and objectives of the library.

(Note: Further stratification of adult and juvenile non-fiction collections should be worked into this calculation if norms for distribution can be determined.)

The present percentage distribution of adult non-fiction (including reference) in Library B is 33%. The Librarian believes that this distribution should be increased to the 40% level.

Library B is experiencing a marked decrease in use of the juvenile collection as a result of the recent build-up of school library resources in that community.   Until a redefinition of role and objectives is formulated, the Librarian suggests that the present percentage distribution of children's materials should be used.   The tentative distribution formula for Library B works out to:

Adult non-fiction and reference	40%
Adult fiction	45%
Juvenile fiction and non-fiction	15%

(Note: In smaller libraries, with collections of 6, 000 volumes and under, the percentage of adult non-fiction might be dropped as low as 10% to reflect the different role of the very small agency.)

3. On the basis of (1) and (2) above, determine the number of volumes necessary to meet the "norms" tentatively adopted for the purpose of this study:

Adult non-fiction	75-90% within last ten years
Adult fiction	52% within last ten years
Juvenile	45% within last ten years

4. Subtract the number of volumes of appropriate date the library presently holds from the above ranges.

5. The difference is the number of volumes needed to achieve the level suggested in this report.   This

Example of Method and Cost Factors

Application of Recommended Standards for Age Distribution of Collection: Library B

ACQUISITION

Collection and Present Size	Recommended Size and Distribution		Recommended holdings copyrighted within last ten years		Library holdings copyrighted in last ten years (Volumes)	Needed Acquisitions (Volumes)	Avg. Cost per Vol.	Total Cost
	%	Volumes	%	Volumes				
Adult Non-Fiction 3447 (36%)	40	5672	75-90	4254-5105	1228	3026-3877	$6.00	$18,156-23,262
Adult Fiction 4883 (51%)	45	6382	52	3319	945	2374	$4.52	10,730
Juvenile 1250 (15%)	15	2127	45	957	705	252	$3.46	871
								$29,758-34,864

WEEDING

Collection and Present Size	Recommended Size and Distribution		Recommended holdings copyrighted prior to 1956		Library holdings copyrighted prior to 1956 (Volumes)	Weeding Estimation (Volumes)	Avg. Cost per Vol.	Total Cost
	%	Volumes	%	Volumes				
Adult Non-Fiction 3447 (36%)	40	5672	10-25	567-1418	2219	1652-801		
Adult Fiction 4883 (51%)	45	6382	48	3063	3938	875		
Juvenile 1250 (15%)	15	2127	55	1169	545			

difference multiplied by the average cost per volume will give a cost range.

6. The same type formula applied to the remainder of the book stock may result in a positive difference (surplus of volumes), and the amount of weeding necessary will fall somewhere within the range indicated by this positive difference.

(Note: The cost of weeding--i. e. , actually selecting and removing items from the collection--should also be added to get a complete picture of cost. This cost factor will vary widely from library to library, and even from one classification to another within one library. Variants include the salary level of the librarian reviewing the collection, the number of entry cards to be removed from the catalog, salary and performance rate of clerical staff. Thus, the costs of weeding have not been calculated here.)

The data presented for Library B, page 694, indicates a cost range (excluding cost of weeding) of $29, 758 to $34, 864 to effect a desirable date distribution level. When one puts the problem this way, recalling that there are over 400 public libraries in the state, or even that there are 305 libraries receiving state aid, it seems entirely unlikely that expenditures of this magnitude could be covered by the state at the present rate of aid. The problem is very much larger, in scope and scale, than has yet been suggested.

Evaluation of a Research Library Collection

by Robert Peerling Coale   Deputy Chief Cataloger, Newberry Library, Chicago. This
paper was drawn from the author's Master's thesis at the
Graduate Library School, University of Chicago

From his "Evaluation of a Research Library Collection: Latin-American Colonial History at the Newberry," Library Quarterly 35:173-5, 184, July
1965; Reprinted from Library Quarterly by permission of the University of Chicago Press, (c) 1965
by the University of Chicago.

The systematic evaluation of the book collection of a
large library is rarely undertaken. Such evaluations as are
made are usually subjective in nature, based upon the opinions of librarians, faculty members, and occasionally students. Yet the objective evaluation of the book collection of
a large library is highly desirable for the formulation of an
intelligent acquisitions program, because the librarian needs
to know both where his collection is strong and where it is
weak in order to plan its growth reasonably and well.

The attempt to find an objective method of evaluation
raises problems. No standard list exists of books and materials that should be in a research collection of any breadth.
If there were such lists they would probably be so lengthy
that the cost of checking them against holdings would discourage their use. One alternative open to the librarian is to
compare the library holdings with many specialized subject
bibliographies. This procedure is quite expensive in time
and effort, however, and the surveyors of the Indiana University Library in 1940 contented themselves with using a
few brief checklists. [1] Another method that has been utilized
by university libraries is to enlist the co-operation of the
faculty. This procedure was used in the self-survey con-

ducted by the University of Chicago libraries in 1930, which involved the critical examination and checking of some four hundred bibliographies by about two hundred faculty members. [2] This experiment has not been repeated frequently, perhaps for obvious reasons concerned with faculty time and good will. At any rate, that method cannot be followed by an independent research library such as the Newberry Library, which has no faculty. Consequently, in spite of the difficulties, bibliographic checking seems to be the most feasible way to evaluate its holdings.

The Newberry Library, in accord with an agreement established in 1896 with the Chicago Public Library and the John Crerar Library, has specialized in the humanities. Such specialization reduces the task of using subject bibliographies, but the problem remains very large. In order to reduce it to a manageable size, it seems necessary to consider only a part of the total collection at a time. That is, a series of investigations aimed at evaluating certain subjects in the library's holdings could be pursued separately and at different times.

A pilot project was set up to survey the Newberry Library holdings in the colonial history of certain key areas of Spanish America--Mexico, Peru, Chile, and Colombia and Venezuela. An attempt was made to determine not only how strong the Newberry is in the general subject of Spanish-American colonial history but also how strong it is on a century by century basis in each of the areas concerned. The results of the survey helped show the Newberry in which areas and centuries it has the strongest foundation on which to build and also indicated obvious gaps which should be filled.

Two questions were asked regarding the colonial history of each area: (1) Does the collection contain the primary printed source material and the important secondary accounts? (2) Has the library kept up with the acquisition of the current scholarly output in the field?

The first of these questions is the most difficult to answer. In most cases there is no satisfactory standard bibliography. A research collection can be put to a series of tests, however, by taking a selected group of scholarly books about a subject and checking the bibliographies of these books against the library holdings. This is the method chosen for evaluating the Newberry collection in Latin-American

history.   In effect, the question is asked: Could these books
have been written at the Newberry?

In this sampling technique the bibliographies utilized
are not theoretical lists of "best" books.   Instead, they are
lists of the actual works consulted or examined by the author.
They test not only the strength of the special collection but
also, to a certain extent, the strength of the general library,
because many of the books listed in the bibliographies used
do not pertain entirely to Spanish America but concern the
European political, economic, or religious background.   A
library might have quite a good special collection and yet be
a poor place for a scholar to work if many necessary titles
tangential to his subject are lacking.

In choosing the bibliographies to be checked an attempt
was made to secure those that would permit a measure of the
book collection in each of the three centuries of colonial rule.
Bibliographies of substantial size were sought (usually between one hundred and four hundred titles in each), confined
to the colonial era, listing both contemporary sources and
later scholarship, and compiled by recognized scholars in
the field.

In order to determine the Newberry's relative standing among other libraries with widely recognized collections
in the colonial Spanish-American field certain bibliographies
checked at the Newberry were also checked at the University
of Texas and the University of California at Berkeley, in addition to the Library of the Hispanic Society of America.   Of
course, there are other notable collections of Spanish-American materials in libraries such as the New York Public Library, the Library of Congress, and the Library of Yale
University, but to keep the study within reasonable bounds it
was decided to hold the survey to comparisons with three
other libraries.

Time did not permit checking all the bibliographies
used at the Newberry in the other three libraries.   Only the
bibliographies for which the Newberry scored best and worst
for each area were checked in the other libraries as well.
In the case of Texas the bibliographies were compared both
with the public catalog of the University and the special catalog of the Latin-American collection.   At California the checking was done in the public catalog at the Berkeley campus,
which includes cards for printed materials in the Bancroft
Library.   In addition, these same bibliographies were checked

against the 1962 catalog of the Library of the Hispanic Society of America (New York) and its earlier catalogs of books printed before 1700. Because it is usually impossible to tell from a catalog card whether a particular issue of a periodical is in the library or not, and also because the printed catalog of the Hispanic Society of America does not include most periodicals, the comparative statistics among the four libraries refer only to books and do not include periodical articles.

The question of whether the Newberry Library has been keeping up with the current scholarship in the field is a little easier to answer, thanks to the Handbook of Latin American Studies. [3] This approximately annual bibliography, which Howard Cline, Director of the Hispanic Foundation at the Library of Congress, calls "absolutely indispensable for following current production,"[4] is broken down by subjects, such as history, art, geography, etc., and is further subdivided by country or region. By checking in sample volumes the entries for History under each country or area against the holdings of the Newberry Library it is possible to determine to a certain extent how well acquisition of current books and periodicals has been proceeding since 1936. The volumes of the Handbook were not chosen at exactly equal time intervals, because in certain years there was a comparative paucity of pertinent titles listed. Instead, beginning with the volume for 1936, every fifth or sixth volume was selected, except for the last volume utilized, the latest published at the time of the survey.

The results of these two types of bibliographic checking furnish information on which to base an evaluation of the strength of a collection and indication of significant gaps. As the evaluation is concerned only with the value of the collection for historical research, the rarity or monetary value of a specific edition of a title is not considered. The only thing of interest for the purposes of the study is whether a title is or is not in the library. A title was counted as present in the library whether it was an original reprint or facsimile edition.

To sum up, the results of these surveys indicate that the Mexican collection is the superior one at the Newberry, with the Peruvian collection in second place. In addition, the Mexican collection remains quite strong over the entire colonial period, while the quality of the Peruvian collection drops decidedly in the seventeenth and eighteenth centuries.

The Newberry collections in the Chilean and Colombia-Venezuela region are inferior to those for Mexico and Peru, but
the library has substantial materials in all of these areas.

The strength of the Newberry collection is greatest
for the sixteenth century. With respect to printed materials
the Newberry collections in Mexican and Peruvian history in
the sixteenth century are approximately equal to the fine collections at the Universities of Texas and California. In the
later centuries of Spanish rule in Mexico and Peru, the Texas and California collections are quite superior, as they are
in Chilean colonial history. The Newberry is somewhat superior to the University of Texas in the colonial history of
the Colombia-Venezuela region, but it is a little inferior to
the University of California.

The Newberry collections in the colonial history of almost all of the areas and time periods surveyed are greatly
superior to those of the Library of the Hispanic Society of
America. This low position occupied by the Hispanic Society
with respect to this survey is, of course, partially due to the
fact that the Hispanic Society is not a general library and
therefore makes no attempt to acquire much background material outside of its declared fields of interest: the art, history, and literature of Spain, Portugal and colonial Hispanic
America.

Even though selected, relatively short bibliographies
were checked instead of the nonexistent "standard" bibliographies in each subject area, the time involved in tedious checking was still considerable. But an advantage of the method
presented above is that the bulk of the checking can be done
by a reliable searcher, with an experienced catalog librarian
to review the titles not found by the searcher. It need not
involve the participation of the faculty or other academic personnel. In effect, through this survey method the book collection is subjected to a series of probes which do not examine it in its totality but which do examine it in depth.

Notes

1. Coney, Donald Report of a Survey of the Indiana Univer-
      sity Library for the Indiana University, February-
      July, 1940. Chicago, American Library Association,
      1940.

2. Raney, M. Llewellyn The University Libraries Chicago, University of Chicago Press, 1933.

3. Cambridge, Mass. , Harvard University Press, 1936--.

4. Cline, Howard F.   "Latin America" Guide to Historical Literature.   New York, Macmillan Co. , 1961, p. 656

Faculty Evaluation of Resources

From Columbia University. President's Commit-
tee. The Columbia University Libraries: A Re-
port on Present and Future Needs. New York,
Columbia University Press, 1958. Appendix II.
Faculty Evaluation of Resources, p. 263-75 (sel.);
Reprinted by permission of Columbia University
Press, New York City

Business. Thirteen faculty members from Business
furnished opinions on the collections. In such fields as accounting, transportation, business law, taxation, and business
management, there was agreement that present holdings are
at the general research level and should be retained at that
point. Attention was called to other business collections in
New York City that are used by students and faculty members. In other fields, such as insurance and traffic management, the present holdings are considered at the working collection level, and recommendations indicated that they be
kept there. Improvement was suggested for consumer market behavior, retailing, market research, and pricing. Improvement also was indicated for such fields as general administration, human relations in business, and the modern
corporation. One faculty member, writing of these three
fields, stated:

> I feel sure that there will be greatly increased in-
> terest in these fields during the next 25 years.
> There are strong indications that professional busi-
> ness education will move its emphasis from func-
> tional fields (sales, finance, etc.) to these fields.
> If we are to play a leading role in this develop-
> ment we must have good library resources.

These fields are predominantly American in character, and
foreign publications are limited.

Business holdings should be correlated with those of
economics, and there were observations on improving the

collections of economic geography in the Far East and of progress in underdeveloped areas. Foreign, as well as American, publications were suggested.

Engineering. The field of engineering was represented by 25 faculty members, divided as follows: civil (9), chemical (3), electrical (5), industrial (2), mechanical (3), and mining (3).

In civil engineering, there was enough variation in evaluation of present resources to summarize the responses as suggesting moving toward general research or comprehensive collections in structures, applied mechanics and mathematics, hydraulic and fluid mechanics (excluding sanitary and marine engineering), and heat transfer. The common European languages are needed, as is also Russian, and, if possible, the latter in translation. Chinese and Japanese were recommended for exclusion.

There was also a difference of opinion regarding the present status of chemical engineering, but all three faculty members regarded the goal as comprehensive. It was noted that materials in Russian were desirable.

Appraisal of the present collections in electrical engineering indicated ranges from working to general research collections. Four of the five recommended working towards a comprehensive collection. Among the areas which were indicated as weak were military communications, information transmission, and industrial measurement and control. It was suggested that perhaps too much collecting was being done in power uses. Emphasis was placed on German, Russian, and French publications, although Italian and Scandinavian received some support. Among the language materials indicated as not needed were Spanish, Chinese, and Japanese.

Comprehensive collections were recommended for operations research (now a working collection) and for organization and management. It was pointed out by a faculty member in industrial engineering that organization and management represented an interdisciplinary field that resulted in scattering of the materials in various libraries. Research reports, journals, and dissertations are considered important in the field of organization and management. Trade publications, small pamphlets, and advertising materials are not needed. Attention was called to the collecting and cataloging of much commercial material that might well be avoided.

In mechanical engineering, one faculty member considered the collections "adequate" and recommended retention at that level, and another felt it should approach the comprehensive level. A third faculty member saw the collection on kinematics and mechanisms as poor and in need of considerable attention in so far as books, journals, and dissertations were concerned. Among the languages for the general field of mechanical engineering, attention was called to German, French, Russian, Scandinavian, and Italian for machine design, but not Scandinavian for metal working. Manuals and trade school publications should be avoided. Russian, German, and English were considered the basic languages for kinematics and mechanisms.

Three faculty members commented on the present coverage in various areas of mining. In physical metallurgy, the holdings were considered at the general research level in English and German, with a working collection in French. Materials are nil in Russian. It was recommended that the English, French, and German collections be comprehensive and that a general research collection be developed for Russian works. Primary materials are books and journals in the field.

General research collections are available, according to the faculty, for mining methods and sampling and statistics, and a working collection is now held in explosives. General research collections are needed in all three, with emphasis on American, Canadian, English, French, German, South African, and Australian publications. The major materials are books, journals, handbooks, and government publications.

In mining exploration, there is a suggestion to move from a working collection to a level between general research and comprehensive. Similar collections are needed in mineral economics. In addition to materials in the languages specified above for other areas in mining, Russian materials were also suggested as desirable. Especially needed are transactions of mining engineering societies, journals, important textbooks, and reports on international conferences. When possible to obtain, English translations of foreign international conferences should be acquired.

<u>Library Service</u>. Eleven faculty members returned questionnaires in the field of library service. In many areas the collections are comprehensive and should be continued at

that level.   Areas which appear to be in need of improvement include rare book bibliography and communications.   It
was observed that examples of standard reference works
should be considered expendable and paid for from the instructional budget to allow more duplicate copies for circulation.   Because librarianship goes into all fields of knowledge, the question of materials in other areas is a constant
problem.   The suggestion is made that the Library School
Library have basic materials in the humanities and social
sciences.   There is no effort to resove this problem at this
time, but it warrants the attention of the library administration.

Music.   There was general agreement among the four
faculty members as to the need for improvement of the following fields: folk, primitive, and Oriental music, the theory of music, and scores.   The faculty regarded the collections in music history, musicology (including comparative
musicology), and ethnic-music studies as comprehensive and
felt these should be kept to that level.   Slavic and Scandinavian music were not considered essential, but translations
from Chinese, Japanese, and Hungarian were regarded as
desirable.   The major European countries and Latin American countries should be represented.

According to one faculty member,

> ... the record collection is quite good, but in many
> cases, various readings of the same work are de-
> sirable.   Various series of historical surveys of
> music, on records, must be continued.   Coverage
> of major composers should be as complete as pos-
> sible, in some cases more so than the present.
> Many minor composers should be represented for
> historic studies.   Certain areas need strengthening,
> either from currently available sources, or as new
> records become available, as follows: (1) 17th
> and 18th century operas;   (2) 17th and 18th century
> sacred choral music; (3) 15th and 16th century
> sacred and secular vocal music, and (4) organ mu-
> sic, 15th-18th centuries.   In some cases, the re-
> cording on hand was the first of the composition
> available; subsequently new versions have been re-
> leased that are superior in performance or engi-
> neering, but cannot be acquired because of budget
> limitations, and the fact that the title is already
> in the collection.   This should be corrected.

Editor's note: See the article on p. 647 for a brief outline
of the levels of collecting used in this study which
was under the direction of Dr. Maurice F. Tauber.

An Evaluation of the Ghana Collection in the
Rutgers University Library

by Janet Martin Welch   Mrs. Welch is Assistant Director, Technical Information Cen-
ter, National Lead Company
Research Labs, Hightstown,
N. J. Her paper was prepared
as a student assignment at
Graduate School of Library Service, Rutgers University

From her "An Evaluation of the Ghana Collection
in the Rutgers University Library." New Brunswick, N. J., Graduate School of Library Service,
Rutgers-the State University, 1967. Unpub. ms.
p. 9-12, 17-19; Reprinted by permission of the
author.

General
Evaluation of the Collection

The most immediate and dominant impression one
gains of the Ghana collection is its age. Even at first glance
few of the titles have the fresh appearance of current titles.
Most titles use the term "Gold Coast" rather than "Ghana,"
indicating a preponderance of pre-independence (1957) titles.
A more thorough examination of the collection substantiates
the immediate impression of old age. Almost 40% of the
books were published before independence ten years ago and
almost 60% were published before 1960. Even more revealing is the fact that in terms of content only 27% of the books
deal at all with post-independence Ghana.

If one views the collection in terms of coverage of
the topics which, according to the Library of Congress classification appearing on the books, should be included--his-
tory, ethnography, social life and customs, biography, description, and travel--definite inadequacies and imbalances
become apparent.

The collection is adequately stocked with books on Ghana's history before 1957 from British, American, and Ghanaian viewpoints, but other viewpoints, such as the Russian one, are largely ignored. Many countries have influenced and continue to influence Ghana and scholars of many lands have studied the country. Books such as the following ones should be added to the collection to represent these divergent viewpoints:

1) Aleksandrovskaia, L. Gana. Moska. , Mysl. 1965.
2) Alvarez del Vayo, Juilo. Ghana Triumphs. Tr. from Spanish by William Rose. New York: Monthly Review, 1964.
3) Tixier, Gilbert. Le Ghana. Paris: Libraries Génerale de Droit et de Jurisprudence, 1965.

As has already been mentioned, the post-independence history of Ghana has been sadly under-represented in the collection. Only one work has been added to the collection (Afrira's The Ghana Coup) since the fall of Nkrumah almost two years ago. The rapidly developing and changing nature of new nations like Ghana makes the need for current material particularly acute, and the absence of such material in the Rutgers University library turns the Ghana collection into an archive of some historical importance, but little current use. New scholarly works on Ghana's most recent political and economical development are admittedly difficult to locate, but at least three titles could be added to the collection to help fill the gap:

1) Birmingham, Walter, I. Newstadt, and E. N. Omaboe, eds. The Economy of Ghana. Evanston: Northwestern University Press, 1966. First in a two volume series, A Study of Contemporary Ghana originating at the University of Ghana. According to the Bibliography of Current African Affairs it is "indispensable" and "highly recommended for college and university libraries. "

2) Brokensha, David. Social Change at Larteh, Ghana. New York: Oxford University Press, 1966. A systematic and comprehensive study of changing social institutions in a rural Ghanaian town. "Highly recommended" by the Bibliography of Current African Affairs.

3) Harvey, William B. Law and Social Change in Ghana.

Princeton: Princeton University Press, 1963. A
substantially documented study of an evolving legal
order. "Highly recommended" by the <u>Bibliography of
Current African Affairs</u>.

These books also help fill some other gaps in the collection.
For example, there are books of political observation in the
collection already, but no carefully researched study of
Ghanaian law. The Harvey book helps alleviate this problem.

Other areas in which the collection is weak are geography and demography. The only definitive geographical
work in the collection is the Boateng book. However, careful searching reveals that, as yet, there is no worthwhile
geographical supplement or replacement for this work. In
the area of demography, however, much work has been done.
There is no excuse for the fact that the Rutgers University
Ghana collection does not contain a single demographic
study. A few books which might be added to begin to correct this dismal situation are:

1) Barbour, Kenneth Michael and Prothero Mansell.
   <u>Essays on African Population.</u> London: Routledge
   and Paul, 1961.

2) Gil, Benjamin. <u>Demographic Statistics in Ghana.</u>
   Seminar on African Demography. Paris, 1959.

Biography is another topic which, according to the
Library of Congress Classification numbers, should be covered in this collection. Yet, the only biography in the collection is Timothy's acceptable but twelve-year-old biography of Nkrumah. This lack of material on Nkrumah, still
a political figure of international importance, is disturbing.
However, the problem becomes more acute when the librarian searches for a more recent authoritative work on Nkrumah for, surprisingly, little has been published on this man.
The best supplement for the 1955 biography available is
Sophia Ames' <u>Nkrumah of Ghana</u> (Chicago: Rand McNally,
1961). Certainly Nkrumah's own work, <u>Ghana, the Autobiography of Kwame Nkrumah</u> (Nelson, 1957) should also be
added to the collection. Furthermore, there are non-
Ghanaians who have influenced Ghana's history and should be
given biographical coverage in the collection. For example,
at least one definitive biography on Dr. Aggrey, such as
W. M. Macartney's <u>Dr. Aggrey, Ambassador for Africa</u>

(S. C. N. Press, 1949) should be included.

This analysis of the subject content of the books points to a basic imbalance in the collection--the disproportionate number of books which are based on personal experience or travel in Ghana rather than on extensive research and study of the country.   While subjective personal accounts by skilled observers add a new and valuable dimension to the collection, too many such works, particularly those written by observers who are less than skilled, weaken the collection by making it impossible for the student and researcher to obtain the empirical data and objective analysis he needs.   The books already suggested for purchase are all scholarly, objective works and would help alleviate this imbalance.

It is necessary to add that the collection does have some strong points.   As was mentioned earlier, there appears to have been a definite attempt to include books which see Ghana through Ghanaian eyes.   Furthermore, most of the major pre-independence classic or standard works on Ghana, such as Ward's History of Ghana, are included in the collection, along with Boaten's book which is still the major geographical work on the country.   A number of the books included in the collection such as Afrira's and Alexander's works are first-hand adventure stories which might spark the interest of a beginning student who would be bored or discouraged by more scholarly works.   This area of extracurricular reading is an important one which is often overlooked by college libraries, and it is to Rutgers University Library's credit that this need has been taken into account in its book selections.   Yet, all of these strong points do not compensate for the basic weaknesses of the collection: lack of current material, imbalance in subject content, lack of scholarly research studies, and lack of diverse viewpoints.

Policy Recommendations

The Rutgers University Ghana collection, as it now stands meets, at best, only the needs of undergraduates.   It provides general college level introductory materials and a few in depth studies for those whose major area of undergraduate concentration may involve the historical, or political study of Ghana.   However, the absence of current material even throws some doubt on the collection's overall ability to meet the needs of undergraduates.   In terms of supporting faculty and graduate student research, the collection does not even begin to do the job.

The immediate task of the librarian is to purchase those titles needed to bring the present collection up to the level of a good college level working collection. The addition of those titles mentioned earlier in this paper will help to do this.

However, with the research going on at Rutgers in political science, history, and geography, with doctorates given in these three fields, and with graduate courses offered in African geography, the future policy of the library should be to build its basic working collection on Ghana into a strong general research collection. * The Ghana collection should not be a slave to any one department or discipline, but should provide the interdisciplinary background and research material which is needed by the scholar no matter what viewpoint he uses in approaching the collection. It is only through such a broad collection capable of supporting research that the library will begin to meet the current needs of all its students, including graduate students, and to meet the current needs of faculty researchers. And, it is through such a collection that Rutgers will be able to support the kind of research which distinguishes large major universities from small state colleges.

In addition, the future needs of the university community must be considered. By all indications, the nations of Africa are likely to play an increasingly important role in the world and may be vital in the power struggle among nations. Therefore, the Ghana collection should be built into a strong resource for research not only to meet current needs but also to meet the probable future needs and demands of the university community.

In order to meet these present and future research needs a five-point selection policy for the Ghana collection should be initiated:

1) All quality materials of current or enduring research interest on Ghana published in any country, in the latest and best editions, and in the original language (if not available in translation) should be purchased. Emphasis is to be placed on original sources of information, such as letters and works of Ghanaian leaders, Ghanaian government publications and statistics, and historical records, which

supplement the basic working collection. The aim is not to
create a comprehensive or exhaustive collection, but to provide a collection capable of supporting most research.

2) New books of importance to Ghanaian research or
requested by faculty or students and judged to be worthwhile
are to be purchased immediately after publication in order
to keep the collection up to date. Those which later prove
to have no enduring or historical value or are superceded
should be weeded mercilessly after a few years.

3) The Ghana collection should expand to include information in journals, newspapers, and films, or in whatever new forms it may appear. Bibliographies, dictionaries,
handbooks and encyclopedias in the field should also be purchased.

4) Duplicate copies should be purchased of definitive
works or those in great demand.

5) Faculty and student evaluations and suggestions on
the collection should be actively sought and carefully considered along with changes in topics of study and faculty and
university policies. The aim is to build a versatile collection which can be adapted to new needs and demands as they
arise.

* In an actual library situation the establishment of such a
    policy would involve a university statement on educa-
    tional research aims in this field. Since such a
    statement is not available, I have made inferences
    on university policies, aims, and objectives from
    courses and programs described in the University
    catalogs.